The Victorian Periodical Press

The Victorian Periodical Press: Samplings and Soundings

Edited by Joanne Shattock and Michael Wolff

Leicester University Press
University of Toronto Press
1982

First published in 1982 by Leicester University Press
First published in Canada and the United States 1982
by University of Toronto Press, Toronto and Buffalo
Copyright © Leicester University Press 1982

Designed by Douglas Martin
Phototypeset in Linotron Aldus by
Western Printing Services Ltd, Bristol
Printed and bound in Great Britain
at The Pitman Press, Bath

British Library Cataloguing in Publication Data
The Victorian periodical press.
1. English periodicals—History and criticism
I. Shattock, Joanne   II. Wolff, Michael
052   PN5124.P4
ISBN 0-7185-1190-5 (Leicester University Press)
ISBN 0-8020-2463-7 (University of Toronto Press)

Contents

List of illustrations   vii
List of abbreviations   viii
Notes on the contributors   ix
Introduction   xiii

PART ONE: THE CRITIC AS JOURNALIST

Walter E. Houghton   1   Periodical literature and the articulate   3
                            classes

Brian Maidment   2   Readers fair and foul: John Ruskin and   29
                            the periodical press

Ann P. Robson and   3   'Impetuous eagerness': the young   59
John M. Robson   Mill's radical journalism

Helene E. Roberts   4   Exhibition and review: the periodical   79
                            press and the Victorian art exhibition
                            system

John Woolford   5   Periodicals and the practice of literary   109
                            criticism, 1855–64

PART TWO: MANAGEMENT AND MONEY

Joanne Shattock   6   Problems of parentage: the North   145
                            British Review and the Free Church of
                            Scotland

Sheila Rosenberg   7   The financing of radical opinion: John   167
                            Chapman and the Westminster Review

Maurice Milne   8   Survival of the fittest? Sunderland   193
                            newspapers in the nineteenth century

Scott Bennett   9   Revolutions in thought: serial   225
                            publication and the mass market for
                            reading

PART THREE: THE NEW
READERSHIP

Brian Harrison   10   Press and pressure group in modern   261
                        Britain

Aled Jones   11   Workmen's advocates: ideology and   297
                        class in a mid-Victorian labour
                        newspaper system

Donald J. Gray   12   Early Victorian scandalous journalism: 317
                        Renton Nicholson's *The Town*
                        (1837–42)

Louis James   13   The trouble with Betsy: periodicals and   349
                        the common reader in
                        mid-nineteenth-century England

Michael Wolff   14   *The British Controversialist and*   367
                        Impartial Inquirer, 1850–72: a pearl
                        from the golden stream

                        Index   393

List of illustrations

BETWEEN PAGES 142 AND 143

Plate 1. The Great Room of the Royal Academy, 1843

Plate 2. Portraits in the Great Room of the Royal Academy, 1845

Plate 3. The Grosvenor Gallery, 1877

Plate 4. The 'Patent Penny Knowledge Mill': cartoon from *McLean's Monthly Sheet of Caricatures*, 1 October 1832

Plate 5. Title page of the Monthly Supplement of the *Penny Magazine*, II (1833)

Plate 6. Title page of the *London Temperance Intelligencer*, 31 December 1836

Plate 7. 'The Man about Town', from *The Town*, 3 June 1837

Plate 8. Masthead of *The Town*, 2 June 1838

Plate 9. Title page of Joseph Livesey's *The Struggle*, no. 7 (1842)

Plate 10. Title page of the *London Journal*, 29 April 1848

Plate 11. Title page of the *Band of Hope Review*, January 1851

Plate 12. Title page of *Bow Bells*, 6 April 1864

Plate 13. Title page of the *Sunderland Daily Echo*, 22 December 1873

Plate 14. Title page of the *Workman's Advocate*, 23 July 1875

List of abbreviations

Note: Places of publication are given only for works published outside the United Kingdom. In abbreviating titles of periodicals, the commonly accepted usage of, e.g., *J.* for *Journal*, *Mag.* for *Magazine*, *Rev.* for *Review* etc, has been adopted. Other abbreviations are listed below.

BL	British Library
Blackwood's	*Blackwood's Edinburgh Magazine*
Bod.	Bodleian Library
Chambers's	*Chambers's Edinburgh Journal*
ILN	*Illustrated London News*
PRO	Public Record Office, London
RO	Record Office
VPN	*Victorian Periodicals Newsletter* (now *Victorian Periodicals Review*)
VS	*Victorian Studies*
WI	*The Wellesley Index to Victorian Periodicals, 1824–1900* (Toronto, 1966—)

Notes on the contributors

Scott Bennett is Assistant University Librarian for Collection Management at Northwestern University. He has published on W. D. Howells and textual editing, on nineteenth-century publishing history and on serials bibliography. He is currently working on a biography of Charles Knight and on problems in the bibliographic description of Victorian serials.

Donald Gray teaches English at Indiana University. He has served as Book Review Editor and on the editorial board of *Victorian Studies*, written on Victorian humour and nineteenth-century representations of the city in pictures and print, and edited an anthology of Victorian poetry. He is the editor of *College English*.

Brian Harrison has been Fellow and Tutor in Modern History and Politics at Corpus Christi College, Oxford, since 1967. He has published *Drink and the Victorians. The Temperance Question in England 1815–1872* (1971), *Separate Spheres. The Opposition to Women's Suffrage in Britain* (1978), and several articles on social and political history. He is now studying the history of British women's organizations since the 1840s.

Walter Houghton was a tutor in the Department of History and Literature at Harvard University and later taught English at Wellesley College, where he is Professor Emeritus. His principal work is *The Victorian Frame of Mind, 1830–1870*, (1957). He is the General Editor of *The Wellesley Index to Victorian Periodicals* (1966—) and is also writing a book to be called 'Matthew Arnold's *Culture and Anarchy:* an Essay on Reading the Text'.

Louis James is Reader in Victorian and Modern Literature, University of Kent at Canterbury. His books include *Fiction for the Working Man* (1963), *Print and the People* (1976) and *Jean Rhys* (1979). He is particularly interested in literature as it relates to society, and is engaged in writing a social history of the early Victorian novel.

Aled Jones teaches history in the University College of Wales, Aberystwyth.

A graduate of the University of York and the Centre for the Study of Social History, University of Warwick, he is currently working on a doctoral thesis on mid-Victorian provincial working-class journalism in England and Wales.

Brian Maidment teaches English at Manchester Polytechnic. He has published a number of essays on Ruskin, Victorian publishing, and nineteenth-century popular literature. He is completing a study of popular fiction, publishing, and social concern in the 1860s.

Maurice Milne is a senior lecturer in the School of English and History at Newcastle Polytechnic. He has published *The Newspapers of Northumberland and Durham* (1971) and a number of articles on provincial newspapers, as well as contributing to the *Dictionary of Labour Biography*. He is at present working on a study of *Blackwood's Magazine*.

Helene E. Roberts, the Curator of Visual Collections in the Fine Arts Library, Fogg Art Museum, Harvard University, has compiled bibliographies of English and American eighteenth- and nineteenth-century art periodicals and is the author of articles on Victorian art and art criticism.

Ann P. Robson, Associate Professor of History, University of Toronto, is co-editing, with Francis E. Mineka, the newspaper writings for the *Collected Works of J. S. Mill*. She has published articles on Victorian social history.

John M. Robson, Professor of English, Victoria College, University of Toronto, is General and Textual Editor of the *Collected Works of J. S. Mill*. Author of *The Improvement of Mankind: The Social and Political Thought of J. S. Mill* (1968), he has published extensively on Victorian prose.

Sheila Rosenberg is a part-time tutor for the Department of Extra-Mural Studies, University of London. She has edited, with Henry Rosenberg, the section on 'Newspapers and Magazines' in the *New Cambridge Bibliography of English Literature*, III (1969), and is an editorial advisor to the *Wellesley Index to Victorian Periodicals*.

Joanne Shattock is the Bibliographer at the Victorian Studies Centre, University of Leicester. She has contributed to the *Wellesley Index to Victorian Periodicals*, and to *Victorian Periodicals: a Guide to Research* (1978), and has published articles on Victorian quarterlies, literary reviewing, piracy and nineteenth-century publishing.

Michael Wolff is Professor of English at the University of Massachusetts at Amherst. He was a founding co-editor of *Victorian Studies*, the founding president of the Research Society for Victorian Periodicals, and the founding editor of the *Victorian Periodicals Review*. His books include, with P. Appleman and W. Madden, *1859: Entering an Age of Crisis* (1959); with H. J. Dyos, *The Victorian City: Images and Realities* (1973), and with John North and Dorothy Deering, *The Waterloo Directory of Victorian Periodicals* (1976).

John Woolford is a lecturer in English at King's College, London, and formerly Research Fellow, King's College, Cambridge, and Fellow and Director of Studies in English, Fitzwilliam College, Cambridge. He has edited (with D. R. Karlin) the forthcoming edition of the poems of Browning in the *Longman's Annotated* series and is the editor of the *London Browning Society Notes*.

Introduction

Nobody who reads about or studies Victorian Britain nowadays needs to be reminded of the importance and inescapability of the Victorian periodical press. There is surely no monograph or scholarly article, scarcely a popular biography or general history which does not refer to or cite some portion of the tens of thousands of newspapers and magazines which constituted that press and which were, in effect, the first of the mass media.

Nevertheless the systematic and general study of that press has hardly begun. We have had a series of treatments of individual papers and editors; *The Times* and the more famous reviews and magazines are consistently used to provide documentation; the reputations of major authors are being traced through the press; innovative indexing and the identification of anonymous contributors for some of the best known journals of opinion has proceeded apace; scholars writing about particular movements in Victorian politics or literature or crucial episodes in Victorian science or religion search out the periodicals most relevant to their topic. Examples of this sort are innumerable. Yet, for the press as a whole, we appear to have little choice except to be satisfied with a casual or glancing knowledge, believing that anything broader or deeper or more systematic is beyond the bounds of reasonable humanistic ambition.

The sheer bulk and range of the Victorian press seem to make it so unwieldy as to defy systematic and general study. Given the inadequacy of most existing reference works, the uncertainties of cataloguing, and that vague but all-too-familiar feeling that there are literally millions of serial articles out there whose allure we dare not admit, we can barely grasp the dimensions of the subject, let alone come to grips with its content. And yet, despite what prudence and common sense would tell us, a case can be made that the very impenetrability of the Victorian press requires of us that we attempt a systematic and general study. Perhaps we are not yet ready to deal with the press in general because we are still so busy exploring its specifics. Perhaps the trees prevent us from seeing the forest. But perhaps also, although we know a few of the most interesting trees and are aware of thousands of others, we do not really believe there is a forest, just a gathering of trees.

Not that the most interesting trees are not worth our sustained attention. We must, of course, continue to study that part of the press which was the forum, the arena, the pulpit and the stage of the most extraordinary writers of the time, from those with the greatest literary gifts to the honourable rank and file of expert journalism, both the enthusiastic amateur and the skilled professional. All these men and women of letters, sages, polemicists, educators, wrote in quite unprecedented quantity for each other and for their publics on every conceivable topic and from every conceivable point of view. What in particular might be called the 'opinion-forming' press reached an equally extraordinary audience which was in turn critical, articulate, influential, and, at least for most of the reign, homogeneous to a degree scarcely recognizable in its late-twentieth-century counterpart.

But the emerging need for a more general study of the press is part of the same historiographical development that calls us to the more general study of Victorian life, to the recognition of a great many more or less hidden lives which have until recently escaped the close attention of the historian and the litterateur. In the same way, the Victorian press, seen as a whole, is more than a collective term for those magazines to which our interest in particular figures and particular topics draws us. It is worth study in its own right because it represents and articulates, as nothing else does, what was ordinary about Victorian Britain, and we cannot understand Victorian Britain without understanding the ordinary, which is, moreover, also the environment of the extraordinary.

We need therefore to know much more than we do about Carlyle's and Feargus O'Connor's and Gladstone's and Florence Nightingale's neighbours, not only because they were also Victorians, but, because without some better sense of who they were, we have to settle for a needlessly partial and unbalanced view of the well-known figures. That means that we need to know much more about Charles Knight, John Chapman, G. W. M. Reynolds, Alexander Campbell Fraser, Samuel Storey, William Owen, Renton Nicholson (to name only 'minor' figures prominent in our chapters), not just as individual proprietors or editors but as representative of those thousands of people who put together the new reading material of the first modern society.

We are familiar with Victorian Britain as the first urbanizing society. Journalism is the verbal equivalent of urbanism and Victorian Britain was also the first 'journalizing' society. The first generations of city-dwellers were also the first generations of newspaper readers. The mass media, however carefully some Victorians tried to insulate themselves, are the inescapable ideological and subliminal environment of the modern world. The press, in all its manifestations, became during the Victorian period the context within which people lived and worked and thought, and from which they derived their (in most cases quite new) sense of the outside world.

The Victorians themselves were more aware of this change and of its irreversible importance than are we for whom it has the dimness of habitude. They were constantly exclaiming, whether with pleasure or regret, at the difference that the press made in their lives. The following quotation illustrates both this sentiment and (because it was stumbled on by one of the editors of this book just as this Introduction was to be written) the serendipity of working with Victorian journalism.

> The future of the press has induced men of enlightened minds to contemplate a general absorption of intellectual power in its columns, and that the periodical will supersede the well printed volume is illustrative of our increasing intellectual development. . . . This is certainly within the range of probability, as there are but few subjects of a practical character which cannot be treated in the columns of a newspaper, even more effectually than in the expanded form of a heavy volume, and even subjects requiring deep research are capable of ventilation more readily than by any other means. Take as an illustration any subject on practical husbandry. Let the result of a well tested experiment be published in our 'Monthly Agricultural Supplement' and in a few days it will engage the attention of 10,000 or even 70,000 practical farmers whose personal knowledge will be compared with that of the writer, and at once the merit of the article in question is determined, and the store of public knowledge increased. If of value it will obtain in a few days a reputation which it might never have received.

Thus on 16 January 1866 the twice-weekly *Sussex Agricultural Express, Surrey Standard, Weald of Kent Mail and County Advertiser* announced its intention to add a monthly supplement. Periodical and especially newspaper publication had by that time clearly attained an almost commonplace significance whereby practical men could address one another on practical subjects with speedy and reliable results. The opinions expressed are neither mandarin nor radical; the prose is undistinguished, even clumsy. If the quotation appeals to us it is for its sheer ordinariness. What it takes for granted in a middle-brow, middle-class, John Bullish way is that the press made sense, that it was useful and efficient, that it was available to bring anything within reach of anyone, that it had become an essential and powerful element in everyday life.

The idea for this book came in the autumn of 1976 during a conference on

Victorian periodicals organized by the Victorian Studies Centre at Leicester University. Michael Wolff, chairman of the conference, and Joanne Shattock, of the Victorian Studies Centre, agreed that the time was ripe for a volume on the Victorian periodical press. Having received encouragement from Leicester University Press, we found ourselves both excited and nervous about the project. On the one hand we were sure that if anything the book was overdue; on the other we were apprehensive of the state of the subject. The Research Society for Victorian Periodicals had been founded in 1968 and with it the *Victorian Periodicals Newsletter* (now the *Victorian Periodicals Review*). The *Wellesley Index to Victorian Periodicals* had since 1966 been opening up the major periodicals to scholars by identifying authorship. The resulting research had shown how fruitful the subject was, but also how daunting.

We knew that ideally what was wanted was a history of the Victorian press embracing all its constituent parts from the newspapers – London and provincial, daily, weekly and Sunday – through the literary journals – monthlies, quarterlies and weeklies – to the more specialized areas like children's periodicals, women's magazines, the labour press, comic publications. We also knew that given the present state of research this was simply not possible. The task was too vast and the amount of groundwork left to be done too great for such a comprehensive history to see the light of day in the foreseeable future. It was a project for the next decade, and it was the work of several volumes, not one.

After some discussion we decided that if such a history was not possible the best alternative was a series of original essays by scholars currently doing research on various aspects of the subject, each of which might act as a kind of model for other studies which could be undertaken on similar material. Hence the 'samplings' and 'soundings' of our title.

We also knew that if we were to demonstrate the importance of the periodical press to an understanding of the Victorian period we needed to engage the help not only of those who were doing research on aspects of the press itself but also of historians and students of literature and fine art who were making use of periodicals in their work. Our aim was to be as wide-ranging as possible, to be both specialist and yet deliberately non-specialist.

The present table of contents is the result. Apart from the essay by Walter Houghton, all the chapters have been written expressly for this book. Houghton's essay is a revised and expanded version of one published in the Summer 1979 issue of *Victorian Studies*.

We make no pretence to inclusiveness. Indeed we are all too aware of omissions. We would have liked a chapter on illustrations in the periodical press, one on the technical aspects of periodical production, one on the way the press influenced or reflected major issues of the day such as foreign policy, one on the women's press – the list could be extended indefinitely. Perhaps these or similar chapters might one day form the contents of a second volume. Nor have we been particularly strict in our chronological definition of 'Victorian'. At least one contributor stretches forward into the twentieth century, arguing that the history of the press is not naturally a nineteenth-century or Victorian subject but that it extends beyond that period at both ends. Most of the chapters, however, deal with one or more decades, ranging from the 1820s and early 1830s, technically pre-Victorian, through to the 1890s, with the bulk of concentration on the five central decades of the 1830s to the 1870s.

The chapters fall nicely into three sections. Part One, which we have sub-titled 'The Critic as Journalist', deals with the rich and complex interaction of the periodical press and the major literary and intellectual figures of the period. Walter Houghton writes of the heavyweight literary periodicals and shows how they had become the natural medium of publication for these major figures, a genre in their own right, and a collective mirror of the conflicting and converging views of the Victorian 'clerisy'. Brian Maidment describes how Ruskin audaciously substituted for the orthodoxy of volume format the greater immediacy of serial publication so as to extend his influence through more direct address. Ann P. Robson and John M. Robson reveal a young and energetic John Stuart Mill also taking advantage of the periodicals, in this case newspapers, to comment on current political events. Helene Roberts demonstrates how art criticism in the periodicals had become a vital element in the workings of the Victorian art world. John Woolford traces and explains quite sudden and important shifts in poetics and the criticism of poetry which were registered in the pages of mid-Victorian magazines and reviews.

Part Two, 'Management and Money', is concerned with the production and day-to-day operation of the periodical press. Joanne Shattock uses the sectarian press to illustrate the complexities of the actual control of periodicals, of the relative influence of proprietor, editor and sponsor. Sheila Rosenberg's chapter shows the energy, ingenuity and pertinacity necessary to maintain an influential but heterodox journal – in this case the *Westminster Review* – despite consistent unprofitability and internal discord. Maurice Milne discloses the essential links between politics and the birth, survival and death of provincial newspapers. Scott Bennett's study of the early years of the Society for the Diffusion of Useful Knowledge deals with the opportunites and problems of a pioneering effort to create and reach a mass readership.

Part Three, 'The New Readership', takes some particular instances of this readership and discusses ways in which journalism was important both to the readers and to those who wished to influence them. Brian Harrison explores the complicated relationship between the press and reform movements generally and examines the use of the press by a variety of pressure groups in the Victorian and Edwardian periods. Aled Jones reveals a hitherto unknown activity of the labour press of the 1870s, the transformation of local trades union news-sheets into an impressive though shortlived network of labour newspapers. Donald J. Gray writes of 'fast' or scandalous journalism and its extraordinary popularity in the 1830s and 1840s, and places it in a journalistic tradition which stretched from the Regency through to the end of the nineteenth century. Louis James looks at some of the periodicals available to a particular readership, in this case female domestic servants, and speculates on the impact of the physical quality of periodicals both on the contemporary reader and on the historian of the press. Michael Wolff describes a particular periodical as a representative of the thousands of hitherto unexamined titles and also as a unique forum for the articulation of one strand of mid-Victorian opinion.

These 14 'samplings' and 'soundings' are precisely that – 14 explorations of particular kinds of periodicals, their readerships, their impact, their contents, the problems of conducting them. Yet diverse as the subjects and the approaches are, certain common ideas and themes emerge. Scott Bennett and Walter Houghton, from either end of the spectrum, deal with the 'revolution' brought about by periodicals. As Houghton suggests, periodicals displaced books and at the same time created them. For Bennett the economics of mass serialization made it possible to reach an entirely new section of the population, an audience which previously would not have been dreamed of. Louis James adds to this picture of the impact of the press by his speculations on the physical qualities of the periodical as opposed to the book, qualities which carefully and even subconsciously determined the attitudes to these periodicals.

Maurice Milne and Scott Bennett both underline the importance of the mass market for the survival of certain periodicals. Michael Wolff, Louis James and Scott Bennett each deal, at different periods, with the periodical as an instrument of instruction. Aled Jones and Brian Harrison are concerned with a branch of the press which among other things articulated working-class feelings which had hitherto been unexpressed. Harrison, Jones and Milne all underline the close links between politics and the newspaper press. Louis James and Donald J. Gray both explore the subculture created by the Victorian press and illustrate the uses the study of such a subculture has for students of the period.

Walter Houghton, Joanne Shattock and Brian Harrison shed light on the curious chemistry of periodicals which are organs of particular groups.

Sheila Rosenberg and Joanne Shattock emphasize the extraordinary precariousness of the finances of major quarterlies, and of the important role of the proprietor, points which are echoed in Milne's discussion of the proprietors and finances of provincial newspapers.

Brian Maidment and Ann P. Robson and John M. Robson present a major literary figure, known for solid publications in volume form, who turns to the periodical press to meet a particular need at an important point in his career. Helene Roberts and John Woolford demonstrate the periodical press as the medium for the emergence of critical theory – a testimony to the formative influence and creativity of this press.

We hope that these 14 'case-studies' collectively and individually will point the way to further research. In some respects they represent a milestone, a concrete testimony to the enormous strides which have been taken in research on Victorian periodicals over the last 20 years. And yet, if they are a milestone, it is of a very early stage in the journey. There is still a very long way to go.

August 1980

Joanne Shattock
Michael Wolff

Part One

THE CRITIC AS JOURNALIST

Walter E. Houghton   Periodical literature
and the articulate
classes[1]

Looking back in 1896 on the literary history of the century, George Saintsbury thought that 'perhaps there is no single feature . . . not even the
enormous popularization and multiplication of the novel, which is so distinctive and characteristic as the development in it of periodical literature.'[2]
It is a measure of its subsequent decline, in quality and quantity, that these
and similar statements still seem rather surprising. Only recently have we
come to realize that the Victorians published not only over 25,000 journals of
all kinds including newspapers, but also – at a guess – several hundred
reviews, magazines, and weeklies that could claim to be 'literature' because
they published literary genres (fiction, poetry, familiar essays) and critical
and historical papers in which the form of expression was an integral
element, in which the thought was experienced, crudely or subtly. This
periodical literature was addressed, at one level, to the common reader, and
at another to 'the articulate classes, whose writing and conversation make
opinion'.[3] Those periodicals devoted to the serious discussion of ideas in all
fields of knowledge or to a good grade of entertainment commanded an
influence and prestige without parallel, earlier or later.[4] Even a short list of
contributors bears this out: Gladstone and Disraeli, J. H. Newman and
Cardinal Manning, both The Mills, Sir Charles Lyell and T. H. Huxley,
historians like Macaulay and Lord Acton, the economists McCulloch,
Jevons and Nassau Senior, Carlyle, Matthew Arnold, Leslie Stephen
and Walter Pater, all the major novelists, generals and captains in the
army and navy, diplomats, judges, bishops, travellers – Layard, Richard
Burton, and the African explorers Samuel Baker and John Speke. To imagine
a similar array of our own outstanding contemporaries writing for our few
general periodicals is laughable. How did it happen? What conditions of the
time made it not only possible but essential? What did it do for the Victorians, both readers and writers? To provide all the answers would require a
monograph. I have therefore focussed on the 1850s and 1860s, adopted an
essay by Bagehot (1855) and another by Arnold (1864) as central texts, and
glanced before and after.[5]

1. SOME FERTILE GROUNDS

To begin with, there was a growing middle class, born of the Industrial Revolution and coming of age with the 1832 reform bill, that was eager to acquire the education that it lacked. John Morley explained the popularity of Macaulay's *Essays*, first published in 1843 and often reprinted:

> Macaulay came upon the world of letters just as the middle classes were expanding into enormous prosperity, were vastly increasing in numbers, and were becoming more alive than they had ever been before to literary interests. His Essays are as good as a library: they make an incomparable manual and vademecum for a busy uneducated man, who has curiosity and enlightenment enough to wish to know a little about the great lives and great thoughts, the shining words and many-coloured complexities of action, that have marked the journey of man through the ages.[6]

And if curiosity was lacking, the political standing and social opportunities of the new captains of industry suggested the importance of at least a veneer of culture.

But to know the past was scarcely enough in an age of increasing knowledge in all fields of learning. Educated and would-be-educated alike wanted accounts of new or rapidly developing subjects like geology, political economy, biblical criticism, anthropology, and sociology. They needed to be told what was meant by Benthamism, Puseyism, positivism, evolution; and to know what might be their political, moral, and religious implications. In the parallel area of action, a succession of radical and difficult problems – catholic emancipation, reform bills, poor laws, corn laws, factory acts, chartism, the Crimea, home rule – provoked wide discussion.

But to discuss was to question, and to question, in an age when traditional thought was being challenged by new ideas and traditional institutions transformed, was to threaten the very convictions and social foundations on which life had been built. What was said of the 1850s and 1860s applies to the entire period, though with greater intensity and wider repercussions as the years passed: 'It was the age of science, new knowledge, searching criticism, followed by multiplied doubts and shaken beliefs.'[7] Especially in religion. The alternatives were baffling: Is true religion Christianity or theism? And what is Christianity? Roman catholicism or protestantism? And if protestantism, is it anglicanism or dissent? And if one or the other, which kind? High church? Low church? Broad church? Congregationalism? Unitarianism? And if unitarianism, orthodox or liberal? Above all, is it possible to reconcile science and religion? Similar questions invaded ethical theory and the very conception of man, the son of God – or a descendant of the apes? Perhaps a human automaton. We see why doubt, whether intellectual or political, was so painful to the Victorians: they experienced the collapse of their childhood certitudes, with the result, as early as 1838, that the age was 'at once destitute of faith and terrified at scepticism'.[8] We can hear the agonized cry for reassurance, or for something – anything – one could cling to.[9]

2. THE GROWTH OF THE REVIEWS – AND REVIEWERS

These are the basic needs that were answered by scores of books and many thousands of articles. They underlie the central statement that Walter Bagehot made in the *National Review* for October 1855:

> It is indeed a peculiarity of our times, that we must instruct so many persons. On politics, on religion, on all less important topics still more, every one thinks himself competent to think, – in some casual manner does think, – to the best of our means must be taught to think – rightly. Even if we had a profound and far-seeing statesman, his deep ideas and long-reaching vision would be useless to us, unless we could impart a confidence in them to the mass of influential persons, to the unelected Commons, the unchosen Council, who assist at the deliberations of the nation. In religion the appeal now is not to the technicalities of scholars, or the fiction of recluse schoolmen, but to the deep feelings, the sure sentiments, the painful strivings of all who think and hope. And this appeal to the many necessarily brings with it a consequence. We must speak to the many so that they will listen – that they will like to listen – that they will understand. It is of no use addressing them with the forms of science, or the rigour of accuracy, or the tedium of exhaustive discussion. The multitude are impatient of system, desirous of brevity, puzzled by formality.

There follows a contrast between the books of a more laborious age, treatises of scholars 'analysing all difficulties, discussing all doubts,' and those of our modern age written by educated men of the world, 'exhausting nothing, yet really suggesting the lessons of a wider experience', on to the explicit conclusion: 'In this transition from ancient writing to modern, the review-like essay and the essay-like review fill a large space.'[10]

The double terminology should be noted. They are the two forms of 'the essay-like criticism of modern times . . . The *Edinburgh Review*, which began the system,' became a model that affected the whole development of the Victorian 'review', including the *National Review,* including this very article. There the focus was first shifted, partially or entirely, from the book itself to what the book suggested. In place or critical examination, the 'review' might become a series of observations woven into an essay that is illustrated, here and there, by reference to the text, of that combines currents of thought drawn from one passage or another. In either case, there is a movement out and in, away from the book and back to it. This is the typical essay-like review. Bagehot's own paper is quite different. At its head stand the titles one might think he was to deal with: *A Memoir of the Rev. Sydney Smith, Lord Jeffrey's Contributions to the 'Edinburgh Review', Lord Brougham's Collected Works,* vols. I, II, III, and *The Rev. Sydney Smith's Miscellaneous Works.* The first half of the paper, however, is on Reviews, Lord Eldon, Conservative scepticism, and Whiggery; then, when at last the first *Edinburgh* reviewers are reached, Bagehot devotes the remainder of the article to the temperaments of Francis Horner, Francis Jeffrey, and Sydney Smith. The books are not so much as mentioned. This is the review-like essay. To the best of my memory, none of the 'reviews' of Stanley's *Life of Thomas Arnold* ever discussed it as a biography; it was simply a point of departure from which to consider Arnold's ideas on religion and education, with some quotations from the letters.

From here it is only a step to an out-and-out essay, standing alone. This was first taken, apparently, in the fall of 1833 when Mill and J. A. Roebuck determined that the new *London Review* should discard 'the lie of pretending that all the articles are *reviews,* when more than half of them are not',[11] with the result that the opening issue (April 1835) contained three articles and seven essay-like reviews; the second, six of each; and so on, combining both, through the April 1837 number of the *London and Westminster,* after which the reviews regained their dominance. The experiment was premature. In the early 1860s eight articles appeared in Bagehot's own *National Review,* two of them by Arnold: 'Joubert: a French Coleridge' (January 1864) and 'The functions [*sic*] of criticism at the present time' (November 1864). Three years later (July 1867) another article slipped into the *Westminster,* followed by more and more, leading eventually, when the journal became a monthly in 1887, to an all-article review. In the meanwhile, the three great reviews of the later century established the pattern. The *Contemporary,* beginning in 1866 without articles, in 1868 (vol. VIII) carried 18 out of a total of 30 papers, and in 1875 (vol. XXVI), 45 out of 48. From the start (1865), the *Fortnightly* published only about three or four essay-like reviews every six months, and very few at all once Frank Harris became editor in July 1886. The *Nineteenth Century* (1877) contained almost nothing but essays. In addition to Mill's argument, I imagine that the article, untied to any book, offered authors a freer choice of subject and editors more variety. If anyone felt like writing on Handel or the cost of elections, he could do so without having to have a book to hang it on, or discuss Pascal's *Provincial Letters* without a new edition. Also, subjects of immediate concern, like 'Progress of events in Canada', could be handled at once.[12]

Reviews in the strict sense of the term, however, continued to appear throughout the period, especially of abstruse publications like *The Origin of Species* which demanded exposition and argument; or reviews that were essentially descriptive, using extensive extracts, notably in the *Eclectic Review*, 1824–*c*.1840. (Founded in 1804, the *Eclectic* was too young to appreciate the *Edinburgh*'s break with the eighteenth-century tradition.) And a section containing brief notices of recent books was almost standard. Nevertheless, the Victorian reviews consisted largely of essay-like criticism and of articles.

Bagehot's 'multitude', we notice, is 'the mass of influential persons', which would cover the ministries, the London clubs, the country houses and country rectories, the town councils and holders of the suffrage in the boroughs and counties, the universities, the Bench and Bar, the leaders of industry, the chiefs of political parties; to which may be added members of parliament, who sometimes quoted the reviews.[13] Indeed, Bagehot includes even all who think about intellectual matters, however casually. How large was this group? A few years later, in 1860, the estimated circulation figures are unexpectedly small: The *Edinburgh Review* 7,000; the *Quarterly Review* 8,000; the *Westminster* 4,000; the *North British* 2,000; *Blackwood's Magazine* 10,000; *Fraser's* 8,000; and Bagehot's *National Review*, 1,000.[14] Of course, there is a great difference between circulation and readership. Every member of the Carlton Club who was not himself a subscriber read the club's copy of the *Quarterly*; many of the middle class used the circulating libraries; the ambitious artisans took turns at the Mechanics' Institutes. Nevertheless, when all allowance is made, we have to realize that Bagehot's 'multitude' – as it seemed in comparison with eighteenth-century readers – was a small minority even of the literate; small, but important – and confused.

These '*we* must instruct'. The sense of obligation was a central strand of Victorian earnestness, reinforced by the contemporary crisis.[15] On no account was the writer to live a selfish life of aesthetic pleasure; it was his moral duty to meet the intellectual needs of the time. With earnest solemnity John Morley spoke of the contributors to the *Fortnightly* as being entrusted with nothing less than the 'momentous task of forming national opinion'.[16] With the *Edinburgh* in mind, Bagehot reiterated the sense of mission: 'The modern man must be told what to think – shortly, no doubt, but he *must* be told it.'[17]

The needs were various. To keep abreast of the expanding development in many areas of learning, even the educated person – even a graduate of the universities where the formal studies were limited to the classics and mathematics until well on in the century – could profit from the range of material found in the reviews. In *The Idea of a University* (1852), Newman defended 'that superficial acquaintance with chemistry, and geology, and astronomy, and political economy, and modern history, and biography, and other branches of knowledge, which periodical literature and occasional lectures . . . diffuse through the community,' as 'a graceful accomplishment, and a suitable, nay, in this day a necessary accomplishment, in the case of educated men'.[18] Newman seems to be thinking of gentlemen. The 'multitude' who were not educated and cared little about graceful accomplishments would never have gained a glimpse of the range of human thought without the periodicals. In 'Reviews and reviewers', in the *Literary Gazette* for May 1860, a critic claimed that many who would have 'read nothing beyond a trashy novel or political journal . . . may now . . . become fairly acquainted with the leading subjects in science and general literature; and though review-reading will never produce a scholar . . . it may make an intelligent and well-informed man.'[19] At a lower level there was the necessity, under pressure of novel theories and rival interpretations, of having an opinion on scores of contemporary questions. Not to do so was shameful; for anyone who was a person of importance, or professed to be (that is, any member of the middle class), ought to know what he thought about the Oxford Movement, or Mesmerism, or Victor Hugo. But to think is never easy. Newman drew the deduction: 'Hence the extreme influence of periodical publications at this day [1850], quarterly, monthly, or daily; these teach the multitude of men what to think and what to say.'[20]

Though he may not have mentioned it, Bagehot had suggested that those who considered themselves competent to think, and perhaps did so casually, must be taught to think. They must be shaken out of the 'stock notions and habits' they 'now follow staunchly but mechanically' by the challenge of fresh ideas they never dreamed of in heaven or earth, like the abolition of capital punishment or the decline of marriage; or by the defence of ideas they thought indefensible, like democracy, socialism, or agnosticism. In short, readers must be made to use their minds, if only feebly. The *Edinburgh Review*, wrote Lord Cockburn, 'taught the public to think. It opened the people's eyes.'[21]

Bagehot, however, added one more word: the public 'must be taught to think – rightly'. They must be told the truth. The assumption of an élite with supreme insight and therefore of the authority that went with it was nearly as Victorian as earnestness and was readily accepted – welcomed – by readers genuinely eager for education, guidance, and the resolution of doubt.[22] The writer, in an age when the clergy no longer spoke with the old credibility, became a priest or prophet. Two things seemed very plain to Carlyle in 1842: 'first, that there is at present no preaching in England, and a visibly growing appetite (the sternest *necessity* there has long been) to have some: and second, that the Printing Press is the only, or by far the chief, Pulpit in these days'; and he proceeds to wonder if it were possible for authors to unite and publish some 'Magazine, Review or Periodical Publication' of their own, 'and so preach nothing but the sound word'.[23] Arnold spoke more soberly but with equal confidence. His dictum that it was the business of criticism, 'in all branches of knowledge, theology, philosophy, history, art, science . . . to establish an order of ideas, if not absolutely true, yet true by comparison with that which it displaces; to make the best ideas prevail', is simply Bagehot's commitment to teach the right ideas, right for our time, and Carlyle's to preach the sound word.[24] In a passage of *Culture and Anarchy* the men of culture are the critics: 'The great men of culture are those . . . who have laboured to divest knowledge of all that was harsh, uncouth, difficult, abstract, professional, exclusive; to humanize it, to make it efficient outside the clique of the cultivated and learned, yet still remaining the *best* knowledge and thought of the time.'[25] Think of Acton, Bagehot, Carlyle, Huxley, James Martineau, Mill, John Morley, Mark Pattison, Fitzjames and Leslie Stephen, G. S. Venables, and Arnold himself, to name only some extensive contributors to the reviews. Many writers of like calibre – George Eliot, George Grote, Frederick Pollock, and others cited in my initial list – contributed less often. Though by no means agreeing at every point, these critics as a group may be said to represent the best thought of the age. What Gertrude Himmelfarb wrote of Mill's essays after the death of his father could be said of theirs: 'They are that peculiar amalgam of philosophy, history, politics, and sociology that was the distinctive quality of the English essay in the age of the great Reviews. They are the product of a lively, cultivated, interested, and engaged mind, in which all the resources of thought are brought to bear upon any subject, and in which any subject may be made to bear the burden of truth.'[26] In this light, to talk of instruction or guidance is to belittle the periodical achievement. It conferred, in addition, 'that large-mindedness and general breadth of view which are so constantly found missing in deeply-read theologians, in erudite philologists, and profound philosophers'.[27] It was not possible, of course, that a great body of articles could attain such distinction. In many cases no doubt, a bright young man from the University dashed off a review by throwing together social conversation and a little reading without pausing to reflect. But the very fact that people like those just named were writing for the periodicals was a persuasive invitation to lesser minds to do likewise, so that the average level of serious writing was remarkably good, especially in the later century when increased knowledge raised the quality of performance.[28]

The critic, conceived in ideal terms, had to possess a broad education in the 'great books' of the past and a continuing grasp of the latest thinking, both at home and abroad; he had to have first-hand acquaintance with contemporary events and social opinion; he had to think for himself before he could tell others what to think – and he had to think disinterestedly, free from the distortions of practical, party, or personal considerations. Thinking meant deciding, in the light of all that he knew, by reason and intuition, what seemed closest to the truth, and on that basis judging the subject of his essay, whether book or man, theory or movement. But

> the judgment which almost insensibly forms itself in a fair and clear mind, along with fresh knowledge, is the valuable one; and thus knowledge, and ever fresh knowledge, must be the critic's great concern for himself. And it is by communicating fresh knowledge, and letting his own judgment pass along with it, – but insensibly, and in the second place, not the first, as a sort of companion and clue, not as an abstract lawgiver, – that the critic will generally do most good to his readers.

All this is Arnold.[29] In other phrasing it could be Bagehot or Mill or the early Carlyle, for they too wrote in this spirit. So, to a lesser degree, did hundreds of critics who contributed to the Victorian reviews.

3. SECTARIANISM

It might be argued that the sectarian organization of the reviews made the necessary detachment for writing of high calibre scarcely possible. Certainly the party spirit that created most of them was only too likely to destroy the disinterested mind, or at least to colour its thinking. Arnold was well aware of the enemy: 'We have the *Quarterly Review*, existing as an organ of the Tories, and for as much play of mind as may suit its being that; we have the *British Quarterly Review*, existing as an organ of the political Dissenters, and for as much play of mind as may suit its being that . . . And so on through all the various fractions [*sic*], political and religious, of our society.' But the conclusion seems to deny, or at least ignore, any free play of mind at all: 'It must needs be that men should act in sects and parties, that each of these sects and parties should have its organ, and should make this organ subserve the interests of its action; but it would be well, too, that there should be a criticism, not the minister of these interests, not their enemy, but absolutely and entirely independent of them.'[30]

Apart from the fact that there had already been some periodicals without party affiliation, there was more free play of mind, more currents of independent thought, in the sectarian journals than Arnold implies. Consider two numbers of the *Quarterly* and the *British Quarterly* that just preceded the publication of Arnold's 'Function' in November 1864.

The Quarterly Review, July 1864
1 *Words and places* [or, *Etymological illustrations of history,
ethnology and geography*, by Isaac Taylor]
2 Ludwig Uhland
3 Free thinking – its history and tendencies [on the Essayists and
Reviewers as descendants of Locke and the deists]
4 The Circassian exodus [to Turkey]
5 Lacordaire
6 Christian art
7 Public schools
8 Travelling in England
9 The House of Commons

No. 9, of course, is the Conservative political article that normally closed each issue; no. 3 ends with a rejection of *Essays and Reviews* and an affirmation of the traditional doctrines of the Church of England. But nowhere else is there any sign of bias. Indeed, no. 2 supports the political liberalism of Uhland and no. 5 defends and praises the liberal catholicism of Lacordaire and Montalembert. As a matter of fact, the authors of nos. 1, 2, 6, 7, and 8 also wrote for the rival *Edinburgh* (see the *Wellesley Index*).

The British Quarterly Review, October 1864
1 William the Conqueror
2 Hansell's *Greek Testament*
3 *The Dolomite mountains*
4 Chevalier's *Mexico*
5 Our foreign policy
6 Charles Knight's *Personal Recollections*
7 Mind and brain
8 Tennyson's poetry
9 Projected reforms in Germany
10 Epilogue on affairs

No. 2 is a scholarly piece of biblical interpretation with a mild criticism of Dean Henry Alford, which is offset by quotations from the Anglican *Record*. No. 8 is plainly hostile to Tennyson on religious, social, and aesthetic grounds: his 'muscular divinity' and 'perfumed morality' are addressed only to the 'high bred'. No. 10 is the party line. But the other seven reviews are entirely free of nonconformist attitudes, and for no. 5 the editor (Robert Vaughan), though not himself in complete agreement, has allowed the writer 'full liberty of utterance'.

These two examples, chosen because of their date, suggest that it might be more correct to say that the *Quarterly* and the *British Quarterly* exist as organs of free thought, with as much toryism and dissent as their public profession required. But one must add 'at this time'. Earlier in the century the political debate that had its roots in the two revolutions, French and Industrial, was so sharp that sectarianism in the *Edinburgh*, the *Quarterly*, and the *Westminster* was dominant. So too in Tory magazines like *Blackwood's* and early *Fraser's*. And this was especially true of the religious periodicals – the Anglican *British Critic*, the nonconformist *Eclectic Review*, the catholic *Dublin* – as well as of the religious articles in the secular reviews and magazines. Longstanding hostilities, bred of the Reformation and in the eighteenth century by deism and the evangelical revival, were heightened by the desire of each church, or church party, to insist the louder on its own doctrine in the face of growing controversy and doubt.

In the 1830s there were signs of revolt. They began, as we might suppose, at one of the universities, where search for truth and pride of learning might well find the sectarian voice of the periodicals unacceptable. The university was Oxford and the journal the *London Review* of 1829, founded by Nassau Senior, professor of Economics, and Richard Whately, principal of St Alban's Hall, edited by Blanco White of the Oriel common room, and written for the most part (two-thirds of its articles) by Oxonians. In 'Art. I. – *The Times*, the *Morning Chronicle*, &c. &c. *The Edinburgh Review*, *The Quarterly Review*, &c. &c.' with 'Journals and reviews' as running-title, the editor announced that the time had come when 'men of sense and substance' had 'little to gain and much to lose by party squabbles'; when private individuals were 'shy of pledging themselves to any more specific party than their country and their common interests [as men], and adopt no other rule of judgment than the merits of each individual case' (p. 7; also see pp. 8–9). Three years later when W. J. Fox took over the *Monthly Repository*, he began at once to divest it of its unitarian character.[31] Partly under the influence of these two examples[32], J. S. Mill, after his father's death in 1836, was able to do for the *London and Westminster* what he had wished to do for the *London Review* (1835–1836): to get rid of its role as an organ of the old Philosophical Radicals and to open it eventually to everyone who believed in 'political & social improvement'.[33] Moreover, condemning 'all exclusiveness & sectarianism in religion as well as in philosophy', he hoped 'to draw its contributors from persons of every religious belief who hold that belief in a truly catholic spirit.'[34]

But these anti-sectarian beginnings were abortive. In 1840 the *Westminster* under W. E. Hickson returned to its earlier utilitarianism, and the other reviews and magazines continued on their party ways. This means that if we focus on the 1840s when Arnold was beginning his career, we find that what he said in 1864 was then true. Of the eight articles in the *Quarterly* of October 1844 only three are products of a free play of mind; and out of eight in the first issue of the *British Quarterly* (January 1845), only two. Can we account for this striking difference? In 1869 Henry Sidgwick observed that during the last 20 years 'we' have been 'growing year by year . . . more sceptical in the proper sense of the word: we suspend our judgment much more than our predecessors, and much more contentedly: we see that there are many sides to many questions; the opinions that we do hold we hold if not more loosely, at least more at arm's length . . . We are gaining in impartiality and comprehensiveness of sympathy.'[35] Certainly, through this period the *Edinburgh* and the *Westminster* (after Chapman and Marian Evans took over in 1852) lost much of their old partisanship; the *National Review* (1855–64) was more national than unitarian; the *Saturday Review*, beginning in 1856, and its offshoot, *Bentley's Quarterly Review* (1859–60), were frankly non-sectarian; so was Acton's *Home and Foreign Review* (1862–4), followed in 1865 and 1866 by the *Fortnightly* and the *Contemporary*. The *Fortnightly* was founded as 'a platform for the discussion of all questions by the light of pure reason, on lines agreeable to impartial intellect alone'; and though under Morley it became markedly liberal, supporting trade unionism and non-religious teaching in the national schools, this was a change in emphasis, in what Mill had called 'spirit' or 'tone'; not an adhesion to the Liberal Party.[36] A year later (1866) the Dean of Canterbury banished 'all sectarian and class prejudices' from his *Contemporary Review*.[37] By 1877 the *Nineteenth Century* was deliberately printing 'Symposia' in which people were invited to express their contrary opinions. Once this development had occurred, the *raison d'être* of anonymity – that articles represented the position of the review and not that of the individual – was destroyed, and the open platform led to the increasing use of signature. The *Nineteenth Century*, in particular, capitalizing on the 'big name', insisted on every article being signed.

It is ironic that Arnold, generally so sensitive to his time, should have attacked the sectarianism of the reviews just at the moment when the tide had already turned and the *Home and Foreign*, far from being a welcome oddity soon extinguished for violating the custom of fractional journals, as he implies (it was stopped by papal influence for being too liberal), was in fact another sign of an age of free inquiry that soon came to maturity with the *Fortnightly* and the *Contemporary*.[38]

4. THE FOREIGN REVIEWS

The 'British foreign reviews', as they were called, require a separate treatment, for they had a distinct focus – on modern Europe and its relevance to English thought and literature. This at once freed them from the party bias so common in the period when they were published, between the early 1820s and the mid-1840s. Moreover, the book reviewed was here more important: many articles were essentially bibliographical tools calling attention, through descriptions and extensive extracts, to a foreign work the reader could buy or borrow, or providing useful summaries of political, commercial, and literary conditions abroad through a survey of recent publications. In addition, they printed sizeable essays on important figures – Goethe, Mazzini, Comte, and others. But in the best of the dozen or so journals of this kind – the *Foreign Quarterly Review* (1827–46), the *Foreign Review* (1828–30) and the *British and Foreign Review* (1835–44) – the range exceeded the focus to include foreign subjects of any date for their own sakes (Greek romances, Medieval France, Anglo-Latin poets of the twelfth century), or simply general essays on demonology or modern architecture and architectural study, which might deal only with England. The *British and Foreign* especially, as its title would imply, accepted many articles confined to domestic affairs. (The *Home and Foreign Review* of 1862 to 1864 was both too late and too free of any primary focus to belong to this group.)

After the Revolution and the Napoleonic Wars had isolated England for 25 years, a new generation was eager to learn something of the culture and politics of the Continent; and since foreign travel in the days of coaches was expensive, the medium of periodicals promised a potential, if small, audience. In 1831, 'among the signs of improvement, at least of extended curiosity', Carlyle cited 'our British Foreign Reviews, a sort of merchantmen that regularly visit the Continental, especially the German Ports, and bring back such ware as luck yields them, with the hope of better.'[39] And for sailors, to pursue the metaphor, there was a sizeable body of temporary or permanent refugees available in London to support such ventures, and only too ready to eke out their bare subsistence by writing of their homeland. In another image this incentive, which might be called enlightened self-interest, appeared in the introduction to the *British and Foreign* (July 1835, p. 5) with its promise to 'collect the gleanings of literary research, and bring into one storehouse the dispersed grains of science, as fast as they are brought to maturity by the intellectual industry of Europe.' But to profit from foreign knowledge demanded an open mind, which was something the insular parochialism of England, regarding 'its own modes as so many laws of nature', tended to lack. Hence Carlyle's shrewd erection of thinking justly of our neighbours into a duty implicit in an age of conflict – namely, to heed whatever light one could find from any quarter.[40] But the highest contribution that foreign literature could make to English life was analogous to that of living abroad, the enrichment of intelligence. It could bring to Britain a current of fresh and free thought, foreign thought, free of English assumptions and presumptions; for Arnold, of course, was quick to point out that 'to learn and propagate the best that is known and thought in the world' automatically includes foreign nations.[41] To similar effect, Goethe had spoken of how much of one's education one owes, if one stops to think of it, to the impact of foreign culture.[42] But how well did the foreign reviews serve this objective? It seemed to Mill that their scattered articles failed to provide the systematic attention that such impact would require, and he therefore started to publish a series of essays in his *London Review* on 'Society and civilization in France', written by distinguished Frenchmen like Nisard and de Tocqueville.[43] Nothing so good as that appeared in the foreign reviews, but in some degree they must have contributed to the same end.

Finally, the incentive of self-interest took a different turn, to some extent, in the *British and Foreign*. Unlike its companions, it was partly a political journal. The restoration of the independence of Poland and the spread of liberal views in foreign affairs, together with fierce hostility to Russian imperialism, were a frequent concern in the early volumes. David Urquhart and John McNeil combined to spread their Russophobia in its pages. Furthermore, its national articles were often political. 'Corporation reform', 'Taxes on knowledge', 'Parties and public opinion' [on Robert Peel] all appeared in the first number, followed by similar themes throughout its existence. But this trend stopped short of sectarianism. Mill later proposed on one occasion to merge his *London and Westminster Review* with the *British and Foreign* on the grounds that both were 'promulgating extensive views of political & social improvement, freed from party trammels'.[44]

Though I can find no statement of such an intention, the foreign reviews were useful not only to Englishmen but also to foreigners. In praising J. G. Cockrane, the editor, for admitting conflicting opinions into the *Foreign Quarterly*, Mill concluded – perhaps to Cockrane's surprise – that 'his Review the better fulfils its *mission*, by representing the more correctly the attitude which English minds of all parties and sorts have taken up towards foreign nations'.[45] Four years earlier, commenting on the *Edinburgh* as well as the *Foreign* and *Foreign Quarterly Reviews*, Goethe had written: 'We continentals can learn from them the intellectual background of the time across the channel, what they are thinking and what their judgments about things are'; in particular, what they think of the Germans, their 'reception of our productions'.[46]

In the same passage, on the same journals, à propos of his famous idea of a world-literature evolving in time through closer and closer communications into a unanimity of feeling and thought, Goethe qualifies this by saying: 'not that the nations shall think alike, but that they shall learn how to understand each other, and, if they do not care to love one another, at least that they will learn to tolerate one another'.[47] (The date is only 13 years after Waterloo.) This reciprocity is the third role of the foreign reviews – of all foreign reviews. Under Goethe's influence Carlyle foresaw 'a universal European Commonweal' in which 'the wisest in all nations will communicate and cöoperate; whereby Europe will again have its true Sacred College, and Council of Amphictyons'.[48] There is no reference here to periodicals but on p. 10 of its July 1835 issue the *British and Foreign Review* announced: 'We are desirous of seeing established, through the intervention of the press, a common standard of taste and public opinion among the enlightened and polished nations of Europe'. What is this but the criticism advocated a generation later by another disciple of Goethe – 'a criticism which regards Europe as being, for intellectual and spiritual purposes, one great confederation, bound to a joint action and working to a common result'.[49]

Always in danger of financial collapse because of a limited audience and the shortcomings of exiles with little command of English, or Englishmen who sometimes knew little about Europe, the foreign reviews came to an end in the mid-1840s, the *British and Foreign* in 1844 and the *Foreign Quarterly* in 1846, the latter with a whimper, reduced to publishing a section called 'Foreign literature' in the *Westminster Review*, renamed for the moment (1846–51) the *Westminster and Foreign Review*. By 1845 the European railways were in place, providing easier and cheaper travel,[50] and the standard reviews, partly under the influence of the foreign ones, were paying more attention to European matters. Presently, when Chapman and Marian Evans took over the *Westminster* in 1852, they at once instituted three long sections on contemporary French, German, and American literature.[51]

5. DICHOTOMIES

Some mention should be made of the inadequacy of the usual dichotomies – quarterlies and monthlies or reviews and magazines. To begin with, the first is sometimes thought to be the equivalent of the second: the quarterlies are the reviews and the monthlies the magazines. This was true enough (with the exception, primarily, of the monthly *Eclectic Review*, 1804–68) until the 1860s, when the increasing pace of fresh knowledge and debate, spurred on by *The Origin of Species* (1859) and *Essays and Reviews* (1860), turned the major reviews into monthlies and all but ended the establishment of new quarterlies. By 1877 Mark Pattison could say: 'Those venerable old wooden three-deckers, the *Edinburgh Review* and the *Quarterly Review*, still put out to sea under the command, I believe, of the Ancient Mariner, but the active warfare of opinion is conducted by the three new iron monitors, the *Fortnightly* [1865], the *Contemporary* [1866], and the *Nineteenth Century* [1877].'[52] Thus, 'quarterlies and monthlies' tells one little more than the intervals between publication, the 'more' being the implication that the former were weightier and more authoritative, which in general was the case.

'Reviews and magazines' is more pertinent, but it implies a contrast that is only half true of both: that the former are devoted to serious discussion and the latter to entertainment. As early as 1806 Francis Jeffrey was telling a would-be contributor to the *Edinburgh*, 'To be learned and right is no doubt the first requisite, but to be ingenious and original and discursive is perhaps more than the second in a publication which can only do good by remaining popular';[53] and 50 years later Walter Bagehot, we recall, was saying that if we wish to teach people to think rightly, we must speak to them 'so that they will listen – that they will like to listen'. Macaulay's essays, mainly published in the *Edinburgh*, owed their remarkable success more to their style than to any interest in history and literature – their brisk movement, the cut and thrust of skilful debate, even their ridicule when free of malice (as in his review of Southey's *Colloquies on the Progress and Prospects of Society* in 1830). And no one can read Bagehot without appreciating his wit. Furthermore, the *Literary Gazette's* report in 1860 that 'review reading is the amusement', as well as the instruction, 'of a large majority of the intelligent public'[54] allows for a difference in kind – for articles like 'Travelling in England' or 'The Dolomite mountains' as distinguished from 'Lacordaire' or 'Mind and brain'. When J. B. Mozley, the theologian, wrote to a friend that 'one naturally looks into a review for amusement first, and then edification in due time', he meant, I suppose, looks at the lighter articles first and the learned ones later.[55] On the other hand, George Eliot, in a threnody of 1859 on the death of Old Leisure, found that 'even idleness is eager now – eager for amusement; prone to excursion-trains, art museums, periodical literature, and exciting novels', in which the context points mainly to the magazines.[56] Published monthly, they contained, in addition to articles and an occasional review, poetry (original and translated), short stories and serialized – often sensational – fiction, sometimes with illustrations by men like Cruikshank, Leech, Hablôt Browne ('Phiz') and the painter John Millais; and *their* first requisite was to amuse. (It is true that the *Fortnightly Review* printed some verse and fiction of high calibre – Swinburne, Trollope, Meredith – but this was infrequent.) In the very year of George Eliot's remark began an outburst of shilling magazines, starting with *Macmillan's*, and followed rapidly by the *Cornhill, Good Words,* and *Temple Bar* (all in 1860), *St James* (1861), the *Victoria* (1863), the *Argosy* (1865), *Belgravia* (1866), *Tinsley's, St Pauls* (*sic*), and *Broadway* (all in 1867). In the same period the principal older magazines were continuing: *Blackwood's, Bentley's Miscellany,* and the rest.

However, even a cursory glance at these journals is enough to expose a broad division. If all were designed to entertain, some were also concerned, like the reviews, with the formation of opinion. One thinks of the *Monthly Repository, Blackwood's, Fraser's, Tait's,* the *Dublin University,* the Pre-Raphaelite *Oxford and Cambridge, Macmillan's, Good Words,* and *St Pauls.* By contrast, the *New Monthly, Bentley's Miscellany, Ainsworth's Magazine,* for the most part the *Cornhill,* and the other new journals of the 1860s were often so firmly committed to amusement as to banish politics and religion altogether, either explicitly or by omission; and they tended to devote their prose, apart from fiction, to familiar essays, travel journals, reports on current affairs, biographical sketches, and elementary lessons in science, written in what Bagehot called 'the light, frivolous style of merely amusing literature'.[57] Their vogue was explained and defended in 1854 by Dickens' explosive reply to Charles Knight on his desire to raise the level of popular reading: 'The English are, so far as I know, the hardest-worked people on whom the sun shines. Be content if, in their wretched intervals of pleasure, they read for amusement and do no worse . . . Good God, what would we have of them!'[58] It follows that the articles, however valuable for relaxation, were only rarely the work of the critical, reflective mind that to a considerable degree was present in the more serious magazines. The same division is apparent in the weeklies. To the first group, which might be described as short reviews because they rarely contained any fiction or verse, would belong the *Examiner* (1808), the *Literary Gazette* (1817), the *Athenaeum* and the *Spectator* (1828), the *Guardian* (1846), the *Leader* (1850), the *Saturday Review* (1856), and the *Academy* (1869). In the second group the leading weeklies were Dickens' *Household Words* (1850) and *All the Year Round* (1859).

Keeping in mind that the reviews had also to be entertaining and that starting in 1865 they became increasingly filled with articles, one begins to suspect that in the later century they and the more demanding magazines drew closer together. Consider the make-up, at a six-year interval, for the same issues in two reviews and two magazines of high calibre.

In these samples, the reviews and magazines carry and omit the same forms of writing, with almost no difference of amount in 1878, and minor differences for both years together, the magazines having fewer reviews but slightly more articles, fiction, and poetry, as we should expect. Later on, the

New Review (1889–97), in addition to six novels, printed almost 50 short stories. Of course, if we dropped back to 1832 and 1838 and used the *Edinburgh* and *Quarterly Reviews* with *Blackwood's* and *Fraser's Magazines*, the difference would be striking, for these reviews published no fiction and no articles. And in all periods, of course, the line between the reviews and the magazines of amusement was clear.

	Articles		Essay-like reviews		Serialized novels		Short stories		Poems	
February 1872										
Contemporary Review	5	}11	2	}3	0	}1	0	}0	0	}0
Fortnightly Review	6		1		1		0		0	
Fraser's Magazine	9	}17	0	}0	1	}2	0	}0	0	}2
Macmillan's Magazine	8		0		1		0		2	
February 1878										
Contemporary Review	9	}17	1	}2	0	}0	0	}0	1	}1
Fortnightly Review	8		1		0		0		0	
Fraser's Magazine	11	}17	1	}1	0	}1	0	}0	0	}2
Macmillan's Magazine	6		0		1		0		2	

On the whole, then, this dichotomy makes sense, but one must use it with awareness of the full meanings of both terms, and of the gradual breakdown of the formal distinctions after 1864.

6. THE PERIODICAL AS CREATIVE FORCE

The influence of periodicals on authors was varied and wide. On one level, they could keep the writer alive, in body and mind; for the difficulties of publishing books were daunting. The fact that most authors of poems, sermons, and works on morals or metaphysics could expect no return from a publisher – if they could find one – and that others might have to make an advance varying from £50 to £200 to protect the publisher from loss, made periodicals with their usually prompt payment attractive.[59] In October 1832, when he had been unable to bring out any literary work of his own, Carlyle realized that 'My Editors of Periodicals are my Booksellers [Jeffrey and Napier of the *Edinburgh Review*, J. G. Cockrane of the *Foreign Quarterly*, William Fraser of the *Foreign*, and James Fraser of *Fraser's Magazine*], who . . . purchase and publish my *Books* for me; a monstrous method, yet still a method'.[60] *Sartor Resartus* might never have appeared in Carlyle's lifetime after James Fraser's demand for a prepayment of £150 was indignantly rejected and the manuscript was refused by Longmans, by Colburn and Bentley, and by John Murray, had not Fraser finally agreed to print it in his *Magazine* (May 1833–August 1834), and Emerson read it there with so much enthusiasm that he arranged for the first edition in Boston in 1836.[61]

More important than solving the problem of publishing books was the creative role of the magazines. They made it possible for individuals to write an article on a special subject that was too narrow for longer treatment or beyond their power to treat at length. Take the year 1862, chosen at random, in *Fraser's Magazine*. Here one was offered Early Scottish poetry, West-borough Fair, the secret writings of the Indians of Central America, notes on Numidia [ancient Algeria], Mrs Delany – a lady of quality in the last century – humming-birds, indigo-planting in Bengal, Romney Marsh in Kent, Bo-hemian Jews, and what to do with our old maids. A similar list could be found in the other magazines mentioned above that were published in 1862, as well as in eight more by 1870. Hence the extraordinary range of subject matter in the Victorian journals. And apart from out-of-the-way material, a writer had the same benefit in familiar fields: 'How many of us are there who feel quite capable of saying something worth listening to on several topics of art, philosophy, or history; but would shrink from undertaking a work on any of these subjects? Without a periodical literature we should . . . let what small insight we may have attained to die with us.'[62] Insights of this kind could be sent to the reviews that published articles as well as to the magazines. As Michael Wolff has observed, à propos of the periodicals, 'vastly more people were involved . . . in [Victorian] culture, than in any previous age.'[63]

From a different perspective, the periodical had a much stronger influence on contributors than the publication of books on authors. Because of its intermittent appearance, readers had an opportunity to send criticism or suggestions to the writers of serials, whether fiction or prose, directly or by way of the editors; and in general the editors, in deference to the clergy and Mrs Grundy, and to possible alarm over unorthodox economic and social views, often felt forced to interfere with what was said or how it was said. We know, for example, that in his novels Hardy had to yield to editorial controls and could speak his mind freely only when they were published later as books.[64] Moreover, serial publication of a novel affected its form because the chapters had to be fitted into more or less prescribed limits, ending if possible at a moment of sufficient suspense to encourage the reader to buy next month's issue. Even the subjects of articles, like most of those just cited, were chosen not only because of an author's specialized knowledge but also because of the readers' attraction to something strange or slightly bizarre: the secret writings of Central American Indians, indigo-planting, notes on

Numidia, what to do with our old maids. In such ways writers had to shape their work to the requirements of periodical publication.

In a wider sense, scores of writers shaped their whole work to periodical publication. Except for the romance of *Klosterheim*, almost the entire 20 volumes of Masson's edition of De Quincey consist of essays reprinted from the magazines, mainly the *London*, *Blackwood's*, and *Tait's*. Walter Pater wrote only one original book, *Marius the Epicurean*; everything else, except for some of *Plato and Platonism* and three of the *Studies in the History of the Renaissance*, first appeared in the *Westminster*, the *Fortnightly*, *Macmillan's*, the *Contemporary*, and the *New Review*. Most surprising of all, the bibliography of Matthew Arnold, barring his reports on English and Continental education, contains only four books that had not first been published in periodicals: *England and the Italian Question, On Translating Homer* and *Last Essays on Translating Homer*, and *Literature and Dogma*. And the last was planned as three essays, two of which actually appeared in the *Cornhill*. All the volumes that look like books, that would have been books before the Victorian period – *A French Eton, On the Study of Celtic Literature, Culture and Anarchy, St Paul and Protestantism, God and the Bible, Civilization in the United States* – together with *Friendship's Garland*, the first lecture of *Discourses in America*, and of course the *Essays in Criticism*, first and second series, *Mixed Essays, Irish Essays*, and *Last Essays*, all were reprinted from major reviews and magazines. Plainly, Arnold's creative mind was formed in the periodical mould. Like De Quincey and Pater and many other critics, notably Richard Holt Hutton, Andrew Lang, and George Venables, Arnold was not a writer of books; he was a writer of periodical literature.

Finally, if the wide appeal of the periodicals discouraged the writing of books, it greatly increased their publication, as the case of Arnold shows. The obvious motivation to print a collection of articles was the second sale of the same material, but often more persuasive was the opportunity of preserving them in less ephemeral form and of picking up new readers who had overlooked their original appearance. Nor should we forget the author's pride in a new book, advertised and reviewed and discussed as few of its articles had been. All these factors, no doubt, lay behind the most famous example of republication: Macaulay's *Critical and Historical Essays, Contributed to the 'Edinburgh Review'* (3 vols., 1843).[65] By 1877 Mark Pattison could report that 'books now are largely made up of republished review articles. Even when this is not the case, the substance of the ideas expanded in the octavo volume will generally be found to have been first put out in the magazine [i.e. periodical] article of thirty pages'.[66]

The periodical creation of books was sometimes accidental. As many authors knew, they tried out an idea in an essay only to discover that fresh angles of the subject sprang up demanding another essay, and so on until the collection, perhaps with some fresh links, became a book. The best example for which we have documentation is *Culture and Anarchy*. In the *Cornhill* for July 1867 Arnold published his last lecture as Professor of Poetry at Oxford, 'Culture and its enemies', with the intention of following it in August with another paper 'to say several things which need to be said in accompaniment to what has been said here'. But various criticisms of the lecture in the daily and weekly press led him to postpone the additional material and wait until he could 'gather up all the murmurings into one and see what we come to'. However, the murmurings were so numerous and telling, especially Henry Sidgwick's in the August *Macmillan's* and Frederic Harrison's in the November *Fortnightly*, that the second article, 'a sort of pendant to *Culture and Its Enemies*' called 'Anarchy and authority', did not appear (in two parts) until January and February 1868, by which time further thought dictated a third – 'but the third will certainly end it'. Then the third, which did not come out until June, was followed by two more in July and August. The earliest mention of a volume, I believe, was on 25 July when Arnold told his mother that the whole series might be reprinted. With some revisions and a sizeable preface, the five articles became the famous book of 1869.[67] It is fair to conclude that *Culture and Anarchy* would never have been written had there been no periodical to provide it with growing space. No doubt similar evolutions lie behind other books.

Because of the contemporary popularity of the novel, the indispensable staple of the magazines, after about 1840, was at least one piece of serialized fiction (sometimes two at once), and for the same reason a vast majority was reprinted in a three-decker or one-volume edition; and in any event an author would have been reluctant to leave his work in fragments. As a matter of fact it would be more accurate to say that novelists consciously planned a double publication from the beginning; indeed, more often than not were writing the novel month by month. It must not be assumed, however, that the publication of a serial in book form was an exact reprint. Quite apart from an author's revisions, there was sometimes – I suspect often – considerable alteration by a publisher, as with 'The luck of Barry Lyndon' (*Fraser's*, 1844) which was revised (whether by Thackeray or not is unknown), and published as *The Memoirs of Barry Lyndon,, Esq.* (1856), with the result that all subsequent editions (except Anisman's in 1970) reproduce the *Memoirs*. Thackeray's 'Catherine: a story' (*Fraser's*, 1839–40) did not appear as a book until 1869, at Boston and London; and virtually all reprints follow these two first editions by 'cutting out the most ghastly episodes'. Further research will undoubtedly show that editorial omissions designed to save space or spare Victorian scruples have made many serials the definitive text.[68]

In the field of the short story we can find developments analogous to that of *Culture and Anarchy*. Thirty years after its publication in the *Dublin University Magazine* for October 1839, Sheridan Le Fanu expanded his 'Chapter in the history of the Tyrone family' into *The Wyvern Mystery* (1869); and his 'Some account of the latter days of the hon. Richard Marston of Dunoran', beginning as a three-part story, April to June 1848, was first reprinted as the 'Evil Ghost' in *Ghost Stories* (1851), later amplified into a full-length serial for *Temple Bar* (May 1867–May 1868), entitled 'A lost name', and finally published as a three-decker in 1868.[69] Nor are these isolated cases. Many short stories provided the précis of a later novel.[70] Also, of course, like volumes of collected essays there were volumes of collected stories, the best of hundreds being George Eliot's *Scenes from Clerical Life* (1858), reprinted from *Blackwood's*.

Had it not been for periodicals, Saintsbury thought that 'more than half the most valuable books of the age in some departments, and a considerable minority of the most valuable in others, would never have appeared as books at all'.[71] This may be exaggerated, but not much. The periodicals displaced books and created them.

NOTES

1. This essay is a revised and expanded version of an article with almost the same title in *VS*, XXII (1979), 389–412, adapted by permission of the Editor.

2. *A History of Nineteenth Century Literature, 1780–1895* (New York and London, 1896), 166.

3. *The Waterloo Directory of Victorian Periodicals, 1824–1900*, Phase I, ed. Michael Wolff, John S. North, and Dorothy Deering (Waterloo, Ont., [1976]), suggests the number I give; Richard D. Altick, *The English Common Reader: a social history of the mass reading public, 1800–1900* (Chicago, 1957), chs. 14, 15; G. M. Young, *Victorian England: portrait of an age* (1936), 6. For a breakdown of the articulate classes, see p. 7 below.

4. I give no list of these periodicals because it would consist of nearly 100 titles; 52 are mentioned below. Besides, such a list could only be one scholar's opinion.

5. In the overall view that follows, I think that, barring finances and circulation, the only important aspect not discussed is the tradition of anonymity, with the resultant debate between its supporters and those who insisted on signature. This has been summarized in *WI*, I, xvii–xix, and II, xvi, and dealt with at length by Oscar Maurer, 'Anonymity vs. signature in Victorian reviewing', *University of Texas Studies in English*, XXVII (1948), 1–27. Also see Christopher Kent, 'Higher journalism and the mid-Victorian clerisy', *VS*, XIII (1969), 181–98, where the topic is linked to the increasing number of educated men who began to write for the top periodicals in 1850–70.

6. 'Macaulay', *Fortnightly Rev.*, n.s. XIX (1876), 499, repr. in *Critical Miscellanies* (3 vols., 1886), I, 264–5.

7. John Morley, *Recollections* (2 vols., 1917), I, 100.

8. Thomas Carlyle, 'Memoirs of the Life of Scott', *London and Westminster Rev.*, VI/28 (1838), 315, reprinted in *Critical and Miscellaneous Essays* (4 vols., Boston, 1838) (hereafter cited as Carlyle, *Essays*), being the first five volumes of his *Works* (ed. H. D. Traill, 30 vols., New York, 1896–1901), IV, 49. Quoted with

agreement by J. S. Mill, *On Liberty* (1859), ch. 2, in *The Collected Works of John Stuart Mill*, ed. John M. Robson (Toronto, 1963—), XVIII, 233.

9. See, for example, Charles Kingsley, in December 1846, in *His Letters and Memories of His Life*, edited by his wife [Fanny Grenfell Kingsley] (2 vols., 1877), I, 141; or in the abridged edition (2 vols., New York, 1900), I, 113.

For this quick survey of what are now established facets of the age, I have used my *Victorian Frame of Mind, 1830–1870* (New Haven, 1957), hereafter cited as *Frame of Mind*. For more discussion and documentation see the index to that book, under education, middle classes, and doubt.

10. 'The first Edinburgh reviewers', reprinted in *Literary Studies*, ed. R. H. Hutton (3 vols., 1898), I, 146–8, and in *The Collected Works of Walter Bagehot*, ed. N. St John-Stevas (Cambridge, Mass., 1965—), I, 311–12. The next quotation is on pp. 149 and 313 respectively.

11. Mill to Carlyle, 22 Dec. 1833, *Earlier Letters*, ed. Francis E. Mineka (2 vols., Toronto, 1963) (hereafter cited as Mill, *Earlier Letters*), I, 202, being vols. XII and XIII of *The Collected Works of John Stuart Mill*, ed. cit.

12. It is worth recording that when J. R. McCulloch was writing for the *Edinburgh Review* in the 1820s, he felt obliged to invent fictitious books in order to make articles appear to be reviews. At the head of Article IV in June 1829, which McCulloch claimed on his own List (see *WI*, 1182), stood *'Maltster and Brewer's Guide. Pp. 170. London, 1829.'* Years later Augustus De Morgan, in *A Budget of Paradoxes* (1872; 2n edn, 1915), 319, recalled: 'About the year 1830 a friend showed me the proof of an article of his on the malt tax, for the next number of the *Edinburgh Review*. Nothing was wanting except the title of the book reviewed; I asked what it was. He sat down, and wrote as follows at the head, "The Maltster's Guide (pp. 124)," and said that would do as well as anything.' The same subterfuge was resorted to by McCulloch in the March issue (no. 97) for an article with

the running title, 'Census of the population – law of mortality, &c.', also claimed on his List. This was: 'Art. I. – *Proposals for the Improved Census of the Population. Pp. 37.* London, 1829.' John Rickman wrote to Robert Southey, on 25 Sept. 1829 (quoted in *Selections from the Letters of Robert Southey*, ed. J. W. Warter, 4 vols., 1856, IV, 151n.): 'I must tell you a whimsical story of the Blue and Yellow Review. Some M.P. before the end of the Session, asked me if I had seen the Population Pamphlet reviewed in the March No. XCVII? I said I would procure it, but no London bookseller knew of it; and on making irresistible inquiry in Edinburgh, the editor acknowledges "that no such pamphlet exists, but they had an article ready," which I see is 34 pages, and which I suspect was thus suddenly thrust into the world to anticipate a House of Commons paper then in the press, containing a quotation from the 'Pandects,' which our Edinburgh thus adroitly appropriates (p. 25.), as a mark of extensive reading, and of an unexpected ancient authority on a very modern topic; I think I know the M.P. who helped Macculloch to this quotation, for I am told the article comes from the Professor of Political Economy.' One wonders if other pamphlets such as *Remarks on the Financial Situation of Great Britain*, heading the issue for October 1827 and reviewed by McCulloch (see his List), were not fictional. Bagehot noticed (p. 145) that the manoeuvre had been suggested by Hazlitt but thought it had never been carried out, which implies that it was not a common practice. I am grateful to Professor William H. Kruskal of the University of Chicago for calling some of this material to my attention.

13. 'Colonisation . . . Mr. Charles Buller's speech', *Fraser's Mag.*, XXVII (June 1843), begins on p. 735: 'Mr. Charles Buller, M.P., is a very lucky person. He has read with attention, and cleverly digested, sundry elaborate essays in the *Quarterly Review*, as well as two or three papers in *Fraser's Magazine*, and some articles in the

Colonial Gazette and in the *John Bull* newspaper; and out of these he has contrived to manufacture one of the most taking speeches that have been uttered for some time past in either house of parliament.' For William Molesworth's use of the *London Review*, see *Mirror of Parliament*, 11 March 1836, 599–600.

14. Alvar Ellegård, 'The readership of the periodical press in mid-Victorian England', *Göteborgs Universitets Årsskrift*, LXIII (1957), no. 3, 27, 30, 32; reprinted in *VPN* (Sept. 1971) 13, 16, 18.

15. See the description of Dr Arnold's mind by W. R. Greg, *Westminster Rev.*, XLII (1844), 380, cited in *Frame of Mind*, 221.

16. *Fortnightly Rev.*, n.s. II (1867), 292.

17. See end of n.10. The italics are Bagehot's. But those in the first line of the paragraph are mine. For a qualification of these claims, see the last part of n.29.

18. New impression (1901), Discourse VI, 143–4.

19. n.s. IV (5 May 1860), 555. Michael Wolff called this article to my attention.

20. 'Christ upon the Waters' (1850), *Sermons Preached on Various Occasions* (1881 edn), 149.

21. Henry Thomas Cockburn, Baron Cockburn, quoted in R. G. Cox, 'The great reviews', *Scrutiny*, VI (1937), 2. Cf. 'Journals and reviews', *London Rev.*, I (Feb. 1829), 6: We aim 'to stimulate . . . curiosity' and 'instead of manufacturing thoughts for the reader, to induce him to think for himself.'

22. See *Frame of Mind*, 144–54, on 'The rationale of infallibility', especially 152–4.

23. Letters to Sterling, 2 Nov. 1842, and to Mill, 16 Oct. 1832, in *Letters of Thomas Carlyle to John Stuart Mill, John Sterling, and Robert Browning*, ed. Alexander Carlyle (1923), 259 and 21.

24. 'The function of criticism at the present time' (Nov. 1864), in *Essays in Criticism* (1865; 1875), 6–7, or in *The Complete Prose Works of Matthew Arnold*, ed. R. H. Super (11 vols., Ann Arbor, 1960–77) (hereafter cited as Arnold *PW*), III, 261.

25. *Culture and Anarchy* (1869), ed. J. Dover Wilson (1932), 70, or Arnold *PW*, v, 113.

26. *Essays on Politics and Culture: John Stuart Mill* (New York, 1962), xxi–xxii. Cf. Leslie Stephen, *Some Early Impressions* (1903; 1924), 118; speaking of G. S. Venables' articles: 'They seemed to be judicial utterances from the loftiest regions of culture, balanced, dignified, and authoritative.'

27. *Literary Gazette*, 5 May 1860, 555.

28. On 15 December 1865, Harriet Grote wrote to Abraham Hayward, Beinecke Library, Yale University, à propos of an article by Bulwer Lytton of 1834: 'Such a production would never go down, now. Surprising how exigent the present race of readers has become. The competition among writers of passing criticism seems to have sharpened up the quality of periodical writing to a degree of which one is really not always conscious, unless you recur to things of 30 years ago. Modern writing is, now, so able, that I begin to tire of cutting out articles!' For one explanation see the last sentence of n.5 above. Cf. Leslie Stephen, 'The first Edinburgh reviewers', *Cornhill Mag.*, XXXVIII (1878), 222, repr. *Hours in a Library* (3 vols., New York, 1899), II, 248–9, where he speaks of the standard then being 'so low that writing which would now be impossible passed muster without an objection.'

29. The description is a combination of remarks in 'The Function of Criticism', from which the quotation is taken (*Essays in Criticism*, 43–4, or Arnold *PW*, III, 283), with assistance from the preface to *Culture and Anarchy* (pp. 6–7, or Arnold *PW*, v, 233–4, 529–30); and from 'Sainte-Beuve' (*Academy*, I, 1869, 31–2, also in Arnold *PW* v, 306–7). I have inserted the remarks about contemporary events and social opinion because the élitists sometimes talk as though they themselves, like geniuses, created public opinion ('we must tell them what to think' is the burden of the earlier quotations from Bagehot, Morley, Carlyle, and Arnold), when the truth is, as they themselves

realized, that in part they were giving form and expression to what they had learned from observation and intelligent conversation. Arnold refers to observation along with reading and thinking in *Culture and Anarchy*, but does not mention conversation, though that too, of course, may contribute to 'the best that is known and thought in the world'. Cf. Leslie Stephen, *Some Early Impressions*, 119: 'What Venables' articles really did, I suppose, was to embody in finished and scholarlike style the opinions prevalent among the most intelligent circles of the London society, of which Holland House had been the centre in the preceding generation.'

30. *Essays in Criticism*, 22–3, or Arnold *PW*, III, 270–1.

31. Francis E. Mineka, *The Dissidence of Dissent: The 'Monthly Repository', 1806–1839* (Chapel Hill, 1944), 248–9, 255.

32. Mill, *Earlier Letters*, I, 248, 210.

33. *Ibid.*, II, 369–71, 410.

34. Under 6 April 1836, *Later Letters*, ed. Francis E. Mineka and Dwight N. Lindley (4 vols., Toronto, 1972), IV, 1963. In his *Autobiography* (1873), ed. Harold Laski (1924), 88–90, Mill describes the 'Philosophic Radicalism' of the early *Westminster*. For other material on Mill's periodical theory from 1834–40, see Mill, *Earlier Letters*, I, 364; *Autobiography*, 168–70, 174–5; the Note in *London Rev.*, II [*Westminster* XXXI] (1836), 389, and one in *London and Westminster Rev.*, XXXIII (1839), 68.

35. 'The poems and prose remains of Arthur Hugh Clough', *Westminster Rev.*, n.s. XXXVI (1869), 363–4, reprinted in *Miscellaneous Essays and Addresses* (1904), 60. See the section 'The open and flexible mind' in *Frame of Mind*, 176–80, for other testimony from the 1850s to the 1870s.

36. T. H. S. Escott, *Anthony Trollope* (1913), 178; see Mill's Note, *London Rev.*, II (1836), 389. 'The Liberal programme', signed 'Editor', appeared in September 1867.

37. John Stoughton, quoted in *Life, Letters, and Journals of Henry Alford*, edited by his widow (3rd edn, 1874), 511.

38. For a different road leading to the same critical view of Arnold's passage, see Joanne Shattock, 'Editorial policy and the quarterlies: the case of *The North British Review*', *VPN*, (Sept. 1977), 130–9. Indeed, this article complements the previous paragraphs of this essay.

39. 'Historic survey of German poetry', *Edinburgh Rev.*, LIII (1831), 154, reprinted in *Essays*, II, 336.

40. 'State of German literature', *Edinburgh Rev.*, XLVI (1827), 306–7, reprinted in *Essays*, I, 29–30, which includes the remark about 'laws of nature'.

41. *Essays in Criticism*, 43, or Arnold *PW*, III, 282.

42. 'Goethe's theory of a world literature' (first published as five articles in his own periodical, *Über Kunst und Alterthum*), translated in *Goethe's Literary Essays*, ed. J. E. Spingarn (New York, 1921), 92.

43. Note, *London Rev.*, II (1836), 389 Also, for Mill's eagerness to print 'the best articles possible' on France and Greece, see *Earlier Letters*, I, 239, 242–3.

44. Mill, *Earlier Letters*, II, 410.

45. *Ibid.*, I, 132; my italics.

46. 'Goethe's theory of a world literature', trans. Spingarn (see n.42 above), 92, 97.

47. *Ibid.*, 92.

48. *Essays*, II, 370.

49. *Essays in Criticism*, 46, or Arnold *PW*, III, 284.

50. In 'our day', wrote Charles Lever in March 1845 (*Dublin University Mag.* [XXV], 265), travel has become 'des plus nécéssaires . . . Man is but a living locomotive.'

51. In this section I am partly indebted to Eileen Curran's 'Reviews of foreign literature: some special problems', *VPN* (June 1973), 1–7; to her introduction to the *Foreign Quarterly Review* in *WI*, II; and to that by H. B. de Groot to the *British and Foreign Review* in *WI*, III.

52. 'Books and critics', *Fortnightly Rev.*, n.s. XXII (1877), 663. *The Times*, 20 Aug. 1859, 7, announced the decline of the quarterlies. Also see *WI*, II, 7–8.

53. Jeffrey to Dr Charles Koenig, 20 Jan. 1806, BL Add. MS. 32439, f. 235. 'Discursive' means 'passing rapidly and

irregularly from one subject to another' (*OED*).

54. 5 May 1860, 554.

55. *Letters* (1885), 93, under date of 10 July 1839. Cf. Mill, *Earlier Letters*, I, 248, speaking on 26 February 1835 of the coming issue of the *London Review*: 'I fear its fault will be, a deficiency of literary & other light matter & a superabundance of politics.'

56. *Adam Bede*, end of ch. 52, 'Adam and Dinah'.

57. Editions cited in n.10, I, 163 and I, 323 respectively.

58. *The Letters of Charles Dickens*, edited by his sister-in-law [Georgiana Hogarth] and his eldest daughter [Mary Dickens] (2 vols., 1880), I, 352.

59. G. H. Lewes, 'The condition of authors in England, Germany, and France', *Fraser's Mag.*, XXXV (1847), 290.

60. *Letters of Thomas Carlyle to John Stuart Mill, John Sterling, and Robert Browning*, ed. cit., 21.

61. *Thomas Carlyle: Letters to his Wife*, ed. Trudy Bliss (Cambridge, Mass., 1953), 55 and 72; 56 and 61; 73; 72, 80, 83, 84.

62. Lewes, *op. cit.*, 289.

63. *J. English and Germanic Philology*, LXVII (1968), 532. Upon completion the four volumes of the *Wellesley Index*, covering only 47 reviews and magazines, will contain about 12,000 different contributors.

64. See Oscar Maurer's well-documented article, '"My squeamish public": some problems of Victorian magazine publishers and editors', *Studies in Bibliography*, XII (1959), 21–40. Hardy is discussed on pp. 38–40. Hardy's own protest, 'Candour in English fiction', appeared in the *New Rev.*, II (1890), 15–21. According to Michael Sadleir, *Things Past* (1944), 105, Rhoda Broughton, by publishing her novel *Nancy* as a book in 1873, 'was spared the tortures' she had endured from the serial publication in *Temple Bar* of her

two previous novels, 'which provoked opinions from friends and strangers with each instalment.'

65. Such books also had a special value for readers beyond convenience and the discovery of 'new' essays missed before, as a reviewer of Kingsley's *Miscellanies* pointed out: 'There are very few descriptions of reading so interesting as a collection of anonymous essays by an eminent writer. It is a kind of book almost peculiar to the present generation; and a more complete picture of the author's mind than it usually presents would in most cases be impossible . . . When we know what a man has been writing in reviews and saying in lectures for the last ten years, we understand pretty well what he has been thinking and feeling during that time' (*Fraser's Mag.*, LXII [1860], 372).

66. 'Books and critics', *Fortnightly Rev.*, n.s. XXII (1877), 663.

67. The evolution and the quotations are taken from *Prose Works*, v, 410–12.

68. See Robert A. Colby, *Thackeray's Canvas of Humanity* (Columbus, Ohio, 1979), 224, n.3 and 168 n.2. The original text of *Catherine* can be read only in the Oxford Thackeray, ed. George Saintsbury (1908), III, and the Harry Furniss Century Edition (1911), VI. Of the eight biographies in vol. II of Samuel O'Sullivan's posthumous *Remains* (Dublin, 1853) which were 'written for the *Dublin University Magazine*', some were very considerably abridged by the publisher in order to hold the complete work to three volumes (see *Dublin University Mag.*, XLII [1853], 354).

69. Montague Summers (ed.), *Victorian Ghost Stories* [1936], xxxvii.

70. For an excellent example see the evidence for the stories of Selina Bunbury given in the Appendix to *WI*, III, and cited in its index under her name.

71. Saintsbury, *op. cit.*, 166.

2

Brian Maidment   Readers fair and foul:
John Ruskin and the
periodical press

1

Victorian critics were fond of calling Ruskin a 'voluminous' writer. The word
must have seemed entirely appropriate to the commonly held understanding
of Ruskin's work: leisurely, expansive, unorganized and eccentric. But
voluminous also implied another meaning, for the 'voluminous' Ruskin was
also the writer of many volumes. This double implication of spaciousness
and book form is an important element in explaining the way in which
Ruskin's work has been mediated into literary and intellectual consciousness
over the last 100 years. Indeed, the widespread notion of the major Victorian
writers as prolific producers of works in book form (instant collected editions
as it were) has only slowly been broken down by study of such crucial
matters as serial publication, the development of cheap and popular literary
genres, and the range and variety of readerships in Victorian England. From
defining the major scholarly need as that of establishing a fixed, single text,
recent criticism has tended to focus on the way in which a text is produced
and read by a society. Such a shift has inevitably led attention away from the
book towards study of the genres and occasions of literature, and the way in
which a text is formed out of such pressures. The text, in other words, is seen
not as a fixed object, but rather as a series of occasions or even transforma-
tions. As I hope to show, some sense of the variety of literary occasions is a
necessary factor in understanding Ruskin's work, yet the idea of the 'many-
volumed' Ruskin has died hard. While it is generally accepted that we make
important qualifications to the notion of the novel when we describe Dickens
as a *serial* novelist, or Hardy as a *periodical* novelist, there has so far been no
critical attempt to describe Ruskin's books in such ways. Admittedly, any
such attempts have been largely forestalled by the publishing history of
Ruskin's works since 1870. A great deal of effort has gone into the creation of
a Ruskin canon – that is, a series of uniform volumes in which the texts have
been established and re-organized into an apparently coherent book form.
The partial codification of Ruskin's writing began with a 'Works' series

from 1870 on, containing Ruskin's main volume-length works on social and ethical matters, and published either in frail grey paper boards or in even more fragile purple calf at considerable expense.[1] From this series Ruskin appears as a surprisingly brief and reasonable writer on political economy and social ethics. But the 'Works' series was only a half-hearted attempt to publish Ruskin in mass multi-volume format. In effect, the venture was an effort by Ruskin himself to focus attention on a limited area of his thought, an area which had become of intense emotional importance to him during this period. The first attempt to see Ruskin whole emerged, significantly, after Ruskin himself had withdrawn through illness from control over the publishing of his own books. From the late 1880s up to his death in 1900 Ruskin's vast output began to appear in uniform green cloth octavo reprints, which often collected occasional and fugitive pieces into volume form. From this time on, successive editions of Ruskin's works have been almost entirely in such formats – multi-volume uniform series.[2] The apotheosis of the many-volumed Ruskin came with the publication of the great Cook and Wedderburn edition familiar to all scholars of Victorian literature – 39 huge red buckram volumes published between 1903 and 1912.[3]

It is worth considering briefly the effect of the prevalent volume mentality on one or two of Ruskin's works, because an understanding of the differences between serial texts and volume reprints is central to my argument. Of the four volume-length works on political economy which Ruskin initially published as series of periodical articles, two underwent enormous change between initial publication and volume reprint. The first of these, *Time and Tide* (1867), was deliberately and selfconsciously rewritten for volume publication by Ruskin himself, so that Cook and Wedderburn's decision to print the text in the last volume revision undertaken by the author himself seems eminently fair and reasonable,[4] especially as the editors give a full bibliographical account of the text as well as six close-printed pages of the variations contained in the original serial text. But despite this exemplary scrupulousness in editorial policy, Cook and Wedderburn's decision is heavily influenced by a sense of the superiority of the considered, revised volume format over the more improvised, more fluid, and occasional form of original publication. Which text is the reader to reconstruct? Do the successive texts show sufficient differences in form and intention to constitute different meanings? These kinds of questions form the substance of this paper.

The status of the texts of *Fors Clavigera* (1871–84) presents different, but even more startling, problems. The work was written as a discursive experiment in serial form, and was made alternatively available in an unaltered volume form. But when a cheap reprint was required in the mid-1890s, Ruskin was too ill to undertake the revisions. The original eight volumes

were revised and squeezed into four. Much personal and introspective
writing was eliminated, and nearly all the symptoms of the original serial
form were destroyed. The result was a totally different book: the *Fors*
known to a whole generation of Ruskin readers. I want to quote at some
length one reader's understanding of the differences between the two *Fors*:

> And now, as one who has deeply enjoyed *Fors*, and, perhaps,
> somewhat excessively rated it as Ruskin's central work, I am bound to
> make a personal confession – almost a belated recantation. Like the
> rest of the world, even the Ruskinian world, I was myself far too busy
> between 1871 and 1878 to be sending 7d. every month to Keston and
> to read through the pamphlets regularly, even when they contained
> paternal rebukes on myself. The only *Fors* I ever really read and knew
> was the edition in four volumes, small cr. 8vo., 1896. This handy
> edition reduced the eight full volumes to four moderate volumes of
> 500 pages, omitted all the Appendices, and much curtailed sundry
> parts of the ninety-six letters. I am free to confess that I greatly
> prefer the abridged *Fors* to the unadulterated torrent we now get,
> overlaid with cuttings from the *Daily Telegraph* and provincial prints,
> stuffed with silly letters from anonymous correspondents and the
> gossip of aesthetic old ladies. The abridged and bowdlerised *Fors* was
> trivial and desultory enough in all conscience. But the 'pure milk' of
> the Ruskinian word is to me a *purée* which my palate declines to
> approve . . .[5]

In the context of Frederic Harrison's readings of *Fors* – rational, retrospec-
tive, appraising – it is hardly surprising that he found the activity and
overstatement of the serial form incomprehensible. Yet underlying his
attitude is again a sense of the supremacy of the volume format, an assumption that the only significant literary discourse lies between cultured men in
considered, revised, tidy, rational books. Ruskin's challenge to the volume
format was too alarming to survive his editors and apologists.

I have already pointed to the irony by which the 39 volumes of Cook and
Wedderburn have become the starting place for the 'de-voluming' of Ruskin's work. Yet from the bibliographical notes in the *Works* emerges a sense
of Ruskin's writing which would have been immediately apparent to any
mid-Victorian reader: that only a few of Ruskin's works were specifically
written for volume publication, and the majority were in the form of
lectures, serials, periodical articles, or advanced and self-conscious experiments in popular literary genres. Indeed of all Ruskin's books only the three
great early art books, *The Seven Lamps of Architecture*, *Modern Painters*,
and *The Stones of Venice* were written deliberately in volume form without

Ruskin having any real sense of a particular readership, and even here the five volumes of *Modern Painters*, spread over 17 years, are a kind of exaggerated or perverse serial publication. The vast bulk of Ruskin's work comprises lecture texts (at least 15 volumes), educational text books, popular guide books, controversial pamphlets on art and religion, books of popular science, exhibition catalogues, extended didactic dialogues, and a fairy tale. Not least important among these are a large number of periodical articles. In other words, nearly all of Ruskin's work is *occasional*, written for the specific needs of a specific readership on a specific occasion. This is not to deny that Ruskin's work has a value beyond its immediate context – this, too, was part of his purpose – but rather to stress the enormous range and grasp of literary forms and publishing methods which Ruskin had, a grasp which does much to rescue his work from charges of formlessness, whimsicality and in-dulgence. Far from being detached by class, wealth, and inclination from Victorian literary discourse, Ruskin showed an awareness of formal and generic possibilities which is far in advance of that of many of his contempor-aries. That the subtitle of one of Ruskin's books should direct it to 'little housewives' (*Ethics of the Dust*) while another (*Fors Clavigera*) was aimed at 'the workmen and labourers of Great Britain' suggests the variousness and specificity of Ruskin's literary intentions.

Ruskin's knowledge of the literary market-place and its forms liberated his work in several ways from conventional literary contexts. Firstly, Ruskin realized that popular literary genres had both a form and a readership ready made, which enabled a writer to utilize the vigour of the form without necessarily using the genre for conventional purposes. For example, Ruskin turned the idea of a utilitarian exhibition catalogue for the Royal Academy into the place for a polemic on contemporary painting. Thus the prescribed, but very specific and quite substantial, readership created by the form had its expectations affronted by an unexpected use of a format more usually informative than argumentative. One of the most radical tendencies in Ruskin's work is this ability to subvert conventional forms while at the same time exploiting the readership and the occasion already established by that form. Ruskin's own version of the 'Cottage Libraries' and 'Books for the People' series widely distributed in the north of England is a typically perverse example. Ruskin called his series 'Bibliotheca Pastorum' ('the Peasants' Library'!), produced it with exquisite care and at great expense, published three volumes, and abandoned it as soon as he realized it had no readership. The people who needed the series could not afford it, and those who could afford it did not need it. Many critics have seized gleefully on Ruskin's impractical and paradoxical betrayals of the need for popular cheap literature, focussing attention particularly on the wilful difficulties of *Fors*

Clavigera. But it is equally important to stress Ruskin's splendidly pragmatic and successful development of other popular genres. Think of the good sense and practical virtues of the original part issues of *Mornings in Florence* (1876–7), for example. Ruskin's six stout canvas-backed pamphlets, each containing a morning's activity, are both a charming and a perceptive response to the need for a popular portable guide. Such persuasive use of a popular format is clearly lost by subsequent bulky volume reprints. That the guidebook genre, exploited again by Ruskin in *St Mark's Rest*, was successful in gaining a hold on the market can be gauged by E. M. Forster's need to ridicule the Ruskinian guide book, in the interests of 'life' and 'imagination', 30 years after its original publication.[6] Ruskin's essays in popular genres, then, often succeed in exploiting *and* subverting a ready-made form, and also show a practical, vigorous, and original grasp of the opportunities of publication outside volume format.

Secondly, Ruskin grasped very clearly the differing readerships available in Victorian England, and the way in which these were defined by the genre, the periodical, or the occasion which the writer used. I want to trace the progressive redefinitions of readership Ruskin made in his writing career later, but it is important to stress here that volume publication was the mode of publication in which readership could be *least* clearly identified. Implicit, though not necessarily fully realized, in all magazines, serial publications, and popular genres is a fairly detailed sense of who, and how many, are going to buy and read such literature. All available evidence suggests that no magazine could be launched without considerable thought about the relationship between content and readership, even though the readership might be as large and ill-defined as that of the *Cornhill* in 1860 or as specific and limited as the *Papers of the Manchester Angling Society*. One of the main forces propelling Ruskin into serial, periodical, and popular literature was the realization that here were identifiable readerships with identifiable literary expectations which Ruskin could subvert to his own purposes.

These arguments, then, all point to the main theme of this paper, which is an attempt to describe the extemely advanced selfconciousness that one major Victorian writer had of the modes and occasions for literary expression available to him. This extreme sensitivity to readership and context gives a very different view of Ruskin from that of the digressive eccentric pouring out volume after volume. Instead we have an urgent, witty writer forced by the need to find the most appropriate context into startling and even inappropriate forms of literary expression. There is a need to see Ruskin's periodical writing as just one area of a literary output which reveals an advanced awareness of literary possibilities – as one front in the war against the reader's complacency and conventional expectations.

2

The above brief description of Ruskin's work suggests that his awareness of the contexts of periodical literature was, in addition to being particularly acute, also extremely unusual. The motives underlying Ruskin's considerable periodical contributions have less to do with money and self-advertisement, and more to do with the development of literary forms, the understanding of the needs of varying readerships, and the pressure of social and political events than is usual among Victorian writers. To some extent this apparent freedom is the result of a deliberate and sophisticated understanding of the social force of periodical literature. But to some extent it is happily accidental – Ruskin's family wealth and gift for non-literary self-publicity freed him from many constraints endured by less privileged and less famous authors. This being said, Ruskin's periodical writings still provide unrivalled evidence of the overlapping pressures which direct authors towards magazines and newspapers. It is worth considering how the opportunities and constraints of periodical writing relate to Ruskin's work in more detail.

One immediate distinction which affects the study of periodical writing is that to be drawn between *freely submitted* and *commissioned* work. Any attractive notion about the freedom of the author in choosing and developing the nature of his or her article-length writing has to be tempered by close consideration of the effects which editors and publishers have in the conception and development of an author's oeuvre. Commissioning work is another literary relationship which is far more common in periodical than in volume publication, and certainly played an important role in the shaping of Ruskin's literary output. Even though Ruskin was largely, and unusually, in control of the locations and publishing modes of his work, several key works have their origin not so much in his own selfconsciousness as in the understanding of his thought, interests, and market value which existed in the minds of editors, publishers and literary advisers. His father, too, had an important role in the shaping of Ruskin's early writing. As we shall see, several books which seem to occupy a crucial place in the development of Ruskin's thought do not proceed solely from internal compulsions, but from outside promptings and solicitations.

Immediate financial gain is the most obvious motive for writing contributions to magazines. Although some forms of occasional writing might have been slow to pay,[7] most magazine articles combined the advantages of quick financial returns for relatively little outlay of either time or money on the author's part, and accordingly a day-to-day income could be assured between more extended exercises in the major literary genres, which were largely dependent on the slow process of volume publication. The sometimes slow accumulation and payment of royalties, the dangers of an outright sale of a manuscript which might meet with an unexpected success, the investment of large amounts of unpaid time in writing lengthy books without any sure rewards, the lack of proper copyright protection, and the uneasy relationships between publishers and authors all made volume publication the reserve of either established writers, or those supported by inheritance, husbands, wives, patrons or a non-literary profession. The development of popular journalism throughout the mid-Victorian period, while not generally allowing writers the journalistic independence which became possible in the 1880s and 1890s, did make connections with magazines, which generally maintained a small stock of 'house' writers, a necessary resource in a writer's financial organization. The money available to successful contributions undoubtedly led to the cynical submission of trivial, second-rate, or hurried articles on many occasions, but it also led to the serious consideration and development of certain forms of article and review as distinct and important literary genres. This is clearly not the place to go into the huge subject of the relationships between magazines, literary forms, and the financial constraints of Victorian authors. The point to be made is that Ruskin, even late in his life when his income was almost entirely dependent upon his literary output, did *not* have to rely on an income from periodical contributions. His vast inheritance and the increasingly prolific and continuous sales of his books freed him from the necessity to write occasional pieces, and he enjoyed a freedom of choice in the kind of work he wrote not available to those Victorian writers who combined a repeated success in one literary genre (usually published in volume form) with the quicker returns of occasional journalism.

A second way in which authors combined journalism with volume publication was in the use of magazine articles to publicize the supposedly more substantial or serious volume publications. This volume/article relationship varied from the direct to the oblique. At the most direct level, a series of magazine articles were republished as a volume, perhaps with additional textual material, annotations, or illustrations, to cater for readers who wanted the text in a more permanent form, or who had missed parts of the serial issue, or who did not subscribe to the magazine at all. Such an article/book connection was the non-fictional prose equivalent of the serial novel, and many important works of social analysis appeared in such a form, including *Unto This Last* and *Munera Pulveris*. Even with the widespread practice of abstracting articles from magazines for individual binding as a volume – a practice still financially possible for middle-class Victorians until the total domination of mass-produced publishers' cloth late in the century –

it is clear that serial publication in magazines did not necessarily destroy the market for volume reprints, and seems on many occasions positively to have helped book circulation. At the more oblique level, constant periodical publication kept the author's name before the public, and served as a reminder of his or her work in other fields and genres. So periodical writing was largely used by authors to *increase* their readership.

Ruskin, it is fair to say, never willingly used the periodical press in this kind of way, even with the serializing of *Unto This Last* in early issues of the *Cornhill*. Indeed, the relationship between articles and volume publication is particularly interesting here, as the circulation figure for the *Cornhill* is quoted at over 120,000 for the first issue (Ruskin himself put it at 80,000), while *Unto This Last* sold under 900 copies in the first ten years of volume publication. Such an unequal readership between articles and books is typical of Ruskin, if not of other Victorian writers, because he always used magazine articles not for the effect they might have on the wider diffusion of his work in general, but for specific reasons of occasion and form. Ruskin's hatred of the self-advertisement and publicity supposedly fostered by popular journalism was notorious and should not be confused with his genius for creating localized controversy. Ruskin was famous and eccentric enough not to need ephemeral notoriety and although there can be no doubt that the serial publication of *Unto This Last* and *Fors Clavigera* at least did have the effect of publicizing Ruskin's other work, this was not an effect which Ruskin had calculated or even wanted. As a matter of consistent policy Ruskin never permitted his own volume publications to be advertised in magazines or newspapers, allowing only plain listings of his works to be circulated by post or printed at the back of his books. It is worth pausing to consider Ruskin's critique of Victorian popular journalism in more detail.

3

Ruskin deplored above all the *quantity* of Victorian popular journalism. Quantity, he felt, implied a lack of discrimination and judgment on the part of the author, and also created a baffling proliferation of information or opinion which confused readers. How was an ordinary person to choose what to read? How could the true and the worthy be distinguished from the corrupt and ill-informed? Linked to this belief that quantity inevitably affected quality was a growing anxiety over the decline in aesthetic quality which Ruskin associated with mass production. This aesthetic revulsion was both a matter of personal taste and a wider attack on the aesthetics of machine production. Ruskin's distaste for shoddily written, poorly printed, badly laid out, cheaply illustrated periodical works was at one level snobbery, at another an appreciation of the symptoms of what he saw as moral and economic decline. Ruskin also fulminated against sensationalism, though it was sometimes hard to distinguish between Ruskin's own manner and that which he was abusing. Nonetheless, Ruskin believed sensational journalism to be a kind of lying. All these views were most vigorously expressed in *Fors Clavigera*, a publication which was in many ways intended to embody the potential in periodical writing for the true, the socially concerned, and the useful:

> For you will find, if you think deeply of it, that the chief of all the curses of this unhappy age is the universal gabble of its fools, and of the flocks that follow them, rendering the quiet voices of the wise men of all past time inaudible. This is, first, the result of the invention of printing, and of the easy power and extreme pleasure to vain persons of seeing themselves in print. When it took a twelve-months, hard work to make a single volume legible, men considered a little the difference between one book and another; but now, when not only anybody can get themselves made legible through any quantity of volumes, in a week, but the doing so becomes a means of living to them, and they can fill their stomachs with the foolish foam of their lips, the universal pestilence of falsehood fills the mind of the world as cicadas do olive-leaves, and the first necessity for our mental government is to extricate from among the insectile noise, the few books and words that are divine.[8]

Only Ruskin could have assumed in the late nineteenth century that writing should be an unrewarded moral duty rather than a paid profession. But beyond his contempt for writing as a livelihood, his hatred of the undifferentiated plenty of Victorian occasional writing, and his distrust of sensational journalism, Ruskin did half-grasp the possibility of the ideological control which might be exercised by an advanced and persuasive popular press:

> And the double and treble horror of all this, note you well, is not only that the tennis-playing and railroad-flying public trip round the outskirts of it [the slums], and whirl over the roofs of it, – blind and deaf; but that the persons interested in the maintenance of it have now a whole embodied Devil's militia of base littérateurs in their bound service; – the worst form of serfs that ever human souls sank into – partly conscious of their lying, partly, by dint of daily repetition, believing in their own babble, and totally occupied in every journal and penny magazine all over the world, in declaring this present state of the poor to be glorious and enviable, as compared with the poor that have been. In which continual pother of parroquet lie,

and desperately feigned defence of all things damnable, this nineteenth century stutters and shrieks alone in the story of mankind.[9]

In this gloriously splenetic, and selfconsciously sensational, vision of the 'shrieking and stuttering' popular press, Ruskin brilliantly equates journalism and the social *status quo* through a clear grasp of the way in which the printed word has become a major political force. Ruskin's most selfconscious manner here, which almost parodies popular journalism by its advanced use of sensational and melodramatic language for entirely serious purposes, also shows Ruskin's own determination to use all available methods in pursuit of his own political and social aims. His horror at what he thought to be the unselfconscious ideological strength of the popular press did not prevent Ruskin from using popular rhetoric in pursuit of his own ideological purposes. Indeed, the main difference between Ruskin in passages like these, and the magazines and newspapers which he depised, is not so much in opinion as in manner – the quality of Ruskin's writing is effective as both enjoyable parody of a widely used kind of sensational manner, and in conveying social insights with imagistic insistence and verbal drama. The *quality* of the writing is thus a crucial element in the success of Ruskin's periodical journalism.

Ruskin's hatred of paid journalism is given a further level of seriousness by reference to the theory of 'worth' outlined in the 'Nature of Gothic' chapter in *The Stones of Venice* and elaborated in *Unto This Last* and *Munera Pulveris*. In attempting to link the value of labour not to market conditions but the moral and physical effort and quality involved in the production of an object Ruskin inevitably found reasons for indignation at the disproportionate rewards of occasional writing:

> Just think what a horrible condition of life it is that any man of common vulgar wit, who knows English grammar, can get for a couple of sheets of chatter in a magazine, two thirds of what Milton got altogether for *Paradise Lost*! all this revenue being of course stolen from the labouring poor, who are the producers of all wealth.[10]

Ruskin can, of course, afford this Olympian contempt. Nevertheless his total dismissal of hack writing is enacted here not only intellectually (through the provocatively imported reference to theories widely expressed in Ruskin's works) but *verbally*. By his brilliantly evocative (but quite unfair) yoking together of Milton and hack journalists, utter contempt ('sheets of chatter') and spitting consonants (especially 'c'), Ruskin asserted his own imaginative and verbal superiority to vulgar journalism, and established his right to be heard. It is this immediately apparent verbal quality which enabled Ruskin to write unscathed by the degradation and vanity he found in Victorian popular journalism.

4

On the far-reaching grounds of bad production, sensationalism, over-production, the creation of false ideologies, and theft from true productive labour Ruskin thus attacked popular journalism. What compulsions, then, could have driven such an avowed opponent of commercial and self-advertising motives so prolifically into magazine and newspaper publication, defended only by his literary style from being taken for a gabbling, insectile, cicada-voiced, trivializing, self-advertising journalist? The main reasons are threefold: firstly, a wish to change or redefine his readerships; secondly, a need to write in genres only available in magazines and newspapers; and thirdly, through the extreme urgency of the occasion. Ruskin's wish to change or re-define his readership must be sharply differentiated from the more usual, but less disinterested attempts of most writers to increase their readership through their periodical contributions. As I have already suggested, periodical literature has a somewhat sharper and more specific sense of readership than most volume publication, a readership defined by content, price and editorial policy. This enabled an author to choose a fairly specific section of society as his or her readers when writing for magazines or newspapers. Contributions to specialist publications provide obvious examples, and Ruskin in the course of 50 years of writing wrote for specialist geological, natural-historical, architectural, economic and art magazines, to say nothing of local newspapers. He also wrote for such heavyweights as *Fraser's*, the *Cornhill*, the *Quarterly* and the *Contemporary Review* with much larger, but less clearly differentiated, readerships. Yet however precise or vague the nature of the readerships for such magazines may have been, Ruskin was always aware that there were profound differences to the discourse in, say, the *Geological Magazine* and the *Cornhill*. This notion that the author had a *choice* of readers is an extremely important one for the understanding of Ruskin's work as he strove to *create* kinds of readerships not available even to the periodical market. In his search for the appropriate periodical readership for his work (that is to say a readership not dependent on size but on the author's choice of who *ought* to read his work) Ruskin was ultimately driven to establish his own forms of periodical.

The issue of the specific literary genres and styles only available in magazines and periodicals clearly needs detailed illustration which I hope to provide by discussion of *Unto This Last*, *Time and Tide*, and *Fors Clavigera*. It is worth saying, however, that for the possibilities of literary form in periodicals to be realized, the author needs both an advanced formal selfconsciousness and a willingness to experiment to the point of rejecting widely held conceptions of what articles might be like. In particular, Ruskin re-appraised the necessity for brevity and concision forced upon him by limited space, on some occasions deliberately changing his style for immediate effects, but on others refusing to accept that articles should be brief and pointed. The extremes of Ruskin's style – on the one hand epigrammatical, heavily imagistic, covering vast ranges of ideas in metaphors, similes, allusions and comparisons, and on the other fragmented in syntax, discursive, personal and unshaped, giving an air of dangerous spontaneity – are well represented in Ruskin's occasional writing.

The occasional pressures which operate on a writer are obviously of many kinds, and Ruskin is entirely right to stress how powerful a motive public events are in the shaping of his work. In the preface to *The Arrows of the Chace* (1880) he acknowledged that: 'all these letters were written with fully provoked zeal',[11] a conviction emphasized by the further declaration that 'I never was tempted into writing a word for the public press unless concerning matters which I had much at heart'.[12] Ruskin acknowledges here that urgency of occasion is actually a defining feature of a periodical contribution, in distinction from the 'large book' where 'an indulged diffuseness weakens the fancy, and prolonged strain subdues the energy'.[13] Depth of feeling, immediacy, topicality, and energy are all characteristic of short newspaper contributions, Ruskin argues, and create a separate literary style.

Ruskin was, in addition, often stirred by the publication of other people's periodical articles which drew a written response from him, often developing into a kind of improvised or self-generating controversial occasion in serial form. This process, at which Ruskin was uniquely adept (turning even the flooding of the Tiber into a public controversy[14]), is well described by Ruskin in the preface to his collected letters to the press:

> It is to be remembered also that many of the subjects handled can be more conveniently treated controversially, than directly; the answer to a single question may be made clearer than a statement which endeavours to anticipate many; and the crystalline vigour of a truth is often best seen in the course of its serene collision with a trembling and dissolving fallacy.[15]

'Serene collision' is a splendid description of Ruskin's public letter writing method – the serenity deriving from literary skill as much as intellectual conviction on many occasions. Underlying all such occasional pressures on Ruskin to enter the lists of periodical controversy was always the compelling need to release overwhelming psychological and intellectual energies and compulsions, and often it is very hard to distinguish selfconscious and more or less controlled polemical method from nervous breakdown. Nonetheless, these distinctions have a necessary function in showing the selfconsciousness of Ruskin's literary method.

5

The fivefold complex of motives which, I have proposed, press authors towards magazine publication – money, increasing readership, changing readership, the possibility of using new forms and styles, and the pressures of occasion – all suggest the sense of vigour and opportunity offered by Victorian periodical publication. Ruskin was undoubtedly unusual among Victorian authors in his highly developed sense of the latter three possibilities and his rejection of the first two. In holding this particular balance of motives, Ruskin put a great deal of weight on the *riskier* potentialities of periodical writing – on new forms and styles, on experimental and varied definition of readership, and on the hasty, improvised, responses of intense moments of public controversy. With no financial risks to run, and a huge reputation, Ruskin was free to use the periodical press in a startlingly adventurous way, even running the risk of public ridicule for the embarrassing personal urgency of his periodical writing. Such experimental opportunities, as well as the respect occasioned by his fame, partially freed Ruskin from the constraints of periodical writing, constraints which were for most writers as evident as the opportunities. As a famous, circulation-increasing writer, Ruskin was likely to be allowed all the space he required, although he was fully conscious that the energy and eccentricity of his views put even his work at risk: 'they [letters to the press] were likely almost, in the degree of their force, to be refused by the editors of the adverse journals.'[16] Luckily for Ruskin, his periodical articles and letters were only, as he notes rather smugly, 'almost' refused. As the scope and nature of Ruskin's periodical writing grew, he was increasingly able to find freedom from editorial control over the length, content, and manner of his periodical writing, even developing in *Fors Clavigera* a form of magazine which allowed him the maximum amount of freedom. Ruskin's bitter experience of editorial interference from his early *Cornhill* days was clearly one of the factors which urged him towards a more experimental use of periodical forms. The other prevailing constraints of the periodical format – the pressure of readers' expectations expressed both through sales figures and hostile criticism, the need for hurried writing with a consequent lack of time for careful revision, and the lack of clearly defined genres and styles of writing – Ruskin positively welcomed, and regarded as strong intellectual, practical, and temperamental arguments in favour of periodical writing. In weighing up the forces bearing upon him, which was, of course, never an entirely conscious process, Ruskin found himself able to reject commercial arguments, to develop methods of avoiding the constraints of editors, publishers, and even to some extent readers, and to exploit a rich variety of opportunities in form, style, and readership opened up to him. With such an understanding of the periodical press, Ruskin's large output of periodical writing becomes less surprising. It is the energy, experiment, and unusual mode of address of Ruskin's periodical writings which impress the modern reader, an energy which derives from a bold belief in the paradox that newspapers and magazines were a considerable social evil in the hands of other writers, but an untried opportunity for a man of Ruskin's social principle and literary skill. As Ruskin had put it in his notorious preface to the second edition of volume 1 of *Modern Painters*: 'I do not consider myself in any way addressing, or having to do with, the ordinary critics of the press. Their writings are not the guide, but the expression, of public opinion.'[17] This apparently arrogant discrimination between his own work and that of all other critics, stated at the onset of his literary career, was, one might claim, ultimately justified by Ruskin's subsequent periodical writings.

6

Thus far I have deliberately considered Ruskin's periodical writings as an undifferentiated body of work in order to suggest their place in his work as a whole and to show conditions which prevailed for all his occasional writing. Yet necessary distinctions have to be made, and the apparently simple task of *describing* Ruskin's periodical writing brings the problem of such definitions into immediate focus. Chronological description identifies changes in subject matter – the early articles on natural history and architecture, which are really treatises on close observation and visual sensitivity, give way to controversial discussions of contemporary painting, which are in turn overshadowed by a substantial body of work on political economy, produced in serial form in major periodicals during the 1860s. In the 1870s these strands of interest are maintained, but they are augmented by increasing use of controversial letters to the press on topical matters, by fragmentary articles on art, architecture, and social ethics, and by the journal and magazine *Fors Clavigera* which was published through most of the 1870s and erratically extended on into the next decade. The conclusion to be drawn from such a bald description is little more than that of establishing that Ruskin's periodical writings follow and reflect the overall course of his intellectual and psychological development in a very close way. A more explicitly psychologically-based description of the same material would only add further evidence for the interdependent nature of Ruskin's personality, biography, and works. The extent and variety of the periodical contributions stress the

links which exist between temperament and a predisposition towards occasional writing. Anyone as restless, as quick to respond to controversy, as
conscious of his social responsibility as a sage, as increasingly physically and
mentally incapable of sustained work is likely to express himself widely in
concentrated and occasional forms. In this way, too, it is possible to see
Ruskin's periodical writings as an undifferentiated confirmation of the
general development of his work.

Thematic classification, however, begins to suggest the distinctiveness of
the periodical writings, by throwing into relief the prominence of political
economy as the main subject for Ruskin's periodical writing. *All* of Ruskin's
book-length writings on political economy appeared first in periodical form,
while his central works on art and architecture used initially the volume
format, and then, increasingly, the lecture as the dominant form of publication. Yet as useful as a thematic description might be as a way of
approaching Ruskin's periodical writing, such an approach still leaves un-
stated the relationship between content and literary form. Why did some
subjects fit readily into periodical modes? Was the use of such modes a
conscious choice, or merely the accident of the occasion? This central relationship can only be described generically and formally.

7

Ruskin once wrote, in all sincerity, that he 'never wrote a letter in my life
which all the world are not welcome to read if they will',[18] and a public
manner certainly permeates many of his private letters. Public and semi-
public letters to the press in fact form the most numerous, if not the most
voluminous, aspect of his periodical writing. The two-volume collection of
his letters in the press, *Arrows of the Chace* (1880), was a response to
considerable public demand for such an anthology, and comprises well over
100 letters, arranged thematically, but complemented by a chronological
chart which gives considerable bibliographical detail. Further letters were
published in *Ruskiniana* (1890) and in the magazine *'Igdrasil'* – all are to be
found in vol. xxxiv of the *Works*. In addition to such an obvious contemporary recognition of the importance of this aspect of Ruskin's work, many of
Ruskin's apparently non-public letters, especially where they were addressed to clubs or institutions rather than individuals, were turned into public
letters through being reprinted in newspapers. I have an entire volume of
such cuttings, compiled anonymously in the 1880s, in which Ruskin's letters
to individuals, newspapers, and groups alike are reprinted under such headlines as 'Mr Ruskin on Cycling' or 'Mr Ruskin and the Socialists'. Such
dislocation of letters from their original contexts and controversies may well
not have pleased Ruskin, but such acts of metamorphosis from private

correspondence into public statement do mark a recognition by late-Victorian readers of the importance attached to the *letter* as a way of maintaining public discourse in a distinctive language and form. Cook and Wedderburn make very similar use of Ruskin's letters in the editorial matter in the *Works*.

There can be no doubt that Ruskin acknowledged that his letters to the press displayed generic similarities of style, manner, and occasion which were as important as specific content. The preface to *Arrows of the Chace*[19] sets up a clear formal paradigm for the Ruskinian public letter by differentiating positively between a volume and a periodical manner. First of all the letter to the press had to proceed from a deeply felt source. It should never be casual or trivial. In part this insistence on the seriousness of the occasion offered Ruskin further protection from the charge of opportunist or sensational journalism. But this 'fully provoked zeal' also implied disadvantages: the deeply felt article was likely to be hurried and exaggerated in tone, liable to intemperance or hysteria. Second, the newspaper letter had to be 'controversial rather than direct' – that is to say, provocative and requiring further reply. This notion of the public letter being a *dialogue* rather than a *statement* is a very important element in the development of Ruskin's late work, and the number of his letters which generated extended exchanges is understated by *Arrows of the Chace* which only prints Ruskin's side of the correspondence. The press letter was a literary mode which put Ruskin in direct contact with at least some of his readers, a kind of discourse which prompted many of his later experiments in literary form. Third, the letter to the press, while being too urgent and too short to allow the writer to become selfconscious about literary form, did make him acutely conscious of style. The brevity and simple purpose of the newspaper letter demanded what Ruskin called 'deliberate precision'. This precision, Ruskin felt, was principally to be found in startling imagery, and especially in the concentrating effects of the wide-ranging allusion and the vigorous simile:

> At the time of my life in which [my letters to the press] were composed, I was fonder of metaphor, and more fertile in simile, than I am now; and I employed both with franker trust in the reader's intelligence. Carefully chosen, they are always a powerful means of concentration; and I could then dismiss in six words, 'thistledown without seeds, and bubbles without colour', forms of art on which I should perhaps spend half a page of analytic vituperation; and represent, with a pleasant accuracy which my best methods of outline and exposition could now no more achieve, the entire system of modern plutocratic policy, under the luckily remembered image of the Arabian bridegroom, bewitched with his heels uppermost.[20]

The strikingly allusive and wildly imagistic style described here is to be widely found in Ruskin's work (as are deprecatory remarks about his failing literary powers). Here is a famous short letter, initially addressed to a group of Conservative students who had asked Ruskin to stand for the rectorship of Glasgow University, but provocative enough to demand wide reprinting in the press:

> What in the Devil's name have *you* to do with either Mr D'Israeli or Mr Gladstone? You are students at the University, and have no more business with politics than you have with rat-catching. Had you ever read ten words of mine with understanding, you would have known that I care no more either for Mr D'Israeli or Mr Gladstone than for two old bagpipes with the drones going by steam, but that I hate all Liberalism as I do Beelzebub and that, with Carlyle, I stand – we two alone now in England, for God and the Queen.[21]

It may seem here that the literary method is largely aimed at distracting attention from the reactionary social perspective, but in fact the literary intention is more sophisticated than that. Ruskin gains his moral victory by the startling energy, almost venom, of his reply – an apparently inappropriate, but deliberately and mischievously contrived, over-reaction to a polite request. The antitheses are equally carefully handled – politics/rat-catching, Liberalism/Beelzebub, Carlyle and Ruskin/God and Queen/Disraeli and Gladstone – and brilliantly underlined by the simile (or should it be personification ?) of the bagpipes. Ruskin even manages to import, by extending the bagpipe image, a key word – 'steam' – which resonates throughout his works. Thus, by allusion, Ruskin invokes a connection between a totally dehumanized, regulated, steam-driven society and the unceasing mechanistic rhetoric of political debate, a 'drone' which stands in damaging contrast to Ruskin's own pointed brevity here. The total trivializing of Disraeli and Gladstone is an almost incidental benefit. No wonder the public enjoyed the unpredictable energy of Ruskin's newspaper letters, and insisted on their wide appearance. The extent of this pleasure can be gauged by a wittily conceived parody of the above letter, contained in an article which has the wider target of letter-writing manuals for the aspiring social climber as its main source of ridicule:

To the Secretary of a Working Men's Constitutional Association, on being requested to become President of the same.

> MY DEAR SIR,
>   May I politely inquire of you what, in the Devil's name you mean by calling yourselves a 'Working Men's Constitutional Association'?!

> You are working men; and as such you have no more do with the
> Constitution – of which, by the bye, T. C. and myself are the only
> true guardians and supporters left in all broad England, especially
> myself – than you have to do with the fine old sport of bear-baiting. *I
> am a Constitutionalist, and the best of the lot*; but, dash my buttons,
> if I see what right you have to put yourself on a level with me and
> T. C. Read my books. If you say you can't afford them, I beg to
> remind you that by abstaining for five years from bread, beer, spirits
> and tobacco, you will be quite able to afford a volume of *Fors
> Clavigera*.[22]

The appreciation and delight in Ruskin's allusive, energetic, and concentrated style testifies to his success as a public letter writer. The constant use
of key words like 'steam' to invoke concepts widely analysed in his work, and
the deliberate verbal play all point to Ruskin's grasp of the 'concentration'
imposed by the Letters Page.

The bulk of Ruskin's letters to the press appeared, as might be expected, in
The Times, the *Daily Telegraph* and the *Pall Mall Gazette*. Many others
appeared in appropriate specialist journals – the *Artists' and Amateurs'
Magazine*, the *Builder*, the *Monetary Gazette* – as the subject demanded. A
considerable number appeared in local papers, although generally large-
circulation local papers, often in response to cuttings which had been sent to
Ruskin. Local papers in Liverpool, Birmingham, Leicester, Kidderminster,
Sheffield, and Glasgow all published contributions by Ruskin, perhaps suggesting the connection of his interests with major manufacturing areas of
Britain. The subject matter of Ruskin's letters to the press ranged across an
enormous variety of topics: art, architecture, geology, natural history, wars,
political economy, railways, servants, education and women, to use only the
categories adopted by *Arrows of the Chace*. Yet a reading of these disparate
occasional writings does not identify any particular consciousness in the
author of the differing readerships for which he is writing. Much more
striking are the similarities in tone, method, and stylistic strategy which
underlie the variety of purpose. The *generic* coherence of the letter to the
press, based on the factors outlined above, seems far more important to
Ruskin than the *occasional* differences. This coupling of advanced literary
awareness and occasional indifference is not to be found in Ruskin's more
extended, but stylistically less extreme, periodical contributions.

8

An important initial distinction to be made among Ruskin's more extended
periodical writings is that between single articles, series of articles, and series

of articles deliberately intended to form book-length studies. The number of Ruskin's single articles is amazingly few for such a fluent, prolific, and famous writer. Less than 20 articles were published under his name, and of these less than a dozen were unsolicited. Clumsy as it seems, it is worth listing the most important of these articles in order to suggest the coherent and self-conscious policy which underlay the apparent variety of Ruskin's periodical writings. Ruskin wrote the following articles: four short articles for Loudon's *Magazine of Natural History* (1834–6); an article on the state of meteorological studies for the first volume of the *Transactions of the Meteorological Society* (1839); two long review articles on art books for the *Quarterly* (1847 and 1849); 'Samuel Prout' for the *Art Journal* (1849); 'Sir Joshua and Holbein' for the first issue of the *Cornhill Magazine* (1860); a short article on knowledge for the *Contemporary Review* (1871), where he also published 'The nature and authority of miracle' and 'Home and its economies' in 1873; 'The three colours of Pre-Raphaelitism' in the *Nineteenth Century* (1878); and 'Usury' again in the *Contemporary Review* (1880). To these might be added 'An Oxford lecture', intended as a lecture, but reprinted unaltered in the *Contemporary Review* in 1878. All these periodical contributions were reprinted in successive editions of *On the Old Road* among various pamphlets, lectures, and prefaces to other writers' works. A few other short articles are to be found in vol. xxxiv of the *Works*.

Such a remarkably small total of articles poses the question of why Ruskin published even these few. Some answers are easily supplied. 'Sir Joshua and Holbein' was commissioned by the new and immensely prestigious *Cornhill*, which was to be published by Ruskin's own publishers, Smith Elder & Co., whose literary adviser was W. S. Williams, a personal friend of John James Ruskin and one of Ruskin's earliest patrons. The article, in short, was written as a personal favour, and although published anonymously, the authorship was an open secret. The early group of natural history articles, too, had their origins in the literary world inhabited by John James Ruskin and his cultured friends. Ruskin was only 15 when he began to publish in Loudon's journals, and while his work was not without merit or interest, his early break into print was carried out under the patronage and parental sponsorship of John James Ruskin.[23] The two long *Quarterly* reviews are more interesting and revealing. Both were commissioned by the editor J. G. Lockhart and published anonymously (or at least under Ruskin's honorary pseudonym of 'A graduate of Oxford') the first largely out of regard for Lockhart's daughter.[24] In their anonymous dogmatism they represent the kind of journalism which the later Ruskin most despised, for, as reviews, they derived their energy from the work of others, were concerned with making or destroying reputations, and fulfilled a transient interest in new books. The seriousness of tone and the measured rolling paragraphs of the review of Lord Lindsay's *Christian Art*, for example, cannot conceal the fact that the essay is extremely hostile, and capable of breaking the book's reputation. The overall tone is one of sustained and faintly indignant scepticism, a worldly tone unenlivened by Ruskin's more urgent invective or caustic contempt. Such a tone – Osbert Lancaster might call it 'Reviewer's sophisticated' – is one only found in the young Ruskin, and, in the light of his later tirades against the clever insincerities of paid reviewing, it is much to Ruskin's credit that he not only deliberately refused further commisions for reviews (many of which must have come his way), but actively renounced his anonymous, assured, dogmatic *Quarterly* mode: 'I never felt at ease in my graduate incognito, and although I consented, some nine years ago, to review Lord Lindsay's "Christian Art" and Sir Charles Eastlake's "Essay on Oil Painting" in the *Quarterly*, I have ever since steadily refused to write even for that once respectable periodical.'[25] Ruskin wrote this in 1856, early in his career, and already he was formulating, and enacting, principles from which he never wavered.

As far as I can tell, the article on meteorology, 'Samuel Prout' (published anonymously), and the brief but ambitious 'The range of intellectual conception proportioned to rank in animated life', were freely submitted by Ruskin to their various places of publication. 'The nature and authority of miracle', too, was freely submitted to the *Contemporary Review*, prompted only by widespread newspaper controversy and Ruskin's belief in the urgency of what he was saying. More interesting than those occasional pieces, however, are the generic confusions and developments of three late articles 'Home and its economies', 'The three colours of Pre-Raphaelitism' and 'Usury'. 'The three colours of Pre-Raphaelitism' was planned as a lecture (Ruskin's most frequently used literary mode in the 1870s), part of a series he was giving during his second tenure of the Slade Professorship of Art. Serious illness intervened, and Ruskin's lecture, an account of Pre-Raphaelite imaginative power in distinction from naturalistic technical accomplishment which unfolded from a typically Ruskinian insight into a chance combination of pictures hanging together in a country-house drawing-room, found its way in the *Nineteenth Century* under the following conditions:

And for many reasons I would fain endeavour to tell my Oxford pupils some facts which seem to me worth memory about these six works of art; which, if they will reflect upon, being, in the present state of my health, the best I can do for them in the way of autumn lecturing, it will be kind to me. And as I cannot speak what I would, and believe my pupils are more likely to read it if printed in the

Nineteenth Century than in a separate pamphlet, I have asked, and
obtained of the editor, space in columns which ought, nevertheless, I
think, usually to be occupied with sterner subjects, as the Fates are
now driving the nineteenth century on its missionary path.[26]

Ruskin's apologetic tone is instructive: a magazine article, he suggests, is a
less effective discourse than a lecture, but, if necessity presses, reaches a
wider audience than a pamphlet. The apologies go even deeper, including the
apparently timid and ingenuous 'request' to the editor (which editor would
have been unwilling to include a lengthy article by Ruskin, especially if it
was not about economics?), and hesitant sequence of qualifications: 'ought'
. . . 'nevertheless' . . . and 'I think'. The weight of Ruskin's anxiety,
however, lies in his belief that magazines should be devoted to 'sterner stuff'
than art criticism. Such a belief might appear conventional modesty on
Ruskin's part if 'The three colours of Pre-Raphaelitism' had not been a rare
exception among his works – an occasional, article-length publication submitted freely to a magazine in the hope of a wider readership. In fairness to
Ruskin, it seems right to accept the sincerity of his apologies.

'Home and Its Economies' and 'Usury' are interesting not so much as
re-statements of Ruskin's views on the moral basis of economics as exercises
in popular polemic. 'Home and its economies' had as its sources an article by
Herbert Spencer, previously published in the *Contemporary Review*, and an
article by W. R. Greg in the *Pall Mall Gazette*. Ruskin also drew on other
articles in the *Cornhill*, and made considerable, if unspecified, allusions to his
own works. Although the manner of the article is that of the experienced
controversialist – now wounded by the misunderstanding of others, now
triumphantly assertive, now icily polite, and always energetic, concerned,
rational, – the mode of address is more unusual, largely because Ruskin
assumes continuing debate to be a normal literary method. With a small
group of intellectual disputants as his readership, such a manner would be
expected, but in this article Ruskin is beginning to open his dialogue by
including comment and quotation from a wide range of sources, often
only made relevant by a striking allusion, a strained metaphor or a verbal
resonance. Thus Ruskin alludes to letters he has received from various
correspondents, cites Dick Turpin as a metaphor for a certain economic
system, quotes lengthily from *The Times* and the letters of Walter Scott.
This apparent randomness and lack of concentration on a single, developed
argument in fact creates an interesting effect of activity and process. Argument is to be created from material culled from all levels of discourse – the
stray thoughts of a clergyman correspondent are given the same prominence
as the ideas of W. R. Greg, Sir Walter Scott is presented as a more incisive

social critic than Mr Goldwin Smith. In this cumulative, allusive, democratizing polemical method, Ruskin manages to create an active, unfinished, untidy, but open kind of dialogue.

'Usury' has an even more improvised, more allusive structure. A letter from Ruskin to the Rev. F. A. Malleson was published in the *Contemporary Review* which provoked the Bishop of Manchester to write a long reply to Ruskin who promptly incorporated it into 'A reply and a rejoinder' in the same magazine. The allusiveness of Ruskin's rejoinder is typical. He preserves the energy of a violent tirade against contemporary social evils, as he begins to find his verbal resources failing, by quoting at length from an anonymous, simple-hearted, less subtle correspondent, and actually makes us believe that the letter arrived on his desk just as he was writing the letter, and was immediately assimilated into it. This improvisational quality – in fact a carefully wrought spontaneity – is furthered by the range of material incorporated in the article, from books on polar exploration to Bishop Jewell writing in the *Contemporary Review*, to a calculated self-revelatory anecdote. Again equal status is conferred on a wide range of authorities, from a simple-minded correspondent to a bishop. Again there is the sense of openness, of continuation, of work left unfinished and unshaped to allow further contribution. It is the sense of possible *discourse*, increasingly evident in Ruskin's work on political economy in the 1870s, which makes the heavyweight magazines, with their largely well-informed and cultured readership, untenable for Ruskin's intentions. Ruskin had clearly meant what he had said in his denunciations of opportunist journalism, and the dearth of his periodical articles suggests his integrity in refusing the tremendous opportunities he must have had to appear in wide-circulation periodicals, especially as an influential reviewer. Under heavy occasional pressure, he was prepared to use magazine articles, especially to create or prolong controversy, but only when his other, deliberately fostered, literary discourses were inappropriate. Ruskin acknowledged that using magazines increased his readership – he talked of the 'large circle' of the *Contemporary Review* readers,[27] and the 'more likely' readership of the *Nineteenth Century* – but also knew that the kind of readers he would gain were not those he really wanted to impress. Yet even in his single magazine articles, Ruskin began to develop his controversial dialogue forms which dominated his later writing, and gave rise to the *serial* article as his major chosen genre for works of political economy and social criticism.

9

Six of Ruskin's volume-length works had their origin in series of periodical articles, seven if one includes the ten short tirades on the moral failings of the contemporary arts published in the *Art Journal* (1865–6), and partially reworked in *The Queen of the Air* and *Ariadne Florentina*. These somewhat extreme examples of Ruskin's more hectoring style go under the name of *The Cestus of Aglaia*. Of the other six, *The Poetry of Architecture* (published in book form in 1893) belongs to the youthful articles published by J. C. Loudon, sponsored by John James Ruskin, and republished by George Allen nearly 60 years after they were written. The articles were never intended to form a coherent book, for they were organized around a sensibility rather than a theme, but the overall result is a surprisingly effective essay on early-nineteenth-century associationalism. *Fiction Fair and Foul* appeared as five essays in the *Nineteenth Century*, four in 1880 and one in late 1881, and these essays reflect the discursive, almost chaotic, spontaneous, associative style of Ruskin's last work. Ruskin attempted to organize his judgments on the novel (including his boundless contempt for George Eliot) but the blend of over-indulgent style, especially revealed in the leaden humour of the essays, and disintegrating critical faculties, failed to do Ruskin's literary criticism proper justice. Without discounting these three works, I want to concentrate attention on the four works which show Ruskin's central use and development of the serial article form: *Unto This Last* (1860), *Munera Pulveris* (1862), *Time and Tide* (1866–7) and *Fors Clavigera* (1871 onwards).

I have already pointed out that these four works form Ruskin's main writing on political economy specifically differentiated as a subject from social ethics or political and educational reform. As Cook and Wedderburn say, the first three of these works were 'written in the same temper; they deal, from different points of approach, with the same topics',[28] but they also go on to point out, in defence of their own grouping of all three works and related letters in one volume, that 'his teaching is discursive in method, and is scattered through many books and papers'.[29] It is these links between theme, occasion, and method which need elaboration here. It is tempting to jump to the conclusion that there is an obvious and close relationship in Ruskin's work between political economy and the serial article form. Certainly the serial article in wide-circulation and influential magazines would seem an obvious place for major work on such a subject. The dialectical method was central to Victorian economic writing, and the statement and rejoinder form of the periodical discussion was suitable for clarifying ideas prior to larger attempts at systemization. Many Victorian social critics were principally periodical contributors rather than writers of volumes – Morley, Huxley, Hutton, and Frederic Harrison, in slightly differing fields, come immediately to mind. Then again the advantages of large circulations for what in volume form was likely to become a technical treatise with a tiny, specialized readership, meant that the periodicals had a high claim on the political economist's attention. I have assumed, in default of more extended study of economic writing in the periodicals, that the wide-circulation, serious periodicals pre-existed Ruskin's work as an appropriate place for economic discussions, and that the dialogue mode of continuing riposte and highly developed polemical styles also pre-dated *Unto This Last*. Why then, did Ruskin, having himself developed such pre-existent forms of discourse to a high degree of polish, abandon the heavyweight periodicals for, on the one hand, provincial newspapers, and, on the other, his self-evolved, experimental format *Fors Clavigera*? Instead of seeing political economy and the serial article as interdependent in Ruskin's work, it is necessary to look more closely at the modes and occasions of his work in this field.

Ruskin's first attempts to elaborate more formally the implicit economic analysis which underlay the 'Nature of Gothic' chapter in *The Stones of Venice* were two letters to *The Times*, written in 1852, which, due to John James Ruskin's disapproval, were not published until the *Works* edition. The two letters give a clear insight into the procedure of Ruskin's economic works. In the process of a brief letter on taxation, Ruskin suggested that basic principles could be defined for taxation, election, and education, a division which generated the progress and shape of subsequent letters. Such a group of self-contained articles, shaped by the needs of a developing argument, and locking into a series, gave Ruskin both a concentrated and a spontaneous, discursive form, free to develop in any direction. With the general movement of the work loosely defined, but each essay capable of generating its own shape and that of subsequent essays, Ruskin's choice of the serial article for what he saw as his most important subject was thus made before any sustained work in the field had appeared in print. Yet such a choice was not as free or as conscious as it may seem, for Ruskin in the 1850s was still very uncertain of his abilities as a political economist even as he became convinced of the centrality of the subject. The serial letter or article form enabled him to test public response, and to withdraw if hostile opinion compelled. In addition, through his choice of *The Times* as the place to display his political economy, Ruskin made a crucial psychological break from the literary relationships of patronage into the world of 'worth' where what he wrote was subject to scrutiny, and criticism, from a wide range of informed opinion. The quality of Ruskin's work was being put to public test, an ordeal which he came later to welcome, but which caused a great deal of initial anxiety. That his attempted correspondence with *The Times* was a radical gesture can be gauged from the violence of John James Ruskin's response. He wrote to his son that criticism of his writings on art 'was as the waves beating on Eddystone lighthouse' while his work in political economy was 'slum buildings, liable to be knocked down'.[30]

Over the following eight years, increasing conviction of the importance of the subject matter drove Ruskin to a further redefinition of the modes and occasions for his political economy. He again chose the serial periodical article format, largely through a need to reject entirely the uncontroversial, complacent literary values of his father's circle of friends. The new *Cornhill* was the perfect place for such theatrical gestures, as it represented exactly the genteel discourse Ruskin was attacking. Having been asked to contribute 'Sir Joshua and Holbein' to the first issue, as befitted a prestigious Smith, Elder author, Ruskin knew that he could use his standing to find a wider audience for his political economy which was not available elsewhere. The psychological and intellectual urgency of the matter can easily be seen in the accompanying letter he sent with the first instalment of *Unto This Last* to his old, and alarmed, patron W. Smith Williams: 'I send you some Political Economy, which, if you can venture to use in any way for the *Cornhill*, stigmatizing it by any notes of reprobation which you may think necessary, I shall be very glad. All I care about is to get into print, somehow.'[31] As Ruskin reveals here, he felt compelled to find a new, far larger audience for his insistent subject, regardless of consequent censorship or hostile criticism. The subsequent history of the serial publication of *Unto This Last* is well enough known. Combined editorial, parental, and public pressure (though it is not clear that Ruskin really outraged half of England, as was later claimed), caused *Unto This Last* to be stopped after four appearances with the editorial concession of an extended final instalment to allow Ruskin to impose something like his intended shape on the essays. It is difficult to judge whether it was the 'socialistic' tendencies of the essays which shocked some readers, or the passion which Ruskin imported into supposedly rational and objective discourse, but what is clear is that Ruskin firmly succeeded in breaking the proprieties of magazine articles through the personal urgency which he brought to his beliefs and the violence of his style. By using the *Cornhill* at all for such work Ruskin deliberately redefined his readership and broke with the conventions of genteel discourse. By using the *Cornhill* as he did, for an inappropriately passionate discourse on a 'scientific' subject, Ruskin alienated and offended the propriety of serious mass-circulation journalism. The necessity of finding a place to publish free from psychological anxiety or obligation, editorial control, and a predetermined politeness towards one's readership had to be weighed against the potentiality of the serial article form and the urgency, as Ruskin saw it, of the subject matter which drove him, against his judgment, towards the periodicals.

Munera Pulveris was initially a less traumatic experience, but finally left Ruskin even more dissatisfied with the nature of economic discourse. *Munera Pulveris* was commissioned by J. A. Froude, editor of *Fraser's*

Magazine, who was not only sympathetic to Ruskin's ideas but also realized the incomplete and unbalanced nature of *Unto This Last*. The serial article form and extensive readership offered by *Fraser's* still held its attractions for Ruskin, and he embarked on the book in the hope that it could be better organized and as extensive as he wished. The outcome is well described by Cook and Wedderburn:

> The long interval which elapsed between the appearance of the essays in *Fraser's Magazine* and their publication as a book was due to a rebuff of the same kind which had cut short the earlier essays in the *Cornhill*. The fourth paper was sent to *Fraser's Magazine* from Mornex in March 1863, and duly appeared in the number for April. 'The present paper', wrote Ruskin at the end of it, 'completes the definitions necessary for future service. The next in order will be the first chapter of the body of the work.' But the next in order was never to come. Froude . . . 'had not wholly lost courage,' but 'the Publisher indignantly interfered, and the readers of *Fraser*,' says Ruskin, 'as those of the *Cornhill*, were protected for that time from further disturbance on my part.' This second veto was a bitter vexation to Ruskin. . . . he paced his terrace-walk for hours like a caged lion, and deep gloom gathered upon him.[32]

Cook and Wedderburn go on to describe both the public outcry created by *Munera Pulveris* and the anxiety which this caused John James Ruskin. The censorship of a *commissioned* work which Ruskin had clearly conceived as stretching on serially into a very large-scale work confirmed his long-standing belief in the difficulties of mass-circulation journals for authors as well as readers. The conventional discourse of mid-Victorian England clearly did not correspond to the ideas, forms and readerships which Ruskin's political economy required.

The period between the appearance, or rather non-appearance, of *Munera Pulveris* in *Fraser's* and the writing of *Time and Tide* produced no major work of political economy, but the death of John James Ruskin in 1864 freed Ruskin to write as, and where, he chose. *Unto This Last* and *Munera Pulveris* had provoked a great deal of both public and private correspondence and, as Cook and Wedderburn put it, 'his frequent letters to the newspapers did a great deal to call attention to his views.' In addition 'these discussions introduced, to a wider circle than was as yet reached by his books, the theories and principles which he had closely at heart',[33] and gave Ruskin a sense of possible untapped readerships. The genesis of *Time and Tide*, Ruskin's next work of political economy, and its shape, were brilliantly improvisational. The book was written as a series of 25 letters to Thomas Dixon, a Sunderland cork-cutter, whom Ruskin regarded as an ideal of a socially and culturally active, respectable, and hard-working working man. Dixon was prone to extensive correspondence with famous writers,[34] and *Time and Tide* was begun as an attempt to extend Ruskin's work on political economy beyond *Munera Pulveris* through an unamibitious series of simply-phrased letters to Dixon. The 'vehicle of familiar correspondence'[35] was chosen ostensibly because Ruskin was in poor health and unequal to sustained literary work. The more serious reason, however, was that Ruskin was so disillusioned with the hostile response to his work that he had begun to feel that an audience of *one* reader of Dixon's quality and commitment was preferable to thousands of *Cornhill* readers. In addition, Ruskin gave Dixon a free hand to reprint the letters serially in journals or newspapers of Dixon's choice. By this means, Ruskin was clearly trying to create an audience of many Dixon-like readers. In some ways it may seem as if Ruskin was thus attempting to avoid controversy by speaking only to readers whose status and experience predisposed them to be lectured at in silence. But this, I think, is to ignore the brilliantly improvisational way in which Ruskin used the initial occasion of *Time and Tide* to create a genuinely alternative readership to the *Cornhill* or *Fraser's* – a readership dissipated by the volume reprinting of the work. It is interesting that Dixon chose old-established provincial newspapers (the *Leeds Mercury* and the *Manchester Daily Examiner and Times*) for the serialization of *Time and Tide*, seeing such readers – the informed, socially aware working men of the manufacturing districts – as those best suited to Ruskin's intentions.

Although the subject matter of *Time and Tide* is largely an utopian extension of previously articulated ideas, I think the originality of the book has never been fully appreciated. The mode – letters of advice to an aspiring social inferior, to put it cruelly – is by no means unusual, but the relationship between private letter and public statement is uniquely defined by asking the *recipient* to delineate the most effective readership for the letters. Comments and replies by Dixon are also incorporated into the text, and although it is always clear that Ruskin is to dominate any discussion and runs little risk to his authority as author, he is still moving towards a more immediate and topical form of literary dialogue. Ruskin gains a quiet, reasonable tone through the elimination of the sense of strident opposition between author and reader which characterized *Unto This Last* and *Munera Pulveris*, admittedly a gain only possible with a co-operative and subservient readership. (Dixon is continually addressed as 'my friend'.) The combination of this gentle tone, of the effect of the self-contained but cumulatively related letters, of the sense of spontaneity created by the format, of ideas growing and being shaped in the act of writing and discussion, and of the manipulation of the public/private ambiguity of the letter mode all suggest the originality of the book's discourse and begin to define Ruskin's literary intentions when free from parental censorship, editorial control, and the pressures of satisfying a mass readership. The difference in tone between the original letters and the rewritten volume text has never been properly explored, but I suspect any such comparison would only confirm the carefully created spontaneity and deftness of Ruskin's exercise in improvised and familiar political economy.

Fors Clavigera represents Ruskin's least inhibited attempt at combining serial publication format and unconventional definitions of readership. The book is usually regarded as the occasion when emotional and intellectual pressure finally conspired to destroy Ruskin's coherence, and it is certainly not true that Ruskin was always in conscious control of his intentions. But the deliberate attempts which Ruskin had already made to redefine his readership and reconstruct his discourse with Victorian England suggest that *Fors* was the culmination of long experience and considerable understanding of the deficiencies of periodical literature. Such deliberate intentions are confirmed by Ruskin's use of *Fors* as an attack on the dominant modes of bookselling and publishing. *Fors* was issued as a monthly periodical, though whether 'periodical' is an adequate word to describe a magazine whose publisher, editor, sole contributor and most ferocious critic were all the same person is open to doubt, especially as *Fors* could not be obtained except, expensively, by post, from the middle of a field in Kent. Even more bizarre than the uniquely eclectic journal-cum-confessional literary mode adopted by *Fors* is the way in which Ruskin strove to define his readership. The chosen distribution system, the expense, and the lack of publicity all seemed to preclude the precise readership delineated in the famous sub-title dedication: 'to the workmen and labourers of Great Britain'. The paradoxes of Ruskin's position were widely obvious. The Manchester Ruskin Society produced a forlorn pamphlet in 1880 called 'Is it true that Mr Ruskin's books are scarce, dear, and difficult to obtain?', and *Punch* could barely conceal its glee ('I beg to remind you that by abstaining for five years from bread, beer, spirits and tobacco, you will be quite able to afford a volume of *Fors Clavigera*'[36]). But the above account of Ruskin's experiences with the periodical press has suggested the inevitable paradoxes of his position – on the one hand the virtues of wide or well-defined readerships, volatile and exciting literary possibilities and stylistic concentration, on the other the vices of cynical, commercial, unthinking ephemerality on trivial subjects written to divert the lowest tastes of ill-informed people from serious issues.

Such a narrative of the publishing history of Ruskin's articles/books on political economy is inevitably inadequate, particularly in focussing attention on the close relationship between form, occasion, style and content. But I hope I have said enough to suggest the unusualness and importance of Ruskin's experiments in periodical forms, especially in *Time and Tide* and *Fors Clavigera*. Nowhere near enough stress has been placed on Ruskin's selfconscious development of periodical modes for his economic writing, nor on his rejection of polite discourse for riskier, and in many ways less effective, dialogues with different readerships. At this level Ruskin's works provide considerable insight into the ideological relationships of Victorian literary discourse. Equally, the essential link between periodicals and political economy has been largely left unexamined. Ruskin's recognition of the pre-existing dialogues in this field, his sense of the occasional opportunities and formal possibilities of the serial article format, above all his belief that the *seriousness* of the subject protected him from the persecution of mass readerships, all met with total disillusion as instructive to us as it was devastating to Ruskin. His recovery from these terrible experiences led him, with typical energy and determination, to exploit periodical literature in an unique and radical way. *Fors Clavigera* alone represents Ruskin's indictment of the appalling constraints which were created and sustained by the Victorian periodical press.

NOTES

1. A full account of the 'Works' series is given in *The Works of John Ruskin*, ed. E. T. Cook and A. D. O. Wedderburn (39 vols., 1903–12), XVIII, 10–11, and XXXVIII, 26. All references to Ruskin's works are to this edition, hereafter abbreviated to *Works*.

2. By 1909, when most of Ruskin's books were out of copyright, Allen was publishing a 1s., a 1s.6d., a 2s.6d., and a 5s. uniform edition of most of Ruskin's works in addition to the *Works*. Dent were publishing an Everyman's Library edition, and Routledge a Universal Library collection.

3. Published 1903–12, but planned in various forms from the early 1890s.

4. See *Works*, XVII, cxiv and 302.

5. Frederic Harrison, *Realities and Ideals* (1908), 365–6.

6. E. M. Forster, *A Room With A View* (1908), ch. II.

7. Worst of all were the Annuals to which Ruskin contributed poems as young man. It is hard to forget the stories of John Clare, in desperate financial need which he hoped that hurried submissions to the Annuals would solve, discovering that such publications tended to pay contributors their accumulated earning once every *few years*. See F. Martin, *Life of John Clare* (1865), 209 et seq.

8. *Works*, XXIX, 205.

9. *Works*, XXIX, 470.

10. *Works*, XXIX, 205. For other denunciations of the popular press see also the preface to the second edition of vol. I of *Modern Painters*.

11. *Works*, XXXIV, 470.

12. *Works*, XXXIV, 471.

13. *Works*, XXXIV, 470.

14. *Works*, XVII, 547 et seq.

15. *Works*, XXXIV, 470–1.

16. *Works*, XXXIV, 471.

17. *Works*, III, 16.

18. *Works*, XXVIII, 449.

19. *Works*, XXXIV, 469–71.

20. *Works*, XXXIV, 470.

21. *Works*, XXXIV, 548–9.

22. *Punch*, 23 Oct. 1880. See my own article, 'Ruskin and *Punch* 1870–1900',

Victorian Periodicals Rev., xii no. 1
(1979), 15–24

23. My article '"Only Print" – Ruskin and
    the publishers', *Durham University J.*
    (June 1971), 196–207, contains an
    account of the literary world of John
    James Ruskin.
24. *Works*, viii, xxiv.
25. *Works*, xiv, 44.
26. *Works*, xxxiv, 147–8.
27. *Works*, xxxiv, 401.
28. *Works*, xvii, xix.

29. *Works*, xvii, xx.
30. *Works*, xiii, lxxxiv.
31. *Works*, xvii, xxvi.
32. *Works*, xvii, lxviii – lxix.
33. *Works*, xvii, lxviii.
34. The Sotheby's sale catalogue of Dixon's
    papers (6–7 July 1970), gives a good
    indication of the extent of such
    correspondence.
35. *Works*, xvii, lxxx.
36. *Punch*, 23 Oct. 1880.

Ann P. Robson and
John M. Robson

'Impetuous eagerness':
the young Mill's
radical journalism

1

In the *Traveller* for 6 December 1822, over the signature 'S' and under the heading 'Exchangeable value', appeared a letter to the editor which began: 'Sir, – In your notice of the late Meeting of the Political Economy Club, you have inserted a disquisition, which professes to be a refutation of Mr Mill's theory of value. I take the liberty of submitting to you several remarks which occurred to me on reading your article.' Almost exactly 50 years later, in the *Examiner* for 11 January 1873, over what had become one of the best-known names in England, and under the heading 'Should public bodies be required to sell their lands?', appeared a leading article which ended: 'the time has come for announcing with the utmost decision, and we hope to see land reformers uniting as one body in the demand, that no private appropriation of land, not yet private property, shall hereafter take place under any circumstances or on any pretext. J. S. Mill.' These two contributions are the alpha and omega of John Stuart Mill's newspaper writings.

Mill's reputation was founded on, and he remains best known for, such major books as his *System of Logic, Principles of Political Economy, On Liberty, Utilitarianism,* and *Considerations on Representative Government.* A smaller audience knows him also as a major contributor to nineteenth-century quarterlies and monthlies, both as editor and author; their awareness comes mainly through his *Dissertations and Discussions,* a collection of articles mostly from the quarterlies, and through a few other reprints of some of his more influential essays. His third string, however, that which vibrated in the daily and weekly press, is little known today, though it sounded often and tunefully enough to establish him as one of the most interesting journalists of his time.

In all, about 450 items by Mill appeared in newspapers, the great bulk in volume as well as a number being leading articles, the rest being an interesting mixture of letters to the editor and reviews, with a few miscellaneous bits and pieces.[1] These items, especially those written in his early 20s, show a side of

Mill that did not reveal itself conspicuously in his major works, though it colours them. He was not, as is often asserted, a cold and unfeeling man, although on the surface the prose of his books appears only that of the practised logician. And he is misunderstood when the depth and impetuousness of his feelings are ignored. To see Mill vigorously employing and obviously enjoying the vituperation common to the British press, especially in the 1830s, is to appreciate more fully both the man and his journalistic contemporaries.

It must be remembered, of course, that Mill was not primarily a journalist, for he had (thanks to his father) a canny sense of the need for regular employment, as well as a commanding desire for lasting fame:

> Writing for the press, cannot be recommended as a permanent
> resource to any one qualified to accomplish anything in the higher
> departments of literature or thought: not only on account of the
> uncertainty of this means of livelihood, especially if the writer has a
> conscience, and will not consent to serve any opinions except his own;
> but also because the writings by which one can live, are not the
> writings which themselves live, and are never those in which the
> writer does his best.[2]

His career as a newspaper journalist was, consequently, sporadic. In 17 of the 50 years between his first and last writings nothing appeared in any newspaper, and most of his contributions came in three short periods: the first in 1823 when, trying his hand at the craft, he published 27 items, 19 of them letters to the editor (many of them, especially those to John Black of the *Morning Chronicle*, were, if not commissioned, certainly expected); the second from mid–1830 to 1834, when the number rose to more than 200 (the great majority being commissioned leaders in the *Examiner*, and of these the largest number on France); and the third in 1846 and the first part of 1847, when he published a substantial series (almost all leaders) on Ireland in the *Morning Chronicle*. It is on the writings of the middle group, when Mill was in his mid-20s, that we shall concentrate in this necessarily limited examination of the exuberantly radical Mill and the press for which he wrote.

In virtually all his works, Mill is consciously polemical, but in those of his writings which he expected to have a long life (one is tempted, in contemporary jargon, to say a 'long shelf life', like that peculiar form of milk that is sent to warm climates from Cheshire) he muted the argument in a consummately moulded rhetoric. Concerning newspapers, however, he saw, even during the period of his own most intense journalism, that his father's comments on the fickle qualities of quarterly reviews[3] applied *a fortiori* to sheets, even more creatures of a day. For example, in 1837, praising Albany Fonblanque, the editor of the *Examiner*, for which he had written so extensively, Mill asserts that Fonblanque's genius separates him from the merely talented, who do nothing to relieve 'the insupportable tediousness of gone-by politics'. He continues:

> The Spartan in the story, who, for the crime of using two words where one would have sufficed, was sentenced to read from beginning to end the history of Guicciardini, and at the end of a few pages begged to commute his punishment for the galleys, would have prayed to exchange it for death if he had been condemned to read a file of English newspapers five years old. . . . If the interest [in reading Fonblanque's collected articles] anywhere flags, it is towards the end of the last volume, where the contents are recent, and we come in contact with the exhausted controversies of the present day and hour.[4]

Perhaps thinking of his now as-yet-unfulfilled ambitions, he describes Fonblanque as 'a great writer, who happens accidentally to be a journalist', and who has more than the talent most valuable to a mere journalist, that of 'being skilfully common-place'.[5] But for the best, the craft has well-marked limits:

> Even when pursued with higher objects, newspaper writing is subject to the same condition as popular speaking – it must produce its impression at once, or not at all; and he is the most effective newspaper writer, as he is the most effective speaker, who can, without being irksome or offensive, declaim upon one idea long enough to make it sink into the mind.[6]

And he need not be too nice about principles and consistency, as Mill had said three years earlier in one of his 'Notes on the newspapers': 'a newspaper-writer nobody knows; nobody thinks about him, or inquires who he is; nobody remembers to-day what he wrote yesterday, nor will remember to-morrow what he may choose to write to-day. He can afford to praise a ministry up to the last moment, and then turn round upon them.'[7]

While it would be unwise and unfair to use Mill's own words in an indictment of him as a journalist, or of journalism as a whole, these passages indicate that he was aware of tendencies inherent in writing for the daily and weekly press from which neither he nor those he would consider the best could escape. When he became a 'popular speaker' during his parliamentary career (1865–8), these tendencies – parliamentary debate and polemical journalism not being much different – appeared again. *The Times*, not without some relish, remarked in a leader on his defeat for Westminster that though Mill had formerly been admired by men of all parties, he had 'estranged many even of his best friends . . . by his vehement, narrow partisanship, and apparent inability to see a redeeming point in a political adversary.' Perhaps, *The Times* continued, in retirement he might regain his popularity, but only if he resumed 'his old attitude of dignified reserve,' selecting – if he felt compelled to interfere at all in public matters – only 'occasions worthy of his interference, and not be perpetually rushing into the fray with an impetuous eagerness.'[8] The 'old attitude' had, however, been preceded by 'vehement, narrow partisanship', a fact *The Times* forgot, although its collective memory of Mill's early opinions about it might have added relish to the present castigation. If one looks only at the earlier part of Mill's career as a journalist, remembering that virtually everything of his then published was anonymous in fact as well as in theory,[9] one could without major distortion see him, particularly when compared with his public 'sage' self, as given to 'rushing into the fray with an impetuous eagerness'. There is a marked difference in tone between his writings for the daily and weekly press and those for the monthlies and quarterlies, even when the latter are informed by political urgency, as in his calls for radical action in the *London and Westminster* between 1835 and 1839. The difference is even more marked when one looks at the articles Mill, thinking more *sub specie aeternitatis*, chose to reprint in *Dissertations and Discussions* (nothing in the three volumes for which he was responsible originated in a daily or weekly), and *a fortiori* when one looks at his books.

The tendency to rush into the fray was of course reinforced by the circumstances surrounding Mill's entry into the field. As was normal in a small radical circle, he began writing for papers whose editors or owners were acquaintances (initially of his father and of Jeremy Bentham), a group predominantly concerned with the propagation of correct views in the face of determined and entrenched political and religious opponents. Mill's own account of his journalistic beginnings in the *Autobiography* is a dispassionate survey of papers and editors, but no more than that; its measured reconstruction merely encompasses the main topics, and gives but hints of the passions, the accusations and demands. His subject matter was wide, including, as favourite targets, the law and mistaken ideas and practices concerning economics and population. Though these were important to him, it would nonetheless appear that his major purpose up to 1824 was to develop his argumentative skills. As a junior member of a radical team, he of course wished to inform the English public, but he does not seem to have thought that newspaper journalism could reform it.

Perhaps the small readership of his section of the radical press did not measure up to the dream of the young utilitarian with utopian visions.

J. A. Roebuck, looking back on these years, gives more sense than Mill of the messianic fervour that illuminated their youthful discussions, and which undoubtedly found daily or weekly journalism a low and unworthy soapbox compared to the lawgiver's mountain:

> I often laugh now at our splendid plans of moral & political regeneration. We frightened all the old people, by our daring doubts and conceptions, and puzzled them with a severe, and cogent logic drawn from the armoury of the schools. . . . [W]hile the fervid fit was on us, we carried on our studies with a spirit and efficiency, that produced at once marked and lasting effects. . . . The chief of these [persons] . . . has had a remarkable influence in the framing of my intellectual character. I mean John Mill. . . . [I]n this fellowship I worked on, we fell in with no reigning opinion, we opposed ourselves (and in those days, this was no promising game) to everything powerful in this country. We were known as the open foes of its aristocratic government – of its priesthood. We spurned the popular ignorance, as much as the aristocratic despotism, and thus raised up enemies in every quarter.[10]

As the decade proceeded, this fervour spread in one of those periodic recrudescences of youthful certitude and rebellion that seem to capture a whole generation; it was, for example, to send such young idealists as Trench and Kemble on a tragic mission to liberate Spain, as well as to give finally irresistible energy to the movement for reform in Britain. In this mood, and to restrict the case to the young Benthamites, a series – even a stream – of letters to editors would seem a less than effective and worthy way to lead England to that secular Eden where pleasure was pleasure, pain was pain, and people lived by universal principles.

There are more concrete reasons for Mill's near-abandonment of the newspaper press after early 1824. Even for one who seemed to have no moving parts susceptible to strain and fracture, the day had only 24 hours. In baldest summary, he was working at the East India House (1823 on), writing for the *Westminster Review* (1824 on), editing the three manuscripts (five volumes) of Bentham's *Rationale of Judicial Evidence* (1825–6), teaching his younger siblings (all the time), founding and taking a leading part in various societies and groups,[11] and continuing his own education (for example, learning German). And, as everyone knows, he did not feel it necessary to take time out to have a 'mental crisis' in 1826–7; had he been living in our times, he would subsequently have had to deduct one 50-minute hour from each day. By 1830 these passing years full of labour and intense introspection had produced a more sober, uncertain, and mature Mill, but only somewhat more so; he was even now only 24 years old, and the reforming zeal had been not reduced but transmuted: he was, if anything, more determined to hold a light for man's progress and was certainly capable of outbursts of impetuous eagerness.

2

The occasional cause of Mill's first major and sustained outburst was the political excitement in France in the early summer of 1830, whence infectious enthusiasm once again spread through Europe. The French election pitting the liberals against Charles X and his reactionary ministry under the Prince de Polignac inspired Mill to write an article explaining the situation to his compatriots for the *Examiner* of 18 July. By the end of 1834 he had written well over 200 pieces for the *Examiner*, more than half of which were on France.[12] His interest in France was not adventitious or new: he retained vivid memories of the scenery and society of France from his visit in 1820–1; he had long been intrigued by the Revolution of 1789; and during the previous years of intense activity, he had begun to look for answers beyond the circle of the Philosophic Radicals (as Roebuck said in the letter quoted above, he had become 'tainted with a mystic philosophy'). Some of the most appealing answers had come from the French socialist school of Saint-Simon, particularly through the evangelical fervour of Gustave d'Eichthal and the earliest writings of Auguste Comte. The conclusion of Mill's account in the *Autobiography* of this period is again muted but indicative:

> Their [the Saint-Simonians'] aim seemed to me desirable and rational, however their means might be inefficacious; and though I neither believed in the practicability, nor in the beneficial operation of their social machinery, I felt that the proclamation of such an ideal of human society could not but tend to give a beneficial direction to the efforts of others to bring society, as at present constituted, nearer to some ideal standard.[13]

After the elections, all was uncertainty in France until at the end of the month the July revolution – the glorious three days – toppled Charles X and set up Louis Philippe. Mill's hopes were raised, his fervour roused, and, full of bliss, he set out for Paris with Roebuck. The Parisian uprising, the spontaneous action (as Mill saw it) of a people peacefully asserting its rights and imposing its will, fitted neatly with the thoughts about English democracy that had been occupying Mill for some time, and with new force after Macaulay's attack in 1829 on James Mill's essay on government. The tide of progress, the determination of institutions by shifts in power (rather than the reverse), the Saint-Simonian view of periodicity, all probably seemed to Mill to be finding embodiment in the France of 1830.

And the message was an urgent one for Britain. If reform did not come, William IV and Wellington would go the way of Charles X and Polignac. Reform was not to be feared: the people of Paris had shown that the lower classes were to be trusted; they had proved their worth by their restrained and amicable behaviour during the July Days, as Mill reported in a near-rapture:

> When the workmen of Paris, after three days' fighting, had driven out Charles and dispersed his army, they were absolute masters of the city. In the midst of their highest excitation, in the moment of victory, surrounded by their dead and wounded brothers, fathers, aye, and children and wives and mothers – these men, these ignorant, despised, and long-abused people shrunk from all unnecessary carnage – the moment resistance ceased, that moment they abstained from assault – they took equal care of the soldier who had opposed and of the citizen who had aided them. Surrounded by every temptation that perfect licence could offer, not one excess was committed. Vast treasures passed through their hands untouched, and signal punishment was immediately the lot of any one who for one instant departed from the strictest honesty and decorum. (One man was shot by his comrades for stealing a melon.) These men were actually starving, and yet they would take no recompense. Having effected their glorious object, they calmly retired to their homes and resumed their accustomed avocations. The *educated* and the *rich* now came upon the stage. The hour of danger was passed, one government was overthrown, another was to be formed. Compare the conduct of this party with that of the people, the mob, who had fought during the ever memorable three days.[14]

The implications for the British middling and upper classes are obvious.

Mill does not aspire to a balanced account of these early days of the revolution. Not the philosopher, but the preacher: his pulpit, the *Examiner*, and his text, the French great leap forward. Under the heading, 'Prospects of France', Mill poses two questions, and answers them in a fashion that only the most *engagé* would think disinterested:

> How will the Revolution terminate? This is the question, which every person in England who reads a newspaper has asked, and still continues to ask himself every day. But all do not ask this question in the same spirit, nor with the same hopes and fears.

Those who feel interested in an event which changes the face of the world, chiefly as the security of their own commercial speculations may happen to be affected by it; and those, an equally large class, whose sympathies with their species are of such a character, that in every step which it takes towards the achievement of its destiny, they are more keenly alive to the dangers which beset it, than to the glory and the happiness towards which it is irresistibly advancing; these classes anxiously enquire, whether there will be *tranquillity?*

Those who feel that tranquillity, though of great importance, is not all in all; that a nation may suffer worse evils than excessive political excitement; that if the French people had not valued something else more highly than tranquillity, they would now have been the abject slaves of a priest-ridden despot; and that when tranquillity has once been disturbed, the best way to prevent a second disturbance is to prevent a second disturbance from being *necessary;* with these persons the subject of principal anxiety is this, Will the French establish a good government? And grievous will be their disappointment if, when every thing has been put to hazard, little or nothing shall prove to have been gained. . . .

We believe . . . that there will be tranquillity; that there will not be another insurrection; and that there will be no outrages on property, or resistance to the operations of Government in detail, but such as will with the utmost facility be put down, and that, too, by the people themselves, if necessary. But we are also convinced that France is threatened at present even with a greater evil than a second insurrection; and that if the people were to follow the advice of some of our contemporaries, by abstaining from all political agitation, and leaving their destinies to the quiet disposal of their present Ministers and Chambers, they would speedily find that all they had gained by the revolution was, to exchange a feeble despotism for a strong and durable oligarchy.[15]

Other English journals were of course responding to the French turmoil, and Mill's attempts to set right the facts in opposition to his *bête noire, The Times,* show something of the spirit of the day, and more of his embroilment in the habitual rough-and-tumble of the journalistic game. Believing that national ignorance about French affairs made readers particularly susceptible to *The Times's* misinterpretations, he infuses some of his articles with a partisan gusto:

The crazy outcries of our newspapers against the changes in the French ministry, are not calculated to do much honour to England in foreign countries. They will not, however, make so unfavourable an impression upon the French, with regard to our national mind, as might be imagined, since that people, with their usual misapprehension of every thing English, will probably conclude that our daily press is in the pay of the Duke of Wellington. They are by no means aware of the true state of the case, namely, that there is a fund of stupidity and vulgar prejudice in our principal journalists, which needs no extraneous inducements to call it forth; and that our journals, speaking of them generally, are faithful representatives of the ignorance of the country, but do not represent, in any degree, its knowledge or its good sense. One would imagine that, among journalists, a moderately accurate acquaintance with France for the last fifteen years, ought not to be a very rare endowment: if a writer in the newspapers does not know the history of his own times, what, in the name of heaven, does he know? Yet, during the recent struggle in France between the men who made the revolution and the men who were seeking to profit by it, the small number among our journalists who dreaded giving a false and mischievous opinion, dared not to give one at all; while the larger number, who were utterly reckless of the consequences of what they wrote, have made a display of ignorance such as all who knew them would naturally expect. At the head of these was the blundering newspaper which recently asserted that Charles de Lameth, a man who was with difficulty saved from the September massacres, was a conventionalist: we need scarcely say that we allude to the *Times*, a paper which seldom lets a week pass without affording satisfactory evidence that for it to have any opinion at all on French affairs, is a piece of presumption which nothing can excuse.[16]

Here one has an example of the acrimony of occasion. The events which had taken place in France had contributed to conservative fear and radical fervour. At the Rotunda during the preceding weeks, Jacobin speeches were constantly heard and tricolour cockades distributed. The attendance of Wellington and William IV at the Guildhall Banquet on 9 November was cancelled for fear of the hostile demonstrations planned by the radicals, and Peel was rumoured to be arming his police with cutlasses to face the feared radical revolution. The Duke of Wellington resigned on 16 November, two days after the appearance of Mill's article (though, needless to say, not because of it). In these circumstances Mill's immediate attitudes are readily understandable; he was desperately anxious to show that popular demonstrations need not entail violence and destruction. This understanding, of course, will make it also readily apparent that his articles exemplify radical thought and attitude, not an objective account of events and people.

What has been said thus far might suggest that Mill was following a simple and steady line; in fact it was a complex and moving line. He had early been made uneasy by the actions and attitudes of the *'educated'* and *'rich'*, and was later to become disillusioned and frustrated by the ineffectualness of those whose idealism he found so stirring. For in these early days of the new France, Mill's admiration was focussed on the Paris 'mob', his hopes on the young men of the left, and his criticism on the greater number of the Deputies, chosen in June before the three glorious days by a restricted electorate, and therefore anachronistic. It was a taxing task to explain clearly to his British public just who was responsible for what and to make sure that opprobrium fell on the right persons and not on the left.

> The debate in the French Chamber of Deputies, on the motion for reducing the stamp duties on newspapers, is disgraceful to the Chamber. . . . So rapidly has the new oligarchy succeeded to the worst feelings, and even to the silliest catch-words of its predecessors.
>
> The new ministers, we lament to say, did not support the motion, alleging that they were not prepared to consent to any sacrifice of revenue. This temporizing is very deplorable. . . .
>
> Several of our newspapers, and their correspondents at Paris, continue to heap abuse upon the popular party. There are no wise and moderate men, according to them, but those who think that 88,000 men should have the power of dividing among them, at discretion, a revenue amounting (independently of the interest of the public debt), to thirty millions sterling; all the rest are firebrands, who seek to throw the world into disorder. The 88,000 electors are the nation. The nation is declared to sympathize with the Chamber, because the 88,000 have generally re-elected the old members: although even the 88,000, when they had no old member to re-elect, have in many instances elected new ones of a very different complexion.[17]

He continued to portray the popular party, especially its younger radical wing, in as favourable a light as possible, but the possible needed as much argumentative help as it could get. Expressing pleasure at having secured for the *Examiner* a French correspondent, Mill walks with as little grace as caution on the casuistic waters:

> The letters of our correspondent will be a faithful picture of the opinions, the feelings, perhaps even the errors, of the younger and more ardent portion of the popular party. Whatever they know, he

knows; whatever they feel, he feels; whatever he believes, is believed
at least by many of the most active and influential in a party of which
he himself is not one of the obscurest members, and of which his
position and his sources of information render him an adequate
representative.

We are not responsible for all the opinions of our correspondent,
nor do we expect that he will never express any sentiments in which
we should disagree. But we can answer for the purity and excellence
of all the public objects, which he, and his friends, have in view. We
cannot, of course, guarantee all the facts which he relates, especially
those which are of the nature of anecdotes; but we are certain that he
will affirm nothing as true, but what is at least, very generally
believed; and it is often of as much, or even of still greater importance
and interest, to know what is thought to be true, than what really is
so.[18]

Mill, it will be obvious, is not an apologist of the type made notorious by
Helen Maria Williams during the first French Revolution.[19] He is concerned
to inform English readers about French politics, but the information is
interpreted usually in English terms; the method is that of comparative
politics, with lessons both from similarity and contrast. But the differences
receive more emphasis, for Mill, an advocate of reform and not revolution at
home, wishes both to excuse French radical extremism and to assure Englishmen that the native radicals would be less demanding and vociferous. These
points may be illustrated by extracts from 'The municipal institutions of
France':

Debates of great interest and importance are now taking place in the
Chamber of Deputies, on the proposed municipal law. Our daily
journalists, being altogether unaware of the importance of this as of
almost every other topic beyond the range of every-day conversation,
allow the public to remain utterly unacquainted, both with the debates
themselves, and with the facts necessary to understand them. We
shall briefly state the nature of the existing municipal institutions of
France, and of the alterations proposed to be made in them by the
present Bill. . . .

[The nomination] of the various local councils . . . emanates
exclusively from the executive. They are named in every case by the
Crown, or its delegate and representative, the prefect. Such were the
liberties of France under the restoration! and yet there are slaves, both
in this country and in France, who aver that the charter of 1814 was
faulty by not giving sufficient power to the Crown! . . .

> The debates on the bill afford a tolerable foretaste of those on the approaching electoral law, and it might be added, of those in our own House of Commons on the bill for Parliamentary Reform.

He continues with a reference to the 'stale common-places' that are always heard, as they have been in France, whenever attempts are made to justify irresponsible power: 'that men of considerable property are alone fit for managing any of the affairs of the public, they alone having a stake in the country, and being the exclusive possessors of intelligence.' He concludes by assuring his readers that 'These insolent assumptions, which we fear mankind will be condemned to hear for a considerable time longer, were refuted by the speakers on the popular side, with an ability and soundness which we wish we could expect to see equalled in our own Honourable House next month.'[20]

As time went on, Mill found it more and more difficult to hold to this defensive line. There is not space to trace the development of his disillusionment; suffice it to say that the appointment of a conservative ministry in Paris in March 1831, the bitter riots that continued to rock France, the failure of the Chamber of Deputies (especially the left) to organize itself into constructive parties and put through needed reforms, and the increasingly apparent impracticability of Saint-Simonism, all these combined to evaporate Mill's hopes. Although he continued to defend the actions of the French radical press during the government prosecutions under strict censorship laws, and to sympathize with abortive popular movements, his enthusiasm visibly dwindled; he exhibits what in other journalists he would probably see as inconsistency, as his support withdraws from groups to principles, and from principles enunciated by others to principles enunciated by himself. Henry Cole's diary reports Mill as talking privately, on 5 March 1832, 'at great length – to show when a nation is in a state from revolution subsiding, it is requisite for it to pass under a despotism – either of one or many – to restore obedience.'[21] And publicly, in the *Examiner* for 24 June, his article commences: 'The longer we reflect upon the present deplorable measures of the French Government, the more pregnant they appear to us with the most fatal consequences.' Tragically it is not only the government that is to blame: the French people seemed incapable of working within the constitution to bring about needed reforms, and in April 1832 there was a serious if futile armed insurrection. In contrast, the British Parliament had just accepted the Reform Bill, amid much excitement and many threats, but without violence.

> How many years, rather how many ages, of legal protection seem necessary to engender that habitual reverence for law which is so

deeply rooted in the minds of all classes of Englishmen, from the prince to the pauper! Never can we too much rejoice that we have accomplished the first and hardest stage of our national emancipation, and have therefore a reasonable chance of accomplishing the succeeding stages, without any sensible weakening of that salutary association; the first and fundamental condition of good government, and without which any people, however civilized they may imagine themselves, are little other than savages.

Is it not the vainest of fancies to look for any sensible improvement in the government or in the condition of the people, while even honest men are apt to consider any misconduct on the part of the Government a full justification for civil war, and when every King, every Minister, considers every act of resistance to Government a justification for suspending the constitution and assuming dictatorial power?

Yet he still plays on the defensive line, though with noticeably less heart, and indeed less need, there being no real fear of disturbances in England.

Of the two parties who are guilty of the present and of the impending mischief, incomparably the most guilty is the Government. That small part of the people of Paris who planned, or who joined the insurrection [earlier that month], are not without considerable excuse. To compare them with our own people under recent circumstances, would be to judge them unfairly. If we English could neither have formed Political Unions nor held public meetings, how could we have escaped the same extremity? . . .

It is not many weeks since we idly amused ourselves and our readers with dreams of progressive improvement, and the growth and strengthening of the national mind, by sober study and manly discussion of the art of government itself, as distinguished from the mere instrument of government. It is no time now for such thoughts. One of the smallest evils of the present tyranny is, that all such prospects are now, for a season, overclouded. As the French themselves would say, *tout est remis en question*. The forty years war, which we did think was terminated by the final rupture with the fallen dynasty, has broken out afresh. The prize to be contended for is still, as heretofore, whether France shall or shall not have a constitutional government: the skeleton of absolute monarchy has been taken from its grave, clothed once more in flesh and blood, and re-enthroned in the Tuileries. Manuel, and Foy, and Constant, have lived, and the martyrs of the Three Days have died, in vain.[22]

It is not astonishing, then, that Mill's reports on France became both shorter and less frequent during the latter half of 1832; and only slight surprise follows on reading, in the spring of 1833:

> We have discontinued of late our usual notices of French affairs, because all which has been doing in that country is so paltry, so devoid alike of any importance in the immediate result, and of any indication respecting the future, that we felt no inducement to record in our columns, in addition to the trivialities of our own country, the still smaller trivialities of another country, which, as foreigners, we have so little power of shaming into better things.[23]

A full explanation of this sentence would require an excursion into Mill's other interests at this time, which were being expressed in essays and reviews of poetry, and in correspondence with Carlyle and others. He did not lose interest in France (he lived there for about one-half of each of his last 15 years), and he continued, though sporadically, to write about its political affairs. But even in the leaders written after his six-week visit in 1833 there is an underlying tone of sadness, explicable perhaps by the insufficiency of the reforms (in municipal institutions and national education, for instance), and by their being brought in by the conservative ministry of Soult, de Broglie, Guizot, and Thiers, against which the disorganized radicals were powerless. His high fervour of 1830 had gone never to return; the Revolution of 1848 revived his enthusiasm, especially with reference to the socialist experiments, but he certainly did not consider the events of a sufficiently exemplary nature for him to contribute regular discussions to the newspapers.

3

Although to concentrate as we have, not only on one newspaper, but even on one section of that paper within a limited span of years, may make clearer one of Mill's activities, it also gives a distorted reflection of his interests and those of the *Examiner*. The distortion can be at least slightly corrected by reference to his writings in that paper on other subjects. During the first five months of 1831, for example, he combined his interests in the Saint-Simonians and in British intellectual, political, and cultural life to produce his five long articles entitled 'The spirit of the age'.[24] He wrote in these years occasional pieces on various aspects of public and political life, pieces often prompted by specific acts of the government, moving from the truck system to the ballot to the budget to emigration to economics and the poor law. (Rare glances across the Atlantic are somewhat inexplicable, viz., 'Conduct of the United States towards the Indian tribes'.[25]) In the autumn of 1833, a particularly strong series of articles critical of the achievements of Grey's ministry appeared,[26] prompted by the publication of a Whig eulogy by Denis Le Marchant, *The Reformed Ministry and the Reformed Parliament*. It is interesting, though not in the line of our argument here, to note that Mill wrote only on England during September, October, and November of 1833, though he was in Paris for six weeks during the latter two months – with Harriet Taylor, on a trial separation from her husband.

The book reviews he wrote during these years include notices on political economy and philosophy; those on artistic and literary matters are (as less typical of his main *œuvre*) more engaging. They deal with French theatrical productions in London, Italian opera and poetry, and with the publications of close friends. One quotation from a theatrical review will indicate the range Mill attempted:

> A great actor must possess imagination, in the higher and more extensive meaning of the word: that is, he must be able to conceive correctly, and paint vividly within himself, states of external circumstances, and of the human mind, into which it has not happened to himself to be thrown. This is one of the rarest of all endowments; which is the reason why there are so few great dramatists and great actors. But he who is thus endowed, if he can act one character, can act all characters; at least, all which are in nature. And this is what is meant by the universality of genius. Let him who wishes it to be practically illustrated, go [to the French Theatre, Haymarket] to see Mademoiselle Leontine Fay.[27]

On the works of close friends, one is at least maliciously pleased to find Mill, in the spirit of the age, indulging in puffery: Eliza Flower, author of *Musical Illustrations of the Waverley Novels*, was intimate with W. J. Fox, and Harriet Taylor's greatest confidante. Of her work, Mill wrote:

> We omitted to notice this publication among the musical novelties of the last month. Our apology is, that the music is of too high a character to be judged of hastily. Much of it, indeed, cannot fail to please, even at the first hearing: but, at the first hearing, it would most surely be underrated. . . . Nothing can be conceived more unlike the everyday music which the composers for the common market copy from one another. So little are this lady's compositions the result of imitation or memory, that they do not even resemble the works of the great masters. They have a character of their own; distinctly and strikingly individual; compounded, it should seem, of the peculiarities of the poetry, and those of the composer's mind: founded on a strong conception of the meaning and spirit of the poetry; but adding so

much to it, that the inspiration she gives is almost equal to that which she receives.[28]

And of her *Hymn of the Polish Exiles by the Siberian Sea*, a musical setting of Harriet Martineau's *The Charmed Sea*, Mill says:

> The words of this hymn or prayer, notwithstanding some faults, were not unworthy to be chosen by Miss Flower, as the vehicle of one of her inspired strains: and Miss Martineau, or any one else who writes with a meaning, may be congratulated on meeting with a composer who is able and resolved to make that meaning *felt*, even when the collocation and rhythm of the words renders this a task of some difficulty.[29]

(Harriet Martineau, it may be said, never received her full due from Mill, though here he is more judicious about her than about Eliza Flower.) Another example of impetuosity, not in a bad cause, but also not in one of the highest purity.

Mill's journalism in the succeeding years was more in the nature of forays and occasional supplies to the troops than a planned and sustained campaign. His attention was drawn to government policy (especially the Bank Charter Act), and various radical activities (those of Durham and Molesworth); he also contributed some reviews, but in the 11 years from 1835 to 1845 inclusive, he wrote fewer pieces in total than the annual average for his most active period, 1830 to 1834.

In 1846 and the early part of 1847, prompted by the appalling conditions in Ireland, Mill again became a resolute campaigner, this time as a leader writer for the *Morning Chronicle*. Here one finds a more mature Mill, with an established reputation as a philosopher. We suspect, though we have no hard evidence, that his authorship of the series on Irish land must have been known at the time;[30] it is somewhat surprising, in fact, that the series was not published as a book immediately. Formally, these articles are most clearly marked by their unity: not only through concentration on the central idea (the need immediately for intensive cultivation of the Irish waste lands, after which other, ultimately more fruitful, measures might be introduced), but also through various devices typical of Mill, if not of the journalism of the period (or of ours). For example, he uses extensive evidential and corroborating quotations from authorities in what is certainly a scholarly fashion;[31] one would be staggered by such diligence even by the most dedicated of modern investigative journalists – however, Mill (as he indicates in his *Autobiography*, p. 243) interrupted the writing of his *Principles* to compose this series, and he had been using these materials in that work. Perhaps it was his desire to give a full discussion of land tenure in the *Principles* that made him unwilling to publish separately the specifically Irish matter.

Another feature of the series is the sense of continuous argument that reflects the intense public interest in the subject and its pressing importance: Mill takes time to answer a correspondent (21 October), and dash off quick responses to arguments appearing in other journals,[32] including once more *The Times*. He argues, for instance, that Irish indolence – a fact he accepts – cannot be 'racial' but must be environmental and cultural, for otherwise their fellow Celts, the French peasants, would be equally indolent.[33] The periodic nature of the campaign leads to repetition, but not of a kind harmful either to sense or sensibility, for, given Mill's skill in such matters, it increases the sense of urgency.

Apart from what this series, demonstrably a unit from internal as well as external evidence, tells us about Mill's ideas and about his journalism, it also illustrates further the strength and combativeness of the *Morning Chronicle* in these years, justifiably best publicized in the extraordinary series on London labour and the London poor by Henry Mayhew and his colleagues. Mill on Ireland does not rank with that uniquely prolonged and broadly-based joint endeavour, but it certainly deserves more prominence as a rare instance of a sustained and thoughtful journalistic series. Thoughtful as it is, however, it is far from dispassionate; the polemic is as strong as the occasion demands, and the balance is of the kind that pivots on a point not in the centre.

In the remaining years of his life, Mill was never again a regular leader writer; rather, as his public recognition grew, he appeared most frequently in the press as a writer of letters to the editor, now unsolicited, but welcomed in spite of what was often still a disturbing note. His most impassioned letters were written in the mid-1850s jointly with Harriet Taylor, by then his wife, on cases of domestic brutality, in which the expression of outrage is as strong as in anything else he wrote.

The rest of his career must be dealt with summarily: nothing of his has been discovered in newspapers from 1859 to 1862, a period of intense writing and publication in other forms. From 1863 till his death, all but five items are letters, most of them prompted by his parliamentary campaigns and positions he adopted in the House of Commons; the major exceptions are the three pieces that appeared in the *Examiner* in 1873, the year of his death, on land tenure reform, the subject that, with the emancipation of women, most occupied his final years. All of these items appeared over his signature, which was, of course, more than just an identifying mark by that time. It was also a signal to the knowing that the voice was that of a crusader, of one given to unpopular causes who believed that right was on his side, and who would rush eagerly into the fray, if not with the impetuosity and blindness that his opponents attributed to him. His own characterization of the public speaker,[34] the journalist's twin, is not entirely a likeness of him, but certainly his outlines can be seen in it: never irksome, offensive only within the limits accepted by nineteenth-century journalism, and superb in declamation.

NOTES

1. Very few of these have received critical attention: unquestionably the best known is the series of leaders entitled 'The spirit of the age', which was printed as a book by F. A. Hayek (Chicago, 1942) and has since been reprinted. Some notice has been taken of the letter on exchangeable value quoted above, and its companion piece of a week later, which have also been reprinted; and various other articles, such as two on political pledges, have been cited by critics.

   Work on Mill's newspaper writings is made enviably easier by the list he kept of his publications, made available in the *Bibliography of the Published Writings of John Stuart Mill*, ed. Ney MacMinn, J. R. Hainds, and J. M. McCrimmon (Evanston, Ill., 1945), in which all the items here mentioned can be found.

2. *Autobiography and Literary Essays*, ed. John M. Robson and Jack Stillinger, *The Collected Works of John Stuart Mill*, 1 (Toronto, 1981), 85.

3. See James Mill, 'Periodical literature – *Edinburgh Review*', *Westminster Rev.*, I (1824), 206–49.

4. 'Fonblanque's *England under Seven Administrations*', *London and Westminster Rev.*, v and xxvii (1837), 66.

5. *Ibid.*, 65.

6. *Ibid.* The passage continues with one of his running asides against *The Times*, in a battle that may have eventually led to The Thunderer's criticism of him late in his career, which damaged his reputation in some circles: 'Such was the secret of the good writers in the *Times*, when the *Times* had good writers.'

7. *Monthly Repository*, n.s. VIII (1834), 243.

8. 23 Dec. 1868, 9.

9. As every close student of the period knows, the authorship of many apparently anonymous articles in the quarterlies and monthlies was known to some (but how many?), and some newspaper journalists, for one reason or another, implicitly signed some of their work. We have, however, made no attempt to establish whether or not Mill's early journalism was known to be his, outside his immediate circle; our assumption is that it was not. While engaged in this aside, we may also admit that we have no information on an equally crucial question, that of how much Mill (who had a small salary in his early years) earned by his newspaper journalism.

10. Bod., MS Eng., Lett. c. 295, fos. 41–2. Quoted in Sarah Wilks, 'The Mill-Roebuck quarrel', *Mill News Letter*, XII no. 2 (Summer 1978), 9.

11. Including the Mutual Improvement Society, the Utilitarian Society, the London Debating Society, a group that debated the theory of elocution, and the Society of Students of Mental Philosophy.

12. Between 18 July 1830 and the end of 1834 Mill contributed about 230 items to the *Examiner*, just over 140 of which were on France; of those 140, more than 100 had appeared before the end of 1832. The greatest concentration was during the first 18 months of this period, when nearly three-quarters of his contributions concerned France. In 1833, as we shall see, Mill's increasing disillusionment with French political behaviour, amongst other things, led to a shift in his interest and activities and he wrote only 34 pieces, a mere six of which were on France; in 1834 he wrote 45 articles, more than half of them on France. But then his energies turned

away almost totally from journalism until 1846, when he concentrated on Ireland, and he never again wrote regularly on French politics.

13. *Autobiography and Literary Essays*, ed. cit., 175.
14. *Examiner*, 29 Aug. 1830, 547.
15. *Ibid.*, 14 Nov. 1830, 723.
16. *Ibid.*
17. *Ibid.*, 21 Nov. 1830, 745.
18. *Ibid.*, 23 Jan. 1831, 55.
19. *Letters on the French Revolution* (1791); *Letters from France* (1794).
20. *Examiner*, 13 Feb. 1831, 98–9.
21. Quoted from the MS diary in the Victoria and Albert Museum in Anna J. Mill, 'Some notes on Mill's early friendship with Henry Cole', *Mill News Letter*, IV no. 2 (Spring 1969), 7.
22. *Examiner*, 24 June 1832, 408.
23. *Ibid.*, 31 Mar. 1833, 201.
24. *Ibid.*, 9 Jan. 1831, 20–1; 23 Jan., 50–2; 6 Feb., 82–4, and 13 Mar., 162–3; 3 Apr., 210–11; 15 May, 307, and 29 May, 339–41.
25. *Ibid.*, 9 Jan. 1831, 25.
26. *Ibid.*, 22 Sept. 1833, 593–5; 29 Sept., 609–11; 6 Oct., 625–6; 13 Oct., 643–4; 20 Oct., 659–60; 27 Oct., 675–6; 10 Nov., 706–7.
27. *Ibid.*, 22 Mar. 1831, 325.
28. *Ibid.*, 3 July 1831, 420.
29. *Ibid.*, 17 Feb. 1833, 101.
30. The series proper ran through October (12 leaders), November (12), December (15), and the first part of January (4), with a few later related pieces. Three of these (11, 13, and 16 Jan.) were identified as Mill's in the next year, when they appeared, in slightly modified form, as an appendix to vol. I of his *Principles of Political Economy*: see *Collected Works of John Stuart Mill*, II (Toronto, 1965), 433–51.
31. For example, he cites William Blacker (2 Nov.), Arthur Young (19 Nov.), William Howitt (30 Nov.), Henry Inglis (9 Dec.), *Historisch-geographisch-statistisches Gemälde der Schweiz* (24 Dec.), William Wordsworth (9 Nov.), the Devon Commission (25 Nov.), Karl Rau (3 Dec.), and Jean Charles Sismondi (11 Dec.) – all being used in his *Principles*.
32. See, for example, his responses to the *Edinburgh Review* (*Morning Chron.*, 3 and 11 Nov. 1846), the *Spectator* (16 and 17 Dec.), and the *Globe* (6 and 7 Jan. 1847).
33. See *Morning Chron.*, 2 Dec. 1856, 4.
34. See p. 61 above.

4

Helene E. Roberts   Exhibition and review:
the periodical press and
the Victorian art
exhibition system

Much of traditional art history consists in tracing stylistic development
through a canon of selected works. This approach, however, often assumes
the sensibilities of the contemporary world rather than the sensibilities of
the period being studied and it ignores the historical, economic and social
context in which works of art were created. For the art of Victorian England
these sensibilities and these contexts can nowhere be better studied than in
the pages of its periodicals. Any comprehensive history of the Victorian art
world must investigate the many articles in these periodicals on art,
architecture and aesthetics, and must peruse their many reviews of exhibitions. These articles and reviews define Victorian taste and attitudes toward
art, reveal aesthetic criteria by which art was judged in the Victorian world,
and describe the workings of Victorian art patronage.

This essay will look at one aspect of the Victorian art world, that of the
exhibition system, through the eyes of the art critics writing in Victorian
periodicals. The periodicals chosen are those published between the 1830s
and 1890s which had a wide circulation among the educated classes and
whose art critics wrote about the exhibition system and were concerned with
its effects. The examination of these periodicals should reveal not only the
relationship between the press and the art world, but how periodicals provide
the context necessary for a full understanding of institutional influence on
artistic taste and creativity in Victorian England.

A large and diverse number of periodicals commented on the events of the
Victorian art world. Both serious intellectual periodicals like *Blackwood's
Edinburgh Magazine* and the *Fortnightly Review*, and those periodicals
essentially concerned with reporting newsworthy events like the *Illustrated
London News*, reviewed art exhibitions. The fashionable world read the art
critics of *Fraser's Magazine* and *Belgravia* while the more earnest lower
middle class learned about art from the pages of *Chambers's Edinburgh
Journal*. The *Art Journal* and the *Magazine of Art*, although limited in

their subject matter to art, reached a wide circle of readers. Quarterlies like the *Contemporary Review,* monthlies like the *New Monthly Magazine,* and weeklies like the *Athenaeum* and the *Spectator* all regularly devoted space to columns on art. The attention that Victorian periodicals paid to art was formidable and the information they contain about the Victorian art world is remarkably informative.

The periodicals reveal that to Victorians a work of art was not usually a hallowed object evoking awe; art more frequently was looked upon as an entertainment, a show and a commodity to be bought and sold. To the critics writing for the Victorian periodicals the artist seemed not so much a lonely genius, unknown and unappreciated, but a producer of goods that brought enjoyment and edification, and that, if purchased, would embellish the home and bring pleasure to its inhabitants. An artist's works should be taken out of the garret and brought to the market place. 'His works must be seen to be appreciated', declared the *New Monthly Magazine* in 1833, 'and unless he has the means for exhibiting them, they must rot and he must starve.'[1] The artist, to make a living by his art, had to depend on more than creative inspiration, he had also to be concerned with the showing of his wares and the making of his reputation.

The Victorian periodicals described several different ways by which an artist could exhibit his works: he could exhibit in his own studio, he could rent exhibition space in the various establishments maintained for that purpose, he could sell or consign his works to picture dealers, or he could send his works to the annual exhibitions organized by art societies. Many factors affected the artist's choice between these four alternatives. What was important is that his works should be exhibited where they could be seen by the right people and noticed favourably in the press.

In the art market, where the artist and patron sought to effect a mutually agreeable exchange, the Victorian periodicals played a complex role. They acted as recorders of events, announced meetings, described sales and reported the openings of exhibitions. They not only recorded events, but passed judgments on art and artists. In their reviews of exhibitions, critics in the periodicals praised some paintings, condemned others; they foretold success for some artists and predicted failure for others. Although the periodicals did not always speak with a single voice in the making of aesthetic judgments, they discussed similar issues and reviewed the same exhibitions. The critics were read and their opinions were discussed; they influenced taste and they affected sales. The periodicals in their reviews of exhibitions and in their evaluations of works of art become an important part of the exhibition system.

Although many periodicals reported art activities and many reviewed exhibitions, only a few also fulfilled the third function of criticizing the very workings of the exhibition system, including their own role in it. These few went beyond the reviewing of exhibitions to criticize the practices of exhibiting societies. Not satisfied with merely judging a painting's merit, they criticized the role played by critics. They examined the symbiosis between artist, exhibition, critic and patron, and in doing so displayed unusual insight into the influence that an exhibition society could exercise over what an artist painted, what a patron acquired and what a critic wrote. The critics appreciated that a different class of patron could affect the size, the finish, the style and the subject of paintings, and they noted that the purchases of important patrons were reported in the Victorian periodicals and thereby had the potential to influence both the future prosperity of the individual artist and the trend of collective public taste.

The critics writing in the periodicals were aware that the artist might change his painting to accord with what the exhibiting societies, the critics and the purchasing public considered acceptable. The public depended upon the exhibitions and the press to guide them in making their purchases. The press and the exhibiting societies, although seemingly powerful, were themselves influenced by a complex network of influences. This symbiotic relationship between artist, patron, press, and exhibitor was observed and documented in all its subtle ramifications by the periodicals themselves. The critics described how the exhibition system influenced not only the sale of individual works, but the progress of the British school. Periodical critics worked from an unique perspective. They understood the predicament of the artist, the practices of the exhibitors, the changing tastes of patrons, and their own role in the system. Their observations and analyses of the exhibition system scattered through many issues of Victorian periodicals provide an important dimension in the history of Victorian art and taste.

Those art critics who discussed their own role in the exhibition system focussed on three issues: the qualifications of critics, the form of exhibition reviews, and the relative influence of this criticism. All agreed that the art critic should be well trained. A critic's training, suggested F. P. Verney in the *Contemporary Review*, should include 'historical, scientific, mechanical' studies. 'Good criticism', he declared, 'demands at least as long and severe an apprenticeship as that in ironmongery.'[2] The aspect of this issue most frequently and most vociferously discussed, however, and the one which reached its most dramatic moment in the trial of Whistler *v.* Ruskin, was the question of whether the critic's training should be artistic or literary. The critic must be an artist, argued some. The artist alone, they explained, knew how to create art, and thus he alone could understand and judge it.[3] Furthermore, the artist was the only critic enjoying the respect of other artists.[4] Others objected that the very closeness of the artist to what he was criticizing would distort his judgment. he would be lost in admiration for technique, 'doat to nausea on the mechanical dexterity', they predicted, and set too high a value on 'mechanical qualifications'.[5] Because of the artist's emphasis on technique, he would undervalue the importance of subjects and themes.[6] The artist critic would also be guided by feeling rather than reason and would have 'passionate likes and dislikes for particular styles'.[7] His friends would lead him to become too involved in a single point of view and he would become a 'faithful slave' to his friends.[8] 'Enthusiasm for his own little game in art', Elizabeth Pennell warned in the *Fortnightly Review*, 'may leave him indifferent to all who do not play it with him'.[9] Furthermore, the defenders of the literary critics asserted, most of the artists are too narrow-minded and too wedded to dogma.[10]

The literary art critic, on the other hand, argued his defenders, had broader experience and would thus judge more justly.[11] The literary critic would not only be more 'sympathetic' and 'appreciative', he could write with a fuller understanding of the subjects and themes of painting.[12] The literary man would also have a greater flexibility and skill in his manner of present-ation and thus would appeal to a wider readership. 'He must interest Tom, Dick and Harry, *et al.*', declared Harry Quilter in the *National Review*, 'or he will receive short, sharp shrift from his editor and his public.'[13] The public prefers the literary critic as he has a better writing style. 'It is more agreeable to be misled pleasantly', argued William Sharp in the *National Review*, 'than to be instructed with much weariness of the flesh.'[14] But such 'pleasant' reviewers, warned the *New Monthly Magazine*, could easily spout 'whole pages of twaddle written, not on the picture, but on supposed beauties and intentions never intended by the artist'.[15] The literary man could obfuscate what was important in art, carrying 'a torch rather fuliginous than luminous into Art's obscure recesses'.[16] Clearly both artists and literary men had strengths and weaknesses as critics, a conclusion reached by William Alling-ham, writing in *Fraser's Magazine* in 1875. Allingham argued that, although an artist could do justice to the technical aspects of art, he could not give sufficient analysis of the subject and theme of a painting. The literary critic, on the other hand, who could analyse the subject, could not do justice to technique. Both were necessary, Allingham concluded; technique was the life of the painting, but the subject was its soul.[17] Years earlier the *Athenaeum* also had written of the 'double power' necessary to those who would practise art criticism.[18]

Who were the critics? Were they sufficiently qualified with the 'double power' necessary for good criticism? The anonymity of many of the reviews, of course, hid the reviewer's identity and, it was argued, diminished the

effectiveness of the criticism. 'The anonymous system', declared the
National Review in 1887, 'is a crying abuse.' No criticism 'worth the name',
predicted the author, William Sharp, could occur until reviews were signed.[19]
The critic, however, especially the amateur, usually preferred the protection
of an unsigned review.[20] As the century progressed the level of criticism
improved. The art critic became an established professional who was willing
to sign his work. In the early part of the century the *New Monthly* had
deplored the situation where 'raw Irish or Scotsmen', more skilled at reporting parliamentary debates, were assigned to review exhibitions.[21] Near the
end of the century the *National Review* estimated that 'nine-tenths, most
certainly seven-tenths, of our art-writers are literary men'.[22] Artists like
William Bell Scott, F. G. Stephens, William Sickert or P. G. Hamerton, who
also acted as critics, were in the minority. William Michael Rossetti, though
not himself an artist, was closely associated with the Pre-Raphaelites. Ruskin
was an accomplished draughtsman. Other critics, like Hazlitt or Thackeray,
had at one time aspired to be artists and had acquired some formal training in
art. E. P. Rippendale, the editor of the *Artist's and Amateur's Magazine*,
and 'a wielder of both pen and pencil' gained the *Athenaeum*'s praise for the
'double power' he possessed as a critic.[23] Most writers on art in Victorian
periodicals had a literary background and wrote literary as well as art
criticism. This orientation, as the periodicals themselves noted, produced
reviewers who emphasized the subject matter over technical qualities and
who gave prominence to those paintings with the more interesting subjects.
To those who read the reviews and who were influenced by them it soon
became clear that paintings with narrative subjects attracted the critics'
attention and gained their approval.

   The critics proved to be aware that their training, background and associates affected the substance of their reviews. They were also aware that the
type of periodical for which they wrote exerted some influence over them.
The general mood and political bias of course played a part, but the periodicity of the newspaper or journal may have had a greater effect. The large size
of the exhibitions (several of them displayed more than 500 works in their
annual exhibitions; the Royal Academy often exceeded 1500) meant he
needed time to take it all in. The crowds of people who distracted his
attention and obscured his views did not make his job easier. The reviewers
in the daily newspapers had the shortest time to write their reviews; their
reviews were also the briefest. 'The weekly critic of art is happy in comparison with his daily brother', wrote the critic of the *Illustrated London News*
in 1846, 'he has not to struggle with the crowd.' The critic of a weekly or
monthly journal could allow more than a 'half-minute survey' and could
'secure a second thought' before scribbling a review to meet the deadline. 'He

can let the influence of a fine picture work upon him', he continued, 'before he presumed upon it.'[24] The critic of the *Spectator* also felt that only by returning to the exhibition 'after the gloss of novelty had worn off' could one gain a 'satisfactory impression'.[25] R. St John Tyrwhitt, the critic for the *Contemporary*, felt it would take at least two months to view the Royal Academy exhibition, while Henry Morley in the *Fortnightly* estimated that if a critic gave merely one minute of time to each work in the 1872 exhibition, it would take 25 hours to see them all.[26] With such a schedule even the critics of the monthlies and quarterlies would have barely enough time to do justice to the exhibition's numerous paintings and statues. They too would have to depend on quick impressions. Reviews in the quarterlies were generally more thoughtful, made more comparisons and were more frequently organized around a central, often controversial, theme. It was the kind of criticism, the *Saturday Review* pointed out, that was more likely to be read by those with some knowledge of art and those who could not see the exhibition.[27]

The size of the exhibitions and the politics of the exhibition system as well as the periodicity of the magazines had their effect on the form of the exhibition review. In the larger exhibitions hundreds of works lined the walls.[28] The critic could not do justice to this number of works in the space allotted by his editor.[29] Reviewers usually tried to choose those works which were the most interesting to comment on in detail, and to include, even though they might not merit it, those painted by the most revered artists. The typical review thus had a short introduction, usually comparing the exhibition to those of former years and commenting about the injustices of hanging, and then made brief remarks on the 20 or 30 paintings of special interest. Some periodicals deviated from this general form. The *Art Journal*, for example, tried to be more comprehensive. In 1845 it devoted 18 pages to a review of the Royal Academy exhibition. It offered its review to the public as a 'practical guide to the Exhibition' and promised to 'give some notice to every work of interest and merit'.[30] Of the 1470 works exhibited that year, 388 works were noticed individually. This was far more than the 20 or 30 singled out for special attention in most reviews, but still only slightly more than a quarter of the works in the exhibition. The works of many disappointed artists went unnoticed by the press. Several weekly journals which published their reviews in serial form could keep an artist in suspense for months before he knew if he would be praised, condemned or ignored by the press. The *Saturday Review*, for example, planned a series of 12 reviews in 1866 (which actually ran to 13). Sometimes, as in the *Saturday Review* series, each week covered a particular subject: poetic paintings, history paintings, religious paintings, landscapes, portraits, genre scenes, etc. Some periodicals, such as the *Magazine of Art*, did not review each exhibition separately, but were concerned with describing the 'Pictures of the Year' no matter in which exhibition they might be hung.

Although the form of the review might vary and the critics differ about individual evaluations and aesthetic criteria, most of them followed the pattern and selected the most memorable paintings from the vast number exhibited around which to organize their comments. To have one's work among these 'Pictures of the Year' was not unimportant to an artist, nor did inclusion in this select group go unnoticed by the patrons interested in purchasing works of art. To be mentioned in a review the painter must do more than paint a good picture. Many of the 1,500 paintings on the Royal Academy walls were good paintings. The artist must try to do something novel, even spectacular, to attract the critic's eye. 'The evil result of the modern system of exhibitions', grumbled Elizabeth Pennell in the *Fortnightly*, 'is demand for novelty at all cost.'[31]

The critics enjoyed the power they had to influence art and affect taste and they were not modest about their role. 'The press has a vast power at present in the land,' declared the *Athenaeum*, 'it thinks and speaks and criticizes for the multitude.'[32] The *Library of the Fine Arts* asserted that the 'critical voice has a value attached to it which is co-important with art itself.'[33] The *Monthly Chronicle* devoted a whole article by Laman Blanchard to the subject. In 'The influence of periodical literature on the state of the fine arts' he found that influence 'generally admitted to be one of the most striking characteristics of our times' providing a 'gradual but irresistable force in producing and modifying our feelings and opinions.'[34] The press, said Blanchard, could also provide a powerful counteracting force against the interference of government. The power of the press, however, he continued, was not always benign. It could also degrade art by associating it too closely with the other subjects covered by newspapers and periodicals, such as commerce and politics. 'The smoke and dust of party warfare', he declared, 'render invisible the celestial forms floating in a higher region.'[35] The same attitude was echoed later in the century by Ferdinand Rothschild in the *Fortnightly*. He agreed that art had 'a mighty press of its own' but deplored the fact that notices about art were interspersed with advertisements for cocoa, tea and soap. 'Art has become popularized,' Rothschild observed, 'but may also become vulgarized.'[36] The whole exhibition system, indeed, according to the *Saturday Review*, was tinged with the touch of commerce. 'Painting is seen here for the most part under its worst aspects – not as a fine art, ennobling the artist while it instructs and refines and delights the spectator,' the critic declared, 'but as a mere manufacture and a dull routine of trade.'[37]

The cultivated connoisseurs building up their collections needed little guidance from the press, but the new middle-class patrons, purchasing art for reasons of conspicuous consumption or commercial speculation were not so confident of their own taste. To the Victorian nouveaux riches the periodical reviews seemed a sure guide to good taste. In areas where they were not well informed the new patrons readily accepted the 'dogmatic assertions' and opinions of the press.[38] A work of art which has attracted the attention of two or three critics, the *Magazine of Art* reported in 1880, 'creates a little storm of enthusiasm and prophetic augury in the busily-talking world of practical art'.[39] Although the committed artist would work in his own way unaffected by the criticism of the press, 'the man who paints for popularity', warned the critic of the *Fortnightly*, 'cannot afford indifference to press notices upon which it is fed.'[40] A reputation can be made by notice in the press or blighted by neglect. The result is, complained *Blackwood's Magazine* in 1853, that 'outrageous sums' are given for 'really unimportant and mediocre works, provided they be by certain painters'.[41] Recognition by the press, conferred on the artist suddenly and prematurely, could corrupt his aesthetic standards. 'Sale is ready for any work which bears a fashionable name', declared the *Spectator*. 'The temptation', the critic explained, 'is almost irresistable to a young painter to produce as cheaply as possible what is saleable in the market.'[42] A critic in the *Saturday Review* pointed to John Everett Millais as a case in point. 'Mr. Ruskin and the silly people who ape his fiery fanaticism with their own dull cant', he maintained, 'will have something to answer for in hardening this great painter's originality into affectation, his sense of power into frigid conceit and his boldness into insolence.'[43] Ruskin, of course, wielded an influence far greater than that of any of the art critics writing in the periodicals. 'Mr. Ruskin is an English institution', declared John Shelton in *Fraser's*, 'like the House of Lords or the National Gallery'.[44] The periodical critics seemed about equally divided on whether Ruskin's influence worked for good or evil, but none denied his powerful voice. Without 'the brilliant pen of Mr. Ruskin', *Fraser's* asserted, the Pre-Raphaelites would have 'attracted comparatively little notice'. For every person who had seen a work by Hunt or Millais, the critics speculated, a dozen had read Ruskin.[45] If the other periodical critics lacked the critical authority of Ruskin, they had the advantage of writing in a publication of regular periodicity with a stable subscription list. They would be speaking to the same audience of patrons and artists and, over time, could influence them for good or ill.

A critic's praise might lead the artist into false pathways, but a 'cold and fastidious' reception could blunt his spirit.[46] The *Contemporary* described the artist as a 'thin-skinned, impressionable being, with sensitive nerves and perceptions', easily depressed by blame or 'the chill of fashionable indifference'.[47] Many periodicals echoed this attitude. The goal of criticism, they insisted, was not only to point out imperfections, but to encourage the aspiring artist with 'cordial praise'.[48] The role of the critic, through the judicious application of praise and blame, could have a most beneficial effect on art. 'I am convinced we should soon improve our painters', confessed the critic of the *New Monthly*, 'if we could improve our critics.'[49]

Although in general the press had a high opinion of the influence exerted by its art criticism, some periodicals were not impressed with its quality. The problem with most critics, they complained, was that they were ignorant, self-interested, often borrowed from each other, and merely passed along fashionable opinions.[50] They 'echo not only one another's opinions', accused the *National Review*, 'but even one another's works.'[51] With one or two exceptions they showed little capacity for independent judgment. 'The praise or blame is determined by the popularity of the artist', argued the same periodical, 'and the remarks which have been made upon his work in previous years.'[52] On the other hand, they were also criticized for contradicting each other, causing confusion and conflict.[53] Art critics, observed *Fraser's* in 1843, had no vocabulary sufficient for their purposes, but only 'a catalogue of cant terms and phrases, many of them conveying no definite ideas.'[54] Not only do some critics write as if they were prophets, complained the *Saturday Review* in 1862, but they 'splash on their epithets and their metaphors, as if they were making experiments in colour'.[55]

Critics, furthermore, could be bought off with favours. Sometimes, argued the *Monthly Chronicle*, the critic's favourable opinions were 'nothing more than a desire to conciliate the givers of agreeable parties, encourage the willing contributions of engravers and publishers, or retain the small but convenient patronage of numerous free admissions'.[56] Harry Quilter, writing in the *National Review*, recalled his former editor calling him into the office and telling him he must be more lenient in his criticisms. There are 'many papers', Quilter continued, 'in which the great majority of the art writing is connected with and influenced by these commercial considerations.' He described the 'publishers, picture dealers, and proprietors of art exhibitions' who expect 'praise which is in proportion' to the 'monetary importance' of their advertisements. There are many ways that the path of the 'poorly paid' critic, he continued, can be made 'pleasant, or the reverse'.[57] R. St J. Tyrwhitt cynically summed up the pressures impinging on the critic. 'The public says to the journalist, make these fellows paint what we like to buy;' he wrote in the *Contemporary*: 'dealers say, make them paint what we can sell.'[58]

That artists and dealers tried to court or bribe critics was a testimonial to the widespread belief in their influence. It also reflected the enormous wealth that was available for the purchase of works of art. Throughout the middle and later part of the century the public's desire to acquire works of art seemed insatiable. In 1854 the *Art Journal* declared that all pictures of 'merit' had found purchasers. The annual sales from exhibitions, not including the large number of works commissioned or 'forespoke on the easel', had reached £150,000.[59] By the end of the century Harry Quilter in the *National Review* estimated that the amount of money spent on art industries, including decorative arts, was in the millions of pounds. It is, he added, 'greater than . . . any other single department of production'.[60]

The rising middle classes found art the ideal medium for the decoration of their new suburban villas and for the advertisement of their newly acquired status. Art critics wrote frequently of this new class of purchasers, a class furnished with commercial and manufacturing wealth and a class that was replacing the aristocrats as art patrons.[61] Although the new patrons did not display the taste of the aristocracy, they had 'purses that take a pleasure in opening themselves'.[62] Whereas formerly art had been 'indulged in as a luxury or a whim, by a select and exclusive caste', the *Fortnightly* explained, 'it is now the province of the prosperous middle class.'[63] These are, commented *Blackwood's* in 1855, 'most hopeful times for artists.'[64] With the entry of the middle classes into the art market, not only had the number of patrons increased, they were more willing to buy the works of contemporary English artists instead of the old masters preferred by the aristocratic connoisseurs, and they were willing to pay high prices. 'A man may grow fat on the applause of millions,' *Fraser's* observed in 1855, 'but he will surely starve on the praise of connoisseurs.'[65] That the middle classes had reasons, other than the sheer love of art, for acquiring paintings did not escape the critics. R. Folkstone Williams suggested the new patrons were motivated by the age-old desire 'to display the evidence of great riches by an accumulation of expensive articles of luxury'. This critic, writing in *Belgravia*, also suspected that an additional motive existed, that of finding 'an investment for surplus capital which would afford the largest amount of pleasure and the greatest prospect of profit.'[66] W. F. Pollock, writing in *Fraser's*, found 'the excitement of the Stock exchange' had been 'imported' into the pure and formerly unsullied realm of art.[67] Even the less prosperous middle classes and the 'lower orders', through their subscriptions to Art-Unions and their purchases of engravings and reproductions, must be counted in an assessment of changing patronage patterns.[68]

The results of this middle-class patronage, complained the periodicals, was to reduce the size of the canvases, limit the subject matter to landscape and domestic genre scenes, and reduce painting to mere yards of material sold for decorative purposes. The fact that the new patrons bought art to hang in their dining rooms and boudoirs affected both the size and subject of paintings. 'If our dining-rooms approached at all in proportion the halls of our medieval forefathers,' the *Art Journal* predicted, 'small pictures would be ridiculous.' The 'illustration of our history', the critic complained, depends on 'the size of our dining rooms'.[69] The noble historic and religious subjects usually associated with large canvases proved inappropriate in this domestic setting. 'An old man reading his Bible', reported *Blackwood's* in 1869, 'is thought to be more the right sort of thing than a saint gazing into heaven.'[70] Scenes of 'quiet felicity' had replaced those 'high-wrought tragedies or stately histories' of former days.[71] In the modern world, the critic J. B. Atkinson argued, people turn from the 'severe conflict of life' to the 'repose and relaxation' of art.[72] 'Large canvases wholly transcend the dainty sentiments of the boudoir,' he observed in an earlier review, 'they are too extended alike for the thoughts at the artist's command and the space at the patron's disposal.'[73] The critic of the *New Monthly* described the formula for art agreeable to the public: it wants 'pleasing views, of no large dimensions, of its own beautiful country, with its hazy, purple distances and scudding clouds; a poetical transcript of every-day life', he observed, 'with which to decorate its rooms.'[74] The 'lower range of subjects, such as still life, domestic scenes, and comic incidents', reported the *Spectator*, are the subjects 'successfully attempted'.[75]

What had happened to the ideal in art? The *Saturday Review* in 1857 answered that question gloomily: 'pictures are now but a portion of domestic furniture', it stated; 'the home of painting is, with us, the house'.[76] Five years later the critic of the same periodical insisted that he did not object to such subjects being painted, but 'need they be exhibited?', he asked. Why not sell them, not as works of art, but as 'furniture pieces' and 'manufactured goods?'[77] That art had become commercial bothered most critics. *Fraser's*, as early as 1830, complained that 'art has too grovelling and mercantile a spirit; it keeps its ledgers, its debtor and creditor account, and smacks of the counting house'.[78] To the author, 'an artist with the soul of a stock-jobber or a Jew clothes-man, is a monster'.[79] Although there were lingering hopes that art represented something higher and finer, most critics came to accept the realities of the market place, even for art. The same periodical argued in 1860 – 30 years later – that art was a profession as well as a calling and that money matters should not be pushed into the background.[80] 'The painter lays out his imagination, his invention, his idea of beauty, and his technical skill', the critic explained, 'and awaits the effect of his wares on the passer-by.'[81]

Finding the right place to display his wares and to await a potential patron was important to the success of the artist. The wrong choice and the results of his 'imagination, his invention' and 'his technical skill' might go unseen, unappreciated and unsold; the right choice and he might need only mediocre talent to become successful. The most advantageous position, as the periodical critics observed, was to be assured of a place 'on the line' (at eye level) at the annual Royal Academy exhibition. But such assurances, the critics reminded their readers, were limited to only 40 academicians and 20 associates.

No other source documents the alternatives open to the artist as completely as the periodicals do. Their criticisms focus on the Royal Academy, but they also review the exhibitions of other societies where the artist members might have their paintings hung in a favourable position on the wall, but in less prestigious company, with smaller attendance of potential patrons, and less attention by the press. Even though not a member, an artist might choose to send his paintings to the several societies, including the Royal Academy, whose exhibitions were open to non-members, but as a non-member he ran the risk of having his painting hung in a less favourable position where it might not readily be seen.

One of the most frequent observations of the press concerned the injustice of hanging works where, due to the lack of light or the distance away from eye level, they could not be seen. The injustices, real or imagined, often angered and discouraged the artist and he turned to the picture dealers or to renting his own exhibition space. He might also decide to exhibit his paintings in his own studio, if he had an adequate one, where he could control the placement, lighting and audience for his works, but where he might risk losing the important attention the press would give his works had they been hung in public exhibitions. The press did visit and review artists' studios, but only infrequently.

The only artists who escaped the need to show their works or seek approval from the art critics were those who had prior commissions. These were, however, mostly portrait painters or known artists who had already established their reputations by going through the exhibition system and scrutiny by the press. Furthermore, the patron who commissioned the work frequently expected that it would be exhibited upon its completion. 'No picture of Landseer, or Stanfield, or Copley Fielding', complained *Fraser's*, 'ever comes into the general market of art.'[82] They were frequently exhibited, however, but always with the small green ticket which indicated they had already been sold.

Most artists chose to exhibit their works first as non-members at the Royal Academy, with the hope that by being noticed by the press and purchased by a prestigious patron, their works would bring them the fame that would eventually ensure their election to the Academy. It was a long chance. An artist must first be elected to the position of associate, of which there were only 20. The plight of the associates had the critic's sympathy. As an associate the artist enjoyed only part of the prestige and privilege accorded to full Academicians. He might spend the rest of his life in this 'purgatory', the *New Monthly* noted, waiting for the death of an Academician to open a place among the exclusive 40.[83] Associates, in the meantime, Henry Ottley complained in *Fraser's*, must become 'sycophants', ingratiating themselves with the 'despots' who had the power to elect them to full membership.[84] The number of artists painting at any time in the Victorian period far exceeded the number of memberships available in the Royal Academy. In 1852 *Fraser's* counted upwards of 900 artists, while in 1892 Marcus B. Huish writing in *Nineteenth Century* extended the list of exhibiting artists to 5,000 – a number, he wrote, that is 'increasing by hundreds yearly'.[85] The 40 prized places in the Academy formed a nearly unattainable goal for most of the young aspiring artists, or indeed, for the older experienced artists. Many artists, however, did continue to aspire for a place in that exclusive company. The periodicals reported the dashed hopes of many British artists and repeated their embittered accusations of unfair treatment in their columns. Other artists, whose assessment of their talents was more modest, and artists angered by the policies of the Royal Academy, joined together to form societies and organize exhibitions which they hoped would rival the Royal Academy.[86]

These challenges to the privileged and powerful Academy delighted the press. They followed the progress of these upstart societies, but although they could sometimes record survival, they could not always report success.[87] The British Institution in 1825 became the first to establish a substantial and lasting rival exhibition of modern oil paintings that was regularly reviewed by the press. Opening in February, it was the first exhibition of the spring season. In 1852 the *Art Journal* reported that the British Institution had exhibited 544 works.[88] The paintings usually sold well, the *Art Journal* admitted; in 1852 the sum of £16,320 was collected from patrons, but the exhibition did not gain critical respect.[89] 'Mediocrity extends over almost every variety of subject,' complained the *Athenaeum* in 1850, 'platitudes of conception, vulgarity in treatment, and lowness of aim make the rule.'[90] It was an indictment repeated in other periodicals. The critics looked upon the British Institution exhibition as a second-rate Royal Academy show: one critic described the British Institution as being in 'vassalage to the Academy', another called it a mere 'nursing institution for the Royal Academy'.[91] The practice reported by the press, discontinued finally in 1845, of allowing works that had previously been exhibited at the Royal Academy to compete for places in the British Institution exhibition, gave visitors the feeling of staleness and lack of originality.[92] Although it boasted a 'convenient and well-lighted gallery in a conspicuous situation', exhibition at the British Institution was not the artist's first choice.[93] 'The better men reserve themselves, or at least their better works, for the great art-tournament of the Royal Academy,' the *Saturday Review* explained, 'and there are few beginners, we should think, who would not rather win their spurs in the bright sunshine of May [the date of the Royal Academy exhibition] than amidst the fogs and drizzles of February.'[94] Critics blamed the bad management of the British Institution for its steady deterioration. The long list of aristocratic directors cared less about the exhibition, complained the *Art Journal*, 'than if it were a market for the sale of wicker baskets.'[95] Complaints of 'corrupt favouritism' in the selection of pictures were not infrequent.[96] The *Art Journal*, one of the periodicals most ready to expose fraud and corruption, triumphantly printed a letter from an artist who had learned the secret of getting his pictures well hung.

> I commenced sending pictures to the British Institution, but always without success, until I was advised by a friend, deeper in the mystery than I, to have my frames from the son of Mr Barnard, the Keeper of the British Institution. I tried the experiment which was perfectly successful. At first they were hung indifferently, but eventually my pictures got on the 'line'.[97]

Periodicals, especially the *Art Journal* and the *Athenaeum*, recommended that the exhibitions be closed, a recommendation that was carried out in 1867. It had in the meantime provided a place for young untried artists, not yet ready to risk a rejection at the Royal Academy, to hang their works in the sight of prospective buyers.[98]

The Society of British Artists, founded in 1823, held its first exhibition in 1827.[99] It sought, like the British Institution, to rival the Royal Academy. The critics welcomed it because it both opposed the Academy and offered an alternative exhibition space.[100] Unfortunately, as in the case of the British Institution, the critics could not bring themselves to shower liberal praise on its exhibitions. In its early days it was called the 'Refuge of the Destitute' but gained support, despite its poor show of paintings, as a 'useful and laudable institution'.[101] The 'torpedo touch of the Royal Academy', the *Spectator* reported in 1834, was working to undermine its success. Not only did the Academicians prohibit their membership from exhibiting there, but, the *Spectator* reported, 'they secretly discourage it and abuse the ear of the influential patrons of art to thwart the views of another society.'[102] The Society in the 1840s repudiated its former open policy to non-members when 'a parcel of obscure and inferior artists', according to the *Spectator*, usurped control of the society.[103] Although it obtained a charter in 1847, it did not attract the better artists. Its exhibitors, reported *Chambers's* in 1853, 'are mainly composed of the natural overgrowth of artists who prefer a speedy and favourable opportunity for the display of their works in minor galleries to waiting for years and years ere they can work themselves up to a good position on the walls of the Academy'.[104] By the 1870s the Society had become a refuge for the landscapes and genre scenes beloved by the new middle-class patrons. 'One always knows what to expect in Suffolk-street', G. A. Simcox wrote in the *Academy* in 1873: 'a wide expanse of comfortable pleasantness that disdains curiosity and fears aspiration.'[105] By the 1880s the Society had again become hospitable to the more imaginative and avant-garde of painters. It even hung the work of the controversial American James McNeill Whistler on its walls. In 1880 the *Magazine of Art* noted that its 'most distinctive feature is variety', and in 1886 congratulated the Society for voting in Whistler as a member.[106] 'At last real art – art large in aim and worthy in sentiment', the critic applauded, 'is being preferred to mere purblind patience, flimsy pretence and catchpenny cheapness of subject.'[107] Like the British Institution, the Society of British Artists had an attractive exhibition hall, 'well-arranged light', 'warm carpeting' and 'comfortable appointments', but it also shared a reputation of being second rate.[108] Like the British Institution it provided exhibition space for paintings that other-wise might have gone unseen and so unsold. The *New Monthly* reported sales of £12,000 in 1829.[109] In 1832, from the 932 works exhibited, the sales amounted to £18,000.[110] In 1856, during the bad years, the *Art Journal* recorded the number of paintings as 840, the number sold as 200, and the prices paid as £6,000.[111] In 1881 the *Art Journal* reported a total of 1621 works exhibited in two exhibitions, a spring and a winter one, but did not record the sales.[112] The periodicals record the erratic career of the Society of British Artists describing the admirable goal of its early years to offer exhibition space to those refused by the Royal Academy. If, during its middle years, the periodicals denounced the Society for succumbing to that besetting sin of societies, control by an exclusive and narrow clique, they praised its reforms during the later years of the century and applauded its hospitality to the new and avant-garde art that was being rejected by its more prestigious rival.

In 1847 the press welcomed another new exhibition which opened its doors to the young artists excluded from the Royal Academy. Called at first the Free Exhibition, its name was later changed to the National Institution of the Fine Arts. This group is remembered as the exhibition in which the earliest Pre-Raphaelite paintings were exposed to public view. At the time the critics failed to appreciate how remarkable these young artists were; they commented instead on the innovations of the exhibiting society. Admission to their early exhibitions was free, but that practice was soon abandoned. More lasting was their unique practice of renting wall space to the exhibitors.

Their first catalogue, from which the *Athenaeum* printed the following passages, showed a business-like point of view. The exhibitors offered, not art, but 'their manufactures to the world' for sale. 'A picture, a statue, and a shawl are made for exchange', the catalogue stated, 'art has its mercantile, as well as its social value'. They reiterated the need, as the *Athenaeum* approvingly reported, for the artist's works to be seen by the public. 'The artist lives by his works', they stated, 'and the necessity of having a show room for them is evidently paramount to him as to the shawl manufacture.'[113] The admission is free, commented the *Art Journal* but the question is, 'will the pictures sell?'[114] In 1856 the *Art Journal* answered the question: 580 paintings were exhibited with total sale of £3,000.[115] The critics again welcomed a rival to the existing institutions, but could not be very enthusiastic about the works exhibited.

Rival societies formed not only because angry or rejected individuals banded together, the critics noted, but also because the Royal Academy hung few works in certain media such as water-colour, pastel and engravings. In 1805 the formation of the Society of Painters in Water-Colour (also called the Old Society) provided an alternative for water-colour painters. In describing the Old Society the press emphasized the popularity and the high quality of their exhibitions. 'This is the most universally popular picture exhibition of any', reported the *Spectator* in 1835. In 1838 the *Spectator* was still enthusiastic, calling it 'the smallest and choicest of the annual collections'.[116] Here was a real rival to the Royal Academy, at least in quality. The exhibitions included, according to *Chambers's* in 1852, 'works of importance quite equal to those of the Academy'.[117] The *Saturday Review* agreed. 'More fine works are to be found at the Old Water-Colour Exhibition, in proportion to the number on the walls', it asserted in 1854, 'than at any other exhibition in London.'[118] It was not merely the high quality of the works that won praise from the critics, but the fact that the Society preserved intact the old British tradition of water-colour painting. 'The gallery, all but perfect after its kind,' declared J. B. Atkinson in *Blackwood's*, 'may be counted the distinguishing glory of the British school.'[119] At the Old Society the French and German influences so suspect to many Englishmen were absent. Not only was the style of painting uniquely English, but, in large part, so were the landscape subjects depicted. 'This is the exhibition above all others which an Englishman most delights in,' observed the art critic of the *Spectator*, 'and has the greatest reason to be proud of.'[120] Despite their patriotic pride in the British artistic achievement exemplified by the Old Society, the critics did find some faults in this exemplar of societies. The preserving of tradition led to exclusiveness of membership and repetition of manner and subject. 'It cannot be disputed', argued the *Magazine of Art* in 1880, 'that a society which confines itself to the works of its own membership condemns itself to a certain degree of inevitable monotony.' Unfortunately 'much of the work shown by them', the critic confessed, 'is a foregone conclusion'.[121] A beloved tradition with well-known practitioners and their 'prescribed and well-known excellencies' exerted their charm, but they also represented an art that was standing still.[122] 'You can tell a picture of nearly every well-known name at a glance', complained the *Saturday Review*, in 1858, 'by the mannerism of its subject or method.'[123]

Not all water-colourists wished to paint in the traditional manner; neither was there room for them in the small, closed Old Society. The press would soon review a new exhibition organized, not in reaction against the Royal Academy, but against the Old Society. The New Society of Painters in Water-Colours, later called the Associated Painters in Water-Colours, came into being in order to counteract the exclusiveness and narrowness of the Old Society. The members of the New Society, explained *Chambers's*, were more inventive and experimental than the Old Society and tended to paint figure subjects rather than landscapes.[124] The split between the two was almost complete. 'Though there was scarcely a quarter of a mile between the two exhibitions,' the *Spectator* reported, 'it was the rarest sight to see members cross that little bit of road between Suffolk Street and the Guard's Club to look at their rival's paintings.'[125]

The press recorded other societies that formed and sponsored exhibitions, but often their names appeared in the columns of the periodicals for only a few years. *Fraser's* counted 24 exhibitions, including picture dealers, during the 1861 season.[126] Twenty years later, the *Fortnightly* mentioned ten new exhibitions which had 'been opened because of the stupidity and neglect of the Academy'.[127] The list included the New English Art Club, which formed the Academy's chief rival in the last decade of the century.

Despite the 'stupidity and neglect' and many other faults widely denounced by the press, *Fraser's* was forced to record the inescapable fact that the Royal Academy 'remained on the top of Fortune's wheel' throughout the nineteenth century.[128] The periodicals were unanimous in their condemnation of Royal Academy privileges and practices. But critical as the periodicals were of the Royal Academy, they called for reforms, not for abolishing the institution. They realized how central the Academy was to the Victorian art world and to the exhibition system. They demanded a more responsible academy, but they reported, with regularity, on the popularity of its exhibition. 'The opening of the Exhibition of the Royal Academy is one of our annual metropolitan galas,' proclaimed the *Pictorial Times*, 'belonging to the same category as Christmas Day, Easter Monday, and the opening of Parliament.'[129] The press called the exhibition a 'household word'; it was 'hallowed by time' and 'sanctified by tradition'.[130] The exhibition itself was described and satirized many times in the press. The *Illustrated London News* depicted a motley crowd in 1843 (plate 1). 'From ten o'clock till six the rooms are thronged with an interested eager crowd,' reported Margaret Oliphant in *Blackwood's*, 'enduring dust, heat and fatigue with more placidity than in any other haunt.'[131] The floor was a 'sea of bonnets', declared *Fraser's*, and there was a 'Babel of babble on all sides'.[132] The critic of the *Art Journal* found it 'utterly impossible' to perform his duties in such a crowded exhibition. He asked that critics could be allowed admittance to the private showing. Under better circumstances, the critic argued, his review would be likely to be more 'generous'. *The Times* reviewer, the *Art Journal* pointed out with a twinge of jealousy, attended both the private view and the Academy dinner, and he wrote very handsome reviews of the Royal Academy. The Royal Academy did, in fact, let the critics into the private view in 1850, when 'twenty-three cards of invitation were issued to metropolitan journals'.[133]

The press called for many other reforms, usually with less success. The indictments against the Academy dated back to its origins and the manner of its founding. Throughout the nineteenth century the press continued to condemn the Academy for its exclusiveness and its unfairness. The Academy was blamed not only for its current practices, but even for the blight it cast on the English School of painting for years to come. The main indictment in the periodicals during the nineteenth century focussed on the monopolistic position of the Academy and the unfair advantages the Academicians claimed within the exhibition system. The prestige and popularity of the Royal Academy exhibition made inclusion on its walls the goal of most professional artists. 'A good place on its walls', declared the *National Review*, 'is a year's income to a young painter.'[134] That 'good place', however, was not easy to obtain. During most of the century more works were rejected than were accepted.[135] In the later part of the century the press reported that the number of rejections had risen to 6876 in 1885 and to 9861 in 1893.[136] The press was not without its criticisms of the selection process. The Royal Academy could, as the *Spectator* complained, 'exclude what pictures they please without assigning a reason'.[137] The fact that all Royal Academicians received automatic acceptance for eight of their works bothered many critics. The *Art Journal* of 1848 reported the following anecdote which clearly illustrates this advantage enjoyed by the Academicians.

Not long ago a gentleman applied to an artist to paint him 'full length'; all preliminaries being arranged, he said, 'Of course you will guarantee my being hung at the Exhibition.' 'I cannot do so,' replied the artist, 'not being a member, I can guarantee nothing of the kind; but I can pledge myself to send your portrait to the Royal Academy, and it is not likely they will reject it.' The gentleman said he would consider. The result of his consideration is, that his portrait – full length – is now in the Exhibition; painted in a very gay costume, by a member of the Academy, who, of course, did guarantee its being exhibited.[138]

Not only could the Academicians demand automatic acceptance for at least eight of their works, they could claim the best positions on the wall. The consequences of this practice, explained the *Saturday Review*, 'is that "the line" is occupied by huge second-rate productions'.[139] Because many of the Royal Academicians were portrait painters, these 'huge second-rate productions' tended to be portraits. 'Over-dressed women dandling over-dressed children', complained the *Athenaeum*, 'and men standing bolt upright, trying to look dignified, or seated in armchairs trying to look easy'.[140] The portrait painters not only outnumbered those of other genres, but, since the portraits were frequently full-length and life-size, they took up much more than their share of the precious wall space. To demonstrate this point the *Art Journal* critic made a plan of the paintings above the line of what he calls the least objectionable wall of the Great Room, and in it he coloured all the portraits black (plate 2). The wall contained 40 paintings, 28 of them portraits. Seven of the 12 non-portraits, he noticed, were placed at the top of the wall, the other five being pushed into the corners. On the other walls, he reported, the proportion of portraits was even greater.[141]

After the Royal Academicians and the Associates had been hung in the best places on the walls, the hanging committee tried to find places for the other paintings which had been accepted. M. H. Spielmann in the *Magazine of Art* described the hanging committee fitting works into the remaining space like a giant puzzle.[142] The 'hangmen', as the committee had been called by their critics, did not have an easy time. Before the exhibition opened the *Magazine of Art* reported, whole walls might be rehung four or five times; paintings might even be re-framed to fit in smaller places.[143] Although the critic of the *Art Journal* considered the men of the hanging committee of 'unimpeachable integrity', he confessed that there were 'prejudices which upright men cannot always overcome', prejudices which 'often give to well-intended acts the character and consequences of dishonesty'.[144] Other critics were not so sympathetic to the difficulties of the hanging committee, nor so trusting of their good intentions. Another *Art Journal* criticism suggested that the hanging committee might be guilty of arrogance. The paintings of non-members were poorly hung, it suggested, 'by way of lessons to aspiring youths to be humble-minded, and not to HOPE too much.'[145] The *Spectator* suspected even more sinister motivations. The hanging committee, it asserted, exercised the power of 'putting the performances of dangerous rivals out of sight'.[146] Henry Ottley in *Fraser's* quoted David Wilkie's description of the way the hanging committee operated. 'First take care of yourselves, next of your friends', he said, 'and then of the poor devils who have no friends.'[147]

In the several locations occupied at different times by the Royal Academy there existed many opportunities for hanging pictures out of sight – 'among the gathering cobwebs at the ceiling or through the dust about your feet'.[148] A worse fate awaited the luckless artist relegated to the Octagon Room at Trafalgar Square, which the critics dubbed the 'condemned hole' and the 'lumber room'.[149] Many critics described with great poignancy the plight of the young artist on opening day. Not knowing if his painting had been hung or not, he lined up at the entrance on opening day. Proffering his shilling for a catalogue, he frantically flipped through its pages looking for his name. If he saw it there, he would begin the long search to find his painting hanging somewhere among the 1500 or more accepted works. He would eventually find it, predicted the *Art Journal*, 'courting obscurity in some secluded nook, – and by the public never discovered at all'. The labour of an entire year, a labour 'that was perhaps to buy his children's bread', would be utterly wasted. 'Many a wound of the heart', concluded the *Art Journal* critic, 'is carried home from the crowded rooms of the Royal Academy on that first Monday in the merry month of May.'[150]

Another privilege allowed only to the Academicians and one which the reviewers deplored, was the right to add finishing touches to their paintings once they had been hung on the walls. On 'varnishing days' the Academicians could heighten the colour on their paintings so they would stand out from the more subtle paintings hanging near them. 'The very shadow of a cloud is rendered more intensely blue than Byron's classic sea', complained the *Library of the Fine Arts*, 'and the sober gray granite column of a temple blazes prominently brighter than Corinthian brass.'[151] By heightening colours and placing their paintings in prominent positions, the critics claimed, the Royal Academicians assured for themselves the focus of attention; even if a visitor or reviewer attempted to seek out other paintings, he often could not see them clearly in the dark corners or along the floor.

If a young artist became discouraged at being rejected, badly hung, or outshone at the Royal Academy, he might think of exhibiting at one of the other societies, and many critics advised him to do this. But not only would he find himself in less prestigious company, viewed by less important patrons and given less attention by the press, but he could forfeit his chance of becoming a candidate for membership in the Royal Academy. The periodicals considered most unfair the following Royal Academy rule: 'whoever exhibits with any other society at the time that his works are exhibited in the Royal Academy, shall neither be admitted as a candidate for an associate, nor his performances be received the following year'.[152] Although the Royal Academy claimed it did not enforce the rule, the art critics insisted it deterred artists from joining and exhibiting with other societies. It also influenced members of other societies to resign, the critics argued, if the artists thought they were near acceptance as an associate in the Royal Academy. It was one more way, warned the art critics, that the Royal Academy ensured its monopoly of the art world.

The Royal Academy tenaciously grasped the privileges granted by royal sponsorship, but, as the periodicals noted, it also courted men of wealth and power to increase their patronage and to protect themselves from their critics.[153] Not only was the press critical of the actions of the Royal Academy, but various parliamentary commissions throughout the century investigated the Royal Academy. The press enthusiastically reported the charges against the Royal Academy and eagerly awaited the expected reforms. But they waited in vain. All they could do was report the Academy's resistance to change. Diverse though the Academicians were, they all realized that it was to their self-interest to retain a unity in the face of criticism. 'The Academy is only a close borough of trades in public patronage', the *Spectator* explained, 'a knot of mechanics who though hating and envying one another, hang together for the sake of loaves and fishes.'[154]

The Academy's important and powerful friends stood it in good stead when reforms threatened. M. H. Spielmann speculated in the *Magazine of Art* in 1887, that the £40,000 expended for the annual Academy dinner was well spent because by it the Academy ingratiated themselves with the wealthy and powerful. Every year the Academy issued 140 invitations to 'eminent persons'. The *Magazine of Art* described this assemblage of royalty, aristocracy, government officials, rich patrons and men of letters, and how, after they had been well-fed and lulled into good humour by the toasts and after-dinner speeches, the Academicians escorted their guests through the newly-hung exhibition. The dinner, Spielmann argued, promoted the '"bump of acquisitiveness" on the head of John Bull' and impressed the guests 'with a sense of the supreme dignity of art'.[155] The dinner, also, as other critics suggested, impressed the eminent with the 'supreme dignity' of the Royal Academy. It did so at the expense of the non-members whose paintings helped to attract the shilling fees that supported the dinner from which, like the private viewing, the non-members were excluded.

To enhance their image in the eyes of the rich and powerful, the periodicals complained, the Academicians were careful to elect a president who was socially acceptable. 'Either Philips or Shee must be the new president', it was suggested upon Lawrence's death, 'they are the only Academicians that wear hair powder'.[156] *Fraser's*, which reported this anecdote, was one of the periodicals most perceptive about the effects of Victorian social organization and institutions on the art world. Martin Archer Shee, Charles Eastlake, Francis Grant and Frederick Leighton, the reigning P.R.A.s throughout most of the Victorian period, made many influential friends for the Royal Academy and offended no one in power. Of these only Leighton gained a lasting reputation as an artist; the others had talents, however, which were very valuable to the Academy. Shee, observed the *Spectator*, 'has many personal friends in the circles of rank and fashion'.[157] Eastlake had close ties with Prince Albert and Sir Robert Peel. Although the *Saturday Review* accused Grant of making poor jokes about his own profession of artist, they conceded that he was a 'gentleman of the world' and a fox hunter.[158]

The ambiguity of the position of the Royal Academy in the Victorian art world worried the periodicals. They reported that although it was founded in 1768 under the sponsorship of George III, it had never received a charter. Although it acted as an official institution, it was in reality, as many critics explained, a private club. 'The Royal Academy is a private body of artists', the *Spectator* accused, 'usurping title, privilege and power uncontrolled and exercising the functions of a public body without any constituted existence or responsibility.'[159] It was responsible only to the queen, and that responsibility a formality rather than a reality. Most critics recommended that the government exercise more control over its activities. The 'Forty Thieves', as one critic referred to the Academicians, however, successfully fought to keep the status quo.[160] It allowed them privilege and independence without responsibility or accountability. It was the best of both worlds for the Royal Academy, as many critics bitterly observed, and assured the Royal Academy the premier position in the exhibition system.

The periodicals criticized the cliques, the faults and the injustices of the exhibition system, but they had to admit that it was good for business. The *Art Journal* estimated the number of works exhibited during the 1852 season as 4756.[161] Nearly 30 years later, in 1881, the same periodical counted nearly double that number, or 8419 works exhibited.[162] The system was 'a natural and necessary one', declared William Michael Rossetti in *Fraser's* of 1861. Furthermore, he continued, it was better to have many exhibitions than to have only one, as the French did. Rossetti, like the other critics, had reservations about the way the Royal Academy and the other societies managed their exhibitions, and he saw negative aspects to the system. In analysing the effect of exhibitions, he noted that the fact they operated on schedules meant artists hurried to finish their pictures, sometimes submitting them when more work would have improved them, or keeping them for another year, depriving the curious public of the sight of their work and themselves of income from it. Artists also, he observed, tended to paint to the level of the exhibition rather than setting higher goals; they tended to emulate the popular works that sold well, and became involved in the intrigues and petty jealousies which societies seemed to foster. But, he cautioned, it was useless to oppose the system. 'The exhibition is the accepted mart of artistic work', he explained: 'public patronage demands it.'[163]

As discontent with the mismanagement and injustices of the societies grew, the periodicals reported an increasing number of alternative choices. Some artists chose to keep their paintings in their own studios. Ironically Dante Gabriel Rossetti, William Michael's brother, is the artist most cited by the press as an artist who did not exhibit his works publicly. Instead of a large public audience, Rossetti relied, as the critics pointed out, on a small but influential circle of friends and patrons, and the mystique, almost a cult, that surrounded him. It was the rare artist that could rely on his public to seek him out; the press only rarely announced that an artist's work was on view in his studio. Later in the century, as studios, usually functioning as painting rooms, became also used as show rooms, artists paid more attention to their architecture and decoration. Young painters lived in houses like palaces, complained Henry Blackburn in the *National Review* of 1883. Such elaborate studios, he added, suggest very high prices.[164] The periodicals soon began to feature articles on the studios of various artists. The *Art Journal*, for example, discussed the architecture of artists' studios in 1880 and 1881. They printed floor plans and sketched the interiors and exteriors of several studios.[165] Showing works in the artist's own studio, these articles suggest, requires the investment to build one that was conveniently located and attractive. It also required that the artist had gained sufficient fame to inspire his patrons to seek him out and to lure the critics to visit him.

Throughout the nineteenth century periodicals had advertised, announced and occasionally reviewed exhibitions in rooms especially rented by the artist for this showing. He might rent space in exhibition emporiums like Egyptian Hall or the Queen's Bazaar, where his works of art vied with wonders of the natural world, recent excavation finds from the ancient world, curiosities from the New World and new inventions from the scientific and commercial world. By renting exhibition room, the critics pointed out, the artist gained for himself the entrance fees as well as money for the sale of his works. If the paintings exhibited gained sufficient popular attention and were perhaps reviewed by the press, he might be able to sell permission to engrave them as well. *Fraser's* reported an increase in this form of exhibition in 1861, following the success of William Holman Hunt's exhibition of *Christ in the Temple*. Despite the 'throngs of visitors throughout the whole of two successive seasons' the critic does not feel this kind of exhibition is a 'desirable arrangement in ordinary cases'. He did see, however, that these artist's exhibitions would effect the symbiosis between artist, exhibiting bodies, press and patron. Both exhibition in one's studio or in rented space excludes one partner (the exhibiting society) if not two (the press) from the system.[166] William Michael Rossetti, in *Fraser's* four years later, conceded that there could be advantages to viewing only one work or the work of only one artist. There would be no distractions by different artists or styles. The disadvantages, Rossetti observed, would become evident if the works were only of average interest, or if too many artists chose this method.

The number of paintings which the public viewed or the press reviewed in artist's studios or in rented exhibition rooms was small compared to the number of paintings which the societies exhibited. The picture dealer constituted a fourth type of exhibiting agent. In the first part of the century when the press reported the activities of picture dealers, it was almost entirely for the exhibition and sale of old masters. By the middle of the century, however, the pages of the periodicals reveal that picture dealers were playing a significant role in the contemporary art market, and by the end of the century their exhibitions came close to rivalling even those of the Royal Academy. During the first half of the century the press generally adopted a negative and suspicious attitude toward picture dealers. The *Art Journal* in particular warned its readers against those frauds and forgeries that unscrupulous dealers might foist on unsuspecting patrons. By mid-century the *Art Journal*, although still advising patrons to buy directly from artists, admitted that 'dealers in modern art are, generally speaking, fair traders'. The dealers made all the money they could, the *Art Journal* added, sometimes doubling the original cost, by buying paintings before they were exhibited, but the artist usually shared in the profits and gained in reputation by the elevation of his prices.[167] Ten years later, in 1864, the *Art Journal* informed its readers that whereas in former times no contemporary paintings could be seen in the off-season, now they were on show at 'the most eminent picture-dealers'.[168]

R. Folkstone Williams, in the periodical *Belgravia* in 1867, defended the picture dealers. He described the plight of the patron trying to purchase paintings at the Royal Academy exhibition. In the first place, he could not see most of the paintings as the bad ones were hung out of sight and the good ones were obscured by crowds of people. Furthermore, Williams continues, if he finds something he likes it is probably already sold. The patron might leave the exhibition with only aching eyes and a stiff neck for his troubles. At the picture dealer's, on the other hand, Williams argued, the exhibition would be uncrowded, the selection smaller and the quality indisputable. Patrons unsure of their taste could rely on expert guidance. There would be no haggling with the artist over price. To the artist there would also be advantages in dealing with a commercial gallery. The picture dealer would know how best to promote the artist's interests, raise his prices and enhance his reputation. *Belgravia* told its readers that Gambart, Cox, Wallis, Agnew and Morby were the principal dealers, noting that at least one of them (probably Gambart) had a stock of paintings worth £100,000.[169]

In the same year the *Saturday Review* reluctantly confessed that if picture dealers could amass a collection as excellent as that of Henry Wallis in Suffolk Street, the exhibition ought to be reviewed by the press. 'We must either notice Mr. Wallis's Exhibition', the *Saturday Review* argued, 'or ignore some of the best art of the year.' The artist's reputation should not suffer neglect because his painting hangs in a dealer's showroom. 'A good picture does not cease to be good', the critic admitted, 'when it becomes the property of a dealer.' Even though 'we might be advertising the wares of a class of merchants', he continued, 'who as a body, are believed to care more for their own interests than for the advancement of art', he could not pass over such excellent works in silence. The *Saturday Review* did reassure its readers, however, that it would review only those picture dealers who kept the 'shop character . . . in the background', or who would not 'pay court' to one purchaser while showing disrespect to 'simple visitors'. It would not review those galleries where 'the visitor is pestered with commentaries on the merits of the work shown'.[170]

The private exhibition gallery reached new heights of elegance in 1877 with the opening of the Grosvenor Gallery, an event given much attention by the press. The Grosvenor Gallery (plate 3) was partly a commercial venture and partly the personal whim of Sir Coutts Lindsay, an aristocratic and wealthy artist and man about town. The opening of the Grosvenor Gallery, predicted the *Art Journal*, would 'mark an epoch in British Art'.[171] Sir Coutts Lindsay spent over £100,000, said the *Art Journal*, on furnishing the gallery.[172] The artists invited to exhibit, including Burne-Jones, William Holman Hunt, Alma-Tadema, Albert Moore and Whistler, had their works hung on the sumptuous red silk panels of the exhibition rooms. These paintings represented a style of art, as every critic hastened to remark, not welcome at the Royal Academy, but one which the cultivated public was curious to see. The Grosvenor Gallery, reported the *Saturday Review*, was more of a 'complement' to the Royal Academy than a rival to it.[173] Not only did the new gallery display a different style of art from that gracing the walls of the Royal Academy, but its spacious arrangement contrasted, wrote

H. Heathcote Statham in *Macmillan's*, with 'the confusions and weariness which the eye experiences in ranging over the closely packed walls of an average exhibition room'.[174] The real significance of the new gallery was not merely a matter of arrangement or choice of new artists, but a new view 'which regards a painting in reference to the individuality of the artist rather than the mere facts of the subject'.[175] The Grosvenor Gallery did not sustain the promise of its opening, but it did set a pattern that was soon to be followed by the Grafton Gallery, the New Gallery, and others.

The commercial galleries had at last challenged the monopoly of the Royal Academy. The prophecy of the *Saturday Review's* art critic in 1863 had come true. 'The more good men are excluded from the Royal Academy', he had predicted, 'the less does the slur of exclusion become, and the more valueless does the dignity itself appear.'[176] Ironically, the artists who had turned away from the Royal Academy in disgust at its crass mercantilism and abuse of privilege had found a more congenial home in the commercial galleries.

Art critics in the Victorian periodicals chronicled the vicissitudes of the exhibition system, they described the monopolistic practices of the Royal Academy and the attempts to reform it and to compete with it. The more perceptive of the critics saw the exhibition system not merely as an interesting phenomenon providing copy for their columns, but as the primary cause of the mediocrity of the British School. They realized that by turning exhibitions into market places the system elevated those paintings which sold easily and for the highest prices into the models of artistic excellence.[177] Mediocrity was further assured, the critics suggested, by the Royal Academy's habit of choosing financially successful artists for its rare and privileged memberships.[178] The critics further understood that by hanging their members' paintings in the most prominent places in their exhibitions, the Royal Academy helped to create false standards in the public mind.[179] The periodicals realized that instead of seeking to instruct the public the main goal of the exhibitions was to hang as many saleable works as possible in their limited space.[180] The critics also analysed the role of the public itself, formed largely from newly acquired trading and manufacturing wealth and lacking the opportunity for extensive travel and development of a cultivated taste in art, in influencing the course of English art.[181] Their tendency to follow the guidance of fashion or their natural inclination toward the comfortable familiarity of domestic and landscape scenes was documented by the periodicals.[182] The tendency of critics, mainly literary men, to prefer paintings with more narrative subjects to those whose merits lay mainly in composition and colour did not pass unremarked by the press. The system, agreed the critics, left artists the choice of conforming to the popular taste or of seeking patronage outside the established exhibitions.[183] The exhibition system, they explained, led the mainstream of British art away from the grandeur of religious, historical or imaginative subjects toward the detail of small, pretty domestic scenes.[184] In their reviews the critics regretted that originality, poetic instinct and artistic style lacked an appreciative audience and soon diminished until they could no longer be found in the major exhibitions.[185] Artists, in the view of the press, painted down to the level of the public instead of reaching for the ideal.[186] If this yielding to public taste left art cheapened and debased, the critics traced the motivations to the considerable financial rewards.[187]

The periodicals not only present a fairly unified analysis of the workings of the exhibition system, they provide vivid examples and document the consequences on the direction of British art. They are a unique source for the study of factors that influence the formation of art and taste in the Victorian age. The critics, themselves a part of the exhibition system, present an invaluable analysis of its workings. Like no other source, Victorian periodicals explain the social and economic forces affecting the British school.

NOTES

I would like to express my gratitude to Walter and Esther Houghton for all the help the *Wellesley Index* has given in helping to locate the articles used in this essay, and in identifying the critics named.

1. *New Monthly Mag.*, xxxvii (1833), 247.
2. *Contemporary Rev.*, xxxvi (1879), 597.
3. *Fortnightly Rev.*, xi (n.s.v) (1869), 670; *Art J.* (1879). 228; *Fraser's Mag.*, xcii (n.s.xii) (1875), 255.
4. *Ibid.*; *ibid.*, lxvi (1862), 66; *Fortnightly Rev.*, lix (n.s. liii) (1893), 776.
5. *Contemporary Rev.*, xxxvi (1879), 597; *New Monthly Mag.*, xxxi (1831), 578; *Athenaeum*, no. 819 (1843), 629.
6. *Fraser's Mag.*, xcii (n.s. xii) (1875), 258.
7. *Fortnightly Rev.*, lix (n.s. liii) (1893), 776; *Contemporary Rev.*, xxxvi (1879), 597.
8. *Fortnightly Rev.*, lix (n.s. liii) (1893), 775.
9. *Ibid.*
10. *Fraser's Mag.*, xxxi (1845), 161.
11. *Ibid.*, xcii (n.s. xii) (1875), 256.
12. *Ibid.*, lxx (1864), 66.
13. *National Rev.*, xxv (1894), 468.
14. *Ibid.*, ix (1887), 517.
15. *New Monthly Mag.*, lxix (1843), 261.
16. *Athenaeum*, no. 819 (1843), 629.
17. *Fraser's Mag.*, xcii (n.s. xii) (1875), 255–69.
18. *Athenaeum*, no. 819 (1843), 629.
19. *National Rev.*, ix (1887), 517.
20. *Fortnightly Rev.*, xi (n.s. v) (1869), 670.
21. *New Monthly Mag.*, xxv (1829), 567.
22. *National Rev.*, ix (1887), 515.
23. *Athenaeum*, no. 819 (1843), 629.
24. *ILN*, viii (1846), 311.
25. *Spectator*, xviii (1845), 474.
26. *Fortnightly Rev.*, xvii (n.s. xi) (1872), 695.
27. *Saturday Rev.*, xiii (1862), 613–14.
28. *Fortnightly Rev.*, lix (n.s. liii) (1893), 788.
29. *National Rev.*, xxv (1894), 466.
30. *Art J.* (1845), 137.
31. *Fortnightly Rev.*, lix (n.s. liii) (1893), 774.
32. *Athenaeum*, no. 239 (1832), 340.

33. *Library of the Fine Arts*, n.s. III (1833), 160.
34. *Monthly Chron.*, IV (1839), 502.
35. *Ibid.*, 506.
36. *Fortnightly Rev.*, XLIII (n.s. XXXVII) (1885), 67.
37. *Saturday Rev.*, XI (1861), 447.
38. *National Rev.*, IX (1887), 516; *Saturday Rev.*, XIII (1862), 613.
39. *Mag. of Art*, III (1880), 436.
40. *Fortnightly Rev.*, LIX (n.s. LIII) (1893), 775.
41. *Blackwood's*, LXXIV (1853), 103.
42. *Spectator*, LIV (1887), 604.
43. *Saturday Rev.*, III (1857), 452.
44. *Fraser's Mag.*, LV (1857), 619.
45. *Ibid.*, LIII (1856), 686.
46. *Athenaeum*, no. 239 (1832), 339.
47. *Contemporary Rev.*, XXXVI (1879), 597.
48. *Saturday Rev.*, XXII (1866), 331.
49. *New Monthly Mag.*, LXIX (1843), 261.
50. *Fortnightly Rev.*, LIX (n.s. LIII) (1893), 775; *Athenaeum*, no. 819 (1843), 629; *Fraser's Mag.*, LXXXIV (n.s. IV) (1871), 187; *New Monthly Mag.*, XXV (1829), 567.
51. *National Rev.*, XXV (1894), 476.
52. *Ibid.*
53. *Eclectic Rev.*, n.s. XXV (1849), 665; *Blackwood's*, LXXXVIII (1860), 84; *National Rev.*, II (1883), 59; *Saturday Rev.*, III (1857), 452.
54. *Fraser's Mag.*, XXVIII (1843), 72.
55. *Saturday Rev.*, XIII (1862), 614.
56. *Monthly Chron.*, IV (1839), 507.
57. *National Rev.*, XXV (1894), 476.
58. *Contemporary Rev.*, XI (1869), 106.
59. *Art J.* (1854), 312.
60. *National Rev.*, XXV (1894), 466.
61. *Athenaeum*, no. 1124 (1849), 474; *Art J.* (1852), 246; *Blackwood's*, CXXXVIII (1885), 5; *Fraser's Mag.*, V (1832), 709.
62. *Blackwood's*, LXXIV (1853), 89 (American edition).
63. *Fortnightly Rev.*, LI (1855), 708.
64. *Blackwood's*, LXXVII (1855), 585 (American edition).
65. *Fraser's Mag.*, LI (1855), 708.
66. *Belgravia*, II (1867), 290.
67. *Fraser's Mag.*, LXXXVI (n.s. VI) (1872), 21.
68. *Fortnightly Rev.*, XLIII (n.s. XXXVII) (1885), 66.
69. *Art J.* (1859), 274.

70. *Blackwood's*, CVI (1869), 230.
71. *Ibid.*
72. *Ibid.*
73. *Ibid.*, XC (1861), 203.
74. *New Monthly Mag.*, C (1854), 462.
75. *Spectator*, III (1830), 88.
76. *Saturday Rev.*, III (1857), 475.
77. *Ibid.*, XIII (1862), 271.
78. *Fraser's Mag.*, II (1830), 96.
79. *Ibid.*
80. *Ibid.*, LXI (1860), 874.
81. *Ibid.*
82. *Ibid.*, XL (1849), 74.
83. *New Monthly Mag.*, XXXVIII (1833), 79.
84. *Fraser's Mag.*, LXIX (1864), 69.
85. *Ibid.*, XLVI (1852), 228; *Nineteenth Century*, XXXII (1892), 720.
86. *Fortnightly Rev.*, LIX (n.s. LIII) (1893), 887.
87. *Art J.* (1859), 153.
88. *Ibid.*, (1852), 270.
89. *Ibid.*
90. *Athenaeum*, no. 1163 (1850), 162.
91. *Spectator*, X (1837), 114; *Chambers's*, n.s. XVIII (1852), 2.
92. *Spectator*, XVIII (1845), 163.
93. *Saturday Rev.*, IX (1860), 467.
94. *Ibid.*, V (1858), 189.
95. *Art J.* (1846), 15.
96. *Spectator*, IX (1836), 806.
97. *Art J.* (1852), 69.
98. *Fraser's Mag.*, XLVI (1852), 228.
99. *Spectator*, II (1829), 202.
100. *Fraser's Mag.*, LXXXIV (n.s. IV) (1871), 187; *New Monthly Mag.*, ser. 2, XVIII (1836), 194.
101. *Spectator*, X (1837), 282; *New Monthly Mag.*, ser. 2, XVIII (1836), 194.
102. *Spectator*, VII (1834), 999.
103. *Ibid.*, XIV (1841), 307.
104. *Chambers's*, n.s. XVIII (1852), 3.
105. *Academy*, IV (1873), 467.
106. *Mag. of Art*, III (1880), 145.
107. *Ibid.*, IX (1886), 162.
108. *Spectator*, XXI (1848), 376.
109. *New Monthly Mag.*, XXVII (1829), 205.
110. *Ibid.*, XXXVI (1832), 159.
111. *Art J.* (1856), 277.
112. *Ibid.*, (1881), 134.
113. *Athenaeum*, no. 1021 (1847), 528.
114. *Art J.* (1847), 183.
115. *Ibid.*, (1856), 277.
116. *Spectator*, VIII (1835), 424; *ibid.*, XXI (1848), 446.

117. *Chambers's*, n.s. XVIII (1852), 2.
118. *Saturday Rev.*, II (1854), 125.
119. *Blackwood's*, CII (1867), 97.
120. *Spectator*, X (1837), 402.
121. *Mag. of Art.*, III (1880), 159.
122. *Blackwood's*, XC (1861), 202.
123. *Saturday Rev.*, V (1858), 531.
124. *Chambers's*, n.s. XVIII (1852), 2.
125. *Spectator*, LIV (1881), 440.
126. *Fraser's Mag.*, LIV (1861), 580.
127. *Fortnightly Rev.*, LVIII (n.s. LIII) (1893), 887.
128. *Fraser's Mag.*, LI (1855), 707.
129. *Pictorial Times*, IX (1847), 289.
130. *Fortnightly Rev.*, XL (n.s. XXXIV) (1883), 785; *Pictorial Times*, IX (1847), 289.
131. *Blackwood's*, CXIX (1876), 753.
132. *Fraser's Mag.*, LI (1855), 707.
133. *Art J.* (1846), 171; *ibid.*, (1848), 65; *ibid.*, (1850), 165; *ibid.*, (1852), 165.
134. *National Rev.*, V (1885), 458.
135. *Art J.* (1855), 196; *ibid.*, (1854), 157; *ibid.*, (1848), 65.
136. *Blackwood's*, CXXXVIII (1885), 5; *Fortnightly Rev.*, LXIX (n.s. LIII) (1893), 881.
137. *Spectator*, IX (1836), 1189.
138. *Art. J.* (1848), 180 n.
139. *Saturday Rev.*, XV (1863), 593.
140. *Athenaeum*, no. 816 (1843), 570.
141. *Art. J.* (1845), 179.
142. *Mag. of Art*, X (1887), 194.
143. *Ibid.*, 195.
144. *Art. J.* (1852), 165.
145. *Ibid.*, (1845), 180.
146. *Spectator*, XV (1842), 498.
147. *Fraser's Mag.*, LXIX (1864), 71.
148. *Art. J.* (1845), 179.
149. *Spectator*, XV (1842), 499; *ILN*, XII (1848), 299.
150. *Art. J.* (1856), 261–2.
151. *Library of the Fine Arts*, I (1831), 515.

152. *Fraser's Mag.*, XXXI (1845), 583.
153. *Mag. of Art*, X (1887), 231.
154. *Spectator*, III (1830), 544.
155. *Mag. of Art*, X (1887), 231.
156. *Fraser's Mag.*, LXVII (1864), 74.
157. *Spectator*, III (1830), 70.
158. *Saturday Rev.*, XXII (1866), 302.
159. *Spectator*, XV (1842), 498.
160. *Fraser's Mag.*, XXXI (1845), 583.
161. *Art. J.* (1852), 270.
162. *Ibid.*, (1881), 134.
163. *Fraser's Mag.*, LXXI (1865), 737.
164. *National Rev.*, II (1883), 58.
165. Descriptions of artists' studios also became a part of interviews with artists and biographical sketches.
166. *Fraser's Mag.*, LXIV (1861), 583.
167. *Art. J.* (1854), 312.
168. *Ibid.*, 80.
169. *Belgravia*, II (1867), 290–2.
170. *Saturday Rev.*, XXIII (1867), 753.
171. *Art. J.* (1878), 56.
172. *Ibid.*, (1877), 159.
173. *Saturday Rev.*, XLIII (1877), 549.
174. *Macmillan's Mag.*, XXXVI (1877), 112.
175. *Ibid.*
176. *Saturday Rev.*, XV (1863), 593.
177. *Fortnightly Rev.*, XXVI (n.s. XX) (1876), 66; *ibid.*, LVII (n.s. LI) (1892), 828.
178. *Spectator*, VI (1833), 785.
179. *Fortnightly Rev.*, LVII (n.s. LI) (1892), 829.
180. *Fraser's Mag.*, XLVI (1852), 228–32.
181. *Ibid.*
182. *Ibid.*, LXVI (1862), 65.
183. *Fortnightly Rev.*, VIII (n.s. II) (1867), 464.
184. *Blackwood's*, CXXXVIII (1885), 9–14.
185. *National Rev.*, II (1883), 49; *Mag. of Art*, IX (1886), 162; *Blackwood's*, CXXXI (1882), 617–22.
186. *Blackwood's*, LXXXIV (1858), 181–99.
187. *Ibid.*, CVI (1869), 223–30; *ibid.*, CXXXVIII (1885), 5–25.

John Woolford Periodicals and the practice of literary criticism, 1855–64

Various commentators have felt that at some point in the mid-Victorian period a decisive change took place in literary criticism in the periodicals. In his influential essay,[1] Christopher Kent concentrates upon the professionalization of journalism generally in the 1850s, leading to the evolution of what he calls 'the higher journalism' acting as 'the organ of the mid-Victorian clerisy'.[2] He leaves vague, however, the question of the precise timing and motivation of this development, and does not discuss its effect upon literary criticism, though his use of Coleridge's idea of the 'clerisy', a group whose membership was to include, in Coleridge's words, a number 'to remain at the fountain heads of the humanities',[3] necessarily raises this issue. John Gross identifies the nature of the change as one in the tone and style of periodical criticism:

> Most early Victorian criticism was heavily didactic in tone, uncompromisingly moralistic, political and religious in standpoint. By the end of the 1870s, however, a distinct change could be felt in the atmosphere. The winds of doctrine were dying down, the lay sermon was giving way to the causerie, the emphasis had shifted to Appreciation.[4]

Gross discusses neither the historical nor the intellectual causes of this change, however; it was left to Isobel Armstrong, in her admirable study *Victorian Scrutinies*,[5] to draw attention to this area of the subject. Armstrong characterizes the change as a consequence of the critics' belated adoption of Romantic and, specifically, Coleridgean ideas: '[In early Victorian criticism] a few "German", terms such as objective and subjective, are used, but until the sixties, apart from one or two exceptions . . . it is almost as if Coleridge had never been.'[6] She does not, however, pursue this insight, and although she locates a 'change in the sixties', she hesitates to ascribe a single character to it.[7]

I want in this essay to characterize this change more fully than any of these accounts has attempted to do, and to suggest why it happened. I propose to limit myself to the criticism of poetry, and to take as my starting-point reviews of the work of Browning – specifically the receptions of *Men and Women* in 1855 and *Dramatis Personae* in 1864. The contrast between the blistering reviews of the first and the cordial praise of the second remains as surprising now as it was to many commentators at the time, and though various local factors, such as the Spasmodic controversy[8] of the early 1850s, undoubtedly helped to heighten it, it does, I think, typify a general evolution in conceptions of poetry and criticism in this period.

My thesis is that during the 1850s two major changes took place in literary criticism in the periodicals. The critics' conception of their own role, in relation to the poet and in relation to the public, was revolutionized; simultaneously, and concomitantly, their conception of the role of the poet and their idea of poetry were transformed. This is a generalization, and, like any historical generalization, vulnerable to the citation of many exceptions; I have not, however, found any exceptions which seem to me to threaten the general thesis, and most can be ascribed to what might be called the law of untidiness in historical change. A short account, as this is obliged to be, will inevitably be summary, and I have therefore limited my consideration of those exceptions to my case which in a book-length account I would naturally explore in full. Similarly, though I discuss some of the instruments and causes of the change (the influence of the *Saturday Review*; the innovations of the *Oxford and Cambridge Magazine*; Arnold's campaign of cultural reform) I do not claim to have furnished an exhaustive explanation. What I have attempted to do is to focus the discussion of mid-Victorian literary criticism into its most significant historical phase, and to characterize and explain its evolution in terms which have not previously been used.

1. THE POSITION IN 1855

Looking around at the periodical literature of his period in 1864, Matthew Arnold captures what he considers the spirit of mid-Victorian criticism in the phrase 'the note of provinciality',[9] and articulates its character *via* a contrast with contemporary France:

> M. Planché's advantage is that he feels himself to be speaking before competent judges, that there is a force of cultivated opinion for him to appeal to. Therefore, he must not be extravagant, and he need not storm; he must satisfy reason and taste, – that is his business. Mr Palgrave, on the other hand, feels himself to be speaking before a promiscuous multitude, with the few good judges so scattered through it as to be powerless; therefore he has no calm self-confidence and

self-control; he relies on the strength of his lungs; he knows that big words impose on the mob, and that, even if he is outrageous, most of his audience are apt to be a great deal more so.[10]

Unregulated by an institution like the Académie Française, periodical criticism will be characterized by over-intensity of feeling, will 'like and dislike too passionately', will exhibit the 'Corinthian style' which exists 'to get its ends, to damage its adversaries, to be admired, to triumph.'[11] In illustration, Arnold quotes Palgrave: 'It is the old, old story with Marochetti, the frog trying to blow himself out to bull proportions. He may puff and be puffed, but he will never do it.'[12] It is features like the insolent, fleering tone, the verbal acrobatics ('puff and be puffed') and reductive imagery (frog and ox) which this passage exhibits that sound, in Arnold's ears, the 'note of provinciality'; if we turn to another 1864 product, William Stigand's famous review of *Dramatis Personae*, we hear it again:

> It was said of an eminent lawyer that he wrote his opinions in three different kinds of handwriting – one which he and his clerk could read, another which only he himself could decypher, and a third which neither he nor anybody could make out; and into similar categories we are compelled to parcel out the poems of the *Dramatis Personae*.[13]

If the wish 'to damage its adversaries, to be admired, to triumph' is the mark of a Corinthian style, this is Corinthian; looking back to 1855, I can find, in the chorus of disapprobation that greeted *Maud*, *Leaves of Grass* and *Men and Women*, little that is not even more so:

> A strain of puling, incoherent sentiment and disordered fantasy such as might flit through the brain of a love-sick youth in the measles[14]

> Walt Whitman is as unacquainted with art as a hog is with mathematics[15]

> triple rhymes which can only be compared to the painful and spasmodic attempts which a hobbled donkey makes to get out of the reach of a coachman's whip.[16]

These reviewers 'foam at the mouth' so fiercely and continually, their grotesque, 'outrageous' imagery so densely packs every sentence, that the works themselves disappear; simultaneously, the critics' obsessive display of their combined ferocity and wit obliterates the outline of their critical standards as well, and leaves these to be extracted by inference. This latter feature produces what I call an 'adjectival' criticism – a criticism in which performance has usurped the place of principle – and I will add this term to Arnold's collection.

There is no mystery about the origin of this style, for the critics themselves tell us that it derives from the great Regency critics, Jeffrey and Gifford. Stigand's review begins:

> If the shades of Jeffrey and Gifford were to appear among us and to survey the poetic literature of the present generation, they would feel a stern satisfaction and a self-gratulatory delight at the remembrance of the hard-handed castigations which they had inflicted on the young poets of the commencement of this century.[17]

One 1855 reviewer openly calls for a new Gifford to crush the 'Della Crusca of Transcendentalism',[18] and the language of the earlier reviewers is certainly such as to suggest that they might have relished the task:

> The poetry resembles that of a man who has kept company with kept-mistresses. His Muse talks indelicately like a tea-sipping milliner girl . . . with her, indecency seems to be a disease.[19]

> It is a better and a wiser thing to be a starved apothecary than a starved poet; so back to the shop, Mr John, back to 'plasters, pills and ointment boxes . . .'[20]

> We have weighty reasons for believing that *Pauline* is the production of one or all of the Whig ministers. The same folly, incoherence, and reckless assertion, which distinguish their pamphlet on the *Reform Ministry and Parliament*, is visible in each page of the book.[21]

Coleridge, in his discussion of the *Edinburgh Review* in *Biographia Literaria*, called this sort of thing 'the keenness or asperity of its damnatory style';[22] he also drew attention to its important corollary, 'the substitution of assertion for judgment . . . the frequency of arbitrary and sometimes petulant verdicts'.[23] To be assertive and arbitrary while avoiding the fatigue of adducing a 'leading principle'[24] through 'argumentative deduction' is to write adjectival criticism, which in turn aims to use these features to keep the critic's personality rather than the writer's work constantly before the eye. Thus the critic must be 'damnatory' lest he be effaced by the writer; he must be 'extravagant' in order to glitter brightly; he must be arbitrary and dogmatic in order to avoid being effaced by the 'leading principles' he would otherwise have to introduce. It would be false, of course, to suggest that no differences are to be found between Regency and mid-Victorian critical style. As my quotations suggest, the Regency critics were blatant snobs, which their successors were not; the tone in 1855 is altogether heavier and more earnest. Such changes reflect a changing audience for periodicals – in particular the drift from an upper- to a middle-class readership, and from a period in which social revolution was felt as a threat to one whose social fabric seemed more secure. The critic's dominance over his writer, however, essentially survives; the tone continues one of self-display.

The structure of the reviews also contributed to the critic's self-display. James Mill noted that: 'under the guise of reviewing books, these publications [the *Edinburgh* and *Quarterly*] have introduced the practice of publishing dissertations, not only on the topics of the day, but upon all the most important questions of morals and legislation'.[25] Such a procedure allows the critic to by-pass the work he is reviewing, or even to supplant it by turning his review into an essay on the same subject as that of the book he is supposedly criticizing. When, as often happens, he takes not a single work but half-a-dozen or more, and neglects even to mention them until the final page of his essay, it seems safe to say that he is smothering their authors under the cloak of a collective anonymity: it is easy to forget, for instance, that the brilliant early essays of Carlyle and Macaulay are all technically reviews. In reviewing poetry, of course, this extreme is impossible; but a parallel device very popular in the 1850s was to put all the recently published poems together in a single essay and sometimes then shoot them down one by one like clay pigeons at a fair. Mrs Oliphant's essay on the poetry of 1855, for instance, reduces the poets of that year to a 'family'; Tennyson is 'the eldest', 'Mr Dobell is the sulky boy – Mr Browning the boisterous one – Mr Smith the younger brother,'[26] and so on. To shrink serious poets into a squeaking chorus of juveniles is automatically to elevate the critic by contrast.

But what relation does all this self-assertion bear to the fact that these articles were anonymous? That anonymity was not incompatible with the 'note of provinciality' was perceived by Matthew Arnold's father: 'It seems to me that the mischief of our newspapers mainly arises from the virulent language which men use while writing anonymously',[27] and Cardinal Wiseman found in his own case that anonymity 'enable[s] a writer to write with a confidence, and sometimes with a boldness from which he had shrunk if he spoke in his own person.'[28] Against this, however, must be set that curious use of the editorial 'we' instead of the individual 'I' which is so characteristic of the journalism of the period, and which surely deepens the element of anonymity; Wiseman's comment that 'the plural preserves a modesty of tone and a reserve of opinion' would appear to reverse the self-assertion we have found up till now. The periodical writer's 'we' must depersonalize him into what Wiseman calls 'the representative of certain principles embodied in a collective responsibility'.[29]

Whom then does the critic represent? Arnold notes that English journals, unlike 'an organ like the *Revue des Deux Mondes*', form the mouthpieces of the factions, political and religious, which permeate society; 'we have the *Edinburgh Review*, existing as an organ of the old Whigs . . . we have the *Quarterly Review*, existing as an organ of the Tories . . . and so on through all the various fractions, political and religious, of our society'.[30] Jeffrey himself told Scott that: 'The Review, in short, has but two legs to stand on. Literature no doubt is one of them: But its Right leg is Politics.'[31] And the peroration of Richard Simpson's review of Browning's *Men and Women* connects faction to the editorial plural quite openly: 'Though much of their matter is extremely offensive to Catholics, yet beneath the surface there is an undercurrent of thought that is by no means inconsistent with *our religion*.'[32] Simpson's 'we' is unambiguously that of his religious 'fraction' here; usages elsewhere in this essay, however, cannot be ascribed to this source: 'In this *we* do but say that "thought's what we mean by verse, and seek in verse;" poetry of a high order must give us reason, not merely melody. Not that *we* seek reason in poetry as we seek it in a treatise on the differential calculus'.[33] The second 'we' here is of a different order than the first, seeming to represent not the factional collectivity of the Catholic *Rambler*, but the wider collectivity of the public generally, and this usage is very common in the 1850s:

> Our poets now speak in an unknown tongue . . . and the end too often is . . . to the vast world, whom they might assist, they bring only a mystery and recieve nothing but wonder and scorn.[34]

> Our poets would seem this year to have entered into a compact . . . to surprise the world with something new and unexpected.[35]

In both these cases the critic's 'our' becomes identified with 'the world', that is, the public as an entity.

In a period when public opinion was acquiring an unprecedented power over politics and public life, and when newspapers were beginning to see themselves as its legitimate mouthpiece, we should not be surprised to find critics enrolling themselves as the spokesmen of its aesthetic tastes. This move on their part received ratification, however, from a rather unexpected quarter. Victorian aesthetic theorists had, by the 1850s, arrived at the firm belief that popular acceptability formed a test not only of success but even of artistic *merit*: Simpson, for instance remarks that 'the seal of the poet is popular acceptation',[36] G. H. Lewes that 'the prosperity of a book lies in the minds of its readers',[37] E. S. Dallas that 'the true judges of art are the despised many – the crowd',[38] and Ruskin that 'A great painter's business is to do what the public ask of him, in a way that shall be helpful and instructive to them . . . not to consult their pleasure for his own sake, but to consult it much for theirs'.[39] The obvious question as to how such consultation is to be carried out is promptly answered by Dallas's confident assertion that 'no critic worth his salt . . . does not feel with the many';[40] reviews, in that case, will naturally act as the organs of public reaction to a new book. It is interesting to see how readily most Victorian writers assented to this proposition, and were prepared to accept that the critical tribunal really had this authority. Tennyson's acquiescence was notorious; so was Dickens's; so was Trollope's; even Browning, whose relations with his critics became barbed, to put it mildly, regarded them as 'a very few, who act upon the rest', and, as we shall see, paid obsessive attention to their verdicts.[41] It was probably Matthew Arnold who first decisively questioned the entire doctrine, notably by his attack upon the very notion that the public, and through the public the newspapers, constituted the legitimate arbiters of aesthetic practice:

> The *Times* tells us day after day how the general public is the organ of all truth, and individual genius the organ of all error; nay, we have got so far, it says, that the superior men of former days, if they could live again now, would abandon the futile business of running counter to the opinions of the many, of persisting in opinions of their own: they would sit at the feet of the general public and learn from its lips what they ought to say.[42]

In this atmosphere, it can hardly be surprising that the editorial 'we' expanded to allow the critic to assume his role as delegate of the public and custodian of the criteria of artistic judgment. And hence, I suggest, that odd combination of assertive language with anonymous format in Victorian reviews. The anonymity, with its overweening 'we', represents the extent to which the critic has dissolved his individual identity into the collectivity of a wider consensus; his virulence of language stems from the enormous and overbearing authority he derives from this centrality. The paradox was beautifully captured in Bagehot's account of the cultural position of Jeffrey himself:

> Lord Jeffrey, a shrewd judge of the world, employed himself in telling it what to think; not so much what it ought to think, as what at bottom it did think, and so by a dexterous sympathy with current society he gained contemporary fame and power.[43]

Here is a passage that summarizes what we have found so far:

> A new poetical school is springing up, which ought to be brought under the Nuisances Removal Act . . . here is a writer who has got

hold of the very worst mannerism of Keats and the impudence of
Leigh Hunt – who combines the uglier metrical peculiarities of
Tennyson with the inverted gibberish of Browning – who is as dull as
Bailey and as sensual as Alexander Smith – who at once contrives to
be as silly as Greathead and as pert as Tupper. We have had more
than enough of mystics and spasmodics, but this writer, in his
spasmodics, only rises into a gibber, and his mysticism is but
unmitigated nonsense. He simply insults the reader with a cloud of
words, and not an attempt at sense.[44]

This passage from an 1856 review of the *Pinochi* of one Percy Jones seems to
me to typify the kind of criticism I have been examining. It sounds the
authentic 'note of provinciality' by foaming and gesticulating and grimacing
and straining after hyperbolic extravagance; demonstrably, it 'desires to
triumph'; it takes to an extreme the Carlyle-Macaulay privilege of sweeping
together a whole array of different books – or in this case, authors – and
depositing them in a common dustbin. Yet simultaneously it claims to speak
for the public. The reviewer's 'we', together with his venomous language
and inferred critical approach, is transformed, in the course of this blistering
paragraph, into 'the reader': we, it seems, speak these words. It is no wonder
that Arnold saw this kind of thing as essentially pernicious: 'the provincial
spirit', he noted, 'likes in the newspaper just what makes the newspaper such
bad food for it.'[45] It is bad food because it confirms spleen and ill temper, and
frequently foments them when they would not naturally arise, while
consistently claiming merely to articulate and amplify the ubiquitious and
omnipotent 'public opinion'.

Having considered what mid-Victorian critics thought their own role was, I
want now to ask what they thought the poet's role was; what, in other words,
their critical criteria actually were. I have already noted that the adjectival
nature of their style makes it difficult to find out what 'leading principles' are
operative; one is obliged to try to tease out of the adjectives themselves the
criteria which they suggest, and then to triangulate towards some underlying theoretical position – if one exists.

   The first point, which must qualify any conclusions obtained from actual
analysis of the reviews, is that the reviewers are virtually united in their
profound ideological conservatism. The notion of a '*new* poetical school'
seems in itself to shock the reviewer of *Pinochi*, and he thereby audibly
echoes Jeffrey's famous pronouncement, in the first number of the *Edinburgh Review*, that 'Poetry has this much, at least, in common with religion,
that its standards were fixed long ago, by certain inspired writers, whose
authority it is no longer lawful to call in question.'[46] Here is one of the more

intelligent 1855 reviewers: 'we are so dependent on those who have preceded us and who surround us, that originality in any other sense than that of thorough assimilation and reproduction in fresh forms is somewhat absurd.'[47] As usual, Stigand in 1864 supplies an echo: 'Tried by the standards which have hitherto been supposed to uphold the force and beauty of the English tongue and of English literature, his works are deficient'.[48] In Bagehot's view, Jeffrey's conservatism could be attributed to his political Whiggism, which forbade any 'excessive partiality for new, arduous, overwhelming, original excellence';[49] James Mill, more irritable and perhaps more profound, offered an explanation which could be applied more generally: 'Periodical literature depends on *immediate* success. It must therefore patronise the opinions which are now in vogue, the opinions of those who are now in power.'[50]

Mill is speaking of politics, but his argument holds good generally: periodicals are inherently conservative because they dare not risk offending existing opinion by patronizing innovation. 'A new poetical school' is therefore an inherently offensive concept; safety lies in the application of the 'standards which have hitherto been supposed to uphold the force and beauty of . . . English literature', and the likelihood that in private Jeffrey was far more liberal than he ever allowed himself to seem in his public criticism illustrates that safety, the critic's safety and that of his journal, is given precedence over what Arnold was to call 'disinterestedness' and 'curiosity'[51] in the evaluation of novelty, even at the expense of the critic's own personal tastes and preferences.

What then are the standards which mid-Victorian critics struggle to conserve? My examination of the reviews of 1855 has led me to select four which seem both recurrent and to have the potential to contribute towards a poetic theory. Poetry should be

(a) euphonious
(b) lucid
(c) moral
(d) ambitious

These criteria are generally applied *in absentia*. *Pinochi's* exhibition of 'the uglier metrical peculiarities of Tennyson' make it *un*euphonious; and complaints like 'roughness in rhythm',[52] 'harshness',[53] and 'crabbedness'[54] against Browning, or the accusation that Whitman is 'rude and rough, and heedless in [his] forms'[55] generalize the complaint. Similarly, poets are attacked for the *failure* to be lucid: Percy Jones and Browning write 'inverted gibberish' and 'unmitigated nonsense', Browning's 'train of ideas' is 'difficult to follow',[56] he is 'deliberately unintelligible',[57] 'obscure',[58] and 'random';[59] *Maud* is 'incoherent',[60] *Leaves of Grass* is 'disjointed babbling':[61] 'our poets', thundered the *Athenaeum*, 'now speak in an unknown tongue'.[62] Morality, likewise, is found reversed into immorality: Percy Jones is 'as sensual as Alexander Smith', the 'Spasmodics' as a group are 'exceedingly profane', 'very prurient',[63] Browning 'like "Fra Lippo Lippi" cannot get "the value and significance of flesh" out of his mind',[64] while Whitman ought to be 'kicked from all decent society as below the level of a brute'.[65] The category of immorality also includes another kind, definable as the immorality of refusing to gratify the reader, by being either uneuphonious or obscure – Percy Jones is held to 'simply insult the reader', Browning to exhibit 'vanity', laziness', and 'carelessness',[66] to be 'perverse' and 'personal',[67] and to hold an 'Epicurean' philosophy of 'vanity and self-seeking',[68] simply on these grounds. Finally, by the standard of ambition, all the poems of 1855 are found wanting: *Maud* is 'no equivalent for that great master-work . . . which the world expects',[69] *Men and Women* 'does not, indeed, exhibit Mr Browning's powers at . . . continuous stretch and exercise';[70] 'poetic genius' generally seemed to the *Guardian* 'to consist in the power of throwing off at random the phantoms which rise up uncalled in the imagination, without regard to their connection or congruity.'[71] One could give many pages of quotations like these, and yet come no nearer to understanding their theoretical core: to do so, it is helpful to move back briefly to the aesthetic theories – mainly of the early Victorian period – of which they are the garbled echo.

In his deeply influential essays on aesthetic theories, almost all produced in the 1830s,[72] John Stuart Mill defined poetry as taking its origin from *feeling*. *Thought* belongs to a quite separate faculty; it has no place in poetry, or at least, in good poetry; feeling, and feeling alone, must uninterruptedly govern any discourse claiming that title.[73] James Martineau, a sharp-eyed critic of many aspects of Mill's thought, notes, in an essay of 1859, some of the consequences of Mill's formulation:

> Mr Mill's poet must be all loneliness and intensity – a kind of spiritual firework going off by itself in infinite night. So isolating a definition would in no case apply to other than lyric poetry; and our author has the courageous consistency to adopt the limitation, and to consider the drama and epic redeemed from prose only by the intermixture of lyrical elements.[74]

Martineau here notes something which Mill does not admit,[75] that his definition of *poetry* coincides with the customary definition of *lyric* poetry and thereby raises one only of the poetic kinds to unprecedented predominance. Martineau's tone is hardly cordial, and he immediately launches into a vigorous protest:

> it is anything rather than the solitary, self-evolved feeling that constitutes the poet. He more than any goes forth out of himself, and mingles his very being with the nature and humanity around him, entering into their essence by humbling his own, and directing on them the idealising glance which looks in at their eyes and reads their hearts.[76]

The word 'humbling' suggests that his is a *moral* protest: Mill's 'spiritual firework' is *egotistic*; Martineau's model poet uses a Keatsian 'negative capability' to dissolve the poetic identity into the essence of its subject, thereby 'humbling' it.[77]

The two positions, Mill's and Martineau's, could hardly be more incompatible, yet 1855 critics are trying to have both at once, to derive poetry from feeling yet rid it of ego. Thus E. S. Dallas, in his *Poetics* of 1852, begins from the premise that 'by poetry is meant poetic feeling', yet concludes: 'the divine and all that is not Me triumph in the lyric'.[78] The path which connects these two statements is, perhaps not surprisingly, a tortuous one. Clearly, Dallas is anxious to clear poetry of charges like that brought by Mrs Oliphant a little later: 'It pleases the poet to sing of a distempered vanity brooding by itself over fictitious misfortunes . . . and . . . our minds stray away . . . to the labours of this fighting world of ours.'[79] Carlyle had said as much;[80] Dallas's response is to attempt the task of reconciling poetry with moral worth by determining it to be essentially impersonal and therefore unselfish. Unlike Martineau, however, he does not deny that poetry originates from 'poetic feeling'; rather, again unlike Martineau, he neglects to realize that such a definition inevitably confines poetry to the lyric and continues to regard the other two poetic kinds, epic and drama, as perfectly poetic and practicable. Lyric is the highest kind, not surprisingly; but it is lyric into which 'the divine' has been smuggled, and which has therefore, by some unexplained mechanism, become 'not Me'. By contrast, the drama, which would be the obvious exemplification of Martineau's aesthetic, represents the triumph of 'personality or self-hood'.[81]

This startling reversal penetrates nearly all the criticism of 1855, being most neatly encapsulated by the common accusation that Browning, the most 'dramatic' of the 1855 poets, is 'personal'.[82] The norm is lyric (though like Dallas the 1855 critics are generally unaware that what they call 'poetry' is actually 'lyric poetry'); in order to escape the obvious objection that lyric poetry *cannot*, in view of its origins, be called impersonal, critics offer a whole array of different ways of achieving the impossible by conjuring away those origins. It was a matter, to use the jargon of the time, of reconciling the 'subjective' with 'the ideal', of amputating the poet's self from the poem for which it had been responsible.

Thus, some assert or imply what appears in the poem will be, not the poet's own soul, but the face of God. In practical terms, this conception becomes what Ruskin called 'the false ideal', which he defined as 'a fear of disagreeable facts and conscious shrinking from clearness of light . . . terror of all truth, and love of glosses, veils, and decorative lies of every sort.'[83] That is, certain topics – any ugly or unpleasant ones – are declared 'unsuitable for poetry': 'the artist's business', asserted George Brimley in a review of *Men and Women*, 'is not to make people speak and look exactly as they would speak and look, with all the accidents of human weakness around them.'[84] Another way of depersonalizing the lyric is adumbrated by this writer. In addition to purging his poetry of all references to disagreeable subjects, the poet should make its language absolutely clear and euphonious. By this means, he will achieve a linguistic impersonality, an absence of idiosyncrasy, that does duty for self-effacement and is insecurely connected to the representation of the ideal. Thus Browning's 'Epicurean' philosophy, his 'vanity and self-seeking', 'gross self-satisfaction', and all the other moral evils which Brimley finds in his work, is represented not by pornography or sensationalism of content, not, indeed, by any features at the level of content, but by 'vices' (the word is well chosen) of *style*:

> Instead of making God's world more intelligible by unfolding the beauty of meaning of its objects and events with loving care and grateful painstaking, he scrawls down the first rough hints that suggest themselves, and will not even take the trouble to make them legible.[85]

Finally, there is the position outlined by Bagehot, who in 1864 argued that in the lyric 'the poet does not describe himself *as* himself . . . he takes himself as a specimen of human nature; he describes, not himself, but a distillation of himself: he takes such of his moods as are most characteristic, as most typify certain moods . . . of all men'.[86] The absence of any 'ideal', or transcendental element from this version brings it closer to Mill's than any of those of 1855, and Bagehot's use of the word 'moods' suggest that he may have digested Mill's essay on Vigny, which revises somewhat the model proposed by Mill's earlier essays. Mill had already chosen to restrict Wordsworth's desiderated 'powerful feelings' to 'some *one* state of feeling',[87] and when in the essay on Vigny he rephrased this formulation into 'a *mood* of passion',[88] he might seem merely to be refining his terminology. His innovation was to adduce a contrast between a mood and a '*fit* of passion' by proposing that the latter 'had no natural connection with verse or music' and was therefore unpoetic; his object in making this distinction, I believe, was to rid his definition of poetry of the danger of harbouring idiosyncrasy by tolerating *more than one* feeling at its basis, since plurality of feeling will presumably individualize the feeler, while the singularity of a 'mood' offers the poem to any reader whom this mood has engaged and thereby empties it of direct personal application to the poet himself. I fancy that it was this refinement that helped to make plausible the later modes of depersonalization I have adduced, though Mill himself, it is worth noting, makes no claim whatever that the poet should reveal the divine or be involved in any kind of moral system: rather the reverse.[89]

But why was such a combination of poetic mood and poetic impersonality so impossible? The ontological problems involved, and the actual strains of trying to resolve them, emerge in E. S. Dallas's attempt to reinstate the epic as a practicable poetic kind. His problem is that he is unable to abandon the epistemological subjectivity of the lyric even when it becomes, as here, highly embarrassing:

> We tell truth when we represent things as they appear to us; and we tell truth when we represent things as they really are. All art, dramatic, epic and lyrical, must tell truth in the former sense; it belongs to epic to tell truth not only in the former, but also in the latter sense.[90]

His 'not only . . . but also' slides over the real problem, which is that the view of 'things as they appear' and of 'things as they really are' must be, but cannot be, *simultaneous*. They cannot be simultaneous because, in Mill's philosophy as in any Idealist system, only the phenomena of perception can be known, and the noumena which form 'things are they really are' remain unknowable: Mill '[resolves] all our knowledge, "both materials and sources," into *Self*-knowledge; denying any cognitive access to either qualities or bodies external to us; and shutting us up with our own sensations, ideas, and emotions'.[91] Of course, one avoids this problem by repudiating Idealism, but we have seen that Dallas, and the 1855 critics after him, accept an Idealist conception *of poetry*; they cannot, next, add to this a notion of 'things as they really are': where would such a notion come from?[92] Where it appears, as it does in Dallas's definition of epic, it is a mere verbal phantom, incapable of existence, and not even able convincingly to merge itself with the dominant subjective epistemology to form a seeming unity. The pervasiveness and intractability of this difficulty is seen in Brimley's definition of poetry as 'concretions of diverse phenomena organised into phenomenal unity by the pervading vital influence of a subjective idea.'[93] Again, it is a purely verbal unity that is contrived: the phrase 'phenomenal unity' hovers distractedly between the 'diverse phenomena' of the objective world, and the 'subjective idea' which unifies them – is of such extreme ontological uncertainty as to require assigning alternatively to each domain in turn.

That it should prove to be the epic which most visibly exposes the problems of the lyric hegemony is both natural and rather unfortunate. Natural because epic naturally requires an extension beyond that provided by the lyric format; unfortunate because it was precisely such extension that lyric proved unable to accomplish, which converted the continuing and insistent demand for epics into a kind of intellectual suicide. Again, Mill showed 'courageous consistency' in admitting that his own mood-based poetic 'naturally demands *short* poems, it being impossible that a feeling so intense as to require a more rhythmical cadence than that of ordinary prose, should sustain itself at its highest elevation for long together'[94] – sentiment, and a consistency, clearly echoed in Bagehot's assumption that poetry should be 'memorable and emphatic, intense, and *soon over*' (Bagehot's italics).[95] But the generality of mid-Victorian critics felt no need for this consistency. Having demanded that the poet should efface himself in the act of recording his own 'mood of passion', they go on to require that he somehow protract or multiply mood up to long poem proportions, which was impossible because, as Mill noted, a long poem can only be organized by 'consecutiveness of thought',[96] and thought was the first thing to be jettisoned from his definition of poetry.

It is this series of philosophical problems that explains the collapse of mid-Victorian criticism onto the adjectival level; the nightmare of formulation is thereby avoided, and in its place appears, as Arnold notes, a defensive obsession with second-order priorities: 'We have critics who direct their attention merely to detached expressions about the action, not the action itself. I verily think that the majority of them do not in their hearts believe that there is such a thing as a total impression to be derived from a poem at all'.[97] If Arnold's first point (that critics direct their attention to style rather than content) is explicable in terms of the transfer of poetic morality to that level, the second (that this involves implicitly fragmenting the poetic discourse) offers an irresolvable contradiction that really does infest and vitiate the criticism of which he speaks: Stigand, for example, in one breath commends *Paracelsus* as 'the most ambitious in conception' and 'the most complete' of 'Mr Browning's production', and in the next begins 'quoting two or three of the most beautiful passages which it contains';[98] and this characteristic was the one picked out for special reprehension by Browning himself in a comment on Stigand's review: 'The clever creature rummages over the wardrobe of thirty years' accumulation, strips every coat of its queer button or odd tag and tassel, then holds them out, "So Mr Browning goes dressed now!" – of the cut of the coats, not a word.'[99] In another letter, Browning extended censure to his critics generally: 'But what poor work, even when doing its best! I mean poor in the failure to give a general notion of the whole works; not a particular one of such and such points therein'.[100] This inconsistency of critical theory and critical practice may stand for the entire spectrum of inconsistencies which beset mid-Victorian criticism.

2. THE POSITION IN 1864

Even in 1855, however, or at least in 1856, there are signs of a restiveness with the existing practice of criticism which, with hindsight, we can take to herald a coming change:

> It is a fiction, in fact, long religiously maintained in the forms of our reviews, that we write for the benefit of the reviewee. In most cases . . . this didactic figment would be as well put aside. A new work, a body of writings . . . constitutes a subject for investigation; we examine it as we do other matters of interest, we analyse, we dissect, we compare notes about it; we estimate its influences . . . and endeavour to penetrate through the work into some insight into the special genius of the writer.[101]

As my touchstone for the timing and quality of this change, I propose to use the reception of Browning's *Dramatis Personae* of 1864. Amongst the 1855 reviews I have cited have been many of Browning's *Men and Women* of that year, and their hostility typifies the general tone adopted by critics towards Browning's early work in general. The fact that *Dramatis Personae* was very differently received[102] – that something like adulation replaces the contempt to which the poet had by now resigned himself – becomes the more remarkable for the absence of any obvious explanation: no work had intervened to induce such a change by gradations, and *Dramatis Personae* was so little different from its immediate predecessor that Browning could call it 'men and women, but under some other name, to please the publisher'[103] and most critics accepted this: 'it is so much after the author's most peculiar manner . . . that there is little chance that Mr Browning's constituency of admirers will be increased by it, if even it does not provoke, within that constituency, a repetition of old criticisms',[104] thought one, for instance; yet in the event, Stigand was almost alone in reiterating the 'old criticisms'; other critics said things like: 'Mr Browning is one of our very few living poets, and this book is a richer gift than we shall often receive at the hands of poetry in our time'.[105] . . . 'A new volume of poems by Mr Browning is an event of no small importance'.[106] It is rather Browning's earlier critics who receive criticism for their obtuseness: 'the greatest hindrance to a popular appreciation of Mr Browning appears to us to lie in the critical treatment his poetry has hitherto received'.[107] Stigand's article, in which I have found a perfect echo of the style and criteria of earlier criticism, is actually singled out by several reviewers for direct attack; one reviewer describes it as 'the most complete literary fiasco which any of our quarterlies have perpetrated for very many years';[108] another frames his objection in this broader and more suggestive way:

> the position of Mr Browning in our literature and the worth of his poetry are not yet determined. But the subject is of sufficient importance that anyone who proclaims an opinion should at least prove his ability to form one, and his right to possess it . . . A critic of poetry should show some genuine insight.[109]

What we have is, it seems, not just a change in the reception of one particular poet, but a reorientation of the idea of criticism itself; I want now to explore what the change was, and what caused it.[110]

The tone changed. A reflective sobriety replaced the smart, stinging epigrams and epithets of 1855, even adverse judgments assuming a weighty rather than a showy air:

> The expression is universally ordinary and colloquial . . . of that kind which seems to show that the heat of the creative intellectual effort has subsided before the words are chosen at all.[111]

> The pervading idea of the 'Snob Papers' is too frequent, too recurring, too often insisted upon, even in his highest writings; . . . and though it was certainly unworthy of him, it was exceedingly natural that it should be so, with such a mind as his and in a society such as ours.[112]

Analysis replaced judgment. Even the objections I have quoted seem the result of penetrative reflection rather than prejudice, and some critics engage in something very like a modern 'practical criticism':

> The critic said to himself, 'if it is written by Mr Trollope, I shall soon meet with the phrase "made his way", as applied to walking when there is no physical difficulty or embarrassment, but only a certain moral hesitation as to the end and aim of the walking in question'.[113]

> With Mr Browning, it would seem that his sense of music served to put into his verse a greater sense of *accent* than flow of melody; conducing to a kind of *staccato* mental *notation* in words . . .

He is with her, and *they know* that *I know*
Where they *are*, what they *do; they* believe my tears flow
While they *laugh,* laugh at *me,* at *me* fled to the drear
Empty church to pray God in for *them! – I am here!*[114]

The explanation I suggest for this development is that critics now feel
themselves to be *on the poet's side.* That they are no longer on the side of the
public is made especially plain in reviews of *Dramatis Personae:*

It is probable that no man of our times has written so much and so
well without general acknowledgement as Robert Browning.[115]

we think that a writer of Mr Browning's power ought to be better
understood than he is, and the discrepancy lessened between what is
known of him by the few, and what is *thought* of him by the
many.[116]

Gerald Massey, in the second quotation, finds himself so far from representing the public's judgment – what Roscoe calls 'writ[ing] for the
benefit of the reviewee' – that he seems rather to plan to act as his author's
advocate and interpreter. A common illustration of the prevalence of this
new role is critics' new preference for using the author's own words to shape
their definition of his aesthetic: 'he answers to the description he has
incidentally given of a dramatist – "analyst who turns in due course synthet-
ist"'; 'he still "blows through bronze", to use his own description of his own
style'.[117] Gerald Massey cross-breeds Browning's words with his wife's: '[Mr
Browning] "blows through bronze" oftener than through silver . . . a
"medicated music", as it was rightly called by Elizabeth Barrett,'[118] and then
takes the further step of literally speaking for Browning: 'Mr Browning
would say, "Let us have things first, their associations afterwards. Let us
reach the ideal through the real"'[119] – and goes on to show how this
repositioning of the critic might naturally promote the shift towards an
analytical criticism. Speaking of Browning's reputed lapses of verbal
euphony, he remarks: 'The music may not be our music, or Mr Tennyson's
music, or like anything else we ever heard in verse: that is not the point. The
point is whether the music and movement of the verse receive their impetus
and government in any sensible way from the character'.[120] That is, the poet
is entitled to fashion his work just as he sees fit, and the critic accordingly
must seek a justification of the poet's procedure in the inner configuration of
the work, rather than submitting it summarily to some outside criterion. He
will 'endeavour to penetrate through the work into some insight into the
special genius of the writer' on the supposition that genius is allowed to be

special, i.e. individually idiosyncratic, rather than an umpteenth application of the existing standards of art.

Another necessary result of this tolerance of poetic idiosyncrasy is the eclipse of the concept of a poetic norm. It is not just that the lyric, which constituted the norm for 1855 criticism, proves to be less in evidence in 1864; some critics, such as the American Moncure Conway, actually turn lyric into analytic subject-matter, implicitly dismissing its claim to omnipotence:

> A lyric involves two ideas: one of a brief poem complete in itself, and not depending upon external details for the expression of the totality of its beauty . . . It requires not only that a conception shall be beautiful in itself, but that it shall, so to speak, chant itself . . . The mind with which language is 'pure work of thought' as [Browning] confesses it to be in his own case, can scarcely find its full play in the lyric form.[121]

In some critics, this relativized view of lyric has the effect of subverting lyric's associates, the 'ideal' and the 'subjective':

> Mr Browning is not one of those who can look on men as trees walking, and can see all things through a misty glamour or 'a kind of glory' which is really a suffusion of self . . .[122]

> the egotism who would make me see in a tree the double of myself is but the inability to imagine an existence other than my own.[123]

Hence, for E. S. Dallas, from whose 1865 study of criticism, *The Gay Science*, the second of the two above quotations is taken, the lyric forms the haunt of 'second-rate poets' – a far cry from his earlier faith that it harboured 'the divine'. The change we must postulate in order to explain such a reversal was summed up, in the same year, by G. H. Lewes: 'of late years has been a reaction against conventionalism which calls itself Idealism, in favour of *detailism* which calls itself Realism.'[124] And it is in precisely these terms that Gerald Massey had commended Browning's methods: 'Of course, a subjective poet might not have painted in this piercing, keen-sighted way. He might have brooded over the sight until it passed into memory with a sense of rest. [Mr Browing] is describing of the instant – the object itself, and not a dream of it'.[125] Even a critic like Bagehot, who wishes to reserve some position for the lyric, feels obliged to re-christen it the 'type'[126] and to define it in aesthetic rather than spiritual, moral or religious terms: 'There should be a word in the language of literary art to express what the word "picturesque" expresses for the fine arts. *Picturesque* means fit to be put into a picture; we want a word *literatesque*, "fit to be put into a book."'[127] The 'type', that is, forms 'that perfect combination of the *subject-matter* of literature, which suits the *art* of literature.'[128] Bagehot admits that such a formulation reverses the traditional relation between literature and its subject-matter: the 'type of the genus' is nowhere present in reality but rather imperfectly 'mirrored' in it, its true home being the work of art. Bagehot goes on to classify modern literature in terms of its approximation to the 'type': 'pure art', as practised by Wordsworth, approaches 'the type' most closely by describing it 'in its simplicity'; Tennysonian 'ornate' art 'surround[s] the type with the greatest number of circumstances which it will *bear*'; 'grotesque art', whose chosen representative is Browning, 'takes the type *in difficulties*', and 'reminds you of the perfect image by showing you the distorted and imperfect image'.[129] It is a resourceful refinement of the mid-Victorian 'ideal', made the more impressive by Bagehot's refusal to countenance the conception that the 'pure' might be considered the only valid form:

> it does not follow that only the best subjects are to be treated by art, and then only in the very best way. Human nature could not bear such a critical commandment as that, and it would be an erroneous criticism which gave it. *Any* literatesque character may be described in literature in *any* circumstances which exhibit its literatesqueness.[130]

Bagehot was also conscious of the larger change in the conduct of criticism:

> Years ago, when criticism only tried to show how poetry could be made a *good* amusement, it was not impossible that criticism itself should be amusing. But now it must at least be serious, for we believe that poetry is a serious and a deep thing.[131]

Here Bagehot pauses to measure the distance between 1855 and 1864 criticism, and in the process to supply a suggestive explanation for its extent: 'All about and around us a *faith* in poetry struggles to be extricated, but it is not extricated'.[132] Arnold's substitution of poetry for religion, if not Aestheticism itself, is latent in Bagehot's formulation; so too is that veneration of the poet as sage or seer which gave Browning for one such acute embarrassment in later years.[133] The two elements are distinguishable: aestheticism raises the *artefact*, considered as a semi-abstract pattern, to a primacy which sage-worship reserves for the *artificer*; the two co-operate, however, in promoting a solemnized critical tone and an emphasis on analysis rather than judgment which I have just shown to be typical of 1864, and whose prevalence in 1864 they therefore help to explain.

Bagehot notes a further, perhaps even more important effect of this change. Having described the enormous prestige and influence of an old-style critic such as Jeffrey, he concludes: 'Such fame no critic can hope for now. His articles will not penetrate where the poems themselves do not penetrate. When poetry was noisy, criticism was loud; now poetry is a still, small voice, and criticism must be smaller and stiller.'[134] *The Saturday Review* makes the same point: 'No Review, it must be owned, can now hope to make or mar a poet's fortunes after the fashion of the *Edinburgh* and the *Quarterly* in the days of Jeffrey and Gifford.'[135] Necessarily so, since if the critic now speaks for the poet, he will inevitably appeal less to a public whose prejudices he no longer flatters, and whose palate he no longer tickles with profligate witticisms.

Thus the critic joins the poet in isolation from 'this fighting world of ours', and it is perhaps this phenomenon which explains the development, becoming visible by 1864, of what must be called 'creative' criticism; not popular polemics, but principles analogous to those which govern the creative works to which he feels himself to be philosophically committed, furnish the critic with the model for his own procedures. This produces a double movement on one side of which the critic starts to find behind the work he criticizes principles analogous to his own as critic, while his criticism, on the other side, grows a corresponding set of creative features, until work and criticism merge into unity.

At the simplest level, there is a tendency in 1864 for works to attract admiration if and when they *require* the critic to complete or appreciate them: critic after critic observes that

> the reader of Mr Browning must learn first of all that he is one of that class of writers whose finest thoughts must often be read 'between the lines'.[136]

> To follow him in all his ramifications of remote character the reader should be able to meet him halfway at the start.[137]

This perception, so nearly unobtainable in 1855, immediately secures the critic a position in the poet's art by constituting him its mediatory expositor, without whose aid it runs the risk of collapsing into the 'obscurity' of which earlier critics would automatically have accused it. On a slightly higher level, Gerald Massey finds in Browning's work qualities which match those governing his own criticism. Massey's analytic approach has been outlined; his commendation of Browning's 'piercing, keen-sighted way' of describing 'the object itself' effects a transfer of analytic technique to the poet.[138] On another level again, Bagehot's essay as a work of criticism mirrors his conception of the work of art: choosing to treat Tennyson and Browning simultaneously in one essay because 'they are the best possible illustration of something we have to, say on poetical art – because they may give it life and freshness',[139] he models his own theory into a 'type' which the actual works of these artists then imperfectly 'mirror in reality'. A similar drift occurs in Richard Simpson's admirable essay on Thackeray of the same year. Simpson begins from the apparently straightforward determination by analysis to obtain 'some insight into the special genius of the writer' and therefore isolates what he regards as Thackeray's 'greatest characteristic', his 'openness and transparency of soul'. Such a feature

> accounts for many of his peculiarities as critic, historian, artist and thinker. It explains the characters he creates and the circumstances in which he exhibits them. It throws light on his special humour, and on his judgments and theories . . . It is in fact the key-note both of the man and of his works.[140]

The analytic basis is plain enough, being that which affords Simpson an insight of this kind; the insight itself contains the germ of further growth, for it enables Simpson to discover a *critical spirit* in Thackeray's creative work:'There is a point at which Thackeray's ideas of criticism, history, art and philosophy unite and become identical. For their ultimate aim is but one – to discover and display the soul.'[141] His 'critical essays', consequently, form 'historical sketches of authors', his 'novels are fictitious memoirs'; as the critical spirit native to his criticism extends itself through Thackeray's creative work and animates and suffuses it, we have arrived where the two functions abandon their distinctness, and begin to interpenetrate and complete each other. And Simpson's criticism in turn, by deliberately echoing Thackeray's own, is privileged to become a constitutive feature of Thackeray's creative art. As Thackeray's criticism has striven 'to find the man in his works', so by isolating Thackeray's own 'leading characteristic' Simpson has located the man in Thackeray's novels and thus 'completed' them on Thackeray's own principle. There was, Simpson suggests, even perhaps a sense in which, because Thackeray himself proved unable to carry out his own programme, Simpson becomes empowered to do this for him and simultaneously double the idea of criticism into creative art: 'He proves that he has seized the literary soul, by exhibiting his capacity to re-embody it, though perhaps his analytical powers were not active enough to enable him to explain to others wherein that literary individuality consisted'.[142]

I want now to ask how this change in the idea of criticism happened. A useful starting-point is provided by Browning, who attributed his new-found popularity of 1864 to 'young men from Oxford and Cambridge',[143] and thereby directs us back to 1856 and the brief life of the *Oxford and Cambridge Magazine*. The importance of that magazine and of its contributors is that they started a single-minded campaign against the tone and standards of

1855 criticism and supplied a manifesto for the position which by 1864 was generally current:

> Altogether disbelieving, and reprehending with the strongest indignation, the doctrine upon which so many of the critics of the present day seem to act, however they might shrink from maintaining it in so many words, that the reviewer, by virtue of his office, is superior to the writer reviewed, and knowing full well not only at what an infinite height above me is the poet upon whom I have taken it upon myself to pass judgment, but also that a critique on him, which by any partiality might be called adequate, is utterly beyond my powers, it is with the greatest diffidence that I approach my subject. But whatever I advance will have been carefully weighed, and will be the result of several years' almost uninterrupted reading of the Author. Would that every reviewer of a great writer could say as much.[144]

William Fulford here repudiates the approach of the average mid-Victorian critic because it implicitly mounts the critic above the author; instead, he himself steps down into the role of Tennyson's advocate from that of his judge. In his review of *The Newcomes*, Burne-Jones makes the same point in terser language: 'it is time . . . for the critic altogether to take up a new position, descend from his seat of judgment to one of testimony'.[145] That this 'new position' is substituted for the critic's reputed place as public spokesman is implicit in the abandonment, general in this periodical, of the editorial 'we'. A brief existence and a narrow public, however, prevent the *Oxford and Cambridge Magazine* from being seen as a cause of the changes it urged; because *The Saturday Review*, whose longer life had begun the previous year, laid these same changes before a far wider public and proved to be, in addition, both an acknowledged influence on and a uniquely central symptom of the concurrent set of changes overtaking journalism in this period, it is worth describing in more detail.[146]

In its first issue in 1856, the *Saturday Review* claimed for its 'motive in coming before the public', the 'impetus given to periodical literature by the repeal of the Newspaper Stamp Duty'.[147] The duty, chiefly notorious for its function as an instrument of clandestine political censorship, had had the side effect of making it difficult to combine in any one periodical the discussion of news with the criticism of literature and the arts, and it was this deficiency which the *Saturday* was created to remedy. Giving 'no news whatsoever', it would 'consist entirely of leading articles, reviews, comments and criticisms of the various Parliamentary, Social and Literary events and topics of the day'.[148] 'No-one', comments M. M. Bevington in his book on the *Saturday*, 'had as yet attempted the experiment of a journal that would confine itself to criticism and at the same time enlarge the scope of criticism to take in all the political, social and cultural activities of the English nation.'[149] The high-calibre staff for which such an experiment cried out was drawn from the growing ranks of Oxbridge graduates unable or reluctant to find employment at the Bar or in the Church – a class whose later decline is traced in Gissing's *New Grub Street*.[150] In the 1850s, however, these young intellectuals helped the *Saturday* to become 'a significant mile-stone in the social progress of journalism',[151] while simultaneously hav-ing 'excellent effect in raising the standard of criticism':[152] the *Saturday* rapidly became a model for the reform of such established journals as the *Spectator*, the *Athenaeum* and the *Guardian* in the later 1850s, and for such new journals as the *Pall Mall Gazette*, the *Fortnightly Review* and most of all the short-lived but remarkable *Reader* in the early 1860s.[153]

The first campaign into which the *Saturday* allowed its critical spirit to conduct it proved to be a reforming investigation into journalism itself. An early issue commented, perhaps rather defiantly, 'we make no apology for devoting so large a space in our columns to the theory and practice of journalism',[154] and the existence of one issue which contains no less than three articles on the subject seems to warrant the comment. In effect, the campaign crystallized round the *Saturday*'s determination – expressed both in a series of full-length articles and in incidental comments elsewhere – to 'fasten an effectual responsibility on *The Times*'.[155] 'No apology', snapped the leader-writer in the first issue, 'is necessary for assuming that this country is run by *The Times*',[156] and he went on to a suggestive analysis of the causes, or at any rate the typical rhetoric of this injurious hegemony:

> The recent manifesto [in *The Times*] will have it that a daily journal, if not the labour of a single pen, is an emanation from a body of men, fused into the nearest possible approximation to unity . . . Now . . . a theory of this sort . . . is ridiculously false to fact . . . The leading articles of a great newspaper cannot be written by less than six to eight gentlemen.[157]

This passage suggests that the real basis of the assault on *The Times* was the latter's coercive exploitation of its anonymous format as a source of author-ity, and in fact the article directly engages this point: 'We are not for a *loi de signature*, which, for the excessive protection afforded by the present system would substitute an excessive proscription . . . We say to a confiding public – do your best to resolve the "we" into an "I"'.[158] In an article attacking a

Quarterly review of Montalembert, the *Saturday* likewise dismissed the adjectival style of book reviewing:

> Instead of being encountered in that free and liberal spirit of criticism of which his own work furnishes so admirable an example, he has been subjected to that carping style of word-catching cavil with which those who can remember the stupid and ignorant malignity of Quarterly Reviewing twenty years ago must be painfully familiar.[159]

Another article on the same subject puts it that 'to modern readers' the *Quarterly's* tactics 'seemed equally foolish and out of date':

> In the days of Jeffrey and Gifford, it was a regular rule to devil and grill about every alternate author – to eat him bones and all – and ask an applauding public to assist at the spectacle of cannibalism. But as the circle of literature grew wider, public taste softened the manners of reviewers and did not permit them to be fierce.[160]

In view of the general tone of 1855 criticism, and of the fact that the *Saturday* itself had not been always above adopting it,[161] there is something just a little disingenuous about this formulation: its author wants to *bring about* a change which he represents as already accomplished in order to ridicule his adversary the more thoroughly and at the same time to remove the stigma of innovation, perhaps, from his own position. The same formula is adopted with similar effect for Stigand in 1864: 'A critic must assuredly be greatly before or greatly behind his age who now-a-days can venture to assume this style. We doubt whether even in Jeffrey's time, it would have been quite admissable.'[162] Such confident sarcasm would suggest that the *Saturday's* campaign had worked; the examination of Stigand's critical methods which follows illustrates the relentlessly analytical methods of the campaigners: Stigand's 'oracular decision[s]', 'bit-by-bit process [of analysis]', use of the coercive 'we' and lack of any 'poetical discrimination' or 'attempt to judge the author's work as a whole' are berated in a systematic anthology of the faults of mid-Victorian criticism assembled by a journal which had determinedly set itself to reform that criticism, and whose success is attested by the large number of periodicals, notably the *Saturday's* satellite, the *Reader*, now prepared to defend a writer – Browning – against a hostile reviewer – Stigand. It was its role in reforming criticism, presumably, which caused Arnold to describe the *Saturday* as 'an organ of reason'.[163]

It will not do, however, to ascribe the change in critical style which took place in the late 1850s and early 1860s altogether to the arrival of a younger generation of journals and reviewers. For if we take two of the best of the 1864 critics, Bagehot and Simpson, we find not only that both were well established in 1855 but they they wrote then very much in the idiom of that period: 'if, in the following pages', wrote Bagehot near the beginning of his 1856 essay on Macaulay, 'we seem to cavil and find fault, let it be remembered that the business of a critic is criticism; that it is *not* his business to be thankful'.[164] 'True', runs a typical paragraph from Simpson's essay on *Men and Women*,

> a great many sawneys ramble out into the fields, and pluck you a toadstool or a mangle-wurzel, and straightway set it up as a fetish . . . many more, too, will assure you that they read in the gills of mushrooms, or the flakes of the onions 'thoughts that do lie too deep for tears' much more for words,[165]

And Simpson had been capable, in his previous essay, of enumerating amongst 'the characteristics by which we test the poet', 'the felicity of occasional expressions, the melody of individual lines, or the grandeur of detached thoughts'.[166] Again, he affirms in 1857 that 'the seal of the poet is popular acceptation',[167] a position which by 1869 had been reversed into the contention that 'originality accounts not only for obscurity, but unpopularity'.[168] I mention these changes both to illustrate the rapidity with which the transformation of critical methods took place and to raise a further question: what influence brought about this transformation in the case of two able and established critics? The changes in the structure of journalism which I have outlined might help to account for a *general* change of atmosphere, but some more specific and localized influence would seem necessary if we are to account for such a sharp ideological reversal in individual cases, and it is with this in mind that I raise the position of Arnold.

Arnold's attack on his contemporaries' 'note of provinciality', which I have already cited, was only one aspect of his far broader attempt to redefine the activity of criticism in 1864. In the essays which were later grouped into the first series of *Essays in Criticism*, Arnold enriched the phrase 'literary criticism' into unrecognizable splendour: defined as 'the endeavour . . . to see the object in itself as it really is',[169] criticism takes on 'the power to improve the atmosphere of ideas . . . it tends, at last, to make an intellectual situation of which the creative power can profitably avail itself.'[170] Arnold therefore rejects the exercise of old-fashioned 'judgment' – not 'the most satisfactory work to the critic' – in favour of 'a disinterested endeavour to learn and propagate the best that is known and thought in the world, and thus to establish a current of fresh and true ideas'.[171] '[T]he great art of criticism', consequently, is not to obtrude a preemptive judgment but to 'get oneself out of the way and let humanity decide'.[172] Morality is replaced by 'edification'[173] as the appropriate criterion of literary merit and the critic's business is now 'to deal with every independent work as with an independent whole';[174] when we find Arnold publishing his essays in *Fraser's Magazine* because *Fraser's* is 'almost the only literary journal in England where the writer could sign his article',[175] we seem to complete his crystallization into a perfect epitome of the spirit of 1864.

But Arnold was evidently as much an influence as a mere epitome.[176] The definition of criticism first appears in 1860 in *On Translating Homer*; Bagehot's essay on Sterne and Thackeray of 1864 registers its author's assimilation both of this idea and of Arnold's censure of the 'note of provinciality': 'On the whole, therefore, the judgment of criticism on *Tristram Shandy* is [that] it is *provincial*.'[177] Bagehot's very technique, in this essay and the one on 'Pure, ornate and grotesque art', of comparing two writers in order to bring out their contrasting literary characters, is at once an innovation in his own criticism and absolutely typical of Arnold's ('There is no profit for the spirit in such contrasts as this; criticism serves the cause of perfection by establishing them').[178] Simpson takes the further step of assimilating Arnold's even more celebrated claim that art is 'a criticism of life';[179] this provides, I think, the ideological ground for the ventures of the essay on Thackeray, and later supplies Simpson with a consciousness of Jane Austen's 'critical spirit'[180] and Browning's status as 'a critical poet'.[181] Wilde's more radical interpretation of this idea in *The Critic as Artist*, and Eliot's remark that 'probably . . . the larger part of the labour of an author is composing his work is critical labour'[182] both illustrate the power and persistence of Arnold's idea and compel us to see it as the stem of which modern criticism is the flower; yet I want nonetheless to suggest that in some senses Arnold betrayed the revolution of 1864, or rather fitted it to the mould of his own thought, which was at least in part reactionary.

E. S. Dallas noted as early as 1865 that: 'he who in our day is the most hearty in denouncing the weakness of our criticism, Mr Matthew Arnold, is also the most imperious in vaunting the office of the critic',[183] and in the contrast between 'hearty . . . denouncing' and 'imperious . . . vaunting' betrayed his preference for the first rather than the second aspect of Arnold's polemic. And indeed, vaunting the critic's office was very much the inclination of the earlier criticism whose 'weakness' is being denounced. Arnold's critical practice is equally worrying:

> Critics give themselves great labour to draw out what in the abstract constitutes the characters of a high quality of poetry. It is much better simply to have recourse to concrete examples, to take specimens of poetry of the high, the very highest qualities, and to say: The characters of a very high quality of poetry is expressed *there*.[184]

Though a late statement, this adequately describes Arnold's critical practice in the 1860s. Literature is not analysed, nor leading principles established. Instead, the critic points to the texts which constitute, for him at least, classics, and then to the newer work which is to be compared with it, and to which the classic constitutes a 'touchstone', or standard of aesthetic merit. The comparison is carried on by reference to individual passages – 'short passages, even single lines will serve our turn quite sufficiently'[185] – in order to determine how far the junior work shares the senior's 'high stamp of diction and movement': if – as usually happens – it does not, then 'we shall find, also, that high poetic truth and seriousness are absent from [its] substance and matter'.[186] As a critical *method*, I find this indistinguishable from the practice of mid-Victorian critics. Criticism is again stylistic; works are chopped into bits by the critic; close analysis, *any* analysis, is proscribed; and – inevitably – the critic usurps the artist's central position.

Arnold's influence was momentarily a good one in the 1860s. He proclaimed the importance of poetry, of criticism, of the critical element in poetry; his voice strengthened the wider clamour for change, his theories pushed Simpson and Bagehot perhaps into a higher awareness of their own practice then they would otherwise have gained. Simultaneously, the capacity and willingness to engage in detailed analysis which critics like Simpson, Bagehot and Massey, encouraged by journals like the *Oxford and Cambridge Magazine* and the *Saturday Review*, began to develop and exercise, helped lay the foundations of a modern professional criticism. In resisting analysis, Arnold perhaps did not really frustrate this process, but I think he did bequeath to modern criticism a dangerously inflated notion of the importance of the critic which has made the striking of attitudes and proclamation of dogma usurp the place of detailed textual study in the work of Eliot, Leavis and many others. One benefit of the *Wellesley Index to Victorian Periodicals* will be its power to correct this misdirection by removing the spotlight from Arnold and playing it instead over many other fine and serious critics of the 1860s. Their work is the last remaining major anonymous literature; as articles get assigned, certain names start to stand out, and the minds behind the names to grow into three-dimensional individuality and strength. At this point, some will cease to exhibit merely 'period' interest, and take on the character of contributors to the permanently valuable criticism of literature. Richard Simpson has already, since the publication of most of his literary essays in book form, begun to assume this importance; a similar service to Gerald Massey, David Masson, W. C. Roscoe would reveal three more significant critics; while even established names such as Hutton and Bagehot would gain enormously in importance and distinctness from the gathering of their uncollected periodical criticism.

NOTES

1. 'The higher journalism and the mid-Victorian clerisy', *VS*, XIII (1969), 181–98.
2. *Ibid.*, 181.
3. In *Church and State*, ed. J. Barrell (1972), 34.
4. *The Rise and Fall of the Man of Letters* (1969), 131.
5. Isobel Armstrong, *Victorian Scrutinies* (1972). The bulk of this volume is occupied by an excellent selection of Victorian reviews, but there is a long, extremely detailed, and highly suggestive introduction.
6. *Ibid.*, 14.
7. 'There is such a wide spread of critical position in this decade that it would be misleading to say that any one was typical.' (*ibid.*, 50). I think this is over-cautious, and Armstrong adds: 'At the same time, it is indubitable that things were changing'. Unlike her, I believe that there was a 'central core of opinion' in the 1860s 'as in earlier decades', though I agree that this is 'more difficult to define' (*ibid.*, 50–1).
8. See Mark A. Weinstein, *William Edmonston Aytoun and the Spasmodic Controversy* (Yale, 1968). The free use of the word 'spasmodic' in reviews of all the poetry of 1854–6 suggests that a widespread poetic school was believed to exist. This 'school' had totally dissolved by 1864, and no equivalent unification of the poetry of that year was postulated by reviewers. It is likely that the intemperateness of the reviews of 1855 included an element of regression to the tactics of the reviewers of the poets of the 'Cockney' school in the earlier period; the greater peaceableness in 1864 probably reflected in part the absence of anything analogous.
9. 'The literary influence of academies', *Cornhill Mag.*, x (1864), 154–72; Matthew Arnold, *The Complete Prose Works of Matthew Arnold*, ed. R. H. Super (11 vols., Ann Arbor, 1960–77) (hereafter cited as Arnold *PW*), III, 245.
10. 'The literary influence of academies', 169–70; Arnold *PW*, III, 254–5.
11. 'The literary influence of academies', 165, 170; Arnold *PW*, III, 249, 255.
12. 'The literary influence of academies', 169; Arnold *PW*, III, 254.
13. William Stigand, review of *Poems* (1863) and *Dramatis Personae*, *Edinburgh Rev.*, CXX (1864) (hereafter cited as Stigand), 538–9.
14. *Press*, 11 Aug. 1855, 764–5.
15. *Critic*, I (1856); *Whitman: the Critical Heritage*, ed. M. Hindus (1969) (hereafter cited as Whitman *CH*), 56.
16. Review of *Men and Women*, *Guardian*, 9 Jan. 1856, 34–5.
17. Stigand, 537.
18. Review of *Men and Women*, *Saturday Rev.*, I, 24 Nov. 1855, 69.
19. *Blackwood's*, II (1817), 40; Theodore Redpath's *The Young Romantics and Critical Opinion 1807–1824* (1973) covers the ground very well.
20. *Blackwood's*, III (1818), 524.
21. William Maginn, *Fraser's Mag.*, VIII (1833), 670; *Browning: the Critical Heritage*, ed. Boyd Litzinger and Donald Smalley (1970) (hereafter cited as Browning *CH*), 38.
22. *Biographia Literaria*, ch. xxi, in *Complete Works of Samuel Taylor Coleridge*, ed. W. G. T. Shedd (New York, 1853), III, 452.
23. *Ibid.*, 455.
24. *Ibid.*, 458.
25. *Westminster Rev.*, I (1824), 206.
26. *Blackwood's*, LXXXIX (1856), 136.
27. Quoted by E. E. Kellett, 'The Press', in *Early Victorian England*, ed. G. M. Young (1934), II, 19.
28. *Essays on Various Subjects* (1853), preface to vol. I, v.
29. *Ibid.*
30. 'The function of criticism at the present time', *National Rev.*, n.s. I (1864), 240; Arnold *PW*, III, 270–1.
31. *Contributions to the Edinburgh Review* (1844), I, xix.
32. *Rambler*, n.s. v (1856), 71; *Richard Simpson as Critic*, ed. David Carroll (1977) (hereafter cited as *RSC*), 74, My italics.
33. *Rambler*, n.s. v (1856), 55; *RSC*, 59. My italics.
34. *Athenaeum*, no. 1464 (1855), 1327.

35. *Christian Remembrancer*, XXXI (1856), 267.

36. Review of *Aurora Leigh*, *Rambler*, n.s. V (1857), 152; *RSC*, 77.

37. 'The principles of success in literature', *Fortnightly Rev.*, I (1865), 90.

38. E. S. Dallas, *The Gay Science* (1865), I, 127.

39. *The Works of John Ruskin*, ed. E. T. Cook and A. D. O. Wedderburn (39 vols., 1903–12), XXII, 88.

40. Dallas, *op. cit.*, I, 127.

41. Browning himself commented on Tennyson's notorious sensitivity to criticism: 'Tennyson reads the "Quarterly" and does as they bid him, with the most solemn face in the world – out goes this, in goes that, all is changed and ranged . . . Oh me!–': Browning to Elizabeth Barrett Browning, 11 Feb. 1845, *The Letters of Robert Browning and Elizabeth Barrett*, ed. Elvan Kintner (Cambridge, Mass., 1969), 19. Browning's own very complex reactions to criticism will be explored in my forthcoming 'Browning's Development'; the comment quoted above comes from his letter to Ruskin of 10 Dec. 1855: *Life and Work of John Ruskin*, ed. W. Collingwood (1895), I, 199–202. Trollope commented in his *Autobiography* (World's Classics edn, 1961, 232): 'As an author, I have paid careful attention to the reviews which have been written on my own work . . . Among it all there is much chaff . . . but I have also found some corn, on which I have fed and nourished myself, and for which I have been thankful.' In *Dickens and his Readers* (1955), 54, G. H. Ford questions the belief, fostered by Dickens himself, that Dickens was impervious to reviews, and suggests that the poor reception of *Martin Chuzzlewit* 'affected the direction he was to follow in *Dombey and Son*.'

42. 'The bishop and the philosopher', *Macmillan's Mag.*, VII (1863), 243; Arnold *PW*, III, 43.

43. 'Wordsworth, Tennyson and Browning, or pure, ornate and grotesque art in English poetry',

National Rev., n.s. I (1864), 27–66; *The Complete Prose Works of Walter Bagehot*, ed. N. St John-Stevas (1969) (hereafter cited as Bagehot *PW*), I, 322–3. Kellett, in Young, *op. cit.*, II, 6, comments: 'Editors may . . . be pardoned if they believe that by adding the anonymity of Junius to the popular appeal of Cobbett, and by maintaining a pontifical attitude of infallibility, they might exercise an almost unlimited power.'

44. *Saturday Rev.*, II, 23 Feb. 1856, 327.

45. 'The literary influence of academies', 166; Arnold *PW*, III, 249.

46. *Edinburgh Rev.*, I (1802), 63.

47. George Brimley, review of *Men and Women*, *Fraser's Mag.*, LIII (1856) (hereafter cited as Brimley), 108. A truncated version of this major review is to be found in Browning *CH*.

48. Stigand, 565.

49. 'The first Edinburgh reviewers', *National Rev.*, I (1855), 253–84; Bagehot, *PW*, I, 309–41, 329.

50. *Westminster Rev.*, I (1824), 209.

51. 'The function of criticism at the present time', Arnold *PW*, III, 268–71.

52. *Oxford and Cambridge Mag.*, I (1856), 172.

53. *London Q. Rev.*, VI (1856), 495.

54. *British Q. Rev.*, XXIII (1856), 156.

55. *Crayon* (New York, 1856); Whitman *CH*, 53.

56. *Guardian*, 9 Jan. 1856, 35.

57. *Christian Remembrancer*, LX (1856), 281.

58. Brimley, 105.

59. *London Q. Rev.*, VI (1856), 498.

60. *Press*, 10 Aug. 1855, 764–5.

61. *Boston Intelligencer*, 3 May 1856; Whitman *CH*, 61.

62. *Athenaeum*, no. 1464 (1855), 1327.

63. *Blackwood's*, LXX (1854), 534.

64. *Guardian*, 9 Jan. 1856, 35.

65. *Boston Intelligencer*, 3 May 1856; Whitman *CH*, 61.

66. *Spectator*, XXVIII (1855), 1347.

67. *Athenaeum*, no. 1464 (1855), 1327.

68. Brimley, 105.

69. *British Q. Rev.*, XXII (1855), 480.

70. *Ibid.*, XXIII (1856), 156.

71. *Guardian*, 9 Jan. 1856, 34.

72. 'What is poetry?', *Monthly Repository*, VII (1833), 60–70; 'The

two kinds of poetry', *ibid.*, 714–24;
'Tennyson's poems', *London Rev.*,
XXV (1835), 402–24; 'Writings of
Alfred de Vigny', *London and
Westminster Rev.*, XXXI (1838), 1–45.
All these essays were republished in
Dissertations and Discussions (1859);
my text is taken from *Mill's Essays
on Literature and Society*, ed. J. B.
Schneewind (New York, 1965)
(hereafter cited as Mill *LS*).

73. 'The object of poetry is confessedly to
act on the emotions' (Mill *LS*,
103–4); 'All the combinations which
the [poetic] mind puts together . . .
will be indebted to some dominant
feeling, not as in other natures to a
dominant *thought*' (*Ibid.*, 121).

74. 'John Stuart Mill', *National Rev.*, IX
(1859), 495; cf. Mill *LS*, 109: 'All
poetry is of the nature of soliloquy.'

75. Mill does comment that 'Lyric poetry
. . . is . . . more eminently and
peculiarly poetry than any other'
(Mill *LS*, 123).

76. *National Rev.*, IX (1859), 495.

77. There is no need, of course, to
suppose that Martineau's position
derives directly from Keats': it
belongs in the broad tradition of
Romantic *Einfühlung* which,
concentrated in the criticism of
Shakespeare, passed from the German
critics (e.g., A. W. von Schlegel)
through Coleridge and Hazlitt to
Keats and others. Armstrong, *op. cit.*,
8–10, rightly notes the contribution
of the English conception of
'sympathy' within the domain of
ethics, of which Adam Smith's
Theory of Moral Sentiments (1759) is
a key representative; Shelley's
conception of love in the *Defence of
Poetry* as 'a going out of our own
nature, and an identification of
ourselves with the beautiful which
exists in thought, action, or person
not our own', has affinities, though
Shelley's interest in Plato (especially
the *Symposium*) provides an
independent source in his case.

78. *Poetics* (1852), 83.

79. *Blackwood's*, LXXIX (1856), 135.

80. 'there was never a talent even for real
literature . . . but was primarily a
talent for doing something better of

the silent kind. Of Literature, in all
ways, be shy rather than otherwise,
at present! There where thou art,
work, work; whatsoever thy hand
findest to do, do it'
(*Latter-Day Pamphlets*, 1850:
'Stump-Oratory', 50). The attack is
renewed in 'Jesuitism', *ibid.*, 31–43; it
was probably these passages which
caused Arnold to censure the whole
collection as indicating Carlyle's
damaging immersion in 'the sphere
of popular practice'; Arnold's own
conception of the 'disinterestedness' of
'literary criticism' is clearly formed in
antithesis to Carlyle's contemptuous
dismissal of literature.

81. *Poetics*, 83. Dallas shows that he is
aware of the oddity of his statement:
'It may seem strange at first sight
that the lyric, wherein the poet's
individuality is most apparent, should
be the offspring of the law of
unconsciousness; and that the drama,
wherein it is least evident, should
come of that law which is the most
conscious. A second thought will
convince the reader, that we are most
ourselves when we forget ourselves,
and that in becoming self-conscious
we become what we are not' (p. 84).
This position derives from the
Romantic exaltation of
unselfconsciousness in, for instance,
Hazlitt's 'Whether Genius is
Conscious of its Powers?' (*The Plain
Speaker*) and Carlyle's
'Characteristics' (*Miscellanies*, III).
But both these writers regarded the
dramatic art as impersonal: Dallas's
polarization is essentially Victorian.

82. E.g., *Athenaeum*, no. 1464 (1855), 1327.

83. 'Of the False Ideal', *Modern Painters*,
III, iv; *The Works of John Ruskin*, ed.
cit., V, 71. The conception of the
'ideal' in these terms possibly derives
from Reynolds' *Discourses*: [The
artist] 'seeks out an abstract idea of
their forms more perfect than any
one original . . . he learns to design
naturally by drawing figures unlike to
any one object.' Reynolds calls this
'Ideal Beauty', and ascribes to it 'a
right to the epithet of *Divine*'
(Discourse III, *Discourses*, ed. Robert
R. Wark, 1975, 45–7).

84. Brimley, 113.
85. Brimley, 105. One source for this concept is Wordsworth's *Preface to the Lyrical Ballads*: 'Unless . . . we are advocates for . . . that pleasure that arises from hearing what we do not understand, the Poet must descend from this supposed height, and . . . he must express himself as other men express themselves' (*Prose Works*, ed. W. J. R. Owen and J. W. Smyser, 1974, I, 143).
86. 'Wordsworth, Tennyson and Browning, or, pure, ornate and grotesque art in English poetry'; Bagehot *PW*, I, 329.
87. Mill *LS*, 124; earlier, Mill comments: 'whoever writes out truly any one human feeling writes poetry' (p. 118).
88. Mill *LS*, 236–7.
89. Arthur Hallam, in his essay 'On some of the characteristics of modern poetry', *Englishman's Mag.*, I (1831), 616–28; Armstrong, *op. cit.*, 84–101, puts the proposition quite bluntly: 'Whenever the mind of the artist suffers itself to be occupied, during its moments of creation, by any other predominant motive than the desire for beauty, the result is false in art . . . not the gross and evident passions of our nature, but the elevated and less separable desires, are the dangerous enemies which misguide the poetic spirit in its attempts at self-cultivation.' (pp. 85, 88). Mill too emphasizes the 'sensuous' in 'poetry of nature', and though he uses the word 'spiritual' as designating the 'higher' side of poetic activity, he comments in a note that by this 'it is scarcely necessary to say that we do not mean *religious*' (Mill *LS*, 143).
90. *Poetics*, 138.
91. Martineau, *National Rev.*, IX (1859), 496.
92. In bk I, ch. 3, sect. 2 of Vol. I of his *Study of Religion* (1889), Martineau elaborates his objections to Mill's Idealism in a brilliant critique; see esp. pp. 98–106.
93. *Fraser's Mag.*, LI (1855), 160.
94. 'Writings of Alfred de Vigny'; Mill *LS*, 237; Mill adds: 'a long poem will

always be felt . . . to be something unnatural and hollow.'
95. Bagehot *PW*, 333.
96. '[Shelley] had not yet acquired the consecutiveness of thought necessary for a long poem' (Mill *LS*, 123–4). Here ('The Two Kinds of Poetry', 1833) and in his review of Tennyson (1835) Mill betrayed some anxiety to reincorporate thought into his poetics – so incoherently, however, that his recantation in the essay on Vigny is hardly unexpected.
97. Preface to *Poems* (1853); Arnold *PW*, I, 7.
98. Stigand, 537, 543, 544.
99. To Julia Wedgwood, 17 Oct. 1864: *Robert Browning and Julia Wedgwood*, ed. R. Curle (1937), 103.
100. To Isabella Blagden, 19 Aug. 1865: *Letters of Robert Browning*, ed. T. L. Hood (1933), 90. It seems likely that this complaint owes something to Arnold's; it is certain that many of the more thoughtful critics were making similar complaints. George Eliot's review of *Men and Women* (*Westminster Rev.*, n.s. IX, 1856, 295) contains the remark that 'Fra Lippo Lippi' was 'too strictly conservative for any fragments of it to be a fair specimen'; F. W. Marzials' review of Browning's *Selections* of 1862 (*London Q. Rev.*, XX, 1863, 531) objects that the editors 'give as fragments what were meant to be seen as parts of an artistic jewellery in which every stone should not only sparkle with its own light, but with reflected rays from all its brethren.'
101. W. Roscoe, 'W. M. Thackeray, artist and moralist', *National Rev.*, II (1856), 177–213; *Thackeray: the Critical Heritage*, ed. G. Tillotson and D. Hawes (1968), 265.
102. 'we may fairly credit *Dramatis Personae* with having finally awakened his countrymen . . . to the fact that a great creative power had arisen among them.' (Mrs A. Sutherland Orr, *Life and Letters of Robert Browning*, 1891, 269). In two articles, 'Browning's literary reputation at Oxford', *PMLA*, Modern Language Assoc. of America, LVII (1942), 232–41, and 'What Browning's literary reputation owed

to the Pre-Raphaelites', *ELH*,
VIII (1941), 305–21, M. B. Cramer
argues that Browning's reputation
was established by *Men and
Women*, but while he shows
convincingly that Rossetti was very
influential in extending Browning's
reputation among these two groups,
he fails adequately to illustrate how
'the enthusiasm of these men was
slowly, but actually, being extended
to the general public'; nor does he
note the contrast between the reviews
of *Men and Women* and those of
Dramatis Personae.

103. Browning called *Dramatis Personae*
'men and women, but under some
other name, to please the publisher':
5 Sept. 1863, *Browning to his
American Friends*, ed. G. R. Hudson
(1965), 130.

104. *Reader*, 4 June 1864, 704.

105. *Athenaeum*, no. 1910 (1864), 767.

106. *Reader*, 4 June 1864, 704.

107. Gerald Massey, review of *Dramatis
Personae*, *Quarterly Rev.*, CXVII
(1865) (hereafter cited as Massey),
79. A fragment of this major review
appears in Browning *CH*.

108. *Saturday Rev.*, XIX (1865), 15–17;
Browning *CH*, 267.

109. G. Massey, letter in *Reader*, 26 Nov.
1864, 674.

110. One section of Isobel Armstrong's
Introduction to *Victorian Scrutinies* is
entitled 'Change in the 1860s', and
demonstrates a series of changes of
detail in the tone and stance of
various reviewers. However, she does
not offer a general thesis under which
these changes may be grouped;
disappointingly, an earlier hint about
the growing importance of Coleridge
in the 1860s is not pursued. But this
excellent and stimulating essay gives
the impression of having had to be
abbreviated for publication.

111. *Spectator*, XXXVI (1863), 2461.

112. Walter Bagehot, 'Sterne and
Thackeray', *National Rev.*, XVIII
(1864), 523–53; Bagehot *PW*, I, 307.

113. R. H. Hutton, *Spectator*, XI (1867),
329–30; *Trollope: the Critical Heritage*,
ed. D. Smalley (1971), 268. Hutton
was right: Trollope published this
story anonymously in order to test

the capacity of his work to exist
independent of his reputation. He
was forcibly, and not altogether
agreeably, struck by Hutton's 'sagacity',
though he added that 'of all the critics
of my work he has been the most
observant': *Autobiography* (1953 edn),
175–6.

114. Massey, 83. In another passage (p. 85)
Massey, after quoting the last 16 lines
of 'A Grammarian's Funeral',
comments: 'Now, to our feeling, the
movement of this verse . . . conveys
a great sense of going up-hill, and the
weight of the burden – together with
the exultation of the bearers, which
gives them strength to mount; it *toils*
upwards step by step – long line and
short – best-foot foremost, – and
altogether carries out the idea of a
spirit that climbed in life.'

115. *Chambers's*, XIX (1863), 91.

116. Massey, 77.

117. *Spectator*, XXXVII (1864), 711.

118. Massey, 79.

119. *Ibid.*, 87.

120. *Ibid.*, 82.

121. *Victoria Mag.*, II (1864), 311–12.

122. Massey, 79.

123. Dallas, *The Gay Science*, I, 283.

124. 'The principles of success in
literature', *Fortnightly Rev.*, I (1865),
572–89; reprint, ed. K. Tillotson
(1969), 40.

125. Massey, 86–7.

126. Bagehot, 'Wordsworth, Tennyson and
Browning, or, pure, ornate, and
grotesque art in English poetry';
Bagehot *PW*, 325.

127. Bagehot, *PW*, 324.

128. *Ibid.*, 326.

129. *Ibid.*, 333-end.

130. *Ibid.*, 347.

131. *Ibid.*, 323–4.

132. *Ibid.*, 323.

133. The excesses of the Browning Society,
as captured in Beerbohm's admirable
cartoon, are well known, but it seems
to start in the 1860s. 'Few gifts would
be more precious than a book in
which he would lay aside the mask
for once . . . and tell us . . . what he
himself has thought, and believed on
the problems of man's life and the
universe.': *Contemporary Rev.*, IV
(1867), 8.

134. Bagehot *PW*, 323.
135. *Saturday Rev.*, XIX (1865), 17; Browning *CH*, 267.
136. Moncure Conway, *Victoria Mag.*, II (1864), 304.
137. Massey, 91.
138. *Ibid.*, 86–7.
139. Bagehot *PW*, 321.
140. *Home and Foreign Rev.*, IV (1864), 477; *RSC* 157.
141. *Ibid.*
142. *Ibid.*, 159.
143. To Isabella Blagden, 19 Aug. 1865: *Letters of Robert Browning, ed. cit.*, 90.
144. *Oxford and Cambridge Mag.*, I (1856), 7.
145. *Ibid.*, 50. Vernon Lushington's article on Carlyle has a similar passage: 'I do not propose in this Essay to act schoolmaster to Carlyle, look over his exercises, admonish him, run my pen through his blunders, and administer the ferule; no! that would be folly, and worse; nor, on the other hand, need I drug my intellect, but rather keep it wide awake as possible, and approaching reverently the great mind, look well into it, and mark what it is, and what it has done.': *ibid.*, 193. Cf. also Wilfrid L. Heeley's article 'Mr Macaulay', *ibid.*, 173.
146. The primacy of the *Saturday Review* was generally acknowledged. 'The *Saturday Review* quickly attained, and for many years held, the very highest place in English critical journalism as regards literature . . .': George Saintsbury, *Nineteenth-Century Literature* (1896), 381. Kellett, in Young, *op. cit.*, 56–7, acutely notes its symptomatic position: 'the *Saturday* is a new phenomenon. It represents that revolt of the intelligentsia against the bourgeoisie . . . It voices the restlessness of the highly educated under the yoke of people they hold to be inferior. The changes in Public Schools, the expansion of the Universities, the Tractarian movement had formed a new educated class to combat the dominant middle class.'
147. *Saturday Rev.*, I (1855), 18.
148. *Ibid.*
149. M. M. Bevington, *The Saturday Review 1855–1868* (New York, 1941), 6.
150. Bevington *op. cit.*, 13, notes that 'Cook's [the editor's] chief interest was in scholarly, politically minded young men . . . Such men he found among London barristers and in the two universities of Oxford and Cambridge.' Lord Bryce noted that 'among the writers, the man who had not a first-class honours degree from Oxford or Cambridge was a rarity': *Studies in Contemporary Biography* (1903), 360.
151. Christopher Kent, 'The higher journalism and the mid-Victorian clerisy', *VS*, XIII, 187.
152. H. R. Fox Bourne, *English Newspapers* (1887), II, 314.
153. The *Reader* (1863–5) was a weekly newspaper consisting entirely of literary criticism. For the general influence of the *Saturday Review*, see Bourne, *op. cit.*, 250.
154. *Saturday Rev.*, I (1856), 224.
155. *Ibid.*, 402.
156. *Ibid.*, I (1855), 2.
157. *Ibid.*, 3.
158. *Ibid.*
159. *Ibid.*, I (1856), 517.
160. *Ibid.*, II (1856), 56.
161. E.g. in its review of Browning's *Men and Women* (24 Nov. 1855, p. 69), which begins: 'It is really high time that this sort of thing should, if possible, be stopped. Here is another book of madness and mysticism'. Bevington, *op. cit.*, 211, notes the irony of the later attack on Stigand: 'when, in 1864, the *Edinburgh Review* reverted to the tactics and taste of Jeffrey and Gifford to condemn Browning for his obscurity . . . a *Saturday* reviewer could conveniently ignore the fact that his own predecessor of ten years before had laid down the lines that the *Edinburgh* was now following.'
162. *Saturday Rev.*, XIX (1865), 15; Browning *CH*, 264.
163. 'The literary influence of academies', 166; Arnold *PW*, III, 249.
164. *National Rev.*, II (1856), 357–87; Bagehot *PW*, I, 397.

165. *Rambler*, n.s. v (1856), 54–71, *RSC*, 59–60.
166. *Rambler*, n.s. IV (1855), 463.
167. *Ibid.*, n.s. VII (1857), 152; *RSC*, 77.
168. *North British Rev.*, n.s. XII (1869); *RSC*, 207.
169. 'The function of criticism at the present time'; Arnold *PW*, III, 258.
170. *Ibid.*, 261.
171. *Ibid.*, 282.
172. 'Pagan and Christian medieval religious sentiment', *Cornhill Mag.*, IX (1864), 422–35; Arnold *PW*, III, 227.
173. This is stated most clearly in the prolegomena to 'The bishop and the philosopher'; Arnold *PW*, III, 41–4.
174. 'Spinoza and the Bible', *Essays in Criticism* (2nd edn, 1869), Arnold *PW*, III, 174.
175. Quoted in Arnold *PW*, III, 407.
176. Dallas, *The Gay Science*, I, 39, noted that 'his outcry against English criticism for its want of science . . . has been received with the greatest favour'.
177. 'Sterne and Thackeray'; Bagehot *PW*, II, 295–6.
178. 'The function of criticism at the present time'; Arnold *PW*, III, 274.
179. 'Joubert', *National Rev.*, XVIII (1864), 189; Arnold *PW*, III, 209.
180. 'Jane Austen', *North British Rev.*, n.s. XIV (1870), 129–52; *RSC*, 243.
181. 'Mr Browning's latest poetry', *ibid.*, (1869), 97–126; *RSC*, 220.
182. 'The Function of Criticism', *Selected Essays* (1932), 30.
183. *The Gay Science*, I, 65.
184. 'The Study of Poetry' (*Essays in Criticism*, 2nd ser., 1880); Arnold *PW*, IX, 170.
185. *Ibid.*, 168.
186. *Ibid.*, 171.

Plate 1. The Great Room of the Royal Academy (*ILN*, ɪɪ, 1843, 338).

Plate 2. Portraits in the Great Room of the Royal Academy (*Art J.*, 1845, 179).

Plate 3. The Grosvenor Gallery (*ILN*, LXX, 1877, 420).

Plate 4. Cartoon by Robert Seymour from *McLean's Monthly Sheet of Caricatures*, 1 October 1832 (by permission of the British Museum). An attack on the Society for the Diffusion of Useful Knowledge, the cartoon shows Lord Brougham and Viscount Althorp cranking at a knowledge mill which is fed with froth by Lord John Russell and Edward Maltby, Bishop of Chichester. Attorney-General Thomas Denman stirs the mashing vat of 'wonderous condesention & affability' while directing the police to arrest the ragged vendor of unstamped papers (*right*). Charles Knight appears twice, on the left with ass's ears cutting out material to use in S.D.U.K. publications, and on the right cramming John Bull full of twaddle and extracting a huge flow of pennies from his pocket. For more details, see M. Dorothy George, *Catalogue of Political and Personal Satires Preserved in the Department of Prints and Drawings in the British Museum* (1954), XI, 687–8.

Monthly Supplement of
THE PENNY MAGAZINE
OF THE
Society for the Diffusion of Useful Knowledge.

101.]   **September 30, to October 31, 1833.**

THE COMMERCIAL HISTORY OF A PENNY MAGAZINE.—No. II.

WOOD-CUTTING AND TYPE FOUNDING.

[Virgin and Child: after Raffaelle.]

RICHARD DE BURY, Bishop of Durham, who lived more than a century before the introduction of the art of printing, wrote a treatise, entitled ' Philobiblon, or, the Love of Books.' Describing the process by which manuscripts were multiplied, he uses the following words :—" Because everything that is serviceable to mortals suffers the waste of mortality through lapse of time, it is necessary for volumes corroded by age to be restored by renovated successors, that perpetuity, repugnant to the nature of the individual, may be conceded to the species. Hence it is that Ecclesiastes significantly says, in his 12th chapter, ' There is no end of making many books.' " The monks, who were principally engaged in these services, had probably began to weary in their laborious occupation in the time of the good bishop; for in another place he says, " the study of the monks now-a-days dispenses with emptying bowls, not amending books." The account he gives of the industry of their predecessors shows us, however, that the old religious transcribers must have been endued with singular patience and perseverance :—" Many wrote them out with their own hands in the intervals of the canonical hours, and gave up the time appointed for bodily rest to the fabrication of volumes ; those sacred treasuries of whose labours, filled with cherubic letters, are at this day resplendent in most monasteries."

When we compare the multiplication of volumes in our own day with the slow productions of the transcribers described by Richard de Bury, we may say " there is no end of making many books." The copiers of manuscripts, indeed, were many, and their labours were incessant ; but the whole life of the most industrious individual employed in this task would add only a few to the number of volumes in the world. With what ardour must the recluse have been inspired who resolved to set about the transcription of a bible or breviary, or

Plate 5. Title page of the Monthly Supplement of the *Penny Magazine,* 11 (1833), 417 (by permission of the British Library). The wood engraver John Jackson made this cut to illustrate Charles Knight's account of the history of woodcuts in the *Penny Magazine,* 11 (1833), 417–21. Much of the success of the magazine depended on its lavish use of woodcuts. Knight asserted that the demand for the *Penny Magazine* was chiefly responsible for the 'completely changed . . . character of the art of wood-engraving' required by the new commercial circumstances of cheap publication (420).

THE

London Temperance Intelligencer.

UNDER THE DIRECTION OF THE NEW BRITISH AND FOREIGN SOCIETY FOR THE SUPPRESSION OF INTEMPERANCE.

No. 7.]   **FOR SATURDAY, DECEMBER 31, 1836.**   [PRICE ONE PENNY.

"Drunkenness debases and brutifies the intellect so much, that neither moral nor religious considerations have any great effect upon it."—MACNISH.

The readers of the "Intelligencer" cannot fail to recognise the triumphant news which the engraving in this number conveys. Tee-Total Sampson is bearing away the gates of the Gaza of moderate drinking. The breweries are in ruins. The giant Truth is dispelling the delusion. The London Tee-Totalers are resolved, in the strength of Divine grace, to realize this picture to the letter. It is not with societies we war, but with systems and vicious habits; and the cause of truth and holiness will prevail, and the scourge of our beloved land and people be annihilated. Let all join hand to hand and heart to heart; and thus united let every sacrifice be deemed as comparatively nothing when contrasted with the blessed prospect of "snatching as brands from the burning" the victims of intemperance; that the blessings of joy and peace may visit the habitations of cruelty. All admit that Total Abstinence, if adopted, would accomplish this; let none therefore hesitate a moment: the *sacrifice* is *trivial*, the glory immortal. Oh that all who name the name of Christ may live and labour for such a blessed object! ever remembering, "He that converteth a sinner from the error of his way, shall save a soul *from death* and shall hide a multitude of sins." May this blessed motive animate us until a drunkard shall be as difficult to find in our country, as it is now rare to meet with a village or town where there are not numbers of such lost and ruined characters. Let moderate wine and beer drinking be exterminated; and as sure as the giant shoulders of the ancient Nazarite, whose drink was from the brook, bore away the strong holds of the enemy, will we accomplish the freedom of our fellow-countrymen from the direst despot that ever cursed the human race. A long pull and a strong pull, and a pull altogether, and the victory is certain. Let this be the motto of every genuine Tee-Totaler, and a society to *protect moderate* tippling will soon cease to exist, and every good man blush at the long-cherished delusion which could induce him to support such a monstrous folly.

G

Plate 6. Title page of the *London Temperance Intelligencer* (later the *British and Foreign Temperance Intelligencer*), 31 December 1836 (by permission of the University of London Library).

Plate 7. 'The Man About Town', from the first page of the first number of *The Town*, 3 June 1837 (by courtesy of the Lilly Library, Indiana University).

Plate 8. Although the masthead of *The Town* remained in the same style throughout its run, some of the drawings were changed near the end of its first year (in no. 49, 5 May 1838). The central groups of card- and billiard-players were added, replacing drawings of young men flirting with a shop-girl and a group of London street characters. The latter group was moved to the right of the masthead; a coachman and a hod-carrier were dropped, the figure-seller added, and only the guardsmen retained. There is, in short, a somewhat increased emphasis on the recreations rather than on the work of the metropolis (by courtesy of the Lilly Library, Indiana University).

The Struggle.

"We maintain the sacred principle of *Free international intercourse.*"

Though hungry men may weep and wail,
I'll not give up the SLIDING SCALE !

AN AP-PEEL TO HUMANITY.

Sir Robert, as the reader will perceive, has got a *firm* standing ; but many complain that his *justice cap* wants *re-fixing.* The end of Paisley, is in his last " engagement ;" whilst the Old " Buck" is trying to learn the christian lesson, of being " content h *such* things as he has."

These aristocratic necessaries of life called *Turbot, Turtle,* and *Lobsters,* are generously permitted to be imported *duty free,* but a single load of porridge meal, or bread flour, for the use of the starving multitude is allowed to come in on the same terms, till hunger glass falls to the lowest degree, and stands at " stormy." *Wines, Spirits, Mineral Waters, Grapes,* &c., to nourish the der fed bread taxers, are imported in abundance, at a fixed duty. but *bulls, oxen, cows, calves, sheep, lambs, pigs,* and *goats,* are irely prohibited, to prevent over feeding on the part of the poor ! Beef saturated with salt may be brought over at the moderate duty 12s. per cwt. ; but gentlemen's dogs may eat foreign greeves at a duty of two shillings ! *Macaroni* for delicate stomachs, tax 2d.

lb. ; black puddings for clodhoppers, *four pence !*
The duty on *Bacon* is 3d. per lb. ; that on *ox tails,* for fine soups, less than the *eighteenth part of a penny !* *Medlars* only 1s. per hel ; *Onions* 3s. per bushel. Oysters only 1s. 6d. per bushel ; Paddys lumpers *two shillings* a cwt ! Fine *salmon* and all kinds of *fish* l *fowl* take the liberty of importing themselves *duty free ;* but for those who live in cellars and cottags, at eighteen pence a week, ey are quite " out of season."

XTENDED CULTIVATION AND NON-DEPEN-DANCE UPON FOREIGNERS.

We are often told that " there is yet land uncultivated England, sufficient to grow plenty of food for all the eople." True, if we be regardless of the *cost* of pro-iction, and determine to eat no bread but of British cul-re, no doubt by cultivating the bogs and barren parts of the country, we should be able to produce sufficient for all. That is, we could do this as long as our capital would last in pursuing the folly of procuring food under such disadvantages. But we should thus be going to the dearest instead of the cheapest shop, and our food would cost us a great deal more than we can buy it for from our continental neighbours. We might manage, no doubt, to produce all our own wood, hemp, and tallow, as well as food ; nay, if we were disposed to go

No. 7.

Plate 9. Title page of Joseph Livesey's *The Struggle,* no. 7 (1842) (by permission of the University of London Library).

THE
LONDON JOURNAL;

And Weekly Record of Literature, Science, and Art.

No. 166. Vol. VII.]   FOR THE WEEK ENDING APRIL 29, 1848.   [Price One Pe

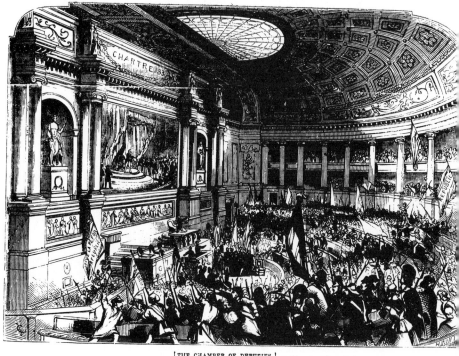

[THE CHAMBER OF DEPUTIES.]

THE FRENCH REVOLUTION.

IN our preceding number we gave an account of most of the proceedings of Sunday, the 26th of March. Continuing our narrative in consecutive order, we now lay before our readers the demonstration of the Poles, which occurred also on that day.

About 3000 of these people assembled in the Place de la Revolution, and proceeded in order, with their national colours (red and white) flying, to the Hotel de Ville. Deputations from the various clubs of Paris preceded them, each bearing its peculiar flag. A considerable crowd accompanied the *cortège*, and loud cries of "Poland for ever!" "Vive la République!" were heard on all sides. At the Hotel de Ville the Provisional Government received a deputation of the main body. M. Godebski, after thanking France for her hospitality, said:—"After so many cruel deceptions, the hour is now come when Poland may decide her own fate by her own hand. It is to concur in this work that we are about to march, and we believe that we have a right to hope that you will aid us to perform our duty as soldiers. We rely upon you, citizens, because we consider you

as the true representatives of the French people, who are our brothers. Vive la République Française! Vive la République Polonaise!"—M. De Lamartine replied :—"Citizens of Poland! the French Republic receives as a happy omen the homage of your adhesion and of your acknowledgment of its hospitality. I have no need to express to you its sentiments towards the sons of Poland. The voice of France has annually declared them to you, even when the monarchy endeavoured to suppress it. The voice and gesture of the Republic are still more sympathetic, and it repeats its fraternal sentiments towards you. Be assured that France will repay you all that she owes you. Only you must leave to her that which she alone can appoint—the hour, the moment, the mode for giving to you, without aggression, without effusion of blood, the place which is due to you in the list of nations. I will make known to you, if you know them not already, the principles which the Provisional Government have adopted invariably for its foreign policy. France is undoubtedly republican. She proclaims this to all the world. But the Republic is not at war, either openly or secretly, with any of the existing nations or governments, so long as these nations and govern-

ments refrain from making war upon it. It w not, therefore, voluntarily commit or suffer to committed any act of aggression or violence up the Germanic nations. They are at this mome labouring to modify by themselves their own inte nal system of confederation. It would be insensa or treacherous to the freedom of the world to d turb and derange their labours by demonstrations war, and thus turn into hostility and hatred th pure disposition to promote liberty which mak them incline with all the best feelings of the hearts towards us and towards you. Look Belgium — Switzerland — Italy — all southern Ge many! Turn your eyes towards Vienna a Berlin! What more is necessary? Even the p sessors of your own land open to you a path to yo country, and call upon you to come and re-establi it in peace! Be not unjust either towards Go towards the Republic, or towards yourselves! Th sympathising states of Germany, the King of Pruss are opening the doors of their citadels to your ma tyrs. The gates of Poland are open. Cracow enfranchised. The Grand Duchy of Posen has aga become Polish. These are the arms which we hav given you in one month. Do not demand any mo

Plate 10. Title page of the *London Journal,* 29 April 1848 (by permission of the British Library).

Vol. I. No. I.]   JANUARY, 1851.   PRICE ONE HALFPENNY.

TO THE
BOYS AND GIRLS OF ALL NATIONS.

DEAR YOUNG FRIENDS.

HAPPY New Year to you all! The year 1851 will be a very memorable one. You have no doubt heard of the Great Exhibition for all Nations, which is to be held in London during this year. If you look into the booksellers' shop windows, you will see pictures of the Great Palace of Glass which is now being built. In a few weeks this wonderful building will be filled with all kinds of curious machinery and costly productions from all parts of the world. The sight will afford a proof of the rich provision which our Heavenly Father has made for his creatures of every clime, and of the skill which he has given to man. Then we shall have people of all kingdoms, and nations, and tongues, walking about the streets of London. The Chinaman with his long tail and wooden shoes; the Hindoo with his white clothes and turban; the Indian with his savage looking face; the Laplander in his bear's skin; and all kinds of curious looking people, such as the Children of England have never yet seen. Oh, what a strange sight, what a great gathering there will be! We hope it will be the means of doing much good, and that it will show to all the world, "how good and how pleasant it is for brethren to dwell together in unity;" for the world is but one family, although a divided one by seas and mountains, &c.; but which should not divide our hearts one from another, nor prevent us from being kind one to another, and dwelling together in peace.

Sometimes a cloud steals over our minds, lest we should not turn this great opportunity of doing good to the best account. We fear that with more people there will be more sin and wickedness committed; but we must pray and labour that *much good* may also be done. Many will turn into our Churches and Chapels, and for the first time join in the service of the true God. Let us daily pray that they may hear something which, when carried back to their own country, will sow the seed of the gospel and bring forth a rich harvest.

In this remarkable year then, which will never be forgotten by any of us, we are anxious to commence another "Great Gathering," not of old people, not of fathers and mothers, but of "Children." We shall not be able to bring you all into one large building, but we want the Children of all nations to unite with their hearts, voices, and hands, in forming a "WORLD'S TEMPERANCE BAND OF HOPE."

A great foe to the world's happiness is now in the midst of us. Not content with slaying thousands of our fellow men every year, and consigning them to a premature grave, he is continually gaining new victims within his grasp. In Great Britain he has placed about 20,000 persons in prisons, and filled the asylums and poorhouses with lunatics and paupers, whom he has robbed of their reason and property. Like a wily serpent he has entwined himself around every family circle in the land, for there is not a household to be found into which he has entered where he has not left a sting behind. The name of this Great Destroyer is INTEMPERANCE. There are now in London alone not less than 20,000 poor ragged children whom this monster has robbed of home, of food, and of clothing. We wish you (*with the consent of your parents*) to promise, by God's help, never to drink any of those intoxicating drinks which lead to Intemperance. Form Temperance Bands of Hope in every city, town, and village, and let us unite in one great army, and never rest until Intemperance falls before our onward march. Let the "BAND OF HOPE REVIEW AND SUNDAY SCHOLAR'S FRIEND," have a place in every Sunday school and family throughout the three kingdoms.

We shall labour to assist the Parent and Teacher in their laborious and responsible duties, and shall gladly receive any suggestions whereby our publication may be promotive of glory to God and good to men.

[REGISTERED FOR TRANSMISSION ABROAD]   A WEEKLY MAGAZINE OF GENERAL LITERATURE.   [THE RIGHT OF TRANSLATION IS RESERVED.]

No. 74. Vol. II.]   WEDNESDAY, APRIL 6, 1864.   [ONE PENNY.

DORA RIVERSDALE.
A TALE OF SORROW.
BY THE AUTHOR OF "WOMAN'S WORTH," ETC.

CHAPTER I.

DORA RIVERSDALE was born in Lancashire, in a dull old town, which I will call Northbrook, and her father was a watchmaker—an humble watchmaker—nothing more.

Samuel Riversdale was fifty years of age when he married his dead wife's sister, then a blooming country girl, who wedded the old man for a home, and because he was reputed to be rich.

As might be expected from such an union of calculation on the woman's part, Samuel soon discovered that he was a wretched man.

Martha's temper, soured by disappointment, by the cares of her numerous offspring, by her husband's parsimonious habits and his irritable disposition, became terrible indeed as the years rolled on; and her wedded life was one long scene of wrangling, discontent, and utter misery.

Dora was the only child Samuel Riversdale's

dead wife had left behind her, and that child was the innocent cause of the greater part of the second Mrs. Riversdale's daily outbursts of temper.

Dora was a plain-looking child—a little fright, Martha said, continually, and frequently in the hearing of the little girl herself—and accordingly Dora was neglected in every possible way, used as a mere household drudge, and driven from pillar to post, as suited the particular humour of those about her, who had the power to command and ill-treat her as much as ever they pleased.

And the bitter words so often repeated by the watchmaker's wife to her motherless niece, sunk deep into the little girl's heart, and there rankled painfully. But as Dora grew older she learned to listen to her stepmother's reproaches just as if the harsh syllables conveyed no meaning to her ears, or as if she really deserved them.

And poor Dora believed that she was plain-looking, that she was unpleasant to behold; and having made up her mind to that fact, she brooded over it in many an hour of loneliness and gloom.

But notwithstanding that the child had steeled her heart to bear much pain, that heart was sometimes so wounded and so torn, that she felt ready to die; and she often prayed to die, too. Dora's were not the petty griefs which a shower of tears will wash away; ah, no! they were such as rankled in her bosom, and time multiplied their number, and likewise their power over her.

Dora was only ten years old, yet she had learned to think upon and study many things. Her affection was repulsed, and she who yearned to love, and to be beloved, had to shut up her little heart, and hide all its best feelings.

She was naturally of a dreamy, poetic temperament, and she hungered for knowledge, even as the parched traveller in the desert thirsts for the water he searches for in vain.

She watched other children go to school, and she wondered why they went thither; and, moreover than that, why it was that she did not go there also.

One day Dora seized courage, and stopping a little girl returning from a neighbouring school, with bag and book in hand, she questioned her.

"What do you learn at school?" she asked, curiously.

The scholar stared at the querist, called her an ignorant dunce, and, laughing, ran away.

Dora's heart heaved tumultuously. She was offended and hurt. She knew that she was ignorant; but it was torture to her very soul to be told so by a stranger.

Creeping to her attic-chamber, Dora produced an old cracked mirror, and placing it in the narrow window, she gazed into it steadfastly and long.

What was it she saw reflected in that looking-glass?

I will tell you.

A pair of large, luminous brown eyes, fringed with long black lashes, which swept cheeks as pale as marble: a brow low, but broad, crowned with a perfect mass of golden-tinted hair, rippling and glistening in the summer light; a nose small and straight, with proudly arched nostrils; eye-

DORA RIVERSDALE UNFOLDS HER TROUBLES TO ESTHER BRIDGEMAN

Plate 12. Title page of *Bow Bells*, 6 April 1864 (by permission of the British Library).

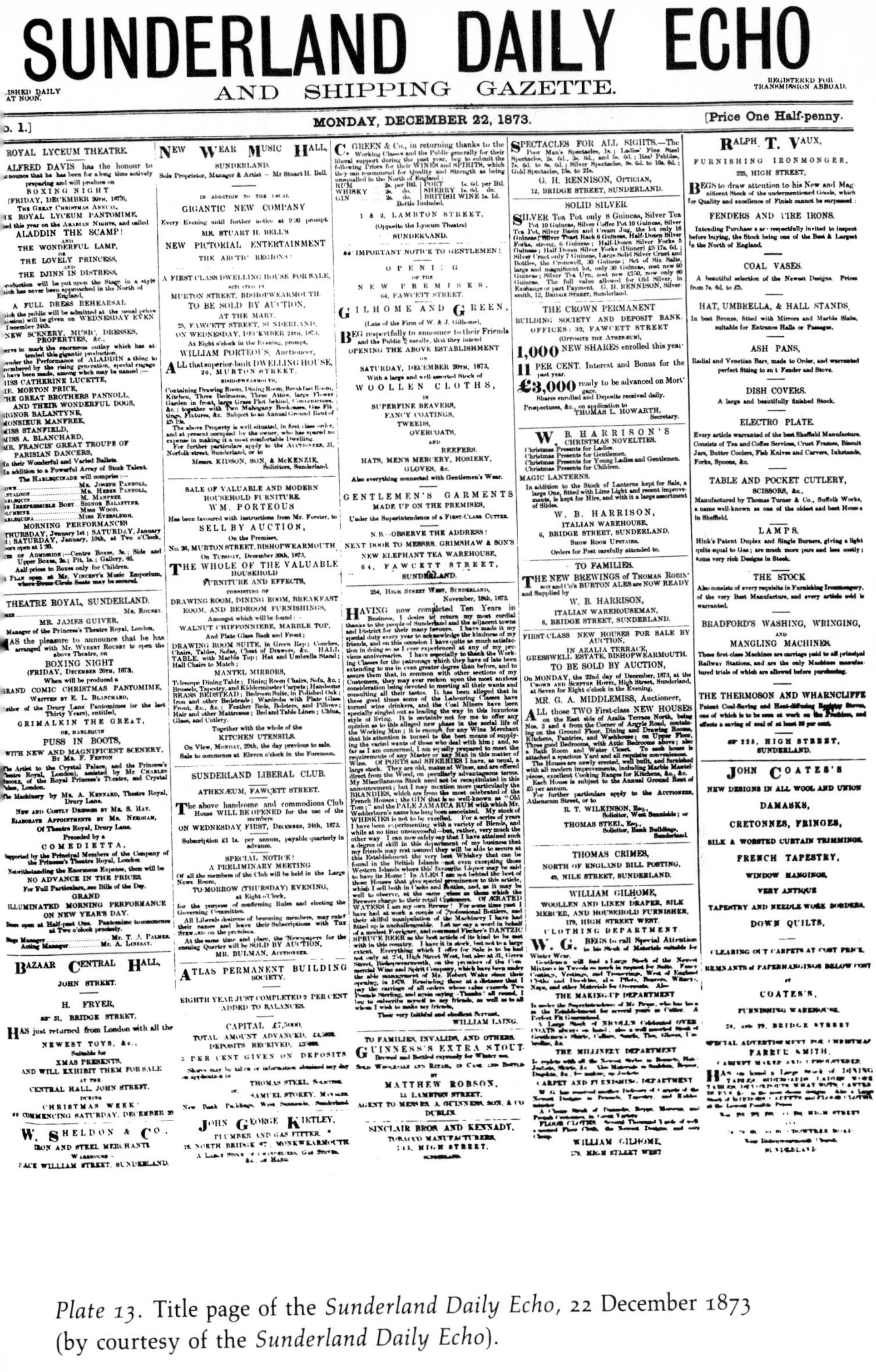

SUNDERLAND DAILY ECHO

AND SHIPPING GAZETTE.

...ISHED DAILY AT NOON. — REGISTERED FOR TRANSMISSION ABROAD.

...o. 1.] MONDAY, DECEMBER 22, 1873. [Price One Half-penny.

ROYAL LYCEUM THEATRE.

ALFRED DAVIS has the honour to ...nounce that he has been for a long time actively preparing and will produce on BOXING NIGHT (FRIDAY, DECEMBER 26TH, 1873), THE GREAT CHRISTMAS ANNUAL ...E ROYAL LYCEUM PANTOMIME, ...ed this year on the ARABIAN NIGHTS, and called ALADDIN THE SCAMP! AND THE WONDERFUL LAMP, OR THE LOVELY PRINCESS, AND THE DJINN IN DISTRESS.

A FULL DRESS REHEARSAL ... will be given on WEDNESDAY EVENING, December 24th.

NEW SCENERY, MUSIC, DRESSES, PROPERTIES, &c.

MISS CATHERINE LUCETTE, MR. MORTON PRICE, THE GREAT BROTHERS PANNOLL, AND THEIR WONDERFUL DOGS, SIGNOR BALANTYNE, MONSIEUR MANFREE, MISS STANFIELD, MISS A. BLANCHARD, MR. FRANCIS' GREAT TROUPE OF PARISIAN DANCERS, In their Wonderful and Varied Ballets. In addition to a Powerful Array of Stock Talent.

MORNING PERFORMANCES THURSDAY, January 1st; SATURDAY, January 3; SATURDAY, January, 10th, at Two o'Clock.

THEATRE ROYAL, SUNDERLAND.

MR. JAMES GUIVER, Manager of the Princess's Theatre Royal, London, HAS the pleasure to announce that he has arranged with Mr. Wybert Rousby to open the above Theatre, on BOXING NIGHT (FRIDAY, DECEMBER 26TH, 1873, When will be produced a GRAND COMIC CHRISTMAS PANTOMIME, WRITTEN BY E. L. BLANCHARD, Author of the Drury Lane Pantomimes for the last Thirty Years), entitled, GRIMALKIN THE GREAT, OR, HARLEQUIN PUSS IN BOOTS, WITH NEW AND MAGNIFICENT SCENERY, By MR. F. FENTON ...

NO ADVANCE IN THE PRICES. For Full Particulars, see Bills of the Day. GRAND ILLUMINATED MORNING PERFORMANCE ON NEW YEAR'S DAY.

BAZAAR CENTRAL HALL, JOHN STREET.

H. FRYER, 31, BRIDGE STREET, HAS just returned from London with all the NEWEST TOYS, &c., Suitable for XMAS PRESENTS, AND WILL EXHIBIT THEM FOR SALE AT THE CENTRAL HALL, JOHN STREET, DURING CHRISTMAS WEEK, COMMENCING SATURDAY, DECEMBER 20

W. SHELDON & CO., IRON AND STEEL MERCHANTS ... BACK WILLIAM STREET, SUNDERLAND.

NEW WEAR MUSIC HALL, SUNDERLAND. Sole Proprietor, Manager & Artist — Mr Stuart H. Bell. GIGANTIC NEW COMPANY ... MR. STUART H. BELL'S NEW PICTORIAL ENTERTAINMENT THE ARCTIC REGIONS!

A FIRST-CLASS DWELLING HOUSE FOR SALE, SITUATED IN MURTON STREET, BISHOPWEARMOUTH. TO BE SOLD BY AUCTION, AT THE MART, 23, FAWCETT STREET, SUNDERLAND, ON WEDNESDAY, DECEMBER 24th, 1873, At Eight o'clock in the Evening, prompt, WILLIAM PORTEOUS, Auctioneer, ALL that superior-built DWELLING HOUSE, 26, MURTON STREET, BISHOPWEARMOUTH ... Messrs. KIDSON, SON, & McKENZIE, Solicitors, Sunderland.

SALE OF VALUABLE AND MODERN HOUSEHOLD FURNITURE. WM. PORTEOUS Has been favoured with instructions from Mr. Forster, to SELL BY AUCTION, On the Premises, No. 26, MURTON STREET, BISHOPWEARMOUTH On TUESDAY, December 30th, 1873, THE WHOLE OF THE VALUABLE HOUSEHOLD FURNITURE AND EFFECTS, CONSISTING OF DRAWING ROOM, DINING ROOM, BREAKFAST ROOM, AND BEDROOM FURNISHINGS ... KITCHEN UTENSILS. On View, MONDAY, 29th, the day previous to sale. Sale to commence at Eleven o'clock in the Forenoon.

SUNDERLAND LIBERAL CLUB. ATHENÆUM, FAWCETT STREET. The above handsome and commodious Club House WILL BE OPENED for the use of the members ON WEDNESDAY FIRST, DECEMBER, 24th, 1873. Subscription £1 1s. per annum, payable quarterly in advance. SPECIAL NOTICE! A PRELIMINARY MEETING ... TO-MORROW (THURSDAY) EVENING, ... MR. BULMAN, AUCTIONEER.

ATLAS PERMANENT BUILDING SOCIETY. EIGHTH YEAR JUST COMPLETED 9 PER CENT ADDED TO BALANCES. CAPITAL £75,000. ... THOMAS STEEL, SECRETARY ... SAMUEL STOREY, MANAGER.

JOHN GEORGE KIRTLEY, PLUMBER AND GAS FITTER, 19, NORTH BRIDGE ST., MONKWEARMOUTH.

C. GREEN & Co., in returning thanks to the Working Classes and the Public generally for their liberal support during the past year, beg to submit the following Prices for their WINES and SPIRITS ... 1 & 2, LAMBTON STREET, (Opposite the Lyceum Theatre) SUNDERLAND.

IMPORTANT NOTICE TO GENTLEMEN! OPENING OF THE NEW PREMISES, 64, FAWCETT STREET. GILHOME AND GREEN, (Late of the Firm of W. & J. Gilhome), BEG respectfully to announce to their Friends and the Public generally, that they intend OPENING THE ABOVE ESTABLISHMENT ON SATURDAY, DECEMBER 20TH, 1873, With a large and well assorted Stock of WOOLLEN CLOTHS, IN SUPERFINE BEAVERS, FANCY COATINGS, TWEEDS, OVERCOATS, AND REEFERS. HATS, MEN'S MERCERY, HOSIERY, GLOVES, &c. ... GENTLEMEN'S GARMENTS MADE UP ON THE PREMISES ... NEXT DOOR TO MESSRS. GRIMSHAW & SON'S NEW ELEPHANT TEA WAREHOUSE, 64, FAWCETT STREET, SUNDERLAND.

254, HIGH STREET WEST, SUNDERLAND, November, 18th, 1873. HAVING now completed Ten Years in Business, I desire to return my most cordial thanks to the people of Sunderland and the adjacent towns and District for their many favours. ... Their very faithful and obedient Servant, WILLIAM LAING.

TO FAMILIES, INVALIDS, AND OTHERS. GUINNESS'S EXTRA STOUT ... MATTHEW ROBSON, 11, LAMBTON STREET, AGENT TO MESSRS. A. GUINNESS, SON, & CO DUBLIN.

SINCLAIR BROS AND KENNADY, TOBACCO MANUFACTURERS, 143, HIGH STREET.

SPECTACLES FOR ALL SIGHTS.— ... G. H. RENNISON, OPTICIAN, 12, BRIDGE STREET, SUNDERLAND.

SOLID SILVER. SILVER Tea Pot only 8 Guineas, ... G. H. RENNISON, Silversmith, 12, BRIDGE STREET, Sunderland.

THE CROWN PERMANENT BUILDING SOCIETY AND DEPOSIT BANK. OFFICES: 39, FAWCETT STREET (OPPOSITE THE ATHENÆUM), 1,000 NEW SHARES enrolled this year. 11 PER CENT. Interest and Bonus for the past year. £3,000 ready to be advanced on Mortgage. ... THOMAS L. HOWARTH, Secretary.

W. B. HARRISON'S CHRISTMAS NOVELTIES. ... MAGIC LANTERNS. ... W. B. HARRISON, ITALIAN WAREHOUSE, 6, BRIDGE STREET, SUNDERLAND.

TO FAMILIES. THE NEW BREWINGS of THOMAS ROBINSON and Co's BURTON ALES are NOW READY and Supplied by W. B. HARRISON, ITALIAN WAREHOUSEMAN, 6, BRIDGE STREET, SUNDERLAND.

FIRST-CLASS NEW HOUSES FOR SALE BY AUCTION, IN AZALIA TERRACE, GRESSWELL ESTATE, BISHOPWEARMOUTH. TO BE SOLD BY AUCTION, On MONDAY, the 22nd day of December, 1873, ... MR. G. A. MIDDLEMISS, Auctioneer, ... R. T. WILKINSON, Esq., ... THOMAS STEEL, Esq., Solicitor, Bank Buildings, Sunderland.

THOMAS CRIMES, NORTH OF ENGLAND BILL POSTING, 49, NILE STREET, SUNDERLAND.

WILLIAM GILHOME, WOOLLEN AND LINEN DRAPER, SILK MERCER, AND HOUSEHOLD FURNISHER, 179, HIGH STREET WEST. CLOTHING DEPARTMENT. ... THE MILLINERY DEPARTMENT ... CARPET AND FURNISHING DEPARTMENT ... WILLIAM GILHOME, 179, HIGH STREET WEST.

RALPH T. VAUX, FURNISHING IRONMONGER, 225, HIGH STREET, BEGS to draw attention to his New and Magnificent Stock of the undermentioned Goods, which for Quality and excellence of Finish cannot be surpassed: FENDERS AND FIRE IRONS. ... COAL VASES. ... HAT, UMBRELLA, & HALL STANDS, ... ASH PANS, ... DISH COVERS. ... ELECTRO PLATE. ... TABLE AND POCKET CUTLERY, SCISSORS, &c., ... LAMPS. ... THE STOCK ... BRADFORD'S WASHING, WRINGING, AND MANGLING MACHINES. ... THE THERMOSON AND WHARNCLIFFE ... 225, HIGH STREET, SUNDERLAND.

JOHN COATES'S NEW DESIGNS IN ALL WOOL AND UNION DAMASKS, CRETONNES, FRINGES, SILK & WORSTED CURTAIN TRIMMINGS, FRENCH TAPESTRY, WINDOW HANGINGS, VERY ANTIQUE TAPESTRY AND NEEDLE WORK BORDERS, DOWN QUILTS, ... COATES'S, FURNISHING WAREHOUSE, ... BRIDGE STREET

Plate 13. Title page of the *Sunderland Daily Echo*, 22 December 1873 (by courtesy of the *Sunderland Daily Echo*).

THE

Workman's Advocate

An Independent Organ advocating the Rights of Labour, Freedom from Class Legislation, Priestcraft, and Tyranny.

Registered at the General Post Office as a Newspaper.]

[Registered for Transmission Abroad.

No. 99 (K.)   FRIDAY, JULY 23, 1875.   PRICE ONE PENNY.

TO SUBSCRIBERS.

The WORKMAN'S ADVOCATE will be posted to any address in the United Kingdom, on payment in advance of the following rates:—

Three Months ... ... 1s. 8d.
Six Months ... ... 3s. 3d.
Twelve Months... ... ... 6s. 6d.

Two copies of the WORKMAN'S ADVOCATE are sent post free to any address for 1½d. 2s. etc. at post free for 6d.; twelve copies 1s.

Post-office Orders to be made payable to J. T. Morgan, WORKMAN'S ADVOCATE Office, Merthyr Tydfil.

A SCENE AT CARNARVON COUNTY COURT.

A scene, in which a Welsh clergyman played a prominent part, was yesterday witnessed at Carnarvon county court. The Rev. Edward Anwyl Jones, a clergyman holding a living near Borth, and who was recently curate of Berriew, Montgomeryshire, was subpœnaed as a witness in one of the causes for trial. He presented himself in court about noon. Addressing Mr. J. A. Hughes, the deputy-registrar, he asked who was going to pay his expenses for attendance. Mr. Hughes referred him to the judge (his Honour Horatio Lloyd), who remarked that he did not think the party who had subpœnaed him had suffered very much by his absence.—The Rev. E. A. Jones: Don't you think so. I do, as the case was a very important one.—His Honour: I will have no insolence. You have your own remedy, and I shall certainly not allow you anything. You are not entitled to nothing since you were not here at the proper time. I see in the papers all sorts of inquiries going on about the clergy, and really one cannot wonder at it if this individual is to be taken as a specimen of the cloth. Who is he?—Mr. Hughes: The Rev. E. A. Jones, of 2, Cambrian-terrace, Borth.—Mr. Jones went out of court, and returning in a few minutes, addressed the judge in a confidential tone, saying—"It's a long journey for me; I have come about 100 miles, and it was a very important... His Honour: I have nothing to do with it, and I have told you so before.—Mr. Jones: Well, I can't be here. It's impossible for me to be here. (Laughter.)—His Honour: But you are here. When did you leave Borth? Last night. I came to Portmadoc, and I have been travelling first class too. (Laughter.) Now then, gentlemen of the bar, you need not laugh like that. (Renewed laughter.)—His Honour: You have evidently spent more time at Portmadoc than you ought to have done.—Mr. Jones: I walked from Portmadoc.—His Honour: I am afraid you called at too many places on your way—to rest, I suppose. So far as I am concerned I will allow you nothing, for reasons which may not be obvious to you, but which are quite apparent to everybody else in court. It you want me to speak plainly, I must tell you that you are not in the condition you ought to be, and that you apparently occupy a most discreditable and disgraceful position.—The reverend gentleman abruptly left the court.

LABOURERS' CONFERENCE AT WESTON-SUPER-MARE.

SPEECH BY MR. ODGER.

It was resolved that the general fund pay all delegates' expenses to the Conference. The auditors' report and balance sheet were adopted. It was unanimously resolved to abolish the present system of double entrance fees for backsliders. A very long discussion next ensued with regard to the future constitution of the governing council of the Association, and at length on the motion of Mr. O'Donnell (Newport) and Mr. Fishlock, it was resolved that the rule should be altered so that in future the General Council should consist of an equal number of Bristol and country members, the Bristol members to form the executive, whose actions should be subject to the approval of the General Council, which shall meet quarterly. It was further resolved that this resolution should take immediate effect, but the members who had not been in the Association for eighteen months, or who were eight weeks in arrears, should be ineligible for seats on the Council. Vacancies are to be filled by the lodge to which the former member of the Council belonged. It was also resolved that the Council should endeavour to organise Bristol, Devon, Cornwall and South Wales.

It was moved by Mr. Peters, seconded by Mr. Clarke, and resolved:—"That this conference views with satisfaction the decision of Leeds Conference to form a national federation of miners, and trusts that other trades will adopt similar steps, believing that no action could be more beneficial to the working men of this country."

Members of the new General Council were then elected, consisting of five Bristol members and one each from Cardiff, Newport, Exeter, Weston and Bath. It was resolved to send a deputation to Clevedon to pay the men on strike. Messrs. J. T. Morgan and M. Robbins were re-elected general auditors.

The Conference resumed at nine o'clock on Saturday morning, Mr. J. T. Morgan (WORKMAN'S ADVOCATE Office), presiding

It was resolved "That in future only accidents which occur whilst the member is actually engaged at work shall entitle him to accidental pay in case the member does not belong to the sick fund branch." Also that members in the accident and trade branches only shall be excluded if their arrears exceed four months.

MR. GEORGE ODGER, of London, then addressed the Conference. He said that he had a desire to see how they conducted business, how, in fact, they governed themselves. The question of labourers governing themselves had been attempted to be used as a handle to do them an injury. He complimented them upon their debates, which had been free from all personalities, and he saw in that assembly pure representative government, free from all dictation. Trades' Unions to-day were in a far different position to what they were years ago. He remembered the time when they had to fight against the law, and a vast amount of prejudice. To-day, however, many of these prejudices had disappeared, and the Home Secretary was found declaring that Trade Unions must be dealt with unfairly, and that the present unjust Labour Laws ought to be amended. This showed that there was a certain amount of respect now accorded to Trades' Unions, and an evident desire to do justice to the working classes. He urged them not to ask for favours from any party, but to ask for justice, and to rely on their own self-effort and their own organisation, and if they did this they were almost sure not to fail. He did not see any reason why labourers should not be paid as fair wages as skilled artizans. He had seen men mowing and shearing sheep, and he thought they had to take care not to out too deep into the mutton. (Laughter.) He had seen the hay and corn stacks after they had been thatched, and their appearance indicate that there

was a certain degree of skill required to do these things. John Bunyan said that he was of a degraded race, a tinker; but he failed to see that a man who mended pots and kettles was any worse than men who preached sermons by the yard. (Laughter.) He did not mean to say that all preachers were of that stamp, but they all knew that there were men who could preach a great deal and yet say nothing—mere wordy men. He also reminded them that if he sneered occasionally at the bishops and parsons he did not sneer at their faith, but rather at their want of faith. (Hear, hear.) There were many good and noble-minded men amongst the parsons—men who were entitled to their highest respect—such, for instance, as Dean Stanley, Archbishop Sandford and others. There was also that good man Canon Jenkins, who lived and laboured in the district in which the President of the Conference resided. (Applause.) But on the other hand, some of the parsons had gone so far as to preach that labourers ought to remain labourers. The motto of these men seemed to be, "Let ignorance and labour go together;" but he contended that education and labour ought to go together. (Cheers.) He looked upon Trades' Unions as a means of education, and in this he agreed with the chairman of the previous night's meeting. He said that the working men of this country had now a good chance before them for with greater facilities for education, and the better laws they were about to have with their own trade organisations, they would soon be able to ameliorate their condition. (Applause.) He was glad to see that they were possessed of such business habits as they had shown in that Conference, and he wished their Association every success. (Applause.)

A vote of thanks was unanimously accorded Mr. Odger for his address and presence at the Conference.

Mr. J. Fox moved that all important resolutions respecting trade disputes shall be decided by the ballot in future.

This was seconded by Mr. Connolly, of Cardiff, and after a short discussion, was carried unanimously.

Mr. FISHLOCK proposed, and Mr. LIMMER seconded, that the code of rules for the sick branch, prepared by the late Executive Council, be embodied in the general laws of the Society. Carried unanimously.

Several minor matters having been disposed of, the Conference was brought to a close with the customary vote of thanks to the Conference officers.

The General Secretary and General Treasurer attended at Clevedon on Saturday afternoon, and paid the labourers who are out on strike their full strike pay of 12s. per week. We understand that another employer there is about to concede the advance.

FLOODS.

The railway traffic between Leicester and Stamford has been suspended. The ballast has been washed away, and the sleepers are afloat for half a mile.

The embankment of the Great Eastern Railway, near Somersham, has given way, and the traffic to Wisbeach has been stopped. Rain in Northamptonshire still falls heavily, the river Nene continuing to rise rapidly. The fens are totally submerged, presenting the appearance of a vast lake.

Plate 14. Title page of the *Workman's Advocate*, 23 July 1875 (by permission of the British Library).

Part Two

MANAGEMENT AND MONEY

6

Joanne Shattock   Problems of parentage: the
North British Review and
the Free Church of
Scotland

The complex question of the control of a Victorian periodical – who guided
and shaped policy, who took the day-to-day decisions, who was responsible
for long-term strategy, who created the image it achieved in the eyes of the
public – is one which poses innumerable problems. The answers are, of
course, nearly as individualistic as the periodicals themselves. Certain specific questions we must inevitably ask. What was the role of the editor in
relation to the proprietor, and of the proprietor to the publisher, when these
were separate individuals? What influence, if any, was exercised by the
group of enthusiasts which almost always surrounded the foundation of a
periodical?

I have elsewhere suggested that the making of policy was a far more
haphazard process than the facts might suggest.[1] What I wish to explore in
this essay is a far less nebulous issue than that of policy. It is, crudely, that of
power.

Dominating editors have become part of the lore of the Victorian periodical press – men like Jeffrey, Lockhart, Delane, G. H. Lewes, J. D. Cook, John
Morley, and James T. Knowles. Almost as well known were the publishers
who frequently doubled as proprietors and occasionally as editors. One
thinks of William and John Blackwood, the Macmillan brothers, George
Smith, Alexander Strahan, John Chapman, and many others. Recent research has shown that conflict between proprietorial control and editorial
independence often became a feature of the life of nineteenth-century
newspapers, except in cases where the posts were occupied by the same
person.[2] It would be surprising if this conflict did not also arise in the conduct
of other periodicals.

But a further element complicated the picture when the impetus for the
establishment of a periodical was not a publishing house like Blackwood,
Bentley, Tinsley or Macmillan, or a loosely-linked group such as the Philosophical Radicals who founded the *Westminster Review*, or the Whiggish

iconoclasts who established the *Edinburgh*, but a recognized organization or institution which founded a periodical as its official organ, its badge of intellectual respectability, its public declaration of having a distinctive 'view' about things.

This essay is an attempt to examine the amount of freedom a given periodical had in the conduct of its affairs when it had such a sponsoring body. I have deliberately selected so-called 'religious periodicals' because it seems clear that it was in this area that the most tensions and problems arose. I am thinking, admittedly, of periodicals rather than newspapers, and of those periodicals, mainly the quarterlies, monthlies and weeklies, which served a highly literate and articulate section of the population. Apart from the *Westminster* and to a lesser extent the *Edinburgh* and the *Quarterly*, there were relatively few periodicals founded in support of a political party or ideology. In contrast there were hundreds of publications spawned by religious groups, from quarterlies like the *British Critic* (high church), the *Dublin Review* (Roman Catholic), the *Home and Foreign* (Liberal Catholic), the *British Quarterly* (Congregational), the *Church of England Quarterly*, the *Christian Remembrancer* (high church), the *Prospective* (Unitarian), and the *North British* (Free Church of Scotland), to monthlies like the *Methodist Magazine*, the *Evangelical Magazine*, and the *Eclectic Review* (dissenting, mainly Congregational), and to weeklies like the *Record* (low church), the *Tablet* (Roman Catholic), the *Guardian* (high church), and the *Rambler* (Liberal Catholic); and from there to the numerous productions of the missionary societies, Sunday school magazines and improving literature generally.

What did it mean, then, to be the official or semi-official organ of the Liberal Catholics, the high church party, the Unitarians or Congregationalists? It depended, of course, on the sort of publication concerned. Many, like the *Guardian*, the *Tablet* or the *Record*, were aggressive in their affiliation, and saw it as their rôle to make their allegiance clear. Others, I suggest, were far more nervous of their origins and quite anxious, given the chance, to shake them off. This was particularly true of publications like the *British Quarterly*, the *North British Review*, the *Prospective* and later the *National Review* – periodicals with ambitions of becoming organs of national standing. To these the term 'religious review' was a burden, a skin to be sloughed off, or more precisely, to be outgrown. A classic example of an earlier publication which had done just that was the *Monthly Repository*, a Unitarian organ which between 1828 and 1836, under the editorship of W. J. Fox, had shed its sectarian character and become a liberal journal of political and social reform.[3] I want now to examine the efforts of one mid-Victorian quarterly to loosen its links with its sponsoring body. A comparison at a later stage with the case of the *Repository* may prove instructive.

The *North British Review* was founded by the enthusiastic supporters of the Free Church of Scotland in 1844, a year after the famous Disruption which drew over one-third of Scottish clergymen out of the Established Church of Scotland, basically over the thorny issue of the Church's cherished spiritual independence – its freedom to call its own ministers and run its affairs independently of the state. This unlikely parentage initially worked to the advantage of the *North British*. The Disruption had engendered a great deal of nationalistic fervour. The *Edinburgh* had long ceased to be a truly Scottish publication, although it continued to be published in Edinburgh until 1847. Supporters of the Free Kirk rallied to what was in fact a quite unrealistic decision to found yet another quarterly for a multiplicity of reasons, of which theology was a relatively insignificant one.

The projectors of the new quarterly made the usual soothing noises regarding its origins. 'It will be distinctly understood from the outset that this is not in any proper sense a religious work',[4] one of them wrote to the first editor. According to its prospectus, the *North British* was a publication 'accommodated to the character of the times'; one which, without being a 'Theological journal' would take into account 'the strong religious feelings of the age'. 'In discussing religious subjects', it went on, 'there will be no attempt to advocate the distinguishing peculiarities of any sect'.[5] It had been brought into being, one of its later editors, William Garden Blaikie, recalled, because neither the *Edinburgh* nor the *Quarterly* had appeared satisfactory to a number of Edinburgh men, the former being too secular, the latter too conservative. They longed, according to Blaikie, 'for an organ of a high class that would be both liberal in politics and Christian in tone'. The projectors were mostly Free Churchmen, he admitted, but it was never designed to be a Free Church organ.[6]

The high command initially was drawn solidly from the ranks of the committed. The editor was David Welsh, the much respected Professor of Ecclesiastical History at Edinburgh, a quiet, scholarly, able man, moderate in his theological views and known to be an 'advanced Whig' in politics. He was also available for the job, having been deprived of his chair as a result of his adherence to the Free Church.[7] The review's proprietor was Charles Cowan, a paper manufacturer from Valleyfield, at this time a vociferous supporter of the Free Kirk and later a Member of Parliament with radical inclinations.[8] Cowan appeared to have provided the bulk of the funds for the initial venture, although other unnamed subscribers were mentioned, and from the beginning he took an active part in the running of the review. The publisher was William Pattison Kennedy, a small Edinburgh bookseller, and another staunch supporter of the Free Church. His connection with the review, which lasted until 1860, was at best an uneasy one, and in the end proved its undoing. The printer was Thomas Constable, the youngest son of Archibald, and his biographer, who was active in Edinburgh literary circles. Constable was a friend and adviser to more than one *North British* editor and his rôle in the running of the review was always far more than a merely technical one.

The initial circulation was encouraging. Nearly 4,000 copies of the first number were sold, not much below the circulation of the *Edinburgh,* and from the beginning it outsold the senior quarterly in Scotland. The number dropped to 3,000 by the end of the year, and Constable's ledgers showed 2,000 to be the normal printing in 1846.[9]

Politically the review was Whig, the party favoured by the Free Church. It had a strong interest in social issues as befitted the evangelical leaning of the founders, and on both social and economic issues its emphasis was decidedly Scottish. The majority of the early reviewers were Scotsmen but by no means Free Churchmen. The Parliament House was the greatest single source of reviewers, and many young advocates proved themselves extremely able literary critics. As a result the *North British* established itself as a leading critical organ from the beginning.

'It is a Free Church review', Lord Cockburn observed crisply at the outset. 'They don't say so in their preface, but rather say the reverse. . . . This may be true in the direct sense, but indirectly the general impression of the work will be against the church.'[10] Certainly a glance at the theology department – the section of the review which dealt with church history, biblical literature, theology proper, and contemporary religious issues – made the review's origins uncomfortably apparent. It devoted only 16 per cent of the total space to these subjects, compared with the 18 per cent devoted to literature and 15 per cent to political subjects, but this was nearly twice the space allotted by the *Edinburgh* (9 per cent) and two and a half times the amount given by the *Quarterly* (6 per cent). It was here that senior Free Churchmen felt able, indeed sought the opportunity to present reviews of current theological works or articles on recent controversies. It would have been a very independent editor indeed who could have refused articles by Thomas Chalmers, the 'Father of the Disruption', his heir apparent, Robert Smith Candlish, and William Cunningham, the principal orator of the Free Church and its major pamphleteer, described by a contemporary as the ablest defender of Calvinism of his time,[11] as well as a host of minor worthies. The topics and attitudes were predictable – anti-establishment, whether Edinburgh, Canterbury or Rome; anti-Tractarian ('semi-papists' as one reviewer referred to them), and, of course, anti-Roman Catholic. The Oxford movement and Newman's conversion followed by the so-called Papal Aggression worked the clerical reviewers up to fever pitch. Other perennial evangelical themes were given an airing – Sabbath observance, baptismal regeneration, and, of course, the infallibility of scripture. The 'menace' of German biblical criticism was not so much challenged and met as dismissed with lofty superiority.

Apart from what could only be described as a lack of decorum in the theology section, the first editor and his colleagues were faced with pressures from outside, from supporters who were anxious that the *North British* position on certain key issues should be made clear and unmistakable. One reader from Dublin wrote to Dr Chalmers requesting that the review's position on support for the Queen's Colleges be made clear as the *North British* 'is generally regarded as an organ of the Free Church'.[12] Another correspondent objected to a political article because it was 'not sufficiently high toned as to Popery in Ireland'.[13] Another reader was critical of an article which he claimed had hinted that politics had nothing to do with religion, and declared that he could not promote the circulation of the review until he could be assured that 'the public will be guaranteed against similar papers in future'.[14] Several authors of theological works wrote to Chalmers and others requesting that they be noticed in 'the Free Church Review'.

For the projectors it was basically a problem of careful navigation, of steering a moderate course. On the one hand the *North British* could ill afford to offend its founders, still at this point the hand that fed it. On the other, if it were ever to achieve a reputation outside this immediate circle it had to indicate independence of thought. Equally burdensome, in its way, was the Scottishness of the review, a factor which initially had worked in its favour. 'Reputation' and 'influence' for a quarterly meant *national* reputation. The bulk of sales of the early numbers had virtually been confined to Scotland. It became a major policy to expand sales outside the country, and firms in London and Dublin were appointed to handle English and Irish sales. A circular, put out by Cowan in 1845, expressed the desire of the conductors to 'make their periodical more generally known in England and elsewhere'.[15]

The finances of the review in these early years were precarious. Circulation wavered between 2,000 and 1,650, stabilizing at the latter figure by 1849 – respectable enough, but not sufficient to make the future financially secure.[16] But despite these worries and in spite of the occasional wrangle with the Free Church the *North British*, in terms of content, flourished. Much of this was due to the editors. Welsh died in 1845, having seen five numbers through the press. He was succeeded by Edward Francis Maitland, a young advocate with literary inclinations, whose position outside the Church made it easier to pursue a non-sectarian policy. (Even Chalmers was called to heel and asked to remove a passage in an article which could have been construed as an opinion on the question of church endowment.) Health and professional obligations forced Maitland to relinquish the post after a year and a half to William Hanna, a clergyman of literary tastes and liberal principles who was also Chalmers' son-in-law.

Both Maitland and Hanna pursued a deliberate policy of expansion, using the name of Chalmers to attract subscribers, and with the added revenue, buying in more eminent reviewers who, it was hoped, would in turn widen the review's appeal. De Quincey, who was by then living near Edinburgh, Coventry Patmore, who was supplementing his British Museum salary by copious reviewing, John William Kaye, John Hill Burton, David Masson, who had left Edinburgh to become a professional reviewer in London, John Kitto, John Robertson, who had been Mill's sub-editor on the *London and Westminster*, Thomas Adolphus Trollope and several others became regular contributors. Together they represented a reasonable cross-section of the professional reviewers of the day and they effectively diluted both the Scottish and Free Church predominance of the early numbers. The *North British* had begun to move into the mainstream of periodicals and away from its sectarian origins and parochial roots.

The financial situation remained the most worrying feature of the conduct of the review. The quarterly was in debt, and Cowan and the other sub-scribers were anxious to recover their original investments. Constable was approached to become a proprietor but could not raise sufficient capital. In the end a joint proprietorship was established, comprising Cowan, Kennedy, Constable, and Hanna. Attempts had been made to offer Hanna a salary – 'the visionary two hundred' as Mrs Hanna referred to it – but towards the end of his tenure he was editing the review without remuneration, and more than one reviewer was submitting articles without payment. Early in 1847 Mrs Hanna commented to a friend that she hoped the review 'will not die a natural death at the end of the year'.[17]

Chalmers, however, died in 1847, and Hanna was entrusted with editing his memoirs and a collected edition of his works. By the end of 1848 he was anxious to relinquish the editorship in order to devote himself to the work full-time. Isaac Taylor of Stanford Rivers, an evangelical particularly popu-lar with the Free Church because of his open support for the Disruption in 1843, was approached as a possible successor but refused. The winding up of the review was proposed as an alternative, but Kennedy in particular was unwilling to abandon the venture. In February of 1850, when the financial situation looked particularly bleak he suddenly announced that he could not go on. Hanna gratefully resigned, and just as abruptly Kennedy changed his mind,[18] and a group of supporters, including Cunningham, Candlish, Mait-land and several others, all Free Churchmen, met in Kennedy's rooms to offer the editorship to Alexander Campbell Fraser, the young Professor of Logic and Metaphysics at New College.

Like his predecessor, Fraser was a member of the Free Church, but his allegiance was as much a matter of family loyalty as personal conviction, and he was also of a younger generation, one which had not been directly involved in the events of 1843. He was academically rather than theologically inclined, able, and had definite ideas about the direction in which he wished to lead the *North British*. It was, he confided to his journal, 'a medium of communion between the Christian church and Modern Society and Philosophy and Literature'. It should 'meet the wants of the earnest, thoughtful, accomplished Christian gentleman and provide for him aids to reflection' – sentiments which would have earned him full marks from the Free Church. But he went further. The *North British* was to advance from among the ranks of 'religious reviews' into the ranks of the leading periodicals, to have 'the place and influence of the National Review of Scotland', and as such was to rival the *Edinburgh* and the *Quarterly* as an organ of public opinion.[19]

The basic requisites of the review as Fraser saw them were 'a more definite aim and function' and a reinforcement of 'fresh blood', of 'rising young men whose credit and reputation might be staked on their productions'.[20] The alleged aimlessness of the *North British* had long been the subject of discussion. The problem might be mitigated somewhat by striving for a more definite aim and character in each number, he thought, but a more pressing problem was the need for new reviewers, and more precisely, English reviewers. These he systematically set about to court. He visited J. C. Hare and F. D. Maurice and offered the pages of the *North British* to the Christian Socialists. J. M. Ludlow and Charles Kingsley became contributors, as did some of the more peripheral adherents of the movement. Fraser secured the support of English churchmen including Archibald Campbell Tait, then dean of Carlisle and later bishop of London and archbishop of Canterbury; William Thomson, then a fellow of Queen's College, Oxford, and later archbishop of York; Richard Whately, archbishop of Dublin; Arthur Penrhyn Stanley of University College, later dean of Westminster; G. E. L. Cotton, then Master of Marlborough College, later bishop of Calcutta. Perhaps most important of all he enlisted John Tulloch, principal and Professor of Theology at St Mary's College, St Andrew's, a theologian of known liberal views and all the more impressive as an acquisition because he belonged to the Established Church of Scotland. Isaac Taylor, having declined the editorship, agreed to become a contributor, a particularly valuable addition as he was considered to possess the necessary detachment for reviewing Scottish theological topics. It was to be hoped that Taylor, Tait, Tulloch and their colleagues would be able to dilute the aggressive evangelicalism of Cunningham, Candlish and their adherents.

It was not only the review's theology section that Fraser set out to widen. Top-ranking professional reviewers like W. R. Greg, E. S. Dallas, Bonamy Price, Abraham Hayward, the young historian E. A. Freeman, Herbert Spencer, and Nassau Senior were secured, as well as Scotsmen like J. C. Shairp and John Stuart Blackie. David Masson, an old friend from Edinburgh University days, proved particularly helpful as both an advisor and contributor.

Fraser's youth and inexperience, together with his rather retiring nature, did not mark him at once as destined for a great editorial career. He grew into the job surprisingly quickly. He was careful not to let his image appear too aggressively that of the new broom. He turned to the review's old friends and contributors as well but took Dr Hanna's advice in not committing himself too readily to any long-standing engagements. His inclination was to establish a formal staff of reviewers, 'an organized band of ten or larger', a 'corps of North British reviewers'[21], as he variously described them, who would meet in the publisher's rooms to thrash out policy, fostering a spirit of unity similar to the early days of the *Edinburgh*. Masson in particular was sceptical of the idea. Fraser did make some attempts to allocate subjects to individuals but the sheer abundance of offerings which resulted from his widespread invitations soon made the scheme impossible. This embarrassment of riches was nevertheless a healthy sign. The new blood was having the desired effect.

One positive indication of the coming of age of the *North British*, and one from which Fraser could derive some satisfaction, was the number of reviewers it shared with the *Edinburgh*. Greg, Senior, Hayward, Tait, Price, Spencer, Freeman, the duke of Argyll and John Hill Burton contributed to both quarterlies, although not always in equal proportions. Greg, as he confessed, reserved the 'cream' of his productions for the *North British*, in the form of political articles, while those in the *Edinburgh* were more general – reviews of history, biographies and the occasional novel.[22] With Hayward and Senior the proportions were reversed. Nevertheless, the fact that a church-affiliated quarterly could command so many professionals was proof that Fraser's efforts had borne fruit, and that the image of a 'religious review' was gradually being dispelled.

Financial troubles continued to dog the review, and actual circulation had declined since Hanna's day. Kennedy's business book recorded 1,650 copies printed up to February 1850 with less than that number, usually 1,550, prepared for binding. The figure then dropped to a constant 1,500 up to the

February 1852 issue, with 1,450 being the usual number of copies bound. The exact sale at this time was probably somewhat less. Fraser based all his calculations in 1850 on an average circulation of 1,340, broken down into 560 copies in England, 740 in Scotland and 40 in Ireland. May 1852 marked the beginning of an upswing, with 1,600 copies printed. The number fluctuated between 1,500 and 1,750 through to the end of 1855. During 1856 there was a tailing off, with between 1,500 and 1,560 copies printed, down to Fraser's last issue in February 1857.[23]

The February 1854 issue marked an important step forward with the inauguration of a system of simultaneous publication in America. The only relevant figures given by Kennedy were those for 1854 which indicated that between 63 and 70 copies of each issue circulated across the Atlantic. The number was not large, but judging by the enthusiastic response Fraser had from American readers the issues managed to reach major literary circles in the East.

Records of English sales, when available, showed that between 650 and 725 copies of each issue were distributed in England during Fraser's editorship. The increase is proportional to the overall increase in circulation. Fraser noted in 1850 that the English copies were taken more by clubs and libraries than individuals. There was no way of discerning the composition of the new English public, but it was clear from correspondence and general comment that the impact which the *North British* made south of the Border under Fraser was of far greater proportions even than indicated by the increase in sales.

Certainly a concentrated effort was made to bring the review to the attention of a larger audience in England, mainly by using the new English contributors. E. A. Freeman offered to publicize the review in the *Guardian* and *Morning Chronicle*, with whom he had connections.[24] J. W. Kaye boosted early numbers with notices in the *Morning Herald*. Kingsley offered to approach the *Spectator, Fraser's* and the *Leader* and assured Fraser that his friends W. E. Forster and the Macmillans would be glad to spread notice of the review in the North and at Cambridge respectively on the strength of his articles.[25] Nassau Senior went to great pains to puff one of his articles by writing to the editors of *The Times*, the *Examiner* and the *Globe*, with the comment: 'That review is so little known in England that any notice of yours wd. do it great good'.[26] This, coming in 1855, can hardly have boosted Fraser's morale. Masson had been annoyed at Fraser's frequent requests for notices in the weeklies, insisting that it was better to ensure that individual copies reached the 'right quarters'. He did arrange for a copy of one of his own articles to be sent to Carlyle and suggested that an issue of the *North British* be sent to the offices of the *Leader*, where it might 'get at a number of the out-of-the-way thinking rascals in England'.[27]

Greg proved the most useful link with government and influential circles. He claimed no openings to the London papers with the exception of the *Examiner* and the *Economist*, but willingly directed copies of the review to Gladstone, Disraeli, Russell, Edwin Chadwick, Palmerston, Sir Arthur Helps, Cobden, the marquis of Lansdowne, the duke of Newcastle, Lord Clarendon. Abraham Hayward likewise sent copies of an article to Robert Lowe, Earl Stanhope, and the marquis of Lansdowne among others, and quoted the favourable opinions of Lord Raglan and the (second) duke of Wellington on an article he had written on the Crimean War. No one could claim that Fraser had not used his new reviewers to the most advantage.

The first reports were encouraging. Greg claimed to have heard the review spoken of with much enthusiasm in many quarters where it had previously been unknown. At the same time, in 1851, William Thomson observed that the *North British* was obviously acquiring influence in Oxford as he had heard its praises from many different sources. The following year, Isaac Taylor assured Fraser that the review was seen and read 'to a considerable extent' in England and particularly in Cambridge 'by the thinking and reading men'.[28] Most of the uncertainty appears to have been dispelled by 1853. Fraser reported to Tulloch in January that the latest number was making a great stir, far more so than any of its predecessors, a fact which was borne out by Kaye, who claimed several weeks later to have heard the same number spoken of highly in influencial circles. As late as 1856 Hayward commented generally that the review had a very high reputation wherever it was known.

The relatively small increase in English sales was obviously not a fair indication of the quite remarkable growth in its reputation south of the Border. But apart from sales and circulation and the encouraging comments of friends, Fraser was anxious to measure the *North British* against its more senior rivals. After the second number Greg declared that in 'sterling ability and interest' it ranked next to the *Edinburgh* and *Quarterly* and perhaps above either in the 'sustained value and attractiveness of the articles as a whole'.[29] The review, in other words, had so far managed to avoid the weaknesses of the other two without quite rising to their heights. Kaye loyally maintained that there was more heart in the *North British* than in all the other quarterlies put together and reported that his publisher had assured him it was more influential in Scotland than the *Edinburgh*, a fact which of course Fraser already knew.[30] According to John Cairns, another old university friend, by 1851 the *North British* had nothing to fear from a comparison with the *British Quarterly*,[31] and the following year Masson insisted that the *Westminster* could not compete with the *North British*, not even in 'what the *Westminster* vaunts most – freedom and thought'.[32] For subject matter, Freeman in 1853 placed it 'a good deal above the *Quarterly* and treading closely on the heels of the *Edinburgh*',[33] and when William Whewell, the eminent Master of Trinity, was secured as a contributor the same year Masson wrote jubilantly that they would 'beat the *Edinburgh* out of the throne, I hope, yet'.[34] The *Edinburgh*, according to Bonamy Price in 1854, was 'getting fit for Dowagers', and he found himself turning with renewed interest to the *North British*. Dr John Anster, an Irish contributor from the days of Hanna, in the same year declared the review unquestionably better than any other, adding that 'nothing could be duller than both the last *Edinburgh* and *Westminster*',[36] all of which was music to Fraser's ears. The *North British* was too good, according to Hayward, for its circulation and 'notoriety' in 1856, but as he shrewdly observed, people 'no longer dashed at [the quarterlies] as they used to do'. It was no easy matter to make a sensation now.[37]

The general problem of parochialism as Fraser had seen it at the beginning of his editorship had virtually been eradicated. The *North British* under his editorship had become better known, more widely read and more influential than ever before. As a result of the new contributors, the quality of articles, particularly on political, social, and literary subjects, continued to rise. The *North British* was no longer regarded as merely a Scottish review.

But the incubus of the Free Kirk remained, and if anything it had become more intractable. Lord Cockburn, writing approvingly of the Disruption in his Journal in 1843, commented shrewdly that the new position of the Free Church would cure all the defects of the evangelicals 'except fanaticism, which it will probably increase'.[38] W. G. Blaikie warned Fraser when he took over that 'a decidedly narrower spirit was now guiding the councils of the church than in the days of Chalmers and Welsh'.[39] An independent and even mildly liberal theological policy was clearly less possible in 1850 than it might have been in 1844.

Fraser was determined to try. He confessed to John Cairns that there would be difficulty in keeping 'the free and essentially literary or at least non-theological character' of the review intact.[40] Less sanguine observers might have wondered if the *North British* indeed possessed a non-theological character which had to be protected. Certainly Fraser's advisers underlined the importance of shedding its theological bias if it were to increase its English public. 'The Tweed is a water at least as wide as the Atlantic'[41] when it came to theology, Isaac Taylor warned him. English readers could not be expected to stomach the *North British*'s existing brand of Scottish evangelicalism. 'English tendencies in literature, as well as in other things are national rather than Catholic',[42] another old friend, who was also a Church of England vicar, wrote to him diplomatically. It was 'almost self-evident that the English will take no interest in Scotch polemics civil or ecclesiastical, sufficient to support or encourage a review', Abraham Hayward reiterated.[43]

In the first few months of Fraser's editorship the Free Kirk made what was virtually a bid for control, offering to promote the sale of the review by an official recommendation 'to the Christian public of Scotland', provided that 'a more explicit account of the design and aim of the review' was given than that contained in Welsh's prospectus. This had of course stated categorically that in discussing religious subjects there would be no attempt to advocate 'the distinguishing peculiarities of any sect'. What presumably was required was some sort of indication that the *North British* was the official Free Church review. This Fraser emphatically rejected, and angrily expressed his deprecation of any such step which would modify the 'original character' of the review or attempt to curb his freedom in the management of it.[44] These were bold words in 1850.

For the first few years he was reasonably successful at keeping the Free Church at bay. For a start the total number of articles on theological subjects was substantially reduced, so that for once social, political, and literary articles each outnumbered those on religious subjects. The sectarian label seemed to have been erased in the minds of most of the review's readers and contributors. George Combe referred sarcastically to a review by the duke of Argyll in 1852 as 'the words of a religious Review'[45] but he seems to have had few sympathizers. George Lillie Craik, whom Fraser recruited in 1853, assured him that the *North British* was no longer regarded 'as a merely sectarian organ but as a first class work of its kind'.[46] The Rev. John Eadie, one of the Free Church theological contributors, known for his stolid articles on biblical exegesis of a somewhat outdated mode promised to keep in mind that 'the N.B. review is non-theological',[47] a promise which unfortunately he appeared never quite to have been able to keep. E. A. Freeman significantly compared the *North British* with the *Christian Remembrancer* which, although it contained some able articles, threw 'too much of a theological shadow over the whole thing',[48] whereas the *North British* presented no hindrance to people of other communions from being both readers and contributors.

In the theological section itself Fraser's efforts at dilution gradually made some headway, but it was uphill work. Dr Cunningham, now Principal Cunningham, of New College, still insisted on rehearsing the argument for the separation of Church and State, virtually a dead issue. The Church of Rome, 'Satan's great scheme for frustrating the leading objects of the Christian revelation', papal aggression, 'a gratuitous and wanton insult to the British sovereign', and 'the gibbering of this medieval ghost called

Puseyism' were still favourite themes, hardly encouraging to Fraser's scheme for a more detached and philosophical approach to theology.

But his new reviewers provided intellectual muscle. Bonamy Price, in an article on reform of the liturgy in the Church of England (August 1852) was highly critical of the evangelicals for not using scripture to support their arguments regarding infant baptism. The neglect of a scientific and accurate exegesis of scripture was the weakness of modern evangelicals, a point which drew protests from Free Church readers and praise from English readers. An article by G. E. L. Cotton (February 1854) took up the theme of the dearth of high quality biblical exegesis on either side of the Tweed but particularly north of the Border. English and Scottish critics could not afford to remain ignorant of the work which was being done on the Continent. It was a duty 'to welcome every help which we can procure towards the interpretation of His Word, and while we lament the evils which pollute the present theological movement in Germany, to regret still more the sluggish apathy into which we ourselves have fallen'. Cotton expressed the hope that the work of Stanley and Jowett would initiate a school of criticism 'at once intelligent and reverential, searching, earnest and believing; uniting the research of Germany with the practical good sense and devout Christianity of England'.

This was hardly a point of view likely to find favour with the founders of the Free Kirk. The work of two other reviewers helped to compound their dissatisfaction with the 'new look' of the North British. John Tulloch took on a review of Bunsen's Hippolytus (May 1853), and warned Fraser that he wanted to compare Bunsen's historical method with the German 'Middle' school of criticism in order to vindicate the superiority of the former, and to show that Bunsen and his school were on the road to truth. He admitted that this might be too free a point of view for the North British and said he would quite understand if Fraser found a more 'competent' reviewer.[49] Fraser demurred either in finding another reviewer or in making any changes in the article despite frequent invitations from the author. The article was duly published, suggesting as Tulloch had warned that the 'animating principle' of the German movement was that of reaching Christian truth.

The article was highly technical, to a degree which must have defeated all but the specialist. Most readers must either have lacked the stamina to plod through the detailed discussion to reach Tulloch's more startling observations, or have been placated by his apparently orthodox conclusions, for the article produced not a ripple of comment either from Fraser's correspondents or the press.

Tulloch in the meantime was at work on an article to be called 'British New Testament Criticism' (May 1856), which was to embrace the unlikely combination of Stanley, Jowett and Dr Eadie. Tulloch confessed that he was having difficulty over Jowett, with whom he entirely sympathized, realizing that his statements would sound unorthodox to a great many people. He confessed himself at a loss, too, on how to include Dr Eadie as there was nothing complimentary he could say about him. Any impression that his work constituted an advance in criticism was scarcely borne out by inspection, and while it was thoroughly learned it had none of the undogmatic tone which he admired so much in the other two writers. The article was submitted, based on an examination of Jowett and Stanley only. Fraser accepted it but after reading the proofs and also Jowett's book, he told Tulloch he felt it went too far to commit the *North British* to the theology of the new Oxford school and in his words 'would seriously modify the independent place we have tried to keep'. He proposed that the latter portion of the article be omitted, and that a final paragraph be inserted maintaining that, as the *North British* differed from many of the conclusions of Stanley and Jowett, it reserved the right of expressing the grounds of this difference on a future occasion. He added that he had a paper in prospect which did just that, and that he would be hampered 'if the free position of the N.B. was not guarded'. The 'free position' of the *North British*, it now seemed, could only be maintained by having no views at all.[50] Tulloch's article was printed in its emasculated form with a final apologetic paragraph together with a consideration of Dr Eadie. 'We recommend them [particular remarks of Stanley] to the attention of our readers, as indeed the whole work, which is always interesting and instructive, even when its views are such as do not entirely meet our assent' (May 1856).

It was a lame conclusion for an editor who six years previously had vowed to maintain his independence of the Free Church at all costs. But Fraser's cold feet were perhaps more understandable in view of his academic position at New College. As the fiery issue of the Disruption faded from memory more students drifted back to Edinburgh University. In subjects like logic and metaphysics the college now appeared to be simply duplicating courses at the university. Attendance at Fraser's classes dwindled, and there was pressure to abolish the post. His journal at the beginning of 1856 recorded that numbers were down to twenty and that his position at the college remained doubtful and 'if possible more unpleasant'.[51]

A possible solution appeared in the spring of 1856 with the death of Sir William Hamilton, who held the chair at Edinburgh. Fraser was a strong candidate for the post, along with James Frederick Ferrier, a known Hegelian who was popularly believed to be of the Continental rather than the Scottish school of philosophy, and several others. The full resources of the *North British* and the Hamiltonian school of philosophy were brought to bear in the general fray. Fraser unabashedly solicited testimonials from all of his emi-

nent contributors, many of whom found themselves profoundly embarrassed by the request. A fairly savage pamphlet war was also waged, some of it in
the pages of the *North British*.[52] The result was a victory for Scottish
philosophy and Fraser was elected to Hamilton's chair in July 1856. This in
effect released one of the holds of the Free Church upon him.

In the meantime the domestic affairs of the review were not happy. This
for the most part was owing to Kennedy. Like other members of the Free
Church he was nervous of some of Fraser's new recruits, men like Greg and
Herbert Spencer, with dubious theological leanings. He was also made
uneasy by the fact that he was now dealing with professional English
reviewers rather than old Edinburgh acquaintances and associates. He caused
a great deal of irritation by the high correction charges he levied, and this was
not the only evidence of his parsimony. The rate of payment for articles was
low, an average of £10 per sheet, which compared badly with the rates of the
Edinburgh and *Quarterly*, who offered between £20 and £25, although it was
not as low as the notorious *Westminster* and compared favourably with
reviews like the *Christian Remembrancer*. The rate operated on a sliding
scale, decided upon by Kennedy, so that Greg, Senior, Hayward and their
colleagues received a higher rate of £15 or £16, while little-known clergymen
had to be content with £8 or less.[53]

A new source of friction between Kennedy and the contributors arose over
the permission to republish articles from the review. This was one of the
perquisites of professional reviewing, the prospect of a collection of essays at
fairly short intervals after their publication in periodicals. Kennedy was
reluctant to consent to republication on the grounds that it threatened the
sale of back numbers on which he claimed to recoup the losses he made on
virtually every number. In fact his intransigence was caused more by
resentment that many of these arrangements were made between Fraser and
the contributor without consultation with him. But, as with the rates of
payment, there appeared to be two classes of contributors. He willingly
allowed Greg, Senior and Freeman to republish articles from the *North
British* in various collections, but alleged that Kingsley had illegally reprinted his *North British* contributions in his 1856 *Miscellanies*. He also dug
his heels in with Isaac Taylor and several more minor contributors. The
show-down came with Masson when after furious exchanges of letters
Kennedy prevented him from republishing an article on Ben Jonson in his
Essays Biographical and Critical (1856). The refusal, which Masson claimed
was a denial of the rights of contributors, was even more galling when he
learned that his standard fee of £12 per sheet was substantially lower than
that of many other contributors.

Kennedy had won that particular round, but the incident served to widen the breach with Fraser. For more than a year there had been a general feeling among contributors, as one of them expressed it, that until the *North British* got a more liberal and spirited proprietor it would not attain the position it deserved.[54] A concerted effort had been made in 1855 to attract a new publisher. Fraser noted in his journal that the review was 'on the eve of a new and more prosperous epoch'.[55] Smith, Elder expressed interest but later withdrew. Thomas Constable was approached to take over as publisher. After negotiations had dragged on for nearly a year Kennedy suddenly announced that he refused to part with the property of the review and the matter was abruptly closed. He had done just this before, of course, in 1850.

Fraser by this time had his chair at Edinburgh. His patience was wearing thin, his academic responsibilities increasing, and the review was beginning to occupy a less central position in his career. He had already allocated the day-to-day running of it to a sub-editor, and he no longer felt obliged either to toady to Kennedy's whims or to placate the Church. Having erred absurdly on the side of caution regarding Tulloch's article, in May of 1856, he now swung dramatically the other way.

In 1852, when Fraser solicited a review of the Chalmers *Memoirs* from Isaac Taylor, Taylor also agreed to undertake a review of the complete works at a later date. Early in 1856 Taylor expressed his readiness to do so, but before proceeding made careful inquiries from Fraser as to whether the readers of the *North British*, the proprietor, or 'the Family' expected an encomiastic article 'setting Dr. Chalmers upon the highest place as philosopher-writer-theologian?'[56] This, he insisted, after a careful consideration of the works, he was not prepared to do. (His first article, in May 1852, had praised Chalmers as a man and as a leader, but had been cautious in its comments on his writings.) As with his former article, Fraser gave him *carte blanche*, assuring him that his own impressions as well as those of Dr Hanna coincided with Taylor's general estimate of Chalmers as a writer. It was almost as if Fraser were deliberately offering a challenge to the Free Church. Even Taylor had cold feet momentarily before publication and insisted that if he had known as much about Chalmers' works four years ago as he knew then he would have asked to be excused from the task of reviewing them.[57]

His opening remarks (November 1856) were deliberately iconoclastic. Chalmers' reputation as a Churchman and Christian leader could never be matched by his reputation as a writer. His works would undergo a sifting through the years and a relatively small proportion of them would survive. He was a popularizer, a man of action, not an analytic or original thinker. He was 'the man to give a healthful impulse to all things around him, but he was not the man to give them altogether a new direction'. Taylor of course was proved correct, and many would have concurred with his assessment even in 1856, but to the majority of Free Churchmen this was undoubtedly sacrilege.

It was not this section of the article, however, which caused the real *furore*. In discussing the major works in turn Taylor made two points which electrified his orthodox readers. The first was the suggestion that Chalmers had not adhered completely and unquestioningly to the canons of Scottish Christianity, that he was implicitly critical of parts of the Westminster Confession and the Larger Catechism, even if he had never directly expressed dissent. If this were not enough Taylor plunged into a discussion of the need for a consistent doctrine of inspiration, one which would allow scope for the freest methods of historical criticism. Chalmers' doctrine of inspiration was 'crude, inadmissible, unintelligible'. With one blow Taylor had struck at two of the most sacrosanct canons of Scottish evangelicalism – the Westminster Confession and the doctrine of the infallibility of scripture.

The impact of the article was undoubtedly greater than either he or Fraser could have imagined. The evangelical press took up the challenge, seething with indignation, and attack was followed by counter-attack. The unfavourable publicity was brought to a climax by Cunningham, who devoted his annual address to the students of New College to a denunciation of the article which he declared 'erroneous and impious' in spirit and tendency and in its views a threat to the faith of every student in the college. Guided by 'a sense of duty . . . to the memory of Dr. Chalmers, and by a sense of what is due to the interests of truth', he launched into a point-by-point refutation of the article and issued a formal warning to the students against being influenced by anything it said.[58]

Fraser by this time had had enough. With this official condemnation by the Free Church the delicate balance which he had tried to preserve within the *North British* was destroyed, and the review as he had conceived of it was no longer in existence. Kennedy, coming out in support of the Church, publicly insinuated that Fraser had departed from the original prospectus. The rupture was then complete.

It was, as Bonamy Price told Fraser, 'a going back in any direction but the right one'[59] and, as John Cairns commented, it was particularly unfortunate that the review should have been wrecked on a 'theological quicksand'.[60] Patrick Fraser, another reviewer loyal to Fraser, commented that neither Fraser nor his predecessors had ever given anything to the Free Kirk, the main factor which had kept the *North British* from ever being called a denominational review.[61] It would be a pity, Freeman wrote to Fraser, if a review which had 'held so high a character' were to sink 'into a mere sectarian organ',[62] a sentiment which was echoed generally among the ranks of its reviewers and supporters.

It was difficult to judge the extent of support for Cunningham and Kennedy. Certainly the hard core of church leaders and the Free Church press had regarded Taylor's article as a direct challenge. Even moderates like Blaikie felt that the review over the years had contained 'a number of almost wanton provocations of the orthodox'[63] and hinted, albeit kindly, that Fraser had brought the catastrophe upon his own head.

Nevertheless most of Fraser's contributors were vociferously on his side. A nucleus of support, centred on Constable, Hanna and Cairns, formed in Edinburgh, and Masson, Hayward, Greg, Freeman, Price and Kaye among others offered sympathy and moral support from a distance. Cairns wanted a public statement, denying Kennedy's accusation of a departure from the prospectus and offering a testimonial to Fraser's editorship. Others felt an official declaration of their reasons for withdrawing from the review was essential. Fraser himself was determined to refrain from any kind of public announcement.

Isaac Taylor, conscience-stricken by the repercussions of his article, suggested that subscribers might be privately circulated to inform them that the author of the offensive article 'had distilled [his] last poison in the pages of the review' and that there would be no more such 'dangerous doctrine' in the *North British*. He offered to qualify anything he had said which might have been interpreted as a reflection on Chalmers' personal merits or reputation, and made a further suggestion that the article might be reprinted with a few pages of explanation, which while not a retraction, would offer certain assurances as regards his attitude to the main tenets of the evangelical faith and 'state a little further what [he] felt was desirable and likely to come about in Biblical interpretation'.[64] All of this Fraser refused to countenance.

Meanwhile rumours as to the future of the review were rife. The May 1857 number, inexplicably, did not appear. Masson, in London, heard that he was to be the new editor. Several supporters in Edinburgh proposed the establishment of a *New North British* with Constable as publisher and Fraser as editor. Support for this venture was alleged to be widespread, but after some deliberation Fraser declined to assume the editorship on the grounds of his academic commitments. John Tulloch was then proposed as his successor.

Once again Kennedy refused to part with the review, despite the generous terms offered by Constable,[65] and began to solicit articles himself from the regular contributors. Further friction occurred when Kennedy then demanded that Fraser turn over all manuscripts currently in his possession, forcing Fraser to place them in the hands of a solicitor.

Despite the efforts of what Isaac Taylor referred to as the 'liberal few',[66] the proposed *New North British* did not materialize. Lack of funds, Fraser's withdrawal, and Kennedy's refusal to sell the original property, were contributing factors. Few of the promoters actually regretted the outcome, for most felt eventually that a counter-review would merely aggravate the mood of extremism and intolerance already prevalent. The happiest outcome, as Cairns reflected, would have been for the existing review to have died of inanition and a new one established on the original grounds and with a sympathetic staff, 'avoiding all just ground of offence but compromising no assertion of liberal sympathies and principles'.[67] But this, due to the intractability of Kennedy and the Church, was impossible.

In what became simply a power struggle the editor was the loser in the dispute and the sponsoring body the clear victor. The Free Church remained an albatross around the necks of successive editors and effectively prevented the *North British* from ever returning to the heights it achieved in the 1850s under Fraser. His confidence that a so-called 'religious review' could shake off its affiliations proved unfounded. The *North British* passed first into the hands of the Rev. John Duns, a Free Churchman who was very much under Kennedy's influence, and in 1860, to W. G. Blaikie, who, although a more enlightened Churchman, kept it very much within the fold. In 1863 Kennedy finally sold it to David Douglas, a small Edinburgh publisher, who turned it into a kind of coterie magazine, centred around a small group of Edinburgh *literati*. In 1869 it became the organ of the Liberal Catholics until its demise in 1871. Its gradual decline in its later years had as much to do with the decline of the quarterlies generally as it had with the quality of its editors and proprietors.

But the role played by the Free Church in the 1840s and 1850s has important implications for the study of Victorian periodicals. And here a comparison with W. J. Fox and the transformation of the *Monthly Repository* is relevant. When Fox took over as editor of the *Repository* in 1828 the magazine was owned by the British and Foreign Unitarian Association and was its official organ. While he was the single responsible editor under these terms, he made no appreciable changes in the magazine. It was only when he purchased it outright from the Unitarian Association that he divested it of its theological character and transformed it into a liberal journal of social and political significance. Fox took care to announce his proprietorship openly, more openly than was usual during the 1830s, ostensibly to free the Unitarian Association from responsibility. The real reason for this openness, it has been suggested, was publicly to release the magazine from its sectarian origins, to make a clean break, and to untie his hands.[68] The comparison of the *Monthly Repository* under Fox and the *North British* under Fraser, in other words, is not a valid one. Fox took a step which was not open to Fraser, that of outright purchase.

Simplistically it could be argued from both cases that the power ultimately resided in the hands of the proprietor rather than the editor, and that when the proprietor's views were synonymous with those of the sponsoring body, any attempt at editorial independence would be likely to fail. But Kennedy was not a powerful proprietor in the same way that the Unitarian Association was. He held the purse strings, and he supported the Free Church position unwaveringly, but the real power lay with the Church, who was the *de facto* proprietor. Kennedy's role in the *North British* débâcle was that of a constant irritant whose intransigence and incompetence coincided with larger issues and helped to bring about Fraser's fall.

A similar study of the publishing history of periodicals like the *British Quarterly*, with its Congregationalist support, and the *National Review*, founded in 1855 with Unitarian links, would undoubtedly produce equally complex tissues of connection between editor, proprietor and the founding fathers. What is clear is that in any study we must take very seriously the fact that a quarterly or monthly or weekly was the protégé of the Congregationalists, the Baptists, or the high church party. Founding fathers, it would seem, were rarely content with a fond blessing, and a gradual loosening of parental ties. To ignore the sponsor is to ignore a vital ingredient in the chemistry of a periodical.

NOTES

1. 'Editorial policy and the quarterlies: the case of the *North British Review*', *VPN*, x (Sept. 1977), 130–9.

2. See George Boyce, James Curran and Pauline Wingate (eds.), *Newspaper History: from the 17th Century to the Present Day* (1978), especially Ivon Asquith, 'The structure, ownership and control of the press, 1780–1855', 98–116; Alan Lee, 'The structure, ownership and control of the press, 1855–1914', 117–29; Philip Elliott, 'Professional ideology and organizational change: the journalist since 1800', 172–91. On the complicated roles of proprietors and editors see Sheila Rosenberg, 'Some further notes on the history of the *Globe*: its editors, manager, and proprietors', *VPN*, xv (Mar. 1972), 40–7; and F. David Roberts, 'Who ran the London *Globe* in the 1830s, 1840s and 1850s?', *ibid.*, xii (June 1971), 6–11. On newspaper editors see also F. David Roberts, 'Early Victorian newspaper editors', *ibid.*, xiv (Jan. 1972), 1–12; 'More early Victorian newspaper editors', *ibid.*, xvi (June 1972), 15–28; and 'Still more early Victorian newspaper editors', *ibid*, xvii (Dec. 1972), 12–26.

3. See Francis E. Mineka, *The Dissidence of Dissent: The Monthly Repository, 1806–1838* (Chapel Hill, 1944), an excellent study of the workings of an individual religious periodical. It contains a useful chapter, 'News from Heaven: English religious periodicals to 1825', 27–97.

4. E. F. Maitland to David Welsh [n.d.; 1843], Alexander Campbell Fraser Papers, National Library of Scotland, TD 471. Quoted with permission of Mr A. C. Fraser. The papers consist of letters, notebooks and Fraser's journals, all of which contain extensive material dealing with the *North British Review*, 1850–7.

5. Prospectus, issued first in February 1844; ledger no. 1, T. and A.

Constable Ltd, Edinburgh, subsequently included with *North British Rev* I (May 1844).

6. *William Garden Blaikie: an autobiography. 'Recollections of a Busy Life'*, ed. Norman L. Walker (1901), 136–7.

7. See *DNB*. On the foundation of New College, Edinburgh, for the training of Free Church ministers Welsh became Librarian and Professor of Church History.

8. He ousted Macaulay from his Edinburgh seat in 1847. Cockburn noted in that year that he was 'an avowed Voluntary and very nearly a Radical': *Journal of Henry Cockburn, Being a Continuation of the Memorials of his Time, 1831–1854*, ed. Thomas Cleghorn (1874), (hereafter cited as Cockburn, *Journal*), II, 192.

9. *Ibid.*, II, 71; Ledger no. 2, f. 188, T. and A. Constable Ltd, Edinburgh.

10. Cockburn, *Journal*, II, 70.

11. On all three see *DNB* entries.

12. R. Dill to Chalmers, 1 Apr. 1846, bound vol. 1846, Chalmers Papers, New College, Edinburgh.

13. A. Johnston to Chalmers, 5 Feb. 1847, bound vol. 1847, Chalmers Papers.

14. E. Smith to Chalmers, 25 Feb. 1847, bound vol. 1847, Chalmers Papers.

15. Bound vol. 1845, Chalmers Papers.

16. W. P. Kennedy, business book, National Library of Scotland MS 3927, fos. 25, 26, 28, 29, 36.

17. Mrs Hanna to Dr Chalmers, undated fragment; Mrs Hanna to Mrs Edward Cardwell, 19 Feb. 1847, Chalmers Papers

18. Entries for the *North British Review* begin in Kennedy's business book in 1849, which suggests that possibly at this time Kennedy had become the sole proprietor.

19. Journal, 5 Mar. 1850, 15 Mar. 1850, 14 May 1851: MS notebook, Fraser Papers.

20. Journal, 19 Feb. 1850.

21. Fraser to John Cairns, 23 Feb. 1850, 'Box 1', Fraser Papers; Journal, 15 Mar. 1850.

22. Greg to Fraser, 5 Jan. 1852, Fraser Papers.

23. Kennedy, business book; Fraser's memoranda book, 'Circulation in 1850', Fraser Papers.

24. Freeman to Fraser, 1 July 1854, Fraser Papers.

25. Kaye to Fraser, 12 Nov. 1850; Kingsley to Fraser [1850], Fraser Papers.

26. Senior to Fonblanque, J. Wilson and Delane, 26 Feb. [1855], copies, Fraser Papers.

27. Masson to Fraser, 23 July and 30 Oct. 1850, Fraser Papers.

28. Taylor to Fraser, 25 Apr. 1852, Fraser Papers.

29. Greg to Fraser, 19 Feb. [1851], Fraser Papers.

30. Kaye to Fraser, 12 Nov. and 21 Nov. 1850, Fraser Papers.

31. Cairns to Fraser, 26 Feb. 1851, Fraser Papers.

32. Masson to Fraser, 5 Aug. 1852, Fraser Papers.

33. Freeman to Fraser, 19 May 1853, Fraser Papers.

34. Masson to Fraser, 23 Apr. 1853, Fraser Papers.

35. Price to Fraser, 3 Nov. 1854, Fraser Papers.

36. Anster to Fraser, 24 Aug. 1854, Fraser Papers.

37. Hayward to Fraser, 2 May and 15 May [1856], Fraser Papers.

38. Cockburn, *Journal*, I, 97–8.

39. Blaikie to Fraser, 6 June 1850, Fraser Papers.

40. Fraser to Cairns, 2 Oct. 1850, 'Box 1', Fraser Papers.

41. Taylor to Fraser, 6 Apr. 1857, Fraser Papers.

42. Robert Couper Black to Fraser, 30 Aug. 1850, Fraser Papers.

43. Hayward to Fraser, 8 June [1857], Fraser Papers.

44. Journal, 7 Oct. 1850.

45. Combe to Fraser, 1 May 1852, Fraser Papers.

46. Craik to Fraser, 14 June 1853, Fraser Papers.

47. Eadie to Fraser, 30 Dec. 1851, Fraser Papers.

48. Freeman to Fraser, 24 May 1857, Fraser Papers.

49. Tulloch to Fraser, 6 Feb. 1853, Fraser Papers.

50. Tulloch to Fraser, 31 Oct. 1855; Fraser to Tulloch, 1 Jan. 1856, Fraser Papers.

51. Journal, 1 Jan. 1856.

52. Ferrier's most famous work, the

Institutes of Metaphysics, was published in 1854 and was generally badly received. Fraser reviewed it unfavourably in the *North British* (Aug. 1855). His solicited testimonials, which were published, included a letter from Sir William Hamilton, 30 July 1855, expressing his approval of this article. In addition, Fraser's friend John Cairns published *An Examination of Ferrier's Knowing and Being*, a robust attack which was generally acknowledged to have damaged Ferrier's cause in the election.

53. On the rates of the *Edinburgh* and the *Quarterly*, see Sir David Brester to Fraser, 4 Feb. and 26 Dec. 1852; on the *Christian Remembrancer*, see Freeman to Fraser, 22 Dec. 1854; on the *Westminster* see, *George Eliot and John Chapman*, ed. Gordon Haight, (1940), 29, where he recalls that 'the name of the *Westminster* became a word of terror in literary ears'. Kennedy's business book records the total amount spent on contributors per number, and Fraser's correspondence indicates specific amounts to contributors for articles.

54. Brewster to Fraser, 10 Nov. 1854 and 8 May 1855, Fraser Papers.

55. Journal, 6 Apr. 1855.

56. Taylor to Fraser, 4 Aug. 1856, Fraser Papers.

57. Taylor to Fraser, 23 Oct. 1856, Fraser Papers.

58. William Cunningham, *Animadversions upon a Recent Review of the Works of Dr Chalmers*, address delivered at the Conclusion of the Session of the New College (Edinburgh, 1 Apr. 1857), 5.

59. Price to Fraser, 9 June 1857, Fraser Papers.

60. Cairns to Fraser, 17 Aug. 1857, Fraser Papers.

61. Patrick Fraser to A. C. Fraser, 30 Oct. [n.d.], Fraser Papers.

62. Freeman to Fraser, 24 May 1857, Fraser Papers.

63. Blaikie to Fraser, 10 July 1857, Fraser Papers.

64. Taylor to Fraser, 6 April 1857.

65. Constable to Fraser, 3 May [1857], stated that Kennedy was asking £1,000 for the copyright and stock but that he thought he would accept £750 or even £500. Constable's plan was for himself and several others including Hanna and Fraser to advance a share of the capital as joint proprietors. Fraser said he could not raise the sum but agreed to forfeit his salary as editor until the equivalent sum had accumulated. After Fraser had finally withdrawn, Sir David Brewster proposed to make it a joint stock effort, and offered to take a share of between £100 and £200: Brewster to Fraser, 26 June 1857, Fraser Papers.

66. Taylor to Fraser, 21 Nov. 1857, Fraser Papers.

67. Cairns to Fraser, 17 Aug. 1857, Fraser Papers.

68. See Mineka, *op. cit.*, 208, 247–8.

Sheila Rosenberg The financing of radical
opinion: John Chapman
and the *Westminster
Review*

By the time John Chapman assumed responsibility for the *Westminster
Review* in 1852,[1] a succession of wealthy backers had already committed
funds, and a host of talented writers had given their labours free, to forward
'the great work of the amelioration of mankind carried on through the
channel of a review of modern books', which had begun in 1828. Jeremy
Bentham had invested a reported £10,000 before he was joined in 1828 by
T. P. Thompson, who used his new inheritance to pay off the review's accumulated debts of £800 and then helped to keep it afloat until 1836. He was
relieved by Sir William Molesworth who paid £1,000 for the *Westminster* in
order to amalgamate it with the *London Review* in which he had already
invested £4,000. From 1838 to 1840 the proprietorship passed to John Stuart
Mill, who passed it then to W. E. Hickson, a retired boot and shoe manufacturer, who had to rely on gratuitous contributions from others. Finally, in
1852, Hickson sold the radical member of the great triumvirate of Victorian
quarterlies for £300 to a man of little formal education and no private income
or family connections who was the most effective and respected radical
publisher and bookseller in London.

It has been, and often remains, fashionable to sneer at John Chapman for
his medical and intellectual pretensions, and to impugn his financial and
sexual integrity. But to rely on facile generalizations is to miss the quality of
the man. No wholly pejorative account of Chapman can explain how, with
no other capital than his own enthusiasm and idealism, and the rich fund of
good will and enthusiasm of men and women committed to fighting for a
wide range of radical causes, he launched the new *Westminster* and kept it
and himself, wife, mistresses and children afloat for the next 42 years. Most
of that time he was both editor and principal proprietor, without any private
income and with at times a very slender salary – if any at all – from his
medical practice. Despite this, it was always his consistent hope to avoid
claiming any salary from the *Westminster*.

Chapman's task was therefore vastly more difficult than that which had faced any of his illustrious predecessors. Mill felt this very keenly, and after an initial coolness, gave Chapman financial aid, contributed articles without payment, and was a ready source of advice and sympathy. He did this because he felt Chapman had remained true to the old ideals, and he recommended the *Westminster* to Lord Amberley in 1866 as being 'willing to print bolder opinions on all subjects than the other periodicals';[2] and writing to Chapman in 1867 that: 'Knowing how little support there is for a Review of advanced opinions, I have always thought it eminently honourable to you that you should have been able to carry it on for so many years, and to make it as good as it has been through all that time.'[3]

A similar enthusiasm made T. H. Huxley prefer writing for his 'favourite organ, the wicked Westminster',[4] rather than the better-paying *Fraser's Magazine,* and encouraged such financial supporters as Octavius Smith and Edward Henry Stanley who wanted 'a free theological press',[5] or an organ of free discussion on all topics.

Chapman throughout his career drew support from the widest range of political, social and theological dissent: ageing 'philosophical radicals', Unitarian polemicists, free-thinking iconoclasts, liberal reformers. But though he survived, he also paid a considerable price in the hostility, opposition and recrimination that he incurred. This was because he was too dependent on the force of his personality alone in forging business or working relationships. They were, therefore, always vulnerable in that they were based on his 'charisma' – an attractive mixture of shared enthusiasm for a cause and admiration for its champions, plus warmth, sympathy and persuasiveness, all in the context of his constant need for financial support and back-up. Many of his closest long-standing relationships ended in bitterness and disillusion, if not on his side, on the other, and this sadly illustrates the vulnerability of his position.

The saddest was probably the end of his friendship with Marian Evans. He tactlessly presumed on their old relationship to insist that she was the author of *Adam Bede,*[6] although at the time she and Lewes were denying it. Despite all efforts to make amends, he was never forgiven and was banished to permanent exile. And a similar tactlessness, as we shall see, finally alienated Harriet Martineau.

Less justified was Helen Taylor's abrupt severance. She rather hysterically accused Chapman of conducting a long vendetta in the *Westminster* against her step-father John Stuart Mill. Despite Chapman's energetic and convincing refutation, he had to repay the £600 mortgage Mill had long ago taken out on the review.[7]

Bitterest of all was Josephine Butler's reaction. As President of the

Association for Obtaining the Repeal of the Contagious Diseases Acts, Chapman's support of her campaign was total and energetic. He gave up space in the *Westminster* to four long controversial articles on prostitution and venereal disease which cost him a great deal in time and labour. They earned him the censure of the *British Medical Journal*, in no way counterbalanced by gratitude from Josephine Butler, who only seemed to have her own prudish antipathy to him reinforced: 'Unfortunately the doctors in London who are prominent on our side are some of them not men of high character. Dr Chapman and Dr Drysdale are both men on whom a shadow sits.'[8]

The briefest acquaintance with Chapman's private life makes it easy to understand how respectable campaigners against political, religious or even sexual orthodoxy found him a dangerous ally. No Victorian campaigner could afford to fight orthodoxy on more than one front at a time. Josephine Butler needed champions of unexceptionable respectability in all other fields, but so did all the others who looked to Chapman for support. His combination of plebeian background, free love, religious unorthodoxy, medical opportunism, financial instability and personal magnetism made him suspect and dangerous to many. And for such as these he was in the end to be used, but not encouraged.

But if his weaknesses and failures are and always have been clear, the strengths which account for his success have been more elusive. It is thus easier to describe what he achieved than to explain how he did it. The following attempt to trace the still imperfectly documented history of Chapman's control of the *Westminster* may do something to explain his skills and talents. More important, it illustrates some of the various methods of financing a form of journalism that never had and never would pay its own way, and it throws light on the complex pattern of intricate relationships and connections among the Victorian champions of heterodoxy who supported the *Westminster*.

When Chapman bought the *Westminster*, he was 30. He had been a publisher of heterodox Unitarian and Transcendental literature for some six to seven years and entertained many English and American men of letters at 142 Strand. He now proposed to use this powerful circle of contacts, plus his own energy and idealism, to buy the *Westminster* and to re-establish its radical identity, restoring it to its former stature as a worthy opponent of the *Quarterly* and the *Edinburgh*.

The decline of the *Westminster* during the 1840s from its former preeminence was generally agreed on. In a series of articles on the periodical and newspaper press in the *Critic*, Herodotus Smith sadly admits:

> On the whole the *Westminster* under Mr Hickson's management cannot be said to have been successful . . . For one thing it has been exposed of late years to the competition of the *North British Review*, the *British Quarterly* and the *Prospective*, all of them liberal.[9]

To re-establish the *Westminster* as a powerful radical organ, Chapman needed all the help he could muster. In Marian Evans he had an editor of sweeping intelligence and unrelenting industry, to whom he could leave the actual preparation of manuscripts. As a publisher he had already worked with F. W. Newman, Harriet and James Martineau, Herbert Spencer, W. R. Greg, Theodore Parker, and others, who could be applied to for material and many of whom became subscribers. But he needed capital. The *Westminster* under Hickson was already being supported by Edward Lombe, a member of the English colony in Florence and a wealthy capricious supporter of George Combe. He now promised 'to assist in the establishment of a quarterly that should go far enough for him'.[10] He was demanding and difficult and Chapman had to make quite clear his intention to maintain editorial independence – Browning refers to Chapman's problems in coping with his 'Lombago'.[11] But he finally made available the £300 with which Chapman could buy the *Westminster*.

Thus began Chapman's long career of shifts and manoeuvres to get money. But it is worth remembering that these – the letters explaining accounts, confirming expenses, assuaging doubts – took their place alongside the other activities of an immensely busy life: soliciting contributions, reading proofs, writing lengthy articles himself, campaigning for free trade in books and for medical reform and a new attitude to prostitution, patenting the spinal ice-bag, writing a dozen thick medical books, carrying on a medical practice, boarding lunatics and enjoying a richly tender love-life. All these bear testimony to an energy outstanding even by mid-Victorian standards.

He understood from the beginning that the *Westminster* at 6s. a copy and with, as far as I have been able to gather, a circulation of 1,620 at its highest, would never pay its way. But it was not only the radical journals that faced financial hazards. In a letter to Lord Derby describing the *Westminster*'s plight he refers to the 'several thousand pounds' spent on the *National* and the reported £10,000 which had been exhausted on the *Fortnightly* by the time G. H. Lewes ceased to be editor.[12]

The search for support for the new *Westminster* illuminates central and continuing dilemmas which faced Chapman as they had faced Mill, and which in different ways faced other conductors of Victorian periodicals: first, how to establish a separate radical identity for the review strong enough to encourage both the financial backing of wealthy sympathisers, and the support of writers who would be prepared to contribute gratis or accept Chapman's lower rates of payment – though he was, in fact, at 12 guineas a sheet offering twice as much as Hickson had; second, how to hold together what must thus inevitably be a variety of opinions and to present some sort of homogenous view-point; and finally, following this, how to allow for the presentation of extreme opinions without appearing to give them editorial sanction. Mill had tried to cope with this last by a system of attributing authorship by initials, and Chapman introduced his 'Independent Section'. Neither was really successful in dissociating the main groups of *Westminster* supporters from controversial opinions expressed in its pages. In addition Chapman had to satisfy the idiosyncratic demands of wealthy backers like Courtauld, who demanded articles opposing church rates, and Lombe, who wanted the *Westminster* to promote 'organic reform'.

Nevertheless he achieved a considerable measure of success in all this by a persuasive energy and enthusiasm. It was probably his very unsophistication, even his less than first-rate intellect, that enabled him unashamedly to admire others and work with enthusiasm on their behalf, while enjoying the warmth and light of reflected glory. He was not lazy; he worked long hours covering page after page in his neat hand-writing, copiously expounding his philosophic faith and doubts, inviting confidence, beseeching advice, and requesting money and contributions; he even from time to time disregarded the advice of Marian Evans and ventured into print himself, writing articles of which he had no need to be ashamed. But he was never truly an initiator; he always depended on others. He always recognized this quality in himself and referred to his 'unduly frequent consultation of others before deciding in each case needing decision instead of quietly deciding at once'.[13] This was perhaps why, in the end, he did achieve a great deal as editor of the *Westminster*. Mill's incisive individuality and his uncompromising radicalism had alienated even his closest sympathizers when he had edited the review. Chapman was incapable of such independence but because of this he was open to, and drew on, the support of nearly all the English radicals and their sympathizers, and a review such as the *Westminster* was completely dependent on such generous support.

In gathering support for the *Westminster* Chapman followed the pattern he had already used as a publisher. He acquired the review in May 1851 and wanted, perhaps foolishly, to mark the beginning of his own editorial reign by a public avowal of political, economic and theological faith to be included in a statement of future *Westminster* policy. He had some seven months before his first number appeared – in fact the final negotiations were completed in October – and he used the time to find contributors and to canvas opinion upon this public statement or 'Prospectus'. Before making the first draft, he sought advice on the form the review should take from several sympathetic spirits: Joseph Parkes[14] of Birmingham, who had headed the committee which financed Marian Evans' translation of *Leben Jesu*, George Combe,[15] and F. W. Newman,[16] and on 22 May he went down to Coventry and began a first draft of the Prospectus.[17] Inevitably the writing passed to Marian Evans, and by working hard – even forgoing meals – she had it finished by 2 June. Chapman 'liked it extremely'[18] and, with a few alterations, sent it to press.

On 4 June the proofs of the Prospectus were ready and copies were sent to Newman, Mill, Hickson, Greg, J. A. Froude, James Martineau, Sir William Molesworth, Thornton Hunt (son of Leigh Hunt, colleague of G. H. Lewes and editor of the *Leader*), Lombe, R. W. Mackay and Dr Ballantyne Hodgson (educational reformer and friend of James Martineau).[19] These were the men who Chapman felt would be prepared to assist his new venture and to whose opinions he deferred. Except for Hodgson and Hunt, they were all either already on his publishing list, or contributing to the *Westminster*, and he recorded their views eagerly: Newman sent a 'letter of objections . . . They are not strong but are pertinaciously maintained';[20] Greg and Froude approved,[21] but Hickson felt strongly that Chapman was being tactlessly premature in issuing a Prospectus for the new *Westminster*, when there were still two issues of the old one to go.[22]

Mill, was withering. Chapman described his letter as 'long, half-sarcastic' and 'containing severe animadversions'.[23] It indicated clearly how far Mill believed at that point that Chapman was from the Philosophic Radicalism which he himself had tried to promulgate.

> The prospectus [wrote Mill] is addressed to 'the friends of philosophic reform'; I think this a bad phrase. 'Philosophic reformers' is a worn-out and gone-by expression; it had a meaning twenty years ago; 'philosophic reform' does not, to my mind, carry any meaning at all unless to signify a reform in philosophy.
>
> The prospectus . . . contains nothing to distinguish the *Review* from any Liberal or semi-Liberal newspaper or periodical, or from anybody who says he is for reform but not for revolution. The doctrine stated, such as it is, I do not agree in. Instead of thinking that 'strength and durability are the result only of a slow and peaceful development', I think that changes effected rapidly and by force are often the only ones which in given circumstances would be permanent; and by the statement that 'reforms, to be salutary, must be graduated to the average moral and intellectual growth of society', I presume is meant (though I am by no means sure about the meaning if any) that the

measures of a Government ought never to be in advance of the average intellect and virtue of the people, according to which doctrine there would never have been the Reformation, the Commonwealth, or the Revolution of 1688; and the stupidity and habitual indifference of the mass of mankind would bear down by its dead weight all the efforts of the more intelligent and active-minded few. The prospectus says 'the *Review* will not neglect that important range of subjects which are related to politics as an inner concentric circle, and which have been included under the term sociology'. I understand by sociology not a particular *class* of subjects included *within* politics, but a vast field *including* it . . . And it seems to me impossible that even the politics of the day can be discussed on principle or with a view to anything but the exigencies of the moment unless by setting out from definite opinions respecting social questions more fundamental than what is commonly called politics. . . . I confess it seems to me the only worthy object of a review of progress is to consider how far and in what manner such objects may be *promoted*, and how the obstacles, whether arising from the cause mentioned or from any other, may most effectually be overcome. . . . My willingness to contribute even occasionally to the *Westminster* under any new management would entirely depend on the opinion I form of it after seeing it in operation.[24]

In his main criticism – that politically and socially the new review would advocate almost nothing that the *Edinburgh* would not approve of – he is at once sensitive to the problems he himself faced in the latter days of his editorship and striking at the root of the comfortable theories of gradual organic reform such as the one that seems to have been advocated by Lombe – theories shared by many *Westminster* supporters. In his criticisms of Chapman's differentiation among politics, philosophy, and sociology Mill shows how much more comprehensive was his own view of the motives of all man's actions within society, and how much more rigorous was his own conception of a basic system to which all political and economic changes could be related.

Hard on Mill's letter came a 'half-sneering cold' one from James Martineau:

I am not so presumptuous as to offer any opinion. You probably aim, and do well to aim, at securing the support of the large and increasing class of men of thoughtful but not regularly disciplined or largely cultivated mind, the class who may perhaps be most influential in determining the next future. Otherwise, if you aim at conciliating the attention of the intellectual and scholarly class who are the main supports of the 'Quarterly' and 'Edinburgh' I should doubt whether the Prospectus is quite the thing. It is very likely impossible to become the organ of the movement party in Politics as it now exists, without descending to a lower literary level. The course of the 'Westminster' for a long time past has seemed to imply this; and there may be commercial wisdom in acquiescing in it.[25]

Despite the unfortunate tone of this, Martineau had emphasized, as Mill had done, one of the main problems facing Chapman: who was going to read the *Westminster*? Obviously the adherents of the *Quarterly* would rarely be tempted, but the relative positions of the *Westminster* and the *Edinburgh* had to be seriously considered if the new organ as envisaged by Chapman was to achieve a separate identity. Martineau's contempt for the intellectual calibre of those sympathetic to many of Chapman's views is scarcely concealed.

The criticisms of two men as important in their own fields as Mill and Martineau were significant. They did not agree on what the review should become, for Mill wanted more uncompromising radicalism, and Martineau, as it turned out, wished to promulgate his own form of Unitarianism, but their two comments exposed the great weakness of Chapman's position if he wanted to enlist the support of strongly committed radicals and free-thinkers: they would want to make the *Westminster* the vehicle for their specific ideals. Chapman was more vulnerable than the editors of almost any other major magazine, because he was completely dependent on the good will and generosity of contributors and supporters; he therefore had to make various editorial compromises to satisfy individuals without compromising any of the general principles strongly upheld by all the contributors. However, many of these contributors and supporters were already well-disposed to-wards the ideas in the Prospectus: George Combe sent a 'kind suggestive' letter; the Unitarian, J. J. Tayler, gave his approval verbally, and Andrew Johnson thought it 'good but tame' – but then he was a friend of Marx. Herbert Spencer 'of course had many suggestions to give.[26] Chapman next turned to Coventry with all these views. Marian Evans had been appalled by the difficulties raised by their precipitate sending-off of a draft of the Prospectus.

I heartily wish the prospectus had been longer delayed and thought over before it was sent out to any of the dons . . . Everything has been too hurried. But you will say, 'After meat, mustard'. Your wisdom comes too late. Still, the moral is not useless. Caution for the future.[27]

In her next letter[28] she corrected in detail the draft of an answer to Mill's 'severe animadversions' which Chapman had sent her. He sent the amended version to Mill, who received it more kindly than he had the Prospectus, though still with significant criticism.

> The reason you give for what you very truly call the air of conservatism in the Prospectus, is intelligible, but does not seem to me to render advisable the use of expressions giving the idea that the West[r] no longer wishes to be considered as professing extreme opinions. The review was founded by people who held what were then thought extreme opinions, and it is only needed as an organ of opinions as much in advance of the present state of the public mind as those were in advance of its then state. Anything less is but child's play after the events of the last three years in Europe & besides, every intermediate position is fully occupied by other periodicals.[29]

Meanwhile another letter to Martineau had also produced more amiable results and the minister now 'spoke frankly and well about the Prospectus'.[30] However a good deal more work was done on it by Chapman and Marian Evans before its publication at the end of August, and the final product was again sent to Mill, who passed his verdict:

> I like the altered Prospectus better than the first; but I should have greatly preferred a simple and plain expression of the plan and principles intended to be followed. The Prospectus still seems to me to rely on sound rather than on sense; the only distinct statement of opinion being on the mere newspaper topics of the day. . . .
>   The first number will show what meaning the writer attaches to the word Progress, and how far the review will be an organ of it.[31]

Mill's criticism of this final version is not unjustified; a careful examination of the form which appeared in the January 1852 issue of the *Westminster* reveals some very woolly thinking, and a total lack of excitement. The consultation had been valuable, not because of the manifesto it produced, but because it had fully involved radical thinkers, writers and supporters in the new *Westminster* and the form it should take.

  In the end the success of the *Westminster* was to depend not on the turgid drawing-up of flaccid generalizations but on solid contributions from old-established radicals like Mill, on the fire and energy of new disciples of heterodoxy like Frederic Harrison, who launched himself with his 'Neo-

Christianity'[32] in the *Westminster*, and on the onslaughts of an old *enfant terrible* like F. W. Newman whose 'Religious weaknesses of Protestantism'[33] may have lost the *Westminster* some circulation but contributed to its unique excitement, causing Walter Bagehot, always acutely conscious of the rivalry between the *Westminster* and the *National*, to complain to R. H. Hutton in 1859: 'A strictly orthodox man told me yesterday there was a "delightful new Westminster out". Quite seriously our heresy is not spicy enough for real believers. Martineau used to have some attractive profanity but he is getting *good*'.[34]

This energy and excitement gave the *Westminster* the impetus to survive from crisis to crisis and was as important as Chapman's personal drive and persuasiveness, and as the fact that the *Westminster* provided the unique vehicle for radical opinion. There was, however, one final factor that materially affected the review's survival, and that was patronage from a network of families who might be characterized as the 'first families of dissent'. Noel Annan has described some members of this 'intellectual aristocracy' in detail, seeing their dynastic connections as 'the poetry of history'.[35] They were the Huxleys, Trevelyans, Macaulays, Darwins, and the descendents of William Smith, the abolitionist M.P. The *Westminster*'s survival owed a great deal to Octavius and Julia Smith, son and daughter of William; to Barbara Leigh Smith, his grand-daughter; and no little to T. H. Huxley and Darwin. Chapman could also draw in the Unitarian families like the Courtaulds and he tried to involve a previous *Westminster* supporter, Edward Fordham Flower, the wealthy Stratford brewer who was still giving help to W. J. Fox. The close involvement of these families is particularly clear in the early years of Chapman's control.

After the initial £300 from Lombe, Chapman opened the first of many subscription lists. George Combe's was the first,[36] and he was followed by his wealthy West Country patron, Thomas Horlock Bastard.[37] Others followed: F. W. Newman, Miss Susan Hughes (sister of Dr Brabant) and Woodfall, the printer.[38] But no subscriptions could cope with the first crisis which came in 1852 soon after the death of Mr Lombe, when Dr Brabant of Devizes, with no dimunition of good will, found he had to ask for repayment, within two years, of the £800 he had lent Chapman.

This demand for £800 came at a very unfortunate time. By May 1852 Chapman also needed £250 to pay for the authorship of the July issue of the *Westminster*; he was still looking for a partner to share his financial burdens, and at the same time he was contemplating a reduction in staff.[39] In desperation he looked round for help. George Combe tried to interest Richard Cobden but to no avail.[40] Then Charles Bray approached his friend, Edward Fordham Flower, who also refused.[41] Marian Evans was growing angry at the indignity of their having to tout for 'these miserable loans'.[42] She did not at first realize the gravity of the situation and still less did she understand at this point that it could not be resolved easily or swiftly. During the whole of the 1850s the financial condition of the *Westminster* was inextricably inter-woven with Chapman's other financial problems – his dependence on a constant flow of boarders for the upkeep of the large Strand house, the loss of goodwill and profit which had resulted from his battle to maintain free trade in books, and, above all, the fact that none of the books he published would ever find a large popular market. This was the background against which he had launched an ambitious programme for the *Westminster*, whereby the frequently makeshift arrangements resorted to by Hickson were to be replaced by a policy of employing and paying the best-qualified people. It was therefore inevitable that he should need subsidizing.

Finally in December 1852 the 'dismal . . . affairs of Chapmandom',[43] as Marian Evans put it, made him go down to Brighton to apply for help to the wealthy silk manufacturer, Samuel Courtauld, who had already settled an annuity of £400 on W. J. Fox.[44]

The relationship between Chapman and Courtauld was to be extremely important to the history of the *Westminster*. Courtauld was a free thinker, a Unitarian, interested in the revocation of the church rates – he paid for the insertion in the *Westminster* of an article on this subject by Harriet Mar-tineau – and a benevolent but anti-socialist employer who seems to have been liked and respected by his employees at Braintree. His nephew, Peter Taylor, and his wife became close friends of Marian Evans. They were both ardent supporters of the Young Italy group in London and friends of Mazzini and the other Italian exiles.

Courtauld's help – it afterwards appeared he gave at least £600 – averted the crisis for the moment. By the following April, however, Marian Evans was looking enviously at the *Edinburgh* which had a reported £700 to spend on the authorship of each issue.[45] By the next November she too had become an expense that Chapman could no longer afford[46] – though he certainly needed her. She continued working, however, without salary, because she apparently believed the *Westminster* had an important part to play in providing a vehicle for the free expression of unorthodox opinion.[47]

The next major crisis was caused by James Martineau. His growing intransigence and opposition to the *Westminster* which led to Chapman's financial crisis in 1854 was in direct relation to his growing hostility towards his sister, Harriet. Their quarrel dated back to 1851 when Chapman pub-lished *Letters on the Laws of Man's Nature and Development* by Harriet Martineau and H. G. Atkinson. James Martineau's scathing review in the *Prospective* led to a permanent breach between brother and sister, and their quarrel had very important effects on the history of the *Westminster*. From the beginning various members of the circle had been uneasy in their relations with James. He seems to have been a difficult and uncompromising person to deal with, especially when his ideals and beliefs seemed threatened. Neither Marian Evans,[48] Andrew Johnson,[49] Mill[50] nor Froude[51] liked him. For his part, James complained of the 'atheistic tendency and Refugee politics'[52] of the *Westminster* under Chapman. Certainly his sister and G. H. Lewes were working on Comte, and there was also a keen interest in the European revolutions in the *Westminster* circle. Chapman's close friend, Andrew Johnson, Principal Bullion Officer of the Bank of England, concealed under his unexceptionably respectable and capitalist exterior a great sympathy and friendship for Marx, Freiligrath and Engels; Chapman met Marx at Johnson's house.[53] The German revolutionaries did not contribute to the *Westminster*, but Johnson's own influence on Chapman was considerable and lasted throughout the decade. The Italian revolutionaries. Mazzini and Aurelio Saffi, actually wrote articles for the *Westminster*,[54] and the Peter Taylors maintained their close relationship with the group.

Martineau was therefore not kindly disposed to the *Westminster* circle when, in 1853–4, Chapman's continual financial embarrassment brought him to the edge of bankruptcy. Martineau tried to amalgamate the *Westminster* with the *Prospective*, but his sister, by assuming the mortgage of the review, prevented him. The story is best told in their own words. Martineau's account shows himself as the model of high-minded innocence being the victim of sharp practice. It is interesting to note that the large sympathetic public, which he said did not exist when Chapman took over the *Westminster*, had suddenly sprung into being at the possibility of an amalgamation between the *Prospective* and the *Westminster*.

> From the known opinions of the Editors, this 'Review' has often been regarded as an organ of the Unitarians, [but] . . . its aim might be more correctly described as anti-Unitarian; . . . And, in point of fact, this breadth of purpose while securing it some circulation and marked respect among studious persons in various connections, caused it to be looked coldly upon by the very people it was supposed to represent. This relative incidence of public favour led to proposals, in 1853–4, to merge it in the 'Westminster Review', which included much of the same ground; but instead of this, to the expansion of the 'Prospective' into the 'National Review', – a separate large Quarterly, embracing the field of Literature and Politics, in addition to the scope of its predecessor. This move was preferred, because the tone of the 'Westminster' was becoming more and more uncongenial with the

philosophical and religious convictions of the Editors of the 'Prospective', . . .

At one moment, indeed, a possibility seemed to present itself of an amalgamation of the two periodicals. In the autumn [summer] of 1854, the proprietor and publisher of the 'Westminster' became insolvent, and the 'Review' – the most important of his assets – passed, with the rest of the estate, to the disposal of the creditors. Had it come into the market, and its value been tested by the offer of a sale, a bid for it would have been made by the proprietors of the 'Prospective' with tolerable certainty of considerable increase to the dividend. With other of the creditors, I was of the opinion that this regular course ought to be followed . . . we, who lived two hundred to four hundred miles off, had no opportunity of taking part in the proceedings. A balance sheet was laid before the local attendants, from which the 'Westminster Review' was omitted; and, to induce the creditors to forgo all claim upon it and leave it in the publisher's hands, a personal guarantee was offered of a definite composition by a friend whose security was perfect. The meeting closed with this proposal; but we absentees, disapproving of the management which had been resorted to, declined to accept the composition, unless a second meeting were called at which a vote should be taken after complete valuation of assets. Instead of conceding this reasonable demand, the publisher's wealthy patron set himself to *buy off* the dissentients by payment in full of their claim on the estate. I refused to listen to such proposals; but I was left alone; . . . Some years after, when the insolvent pressed for my signature to his discharge, I qualified myself for duly giving it, by receiving in exchange his surrender of the copyright of articles which I had contributed to the 'Review' during his proprietorship. On this simple story various fictions were grafted at the time.[55]

He describes in more detail the position he hoped the *National* would take when writing to a friend.

When Chapman's failure seemed certain to throw the 'Westminster' into the market, a fund was raised to provide against its surrender to the mere lottery of a Trade-auction, and to secure it as the organ of a serious but free theology, and an English historical liberalism in politics. The 'Westminster' was saved from the hammer; but only to be delivered into the hands of a Comtist coterie, and to suffer the defection of a whole group of its most reliable contributors. So . . . we proposed to start 'The *National* Review'.[56]

Harriet Martineau's account, on the other hand, shows Dr Ballantyne Hodgson and her brother as ravening wolves ready to tear the frail body of free thought.

> My good friend and publisher, Mr. Chapman, had just failed . . . the 'Westminster Review' was by this time mortgaged to me. It was entirely my own doing; and I am anxious, for Mr. Chapman's sake, that this should be understood. The truth of the case is that I had long felt, as many others had professed to do, that the cause of free-thought and free-speech was under great obligations to Mr. Chapman; and it naturally occurred to me that it was therefore a duty incumbent on the advocates of free-thought and speech to support and aid one by whom they had been enabled to address society. Thinking, in the preceding winter, that I saw that Mr. Chapman was hampered by certain liabilities that the review was under, I offered to assume the mortgage, – knowing the uncertain nature of that kind of investment, but regarding the danger of loss as my contribution to the cause. At first, after the failure, there was every probability apparently that Mr. Chapman's affairs would be speedily settled, . . . but two absent discontented creditors pursued their debtor with, (as some men of business among the creditors said) 'a cruelty unequalled in all their experience'. One of their endeavours was to get the review out of Mr. Chapman's hands; and one feature of the enterprise was an attempt to upset the mortgage, and to drive Mr. Chapman to bankruptcy, in order to throw the review into the market . . . It was the will of the great body of the creditors, however, that Mr. Chapman should keep the review, which he had edited thus far with great and rising success; and his two foes were got rid of by the generosity of Mr. Chapman's guaranteeing supporters. The attempt to upset the mortgage failed, of course . . . but the whole anxiety, aggravated by indignation and pain at such conduct on the part of men who professed a sense of obligation to Mr. Chapman, extended over many weeks.[57]

Martineau was being oblique in suggesting that more creditors than he and Hodgson objected, and the discrepancies in time between the two accounts would seem to indicate that he condensed his account in his own favour. Whatever the details of right and wrong, however, the fact remains that by the end of 1854 Harriet Martineau had £500 invested in the *West-minster* and James Martineau no longer contributed. His claim to have drawn considerable support away from Chapman was exaggerated; F. W. Newman, who was extremely interested in the *National*, still contributed many articles to the *Westminster*, and W. R. Greg would probably have ceased to contribute anyway, since as he grew older his distrust of profound social changes became very strong[58] and he dissociated himself from radical movements. But although it did little permanent harm, while it lasted the 'Martineau-Hodgson' affair, as it was called by Chapman, was something of a cause célèbre. Matthew Arnold, writing to his sister, Mrs W. E. Forster, commented: 'I should like to know what William thinks of this pretty Westminster quarrel. Miss Martineau and her brother James, and their hatreds, remind one of the family of Pelops. She proposed for me to take part in the Review (from Chapman) but for that I have not time.'[59]

During much of 1853 and 1854, Chapman was not only harrassed by enormous financial problems – he had to cope with changes in the support of the *Westminster* which had little to do with money. Early in 1853 George Combe had been alienated after some ill-feeling over the failure of an advertisement to appear in the *Westminster*.[60] Then, after a friendship which had lasted for years, Combe took personal exception to Marian Evans' decision to live with Lewes, and felt he had compromised himself by introducing her to some of his friends.[61] He therefore broke away completely from the *Westminster* circle.

Between 1854 and 1858 those with the greatest financial involvement in Chapman's affairs were Samuel Courtauld, Harriet Martineau and Octavius Smith, and there is a voluminous correspondence with Chapman during that period.[62] Harriet Martineau held the mortgage of the *Westminster* and Courtauld and Smith were major creditors in the publishing business; exactly when Smith, a friend of Herbert Spencer's and a champion of free thought, became involved in Chapman's affairs is not clear, but in 1853 he financed the publication by Chapman of W. R. Greg's pamphlet, *The Great Sin of the Great Cities*.

During 1855, Courtauld's dislike and distrust of Chapman grew so great that he refused to communicate with him personally[63] and he wanted to wind up the business and end all connection with it. Throughout the year Chapman was in constant uncertainty whether he would be able to continue. The reason for Courtauld's dislike does not emerge at this point, but it was not shared by Smith and Harriet Martineau, and Chapman was saved. Courtauld applied to Harriet Martineau to remove the clause in the mortgage agreement – originally inserted to save the *Westminster* from the clutches of her brother – by which the executors could not act upon the mortgage within five years of her death. Courtauld was a major creditor and this clause would materially affect the winding up of Chapman's affairs. However, she was not moved and her close and confiding friendship with Chapman continued.

Smith wanted the business to continue as long as possible because it was so valuable in promulgating unorthodoxy and Courtauld himself was considerate enough not to put the business on the market when it seemed most unpropitious, though he doubted whether a purchaser for the business or the review could ever be found. He refused to involve anyone else in the business and would not accept guarantees offered by Susanna Chapman's brother, Bellamy Brewitt, though why Brewitt came forward is not clear for he does not seem to have liked his brother-in-law. A letter from Courtauld to Harriet Martineau in 1858 both indicates Brewitt's attitude and also gives an important clue to the reason for Courtauld's own attitude to Chapman at this time.

> I had near the commencement of my relations with Dr. Chapman's affairs, some incidental correspondence with Mr. Brewitt which left on my mind impressions of him corresponding with those given by you. I knew his theological antipathies to his brother-in-law, and also his distrust of him as a man of business. I did not know that his distrust extended to his moral integrity, nor do the expressions you quote, determine whether it did or not . . . The Misses Attlebury's case is no doubt a very painful one; and they are not the only exhausted sufferers from Dr. Chapman's parasitical life.[64]

It is significant that Courtauld did not fully communicate these suspicions to Harriet Martineau until she also was unhappy about Chapman.

Courtauld was not the only one to distrust Chapman. In 1854 Joseph Parkes, writing to his daughter Bessie Rayner Parkes, Marian Evans' friend, commented sadly:

> 'As to Mr. Chapman's affairs, all that it is needful for me to say is that his debts are about £9,000 (the £2,500 he managed to extract from his wife's trustees I call the worst). Nearly all the creditors decided to accept 7/– or 8/– in £ dividend in 4, 8, or 12 months. . . . His talents and activities I respect, but he is not a man I would trust. He is so self-opinionated and wilful that no one can be of real use to him in aid of his own judgment. He would have had, I think, a better chance in the present barely-paying state of the 'Westminster Review' had he devoted himself to that work only. He cannot carry on writing, and maintain his business and his own family expenditure. The way he is behaving is, between ourselves, generally the prelude to bankruptcy . . . I have seen so many ups and downs of the 'Westminster Review' and so many thousands of pounds lost on it, that I am not sanguine.[65]

But Chapman did avoid bankruptcy, and, during 1856 and 1857, the business was carried on under the aegis of a Mr Birt, a shadowy figure who is in the background of Chapman's other business communications and is referred to by Courtauld. It seems likely that Courtauld insisted that Chapman should hand over the actual management of the business to someone else while still keeping nominal charge of affairs.

Meanwhile the *Westminster* actually prospered. Chapman always had needed gratuitous articles and they were even more necessary now. Harriet Martineau wrote prolifically for the review, giving freely[66] as W. E. Forster had in the past,[67] and as Harrison, Grote,[68] and Mill were to do in the future. During the period 1855 to 1858 Marian Evans and G. H. Lewes contributed some excellent articles, especially upon literature, Huxley continued to write on science and a new contributor, W. B. Donne, soon to be Examiner of Plays, wrote amiably on a wide range of subjects. A new influence on Chapman personally was Mark Pattison, who undertook various parts of the 'Contemporary Literature' section and also contributed full-length articles.

In 1857, Harriet Martineau, with no diminution of friendliness, felt she could no longer carry on the mortgage of the *Westminster*.[69] Without saying exactly what it was, she claimed that someone else had a greater call upon the money. It was therefore suggested that a fund should be set up to which friends and sympathizers including people like Charles Darwin could subscribe to pay her back; this was done and George Grote consented to be 'banker'. Throughout the first half of 1858 relations between her and Chapman were extremely friendly, as they had been for several years; he confided in her his spiritual troubles, and she told him of her ovarian tumour, though all the world believed that she believed that she had dropsy. He advised her on her diet and other medical matters.

Suddenly in June 1858 the tone changes and this marks the beginning of a voluminious increase in correspondence involving herself, Courtauld and Chapman; she and Courtauld kept all letters and made additional notes on them while Chapman reproduced copies of old letters and extracts from diaries. It is not easy therefore to determine the rights and wrongs, especially as the correspondence is one-sided. Once again the problem seems to have hinged on the inevitably intricate relationships involved in financing the general publishing business and maintaining the *Westminster*. Harriet Martineau canvassed and obtained considerable support to redeem the mortgage on the basis of an original £150 subscribed by a Mr Hippisley. She was therefore extremely angry when she later learned that the sum had originally been given to Chapman personally as a personal testimony to himself and his business. She accused Chapman of duplicity and prevarication and an increasingly frantic correspondence followed, with matters made worse by Lord Stanley also saying at first that he did not realize what the money he had donated was for. On this point at least Chapman was exonerated, for Stanley later admitted that he himself had been confused and had made a mistake. Chapman pleaded for permission to come to Ambleside for a personal interview, but Miss Martineau refused. His injured protestations of innocence, his claims of having been victimized because of his poverty, and his appeals to their long-standing friendship do not convince us that his style in letter-writing had improved. Then he made an unforgivable blunder – he attributed her strong reactions to her medical condition, reducing her right-eous indignation to an ovarian affliction. There was no going back from there, and she sadly wrote him her valediction; she had always supported him in the past against hostile criticism; but that was over: 'I can only repeat what I have before said, – that confidence is not a voluntary matter, & that it cannot be awarded (after suspension) on the judgment of others, even if that judgment were open to no doubt or objection'.[70] How far Chapman was culpable it is difficult to tell, but one of her accusations that she did not know that Chapman had any other creditors, is disproved by one of her own earlier letters. On balance it would seem that he had been devious rather than dishonest, and extremely tactless in his long letters – at one point in June they were writing nearly every day – and she, never one to be ruled by her head rather than her heart, felt a deep personal betrayal that did not have all that much to do with the facts of the case.

Harriet Martineau's opposition was strengthened by Courtauld who in the summer of 1858 was further angered by Chapman, and it was their joint and simultaneous disillusion that nearly ended both the business and the *West-minster*. In July Courtauld discovered that back in 1855, when the business had been heavily in debt, Chapman had drawn out money for his own personal expenses, partly to pay for his costly medical studies. Chapman's reply was that he had applied to Courtauld and been referred to the other creditor involved, Octavius Smith. Believing that Smith had given permis-sion, he had taken the money as – and here again the wording is less than tactful – he had a right to do. Courtauld was furious, claiming that Chapman should certainly not have withdrawn any money at all so long as the business was in debt, and that in any case he had no 'right' to do so.

The fate of the *Westminster* now seemed sealed. When the subscription for the mortgage had been opened, Courtauld had, reluctantly, and as a personal favour to Harriet Martineau, agreed to join Smith in not claiming the £500 as part of the money due to him as Chapman's creditor. Now, with both Harriet Martineau and Courtauld antagonized, there seemed no reason why the agreement should not go and the business *and* review be wound up. There was some move for Octavius Smith to assume Courtauld's claims, but he insisted that Chapman should take over responsibility for the business and this was impossible in the existing financial state. Matters seemed hopeless when on 17 November Chapman wrote a desperate note to George Grote. Grote had become financial executor during earlier arrangements, and Chapman asked him to send copies of the original agreement in which Courtauld had consented to respect the safety and independence of the *Westminster*. It was the review that was causing Chapman such anxiety; the fate of the publishing business seemed sealed, but he wanted to save the *Westminster*. Then Lord Stanley offered £600 with no conditions about the publishing business. Chapman accepted and Courtauld at last agreed to stop any attempts to wind up the business or the *Westminster*, although the sum did not cover the whole of Chapman's debt to him, for the bonds he handed over amounted to £900. He was extremely relieved to be released from responsibility for a situation which he was finding increasingly irksome. Harriet Martineau had accepted the £455 which had been collected and which all the subscribers eventually agreed should be used to redeem the mortgage. Octavius Smith continued the support which he had originally undertaken 'in the general interest of a free theological press'.[71]

The final stage of Chapman's initial proprietorship, from 1858 to 1860, was devoted to plans for the setting up of a Westminster Review Company, with Chapman's chief creditors commuting their claims into shares. Many people were interested and Chapman became a shuttlecock flying between the battledores of opposing factions; he, Grote and Lord Stanley wanted the *Westminster* to remain independent of the company,[72] while Spencer, Octavius Smith and Huxley wanted the company to control the review.[73] Finally the whole plan fell through from a lack of sufficient support – W. B. Carpenter at least withdrew after saying he would join[74] – and in March 1860 the business and review were sold to George Manwaring who already had some money in Chapman's business.[75] Chapman had permission from Smith to act on his behalf[76] and commuted both Smith's claims, and his own claims of £900, into shares in the new business.[77] The diary for 1860 is full of anxious references to his financial troubles; at one point he believed that Manwaring had absconded to America leaving him to bear all the debts.[78] Fortunately he had not, but he seemed no more successful in business than Chapman had been, though the *Westminster* itself was doing well and sales were up to 1,600[79] whereas they had been as low as 600.[80] Finally Manwaring sold out in 1862 to the courageous and lively German publisher, Trübner,[81] but not before a good many people like Sara Hennell had lost money by him.[82]

The details of Trübner's control are not clear. What is known is that while he continued to support the *Westminster* by subscription, Chapman soon resumed and continued to carry financial responsibility for the review until the formation in 1886 of a limited company. To do this he had to maintain the same unrelenting campaign to find financial support. Subscriptions and donations came from a wide variety of sources: John Stuart Mill; an anonymous wealthy Hindu; Mill's friend, Manchester businessman and abolitionist, Max Kyllman,[83] and his friends; and above all, E. H. Stanley. It is from Chapman's correspondence with Mill and Stanley that most is to be learned of the *Westminster's* economic situation between 1860 and 1886. Both men gave substantial financial help and canvassed support from others, and both were involved in Chapman's attempts to make a living separate from the *Westminster*.

Chapman's relations with Mill are very interesting. After his 'Severe animadversions' on the Prospectus, Mill wrote only one article for the *Westminster* in the 1850's.[84] This may have been Harriet Taylor's influence, and indeed the tone of a letter to her from Mill in 1854 seems to confirm this: 'This morning has come from Chapman a proposal for reprinting the article Enfranchisement of Women. How very vulgar all his notes are.'[85] But by 1861 Chapman was able to report to Stanley that Mill was going to write again. His two essays on Comte appeared in 1865[86] and he contributed others.

He refused all payment: 'I cannot think of receiving payment for any paper which I may offer the Review as long as it is not in a position to pay all its contributors'.[87] He continued his support and during Chapman's next financial crisis in 1867 he took out a mortgage for £600 on the *Westminster*.[88] There are frequent letters[89] all bearing testimony to Mill's commitment to the continuation of the *Westminster* and concern for Chapman's own position, and showing how Chapman's search for support was taking him farther and farther afield.

> Any help in my power to give, will go but a little way; and unfortunately my personal connection does not lie among monied people. Most of my radical allies in the House of Commons who are men of wealth, and who are chiefly Yorkshire and Lancashire manufacturers, care for little except practical matters and politics; the most characteristic feature of the Westminster Review, its freedom of speculation in religion and philosophy, would rather be distasteful than a recommendation to most of them; while many who like this, do not like its radicalism. I do not know whether there is any other MP except Mr Stansfield, whom there would be any use in taking into our councils. Him you probably know. The other persons I can think of to consult with are Mr. Grote and Mr. Herbert Spencer.[90]

Mill continued his support through the 1860s and even tried to help Chapman find employment with the Mutual Life Assurance Society.[91] His final act seems to have been in 1869 when he commuted a further loan of £100 into a subscription.[92]

Chapman's longest-standing supporter was E. H. Stanley, 15th Earl of Derby and son of the Conservative Prime Minister. He was successively Colonial Secretary, First Indian Secretary, Foreign Secretary under both his father and Disraeli, Colonial Secretary again in 1882 under Gladstone – after he had left the Conservative party – and finally leader of the Liberal Unionists in the House of Lords. W. E. H. Lecky characterizes him as an old-style radical, belonging comfortably in neither party – though he was always loyal – and more interested in the 'Condition of England Question' than in party political faction.[93]

The correspondence between Chapman and Stanley is in the Liverpool Public Library Archives and extends from 30 March 1858 to 27 October 1892. Once Stanley had become a major supporter he asked for and received regular, detailed reports on the *Westminster*. By January 1860 he had made the £600 he lent in 1858 into a free gift and was subsidizing Chapman at the rate of £200 a year,[94] so he was entitled to the detailed breakdown of the *Westminster*'s fortunes. Some fascinating and otherwise unobtainable material emerges for, apart from sending him regular lists of attributions, Chapman gives a great deal of information about the *Westminster*'s fluctuating income and circulation.

In 1858 he regrets the review's inability to compete with the *Edinburgh*'s payment of £16 a sheet and its dependence on unpaid contributions. This was of course for the perennial and familiar reason that: 'the ideas of which the "Westminster" is the exponent are too far in advance of popular creeds – philosophical, theological and social.'[95] As a clear illustration of this, it was as a direct result of the fall in sales that followed F. W. Newman's 'Religious weaknesses of Protestantism' that Stanley promised £100 a year for the next three years.[96]

A close examination of the balance sheets for 1854–9 which Chapman furnished in October 1860[97] reveals the constant loss at which the *Westminster* operated. Income from sales per issue ran between £374 18s. 4d. and £291 10s., while costs per issue ranged between £438 4s. 7d. and £359 10s. the average being £400.

There are detailed accounts from 1858[98] of Chapman's own financial position in relation to the income the *Westminster* received, the articles he himself wrote, other gratuitous articles he received from elsewhere and the needs of his family. Stanley, while giving help, in 1860 advised amalgamation with the *National*[99] but Chapman was committed to the *Westminster* and tried to find medical employment which would make him independent. In 1861 he asked Stanley to use his influence to help him secure a post with the Medical Council, without success as it turned out.[100]

The correspondence continues with Chapman's frequent requests for advice about articles, and with some considerable details on income and outgoings. He noted with delight when Mudie increased his order from 100 to 150[101] and was hopeful that circulation would increase when the *National* changed from being a quarterly to a monthly.[102] He was equally hopeful of an increase in European circulation when a Leipzig bookseller agreed to take copies of the *Westminster* but was depressed by the loss of income from the sale of plates caused by the American Civil War. However, the abolition of paper duty would reduce expenses.[103]

The painful extrication of the *Westminster* from the morass of Manwaring's affairs in 1862 is given in considerable detail. Once again Chapman opened subscription lists but more substantial help appeared to be available from an unidentified 'wealthy Hindu, a friend of Professor Theodore Goldstücker', in return for articles on India. But this 'temporary help from India' was not as substantial as it had promised to be and the 500 copies of the review that were originally to be taken[104] soon dropped to two-thirds that number,[105] while in the end he appears to have given only £100 for the July and October issues[106] before the agreement came to an abrupt end.

Chapman continued his efforts to build up his private medical practice and was appointed as physician at the Farringdon Dispensary, one of the medical centres to treat the poor. By 12 February 1864 he assured Stanley that he hoped to conduct the *Westminster* without drawing any income from it. How far he managed to do this remains open to doubt. The first positive statement I have found that he and his wife drew no income from the *Westminster* comes in a letter to Stanley in January 1888 when he had had time to establish a successful practice among the English and American communities in Paris. Meanwhile, the correspondence up to 1873, though always indicating financial difficulties, is hopeful, full of suggestions for articles and ideas for his medical works.

Then in 1873 a double crisis arose. The *Westminster* was £800 in debt and Chapman lost his post at the Farringdon Dispensary. To satisfy his creditors, who were willing to settle for a composition of 5s. in the pound, subscriptions of £100 were invited. Chapman sent Stanley the list of those who had already subscribed and they included George Atkinson, Sir James Harman, Sir John Lubbock and W. E. Price, M.P.[107]

The loss of his medical post could not so easily be remedied. He was dismissed not for incompetence or quackery, but for a foolhardiness – or courage – which had always characterized him. He had published in the *Pall Mall Gazette* an outspoken criticism of 'the treatment of outpatients at the London hospitals and dispensaries'. He refused to retract his criticisms and so lost the post.[108]

He then moved to Paris, conducting the *Westminster* from there, and there is a gap in the correspondence until 4 November 1884. Then financial difficulties again prompted Chapman to write. This time he offered Stanley a half-share in the *Westminster*.[109]

Neither Stanley nor anyone else was interested and finally in 1886 Chapman formed the Westminster Review Company, a limited liability company whose records still exist. They show that, besides Chapman and his wife and Stanley, there were a good number of Liberal peers and M.P.s, a sprinkling of manufacturers and professional men and the loyal 'Trübner and Co.' who were interested enough in the *Westminster* to buy shares. Chapman was by then a member of the Liberal Party and he could recommend the *Westminster* to Gladstone as 'a consistent, zealous influential advocate of the doctrines of the advanced liberal cause.'[110]

In his final letters to Stanley there is considerable discussion of topics close to the earl's heart, especially home rule and the colonies. Ever hopeful, Chapman saw a new future for the review as 'the medium for the discussion of colonial subjects both by colonists and writers at home',[111] and he included a long list of articles on Indian and Colonial subjects which had appeared in the *Westminster*.

But even when he had apparently piloted the *Westminster* into the comparatively safe waters of major party political polemics, Chapman was still capable of a dangerous enthusiasm. The *Westminster* was still not 'safe'. In January 1891 he published an article by the American feminist, Elizabeth Cady Stanton,[112] which staunchly defended Parnell, in terms so outspoken that it was immediately seized on by W. T. Stead and his followers. She described them as 'the little set of Social Purity people who are down on my article'.[113] In this article she minces no words in exposing the double standards and the 'many headed cants and hypocrisies' of British public life. As she recorded in her diary, the public view of chastity and patriotism are equally false and are the result of totally misguided education.

As men have not been educated to chastity, why look for it? We might as well require that women, who have never been trained to patriotism, should be public spirited. Let us condemn the system which makes men and women what they are, and not crucify the victims of our false standards of morals. The one lesson these social earthquakes teach us is to cultivate in women more self-respect.

Instead of hounding men, emancipate women from all forms of bondage. But as long as women are slaves, men will be heroes.[114]

In this same entry in her diary she notes how pleased Chapman and his wife were with the article, and this despite the ammunition given to the opponents of Home Rule.

Some of Chapman's old fire survived to the end. From the days of his association with Barbara Leigh Smith, Chapman had made the *Westminster* an early and consistent champion of 'The Cause' and for this, apart perhaps from Mill, he received no patronage, no welcome additions to his subscription lists.

Perhaps, therefore, the most perceptive analysis of those qualities in John Chapman which ensured that the *Westminster* did survive, honourably and even vigorously against all odds, is still Carlyle's. It catches the qualities that evoked equally support from men like Stanley and Mill, and gratitude from new young hopefuls like James Hannay, P. G. Hamerton, John Bridges and Frederic Harrison.

Writing to Browning on 10 October 1851, Carlyle speaks of:

A certain John Chapman, Publisher of Liberalisms, 'Extinct Socialisms' and notable ware of that kind in the Strand has just been here: really a meritorious, productive kind of man, did he well know his road in these times – He has just effected a purchase of the *Westminster Review* . . . his intense purpose now is, To bring out a Review Liberal in all senses, that shall charm the world. . . Poor soul, I really wished him well in his enterprise . . . The man means to pay handsomely; is indeed an honest kind of man, with a real enthusiasm, (tho' a soft and slobbery) in him which can be predicated of very few.[115]

Maybe we might cavil at the 'honest kind of man' but we should also, in the light of the next 40 years of Chapman's career, amend the 'soft and slobbery' to 'tough and resilient'. He was a survivor and it was this that guaranteed the survival of the *Westminster Review*. But it was not just a mediocre survival, and the considerable achievements of the review under his control bear testimony to that 'real enthusiasm' which, after all is said and done, can still 'be predicated of very few'.

NOTES

1. Rosemary van Arsdel's introduction to the *Westminster Review* in WI, III gives a clear picture of the *Westminster* up to 1852. Her bibliography is the best guide to the useful works on the *Westminster*. In her assessment of Chapman himself, however, she unfortunately continues a long tradition of misunderstanding. He certainly had manifest failings,

business was carried on under the aegis of a Mr Birt, a shadowy figure who is in the background of Chapman's other business communications and is referred to by Courtauld. It seems likely that Courtauld insisted that Chapman should hand over the actual management of the business to someone else while still keeping nominal charge of affairs.

Meanwhile the *Westminster* actually prospered. Chapman always had needed gratuitous articles and they were even more necessary now. Harriet Martineau wrote prolifically for the review, giving freely[66] as W. E. Forster had in the past,[67] and as Harrison, Grote,[68] and Mill were to do in the future. During the period 1855 to 1858 Marian Evans and G. H. Lewes contributed some excellent articles, especially upon literature, Huxley continued to write on science and a new contributor, W. B. Donne, soon to be Examiner of Plays, wrote amiably on a wide range of subjects. A new influence on Chapman personally was Mark Pattison, who undertook various parts of the 'Contemporary Literature' section and also contributed full-length articles.

In 1857, Harriet Martineau, with no diminution of friendliness, felt she could no longer carry on the mortgage of the *Westminster*.[69] Without saying exactly what it was, she claimed that someone else had a greater call upon the money. It was therefore suggested that a fund should be set up to which friends and sympathizers including people like Charles Darwin could subscribe to pay her back; this was done and George Grote consented to be 'banker'. Throughout the first half of 1858 relations between her and Chapman were extremely friendly, as they had been for several years; he confided in her his spiritual troubles, and she told him of her ovarian tumour, though all the world believed that she believed that she had dropsy. He advised her on her diet and other medical matters.

Suddenly in June 1858 the tone changes and this marks the beginning of a voluminious increase in correspondence involving herself, Courtauld and Chapman; she and Courtauld kept all letters and made additional notes on them while Chapman reproduced copies of old letters and extracts from diaries. It is not easy therefore to determine the rights and wrongs, especially as the correspondence is one-sided. Once again the problem seems to have hinged on the inevitably intricate relationships involved in financing the general publishing business and maintaining the *Westminster*. Harriet Martineau canvassed and obtained considerable support to redeem the mortgage on the basis of an original £150 subscribed by a Mr Hippisley. She was therefore extremely angry when she later learned that the sum had originally been given to Chapman personally as a personal testimony to himself and his business. She accused Chapman of duplicity and prevarication and an increasingly frantic correspondence followed, with matters made worse by Lord Stanley also saying at first that he did not realize what the money he had donated was for. On this point at least Chapman was exonerated, for Stanley later admitted that he himself had been confused and had made a mistake. Chapman pleaded for permission to come to Ambleside for a personal interview, but Miss Martineau refused. His injured protestations of innocence, his claims of having been victimized because of his poverty, and his appeals to their long-standing friendship do not convince us that his style in letter-writing had improved. Then he made an unforgivable blunder – he attributed her strong reactions to her medical condition, reducing her right-eous indignation to an ovarian affliction. There was no going back from there, and she sadly wrote him her valediction; she had always supported him in the past against hostile criticism; but that was over: 'I can only repeat what I have before said, – that confidence is not a voluntary matter, & that it cannot be awarded (after suspension) on the judgment of others, even if that judgment were open to no doubt or objection'.[70] How far Chapman was culpable it is difficult to tell, but one of her accusations that she did not know that Chapman had any other creditors, is disproved by one of her own earlier letters. On balance it would seem that he had been devious rather than dishonest, and extremely tactless in his long letters – at one point in June they were writing nearly every day – and she, never one to be ruled by her head rather than her heart, felt a deep personal betrayal that did not have all that much to do with the facts of the case.

Harriet Martineau's opposition was strengthened by Courtauld who in the summer of 1858 was further angered by Chapman, and it was their joint and simultaneous disillusion that nearly ended both the business and the *West-minster*. In July Courtauld discovered that back in 1855, when the business had been heavily in debt, Chapman had drawn out money for his own personal expenses, partly to pay for his costly medical studies. Chapman's reply was that he had applied to Courtauld and been referred to the other creditor involved, Octavius Smith. Believing that Smith had given permis-sion, he had taken the money as – and here again the wording is less than tactful – he had a right to do. Courtauld was furious, claiming that Chapman should certainly not have withdrawn any money at all so long as the business was in debt, and that in any case he had no 'right' to do so.

The fate of the *Westminster* now seemed sealed. When the subscription for the mortgage had been opened, Courtauld had, reluctantly, and as a personal favour to Harriet Martineau, agreed to join Smith in not claiming the £500 as part of the money due to him as Chapman's creditor. Now, with both Harriet Martineau and Courtauld antagonized, there seemed no reason why the agreement should not go and the business *and* review be wound up. There was some move for Octavius Smith to assume Courtauld's claims, but he insisted that Chapman should take over responsibility for the business and but his detractors, both nineteenth- and twentieth-century, have as often been guilty of the twin afflictions of snobbery and hypocrisy as he was guilty of deviousness and conceit.

2. John Stuart Mill, *The Later Letters 1849 to 1873*, ed. Francis E. Mineka and Dwight W. Lindley (4 vols., Toronto 1972) (hereafter cited as Mill, *Later Letters*), III, 1007.

3. *Ibid.*, no. 1011.

4. Huxley Collection, Imperial College, London, 19.191.

5. Martineau Collection, University of Birmingham (hereafter cited as Martineau Coll.): Courtauld to Harriet Martineau, 9 June 1858.

6. *The George Eliot Letters*, ed. G. Haight (1955–78) (hereafter cited as Eliot, *Letters*), II, 495, 505, III, 3–4.

7. Helen Taylor to John Chapman, 12 Feb. 1887, London School of Economics, Mill Taylor Collection, IV, f. 57. See also 14 Mar. 1886, f. 56.

8. I am indebted to Ms Jean L'Esperance for a copy of this letter from Josephine Butler.

9. *Critic*, 15 Aug. 1851.

10. G. S. Haight, *George Eliot and John Chapman* (1969 edn), 154.

11. *Ibid.*, 55.

12. Chapman to Stanley, 31 July 1873, Derby Papers, Liverpool RO.

13. Haight, *op. cit.*, 224.

14. *Ibid.*, 167.

15. *Ibid.*, 169.

16. *Ibid.*

17. *Ibid.*, 171.

18. *Ibid.*, 174.

19. *Ibid.*, 175.

20. *Ibid.*

21. *Ibid.*, 176.

22. *Ibid.*, 176, 178.

23. *Ibid.*, 176.

24. Mill, *Later Letters*, no. 53.

25. Haight, *op. cit.*, 176–7.

26. *Ibid.*, 177.

27. Eliot, *Letters*, I, 351.

28. *Ibid.*, 351–2.

29. Mill, *Later Letters*, no. 58.

30. Haight, *op. cit.*, 180.

31. Mill, *Later Letters*, no. 66.

32. *Westminster Rev.*, n.s. XVIII (Oct. 1860).

33. *Ibid.*, n.s. XIII (Jan. 1858).

34. I am indebted to Mr Norman St John-Stevas for this quotation.

35. Noel Annan, 'The intellectual aristocracy', in *Studies in Social History*, (1955), ed. J. H. Plumb.

36. Haight, *op. cit.*, 207.

37. Eliot, *Letters*, II, 33.

38. *Ibid.*, I, 369.

39. *Ibid.*, II, 29.

40. *Ibid.*, 39, 43, 51.

41. *Ibid.*, 55.

42. *Ibid.*, 53.

43. *Ibid.*, 70.

44. Richard Garnett, *The Life of W. J. Fox* (1910), 294.

45. Eliot, *Letters*, II, 95.

46. *Ibid.*, 127–8.

47. *Ibid.*, 237.

48. *Ibid.*, I, 359.

49. *Ibid.*, II, 4.

50. *Ibid.*, II, 47.

51. Waldo Hilary Dunn, *James Anthony Froude 1818–1856* (1961), II, 167.

52. J. Drummond and C. B. Upton, *The Life and Letters of James Martineau* (2 vols., 1902), I, 269.

53. Haight, *op. cit.*, 195.

54. *Westminster Rev.*, n.s. II (Apr. 1852) and n.s. IV (Oct. 1853).

55. Drummond and Upton, *op. cit.*, I, 264–5.

56. *Ibid.*, 269.

57. Harriet Martineau, *Autobiography* (1877), II, 425–7. She also suggests that F. W. Newman gave warning of what Martineau and Hodgson planned to do with the *Westminster*: Harriet Martineau to Chapman, 19 Mar. 1854, Bod. Eng. lett. d.2, f. 117.

58. W. R. Greg, *Enigmas of Life* (1891), xxxvii–xxxviii.

59. *Unpublished Letters of Matthew Arnold*, ed. Arnold Whitridge (New Haven, 1923), 26.

60. Eliot, *Letters*, II, 80.

61. *Ibid.*, 82–3.

62. Martineau Coll. and Bod. Eng. lett. d.2, fos. 213–35 *passim*.

63. In 1858 Courtauld refused to allow Chapman to vindicate his 'plausible representations' by being cross-examined in a personal interview: Courtauld to Chapman, 21(?) July 1858, Martineau Coll.

64. Courtauld to Harriet Martineau, 13 Aug. 1858, Martineau Coll. See also Haight, *op. cit.*, 95–6.

65. Eliot, *Letters*, II, 163.

66. Harriet Martineau, *Autobiography*, II, 427.
67. Thomas Wemyss Reid, *The Life of the Right. Hon. W. E. Forster* (1888), 286.
68. Bod. Eng. lett. d. 122, f. 83.
69. The following account is based on the correspondence in the University of Birmingham Library and the Bodleian Library.
70. Bod. Eng. lett. d. 2., fos. 234–5.
71. Courtauld to Harriet Martineau, 9 June 1858, Martineau Coll.
72. Haight, *op. cit.*, 230, 235.
73. *Ibid.*, 231.
74. *Ibid.*, 233.
75. *Ibid.*
76. *Ibid.*, 235.
77. *Ibid.*, 250.
78. *Ibid.*
79. *Ibid.*, 232.
80. *Ibid.*, 75.
81. Trübner published the *Westminster* until the end of 1889.
82. Eliot, *Letters*, IV, 10–11.
83. Mill, *Later Letters*, no. 1045.
84. 'Whewell's moral philosophy', *Westminster Rev.*, n.s. II (Oct. 1852).
85. Mill, *Later Letters*, no. 140.
86. *Westminster Rev.*, n.s. XXVIII (Apr. and July 1865).
87. Mill, *Later Letters*, no. 556.
88. *Ibid.*, no. 1021.
89. *Ibid.*, nos. 1024, 1026, 1035.
90. *Ibid.*, no. 1018.
91. *Ibid.*, no. 1024.
92. *Ibid.*, no. 1444.
93. W. E. H. Lecky, Prefatory Memoir to *Speeches and Addresses of Edward Henry, XVth Earl of Derby*, selected and edited by Sir T. H. Sanderson, and E. S. Roscoe (1894).
94. Chapman to Stanley, 11 Sept. 1858 and 13 Jan. 1860, Derby Papers.
95. Chapman to Stanley, 11 July 1858, Derby Papers.
96. Chapman to Stanley, 4 Sept. 1858, Derby Papers.
97. Chapman to Stanley, 9 Oct. 1860, Derby Papers.
98. Chapman to Stanley, 11 Sept. 1858, Derby Papers.
99. Chapman to Stanley, 9 Oct. 1860, Derby Papers.
100. Chapman to Stanley, 31 Jan. 1861, Derby Papers.
101. *Ibid.*
102. Chapman to Stanley, 25 Jan. 1864, Derby Papers.
103. Chapman to Stanley, 24 Oct. 1861, Derby Papers.
104. Haight, *op. cit.*, 112.
105. Chapman to Stanley, 4 Aug. 1862, Derby Papers.
106. Chapman to Stanley, 2 Oct. 1862, Derby Papers.
107. Chapman to Stanley, 31 July 1873, Derby Papers.
108. Chapman to Stanley, 19 Oct. 1873, Derby Papers. I have so far been unable to trace a copy of the relevant issue of the *Pall Mall Gazette*.
109. Chapman to Stanley, 4 Nov. 1884, Derby Papers.
110. BL Add. MS 44500, f. 291, Gladstone Papers.
111. Chapman to Stanley, 7 Oct. 1890, Derby Papers.
112. 'Patriotism and chastity', *Westminster Rev.*, n.s. CXXXV (Jan. 1891).
113. *Elizabeth Cady Stanton. As revealed in her letters and reminiscences*, ed. Theodore Stanton and Harriet Stanton Blatch (1922), 269.
114. *Ibid.*, 269–70.
115. *Letters of Thomas Carlyle to John Stuart Mill, John Sterling, and Robert Browning*, ed. Alexander Carlyle (1923), 228–9.

Maurice Milne   Survival of the fittest?
Sunderland newspapers in
the nineteenth century

'For as those prematurely carried off must, in the average of cases, be
those in whom the power of self-preservation is the least, it
unavoidably follows, that those left behind to continue the race are
those in whom the power of self-preservation is the greatest – are the
select of their generation.' – Herbert Spencer, *Westminster Review*,
1852

A pessimist could be forgiven for thinking that to embark upon newspaper
publication in the nineteenth century was to enter into a Hobbesian state of
nature. The history of the newspaper press is littered with the corpses of
Mercuries, Telegraphs, Heralds and *Chronicles*, some still-born, some dying
of inanition, others done to death by rivals. Even in the fertile period
immediately after the repeal of the newspaper stamp tax in 1855, prospects
were uncertain. Of the 25 newspapers known to have been founded in
Northumberland and Durham between 1855 and 1868, nine were already
deceased by the latter date, and only eight entered the twentieth century. Of
the 74 newspaper companies formed, in all regions, between 1856 and 1865,
only four lasted more than 30 years.[1] Writing in 1896, two distinguished
journalists observed that, 'whilst a successful newspaper may be a "mine of
wealth" not easily destroyed, it is terribly true that no class of property is so
difficult to create, and on no kind of enterprise has capital been more
seductively and disastrously expended.'[2]

   Yet the seductions of newspaper ownership proved too powerful to be
resisted. Financial and political fortunes could be made out of a successful
publication. Given the necessary resources and stamina, the initial outlay
could be recouped and the losses of early years could be sustained, until a
sufficient clientèle of readers and advertisers had been attracted. For a
Victorian newspaper with the right combination of winning qualities, life
was far from being 'solitary, poor, nasty, brutish and short'. The successful
publications of the nineteenth century are, in the provinces at least, still

going strong in the closing decades of the twentieth century, albeit often as parts of newspaper chains.

This intermingling of success and failure naturally raises the question of why some newspapers survived while so many others succumbed. It is relatively easy to frame a set of hypotheses. One could reasonably assume that positive assets would include the right politics, the right price, the right brand of journalism, the right location and the right frequency of publication. But what determines what is 'right'? In political stance, is partisanship preferable to neutrality, even if the commitment is to the weaker side? Is it always advisable to bring out a paper at the cheapest price, regardless of the effect on its dimensions and profit margins? Is the 'right' brand of journalism one which conforms to the accepted stereotype for a morning, evening, or weekly paper, or one which experiments? Does location in an expanding town guarantee expanding sales, or merely a proliferation of rivals? Is daily publication always preferable to weekly, and where does the advantage lie between morning and evening publication? Simple hypotheses dissolve into complexity – unsurprisingly, for if there were an easy formula for success, the history of Victorian newspapers would have been very different.

This essay is intended to serve as a contribution to elucidating the problems raised in the preceding paragraph. By means of close attention to the newspapers of one large town, it is hoped that some rough pattern will emerge of the factors most conducive to success in newspaper publication. Whether this pattern is capable of general application will only become apparent after it has been subjected to critical scrutiny by specialists in the newspaper history of other localities. What follows might be the first word on the subject, but it will not have achieved its purpose if it is the last.

1. SUNDERLAND IN THE NINETEENTH CENTURY

Sunderland makes a good location for a case study, both in terms of its socio-economic character and its vitality in the field of periodical journalism.[3] It was the most fertile source of newspaper enterprise in County Durham, although many publications were short-lived. Excluding two publications concentrating on shipping news, at least 20 separate newspapers were launched in Sunderland between 1830 and 1906. By the end of 1906 only the *Sunderland Echo* survived.

The town of Sunderland could well be said to typify the expansion which enterprising industrial centres underwent during the nineteenth century. It became a parliamentary borough in 1832, elected its first municipal councillors in 1835, and its first Poor Law Guardians in 1836. Its growth was based on shipbuilding and coal-exporting. The Wearsiders were relatively slow to change from wood and sail to iron and steam, and local shipbuilding was in the doldrums during the mid-1840s, but after the launching of the Wear's first iron ship in 1852 progress was rapid and impressive. Sunderland claimed to be 'the largest shipbuilding town in the world'. Shipowning, ship-repairing and ship-servicing were allied industries, although local rope-making declined with the demise of sail. The decline of the local pottery industry after 1850, and of glass and bottle manufacturing after 1880, were more than compensated for by the opening of new collieries, at Wearmouth, Ryhope, Silksworth, and Hylton. Sunderland also served as coal-shipping port for the surrounding coalfield. Coal exports quadrupled, to $4\frac{1}{4}$ million tons *per annum*, between 1820 and 1900. The town's population expanded accordingly, from 39,000 in 1831 to 98,000 in 1871 and to 146,000 in 1901.

Impressive as this expansion may be, however, in quantitative terms, qualitative considerations must also be used in gauging the prospects for periodical journalism. Shipyards, docks and coalmines are not necessarily prime locations for the sale of newspapers or the recruitment of advertisers. True, the town had its Athenaeum, its Literary and Philosophical Society, its subscription library and, from 1879, its public library. Also, in banks and commercial offices, and amongst solicitors, schoolteachers, tradesmen and shipping clerks, there could be found the potential readership of a periodical press. But the socio-economic balance was tilted unfavourably towards the lower end of the scale. For instance when, in 1867, the borough franchise was extended from the £10 householder to the artisan householder, the electorate nationally was doubled: in Sunderland it was trebled (from 3,776 to 11,370). The Sunderland School Board found, on its formation in 1871, that there were 18,169 children of school age, but only 11,853 school places available. It is probable, moreover, that newspaper advertising was less forthcoming in a centre of heavy industry than it would have been in a regional economy with a greater proportion of light industries. Certainly this was the view of informed opinion in the neighbouring town of Newcastle upon Tyne. The *Newcastle Daily Chronicle* observed: 'Given the population, Newcastle is perhaps the worst advertising city in the kingdom. This arises from the staple industries being of a kind that do not need newspaper publicity, and from the habits of the people not being to advertise as much as they do elsewhere.'[4] If that observation was true of Newcastle, it was unlikely to have been less true of Sunderland.

The political character of Sunderland underwent a significant change after 1867, partly because of the effect of the Second Reform Act upon the electorate, and partly for reasons more peculiar to Sunderland. Between 1832 and 1867 the alliance between Whigs and radicals, which, despite stresses and tensions, held good nationally, broke down in Sunderland. The Whigs found their social and religious ties with the Tories more congenial than any political affinity they might have with the radicals. The strength of Nonconformity in the borough, with only ten of the 66 places of worship in 1851 being run by the Established Church, helped to make Sunderland a Liberal constituency, as did the presence of the Lambton interest.[5] The Tories, however, who were well represented amongst local shipowners, and who enjoyed the backing of the Londonderry interest,[6] could hope to carry one of the two Sunderland seats if the Whigs and radicals were not combining wholeheartedly. This is precisely what occurred in 1865, when James Hartley, the Conservative candidate, received Whig support in pushing John Candlish, the radical candidate, into third place. The radicals retaliated by capturing the Whig seat in 1866, when its holder, Fenwick, had to fight a by-election on being appointed a Civil Lord of the Admiralty. The radicals drove home their advantage by running an additional candidate, E. T. Gourley, in the 1868 general election, and defeating the moderate Liberal, T. C. Thompson. The radicals now held both Sunderland seats and continued to do so, with one exception, until 1895. These occurrences are significant, not only for their part in determining the general political character of Sunderland, but because they marked the beginning of the active political career of Samuel Storey, the key figure in the history of Sunderland's daily newspapers. It was Storey who helped to form the Monkwearmouth Advanced Liberal Association after the defeat in 1865; Storey who helped to achieve the radicals' revenge of 1866; Storey who became president of the Sunderland Reform League in 1867. A town councillor from 1869, alderman from 1877, and mayor in 1876 and 1877, Storey was Member of Parliament for Sunderland from 1881 to 1895. His entry into the arena, coinciding as it almost does with the effective beginning of Sunderland's daily press, marks a convenient dividing point in the survey which follows of developments in the local periodical press.

2. FROM THE FOUNDING OF THE *HERALD* TO THE FOUNDING OF THE *ECHO*

Of the 21 newspapers published in Sunderland during the nineteenth century, 15 were launched in the period between 1831 and 1873. To discuss each of the papers in turn would be both tedious and, in some instances, unhelpful, given the paucity of information about such periodicals as the *Sunderland Mirror* and the *Sunderland Telegram*.[7] The titles, with other relevant data, are listed in the table on pp. 198-9. Instead, attention will be concentrated upon the question why the *Sunderland Herald* and *Sunderland Times* were able to outlive a dozen local rivals, including two dailies (one of them concentrating upon shipping information) and a cheap weekly.

The *Sunderland Herald* was the first newspaper to be successfully established in Sunderland, and until the repeal of the stamp tax in 1855 it remained comfortably ahead of its challengers. Its subtitle, *Shields and Stockton Observer and General Advertiser*, was clearly aimed at two other Durham towns which lacked newspapers of their own. Indeed a prospectus for the *Herald* issued some weeks in advance of the paper's inception described it as the *Sunderland and Shields Herald*, giving South Shields a share of the main title. The prime target was the maritime interest in both towns: 'The Shipping commerce alone of those places . . . presents a variety and combination of interests, requiring for its advocacy and support the medium of a local and impartial paper.'[8] Mention was also made of the 'mineral and manufacturing commerce' of the district. In politics, the prospectus pledged the *Herald's* support for the Whig's parliamentary reform bill, but cautiously observed that 'it forms, however, no part of our political creed to advocate the unlimited extension of the elective franchise.' In this reservation can be detected the eventual cause of the *Herald's* decline: too Whiggish to move from reform to radicalism, yet never a simply Tory organ, the *Herald* was to be outflanked on both sides. During its first 25 years, however, the *Herald* did well. In 1838 it took the title of *Sunderland and Durham County Herald* and by January 1844 it had doubled its size to eight pages. It was then selling about 1,200 copies a week, rising to a peak of over 2,200 copies in 1854.[9] After an enlargement in January 1848, the *Herald* claimed that its dimensions exceeded the best-known London dailies and any paper in the North of England. It was still claiming to be the largest newspaper in the North of England in 1868, when, in an advertisement in its own columns, it singled out its special merits as follows: 'The *Herald* is the only newspaper published in Sunderland which contains in a single sheet the complete news of the week, and is therefore the most suitable for *families* and for posting to shipmasters and others at a distance.'[10] This was an attempt to turn to its own good the seeming disadvantage of appearing once weekly, as compared with the now bi-weekly *Sunderland Times*. By then, however, the *Herald* had lost the circulation battle within Sunderland itself, although it probably outsold the *Times* in the surrounding county.

There was something of a reversal of roles in this situation, for the *Times* replaced an earlier Sunderland paper, incorporated in its subtitle, the *Beacon*, which had pitched its sales at the landward interests. The *Beacon's* prospectus laid stress upon its intended publication of the latest corn, cattle and provision prices: 'The advantages to the Frequenters of Inns and Public-houses, and of Corn-dealers, Millers, etc. which the *Beacon* will thus possess in a priority of Market Intelligence, need not be pointed out.'[11] Perhaps, however, they should have been pointed out more forcibly, or perhaps they were not advantageous enough, for the *Beacon* was incorporated within the

SUNDERLAND NEWSPAPERS, 1831–1906

First issue	Title*	Initial price	Politics	Last issue
29 Jan. 1831	S. and Durham Shipping Gazette	7d.	Neutral	7 Oct. 1831
28 May 1831	S. Herald (daily from 8 April 1880, price ½d.)	7d.	Whig	3 Sept. 1881 (merged with S. Daily Post)
3 Jan. 1838	S. Beacon	4½d.	Cons.	26 Sept. 1839 (merged with) Northern Times)
5 Oct. 1839	Northern Times, retitled S. Times, from 5 Jan. 1844 (daily from 3 July 1876, price ½d.; the weekly continued as S. Weekly Times, 7 July 1876, retitled S. Weekly Echo, 7 Jan. 1881)	4½d.	Cons. to 1857 Radical from 1857	3 Aug. 1878 (absorbed by S. Daily Echo) 7 Aug. 1914
14 Sept. 1839	S. Mirror	2½d.	Cons.	5 Nov. 1840
5 July 1851	S. News	4½d.	Radical	19 May 1855
2 Jan. 1852	S. Examiner	4½d.	Liberal	7 Apr. 1854
Nov. 1853	S. and Hartlepool General Review and Advertiser			? after 25 Mar. 1854
12 May 1854	Northern Examiner (moved to Newcastle from 1 Sept. 1854)	4½d.		11 Jan. 1856

First issue	Title*	Initial price	Politics	Last issue
Sept./Oct. 1854	S. Daily News	1d.	(Shipping)†	1865
28 Aug. 1858	S. Telegram	1d.	Cons.	18 Dec. 1858
6 Jan. 1865	S. Weekly News	1d.	Radical	27 March 1868
6 Nov. 1865	S. Daily Shipping News	½d.	(Shipping)	31 Dec. 1913
26 Aug. 1867	S. Sentinel	1½d.	Cons.	Nov. 1878
6 July 1870	S. Evening Chronicle	½d.	Cons.	3 May 1871
22 Dec. 1873	S. Daily Echo	½d.	Radical– Liberal	extant
21 July 1876	S. Daily Post	½d.	Cons.	21 July 1906
12 June 1894	Socialist (monthly)		Labour	Jan. 1895
16 Aug. 1897	S. Citizen			22 Apr. 1899
14 Nov. 1898	S. Morning Mail	½d.	Pro-Empire	11 Feb. 1901
10 Dec. 1898	S. Weekly News			6 May 1899
13 May 1905	Wearside Star	1d.		27 May 1905

* S. = Sunderland. Publication is weekly unless stated otherwise; subtitles and price changes are omitted.

† (Shipping) = primarily for shipping information.

Northern Times in 1839. The paper's Conservative politics, however, were less likely to have been a problem in the 1830s than in other, more radical, decades of Sunderland's history. The Conservatives held one of the Sunderland seats, in the person of Alderman William Thompson, from 1833 to 1841. They lost the seat, not at the general election, but at a subsequent by-election, when the Whigs fielded a strong candidate, Viscount Howick of the Grey family. Another by-election, occasioned by Howick's inheritance of the family peerage in 1845, enabled the Tories to recapture the seat through the resourceful candidature of George Hudson. Thus, there was a circulation-base for a Conservative paper in Sunderland at this time, and the Northern Times, retitled the Sunderland Times in 1844, adhered to the Conservative politics of its acquisition, the Beacon. In the late 1850s, however, Sunderland Tories suffered a double blow: Hudson lost his seat in 1859 shortly after the Times had been acquired by the radical Alderman James Williams, a former Chartist. The change of proprietorship and politics proved opportune. The *Times* was well able to respond to the quickening of the radical pulse which occurred in the mid-1860s. Williams recruited a capable editor in William Brockie, formerly editor of the *Shields Gazette*. By converting its mid-week supplement into a full second edition in 1862, the paper became a bi-weekly, costing 1d. on Tuesdays and 2d. on Saturdays (the *Herald's* weekly price was 3d.). If the *Times* had gone on to daily publication in the 1860s, it might have driven home its circulation advantage over the *Herald*, whilst forestalling any attempt by other local radicals to found their own daily. This was what Williams intended, and about 1867, 'the type was bought for the new venture, and other arrangements were made'.[12] Brockie, too, had high hopes of becoming the editor of Sunderland's first general daily newspaper. Williams, however, fell ill, and died in November 1868. His widow continued the business, but the opportunity of conversion to daily publication was allowed to pass. Politically, also, the *Times* missed an opportunity. Although more attuned to the growing radicalism of Sunderland than was the *Herald*, the *Times* aligned itself with T. C. Thompson, the less radical of the two candidates for the seat accompanying that expected to go to the radical John Candlish at the general election of 1868. In so doing, it backed the loser, and it paid the price when the radical activists behind the victorious Candlish and E. T. Gourley resolved to have their own daily organ, the *Sunderland Daily Echo*.

    Although the *Herald* and the *Times* thus entered the 1870s in a vulnerable position, the extent of their achievement should not be understated. Local challengers had come and gone, notably the *Sunderland News* (1851–5), controlled by John Candlish, the *Sunderland Daily News* (1854–5), which brought daily journalism to the town, but mainly in the form of shipping news and advertisements, and the *Sunderland Weekly News* (1865–8). The last-named was probably the most serious threat, particularly to the *Times*. Priced at one penny, it undercut its competitors, whilst espousing the politics of the vigorous group of Sunderland radicals, Candlish, Gourley, and Storey. It had been established by Richard Ruddock, the agent and resident reporter in Sunderland for the *Newcastle Daily Chronicle*, on behalf of his employer, Joseph Cowen. But the paper was terminated apparently as a result of a strategic decision to concentrate upon achieving the highest possible circulation for the *Newcastle Weekly Chronicle*.[13] After going on to assist in the foundation of the *Sunderland Echo*, Ruddock returned to Newcastle to be managing editor of the *Newcastle Daily Chronicle* from 1878 until his death in 1908. The *Sunderland Evening Chronicle* (1870–1), another potential rival to the moderate *Herald*, had no connection with its Newcastle namesake, being one of three papers in a Conservative syndicate which operated briefly in the region at the start of the 1870s,[14] but it could not survive the dominant Liberalism of Newcastle, Tynemouth and Sunderland, particularly in the heyday of Gladstone's first Ministry. The *Sunderland Sentinel* (1867–78) may well have been more successful in attracting Conservative readers away from the *Herald*, particularly as it sold for half the price (at 1½d.) but its abusive editorials, bewildering changes of publication days and slender advertisement basis hardly gave it the foundations for lasting success.[15] Thus, a combination of factors, partly political, partly commercial and partly fortuitous, helped to eliminate the various local rivals to the *Herald* and the *Times*. But this does not suffice to explain why they, in particular, survived. Part of the explanation has already been given, notably the *Herald's* appeal to the shipping interest and the adoption by the *Times* of bi-weekly publication and Liberal politics. Other assets must now be placed in the reckoning, however, if the explanation is to carry more weight.

First, both papers could derive increasing benefit from their longevity. Success in newspaper-management breeds its own reward. A clientèle of readers and advertisers is built up, placing newcomers at a disadvantage. Before 1855 the initial outlay costs of establishing a newspaper were compounded by the advertisement duty (until 1853) and the stamp tax. The neighbouring *Shields Gazette* paid £618 to the Government during its first ten months, in 1849, while the *Sunderland Herald*, with its larger circulation and larger sheet, was paying over £1,000 *per annum* in the early 1840s.[16] These burdens were enough to smother any struggling infant. A second advantage, enjoyed by the *Herald*, was the quality of its typography. The paper prided itself upon its 'chaste and beautiful types' and its occasional wood-engravings were of a very high standard.[17] As other towns on the eastern side of County Durham acquired their own newspapers, notably South Shields in 1849, Hartlepool in 1855 and Stockton in 1857, the concentration of the *Sunderland Times* upon the borough, where its proprietor, Alderman Williams, was a respected political figure, probably proved to be to its advantage. The growth in Sunderland's population and industrial activity, after a lull in the mid-1840s (when, significantly, there were no recorded newspaper foundations), helped to compensate the established Sunderland newspapers for any diminution of extraneous sales. It was, then, in relatively good shape that the *Herald* and the *Times* entered their fifth and fourth decades respectively, during Gladstone's first Ministry. But before Gladstone left office a new era in Sunderland journalism had begun.

3. THE FOUNDATION OF THE SUNDERLAND DAILY ECHO, 1873–8

The *Sunderland Daily Echo* began publication on 22 December 1873 (see plate 13). Priced at ½d. for four medium sides (20 ins by 15 ins), two of its strongest assets were its Liberal politics and its impressive coverage of shipping news. In the first issue, the whole of the third page was devoted to shipping and port information. Although this extensive coverage was subsequently curtailed, maritime news remained a high priority with the *Echo*. In this respect and presumably others its daily publication gave it an obvious advantage over the *Herald*. Of the original 20 columns, eight were occupied by advertisements and four by local news. When the *Echo* increased its columnage to 24, less than a year later, the extra space was taken up by additional advertising and a fuller coverage of general news. The inaugural editorial observed that:

> Of the eighteen or twenty cities and towns in the United Kingdom whose population exceeds 100,000, Sunderland is probably the only one which labours under the disadvantage, not to say the reproach, of not possessing a daily newspaper of its own. For its supply of daily news it is indebted to two neighbouring towns – one a little larger than itself, the other not half so large. Newspapers published in those towns have obtained a foothold here, and from time to time their proprietors have established branches, published special editions, and thus and otherwise sought permanently and fully to occupy the ground with their offshoots; but these colonising ventures have for obvious reasons not been attended with marked success.[18]

The lesser neighbour referred to was South Shields, which was providing Sunderland with daily news through the 3,000 copies of the *Shields Gazette* sent down each afternoon. Coverage of Sunderland news was sometimes inadequate, and although the *Gazette* was Gladstonian Liberal in allegiance, its editorial views were occasionally inimical to 'the new party of constitutional progressives' active in Sunderland.[19] The most active of these 'progressives', Samuel Storey, had also clashed with the *Gazette*'s editor William Duncan, at the previous general election and chafed at Duncan's reluctance to give space for reports of the activities of Storey and his fellow radicals. Storey's threat to establish a rival paper did not appear to alarm Duncan. 'He laughed in my face', Storey later recalled. The threat was given reality, however, with the aid of six other local backers, each of whom contributed £500, as did Storey himself. The initial outlay of £3,500 was soon expended, some of it being used to purchase a small printing business and its plant. The flat-bed press was only capable of producing a maximum of 500 copies per hour, and its steam engine was unreliable. The first day's sale of 1,500 copies was soon followed by a decline to about 1,000 copies. Advertisers were either slow to adjust to the potentialities of daily advertising or dubious as to the circulation prospects of the new paper. The pitying smiles of William Duncan, who lived in Sunderland, must have added to Storey's discomfiture. Another £7,000 was soon needed to maintain and improve the business. Three of the seven co-founders withdrew at this point, so Storey shouldered the additional burden himself. The *Echo's* first anniversary editorial claimed that the circulation had risen from hundreds into thousands, but Storey later admitted that only in its eighth year did the paper begin to make a profit (of £400).

It is worth giving some attention to the prime motive behind the *Echo's* foundation. The inaugural editorial declared: 'Our venture is a purely commercial venture. If we can make it of real use to the busy teeming population around us, it will prosper; not otherwise.' And a year later, emphasis was still being placed upon the *Echo's* value to the local seafaring community: 'That the *Echo* might become the local organ to which anxious wives and families might turn for earliest news of their loved ones, or a sympathetic public for speediest and most accurate news of dreaded disasters, was what we desired, and what in some measure we have fortunately achieved.' In his speech, however, at the 'covering-in' supper of the new *Echo* office, in 1876, Storey declared that 'The proprietors would not be sorry if in the future they made money by their journal, but if they only assisted in the more general adoption of Liberal principles and did anything to better the condition of those around them, they would have achieved the principal portion of their programme.'[20] The two objectives are not, of course, mutually exclusive – the more copies that are sold, the more potential converts that can be reached. There must come a point, however, when either the political or the commercial motive must be given primacy, and there can be little doubt that for the *Echo* the political commitment prevailed. The original founders were united in their Liberal politics, three of them serving at one time or another as Liberal Members of Parliament for constituencies in County Durham. The *Echo* was later to adhere to its Gladstonian standpoint even when this was far from popular, for example at the time of Disraeli's triumph at the Congress of Berlin. Further, the *Echo*, in its early years, refused to indulge the preoccupations of the patrons of the turf, even though the provision of racing tips and betting information was widely regarded as one of the best commercial assets of an evening paper. By the summer of 1876, however, it was publishing racing results.

The task of establishing whether a newspaper was commercially successful is normally aggravated by the haphazard and secretive manner in which newspaper offices kept their files. In the case of the *Sunderland Daily Echo*, however, the survival of the paper's wages book for the period 1875–8 provides a helpful starting-point (see Appendix on pp. 218–22). The total wage and salary bill averaged around £48 per week. Other costs and the income from sales and advertisements can be estimated from data in the *Echo*, supplemented by the ledgers of the *Northern Daily Mail*, a West Hartlepool newspaper which Storey took over in 1884.[21] The *Echo* was claiming a daily circulation of nearly 7,000 copies in the summer of 1876, rising to over 8,000 by May 1877. The circulation accounts in the *Mail* ledgers give an average daily circulation of 5,688 in 1885, rising (after temporarily dropping back) to 6,815 in 1890. The two papers were thus roughly comparable. The *Mail's* wage bill amounted to about 58 per cent of the total running costs, with paper, ink and type consuming 27 per cent, leaving 15 per cent for intelligence, in the form of agency reports and the like. Relating these figures to the *Echo's* wage bill would give weekly running costs of £83, divided between £48 for wages, £22 for paper and ink, and £13 for intelligence.[22] On the income side, a daily sale of 8,000 copies at ½d. per copy would yield £100 per week, less distribution costs and news-agents' commissions, which would probably bring the figure down to around £80. The only other major source of income would be advertising, which, if the *Mail's* ratio is applied to the *Echo*, would have yielded about £60 per week.[23] Against this, however, must be set the costs of constructing and maintaining the premises, the purchase of printing equipment and the depreciation thereon. It is highly probable that such costs swallowed most of the running surplus provided by advertising and sales, at least until major capital items were paid off and sales further expanded. Profitability was then a real proposition. The crucial problem was clearly to survive the pressures of the early years, pressures which were at their most acute in 1876, the decisive year in the history of the Sunderland press.

4. THE DECISIVE STRUGGLE, 1876–81

The year opened with the hearing of a libel action, one of several during the final quarter of the nineteenth century which serve to shed light on Sunder-land newspapers, whilst indicating the heat in which they were conducted. The plaintiff, Henry Ritson, a local Conservative, sued the *Echo* in the person of its publisher, W. A. Brignal, for libel. The case was heard in Liverpool to counteract Samuel Storey's alleged influence over any jury likely to be empanelled in County Durham. The subject matter of the case was the usual electoral badinage of the period and it was not clear whether Ritson was the target, the defence maintaining that the hostile references were to William Williams of the *Sunderland Sentinel*, whose newspaper vilified Storey and the *Echo* in language far more intemperate than that which had brought Brignal before the court. The jury found for the defend-ant, with costs. What is most striking about the case is the calibre of counsel retained. The three counsel for the plaintiff were led by Charles Russell,

Q.C., while the defence was headed by the Solicitor-General. To escape the costs of such a hearing must have been a profound relief to the *Echo's* management, especially as Ritson had allegedly declared, in commencing his action, that he would 'ruin or finish' the *Echo*.[24] The judge, in his summing up, referred to the squibs, abusive letters and newspapers articles, and observed that:

> if that was the usual state of the atmosphere of Sunderland, all he could say was he was very glad he did not live there, for he did not think it could be a pleasant place. A little less speech, a little less letter writing, and a little less article writing would greatly improve the social position of Sunderland.

The judicial advice was not heeded. Instead, the war of words was intensified with the launching of a new daily newspaper, the *Sunderland Daily Post*. The daily advocacy of advanced Liberalism in the *Echo* had placed local Conservatives in an even more disadvantageous position. The *Sunderland Times*, already a bi-weekly and about to become a daily, was staunchly Liberal, and the weekly *Herald* was uncommitted, although it was losing its earlier distrust of Disraeli. Against this formidable array, the weekly *Sunderland Sentinel* was a lone Conservative voice, making up in shrillness for what it lacked in volume. The *Sentinel* was well aware of its inadequacy, and had urged local Conservatives as long ago as 1868 to found their own daily newspaper. The *Sentinel's* wish was now granted, and its own fate was sealed. The Sunderland Conservative Printing and Publishing Company Ltd was formed in June 1876, with a nominal capital of £5,000 in 500 £10 shares. The directors were prominent local Conservatives, including Francis Ritson, Ralph Simey and John Wayman, each of whom held 20 shares.[25] To bring out their new paper they recruited an experienced, if somewhat tarnished, manager – W. A. Brignal, who had recently been dismissed from the *Echo*. The *Sunderland Daily Post* first appeared on 21 July 1876, costing ½d. for four quite large sides (23 ins by 18 ins). It should, in fact, have appeared on the previous day, as an apologetic editorial, headed 'July 20', admitted, blaming a last-minute hitch in the stereotyping department. This inauspicious beginning did not prevent the *Post* from achieving a reasonably tidy lay-out and an improving advertising basis (from four columns in the first issue to ten columns in January 1877). Coverage of horse racing, at one and a half columns in the first issue, was considerably more ample than had hitherto been the case with the *Echo*, although the *Echo* now began, perhaps in consequence, to give a little more space to racing results. The *Post*, however, was not inclined to pander to the sensibilities of potential working-class readers, even though the Conservative Government was busily dis-

covering the Conservative working man. An editorial headed, 'Unthrifti-
ness of the working classes', observed:

> Passing along High Street the other day, we saw a collier riding in a
> cab and smoking a mild Havannah, and taking this man as a type of
> his class, we felt convinced that, sooner or later, the ratepayers of
> Sunderland will have to support him in the Workhouse, with probably
> some other members of his family, to whom he is setting such a
> praiseworthy example. We are not amongst those who are
> everlastingly praising the working classes, as those who do so
> generally have some object in view. We prefer to tell them that which
> is really the truth, however unpalatable it may be. We know that they
> will hate us for being so candid, and pointing out to them the results
> of their folly, in agitating for higher wages. All this we shall
> disregard, and will at once tell them that their sole motive for the
> incessant agitation of the past few years has been to get money and
> spend it.[26]

With editorial homilies such as this, there was little need of the declara-
tions of the *Sentinel*, and it went to its grave in November 1878. The two
senior Sunderland weeklies also succumbed, but not without a struggle. The
Herald and the *Times* had each experienced 40 years of contending for
survival and they adapted spiritedly, but belatedly, to the new situation. The
Times, in fact, became a daily newspaper a fortnight before the birth of the
Post, but its real rival was the *Echo*, now in its third year of daily publication.
William Brockie had retired from the editorship of the *Times* in the year of
the *Echo's* birth, although he continued to contribute leading articles. One
week after the *Times* became a daily, the *Echo* announced its move into new
purpose-built premises, with a powerful new press. The *Times* had acted too
late. The weekly edition, which continued in expanded form alongside the
daily paper, was headed by the borough's motto, *Nil Desperandum Auspice
Deo*. Mrs Williams, however, did despair, selling her newspaper to the *Echo*,
while retaining her general printing and stationery business. The *Times*
ceased publication on 3 August 1878, although the *Weekly Times* continued
under the new proprietary. The *Echo* had not only eliminated a rival, but had
gained a new dimension, in the form of a weekly companion, providing space
for literary material and features which could not find room in the daily
publication.

As the *Times* succumbed five years after the foundation of the *Echo*, so the
Herald gave way five years after the launching of the *Post*. Thomas Carr,
who had shared in a series of co-proprietorships of the *Herald* since the
1830s, had at least the experience of the *Times* to warn him. Carr, however,

'was a firm believer in the old high-priced newspapers', and despised the new halfpenny press in general, particularly as manifested in Sunderland.[27] His partner, H. A. Cave, may have helped to convince him that a weekly could become a daily without losing its soul. Certainly the *Sunderland Daily Herald*, first published on 8 April 1880, at ½d. for four pages (22 ins by 16½ ins), retained the 'quality' appearance of its venerable parent. Shipping news continued to be well covered, with two or three columns daily, and the paper's regular (though not daily) racing coverage included tips as well as results. The question remained, however, whether Sunderland could sustain three daily newspapers. The *Herald* needed both an advertising base and a political base. Commercially, it was one matter to find enough advertising to sustain a weekly paper, but to maintain advertising for six days a week was another problem. Politically, the *Herald* was neither fish nor fowl. Its editorial of 8 April 1880, when the Liberals were winning the general election, managed to cast doubts on the merits of the outgoing Conservatives, while protesting at the suggestion that Gladstone might overstep Granville and Hartington to the premiership. In February 1881, Cave tried to secure financial support from moderates among the local Liberals, notably Sir Henry Havelock-Allan, M.P., the only non-radical to hold a Sunderland seat between 1868 and 1895.[28] Sir Henry, however, resigned his seat at the end of March, to take up a military appointment, and, to add insult to injury, the vacant seat was won by Samuel Storey, without even the inconvenience of a by-election. A moderate Liberal paper, in such a constituency, was truly a voice crying in the wilderness. On 2 September 1881, the *Herald* announced its sale to the *Daily Post*. Out of respect to the senior newspaper in Sunderland, the new publication was entitled the *Sunderland Herald and Daily Post*.

Although the *Post* had absorbed the *Herald*, its own progress had been far from smooth. Conservatism was still too weak in Sunderland to provide good circulation prospects. An attempt to outdo the *Echo* by adopting morning publication, in July 1877, with one edition at 5 a.m. and the other at 5.30 p.m., proved to be more trouble than it was worth and was discontinued. A report in the *Echo*, admittedly an unfriendly source, claimed that the *Post* could not make adequate use of the expensive web-printing press installed at its inception, and so was using 'a small ordinary jobbing machine, capable of producing some six hundred copies an hour'.[29] In October 1878, the directors raised additional capital, calling on each shareholder to increase his holding by half. One recalcitrant shareholder who ignored the call found himself in court, the liability being part of the conditions of shareholding in the company.[30] Another attempt to cut costs led to more trouble. An excessive proportion of juvenile labour was employed in the composing department and the men compositors protested by going on strike. A letter from 'A Compositor', published by the *Echo*, scornfully observed that, if the *Post* could only survive with boy compositors, then 'why not get some smart old woman to do the editing', and do without reporters by copying from other newspapers?[31] The struggle to find a secure footing was clearly proving too severe, and on 31 March 1879 the shareholders agreed to wind up the company, appointing a committee 'to try to induce twenty zealous, self-sacrificing Conservatives to subscribe £50 each to carry the paper on until the General Election comes.'[32] The *Post* was saved by the formation of a new private company, probably headed by John Wayman, one of the directors of the defunct limited company. The new proprietors, with a new editor, James Cuthbert, took over on 1 July 1879, hoping that the *Post* would now 'enter upon a more enlarged field of journalistic action and usefulness than it has hitherto covered.' The paper, which was published at 3 p.m. daily, retained its Conservative politics, but adopted improved typography and more efficient layout, with fuller coverage of commercial news. Wayman was invited to stand as the Conservative candidate at the general election of 1880, but declined because of his business commitments (which included the management of a local building society and the buying and selling of local building land, occupations he had in common with his arch-rival, Samuel Storey). The *Post*, however, was solidly behind the candidate adopted in Wayman's place, Edward Brooke. The *Post*'s eve-of-poll editorial declaimed:

> Men of Sunderland . . . the welfare of our Commonwealth, of ourselves, of our wives, of our children, of our children's children, depends upon your choice. Strengthen the hands of the men who, under Providence, have brought us honour and safety. Let every true Briton *plump* for the Conservative candidate, and get every man he knows to *plump* for the Conservative candidate. The battle is already as good as won. There is trepidation in the ranks of the enemy. God save the Queen.[33]

Brooke finished a disappointing third, leaving the *Post* to lament the feebleness of local Conservatives and the shamelessness of the electorate. A special article in the *Post* for 13 April 1880, entitled 'The next ten years', gave a horrendous, if humorous, set of predictions, beginning with the disestablishment of the Church of England and proceeding via the conversion of St Paul's Cathedral into a warehouse for John Bright and Co., and the conversion of Belgrave Square into artisans' dwellings, to the annexation of Britain by the U.S.A. Given the previous fate of Conservative journals in Sunderland, these predictions were hardly more fanciful than the prospect that the

Post would still be alive in 1890 to witness the truth, or otherwise, of its prognostications.

The acquisition of the *Herald*, however, gave promise of a better future, combining as it did the 'youthful vigour' of the *Post* with 'the mellow experience and wise moderation' of the *Herald*.[34] The dog fight of 1876–81, which saw the elimination of the *Sentinel*, the *Times* and the *Herald*, now gave place to a duel – a straight contest between the *Echo* and the *Post*.

5. *ECHO VERSUS POST*, 1881–96

This period began with an intensification of Storey's proprietorial control over the *Echo*, offset by an increase in his absence. As M.P. for Sunderland from 1881, he was occupied by his parliamentary duties, but the deaths of two of the *Echo*'s co-founders, in 1879 and 1880, enabled him to purchase their shares. The business was then formed into a limited company, with Storey taking three-quarters of the shares. His newspaper activities also expanded with the formation of the Carnegie-Storey syndicate in 1881, an ambitious project which was of significance for the general history of the press but which, having little direct impact within Sunderland, is excluded from the present discussion.[35] The *Echo* was prospering in this period, and in local directories it regularly claimed to outsell the aggregate of all other daily newspapers sold in the borough, whether printed locally or extraneously.

The *Post*, however, was making a fight of it. In June 1882 the *Post* announced that it was in direct connection with the system of the Northern District Telephone Co. and so could receive advertisements and news items by this new medium of communication. Although outsold by the *Echo*, its circulation was sufficient to merit the installation of a four-feeder Hoe printing press in 1885. This year provided another opportunity for a trial of strength, when the Conservatives fielded a candidate for the general election. His name, Austin, combined with his allegiance to the Established Church, which the *Post* saw as under threat, inspired the following grandiloquent editorial:

> To the first Austin who ever appeared in England belongs the fame of having established the Church of England, if that work can be said to have been performed by any one man, or in any one age; and we are willing to regard the victory achieved by St. Augustine over the Pagan darkness and barbarism of our Saxon ancestors as an augury for the success of the present Conservative candidate for Sunderland. *In hoc signo vincet!*[36]

The auguries were, however, wrong. Austin trailed a thousand votes behind Gourley, and Storey headed the poll. Wayman's efforts to promote the Conservative cause, on the platform and through his newspaper, had again proved unavailing. The usual acerbities of the hustings between Wayman and Storey, amplified in their respective newspapers, led to instructions to their solicitors, but apparently not, on this occasion, to court proceedings. In 1886 Wayman suffered a further disappointment when the strategy of fielding a Liberal-Unionist candidate, to rally moderate Liberals to the Unionist side, misfired. Despite the *Post*'s strenuous advocacy, local Conservatives seemed reluctant to go beyond narrow party confines, and the Liberal-Unionist polled fewer votes than the Conservative had obtained at the preceding election. Storey and Gourley were assisted by the sizeable Irish vote, estimated by the *Post* at 2,100, but probably nearer 1,300.[37] In 1885–6, the Irish voters apparently regarded the Home Rule issue as of more pressing importance than the question of voluntary schools, which would have estranged them from the radical candidates. The death of Wayman, later in 1886, placed the *Post*'s future once more in jeopardy. Salvation was forthcoming from an unlikely source: the office of the *Echo*. George Howitt, who had worked there for nearly 14 years, first as reporter and, after Brignal's departure, as manager and editor, now abandoned Storey to take over the *Post*.

The announcement was made in the *Echo*, on 28 February 1887, when it was claimed that the Conservatives had given up, having spent 'some £16,000' on the *Post* in ten years. Howitt, the report continued, had bought the *Post* for a small sum and intended to carry it on as an independent paper, 'without political leanings'. This was substantially confirmed by a statement in the *Post* on 2 March, when it was announced that the paper had 'ceased to be an organ of a political party'. A further statement, on 7 March, observed that:

> Experience has convincingly proven that the Conservative element is not sufficiently numerous in Sunderland to maintain a newspaper devoted to the interests of the party, but in time of need it may depend upon our co-operation in giving due publicity to the opinions expressed on behalf of so large and influential a section of the inhabitants of the borough.

Had Howitt but known it, the 'time of need' was about to give place to a time of opportunity. The long ascendancy of Storey and his radicals was beginning to be eroded. The first sign came in two hard-fought municipal by-elections in 1888, when the radicals were beaten. The *Newcastle Daily Chronicle* suggested that the radicals' defeats might 'indicate a rebellion against their supremacy as much as dissatisfaction with Liberal policy.'[38] In the same month, the *Post* announced a move to 'specially-erected and commodious premises'. Howitt's experience was put to good use in greatly improving the quality of the *Post*. New and clearer typefaces were used, the layout became neater and new features were introduced. Football was promoted to the main news page, reflecting the success of the Sunderland team. In 1891 the paper's contents were enlivened by the inclusion of a 'Humorous column', with cartoon drawings, and a 'Ladies column' with illustrations of fashions. A dialect column, 'Lokal noats in lokal kee', attempted, rather patronizingly, to preach to the working man in the local patois. Howitt's politics were Liberal-Unionist, and his opposition to Home Rule was one motive for his departure from the *Echo*. Another was his frustration at not being made a partner. He bought the *Post* on his own initiative, but then sold it to the publishing company which he formed, becoming its managing director. His two co-directors were both active local Conservatives.[39] The *Post*'s promised neutrality soon gave way to an outright Unionism, and the political, as well as the circulation, battle with the *Echo* was renewed with intensity. Storey later claimed that the *Post* did not 'appreciably' affect the *Echo*'s circulation, 'but competed with us in advertisements and compelled us into larger expenditure in order to hold and stabilise our position.'[40] Much more galling to Storey, however, must have been the sharpness of Howitt's personal attacks on him, backed by the inside knowledge gained during Howitt's years in the *Echo*'s office. In 1892 Storey retaliated by instituting a libel action against Howitt for defamatory material published about him in the *Post*. As in the 1876 libel case, the most distinguished and expensive lawyers were briefed, with Storey's three advocates being headed by Sir Charles Russell, Q.C. (who had led for the opposite side on the previous occasion), while the defendant's trio was headed by the Solicitor-General. It emerged from the evidence that Storey had entrusted the running of the *Echo* to his son, Fred, and would not allow the *Post*'s name to be mentioned in the *Echo*. At length, the jury found for the plaintiff. Storey received £50 compensation and part of the costs. The award displeased the writer of 'Ariel's notes' in the *Post*: 'If the jury meant their verdict as a vindication of Mr. Storey's conduct and character, it was certainly unfair to give him only £50 and leave him responsible for something like £1,000 for costs. If his vindication was not made clear, it was just as unfair to saddle the defendants with twice or thrice that amount.'[41]

The financial blow to the *Post* was softened by a subscription raised by local Conservatives, and, after another electoral defeat in 1892, the political triumph that had eluded the *Post* for 20 years finally materialized. In 1895, the Unionist candidate, W. T. Doxford, a prominent local shipbuilder, captured one of the Sunderland seats, aided by frenzied campaigning in the *Post*. Storey and Gourley were accused of swallowing the socialistic programme of the local trades council in an effort to capture labour votes. 'But they do not seem to have calculated the effect such a surrender would have upon the electors who claim exclusive rights in their wives and families, who demand state protection for freedom of thought and freedom of action, and for the surplus proceeds of individual labour and enterprise.'[42] Worse than depriving a working man of his wife, it was claimed that Storey and Gourley 'would rob a poor man of his beer'. Not surprisingly, Doxford headed the poll and, to make revenge even sweeter, Storey lost his seat. His long political ascendancy in Sunderland was over, and the dominance of his newspaper, already eroded by the *Post*, was about to come under further attack.

6. NEW CHALLENGERS AND NEW ALIGNMENTS, 1897–1906

The late 1880s were a bad period for Sunderland's economy, with depression in local shipbuilding and the coal trade. No newspapers were founded in this period, but in the mid-1890s, with a recovery in local trade, newspaper activity quickened. A monthly periodical entitled *Socialist* appeared in June 1894 and ran for six issues. The *Sunderland Citizen*, frequency uncertain, ran from August 1897 to April 1899, and the *Sunderland Weekly News* from December 1898 to May 1899. Of far greater significance was the publication of the *Sunderland Morning Mail* in November 1898. This was part of the most ambitious attempt yet made to introduce the syndicated system of journalism to the region. It also represented another attempt to succeed, where the *Echo* and the *Post* had both failed, in establishing a morning newspaper in Sunderland. The first *Morning Mail* was launched in Newcastle in May 1898, and after the Sunderland version in November, others appeared in South Shields, Stockton and Middlesbrough. The *Sunderland Morning Mail* combined the attractions of morning publication and size (eight pages) with the more common evening price of ½d. The front page adhered to the convention of concentrating on advertisements, but inside there were signs of modernity. The second page was divided horizontally, with a ladies' feature and some news paragraphs above the line, and a serial story below. The editorial took the form of comments on several topics, rather than a single, lengthy homily. The main news page was well broken up, with numerous headlines and a wide variety of topics. The advertisements on the back page were bigger and bolder than those of the traditional type and the news items were enlivened by the inclusion of small illustrations. The news coverage was comprehensive, and advertisements occupied 11 of the 40 columns. Altogether, the *Mail* was quite an impressive paper, and good value for money.

The *Sunderland Mail* disclaimed political partisanship, professing to be more concerned with the interests of the town and of the nation than with those of any party. In so doing it reflected a national trend in the British press at this time. The era of the penny morning paper, with its clear political coloration and long leading article, was drawing to a close. The politics of Empire, however, represented an exciting arena of debate, and the *Mail*'s involvement therein became increasingly partisan. During the 'Khaki election' of 1900, the *Mail* provided space for articles giving a Liberal viewpoint on the local contest, but the paper's editorial line was vociferously Unionist. The Unionists captured both Sunderland seats – the first time that this had ever happened. The satisfaction of the *Sunderland Post* must have been tinged with some unease at the rapid success of its rival publication. Failing health led George Howitt to dispose of most of his *Post* shares in 1902 to J. S. G. Pemberton, one of the victorious Unionist candidates. By then, the *Morning Mail* had been transformed, first by losing the word 'Sunderland' from its title (although the town's crest appeared between 'Morning' and 'Mail') and then, more fundamentally, by being translated into the *North Mail*, in August 1901. The valedictory editorial emphasized that 'we do not die today. What we are passing through in the interstice between our yesterdays and tomorrows is only the swift episode of transmigration, translation to a larger, more strenuous, more potent life.' The hyperbole was a fitting foretaste of what readers of the *North Mail* could expect under its new owner, C. A. Pearson, the founder of the *Daily Express*. Like the *Express*, the *North Mail* (which was published in Newcastle) put its main news on the front page, and when Joseph Chamberlain launched his Tariff Reform campaign, both papers were loud in their support.

Tariff Reform had an impact upon the Sunderland press as dramatic as its wider political impact. It produced a remarkable realignment, with the *Echo* abandoning Liberalism and free trade, while the *Post* rebelled against both Chamberlain and Balfour. The details have been given in another place.[43] In a discussion about newspaper survival, what is noteworthy is that the *Echo* could terminate more than 30 years' commitment to advanced Liberalism without terminating its own existence in the process. It was not a case of backing the winning side, now that Unionists held both the Sunderland seats. The Unionists in fact lost both seats at the next general election. It could be argued that, as the purveyors of the new journalism insisted, readers were tired of the old party wrangles and had other priorities in choosing their newspapers. The *Echo*'s long experience in supplying daily news to Sunderland was probably more important, by this date, than its political allegiance. The *Post*, too, backed the loser in the 1906 election – its own proprietor, in fact, who stood as a Unionist Free Trader. Deprived of his parliamentary seat, and alienated from the local Unionist organization,

Pemberton decided in July 1906 to let the *Post* die. The *Echo* had seen the end of its last rival.

7. CONCLUSION

Consideration of Victorian newspapers in general, and of Sunderland newspapers in particular, suggests that there were at least 14 positive factors likely to affect survival. Some of these were mutually exclusive, but they can be conveniently grouped into four broad categories: politics, frequency, management, and readership. In the first category, the optimum factor was undoubtedly to adopt the political standpoint of the majority party in the circulation area. A weaker, but still beneficial, factor was to have a recognized political stance of some other kind, at least before the 1890s. Depending on circumstance, this might involve identification with the minority party, or perhaps the expression of a moderate viewpoint which appealed to the less partisan elements in either party. Political content was so integral to a Victorian newspaper that absence of an editorial line was unlikely to command respect, allegiance, or assistance in time of trouble. It was not so much that the leading article would win converts to a political cause, as so many inaugural editorials professedly hoped. It has been shrewdly observed that 'newspapers, when they did preach, almost always did so to the converted, for it is usually only the converted who will abide being preached to.'[44] Rather, it was a case of rallying the faithful, as readers, advertisers, shareholders, and directors. The two most successful Sunderland dailies, the *Echo* and the *Post*, both owed their creation to groups of local politicians. As the paper of the weaker side, the *Post* had more of a struggle to keep going, but local Conservatives were prepared to pay out large sums of money, including the reimbursement of the proprietor after the 1892 libel action. The evidence would suggest that, in Sunderland, it was preferable to be associated with the weaker party rather than to be non-aligned. The *Herald*, which had done well as a Whig paper when the Sunderland Whigs were a significant political force, later found the middle ground between radicalism and Conservatism too constricted to sustain life. Significantly, the *Post's* professed non-alignment under its new proprietor in 1887 soon gave way to an outright Unionism. Perhaps the most interesting example of the connection between politics and survival was that of the *Sunderland Times*, which (with the absorbed *Sunderland Beacon*) enjoyed a 20-year career as a Conservative paper, during a period when the Conservatives generally held one of the borough's seats, followed by another 20 years as a Liberal paper, when Liberalism was gaining in strength. If the *Times* had been able to work with the Storey and Gourley group of radicals, its life might have been considerably prolonged. In the 1890s, however, the importance of having a clear political alignment began to wane. Experienced contemporaries observed that where once 'a paper circulated because of the character and vigour of its opinions' changed conditions 'are tending to eliminate the leader. The evening papers comment on the news of the day by means of the paragraph, *the* type of all modern writing.'[45] The *Sunderland Morning Mail* was a good example of the new kind of newspaper and, but for its translation into the Newcastle-based *North Mail*, might have posed a more serious threat to the established dailies. The *Echo's* ability to abandon its old party-political allegiance without seriously harming its position was further proof of the changed situation.

As regards frequency of publication, four factors can be considered: weekly publication on an independent basis, weekly in conjunction with a daily paper, daily publication, and evening rather than morning publication. Before the 1870s, the situation favoured the weekly paper rather than the daily. The last of the 'taxes on knowledge', the paper duty, was not removed until 1861, the Press Association did not commence operations until 1870, with its daily supply of parliamentary and general news, and it took time for advertisers to become reconciled to the costs of daily advertising. Hence the two longest-lived of all Sunderland newspapers, apart from the *Daily Echo*, were the weekly *Herald* and *Times*. It should be noted, however, that the death-rate was also at its highest in this sphere, perhaps exacerbated by the particular socio-economic character of Wearside. The average life-span of all Sunderland's independent weeklies was just under eight and a half years. If the *Herald* and *Times* are excluded, however, the average falls to less than two and a half years. In these circumstances, there was a case for bringing out a weekly as the companion of a daily paper, with the obvious advantage of sharing the overheads. The *Sunderland Weekly Echo*, arising out of the *Weekly Times*, acquired in 1878, lasted until the eve of the First World War. As a subordinate paper, however, it could be disposed of without affecting the daily publication, and if the daily went down, it went down also, or survived, like the *Weekly Times*, only in a new home. In daily publication, the crucial asset was to occupy the field first. Excluding the abortive *Sunderland Evening Chronicle*, and the shipping papers, it was the prior establishment of the *Echo* and the *Post* which gave them the advantage over their respective rivals, the *Daily Times* and *Daily Herald*. And, in Sunderland, evening publication was clearly preferable to morning publication. Apart from adding to wage-costs, morning publication also meant in the long term bearing the brunt of the competition from the new mass-circulation London newspapers at the turn of the century. For obvious reasons, London evening papers have never achieved the national sales of the London mornings. When the *Echo* began, Sunderland was out of step with the majority of provincial centres in opting for evening rather than morning journalism, the figures, for 1874, being 55 morning papers as against 16 evenings, but by 1906 the morning figures had remained fairly static at 61, while 87 evening papers were now being published in the provinces.[46]

Under the broad heading of management, five factors can be distinguished, of varying utility: a strong proprietor, a cheaper price, group publication, modern technology, and a good advertising base. It was a great asset for a newspaper to be headed by a proprietor of vigour and resourcefulness, and preferably of political standing in the community. Alderman Williams of the *Sunderland Times* and Samuel Storey of the *Echo*, alderman, mayor, and Member of Parliament, are prime examples. Strong individuals tended to fare better than groups of proprietors. Three of the *Echo*'s co-founders soon fell by the wayside, and the *Post* did better when its founding fathers were replaced first by Wayman and then by Howitt, although they both needed the support of company finance. The drawback, of course, is that strong proprietors are not immortal. The death of Alderman Williams prevented the *Times* from going over to daily publication in the 1860s and so from forestalling the *Echo*. Once again the *Echo* had the advantage, as its driving force, Storey, although not immortal, seemed so, surviving to make the main speech at the fiftieth anniversary of his newspaper.

In an age of steadily diminishing newspaper prices, it was an advantage to be ahead of, rather than behind, the trend. The *Sunderland Times*, at 1d. for its mid-week and 2d. for its Saturday edition, outsold, in the 1860s, the *Herald*'s 3d. weekly issue, and was in turn outsold by the ½d. daily *Echo* in the 1870s. The cases, on the contrary side, of the short-lived 1d. *Weekly News* and ½d. *Evening Chronicle*, relate not so much to price as to the nature of their provenance, one as the satellite of a Newcastle paper and the other as part of a Conservative syndicate. This kind of group publication was no asset, but the *Morning Mail*, in a later period, represented the shape of things to come. The *Sunderland Echo* has avoided being absorbed into a chain by itself being the parent paper in a small group, Portsmouth and Sunderland Newspapers, arising out of the dissolved Carnegie-Storey syndicate.

Technology can be regarded as a subsidiary factor in newspaper survival. Obviously the productive capacity had to be sufficient to supply the demand for copies, and was a major item in the expenditure of the daily press. But the *Post*'s inferior circulation meant at first under-utilizing its expensive web press, and its installation of Linotype composition eight years before the *Echo* did not avert its demise. A sound advertising basis was more important, making a vital contribution to profitability. The placing of advertisements in the Victorian period probably owed as much to personal contact and political sympathy as to precise market analysis, although as nationally-placed advertising increased its role later in the period, details of circulation and readership came under closer scrutiny. The modern axiom then began to prevail: advertising gravitates to the successful.

In the final category, broadly termed 'readership', three factors can be distinguished: journalism, interest-groupings and circulation. To a modern journalist, it might seem transparently obvious that the supreme asset of a periodical should be the attractiveness of its contents and layout. Scrutiny of Victorian provincial newspapers, however, does not add much force to this view as applied to nineteenth-century periodicals. Once the classified advertisements, the reports of local courts and committees, the lists of market prices, the near-verbatim parliamentary reports and the long leading article had been inserted, what scope for creative journalism remained? One could at least strive for good printing and tidy layout, but these virtues saved neither the *Herald* nor the *Post*. The *Post* in the 1890s contained a more varied range of features than the *Echo*, but it was the *Echo* that survived. It did so to an important extent because it was secured upon the right interest-groupings. Like the longest-lived of the Sunderland weeklies, the *Herald*, the *Echo* made a special point of appealing to the shipping interests that played such a vital part in the development of the town. It was for news of arrivals and departures, imports and exports, safe-voyages and shipwrecks, rather than for creative writing, that many Wearsiders bought newspapers. Politically, as already noted, the best interest-grouping was the majority party in the locality. Well placed here, the *Echo* had the additional advantage of appealing to most of the local Irish community by its support for Home Rule and its opposition to coercion. Another interest-grouping was the betting fraternity for which all Sunderland's daily newspapers, the *Echo* least readily, provided coverage. Finally, there was the matter of overall circulation. It is a moot point whether this should be regarded as one of the factors in success, or the very proof of success in itself. In the modern period, with advertisers seeking out the best-selling papers in their field, the latter viewpoint makes more sense. For much of the Victorian period, however, a periodical could remain viable, even if outsold, as long as it appealed to a sufficiently large interest-group, or combination of groups. What mattered was that the newspaper, like any other organism, should be in harmony with its environment, and should be capable of adapting when necessary. It would then provide another vindication of that typically Victorian maxim: the survival of the fittest.

APPENDIX: THE WAGES BOOKS OF THE
SUNDERLAND DAILY ECHO

Through the good offices of Miss Patricia Storey (see n. 3) I have been able to consult the wages books of the *Sunderland Echo* for the years 1875–8 and 1899–1903. The survival of these records makes possible an unusually close examination of the staffing and management of a provincial daily newspaper during its formative years. Weekly payments in the 1875–8 book are listed for the compositors, machinists, reporters and commercial staff employed by the paper. The 34 employees included 17 compositors (three of them probably apprentices), 3 machinists (one probably an apprentice), 5 or 6 members of the reporting and literary staff (including, it can be assumed, one proof reader and a junior reporter), and 8 or 9 members of the commercial staff (including 3 or 4 office juniors). The total wage and salary bill averaged around £48 per week, ranging from the lowest point of around £41 in early January of each year (when the New Year's Day holiday reduced compositors' earnings) to a high point of £50 (excluding certain weeks discussed below).

Taking each department in turn, the most obvious characteristic of the compositors is the wide variation in their earnings, both between individual employees and from week to week. The explanation is that compositors were paid piece-rates, except for their overseer, who received a regular wage of £2 5s. 0d. per week, which he could sometimes augment by additional piece-work. The original overseer, Longmuir, had departed before the period of the 1875–8 wages book. The new manager, W. A. Brignal, appointed at the end of January 1874, had decided to abandon the *Echo*'s 9 a.m. edition, in an effort to cut costs. Since the inception of the morning edition in early January, the compositors had been working from 10.30 p.m. until 6 a.m., at a rate of 7½d. per 1,000 letters set, which was below the full rate for a morning paper but better than the normal evening paper rate of 5½d. Brignal arranged to bring out the first edition at 12 noon, with the men starting at 4.30 a.m., and he required the compositors to sign an agreement that they would now work for lower rates, as night work had now been terminated. The men, not unreasonably, regarded the period from 4.30 a.m. to 7 a.m. as being nocturnal rather than diurnal in character, and Longmuir wrote to Samuel Storey to express their concern. Storey claimed that he could not interfere with the manager, but eventually arranged a compromise with representatives of the Typographical Association. The offending form of agreement was withdrawn and Storey used his influence to persuade two non-union compositors, whom Brignal had bought in, to become members of the union. The only victim of the affair was Longmuir, who had objected to Brignal's form of agreement, although not personally required to sign it. Being five minutes late one day, he was instantly dismissed by Brignal, although Storey later paid the wages which Longmuir claimed for wrongful dismissal.

The rates in force between 1875 and 1878 enabled compositors to earn between £1 10s. od. and £2 per week, with the most common figure being around £1 15s. od. The compositors' share of the weekly wage bill came to around £25, or slightly more than half the total. This figure was briefly inflated in August 1878, when the *Echo* took over the *Sunderland Times*, absorbing the *Daily Times* although continuing to publish the *Weekly Times*. Five new compositors were now listed in the wages book, all ex-*Times* and all at first receiving a living wage (averaging £1 13s. od. for the week ending 15 August). By early September, however, two had left and two were receiving only a pittance, leaving only one full-wage employee. Here was the price, in human terms, of a newspaper merger. With the exception of the *Times* staff, a greater continuity of employment was evident amongst compositors in the latter part of the period covered by the wages book. Of the 18 compositors (including apprentices) employed in the week ending 1 July 1875, five had left by December and a further five by December 1876. In 1877, however, only three compositors departed (two of them recruited in 1876). One might surmise that early problems of finding the right calibre of employee were gradually surmounted.

The machining department was much smaller than the composing room. For most of the period, two full-wage machinists sufficed, with one or two assistants or apprentices. The total wage bill averaged only about £2. 10s. od. per week in 1875 and the first half of 1876, but in July it suddenly doubled. One of the existing machinists, paid around £1 per week, was replaced by a newcomer, Spalding, at £2 per week, and Spalding was soon joined by Peterson, also at £2 per week. The explanation can be found in the columns of the *Echo*, where, on 10 July 1876 it was announced that the paper would soon be printed at new premises 'by new and improved machinery manufactured by Messrs. Hoe and Co. of New York and London, and capable of producing 26,000 copies per hour'. Spalding and Peterson were presumably recruited to operate the new press, although Spalding soon departed, leaving Peterson and the existing machinist, Gilchrist, to operate the press, with assistance, for a total wage cost of around £4 10s. od. per week.

The commercial department was headed by W. A. Brignal, who, as the named publisher of the paper, was its highest-paid employee, his salary increasing from £3 per week to £4 from the late summer of 1875. Brignal, who might best be described as the managing editor of the paper, is listed in the wages book with the commercial, not the reporting, staff. At the time of his salary increase, he was joined by a new assistant. Thubron, at a salary of £2 per week. There were about six other members of the office staff, with wages ranging from just over £1 per week down to 5s. The total bill for this section came to just over £10 per week during the Brignal era. The figure for the week ending 10 February 1876, however, leapt to £18, with an additional payment of £7 15s. 0d. being written alongside the names of Brignal and Thubron, jointly – the names, however, being crossed out. In the following week, the overall figure was down to £6 16s. 0d., Brignal and Thubron were omitted and, a fortnight later, a new office manager took over at a salary of £3 per week. For the explanation, one must turn to the news columns of the *Echo* and, as often happens in the history of the Sunderland press, to reports of a legal action. On this occasion, the action was by the proprietors of the *Echo* against Brignal, for the recovery of money improperly retained by him or lost by his negligence. One allegation was that, in breach of an instruction 'not to give credit to any theatrical person, except for a small amount', Brignal had given credit of £138 'to one Whyatt, who was a theatrical person as the defendant knew'. Brignal countered by flatly contradicting all the allegations and claiming £12 missing salary together with six months' salary in lieu of notice, as compensation for his summary dismissal by Storey. The arbitrating barrister found for the plaintiffs on all counts, except that of negligence over the debts of another member of the office staff, Edwards, who had also departed with Brignal and Thubron. Brignal was given leave to apply for a reduction in the total sum awarded, to the amount of Whyatt's debts.

The upheavals in the commercial office proved of benefit to a member of the reporting staff, George Howitt, who, after a period of equal status with another reporter, eventually became editor of the *Echo* at a monthly salary of £15. A pay rise enabled Howitt to earn £205 during the final year of the wages book. Other members of this department included, it would appear, a senior reporter, one or two other reporters, with a junior, and, probably, a proof reader. The total weekly wage bill, excluding Howitt, averaged around £9 10s. 0d. The entries for the week ending 27 December 1877 also record a payment of £100 to Samuel Storey, under 'reporting'.

The Echo at the Turn of the Century

The next surviving *Echo* wages book begins in January 1899 and has been examined for the period between 1899 and 1903. Taking the week ending 23 February 1899 as fairly typical of the first quarter's figures, the total wage bill for the *Echo* was £90 12s. 7d., or about double the 1875–6 figure. Compositors accounted for half the total, as they had done earlier. There were now 24 compositors, joined by two others in March, and their wages varied as before. Common earnings ranged from £2 1s. 0d. to £2 9s. 0d. per week, as compared with a rough average of £1 15s. 0d. in the earlier period. The overseer now received a regular £3 10s. 0d. a week. The same individual, C. Swann, held this post as in 1876, and four other compositors' names are common to the earlier and later wages books.

The literary department had now grown to 12, headed by the editor, George Herring, with £6 a week, and two senior reporters on £3 a week. The chief proof reader received £1 5s. 0d., and the total bill came to a regular £24 18s. 6d. There were no names common to the old book either here or in the machinery department, where two machinists and their two assistants received a total of £5 4s. 0d. a week. There was now a stereotyping section, comprising one employee at £2, and one at £1 10s. 0d. The commercial department was headed by the secretary to the *Echo* company, with a weekly salary of £4, and contained eight other employees, including one survivor from 1876, Mrs Wishart, who had the double distinction of being one of the paper's longest-serving employees, as well as its first woman employee. The wages for staff who brought out the *Weekly Echo* (as the *Weekly Times* had now been re-titled) were entered separately, amounting to £10 11s. 0d. in all. Herring received a further £2 in this category, while the weekly's editor, Spencer, received £2 10s. 0d. The other employees were mostly compositors, receiving £1 12s. 0d. each. The grand total came to £101 3s. 7d. for 57 employees. The recruitment of the two extra compositors in March, the replacement of an assistant machinist by a full-wage machinist, and a salary rise to £5 per week for the company secretary, combined to raise the total wage bill to £114 per week from the last quarter of 1899 to the earlier part of 1901, when, after the *Echo* increased its daily issue from four sides to six, the bill rose to over £120. In July 1902 the page was widened to include an extra column, and at this point the number, and gross earnings, of compositors touched a new peak. A total of 33 compositors (including apprentices) received £68 16s. 8d., pushing the aggregate bill up to £142 6s. 3d. The *Echo's* appearance at this time bore all the signs of health and prosperity; 42 well-filled columns, 18 of them occupied by advertisements, with a tidy lay-out. But the size of the compositor's wage bill must have worried the management. The solution was one which most other provincial dailies had already taken, beginning with the *Newcastle Daily Chronicle* in 1889 and followed, among others, by the *Sunderland Daily Post* in 1894 – the installation of the Linotype.

According to F. G. Storey, speaking in the absence of his father, at the office dinner in February 1903, the decision to introduce the Linotype was 'a wrench on both sides', bearing in mind the inevitable consequences for the old hand-compositors. Those consequences can be traced in the wages book.

In January 1903 there were 30 compositors in employment. Then, with the arrival of the Linotypes, 13 of these employees departed, together with two from the weekly paper. Three new employees arrived, each paid £2 per week and presumably recruited because of previous experience with Linotypes. By the second quarter of 1903, there were 21 compositors employed, at a total wage bill of around £39, the general wage per man having slipped to about £1 17s. od. The installation of the Linotypes must have been costly. The figure for the *Northern Daily Mail* in 1902 was over £1,800.[47] But as an exercise in reducing wage costs the introduction of the Linotype had clearly been a success. In human terms, the provision for redundant compositors was probably better than that generally prevailing in such cases at that time. A long-serving compositor, E. McCready, whose services spanned the wages books but was now at an end, paid tribute to the arrangements made. Each compositor with more than 16 years' service was to receive six weeks' wages when he left, together with 10s. per week thereafter, until his sixtieth birthday, if he did not find permanent employment. This would be apart from his unemployment allowance from the Typographical Association and his eventual superannuation allowance from the same body.[48] Equipped with new technology, the *Echo* went on into the twentieth century, eventually, in the 1970s, discarding the Linotype and hot-metal type as it had once relinquished hand typesetting.

NOTES

1. Alan J. Lee, *The Origins of the Popular Press, 1855–1914* (1976), table 13, p. 282.
2. Sir Hugh Gilzean-Reid and P. J. Macdonell, 'The Press', in *The Civilisation of Our Day*, ed. J. Samuelson (1896), 282.
3. Two uncommon assets aid the researcher in probing the inner workings of the Sunderland press: first, the litigious propensities of newspaper proprietors in the town, giving rise to libel actions and courtroom revelations; and second, the survival of wages books for the most successful of Sunderland newspapers, the *Sunderland Daily Echo*. The latter source was brought to my attention by Miss Patricia Storey, the great-grand-daughter of the founder of the *Sunderland Echo*, Samuel Storey. Miss Storey's M.Litt. thesis, 'Samuel Storey of Sunderland (1841–1925). His life and career as a local politician and newspaper proprietor up to 1895' (University of Edinburgh, 1978), is a mine of information concerning Sunderland and its newspapers. I wish to record my gratitude for the generous collaboration of Miss Storey in this enterprise.
4. *Newcastle Daily Chron.*, 1 Sept. 1888.
5. John George Lambton, first earl of Durham ('Radical Jack'), was a great landowner and colliery owner. The Lambton interest was particularly strong amongst the commercial middle class of Sunderland.
6. Charles Stewart, third marquis of Londonderry, is (perhaps unfairly) best remembered for his opposition to Ashley's Mines Bill in 1842. The family had large coal interests to the south of the town and received political support from many Sunderland shipowners.
7. See, however, P. Storey, 'Sunderland newspapers 1831–73', in *Antiquities of Sunderland*, xxvii (1977–9), 101–16.
8. Prospectus for the *Sunderland and*

Shields Herald, dated 4 Apr. 1831, located in a collection of local newspaper prospectuses at Newcastle Central Reference Library, Lo72/0564.

9. Figures based on stamp returns.

10. *Sunderland Herald*, 17, 24 and 28 July 1868.

11. Prospectus for the *Sunderland Beacon* dated 29 Dec. 1837, Newcastle Central Reference Library, Lo72/0564.

12. *Sunderland Herald and Daily Post* (hereafter cited as *Post*), 20 Oct. 1890, obituary of W. Brockie.

13. *Newcastle Daily Chron.*, 29 June 1908, obituary of R. Ruddock.

14. For details of the syndicate, see M. Milne, *Newspapers of Northumberland and Durham* (1971), 85–7.

15. *Ibid.*, 52–3.

16. *Post*, 28 May 1887.

17. See for instance the special 'Almanack' supplements of 13 Dec. 1872 and 19 Dec. 1873.

18. *Sunderland Daily Echo* (hereafter cited as *Echo*) 22 Dec. 1873.

19. *Echo*, 22 Dec. 1923, report of a fiftieth anniversary speech by Samuel Storey, on which this paragraph is based throughout.

20. *Ibid*, 1 Aug. 1876.

21. Again, I must acknowledge my debt to Miss P. Storey in respect of the *Northern Daily Mail* material. The *Mail's* ledgers, consisting mainly of profit and loss accounts for the period after acquisition by Samuel Storey, are not normally available for inspection.

22. Lee, *op. cit.*, 90, cites a contemporary estimate of £84 17s. od. per week for producing a ½d. provincial daily in the 1870s, taking the recently established *Northern Echo* (Darlington) as a model.

23. This calculation should be contrasted with table IV in A. J. Lee, 'The management of a Victorian local

newspaper: the *Manchester City News*, 1864–1900', *Business History*, xv (1973), 146, where the revenue from advertising consistently exceeds that of sales. The explanation may be due to the fact that the *City News* was a weekly publication.

24. *Echo*, 19 Jan. 1876, report quoting affidavit of Samuel Storey.

25. P. Storey, thesis, 204, citing PRO, BT31 2245/10685.

26. *Post*, 10 Aug. 1876.

27. *Echo*, 5 Jan, 1885, obituary of Thomas Carr.

28. P. Storey, thesis, 397, citing Havelock-Allan papers, Scrapbook, 1880–1, 28 Feb. 1881.

29. *Echo*, 4 Nov. 1878.

30. *Ibid.*, 20 Feb. 1879.

31. *Ibid.*, 3 Mar. 1879.

32. *Ibid.*, 7 Apr. 1879.

33. *Post*, 30 Mar. 1880.

34. *Ibid.*, 2 Sept. 1881.

35. For details, see Milne, *op. cit.*, 124–7, Lee, *op. cit.*, 167–9, and P. Storey, thesis, chap. VI.

36. *Post*, 30 Oct. 1885.

37. An earlier estimate of the *Post*, which P. Storey, thesis, 5, considers likely to be near the mark.

38. *Newcastle Daily Chron.*, 24 Aug. 1888.

39. P. Storey, thesis, citing PRO, BT31 3931/24887.

40. *Echo*, 22 Dec. 1923.

41. *Post*, 15 Feb. 1892.

42. *Ibid.*, 15 July 1895.

43. Milne, *op. cit.*, ch. 8.

44. Lee, *op. cit.*, 188.

45. Gilzean-Reid and Macdonell, *op. cit.*, 279.

46. Lee, *op. cit.*, table 26, p. 289.

47. *Northern Daily Mail*, ledgers, 31 Aug. 1902.

48. *Echo*, 6 Feb. 1903.

9

Scott Bennett Revolutions in thought:
serial publication and the
mass market for reading

'The People' was a protean term in early nineteenth-century Britain. Every
one from Richard Carlile to John Wilson Croker claimed to understand
precisely the needs of 'the People' and wished to speak for them – or at least
to them. The sharpest rivalries of the press were registered in warnings by
one journal that readers should not allow themselves to be misled by other
journals. From this keen competition for the allegiance of 'the People' it is
possible to map the ideological positions of many publications. But no
comparably clear picture emerges of their audiences, 'the People' themselves. For the people who bought and read the outpouring of the periodical
press in the 1820s and 1830s remain largely inaccessible to us. We know
what readers William Cobbett wanted to have, but we do not know in fact
who bought his periodicals or what they actually thought.

The analysis of readership has been one of the most intractable problems
in studies of periodical literature. Where the interest group addressed is
unambiguous – as perhaps was the case with some Chartist journals – the
leap from known editorial stance to the unknown characteristics of actual
readers may not be too hazardous. But when we deal with grey areas of
ideology – what, after all, was the social programme of *Chambers's Edinburgh Journal*? – or allow for the rapid proliferation of serials addressing
specialized trade concerns, or consider the publications that came into existence solely to supply the market for inexpensive serial fiction, our confidence about 'the People' fades. What *can* we say confidently about the
people who read the *Penny Magazine*?

The one certain answer to that question – that some of them bought the
magazine – is the point of departure for this paper. Here 'the People' are
identified not by a supposed ideological allegiance or social status but rather
by demonstrable behaviour: making a purchase in the mass market for
reading matter. This change in focus is a fundamental one because it looks
almost entirely at what 'the People' did rather than what they thought. So
confined a focus does not trivialize the subject, however. The market for

reading matter was one of the earliest consumer mass markets to develop, and it established itself primarily through serial publication. Mass circulation journals became as central a feature of the industrialization and urbanization of Britain as did its coal, iron, and textile industries. For that reason, a careful look at the commercial side of periodical publication is needed and is long overdue. The statistics of mass market publishing will not tell us what 'the People' thought, but they can move us closer to an accurate understanding of the ways in which people satisfied some of their fundamental needs. These statistics also suggest how much richer our historical analysis must be if we are to understand 'the People' properly.

This paper attempts nothing but to open discussion of the commercial side of mass market publishing. And it claims no merit beyond that of beginning with the evident starting point: the Society for the Diffusion of Useful Knowledge. The evidence that exists now suggests that 1825–45 was the take-off period for the mass reading market; that same evidence shows that the S.D.U.K. played a critical role in the development of the market. The S.D.U.K. provides a good as well as a necessary starting point because the Society was from its first day embroiled in ideological matters that threatened its success and have dominated our subsequent understanding of its accomplishments. It is worth looking again at the S.D.U.K., to see what it tells us about the commercial side of the mass market for periodicals and about 'the People' who bought them.

There was a degree of foolhardiness as well as reforming zeal in the creation in 1826 of the Society for the Diffusion of Useful Knowledge. To adopt such a name almost inevitably prompted those with rival views to create a Society for the Diffusion of *Really* Useful Knowledge, while those of a more sceptical cast of mind might simply ridicule the undertaking as one of the 'blunders of a Big-Wig', a 'sixpenny science' affair, the 'steam intellect society'.[1] Because the Society's founder, Henry Brougham, and half its governing body were Members of Parliament – some of them holding Cabinet positions – and because almost all its active members were allied to the middle-class, liberal wing of the Whig party, it is not surprising that the political coloration of the S.D.U.K. has attracted much attention. The evaluation of this connection has seemed straightforward. The Society was part of the great burgeoning of cheap publication meant for the common reader in the 1820s and 1830s – and meant as well to supplant the radical 'blasphemous' and 'seditious' periodicals of the day. This intention was reiterated from time to time as a leading concern of the Society, notably in the founding of its most successful publication, the *Penny Magazine*, and in the *Address* issued by the Society when it closed operations in 1846.[2]

There is no evidence that the S.D.U.K. ever succeeded ideologically. The unstamped periodical press flourished until the reduction of the stamp duties ruined its illegal trade in 1836, and there is ample evidence that many readers of the unstamped press were proof against the attractions of S.D.U.K. publications. Francis Place – himself no admirer of the Society – reported that 'the unionist will read nothing which the Diffusion Society meddles with – they call the members of it *Whigs* – and Whig means with them a treacherous rascal, a bitter implacable enemy'. Charles Knight, the Society's most important publisher, found on a tour of the industrial North that S.D.U.K. publications had an insignificant circulation among the working classes. Street vendors arrested for selling unstamped periodicals told the magistrates they could find no buyers for the *Penny Magazine*. And one of the Society's most active and hopeful supporters, Matthew Davenport Hill, had to acknowledge in parliamentary debate that the Society's publications had not 'penetrated deeply into the masses of the people'.[3]

This apparent failure has dominated evaluation of the S.D.U.K.[4] It has seemed enough to say that the Society began in 1826 with specific social and educational goals and ended in confusion in 1846 with these goals unrealized. In saying this, however, we have missed a probably more important movement of events. For in 1826 the S.D.U.K. – like Archibald Constable, John Murray, and the other publishers who were soon to begin providing for the common reader – had none but the faintest ideas of who their readers might be and how to reach them. Yet by 1846, a mass market for cheap literature had clearly emerged. It is the successful development of this market, which was primarily a market for serial publications, that needs analysis. Knight asserted that the S.D.U.K. was essentially a commercial operation (see plate 4), and the commercial history of the Society does in fact give us a new measure of how useful it was. The Society's financial ledgers can help us make much better sense than we so far have of the zeal that informed its pioneering work in the market for cheap publications. For it is clear that a shrewd commercial sense, as well as confused political enthusiasms, informed Knight's almost millennial description of the impact of the new cheap periodicals:

> They were making readers. They were raising up a new class, and a much larger class than previously existed, to be the purchasers of books. They were planting the commerce of books upon broader foundations than those upon which it had been previously built. They were relegating the hole-and-corner literature of the days of exclusiveness to the rewards which the few could furnish; preparing the way for writers and booksellers to reap the abundant harvest when the 'second rain' of knowledge should be descending 'uninterrupted,

unabated, unbounded; fertilizing some grounds and overflowing others; changing the whole form of social life'.[5]

We have so far attended to assertions like this one in too narrow a political and social context. It is time now to look at what they meant commercially.

When the S.D.U.K. decided to suspend operations in 1846, it issued an *Address* affirming that 'the Society's work is done, for its greatest object is achieved – fully, fairly, and permanently. The Public is supplied with *cheap* AND *good* literature to an extent which the most sanguine friend of human improvement could not, in 1826, have hoped to have witnessed in twenty years.'[6] We can now say this was no empty boast, for the voluminous records the Society created in the course of doing its business have survived and offer quite precise measures of the Society's success.

Cheap books there had always been, but their publication had typically been a specialized business concentrated in special markets (such as those for street ballads or almanacs) and heavily dependent on reprinting works no longer under copyright, on Grub Street writers, or on piracy. What was new in the late 1820s was a conscious policy to publish good original works, especially general non-fiction, by sharply increasing the number of copies printed to achieve a dramatically lower unit cost. It was this new publishing strategy that Archibald Constable so colourfully and so energetically un-folded to Walter Scott in 1825:

'If I live for half-a-dozen years, I'll make it as impossible that there should not be a good library in every decent house in Britain as that the shepherd's ingle-nook should want the *saut poke*. Ay, and what's that?' he continued, warming and puffing, 'Why should the ingle-nook itself want a shelf for the novels?' 'I see your drift, my man,' says Sir Walter, 'you're for being like Billy Pitt in Gilray's print – you want to get into the salt-box yourself.' 'Yes,' he responded (using a favourite adjuration) – 'I have hitherto been thinking only of the wax lights, but before I'm a twelvemonth older I shall have my hand on the tallow.' 'Troth,' says Scott, 'you are indeed likely to be "The grand Napoleon of the realms of *print*."' 'If you outlive me,' says Constable, with a regal smile, 'I bespeak that line for my tomb-stone.'[7]

Constable's Miscellany and the S.D.U.K. took the lead in publishing for the common reader. The S.D.U.K.'s programme was no less expansive, no less Napoleonic than that proposed by Constable. The range of S.D.U.K. publications was phenomenal; it included the two Libraries of Useful and of

Entertaining Knowledge, offering dozens of treatises on the natural sciences, geography, mathematics, history, biography, on the collections at the British Museum, and on the life and manners of such places as Egypt, India, China, New Zealand, and Canada; the Society also published series of books for farmers and young readers; almanacs and companion publications; a famous series of maps; the landmark *Penny Cyclopedia* and *Biographical Dictionary*; a gallery of finely engraved portraits; and two distinguished and pioneering periodicals, the *Quarterly Journal of Education* and the *Penny Magazine* (see plate 5). This plethora of reading matter appeared at stated intervals in serial parts; in marketing terms there were few differences between the Society's 'books' and its 'periodicals'.

Such a publishing programme required massive investments and ran considerable financial risks. It cost more than £25,000, for instance, to produce the *Penny Magazine* in 1833. But even before such sums were ventured, traditional practices of short press runs and high prices for new books looked much safer, especially during the financial crisis of 1825–6. One publisher warned Brougham that the newly proposed Society for the Diffusion of Useful Knowledge should have nothing to do with 'what are called the respectable part of the trade', and John Taylor (who had been publisher of the *London Magazine*) wrote to Brougham at length about the advantage a society would have in initiating cheap publications:

The Establishment of an Association for The Promotion of Useful Knowledge appears to me to afford Facilities for these & similar undertakings which can be hoped for in no other way. A Publisher, if he had the Inclination, has not in general the means to carry into Effect Plans of such Magnitude, where the Outlay is large & the Profit of necessity small. Or if he has the means he looks to the comparative advantages of thus employing his Capital, or of embarking it in other Adventures where the Hazard is less & the expected Profit greater. . . . I have long been of Opinion that in a *Society* alone the proper Power resides. – A Society, while it would be content *not to lose* by its Ventures, possesses an Influence which would ensure the Success of its Plans; & having no apprehension of ulterior Loss needs not the provident Anticipation of considerable Profits. Thus in the most essential Points of Economy of Cost & Lowness of Price, its Production have a vast advantage over those of the individual Trader.[8]

Taylor was right about some of the advantage the Society had in creating a market for cheap literature. The 1846 Address emphasized the editorial flexibility that the absence of the profit motive made possible. But the success of the Society was nonetheless ultimately dependent on the good or ill fortunes of its publications in the market place. As we will see, the non-profit nature of the S.D.U.K. was decidedly not as important as the commercial concerns the Society shared with other publishing establishments. Three activities in particular were common to all and are critically important to our understanding of any publishing venture that required – as most periodicals did – substantial investment and commercial operations on a large scale. These activities are securing the capital needed for the new venture, deciding on the level of profits to be sought, and finding or creating the market in which buyers and sellers of cheap publications could meet.

1. OPERATING CAPITAL

It was not unreasonable to hope that creating a Society whose members subscribed, initially, £1 annually or £10 for life membership would help meet the heavy capital needs involved in publishing for the common reader. One of the most important and characteristic things the Society did in its first years was to send Knight on a tour of the industrial towns of the Midlands and North to promote the interests of the Society. Knight had a twofold charge in 1828. On the one hand he was to visit local booksellers to encourage them to stock S.D.U.K. publications; on the other hand, he was to call upon men of local influence to encourage them to establish local S.D.U.K. committees. These committees would recruit new members and promote subscriptions to the Society's works. The Society's need for subscribed capital forced Knight to give most of his energies on this trip to meeting local leaders and promoting regional committees. Knight thought he had helped establish especially effective committees in Manchester and Derby, and his autobiography recalls cordial meetings on this trip with George William Wood, Edward Baines, the Strutt brothers, Joseph Parkes, and many others. From this beginning, the Society was in time able to establish more than a score of local committees. But it was never able to give them much to do, and from 1830 on membership and subscription income were falling. The Society might complain in its minutes of that year of insufficient capital, and look longingly at the membership income of the British and Foreign Bible Society and the Religious Tract Society.[9] But it was becoming plain that subscription income had not been a significant part of the Society's finances and that the S.D.U.K. would have to depend on its publishers for its capital – or borrow it.

During its first eight years, the Society was able to rely on its publishers for needed capital. Charles Knight and Baldwin and Craddock, the Society's principal publishers, would almost always supply the capital needed for production (typesetting, paper, printing, etc.); they would often pay half or more of the cost of illustrations; and they would sometimes pay for the purchase of copyrights. But this last expense usually fell to the Society, which by 1843 had spent over £30,000 on copyrights.[10] Clearly, such expenses might require considerable operating capital, and given the necessity of advance payments to authors and illustrators and of extended credit to booksellers, the Society and its publishers could often expect no return on their investment for a year and sometimes more. Unhappily none of Knight's records survive, so it is impossible to say how he himself met these capital needs. What the S.D.U.K. records show is the difficulty with which the Society came to terms with the commercial reality of its situation and the extent to which its problems of operating capital were never satisfactorily solved.

At the outset the Society adopted by-laws that prohibited payments to authors until the finished work had been approved for publication. The Society found it could not compete with other publishers on such terms, especially after Knight began the S.D.U.K.'s Library of Entertaining Knowledge in 1829. The Society appointed a special committee to oversee advance payments, and by 1832 the practice had become so routine that it was built into the Society's accounting practices. Knight was allowed an 'advance' account, in which he was credited with capital advances he had made on as yet unpublished S.D.U.K. works in his care. His half-yearly royalty payments to the Society on published works were reduced by the amount in the 'advance' account. The arrangement worked well until the Society found itself without any cash early in 1835 and nothing due from Knight. Knight's 'advance' account at the end of 1834 stood at £3,344, while he owed the Society only £2,667 on his half-yearly royalty account.[11] Under these arrangements, Knight was then, and had throughout his connection with the Society been, its creditor.

The Society's cash flow problems forced it to reconsider the practice that tied up so much capital in unpublished works and denied it a substantial part of its current income. The S.D.U.K. secretary Thomas Coates took up this matter and began to interfere blunderingly in Knight's affairs in 1835, in a way that damaged Knight's commercial credit. Greatly offended and quick to anger, Knight announced his intention to discontinue the Library of Entertaining Knowledge. And though he maintained his connection with the Society to its end, his enthusiasm considerably cooled and he made it his policy whenever he could to purchase for himself financial control of S.D.U.K. publications. A breach thus opened between the Society and its most innovative, energetic, and most profitable publisher. Knight's close friend, M. D. Hill, wrote to Brougham that 'we have lost Knight for ever[.] He may be a Baldwin to us but he can never a Knight to us again – He was devoted to us & has done more for us than any man yourself alone excepted. . . . It gives me great pain to reflect on what we have given him in return – The poor fellow feels it bitterly[.]'[12]

This breach with Knight and the trading difficulties of Baldwin and Craddock deprived the Society of access to its publishers' commercial credit and forced it to look elsewhere for operating capital. To supply the cash needed to pay bills became a pressing and an increasingly preoccupying problem for the Society. From 1835 to 1838 and after 1842, the Society was able to pay only 60 per cent or less, and sometimes considerably less, of its current accounts due; and there was not money enough to invest in new works. Operating capital no longer came interest free from the Society's publishers, but was raised in loans, partly from Committee members themselves but sometimes from the Society's bankers or its printers or bookselling agents. The cash requirements of 1835 were met by Committee members guaranteeing as much as £4,200 to the Society, of which only £1,000 had actually to be borrowed. This indebtedness had almost doubled by the end of 1837.

In 1838 it appeared that the Society had solved its operating capital problems – but it was appearance only. Profits peaked that year because the Society recovered £3,240 from Baldwin and Craddock that had been regarded as a bad debt, and because it sold some of its copyrights (including that of the *Penny Magazine*) to Knight for £630. This income of £3,870 represents, on the one hand, profits that should 'properly' have been spread over several years' figures and, on the other hand, the sale of capital assets. Without these two transactions, the Society showed a £40 loss on operations in 1838. But after so many lean years all this cash produced an illusion of prosperity and made it possible for the Society to pay off most of its loans, to pay all its current liabilities, and to catch up on previously unpaid bills. But doing this only brought it back to the position that prevailed after 1835 and the quarrel with Knight: in the absence of highly profitable publications or the willingness or ability of its publishers to advance capital, the Society had no choice but to borrow the money it needed to continue operating. So dependence on loaned funds increased dramatically again from 1840 onward.

The partial withdrawal of Knight, and the bankruptcy of the Society's other principal publisher, made the Society altogether dependent on loaned capital, and as a consequence the scope of activities had to be constricted. The fact is that after 1835 (and perhaps from as early as 1833), there were no more great bursts of publishing activity from the Society. The excitement and innovation of the first few years was largely gone, so that during the last ten years or so the Society conducted a holding operation. The one exception to this – the launching of the *Biographical Dictionary* in 1842 on a truly heroic scale – was altogether dependent on Lord Althorp's financial support.

When he died in 1845 the Society could no longer avoid the fact that it had no means to continue operation. Some £15,000 was needed to keep the *Dictionary* going, but that was only symptomatic of the general lack of operating funds. In 1842, when the *Dictionary* was first being published, Thomas Coates had defended its success at the same time as he drew attention to the Society's fundamental commercial problem: 'In fact it cannot yet be said that the Dictionary is unsuccessful; 800 copies sold in three months would in former days not be thought want of success. Want of capital for its undertaking the Society may certainly be taunted with.'[13]

Three conclusions emerge from this survey of the Society's efforts to secure adequate operating capital. The first is that the shift from advances made by the Society's publishers to loaned operating capital, especially combined with the withdrawal of much of Charles Knight's good will, contributed significantly to the general slowdown of the Society's activities after 1835. There were doubtless other reasons on the editorial side of the business and arising out of the fact that the Society remained a voluntary one, requiring a great deal of time from the busy men who kept it alive. But even wonderful ideas and boundless energy cannot keep a publishing business going without capital. This impossibility points to the second conclusion, which is how uncertainly those who directed the Society's affairs understood its situation as a non-profit-making organization, all of whose activity took place in a commercial market-place. The Society was always solvent and managed to wind up its affairs with a neat excess of only £8.[14] The requirements of solvency these men clearly understood and met; doing so was, after all, as much a matter of honour as it was good business practice. But the rush to pay bills and reduce debts in 1838 suggests that Committee members never quite understood the broader commercial needs of the Society. It is not surprising that, as Committee members themselves came to provide the Society's operating capital and saw that an additional £15,000 was needed to keep going in 1846, they decided what John Taylor had said 20 years before that any private trader would decide: that other uses of the money would be safer and more profitable.

Profitability thus emerges as the third critical matter. In a sense, the Society defeated itself with its own good intentions. It meant to be and was a non-profit-making organization. As such the Society was never able or willing to extract its operating capital from the sales of its publications; it meant to keep its prices as low as possible and to operate on the thinnest possible margin of profit. Clearly, the Society never succeeded in determining what margin would cover its need for capital. In failing to do that, it failed to provide itself with the only basis that could ensure its continued commercial existence.

2. PROFITABILITY

Profits were vitally important to the S.D.U.K., probably more important than its directing members realized. But profit was possible only if sales could be predicted accurately. Serial publication, more than any other form of publication, enables a publisher to forecast sales with some assurance. A successful serial attracts buyers by its title, by its general reputation; buying and reading it becomes a matter of habit, which is often formalized in a subscription to it. The sale of one number is a more certain guide to the number required of the next issue than the sale of one book is to the sale of the next. Given the uncertainty about the market for the common reader, it is not surprising that the S.D.U.K. adopted serial publication. But it is the two avowed serials published by the Society, the *Quarterly Journal of Education* and the *Penny Magazine*, that epitomize the commercial strategy of the S.D.U.K. From among the plethora of the Society's publications, these two most clearly illustrate how the Society made decisions about production cost, likely sales, and price levels.

A number of contrasts between the two magazines indicate how different S.D.U.K. publications could be from one another and how wide a range of the market-place for reading matter the Society hoped to supply. The *Penny Magazine*, on the one hand, was the cheapest of the Society's publications and was aimed at the broadest, most popular audience. Nearly everyone could afford it, and it addressed the interests of nearly everyone; it was a magazine meant to be universally attractive. The *Quarterly Journal of Education*, on the other hand, cost 5s. each quarter and was, as one impecunious school teacher complained, 'the dearest' of the Society's publications when measured by the 'quantity of matter for the Price'. The *Journal* addressed only those professionally engaged in education, and while it covered the entire range of education, both in Britain and abroad, it concentrated on the education provided to the established classes – those who in turned controlled the education of 'the poorer classes'. So specialized an audience considerably diminished the likelihood of commercial success, and the magazine came close to never being published at all. The idea was first floated in June 1829, and by the following April four different publishers had declined to take it on without a guarantee against financial loss. John Murray declined to take it even with a £200 guarantee. The *Journal* looked commercially impossible until Charles Knight offered to publish it in June 1830, and even then it was not until January 1831 that the first number appeared. By comparison with this 18-month gestation period, it was only eight weeks from the time when M. D. Hill and Knight, walking into the city one morning from their homes in Hampstead, thought of providing a 'weekly penny paper of miscellaneous matter', until the first number was in readers' hands. Their proposal was adopted by the S.D.U.K. on 22 February 1832; the first issue is dated 31 March – a remarkably brief period for so ambitious an undertaking, both editorially and financially, as the *Penny Magazine*. The final contrast between the two serials is the most telling one: the *Penny Magazine* was wonderfully successful, realizing all of Knight's hopes for it and more, whereas the *Quarterly Journal of Education* lost money from the outset. To meet the demand for the *Penny Magazine*, Knight had to start printing three weeks before the issue date, and even then he might run 10,000 copies short. The success of the first month's issues enabled Knight to increase his editorial expenditures for the *Penny Magazine* by 240 per cent. By contrast, the steadily falling sales and accumulating losses of the *Quarterly Journal of Education* forced Knight to cut editorial costs by 18 per cent, leading its editor to observe that he had insufficient funds to secure even the book reviews he wanted.[15]

The financial ledgers of the S.D.U.K. permit considerable refinement of this general comparison of the two magazines, especially on the critical matters of total circulation and profitability. Table 1 sets out what is known of the circulation of the *Penny Magazine* and the *Quarterly Journal of Education*, alongside comparable figures for *Chambers's Edinburgh Journal*, a 1½d. weekly begun a few weeks before the *Penny Magazine*, *Blackwood's Magazine*, and the *Quarterly Review*, a 2s. 6d. monthly and a 7s. quarterly respectively.[16]

The figures for the *Penny Magazine* represent the number of copies actually delivered to Knight by the printer (which might exceed the number ordered by as much as 15 per cent), and they include for each issue an average 5,422 additional copies printed as back numbers during the period for which these figures exist. There was of course no need to reprint back numbers of the unsuccessful *Journal*. Reprinted back numbers are included in the *Chambers's* figures; there are no pertinent figures for the *Quarterly* and no information available for reprintings of *Blackwood's*. The evidence indicates that print runs of the *Penny Magazine* exceeded the number ordered by only about 5 per cent. So all the numbers in table 1 are fairly close to the numbers actually required by the publishers.

These numbers represent copies printed; they also closely approximate – with one exception – the number of copies sold. Nothing is commercially more deadly than a warehouse full of unsold magazines. Given a number of subscribers committed to a journal at least for a year, the guidance provided by previous sales, and the relatively low cost of reprinting that stereotyping made possible, there was little need or incentive for a periodical publisher to print copies much beyond the known demand. This demand might well

Table 1. Average print orders for each issue of five periodicals of the 1830s and 1840s, reported quarterly or annually, and the percentage of the print order actually sold

Year and quarter	Penny Magazine	Chambers's Edinburgh Journal	Quarterly Journal of Education	Blackwood's Magazine	Quarterly Review
1831–1			2,000	—	10,625
2			2,000	—	10,500
3			1,500	—	10,500
4			1,500	—	9,750
1832–1			1,250	—	10,000
2	213,241	25,000	1,250	—	10,000
3	176,866	—	1,250	—	9,000
4	170,335	—	1,250	—	9,250
1833–1	164,522	—	1,250	—	9,250
2	164,522	—	1,250	—	9,250
3	161,397	—	1,250	—	9,500
4	159,522	—	1,250	—	9,250
1834–1	142,647	—	1,250	—	9,250
2	132,647	—	1,250	—	9,250
3	120,335	—	1,250	—	9,000
4	116,522	50,000	1,250	—	9,000
1835–1	109,085	—	1,250	—	9,250
2	104,522	—	1,250	—	9,500
3	102,022	—	1,250	—	9,250
4	98,022	58,000	1,250	—	9,250
1836–1	94,085	—		—	9,250
2	88,585	—		—	9,250
3	85,397	—		—	9,250
4	84,522	—		—	9,250
1837–1	78,255	—		—	9,250
2	69,522	—		—	9,250
3	68,581	—		—	9,250
4	—	—		—	9,250
1838	—	—		7,500	9,250
1839	—	72,000		7,200	9,570
1840	—	70,000		7,000	9,650
1841	—	NA*		7,000	9,750
1842	—	56,365		7,000	9,375
1843	—	53,327		6,583	9,313
1844	—	86,750		6,808	9,275
1845	40,000	86,192		6,000	9,313
1846	25,000	76,096		6,000	9,250
1847		74,653		5,750	9,167
1848		66,096		5,750	9,000
1849		64,288		5,750	9,083

Percentage of print order sold:

range	—	96–100%	41–86%	78–91%	92–99%†
average	c.98%	99%	61/	84%	97%

— Dash denotes figures not available.
* The average print order for the period 1832–41 was 60,956.

† These are the figures for the period Sept.1843–June 1846; the average sold for the period 1832–41 was 97%.

include provision for future sales of back numbers. Knight set aside 10,000 copies of each number of the *Penny Magazine* for this purpose, but that was not adequate, as the evidence of his reprintings indicates. Knight reported that he rarely had more than 200,000 or 300,000 copies of the magazine on hand at a time when he had printed a total of 20,000,000 copies, which suggests that he was selling some 98 per cent of what he ordered to be printed. This may appear a high percentage, but it is certain that a high percentage of sales was critically important to Knight's success in keeping the price low. Blackwood, by contrast, was carrying a stock of some 170,000 back numbers in the mid-1830s against a total number printed that probably did not then exceed 2,000,000 – a tenth the number of the *Penny Magazine* – while between 1838 and 1846 he was selling on the average some 84 per cent of the copies printed. It is likely that so long as the journal was making money for its publisher, current sales would be 85 per cent or greater of the number printed, unsold numbers being held for back issue sales. When a journal was not clearing costs, however, the print run is not a reliable approximation of sales, for the question before a publisher then is not one of matching demand with supply but of how much loss to bear and how effective reducing the print run will be in reducing that loss. Sales of the *Quarterly Journal of Education*, for instance, reached 86 per cent of the print run with the first number but dropped to a dismal 41 per cent for the penultimate issue; the average of this steadily declining sale was 61 per cent. The contrast between that number and the sale of possibly 98 per cent of the copies printed of the *Penny Magazine* gives vivid point to Knight's assertion that the great secret to commercial success is the ability to match demand and supply. 'It is a secret which enables those who possess it to make a fortune with 5 per cent. profit, while those who do not understand it are ruined with 25 per cent. profit.'[17]

These circulation numbers tell us approximately how many purchasers the S.D.U.K. periodicals had; the comparison with *Chambers's Edinburgh Journal* and with a well-established monthly or quarterly demonstrates how massive an audience the *Penny Magazine* won in its first years. There had been nothing like it before, and for a while its circulation was without rival in size.[18] Absolutely how much 'mass' it takes to create a mass market is impossible to say, as the answer is always a matter of comparisons. The comparisons here – with the *Penny Magazine* at first far outstripping either *Chambers's* or the *Saturday Magazine*, with a circulation many times larger than that of any other serial whose circulation is known to me – support the *Penny Magazine*'s claim to be the first mass-market periodical published in Great Britain.

But circulation figures tell only half the story. Periodicals are like any other mass-produced object: the first one produced is very expensive, subsequent copies cost comparatively little, but no profit is made until sales income matches production costs – the break-even point. Profitability was critically important to the S.D.U.K. even as a non-profit-making organization, as we have already seen; as we shall now see, profitability also gives the single most sensitive measure of how large a market, how 'massy' a mass market, the S.D.U.K. and Charles Knight were hoping to create.

Table 2 sets out the production costs, sales income, and the profitability ratios for the same five periodicals cited in table 1.[19] Again the three journals not published by the S.D.U.K. are included to provide comparisons; the figures in isolation from one another mean almost nothing at all. The distribution of the total production cost among its constituent parts is one indicator of the 'character' or 'quality' of the journal. It is instructive, for instance, to know that Knight spent twice as much on the illustrations for the *Penny Magazine* as he did on the text. By taking care to establish proper bases of comparison among journals of different size and frequency of issue, it would be possible to say how different editorial designs are reflected in the comparative costs of executing them. But the point here is not that, but the profits actually earned by the S.D.U.K.'s two periodicals: the *Penny Magazine* returned £1.07 for every pound spent on it, while the *Journal* returned less than half of what it cost to produce.

Profitability changes with the fortunes of the market-place, so the numbers in Table 2 represent the costs and income that at a specific time produced a specific profit or loss in Knight's and the Society's ledgers. More important for the determination of their commercial intention is a permutation of these numbers that reflects the way a publisher might actually weigh the variables facing him – might make the highly uncertain estimates on production costs, unit price, and market size on which the commercial success of the periodical depended.[20] If the relationship among these factors was difficult to predict in any given instance, the theoretical nature of this relationship is perfectly clear. The ratio between costs and income can be represented by a profitability curve that rises sharply at first, as sales begin to cover initial costs, but then flattens out and gradually approximates a straight line as initial costs constitute a smaller and smaller proportion of total production costs. The key decision a publisher must make is where on this curve to place the break-even point. To decide that a publication must recover its costs through a relatively high unit cost and relatively few sales is to put the break-even point in the 'bend' of the curve; doing this involves the fewest financial risks and produces higher profit ratios on relatively modest increases in sales. Alternatively, to decide that a publication should recover its costs through low unit prices and relatively numerous sales puts the break-even point in the 'flat' of

Table 2. Distribution of approximate costs, approximate income, and profitability (*per annum*) of five periodicals of the 1830s

Title and period of publication	Penny Magazine 1833: nos. 49–112	Chambers's Edinburgh Journal ave. annual costs 1832–41: nos. 1–520	Quarterly Journal of Education 1834: nos. 13–76	Blackwood's Magazine 1838–9: nos. 273–84	Quarterly Review 1838: nos. 121–4
Copyright					
Editor	400			1,000	1,300
Contributors	600			832	1,676
Illustration	2,000				6
Total	*3,000*	*520*	*582*	*1,832*	*2,982*
Production					
Typesetting	512	398	162	530	
Printing	2,080	771*	84	471	
Subtotal	*2,592*	*1,169*	*246*	*1,001*	*991*
Stereoplating	160	265	–	–	–
Paper	17,874	2,294*	159	1,534	1,212
Binding	(est) 520	64*	43	726†	416
Miscellaneous	–	–	–	–	9
Total	*21,416*	*3,792*	*448*	*3,261*	*2,628*
Total direct cost	24,416	4,312	1,030	5,093	5,610
Overhead	2,415	431	103	509	561
Total cost	*26,561*	*4,743*	*1,133*	*5,602*	*6,171*
Income from sales	28,451	6,666*	464	7,470	7,893
Income from ads	–	–	60	1,381	–
Total income	*28,451*	*6,666*	*524*	*8,851*	*7,893*
Profitability	1.07	1.41	.46	1.58	1.27

– Dash denotes figures not available.
* During the period 1832–41 only 41 per cent of the total print order was actually printed for Chambers and the costs thereof entered in his ledgers. The other 59 per cent was subcontracted to Chambers's London Agent, W. S. Orr, for whose operations no accounts have been found. Orr's payments to Chambers are however included in 'income from sales': they amounted to 23 per cent of Chambers's total income.
† This figure includes the cost of the advertising section.

the curve; doing this involves much greater financial risks and produces lower profit ratios as sales increase. The difference between these two market strategies is, of course, the difference between the conventional market for printed matter in the 1820s and the mass market that Knight and the S.D.U.K. were trying to create in the 1830s.

Figure 1 sets out the profitability curves of four of the periodicals described in table 2. The curves represent the different profit ratios that result if the conditions that actually obtained in table 2 had obtained at several different levels of sales.[21] These are arbitrarily (but conveniently) set at intervals of 15 per cent of sales above and below the publication's break-even point. *Blackwood's* profitability curve may be taken as representing conventional and conservative marketing practices: rather modest increases in sales (450 copies *per* interval) would produce handsome increases in profitability for some time after the break-even point was passed. It is not surprising that so risky a venture as the *Quarterly Journal of Education* was published on similar terms. But even so conservative a marketing strategy did not succeed. The *Journal* reached its break-even point only in the first number and was thereafter a losing venture for the S.D.U.K. The profitability curve of *Chambers's* is significantly lower than these two journals. What is more, *Chambers's* had a much higher break-even point and so required much larger increases in sales (3,450 copies) for each interval beyond that point. By this measure *Chambers's* was a much riskier venture than *Blackwood's*, and one that (when risk was no longer in question) would have to find 34,500 additional purchasers to yield the return on invested capital (1.37) that *Blackwood's* got by securing only 2,700 additional purchasers. As we saw in table 2, both periodicals were thriving in the 1830s with profit ratios higher than this one. But it is not surprising that *Blackwood's* had the much higher profitability.

The *Penny Magazine* presents a sharply different profile from the other three because its break-even point is much further out in the 'flat' of its profitability curve. The *Penny Magazine* broke even at a much higher number of sales (almost five times that of *Chambers's*), and comparable intervals of increased sales (involving 16,800 copies each) produced much lower profitability ratios.[22] To produce a profitability ratio of just 1.11, the *Penny Magazine* had to find 168,000 readers more than were required to break even, compared to 6,900 additional readers for *Chambers's* and fewer than 900 for *Blackwood's*. One might say that the Chambers brothers – canny Scotsmen that they were – secured the best of both worlds: a fairly 'safe' break-even point and an entry into the mass market.[23] Knight and the S.D.U.K. aimed more single-mindedly at the mass market; their strategy was uncompromisingly one of high sales, low unit costs, and razor-thin

Figure 1. Profitability curves for four periodicals of the 1830s.

Intervals of 15 per cent increase or decrease in sales from the break-even point (BEP)*
−6   −5   −4   −3   −2   −1   BEP   +1   +2   +3   +4   +5   +6   +7   +8   +9   +10
Penny Mag. (BEP 112,000)
.79   .84   .89   .92   .95   .98   1.00   1.02   1.03   1.04   1.06   1.07   1.08   1.09   1.09   1.10   1.11
Chambers's (BEP 23,000)
.30   .48   .63   .75   .85   .93   1.00   1.06   1.11   1.16   1.20   1.24   1.27   1.30   1.33   1.35   1.37
Quarterly J. of Education (BEP 1,700)
.20   .38   .53   .66   .78   .88   .97   1.06   1.14   1.20   1.27   1.33   1.38   1.43   1.47   1.52   1.56
Blackwood's (BEP 3,000)†
.36   .50   .63   .73   .83   .92   1.00   1.08   1.14   1.20   1.26   1.31   1.36   1.40   1.44   1.48   1.52

* The *Quarterly Review* is not included in these figures because its cost ledgers do not permit the separation of typesetting from printing costs – a key discrimination in the determination of profitability curves.

† For the sake of clarity, *Blackwood's* is not charted here. Above the BEP its curve corresponds closely to that of the *Quarterly Journal of Education*, while below the BEP its curve corresponds closely to that of *Chambers's*.

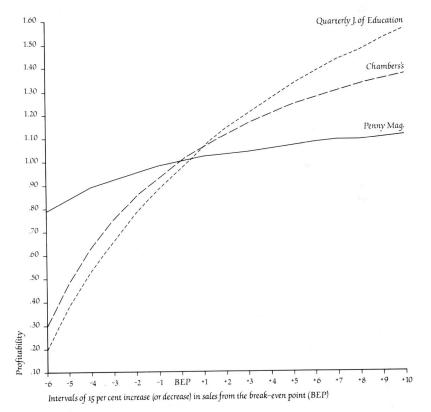

margins of profit. The circulation figures of the *Penny Magazine* establish its claim to be, in fact, the first mass-market publication in Britain. Its profitability curve establishes even more clearly that it was a mass-market product not by accident nor by force of competition, but rather by the conscious and innovative design of the S.D.U.K. and Charles Knight.

3. MARKETING

The success that the S.D.U.K. and Knight aimed for required massive sales that in turn required an effective means for the widest possible distribution of the *Penny Magazine* and the Society's other publications. That the *Penny Magazine* secured broad distribution, even outside Britain, is suggested by the fact that in 1833 in Pictou, Nova Scotia, a schoolboy was eagerly reading the magazine's articles on mineralogy; while on the other side of the world, British missionaries in Canton were translating material from the magazine into Chinese. But it was not breadth so much as depth of distribution that would make the difference between success and failure. Knight knew what every other publisher for the common reader in the 1830s and 1840s knew, that cheap publications required 'more than the usual means & channels' of distribution if they were to find their readers.[24]

Knight and his fellow publishers had three means of getting their wares to market: they might employ special agents solely concerned with their works, they might depend on the established wholesale and retail book trade, or they might try to get to the smaller towns and rural areas in the packs of itinerant pedlars. Knight employed all three means at one time or another, but his main dependence was on the regular book trade.

The book trade was not accustomed to dealing with massive numbers of buyers and narrow margins of profits. It was for this reason, as well as because of their illegality, that the unstamped papers of the early 1830s recruited most of their agents outside of London from among people new to journalism and the book trade. The S.D.U.K., though not involved in an illegal trade, nonetheless felt strongly the need to create its own, new, channels of distribution. It was for this purpose that the Society sent Knight on his tour in 1828 of the northern industrial cities. In Birmingham, on his first night away from London, Knight was asked, 'Pray, sir, what do you travel in?' He answered, 'In Useful Knowledge, sir'.[25]

I have already referred to Knight's success on this trip in establishing several local committees. In visiting booksellers in the same towns, Knight discovered how unwilling they were to co-operate in any scheme that involved local committees in the distribution of the Society's publications. It was intended that the committees would supply the Society's publications directly to local members and perhaps to non-member subscribers; in doing this the committees would act as agents for the S.D.U.K. and as rivals to the local book trade. In Manchester Knight found booksellers unwilling even to tell him how many copies of the Society's publications they sold for fear of competition from the local committee, and he had for the same reason to report that 'there is no disposition amongst *the trade* to promote subscriptions'. He urged that in Manchester and Liverpool the booksellers should supply all local subscribers and be reimbursed by the local committee for those subscribers who were Society members. Such an arrangement would avoid commercial 'jealousies' and would insure that 'no interference should take place with the supply [of S.D.U.K. publications] by the Trade'. Knight felt the Society had much better depend on the trade for the circulation of its works than on specially created committees acting as the Society's agents, especially in the large towns where he found booksellers generally stocked S.D.U.K. publications. It was only in smaller towns – he instanced Loughborough – where the regular trade could not be depended on.[26]

Knight's advice prevailed; the local committees never played a significant role in the financial or commercial affairs of the Society, and during its most flourishing years the Society marketed its publications through the regular book trade. But with the publication of the *Penny Magazine* in unprecedented numbers the very meaning of 'regular' was – at least for a while – stretched. In the spring and summer of 1832, with the *Magazine* only a few months old, the Society once more sent out a traveller in useful knowledge. He toured in the south and west of England, reporting back that 'the interest excited everywhere by the *Penny Magazine* is quite extraordinary; its sale, in almost every town I have visited, is daily increasing.' In London the magazine stimulated the commercial rivalry of

> three or four of the large wholesale Booksellers. Their hostility has been mainly provoked by the wonderful success of the Penny Magazine. They complain that this, and similar works, will absorb all the old trade in books. . . . Upon the subject of their alarms they have had several meetings – Longman and Company have taken a bold step – They have written to all their correspondents begging them to discourage the Sale of the Penny *numbers*, and cultivate that of the *Parts*. . . . I have this within 24 hours and went to another large house to ascertain if they participated in the plot. I found they were too wise to make any such attempt to dictate to the public.[27]

By far most sales of the *Penny Magazine* were in its weekly issues; to change that in favour of monthly part sales would have destroyed the magazine commercially. It is not clear how a shift from numbers to parts would benefit wholesalers, though the ruin of the magazine might benefit a rival publisher such as Longman. But what is clear – even allowing for some triumphant exaggeration on Knight's part – is that the demand for the *Penny Magazine* was so strong that booksellers were not willing to follow the lead hostile to it proposed by one of the most powerful members of the book trade. A new power was making itself felt in the trade, the power of massive numbers of readers.

The strength of the *Penny Magazine* and its newly created mass market is even more dramatically evident in a report Knight made to the Society in June 1832. The S.D.U.K. was considering whether to embark on a penny encyclopedia modelled after the *Penny Magazine*. In urging the encyclopaedia, Knight described the revolution that the *Penny Magazine* was then making in the market-place for reading matter.

> The circulation of the Penny Magazine has opened new views as to the number of persons in the United Kingdom who are desirous to acquire information, when presented to them at a very low price, and at short intervals. The machinery for circulating the Penny Magazine extends to the most opulent bookseller and to the keeper of a stall – to the publisher of the country Newspaper and the hawker of worn-out Reprints. The latter description of dealer, having first set their faces against any publications which should not pay them cent per cent [i.e., 100 per cent profit], have now begun to cultivate the business which the Penny Magazine has suggested to them. For the first time, therefore, all classes may be reached more or less by a work which shall be the cheapest ever published.[28]

Here again the *Penny Magazine* was able to impose its terms on the market-place, rather than conform to it; the success of the magazine and the demand for it were forcing some retail traders to adopt thinner profit margins than those to which they were accustomed. Again it is important to allow for Knight's enthusiasm in describing the success of the *Penny Magazine*, and important to remember that there were at least two other journals – *Chambers's Edinburgh Journal* and the S.P.C.K.'s *Saturday Magazine* – involved in this first burst of the mass reading market in 1832. But these are matters of shading only and do not alter the fact that at least in its first flush of success the *Penny Magazine* was in this specific and concrete way able to enforce the fundamental condition of a mass market – narrow margins of profit – on an unwilling trade. This one report, more than anything else, allows us to put our hand on the pulse of the commercial revolution that made cheap publications possible in Great Britain. This was the way the old conventions of the trade were broken down, the way the market-place for the common reader was created.

The *Penny Magazine* was unable to hold for long its dominant position in the mass reading market, and its ability to force its terms especially on the small dealers accustomed to 'cent per cent' arrangements waned.[29] As early as May 1835 the Society was considering a proposal for improving sales by allowing a 50 per cent discount to a Manchester firm employing pedlars, and in November 1836 the Society agreed to experiment further with sales by hawkers by foregoing its part of the profits. In April and May 1837 the Society considered a proposal from James Miller, a Dundee bookseller, who wanted to employ pedlars to distribute the *Penny Magazine* in 'the remote districts of Scotland' and promised immediate sales of 4,000 copies – rising 'shortly' to 40,000. Miller undertook not to 'interfere with the interest' of Knight nor to supply the regular trade in Scotland himself, but his plan required the larger margin of profit, the 50 per cent that Knight had resisted successfully in 1832.[30] It is not clear how far any of these negotiations went. The Society must have been tempted by this important market not served by the regular trade, and tempted by much larger Scottish sales; but it must also have known that Miller's 40,000 was wildly optimistic, even for Scotland.

Sales by pedlars were essentially a side issue, however. Nine years earlier, in 1828, the Society had committed itself to operating within the regular book trade. Many of its books, its annual almanac, the map series, and most notably the *Penny Magazine*, achieved very large or even unprecedented sales through these ordinary channels – channels made wider and deeper by the very success of the S.D.U.K.'s publications. That widening and deepening had happened most dramatically in 1832 when the *Penny Magazine* was more successful than anyone had thought it might be and could impose its own commercial terms on the book trade. The Society was not able to maintain that success. Knight brought the *Penny Magazine* to an end in 1846, two years after the *Saturday Magazine* had ceased publication. Even the now more successful *Chambers's* was hard-pressed. Chambers' London agent, W. S. Orr, wrote to the Edinburgh publisher in 1845 about the 'unpleasant features' of the magazine's sales ledger and the 'rivals of a formidable character' that they now faced. He added that:

> above all I should not be sorry to see some fresh literary blood if I may use the Phrase infused into its pages. . . . [In the past 14 years] a totally new class of minds have arrived at maturity who require a different *pabulum* to that of *our* younger days. . . . I would not by this hint at any radical change in the Journal but I think we might retain all the solidity of the Journal and yet fall in, in a quiet way with the popular bent of the readers of the day.[31]

The mid-1840s mark a phase in the development of the mass-reading audience, especially with the clear emergence of fiction as the most saleable commodity in that market and with the editorial exhaustion of the *Penny Magazine* and the *Saturday Magazine*. The mass market had changed rapidly since 1832, but unmistakably its take-off point had been the S.D.U.K., Charles Knight, and the *Penny Magazine*.

The question to which we must finally return is the impact of the S.D.U.K. – what sort of success did it have? I have tried to show that the Society's success must be understood in commercial terms and that it has to do not with large profits but with the creation of a mass market for reading matter. Never before had so much new non-fiction been made so widely available at so low a cost. If this is the neglected half of the S.D.U.K.'s history, it is still only half; and the connection between this success in the market-place and the well-known failure of the Society's avowed social and political purposes requires explanation. The connection between the two comes to focus in the dilemma felt by many British publishers and editors during the first half of the nineteenth century. One horn of this dilemma was the need to be politically independent, to avoid partisan politics and religion. The 1846 *Address* acknowledged that almost all the Society's original supporters were Whigs, but insisted that:

> the Society determined, with obvious prudence, to avoid the great subjects of religion and government, on which it was impossible to touch without provoking angry discussion. At a time when the spirit which produced the events of 1828, 1829, and 1832 was struggling with those who, not very long before, had tried to subdue it by force: when religious disqualification and political exclusion occupied the daily attention of the press; and when the friends of education were themselves divided on the best way of adjusting these and other matters of legislation – any interference with theology or politics would have endangered the existence of a union which demanded the most cordial co-operation from all who wished well to the cause.

Yet – and this is the other horn of the dilemma – nothing endangered commercial success more than such independence. In announcing the closing of the *Quarterly Journal of Education*, its editor George Long complained that only those journals that frankly engaged in partisan political or religious controversy could hope for commercial success: 'Periodical publications which are addressed solely to the understanding . . . do not in this country, and hardly perhaps in any country, command an extensive sale.' So bleak a view as this undoubtedly reflects Long's own disappointment, but the dilemma was nonetheless a real one for many publishers trying to find their way in the new market created by and for the common reader.[32]

Charles Knight believed this dilemma crippled his first efforts in the early 1820s to publish for the common reader, an experience that undoubtedly helped to shape his connection with the S.D.U.K. Knight had been a reformer from the outset of his career. Writing to his future wife in 1812, when he was just 21 years old and setting up the *Windsor and Eton Express*, he proclaimed his intention to 'reform many things in this neighbourhood . . . if fair argument can do it . . . . I shall adopt the opinions of no set of men in Church or State; but think for myself on all points.' How much scope for reform Georgian Windsor gave Knight is a question for another time; what is clear is that for the next 15 years – until he took up his connection with the S.D.U.K. – Knight continued to look for a mode of publication that would give full scope to his reforming zeal. In the early 1820s, while continuing as editor of the Windsor *Express*, Knight took over as well the editorship of the *Guardian*, a weekly London newspaper, and began his own monthly, the *Plain Englishman*. Both serials were issued during the turmoil of public feeling following Peterloo, and it must be said that Knight trimmed his reforming sails a good deal. His fear of revolution drove him into the Tory camp. The *Guardian* was directly associated with Liverpool's Government, and Knight could never afterwards find any satisfaction in his actions during these years.

> In my hatred and contempt of the demagogues and profligate writers who were stirring up the ignorant masses to revolt and irreligion, I turned somewhat aside from regarding the injustice that was at the root of a desire for change. I panted for improvement as ardently as ever. I was aspiring to become a Popular Educator. But I felt that one must be content for a while to shut one's eyes to the necessity for some salutary reforms, in the dread that any decided movement towards innovation would be to aid in the work of lopping and topping the sturdy oak of the constitution till its shelter and its beauty were altogether gone. . . . Thence ensued a reticence in writing and in speaking, which looked like a distrust of the progress of improvement even with many of decided liberal opinions. I think this was amongst the worse results of those evil days in which we had fallen in the last months of the reign of the old King. I had to drag this chain of doubtful timidity in my first attempt to address the humbler classes.

Knight does not here say he chose the 'wrong' side in the controversies of the day. The evil was rather that when faced with such divisive controversies, he gave up the brave independence of views espoused in 1812.[33] That left Knight no alternative to the fear-driven responses of the Tories, as they dealt with the civil unrest of the early 1820s. The *Guardian* and the *Plain Englishman* were both unmistakably Tory papers. Such open partisanship was a rule of the day and continued to flourish for many years – the promoters of the unstamped press, for instance, never felt any qualms about it and made it the basis for their remarkable success. But this was not the basis on which a mass reading market was to develop in the 1830s and 1840s in Britain.

The S.D.U.K. offered Knight a new start as a 'Popular Educator' and promised more scope for genuine independence because it offered him a different kind of market-place. The Society meant to address 'solely the understandings' of its readers; it proposed only the diffusion of 'useful' knowledge. What is remarkable is that a Society so thoroughly Whig in complexion succeeded so well as it did in avoiding partisan politics. Such a Society could hardly go through the period of 1828 to 1835 untouched by the pervasive sense of crisis; but in acknowledging that, it is important also to emphasize that the openly partisan publications of the S.D.U.K. are neither representative of its output nor are they very numerous.

The Swing Riots and general conditions of economic hardship drove the Society to action as nothing else did in those tumultuous years. The Society issued pamphlets on machine breaking and on union activity written by Henry Gawler;[34] it brought out Harriet Martineau's tales illustrative of the evils of the old poor law; and it published two books on economic conditions by Knight, the *Results of Machinery* and the *Rights of Industry*. Beyond this the Society approached issues of the day indirectly, as it did when Knight and M. D. Hill visited Paris in August 1830 to collect material on the July Revolution. Hill wrote to Brougham that the Society ought to publish 'the narrative of this glorious revolution in France. But in order to avoid a political complexion, and at the same time to increase the interest, let the work be called "Paris," and let it contain accounts of past transactions, as well as present.'[35] The Society was in this way drawn by its enthusiasm for safe middle-class revolutions, or by its fear of revolution impelled by economic distress, to depart from its policy of avoiding the discussion of public issues. Interesting as these departures are, they should not blind us to the general success with which the Society carried out its policy of disengagement – as, for instance, when George Long refused to include any discussion of Owenite ideas in the *Quarterly Journal of Education* in 1832 because the times were too unsettled for it. The result of this circumspect policy was that critics of the S.D.U.K. were normally left with nothing to scorn but the empty irrelevance of the Society's 'gingerbread dolls', its fascination with kangaroos and dromedaries.[36]

Middle-class radicals were especially unhappy with the Society's policy.

Bulwer, Hume, Place, and Roebuck were disgusted with the Society's failure to deal with political issues and resolved to form their own Society for the Diffusion of Political and Moral Knowledge. Harriet Martineau several years later passed judgment on the Society, one that has stuck ever since.

> The classes addressed by this Society found experimentally that their own Harry Brougham, as well as other Liberal leaders, had not faith enough in them to entrust them with political knowledge, but preferred putting out, in the most critical period of the nation's history, treatises on physical science, as a tub to the whale. From that time forward it was a deep popular persuasion that the Whigs wished to withhold political knowledge from the people.[37]

It is clear that Martineau and the other radical critics of the S.D.U.K. from both the working and the middle classes were still thinking of the press and its social function in much the same terms as did Knight and his backers in the early 1820s. They held that there were fundamental truths (albeit different ones) 'the People' must be taught, and the job of the press was to propagate those truths. There was not a little of this sort of talk, some of it by Knight himself, within the Society, but in fact it counted for very little in the actual operation of the S.D.U.K. over the 20 years of its existence. It was this turn of events, this apostasy, that embittered the radicals against the S.D.U.K. Subsequent accounts of the Society have accepted this view as the whole truth, without looking very closely at what Society was actually doing, and without seeing the genuine alternative to partisan publication for the common reader that it offered.

On what alternative grounds did the S.D.U.K. hope to succeed? Once again Knight is worth listening to:

> [Among the Society's enemies] the most open and avowed are the Radicals, including many of the utilitarians and all the Co-operatives. Some of them are real friends to the Education of the people, but falling into the gross mistake that all knowledge, except what is political, is useless, quarrel with us for leading the people into trains of agreeable thought, and require that we should be always preaching to them the doctrines of political economy – and what is more they insist that we have no right to persuade them that they can find any sources of enjoyment while Tithes and Corn Laws exist.

The simple fact is that the S.D.U.K., as it matured its purposes, gave all its energies to creating a mass market for non-fiction reading matter and believed that to do so it must avoid factional interests. It was looking for a common ground in ideas and interests, not for ideological victories. The measure of its success in finding that common ground was not the number of votes cast, nor the number of signatures on a petition, nor the number of people at outdoor meetings. These were important numbers, but the success at which the S.D.U.K. aimed would be measured by the sales of its publications. The Society was, in its peak period, ordering books printed in runs of four or more times the previous norm for non-fiction, and the circulation of the *Penny Magazine* was unprecedented. When Knight wrote that the circulation of the magazine was 'the extreme point which literature has yet reached,' he was stating the simple but even to him startling truth. [38]

Nothing breeds imitation faster than such success. Surely one of the clearest indications we have that the S.D.U.K. was playing a leading role in the development of a mass reading market is the host of imitators it inspired. Series of cheap books burgeoned mightily in the late 1820s, and the *Penny Magazine* along with *Chambers's Edinburgh Journal* and the *Saturday Magazine* stand at the front of a long line of successors begun in the late 1830s and 1840s. The mass circulation periodical very quickly established itself in the reading habits of the nation. It may be true that S.D.U.K. publications were, with respect to the critical issues of the day, quite colourless and largely non-controversial – simply dull. But these are exactly the characteristics, we are told, of any mass-market product. In focussing on the supposed dullness of S.D.U.K. publications we have avoided altogether the challenge of explaining why the *Penny Magazine* was purchased more than ten million times in 1833. [39]

Charles Knight thought the introduction of the printing machine and the Fourdrinier paper-making machine and the creation of a mass reading market in his own lifetime brought a revolution in the distribution of knowledge comparable in consequence to the revolution of Gutenberg's time. Writing in the *Penny Magazine*, Knight specifically identifies the revolution of his own age with the periodical press.

> It was not till the system of periodical literature was fairly established, and that newspapers first, and magazines and reviews subsequently, had taken hold of the popular mind, that the productions of the press could be said to be in demand amongst the people generally. Up to our own times that demand has been limited to very narrow bounds; and the circumstances by which it has been extended are as remarkable as those which accompanied the progress of the original invention of printing. [40]

Knight and the S.D.U.K. found that to produce this revolution in thought, they had to ignore as much as possible the revolution going on in other spheres of British life. Conditions would be different at later times and in other places, but these were the terms on which the S.D.U.K. won its remarkable commercial success.

This success, not the supposed failure of the S.D.U.K., is the thing that now needs to be understood. I have been primarily concerned in this essay with documenting the commercial foundation of the Society's success in creating a mass reading market; I would like to conclude with three propositions about the long-term consequences of that success.

In the first place, the Society took a leading role in fulfilling a basic need, that for information. Again one knows that in different times and places there have been other ways for supplying this need, but it was through a new mass market for printed material that people's need for information was met in Britain in the 1830s. New books and magazines were a luxury beyond the reach of most people in the England where Knight was born in 1791; that was no longer the case by the end of the 1840s, nor was it ever to be so again. This great increase in the availability of reading matter attracted comment from all quarters, not least from those who before could not afford new books and magazines. Christopher Thomson, writing in 1847, is representative of many working-class autobiographers in noting this major change during his lifetime: 'My great want was books; I was too poor to purchase expensive ones, and "cheap literature" was not then, as now, to be found in every out-o'-the way nooking.'[41] The hunger for knowledge was widespread and deeply felt in the 1820s and 1830s; it was the essential pre-condition for the creation of a mass reading market. But pre-conditions do not bring themselves to fruition. It was the commercial good judgment and daring of Charles Knight and the S.D.U.K., and of the other publishers who followed their example, that brought about this permanent change in the character and quality of British life.

It must be remembered, in the second place, that mass markets can exist only where widely shared interests or values exist or can be created. This is not to say that every individual in such a market is like every other such individual – far from it. But it is to say that mass markets require some common ground, some common feeling, however partial or fleeting it may be in the day-to-day lives of the individuals who make up that market. Such allegiances can be, are indeed likely to be multiform. I suspect that the emergence of mass markets should stand alongside the emergence of class consciousness in our estimation of the new, most socially potent forces of the period. Historians, I sometimes think, regard class consciousness as omnipotent and forget what a highly mixed and often muddled affair day-to-day life is. Surely it is possible for quite intense class feelings to exist alongside an equally vivid sense of the commonalty in things that a mass market creates and on which it depends. We have recently been instructed on the way in which radical, working-class attitudes of the 1830s and 1840s survived in mid-Victorian culture, how they were taken over or absorbed by the larger culture and partially defused.[42] This did not happen in some disembodied ideological sphere, but worked itself out in various market-places. The one for which the most evidence survives is the mass market for reading material. It is here perhaps more visible than anywhere else how this process of penetration and absorption took place, and that it did so not as the result of vigorous intellectual sparring but through a gradual settling on common ground. Too often we have taken conflict and its resolution to be the sole substance of history. Mass markets develop through consensus, not conflict, and if we are to understand their critically important impact on nineteenth-century life we must considerably enrich our tools of historical analysis.

Finally, we must remember that we are dealing with a mass *reading* market – a market that has, I believe, a unique character and a unique importance. For reading is a highly individualistic activity, notoriously hard to control. It may be that the products of a mass market can imprison us in a dreary, pervasive sameness; Knight certainly complained of this late in his career. But it is also possible for reading to free people. Certainly the evidence of British working-class autobiographies from the 1830s and 1840s indicates that reading, for these men, was in the most fundamental sense an assertion of freedom against lives that were otherwise all too often miserably constrained.[43] These writers knew in their bones that knowledge was indeed power, because knowledge carried with it a measure of freedom. It is true that almost everyone publishing for the common reader in the 1830s – whether Richard Carlile, the Chartists, the Philosophical Radicals, John Murray, or the S.D.U.K. – had explicit ideological designs on readers. But it is also true that these designs had to be worked out in a market-place where there were few effective constraints (except commercial ones) on what the reader could choose to read and choose to think. Publishers of all political persuasions had chosen a device for the communication of ideas and values that was predicated on a freedom to choose – a degree of freedom that in other times and places has been thought too dangerous to allow.

One dramatic indicator of this fundamental commitment to freedom in the mass reading market created early in the nineteenth century lies in a letter John Wilson Croker wrote in 1821. He was sending to William Gifford an article on popular education for the Tory *Quarterly Review*, remarking that 'it is a great subject. Whether the mass of men is made better by learning *such* learning as the mass can obtain, or whether (the same question in a more practicable point of view) the *good* effects can counteract the *bad* effects of a free press.' Croker's letter vividly reminds us how certain were the evils of a free press and how seriously its benefits were in question early in the

1820s, at the time of the brief but notorious activities of the Constitutional Association. It takes an effort of will to comprehend how the value of wider education and a free press might seem to hang in so fine a balance. But this is so not least because of the unmistakable and increasingly unquestioned victory that popular adult education won during the ensuing 30 years. The fearful sense of things out of which Croker wrote in 1821 had largely disappeared by 1850. This change, and the confirmation of vital civil and intellectual liberties that it brought with it, was also largely achieved in the span of Charles Knight's professional lifetime; and one of the most important arenas of this change was the new mass market for reading material, to the development of which Knight and the S.D.U.K. contributed greatly. This, I think, is the most remarkable fruit of the enthusiasm with which the Society went about its business. The closing *Address* of 1846 expressed the Society's millennial hopes for the mass reading market by looking forward to the time when 'the *Society for the Diffusion of Useful Knowledge* shall be co-extensive with Society itself'. But it is Charles Knight who deserves the last words about the grand hope for freedom with which, in 1828, he took up the Society's resolve

'to leave nothing undone, until knowledge has become as plentiful and as universally diffused as the air we breathe.' This was a bold declaration – a solemn pledge. I felt carried along with it, to be up and be doing. Even as John Day, one of our great printers of the sixteenth century, took for his mark an emblematic device of the day-spring of the Reformed religion, with the motto, 'Arise, for it is Day,' [so] would I work in the spirit of this pledge, till the wide fields of knowledge should become the inheritance of all.[44]

NOTES

1. Patricia Hollis refers to the Society for the Diffusion of *Really* Useful Knowledge in her *Pauper Press* (1970), 114. For the derisory catchwords, see the attack on Brougham's inaugural volume of the S.D.U.K.'s Library of Useful Knowledge, *The Blunders of a Big-Wig; or Paul Pry's Peeps into the Sixpenny Sciences* (1827), and Thomas Love Peacock's well-known attack on the Society in his *Crotchet Castle* (1831).

2. For the *Penny Magazine*, see Penny Publication Committee Minutes, 8 Mar. 1832, S.D.U.K. Papers 6; and see *Address of the Committee of the Society for the Diffusion of Useful Knowledge* (1846), 15. I am indebted to the Library, University College London, for permission to quote material from the S.D.U.K. and Brougham Papers. I am also indebted to the University of Illinois, the American Council of Learned Societies, and the Victorian Studies Centre, University of Leicester, for their generous support of the research on which this paper is based.

3. Place to Joseph Parkes, 21 Apr. 1834, Place Papers, BL Add. MSS 35,149, f. 281. Knight reported his 1828 findings to the Society's secretary Thomas Coates in a series of letters, 26 May–12 June 1828, S.D.U.K. Papers

25. See Hollis, *op. cit.*, 176 for the street vendors' testimony; for Hill's see *Hansard*, 3rd ser., XXIII, cols. 1216–17 (22 May 1834). Matthew Davenport Hill was one of Knight's closest friends. A member of the remarkable Hill family of Birmingham, Matthew Davenport was an educational reformer, a journalist, and a distinguished lawyer. He was principal counsel in several freedom of the press cases in the 1820s, defending Richard Carlile among others. After 1839 he was Recorder of Birmingham and active in criminal law reform.

4. As in R. K. Webb's *The British Working Class Reader* (1955). Webb's memorable evaluation of the S.D.U.K. is that it was much like a steam engine – both noisy and inefficient (p. 66).

5. *Passages of a Working Life* (1864–5), II, 183–4; Knight quotes Walter Scott's Galeotti Martivalle in *Quentin Durward*, II, ch. 3.

6. *1846 Address*, 13.

7. J. G. Lockhart's colourful account of their conversation in *Memoirs of the Life of Sir Walter Scott, Bart.* (1837), VI, 28–31.

8. John Knight (no relation to Charles Knight) to Brougham, 10 Nov. 1826, Brougham Papers 7,949; Taylor to Brougham, 8 Dec. 1826, Brougham Papers 25,494.

9. See Knight's *Passages*, II, ch. 4–5, for his account of this tour. George William Wood, long a civil leader in Manchester, was the first M.P. to sit for South Lancashire in the reformed Parliament. Edward Baines was editor of the *Leeds Mercury*, one of the finest provincial newspapers in Britain. He was prominent in local affairs, especially in fostering the Leeds Mechanics' Institute, and was elected to Parliament in 1834. The Strutt brothers, William and Joseph, were Derby manufacturers, inventors, and benefactors. Joseph was Derby's first mayor elected under the 1835 Municipal Corporations Act. Joseph Parkes, a Birmingham solicitor, was an energetic proponent of parliamentary reform and supporter of the Birmingham Political Union. After

1833 he was secretary to the parliamentary Commission on Municipal Corporations. On the Society's insufficient capital, see S.D.U.K. Annual Report, 1830, in the British Library collection of S.D.U.K. printed ephemera T.1574 (11), and the comparative statement of income and capital, S.D.U.K. Papers 59. Augustus de Morgan, an active member of the General Committee, refused to pay his annual subscription after 1832, arguing that the Society's affairs were flourishing and in such circumstances any dependence on subscriptions gave the Society an unfair advantage over the rest of the booktrade: see de Morgan to Coates, 10 Oct. 1832, S.D.U.K. Papers 29.

10. See the financial statement in the S.D.U.K., *Address of the Committee, June 1 1843* (1843).

11. See the Journals, S.D.U.K. Papers 77–80, for the most detailed account of Knight's financial dealings with the S.D.U.K.

12. Hill to Brougham, 2 Mar. 1836, Brougham Papers 33, 385.

13. Coates to Brougham, 1 Oct. 1842, Brougham Papers 59. Information in the last three paragraphs about the Society's cash flow problems derives from the ledger of monthly payments, S.D.U.K. Papers 87; information about borrowed capital derives from the General and Finance Committee Minutes and the Minutes of the Financial Sub-Committees, S.D.U.K. Papers 1–8, 15.

14. See the final balance sheet for 1845–8, S.D.U.K. Papers 112.

15. P. Graham to Thomas Coates, 25 Jan. 1832, S.D.U.K. Papers 29, and 'Introduction', *Q. J. Education*, I (1831), 5; John Murray to M. D. Hill, 21 June 1829, S.D.U.K. Papers 26; General Committee Minutes, 28 Apr. 1830; S.D.U.K. Papers 2; Murray to Coates, 31 May 1830, S.D.U.K. Papers 27; and General Committee Minutes, 10 June 1832, S.D.U.K. Papers 2; General Committee Minutes, 22 Feb. 1832, S.D.U.K. Papers 2; Knight to Coates, n.d. [1832], S.D.U.K. Papers 29; General Committee Minutes, 2 May 1832, S.D.U.K. Papers 6; and

George Long to Coates, 9 Jan. 1832, S.D.U.K. Papers 29.

16. The information in tables 1 and 2 and the next several paragraphs derives ´from the Society's Journal accounts with Knight, S.D.U.K. Papers 77–8, from a *Q.J. Education* account 1834–5, S.D.U.K. Papers 92, and from an Aug. 1832 statement of Knight's circulation figures, S.D.U.K. Papers 59. For the *Blackwood's* figures, see the Publication Ledger 1838–47, uncatalogued Blackwood Papers F2, National Library of Scotland. I am indebted to the Trustees of the National Library of Scotland for permission to cite the Blackwood material, and to John Murray and Mr A. S. Chambers of W. & R. Chambers Ltd, Edinburgh, for permission to cite ledgers in the archives of their respective firms.

17. 'The commercial history of a penny magazine', *Penny Magazine*, II (1833), 472.

18. Two possible rivals are Limbird's 2d. *Mirror* (1823–49) and the S.P.C.K.'s 1d. *Saturday Magazine* (1832–44). Limbird's magazine was a pioneering cheap, illustrated weekly periodical, for which no circulation figures are known to me. Its text, unlike that of the *Penny Magazine*, was largely a scissors-and-paste compilation. The annually issued *Report of the Society for Promoting Christian Knowledge* gives the following average weekly sales for the *Saturday Magazine* from its inception in 1832 until 1836, before its sale to its publisher J. W. Parker early in 1837: 1832–3: 81,731 copies (p. 65); 1833–4: 95,329 copies (p. 65); 1834–5: 87,572 copies (p. 87); 1835–6: 74,999 copies (p. 88).

19. The statement of sales income for the *Penny Magazine* in table 2 is based on the S.D.U.K. accounts with Knight cited in n.16. There are no other extant ledgers, from which production costs might be determined with certitude. Reliable production costs can, however, be reconstructed from Knight's own writing about the magazine and about the *Penny Cyclopedia*, which mirrored the *Penny Magazine* as a commercial venture in all things but the cost of copyrights and illustrations. For information about production costs, see Knight's 'Preface' to the *Penny Magazine*, I (1832), iii-iv; 'The commercial history of a penny magazine', *Penny Magazine*, II (1833), 377–84, 417–24, 465–72, 505–11; and *The Struggles of a Book Against Excessive Taxation* (1850). Overhead for all five journals is stated at 10 per cent of the total production cost. Ten per cent of revenue was the standard commission charged in the book trade in these years when one publisher, with no capital at risk, acted as an agent for another. Most of this commission would be absorbed by overhead costs, but doubtless there was some margin of profit in it. It may therefore be that 10 per cent is too high for overhead alone, especially for the *Penny Magazine*. But the 10 per cent figure is used here in the absence of any more reliable figure and on the supposition that it does not alter the overall significance of the figures, except possibly for the *Penny Magazine*.

20. One estimate for the *Quarterly Journal of Education* survives in the Education Committee Minutes, 24 June 1829, S.D.U.K. Papers 5. Some of the assumptions on which this estimate was based changed by 1831, when publication began. Table 2 is based on the costs actually incurred once publication was under way. The computation of the profitability ratios in table 2 and figure 1 is based on the sources cited in nn. 16 and 19, and as in all estimates there is a degree of uncertainty about these ratios. The determination of approximate costs, income, profitability, and of profitability curves is a complex technical procedure that will be described in a separate essay by this author.

21. This is an unlikely assumption, both in fact and economic theory. Specifically it does not allow for the law of diminishing returns and the likelihood that per-unit costs would, in time, increase. These profitability curves do not state what conditions of cost and profit would obtain at different levels of sales; they are, rather,

extrapolations of a given condition of cost and sales that help make clear the commercial strategies pursued by each publisher.

22. The break-even point used here is considerably higher than the 'about 60,000 or 70,000' that Knight himself gives; 'Cheap books', *Penny Magazine*, II (1833), 19. Knight gives only a few rough estimates in this half-page article (such as paper and printing costing 'somewhat more than a half-penny' per copy) and does not allow for overhead expenses. Knight's figures are not self-consistent; they in fact suggest a break-even point at 96,000 copies without allowing for overhead, or something more than 105,600 copies allowing for such expenses.

23. *Chambers's* was, in any event, the only one of the pioneering penny weeklies to survive the 1840s; its continuous publication through nine series until 1956 is a remarkable record in periodical longevity.

24. Frank D. Adams, 'A recent accession to the Redpath Library', *McGill University Publications*, ser. 7 (Library), no. 8 (1926), 3–4; Sir John Francis Davis to Coates, 4 Dec. 1833, S.D.U.K. Papers 30; John Murray to Oliver and Boyd, 6 Apr. 1843, uncatalogued Oliver and Boyd Correspondence, Box 15, National Library of Scotland, cited with the permission of Oliver and Boyd.

25. For the trade's general resistance to encouraging more buyers with thinner margins of profit, see James J. Barnes, *Free Trade in Books: a study of the London book trade since 1800* (1964). See also Hollis, *op. cit.*, 112; and Knight's *Passages*, II, 76.

26. Knight to Coates, 5, 1, and 27 June 1828, S.D.U.K. Papers 25. In time, when the number of subscribers was quite small, the Society's publishers supplied them directly.

27. Thomas Cahusac to Coates, 12 July 1832, S.D.U.K. Papers 29; Knight to Brougham, 29 Aug. 1832, Brougham Papers 10,061 (unavailable for consultation at University College London in May 1979, but transcribed at length in Monica C. Grobel, 'The

Society for the Diffusion of Useful Knowledge . . .' (M. A. thesis, University College London, 1933, 116–18).

28. Knight's proposal for the *Penny Cyclopedia*, 21 June 1832, S.D.U.K. Papers 53. Knight sold the *Penny Magazine* at the regular trade discount, i.e., at c. 67 per cent of the retail price; see Knight's memorandum on Ainsworth & Son, Manchester, 28 May 1835, S.D.U.K. Papers 59.

29. By 1835 the *Penny Magazine* had dropped below the break-even point established in 1833. Doubtless Knight reduced his expenses on the magazine as sales declined, and he was evidently able to do that well into the 1840s, when sales were a sixth of what they had been in 1833. But he almost certainly was operating much closer to his break-even point all these years than he had in 1833 and doubtless had much less leverage on the market. Much of the initial commercial success of the *Penny Magazine* can be attributed to its being the only publication of its sort and scale on the market. The steady decline in sales reflects, most probably, the rapid emergence of effective competitors – especially those who, unlike Knight, were prepared to meet the demand for cheap serial fiction.

30. Ainsworth & Son memorandum; General Committee Minutes, 10 Nov. 1836, S.D.U.K. Papers 3; Miller to Coates, 1 and 17 Apr. 1837, S.D.U.K. Papers 34. As an independent publisher and after his connection with the S.D.U.K. ended, Knight experimented further with sales by pedlars. He describes the system amusingly and asserts that it has many advantages and 'might be redeemed from the disgrace which now too often attaches to it, in the hands of the quacks who are most flourishing in that line' in his *Old Printer and the Modern Press* (1854), 216–17. A recent treatment of the system is Mihai H. Handrea, 'Books in parts and the number trade' in *Book Selling and Book Buying: aspects of the nineteenth-century British and North American book*

trade, ed. Richard G. Landon (1978), 34–51.

31. Orr to Chambers, 3 Jan. 1845, Chambers Papers; quoted in S. M. Cooney, 'Publishers for the People. William and Robert Chambers. The early years, 1832–1850' (Ph.D. thesis, Ohio State University, 1970), 105–6.

32. 1846 *Address*, 4; 'Journal of Education' [closing editorial], *Q. J. Education*, x (1835), vi.

33. *Passages*, I, 124; see John Wilson Croker's correspondence (especially with Charles Arbuthnot) about the *Guardian*, 1818–23, in the Croker Papers, William L. Clements Library, University of Michigan, Ann Arbor; *Passages*, I, 225–6.

34. Brougham undertook to secure Treasury support for the publication and distribution of these pamphlets; see General Committee Minutes, 15 and 21 Dec. 1830 and 11 Nov. 1831, S.D.U.K. Papers 2.

35. Quoted in Rosamond and Florence Hill, *The Recorder of Birmingham. A memoir of Matthew Davenport Hill* (1878), 104.

36. Long to Coates, c. Sept. 1832, S.D.U.K. Papers 29; *Cobbett's Weekly Political Register*, 9 May 1835, col. 367; just how destructive the forbidden ground of controversial politics and religion might be for the S.D.U.K. itself is evident in a pair of letters to Coates from William Allen and Charles Knight on the handling of West Indian slavery in the *Penny Magazine*, 24 Apr. 1832 and n.d., S.D.U.K. Papers 29, and in the General Committee's discussion of a proposal to publish a Penny Bible in 1832: see especially letters to Coates from Anthony Cooper and George Agar–Ellis, both 30 Sept. 1832, S.D.U.K. Papers 29.

37. See Hollis, *op. cit.*, 70–1, and Martineau's *Biographical Sketches, 1852–1868* (1869), 160.

38. Knight to Brougham, 29 Aug. 1832, see n. 26 above; Knight's 'Commercial history of a penny magazine', 378.

39. Webb incautiously asserts that S.D.U.K. publications can 'excite in the modern reader little but disgust', *op. cit.*, 80.

40. 'Commercial history of a penny magazine', 506.

41. *The Autobiography of an Artisan* (1847), 319; cited in David Michael Vincent, 'The growth of working class consciousness in the first half of the nineteenth century: a study of the autobiographies of working men' (Ph.D. thesis, University of Cambridge, 1975), 171.

42. See Trygve R. Tholfsen, *Working Class Radicalism in Mid-Victorian England* (New York, 1977).

43. See Vincent, *op. cit.*, 192, 203, 209–10.

44. Croker to Gifford, 21 Oct. 1821, Croker Papers, William L. Clements Library, University of Michigan, Ann Arbor; 1846 *Address*, 20; *Passages*, II, 66–7.

Part Three

THE NEW READERSHIP

Brian Harrison   Press and pressure group in
modern Britain

The relationship between the British press and public order is sometimes discussed in rather crudely polarized terms. A 'free' press, emancipated from government control, is seen as emerging in the mid-nineteenth century out of a servile press which had been subject to governmental control through monopoly, censorship or other forms of influence. In this heroic story, obscurantists inevitably succumb before the mid-Victorian advance of the enlightened. A recent revisionist compendium on British press history rightly attacks this crude polarity at several points, not least by emphasizing the limitations on press freedom which patterns of newspaper ownership impose. James Curran even argues that between 1800 and 1860, both opponents and advocates of press freedom agreed in seeking a press which would uphold the social order: 'all that had changed was a growing commitment to positive indoctrination of the lower orders through a cheap press, and a growing conviction that free trade and normative controls were a morally preferable and more efficient control system than direct controls administered by the state'.[1]

Yet even this three-dimensional analysis of press freedom fails to capture the full complexity of the sequence. Curran's assertion is misleading in several ways. It understates the extent of the press freedom which is feasible under competitive proprietorship at any time: still more does it understate the impact made by the mid-Victorian press reforms in the eyes of those who witnessed them. The competitive pursuit of profit by newspaper proprietors requires them to engage in an energetic pursuit of readers and (through them) of advertisers; this severely curtails their freedom to dissent from the existing views of their readership. Furthermore, a twentieth-century perspective which is preoccupied with the contest between employer and employee risks ignoring a conflict far more central to nineteenth-century politics: that between aristocracy on the one hand, and a radical alliance between members of middle and working classes on the other. Given the aristocratic predominance within the nineteenth-century political system, the mid-Victorian victory for a free press seemed a major radical triumph at the time. And insofar as proprietor and journalist enjoyed any independent influence, some of them initially used it to undermine those aristocractic and undemocratic institutions which survived in force long after their formal control over the press has been legislated away.

It is with one dimension of the contest between aristocracy and democracy that this essay is concerned. 'Social control', if the term can usefully be used at all, operates in complex and subtle ways. It is not simply a matter of an exploitative government formally imposing curbs and restraints, or even of a spontaneous coming-together of constraining forces from within the community at large; nineteenth-century society witnessed the simultaneous development of several routes to social cohesion, each of which employed the press for its own purposes. This essay discusses only one of them: the growth of the popular pressure group, whose preoccupation with the press has been continuous from the 1780s to the present day, and whose concerns have been far broader than those which arise from the simple polarity between employer and employee. It would be inappropriate to confine this discussion to the Victorian period. The relevant time-span runs from the 1780s to the present day, for not only did the industrialization and political radicalism of the late eighteenth century initiate the developments considered here: those developments are still working themselves out today. There can be no academic *cordon sanitaire* between the study of Britain in the nineteenth century and in the present day in any sphere, and least of all here.

Pressure-group history needs to be seen in the context of a rapidly industrializing society which recognized (if only from observing events in France after 1789) that in modern conditions social cohesion could no longer be taken for granted: it needed to be energetically worked for. In the late eighteenth century the Gordon and Priestley riots, reinforced by the rôle of the crowd in the French Revolution, convinced both conservatives and reformers of the need to forge new links between government and people. Among these, the pressure group played a prominent part; agencies of moral control might appeal more strongly to the conservative, agencies of popular participation more strongly to the reformer – but both developed new and more subtle ways of preventing disorder. Franchise reform and the public meeting were seen by reformers as 'safety valves', releasing pressures which might otherwise produce (in Britain, as in France) recurrent revolution. Even as late as 1917, Earl Russell, continuing a long family tradition during the House of Lords debate on the introduction of manhood suffrage, could still see the vote as 'a substitute for riot, revolution, and the rifle'.[2]

Popular movements and even political parties often promoted something more substantial than their particular reforms: they advertised how easily reforms could be teased out of existing political institutions without resort to violence. In the case of Richard Cobden, this secondary function was overt and self-conscious. Outlining the ancillary achievements of the Anti-Corn Law League in 1845, he included the hope 'that we shall set an example of truth to the working classes, showing them that these questions can be carried by moral means'. Radicals were not alone in this: when refusing office in 1841, that arch-Conservative Lord Ashley spoke of the factory movement's calming influence in the country and told Peel that 'you will some day see and confess the service I have been able to render'. As for the Labour party, its role as a distinct party after 1917 seemed best calculated – in the minds of supporters as different as Henderson and Haldane – to forestall violence and preserve the stability and continuity of British institutions in an increasingly dangerous world.[3]

In using the press, the reformer knew he wielded a very powerful weapon, particularly when governmental restraints on it were removed. But it was a delicate instrument, which could as easily disrupt peaceful political methods as promote them. The preoccupation of the media with sensational reporting is now a familiar theme of contemporary comment; the relationship between the press and public order has always been equivocal, though for different reasons at different times. It is a theme which will recur in the discussion which follows. But the main purpose of the essay is simply to analyse the overall relationship between the press and the popular pressure group in Britain since the 1780s; a rather different picture could no doubt be painted of pressure-group press connections if the focus rested on the more covert interest-group whose major strength does not lie in publicity. The discussion falls into three parts: the first considers pressure-group attitudes towards the non-specialist press which was read by the general public, together with pressure-group attempts at influencing it; the second considers the specialist form of periodical which the pressure group created in its efforts to supplement, or even to counteract, the non-specialist press; finally, there is a brief discussion of the relationship between the popular pressure group and violence, as illustrated by the suffragettes' handling of the press.

1

Any discussion of reformers' attempts at influencing the non-specialist press needs to emphasize three points: the immense importance they attached to the influence of the non-specialist press; the great trouble they took to mould its outlook; and the great importance of press activity within the Liberal party, to which so many reforming leaders were attached.

Nineteenth-century reforming leaders saw themselves as enlightened national schoolmasters, operating outside the classroom on adults as well as on children; for them, the newspaper could be at least as effective as the blackboard. The *Westminster Review* in 1827 felt that popular education would break up that common impulse which lent unity to the mob, and in 1831 Francis Place claimed that a free press, together with other civil liberties, would provide outlets which removed any justification for rural incendiarism.[4] 'Knowledge is the power – knowledge alone – by which we shall bring this foul system to the dust', Cobden declared in 1844; the reforming leader must patiently and continuously work on parliamentary and extra-parliamentary opinion by deploying the reasoned arguments which supported his case. The government was included among the beneficiaries of this educational crusade, for a free and responsible press would keep governments in continuous contact with public opinion; condemning the irresponsibility of the French press in 1851, Walter Bagehot pointed out that 'a really sensible press, arguing temperately after a clear and satisfactory exposition of the facts, is a great blessing in any country'.[5]

A free press was necessary to speakers as well as writers: press and platform were allies in diffusing ideas, as Henry Jephson commented in his pioneering study of the media. 'I go about with the Bible in one hand and a newspaper in the other', Christabel Pankhurst was fond of saying in the 1920s, when she had moved on from suffragette leader to evangelist. Only through the press could the speaker reach those who were unwilling or unable to attend his meetings. Disraeli was as conscious of this as any reformer. 'No newspaper is important as far as its advocacy,' he wrote: 'the importance of newspapers is to circulate your opinions, and a good report of a speech is better than 10,000 articles.' In 1874 Jacob Bright told the annual general meeting of the campaigners for women's suffrage that 'in the country you find that, when an influential meeting is held on the suffrage question, copious and good reports are given, and one of those meetings thus reported is worth a thousand pamphlets. A speech is a living utterance; everybody reads it; there is emotion in it, and we read it with far greater zeal than we read pamphlets.'[6]

The press was no mere adjunct to the platform: there was a circular relationship between the two, whereby the platform publicized ideas drawn from the press. 'Our paper will be a storehouse whence temperance reformers may draw their weapons both for attack and for defence', wrote the *British Temperance Advocate* on 1 May 1861. Robert Lowery, the Newcastle Chartist, recalling his youthful speeches in his autobiography, noted that 'the literature and passing events of the day furnished us with topics. An article in a review, magazine, or newspaper, or speeches delivered in Parliament, would furnish the subject of a discourse.' Furthermore the inexperienced and un-self-confident reformer was exhilarated to see his own words in print, and was sometimes launched on a full-blown career in journalism: 'the platform of a temperance meeting', wrote the pioneer temperance orator (subsequently a newspaper proprietor) Thomas Whittaker in his autobiography, 'was one of the best schools for training any one ambitious of public life this country offered, and the bench and the bar, the pulpit and the press, owe much to it'.[7]

This fruitful interaction applies particularly to the reporting of parliamentary speeches. Among the five functions of the House of Commons specified in his *English Constitution*, Bagehot included the teaching, expressive, and informing functions – reflecting his recognition that Parliament was then 'the great scene of debate, the great engine of popular instruction and political controversy'. He went on to say that 'a speech there by an eminent statesman, a party movement by a great political combination, are the best means yet known for arousing, enlivening, and teaching a people'. The campaigns for free trade, disestablishment, women's suffrage, the ballot, and local option orientated themselves round the parliamentary time-table, and took care to publicize relevant debates in the press. Nationwide petitioning campaigns were organized during the early months of the year in preparation for the great day, with detailed analysis of the division list as the informative denouement. Even if an adverse division was the outcome, said Jacob Bright in the women's suffrage debate of 1873, 'we have accomplished something else. We have taken the best means in our power to instruct the people upon a great public question. The substance of this debate will be carefully reported in the newspapers . . . and therefore we shall secure that, for at least one day in the year there will be a general discussion on a question so deeply affecting the interests and privileges of a large portion of Her Majesty's subjects.'[8]

Reformers' eagerness to stage annual debates on their topic – wearisome to M.P.s and seldom likely to gain a majority – can be understood only by recognizing that the real audience lay as much outside Parliament as in. Close-printed pressure-group periodicals like the *Alliance News* or the *Women's Suffrage Journal* focus eagerly on any parliamentary debate which is remotely relevant to their major concern, and report it at length. A specialist reforming periodical sometimes had to be created to ensure adequate reporting for the debate and adequate public scrutiny of the division list. In 1855, for example, Cobden desired a newspaper favourable to the peace movement, because 'at present, the advocates of peace in the House are literally without support in the Newspaper press of the Metropolis'. The *Morning Star*, which ran from 1856 to 1869, hardly fulfilled his hopes. The reforming movement often seemed almost a mere appendage to its parliamentary spokesman, designed to ensure a hearing for the man of principle when he rose in his seat. In John Bright's ideal world in the 1860s, newspapers would have been devoid of editorial comment, leaving readers to make up their own minds by perusing the parliamentary debates. 'I think the debates on the Second Reading are almost all addressed to the public outside', Lord Robert Cecil told a select committee in 1914.[9]

The parliamentary spokesman for the reforming movement had to be versatile: Wilberforce, T. F. Buxton, Cobden, Ashley, Henry Berkeley, Edward Miall, Wilfrid Lawson, James Stansfeld, John and Jacob Bright, and others like them had to develop a speaking style suitable for the large public meeting without corrupting the intimate and less formal style which alone could influence M.P.s. As the careers of W. J. Fox, Feargus O'Connor and William Cobbett show, several reformers who succeeded in the country failed in the House of Commons. Irish nationalist obstruction in the 1880s illustrates how reforming M.P.s occasionally did not even think it worth their while to try: when faced with the choice between audiences, they chose only the wider audience which could be reached through the press. For them, as for Victor Grayson in 1908 or for the Clydeside Labour M.P.s in the 1920s, Parliament was not the place where the major decisions were reached: rather, it was an arena for advertising the purity of one's beliefs and for gaining publicity in the country at large.

Reforming movements took great trouble to win press support. Thomas Clarkson, collecting evidence against slavery in 1787, cultivated the editors of local newspapers. O'Connell's Catholic Association in the 1820s took care to provide good facilities for reporters at its meetings, and provided them with good advance publicity of the events likely to interest them; O'Connell even cultivated the newspapers in France. No less than 20 members of the Chartist convention in 1839 had press connections, including many of the great names in radical journalism. The Conservative Lord Ashley, leading the factory hours movement at this time, shared the Chartists' preoccupation with publicity: in 1842 he noted in his diary that 'a man having neither an official station nor a party to back him, cannot, humanly speaking, afford to lose the assistance of newspapers'.[10] By the end of the century, reformers' arrangements for press publicity had become quite sophisticated. In 1889 the prohibitionist United Kingdom Alliance established a special press agency to distribute temperance news in London, and by 1911 the non-militant National Union of Women's Suffrage Societies' press department in London could draw on a nationwide network of local correspondents working through the press secretaries attached to its twenty federations of branches. The department simultaneously collected news about the movement from the national newspapers, encouraged well-known suffragist leaders to write for the press, and kept in close contact with the press agencies.[11] And like their anti-suffragist opponents, the suffragist organizations carefully filed away their press cuttings for future use; so did their rank-and-file – as witness the numerous scrapbooks of press cuttings on women's suffrage which often now come onto the antiquarian market.

Most Victorian pressure groups cultivated the press through building up a mass movement which journalists would neglect at their peril. With the militant suffragettes, however, the cultivation of the press became an end in itself. It was a journalist, Charles Hands, who gave the suffragettes their name, and the suffragette leaders developed – and retained into extreme old age – an awareness of the press which often resulted in close personal contact and mutual help. Both reforming leader and journalist were in the same business, the business of publicity, but the suffragette leaders came near to regarding this as their sole preoccupation. Christabel Pankhurst set the tone with her 'major rule of political life', that of never losing her temper with the press.[12] Cicely Hale, as a volunteer in the information department of the Women's Social and Political Union [W.S.P.U.], recalls a daily routine which involved extracting everything relating to the movement from the daily and weekly newspapers, amalgamating the extracts with the cutting received from Durrant's Press Cuttings Agency, indexing them, and sending a book of the day's extracts down to the leaders for their information; they were then all stuck into scrapbooks for future reference. The department also answered the questions of leaders and speakers, which often entailed a visit to the British Museum reading room; the W.S.P.U. even proudly distributed postcards illustrating its editorial department – staffed as it was by rows of young women sitting at desks, wire sorting-baskets to the ready, filing cabinets to the rear.[13]

This involved something more than a utilitarian preoccupation with the press: it reflected a fascination with the glamour of publicity which can nowadays be seen primarily in relation to radio and television. One recalls Robert Lowery, up in London for the first time for the Chartists' great Palace Yard meeting in 1838 and enthralled with the major London newpapers' speed and efficiency in gathering and printing news; his autobiography, published nearly 20 years later, dwells at length on the speaking skills of the famous Chartist orators and is fascinated by the art of communication for its own sake. Or there is W. T. Stead's vision in 1886 of the newspaper editor, 'filled with his central fire, saturated with his ideas', presiding over a national machine for collecting information on public opinion.[14] The Victorians by no means confined their admiration for the new technology to the machinery used in the great textile centres of the North.

Reformers were at least as preoccupied with the press when it was hostile as when it was friendly. The belief of Chartists like Henry Vincent or Robert Lowery that the press was corrupt and misinformed did not prevent them from showing a continuous interest in it; for Richard Cobden by the 1860s, the hostility of *The Times* had become almost an obsession. Beset in the 1850s by the Crimean War, the popularity of Palmerston and the continued vitality of aristocracy, he found in newspapers – especially in *The Times* – the scapegoat he needed, and accused them both of being corrupted by the government and of corrupting the people.[15] The notion that the media are perverting the natural rationality and good sense of the people, who would otherwise enthusiastically enlist in the reformer's ranks, often reappears on the British Liberal and Labour Left. Listing the agents of Russophobia in 1877, William Morris included among the villains the 'desperate purveyors of exciting war-news for the comfortable breakfast tables of those who have nothing to lose by war'.[16] Radical anti-imperialists like Wilfrid Lawson and internationalists like W. R. Cremer believed that journalists fomented wars just as Labour leaders of the 1920s saw the press as the bulwark of capitalism. Nor is this belief in the integration and conscious direction of the media, this fear that the individual cannot resist it, yet at an end. It is a theme often voiced in our own day – by the disciples of Herbert Marcuse, by anti-Marketeers claiming to have been overthrown by the media during the referendum campaign of 1975, and by the trade unionists in search of scapegoats (after the 'winter of discontent' of 1978–9) to explain the Conservative election victory in 1979.[17] Assaults on the media provide that protective shield against the public acceptance of reality which self-respect requires.

Until the 1860s, however, it was still possible for reformers to ascribe the defects of the press to 'taxes on knowledge', and Liberals believed that a free press must inevitably promote progressive causes. They saw themselves as only the latest among the forces of light triumphing over obscurantism and reaction with the aid of libertarian institutions and advancing technology; for them, the pen was mightier than the sword. They stood in the direct line of continuity running from the pioneers of the Reformation, through the Puritan heroes of the seventeenth century to Milton, the champion of press freedom, and on to the men of 1688 and 1832 (with perhaps a pause for Paine and Peterloo *en route*). 'The discovery of printing did a vast deal for the advancement of society', the former Chartist Henry Vincent pointed out in May 1850: the printing press was 'the great friend of everything liberal and progressive' and 'refused to be the vassal of Government or of priestcraft'.[18] It was a strange paradox that those who saw the cheap press as the scourge of obscurantism erected the printing press into an almost magical symbol to be revered, a talisman which could inspire the onward march of mind.[19]

The free press owed much to those provincial and popular pressure groups and reforming movements, often not nominally supporters of the Liberal party at all, which lent such extra-parliamentary impetus to Liberal crusading. Chartism grew out of the campaign for an unstamped press in the 1830s only to merge in the 1850s with Collet's campaign against the 'taxes on knowledge'. The unstamped press was itself largely provincial in nature, and it was O'Connor's distaste for the Whig metropolitan press which led him to establish that great provincial popular paper, the *Northern Star*.

> For despots, though *united*, feel distress,
> And tremble when the thunder of the press,
> Rolls through their kingdoms in the civil storm,
> Proclaiming justice, freedom, and reform.[20]

In 1854 another provincial reforming movement, the United Kingdom Alliance, launched its new periodical, the *Alliance*, in the belief that all taxes on knowledge were 'obnoxious in the highest degree to the interests of virtue and social order'; in 1855, responding rapidly to the repeal of the newspaper stamp, the paper expanded in size.[21] The conviction that cheaper newspapers would broaden the taste for reading and diminish the charms of drink ensured that the prohibitionists were not alone among temperance reformers in championing the repeal of the 'taxes on knowledge'; in 1859 the moral suasionist National Temperance League's executive committee petitioned Parliament for the repeal of the paper duty, which occurred two years later.[22]

Cobden had additional reasons for welcoming the advent of the *Alliance*: the proliferation of unstamped specialist papers like this would force the stamped press into campaigning to remove the newspaper stamp altogether.[23] He told Joseph Sturge in 1853 that 'if we could get rid of the penny stamp we should have more good local papers to counteract this Cockney poison'.[24] The provincial press was less likely to be corrupted by government bribes, he thought, less dominated by London's compromising atmosphere, less changeable in allegiance because its editors, in their smaller communities, were more identifiable. Some of Cobden's hopes were realized; as early as 1862 he could hail the advent of a new, cheaper and much improved provincial and London press;[25] it went on to lend crucially important support to several late-Victorian extra-parliamentary Liberal movements. The contrast in tone between the London and provincial press was often remarked upon in the 1870s and 1880s; the *Daily News* was alone among the greater London dailies in consistently backing the Bulgarian atrocities agitation in 1876, and the failure of the London press to report provincial secularist meetings was a major hindrance to Bradlaugh's movement in the 1880s.[26]

Nowhere were these contrasts clearer than in relation to Josephine Butler's agitation against state-regulated prostitution. 'There is not, I believe, a daily paper in London that has not betrayed you . . . upon this question',

Jacob Bright told a Manchester meeting on the subject in 1870; their editors were 'very much at home in the great clubs of the west end, and in the big houses of great people', but knew nothing of the poor.[27] Mrs Butler felt that the upper classes were colluding to keep news of their immorality from the masses, and believed that 'truth loses nothing, and gains everything by publicity, by being placed on the heart of the people'.[28] She soon found herself in powerful alliance with an imaginative Liberal journalist whose national career had begun (with his launching of the crusade against Bulgarian atrocities) in the provinces, W. T. Stead. The provincial man's indignation at London's corruption is a theme which pervades his exposure of 'Modern Babylon' in the *Pall Mall Gazette* during 1885. At the large indignation meeting held subsequently in Hyde Park, Stead expressed delight that London – 'such a huge, amorphous, anarchic, multitudinous mass of houses and streets' without a heart, soul or voice – had organized 'the nearest possible analogue to a town's meeting in the provinces', and seemed at last about to become articulate.[29]

Yet in the long run, the free press disappointed the hopes of the early Victorian radical. The response to Stead's campaign by the London press proved in the end to be as feeble as during the Bulgarian atrocities agitation nine years before, and in a remarkable article of the following year, Stead fell back on a scheme for appointing Cromwellian major-generals throughout the country who could feed the central editor with instant information on public opinion about any question. Opinion would thereby be more efficiently represented than through Parliament, whose means of eliciting opinion Stead viewed as out of date. Thus informed, the newspaper 'would indeed be a great secular or civic church and democratic university'.[30] The disillusionment of the radical John Morley began earlier. He complained in 1874 that the removal of newspaper taxes had 'done much to make vulgar ways of looking at things and vulgar ways of speaking of them stronger and stronger'. 'See what has become of the struggle to "free the press" for which I went to prison at 17 years of age', exclaimed that fiery Chartist journalist of the 1840s, G. J. Harney, condemning the degraded state of the press in 1878. The educated, pacific and sober democracy dreamed of by Cobden and Bright proved more elusive than had been anticipated. As the retired imperial administrator Alfred Lyall wrote in 1904: 'John Bright's words . . . about popular education and newspapers being a sure antidote to warlike propensities . . . betray a certain superficiality and narrowness of view in his knowledge of the Demos'.[31]

This long-term disappointment of Liberal and radical hopes should not conceal the intimate involvement of the press with the nineteenth-century

Liberal party at several levels. If one analyses the number of London and English provincial newspapers with express party allegiance, Liberal supremacy was assured, even when papers of 'Liberal-Conservative' allegiance are assigned to the Conservatives. In some years Liberal supremacy was overwhelming; in 1874, for example, there were 489 Liberal English provincial papers and 41 Liberal London papers, but only 294 and 25 Conservative papers, respectively.[32] But the 1880s saw significant defections to Conservatism – the *Edinburgh Review* taking its departure on the Home Rule issue, for example – and the twentieth-century Labour party has never been able to recover the supremacy in this area which its Liberal predecessor once possessed. At every general election since 1945, Conservative national daily papers have substantially outgunned Labour papers in circulation – in February 1974 by 8,020,000 to 4,291,000. By the 1970s, however – as James Callaghan pointed out during the 1970 general election campaign – television contributed towards redressing the balance in rather the same way as the Anglican pulpit boosted Conservative resources 100 years before.[33]

At the level of parliamentary representation, the links between nineteenth-century Liberalism and the press were even stronger. At every general election between 1832 and 1895, more Liberal/Radical newspaper proprietors than Conservative were returned to Parliament; newspaper proprietors were even more prominent among the Liberals' Irish nationalist allies after 1886.[34] The Liberal hold over journalist M.P.s was even stronger between 1880 and December 1910; the Liberal journalists, with their Labour and Irish nationalist allies, never fell below 74 per cent of the total number of journalists in the House of Commons.[35] Here the Labour party has inherited some aspects of the Liberal tradition, so that *The Times* in June 1970 could see the contest between Labour and Conservative M.P.s as an argument between different sections of the middle-class Establishment; Labour M.P.s came from teaching or journalism, Conservative M.P.s came from business management and law.[36]

Liberalism and the press were intertwined in other respects; the press was intimately involved at every level in the party's national structure. Journalists' attachment to Liberal causes may owe something to their insecure professional status and their uncertain class location. Journalists were exposed to the same social cross-pressures which influenced those educated men and women from the middle class who became utilitarians, progressive Liberals or Fabian socialists; they can be found in prominent positions, for example, throughout that anguished middle-class crusade of the late 1950s, the Campaign for Nuclear Disarmament.[37] Furthermore, the journalist's occupation so closely resembled that of the pressure group leader, and the two groups came so frequently into contact, that the journalist often found himself sympathizing with the reformer in his many disputes with authority. Recalling his days as a journalist and Chartist in Leicester in 1841, Thomas Cooper vividly described how 'the accounts of wretchedness, and of petty oppressions, and the fierce defiances of their employers uttered by working men at public meetings, kept me in perpetual uneasiness, and set me thinking what I ought to do'. Even his religious faith was undermined: 'I had not spent many months in talking to the Leicester Chartists, before my "religious conscience" began to receive a new "form and pressure" from its new surroundings. I could not preach eternal punishment to poor starving stockingers.'[38]

Resistance to oppression, upholding the rights of the individual, became one of the journalist's weapons in his striving for status. H. W. Nevinson, president of the National Council for Civil Liberties, and self-confessed champion of many lost causes which ultimately succeeded, epitomizes this commitment, which the camera could on occasion powerfully assist. Grace Alderman was impelled into the militant suffrage movement by seeing a press photograph of a policeman with his truncheon raised against a woman on the ground: 'I was baking cakes at the time and Mother came into the kitchen with the paper . . . "just look at this!" she said . . . Until then I'd thought England stood for fair play.'[39] This libertarian tradition is more fully developed in the American press, but its importance even in Britain was stressed by the former Labour cabinet minister Lord Stow-Hill in a debate of the House of Lords on a Bill of Rights recently; the persistent backbencher, the fair-minded judge, the independent-minded citizen and the indignant protestor all feature in Lord Stow-Hill's pantheon of liberty's champions, but he also includes the free press, and praises 'the readiness of a foreign correspondent, for example, to lay down his life on the battlefield in order to purvey news of what is happening to the rest of the world'.[40]

The press is important to reformers in other ways. Newspapers draw together the like-minded, and reinforce their commitment. Readership surveys for the nineteenth-century press do not exist, but the phenomenon can be demonstrated from later examples. When the Aldermaston Campaign for Nuclear Disarmament marchers were surveyed in 1959, 78 per cent were found to read the *Manchester Guardian*, 80 per cent the *Observer* and 53 per cent the *New Statesman*, whereas no popular daily scored more than 5 per cent. And just as the *Daily Telegraph*'s middle- and working-class readers in 1967 were strongly Conservative (69 per cent and 59 per cent, respectively) so the *Sun*'s were strongly Labour (50 per cent and 73 per cent respectively); the newspapers of the Left and Right have at the very least the effect of consolidating the existing commitment of their readers.[41]

Furthermore the press has developed numerous direct connections with

Liberal and radical pressure groups, from anti-slavery to C.N.D. It was the rise of the provincial newspapers in the late eighteenth century which enabled the anti-slave trade movement to make its appeal to public opinion, through inserting its advertisements and correspondence and reporting its meetings. The London and Manchester committees made use of a professional agent, William Taylor, to organize their press affairs.[42] In 1830 a letter in the *Leeds Mercury* was the means of launching the attack on 'Slavery in Yorkshire', Oastler's movement to restrict factory hours. The reforming press also lent stability and continuity to many reforming movements at the branch level by helping to establish supporters as local booksellers and newsagents when the established distributors refused to co-operate.[43] The printed word had a certain magic about it at this time, even for the illiterate, and O'Connell's influence over the Irish press was vital to his success there.[44] For the utilitarians and the free traders – as for the Fabians later – the manipulation of public opinion was central to political success; the Anti-Corn Law League, in addition to publishing its own periodicals, found many ways of subsidizing newspapers sympathetic to its cause.[45]

The role of the press in strengthening the Liberal party received a late-Victorian boost when supposedly non-party pressure-groups (each with their own periodicals) integrated more closely with the party machines. John Morley in the 1870s saw his *Fortnightly Review* as the *Encyclopaedia* which would give the Left the coherence it needed.[46] It was the impetus given from Darlington in 1876 by W. T. Stead's *Northern Echo* which launched the Liberal party on its road to electoral recovery in 1880; Stead, more than anyone else, provided the Bulgarian atrocities agitation with a voice and a strategy.[47] Between 1857 and 1880, the *Alliance News* allotted increasing absolute and proportional space during the four weeks of maximum coverage to reporting general elections, and press sympathy was very important in getting the Crofters' movement launched in the 1880s.[48] Nor did the pioneer socialists of the decade differ from other fringe groups to the left of the Liberal Party in depending heavily on the press; from 1895, *Clarion* vans were travelling the country promoting the cause. The battle for press support, or at least attention, explains much of the strategy adopted by that latecomer among Liberal causes, the movement for women's suffrage. The story of its ultimate triumph is exceedingly complex, but insufficient attention has so far been paid by its historians to the mediating role of the *Manchester Guardian* within the movement and to the crucially important change of sides on the question by *The Times*. Before 1914, *The Times* was resolute, even outrageous, in defence of an exclusively male franchise, whereas by December 1916 Northcliffe had changed his mind, and was complaining to Lady Betty Balfour that 'there is absolutely no movement for

Women's Suffrage anywhere' and urging her to 'try and get up a public meeting on the subject'; the manufacture of 'events' by the media is by no means confined to the age of radio and television.[49]

Some nineteenth-century newspapers even embarked on crusades of their own; Henry Mayhew's famous letters on 'London labour and the London poor' in 1848–9 originated in this way, not to mention Stead's exposure of 'Modern Babylon' in 1885. The Quaker cocoa-manufacturer and newspaper proprietor George Cadbury believed that charity was best promoted, not by individual philanthropic donations, but by subsidizing a reforming newspaper, and in 1904–5 the *Daily News* launched a fund to relieve the unemployed in the East End of London – making daily appeals for cash, food and clothing. On a smaller scale, St Loe Strachey's *Country Gentleman* promoted a cheap cottages exhibition in July 1905 and in the following year the *Daily News* sponsored its famous six-week exhibition on sweated labour at the Queen's Hall.[50] Samuel Barnett might complain in 1906 of the sentimental attitudes to poverty, the degradation of the poor and the duplication of charitable effort involved in such activities,[51] but the promotion of press crusades continues into our own day with the *Guardian's* efforts of 1973 to improve the working conditions of the black population in South Africa, and the *Sunday Times's* campaign to compensate the thalidomide children.

2

Press campaigning has by no means always been employed on behalf of the party of progress: one thinks of the *Pall Mall Gazette's* enthusiasm for naval expenditure in 1884, for example, or of Northcliffe's disclosures on munitions in *The Times* and *Daily Mail* during 1915. And however great the debt owed by particular pressure groups to particular papers at particular times, many of them nurtured an abiding grievance against a press which they felt was constantly maligning them. Their difficulties did not stem simply from the fact that novel causes take time to gain acceptance. So thoroughly aligned with the authorities were many early nineteenth-century newspapers that – far from thriving on threats of disorder – they saw themselves as part of the machinery for suppressing it, and defined such threats broadly. Furthermore, the prestige of the aristocracy was built up through a simultaneous boosting of their prestige and depreciation of their critics. Extensive press reports elaborated on aristocratic parliamentary speeches and public ceremonial. When Chartists actually visited Parliament in 1839 they found the level of oratory there far lower than they had been led to expect; conversely, respectable observers were surprised to discover the respectability of the Chartists, whom the press had convinced them must be monsters.[52]

Cobden in 1851 hoped that a free press would curtail the press misrepresentation which had hitherto been curbed only through public protest meetings. Josephine Butler accused the press of obscuring the reality of social relationships in a second and more direct respect when she claimed to have 'suffered extremely from the inaccuracy of reporters, and sometimes even from their wilful misapprehensions'. For the suffragette leader Annie Kenney, in a naive letter to A. J. Balfour of 1909, the mis-statements of the press were 'all very sickening to the heart'.[53]

Even more galling than any misrepresentation was the sheer failure to report at all. Socialist pioneers were particularly worried by this, and incorporated their concern into their overall analysis of property relations. Discussing the advertiser's control over a paper's content, and the newsagent's control over circulation, Belfort Bax in 1884 pronounced the boasted freedom of the British press a 'snare and a delusion'; as for the journalist who cynically wrote to order, 'we would more respect the defalcating assistant or even the habitual pickpocket than he who sinks to that lowest of all deeps – the office of paid hack of a dominant class'.[54] W. T. Stead deplored the failure of the London newspapers to discuss his researches into 'modern Babylon',[55] and for the Edwardian suffragist perhaps the most infuriating aspect of the male failure to take women seriously was the newspaper's neglect or patronizing tone towards their movement. Totally absorbed in the movements to which they sacrificed so much, suffragists saw the undiscriminating pursuit of the latest news by the press as almost insulting: 'far more notice has been extended by the newspapers of to-day to the trial of some contemptible murderer', the *Common Cause* complained in 1912, 'than to all the public demonstrations for Reform that our streets during this century have known'. The prominent suffragist Mrs H. M. Swanwick warned historians in her autobiography that it would be impossible to found their accounts of women's suffrage solely on press sources, so 'extreme and grotesque' was the censorship the press imposed.[56] In 1911 the *Standard* advertised in *Votes for Women* its claim that its women's section, entitled 'Woman's Platform', would break the 'press boycott' and 'conspiracy of silence' of which suffragists complained.[57] Although by May 1917 the situation was reversed, and the newspapers were by then actually refusing to publish anti-suffragist letters,[58] the press exercised at least as stringent a censorship in the 1920s on a still more important dimension of women's emancipation – the introduction of birth control.[59]

In the last resort, reformers had to embark on the second-best course of creating a periodical under their own control. 'The conspiracy of silence of the press has done us this service,' wrote Josephine Butler '. . . it has forced us to create a literature of our own'.[60] In the first number of his *Northern*

Star, Feargus O'Connor was quite explicit about founding the paper to overcome press silence on Chartism; likewise the *Church of England Temperance Magazine* was launched in 1862 because it was felt that the press had neglected the Church of England Temperance Society's foundation-meeting earlier in the year.[61] The non-militant suffragists saw their *Common Cause* as an essential counterweight to 'the indifference of the daily Press, which is financed and edited by men'. As for Christabel Pankhurst's militant *Suffragette*, 'owing to the Press boycott', it was 'an indispensable means of communication between the [Women's Social and Political] Union and the public'. With situations like these so recently in the memory, it is hardly surprising that one of the justifications in 1920 for launching that important organ of inter-war feminism, *Time and Tide*, run entirely by women, was recognition of the need for a newspaper 'which shall treat men and women as equally part of the great human family, working side by side ultimately for the same great objects . . . a paper which is in fact concerned neither specially with men nor specially with women, but with human beings'.[62]

It is curious that the nineteenth-century pressure-group periodical has not so far been systematically explored. John Vincent does not mention it in his deservedly influential comments on the journalistic springs of Gladstonian Liberalism.[63] This may be because, by Fleet Street standards, the circulation of these papers was not large. But historical significance in this area by no means solely resides in circulation figures or even in readership statistics. Many pressure-group periodicals were directed at the opinion-formers, so that their influence radiated out far beyond their readership. Besides, the figures for periodicals of this type were sometimes large, for their promoters by no means always resigned themselves to writing exclusively for a sect; they often wanted their papers to become major national organs of a more general kind. The *Northern Star* in its peak year (1839) reached 36,000 copies – impressive for a provincial paper largely dependent on a working-class public; its readership was of course far longer, and sales surpassed those of a major provincial newspaper like the *Leeds Mercury*,[64] though they were not maintained for long. Nor should attention focus exclusively on the circulation figures for individual reforming newspapers, for – with Chartism as with temperance, women's suffrage and many other causes – sympathetic periodicals proliferated like mushrooms during a movement's periods of prosperity: their combined circulation, often regional in nature, could be large. Ninety-three Chartist periodicals are listed in a recent bibliography of Chartism, and by the 1850s the British anti-slavery movement (by then in decline) was able to support no fewer than four separate monthlies.[65]

Two aspects of the pressure-group periodical will be considered here: first, its distribution, together with obstacles to circulation and the actual impetus given to reformers by the need to overcome them: and second, its content, together with the threefold contribution it made to the movement's vitality. The pressure-group periodical should perhaps be seen as one dimension of the immense mid-Victorian expansion in the number of specialist newspapers. The production of officially stamped newspapers alone more than trebled between 1801 and 1831, and the cheapness of the printing press made it easy to start up new ventures: the number of letterpress printers in London rose from 124 in 1785 to 316 in 1824 to 500 by mid-century.[66] Few were the areas of nineteenth-century social reform where there seemed to be any conflict between entrepreneurship and social improvement; the same drive and enterprise which built up the great entrepreneurial and commercial concerns also rejuvenated the worlds of charity and social reform – indeed, the same individuals often operated simultaneously in both spheres. Hence what seems incongruous to modern eyes, the Victorians' unabashed union of profit with philanthropy, their shameless competition in doing good. The nineteenth-century press seemed able to reward the enterprising with wealth beyond the dreams of avarice. Reform in twentieth-century Britain has fewer affinities with individual entrepreneurship than it once had. Individual money-making is now often seen as itself the evil which reformers must attack, whereas reformers in the aristocratic world of the nineteenth century aimed at freeing talent to reach its own level, a standpoint fully compatible with individual enterprise and in no way requiring egalitarian attitudes to wealth: the means could in a double sense promote the end.

The *Quarterly Review* in 1880 pointed out that whereas (according to its calculations) in 1851 there were only 53 specialist weeklies, now there were 794; 18 of the 44 in 1851 were religious weeklies, 44 of the 794 in 1880.[67] The temperance movement illustrates the trend; between the mid-1850s and the early 1860s it established or re-established the four major temperance periodicals which were to dominate the late-Victorian temperance scene – the *Alliance News*, the *Church of England Temperance Magazine* (later *Chronicle*), the *Temperance Advocate*, and the *Weekly Record of the Temperance Movement* (later *Temperance Record*). But there were numerous lesser temperance organs, some of them – the *Band of Hope Review*, for instance, with a weekly circulation of 250,000 in 1861 – enjoying very large circulations (see plates 6 and 11).[68] No other reforming cause was as prolific of specialist periodicals, but even the smallest and most specialized movement – the anti-vivisectionists, for example – had their own collection of distinct periodicals, sometimes following one another in close succession, sometimes overlapping and mutually competing: the *Home Chronicler* from 1876 to 1879, the *Anti-Vivisectionist* from 1879 to 1882, the *Zoophilist* from

1881 to 1915, the *Champion* from 1884 to 1887, the *Verulam Review* after 1888, and the *Animals' Guardian* from 1890.[69]

The Edwardian abundance of women's suffrage periodicals reflects the rapid growth in the movement at that time. Some preached the same message to different audiences (the denominational suffrage periodicals, for instance): others preached different messages to the same audience (the militant and non-militant organs, for instance): others preached different messages to different audiences (the politically partisan suffrage organs, for instance, and the adult suffrage periodicals). Circulations sometimes rose quite high. *Votes for Women*, like so much else in the militant suffrage movement under the Pethick-Lawrences' control, went from strength to strength: from 5,000 per month in April 1908 to 22,000 per week in May 1909, to over 30,000 per week early in 1910. The militant *Suffragette*, which became Christabel Pankhurst's organ after the split with the Pethick-Lawrences in 1912, was already laying claim to a weekly circulation of 30,000 in November 1912, though this figure was not sustained.[70]

Schism among reformers often caused a new reforming paper to be launched in parallel with the old; rivalry and intensified effort often ensured that their combined circulations in the short term out-topped the circulation of their parent paper. The hiving off from the W.S.P.U. of the Women's Freedom League in 1907 ensured that by 1909 the Union's *Votes for Women* ran in tandem with the League's *Vote*: in 1912 the split between Pankhursts and Pethick-Lawrences added the *Suffragette*: and in 1913 the divergence between Christabel Pankhurst and her sister Sylvia issued in the *Woman's Dreadnought*. There was rivalry in technique as well as in circulation – though Mrs Swanwick, rational as ever, in her capacity as editor of the non-militant *Common Cause*, tried to resist the temptation: 'I was constantly having it suggested that we should adopt certain features which they [sc. the militant organ, *Votes for Women*] had. But why? If it was being well done by them, why duplicate it?'[71]

These circulation figures are the more impressive, given the numerous obstacles which reforming periodicals encountered. Henry Hetherington's printing business lost much custom because some of his clients disliked its connection with radical periodicals. Thomas Cooper was sacked from his post as a journalist on the *Leicestershire Mercury* because he wrote secretly for the Chartists' *Midland Counties Illuminator*, and had great difficulty in getting local printers to publish Chartist papers.[72] Problems of distribution were also serious. In 1859 the *Ballot* suggested that the newsagents' boycott could be overcome 'only by insisting . . . that the custom of the intending purchasers shall be wholly withdrawn from the purveyor, unless he supply also *The Ballot* when ordered'; likewise the socialist periodical *Justice* in 1884 complained that 'several wholesale Agents have refused to distribute *Justice* to the smaller newsvendors in London'.[73] Edith Fulford remembers going as a young suffragette to Mr Smedley's Post Office in Birmingham for her *Votes for Women* 'in fear and trepidation'; she was greeted with; 'I don't know how you *dare* come in here. You know, you're getting me into a lot of trouble. You know the government has banned this paper.'[74] Militant tactics made a pressure-group periodical's career politically even more precarious, however much their shock-value may temporarily have increased circulation; 'no paper, surely, has ever had a more adventurous and varied career', wrote Christabel Pankhurst of her *Suffragette* in 1913, at the end of its first year.[75]

Not the least of the difficulties was the cost of publication: this was what led Francis Place to discourage the London Corresponding Society from launching a magazine in 1796, and even the Anti-Corn Law League was unable to make its *Anti-Corn Law Circular* pay.[76] In only ten of the 46 financial years between 1854 and 1899 did the United Kingdom Alliance declare a profit on its *Alliance News*,[77] and the Social Democratic Federation's *Justice* had to be subsidized in the 1880s by the voluntary work of its compositors. One response was to retreat from the optimum strategy, profitability, into the second-best strategy of regarding the pressure-group periodical as a legitimate expense: 'ought not each paper to be regarded more as an *agent* for serving the cause', wrote the pioneer teetotaller Joseph Livesey, in his *Staunch Teetotaler* for 1867, 'than as a piece of merchandise for securing profit?'[78] More common was the pursuit of a wider circulation, for if the pressure-group periodical could become a best-seller, the second-best and optimum strategies for publicity might coincide, and a bastion within the non-specialist press might be secured. The optimum stategy was in Richard Cobden's mind in September 1855, when he discussed the creation of a periodical favourable to peace. In a letter characteristically shrewd in its view of how public opinion could best be moulded, Cobden favoured a penny newspaper circulating 30,000 copies daily rather than a paper with 'too much of a sectarian character'. This would gain a wider audience for peace principles, but would require from the editor the 'wisdom of the serpent' in handling the peace question; a readership must first be created, so that 'it may be necessary to temporise a little as to the times and circumstances when and how the peace policy shall be advocated'.[79]

O'Connor's approach to the *Northern Star* was decidedly entrepreneurial; he struggled for years to make a London-based national daily out of it, and distributed free gifts, portraits and medals in the pursuit of profits. 'Like many cheap papers to-day', Mark Hovell complained during the First World War, 'it gave the public exactly what the public wanted'. Hovell saw O'Connor as a pioneer of cheap journalism, yet he used the paper to subsidize his movement, and to serve it in many other ways.[80] Itinerant lecturers often acted as agents for their movement's newspaper, simultaneously promoting the cause in print and by word of mouth. There was seldom any clear distinction in the early Victorian period between the temperance lecturer and the commercial traveller; nor need there have been, for the interests of sobriety and of commercial prosperity were regarded as identical.[81]

Reforming movements found that promoting the sales of their periodical supplied the rank-and-file with something worthwhile to do. It was a way of letting off steam, of venting one's frustration at the slow pace of legislative change; the reformer at least gained the satisfaction of knowing that he was making his small contribution towards gaining the desired reform. Readers were constantly badgered to be more than merely passive: to send in reports of local developments, help finance free distribution and do their utmost to boost circulation. *Justice* regularly requested subscriptions to its 'Propaganda Fund', and pressure-group periodicals often asked readers to pay more than the nominal price for a paper. 'It is not by sitting still and twirling thumbs that any great cause was ever won', wrote *Justice* in 1884, urging every reader to get ten new subscribers in the next three months.[82] Few enthusiasts rivalled the energies of Mrs M'Culloch of Dumfries – praised at her death by the *Women's Suffrage Journal* in 1882 because she annually canvassed for subscriptions, collected them together and sent them up to headquarters with a list of over 100 names from her locality.[83]

Still, it was always possible for urban enthusiasts to stand at street-corners selling the paper, and in 1884 H. M. Hyndman in his top-hat and William Morris in his blue serge suit could be found at their posts. 'Capitalists own almost the whole Press', wrote *Justice* in 1884; 'they are masters of the ordinary means of distribution. We must consequently organise a distribution of our own.'[84] Here, as elsewhere, the women's suffrage movement learned much from the labour movement. In summer 1910, *Votes for Women* promoted a competition among its paper-sellers over who could sell the most copies, and in 1911 the Women's Freedom League *Vote* distributed photographs of Mrs Despard, its leader, to those readers who obtained the most new subscribers during the three months ending 24 June. Sylvia Pankhurst's *Woman's Dreadnought* in July 1914 promised a badge to every reader who sold 1,000 *Dreadnoughts*, with a stripe for every extra 1,000.[85] The paper-seller was a walking and talking advertisement, capable of supplying information to passers-by, and by February 1910 *Votes for Women* had organized sales-pitches in central London. The W.S.P.U. was particularly imaginative in finding new ways of advertising its paper. In October 1909, for instance, the West End witnessed a bus decked out in the suffragette colours, heralded by a trumpeter performing from the roof, delivering supplies to the various paper-sellers in the street.[86] Here again, suffragettes were carrying forward techniques widely used in the socialist societies of the 1880s: the Social Democratic Federation's *Justice*, for instance, had been promoted by a 'justice parade' in the City.

The decision to sell suffragette papers was a symbolic commitment, a small-scale private rebellion which anticipates the subsequent window-smashing, letter-burning and arson: it was an advertised burning of the boats, a way of registering to oneself and to one's public a commitment to the cause. 'The first time I took my place on the "Island" in Picadilly Circus', Kitty Marion recalled, 'near the flower sellers, I felt as if every eye that looked at me was a dagger piercing me through and I wished the ground would open and swallow me.'[87] Paper-sellers often experienced intense cold and got sprayed with mud by passing traffic; they were loaded with insults and even obscene remarks from passers-by, male or female. In this respect, as in so many others where publicity was concerned, the Conservatives were placed at a serious disadvantage; Lady Simon urged anti-suffragists in 1911 to imitate the suffragists in distributing literature, but admitted that 'we are, of course, deterred in this and in much of our work by difficulties which do not exist for our opponents, who will let their women and girls stand about in public places and at street corners, and who have undergone many hardening processes which we do not desire to emulate'.[88] A reforming organization needed to do more than merely co-ordinate existing commitments: the reforming engine developed, cultivated and accentuated commitment by exposing its rank-and-file to continuous contact with the like-minded, and by placing them in situations where they would find their commitment reinforced. Acceptance of the end led on to the means, which in turn reinforced commitment to the end.

Another way of minimizing losses on pressure-group periodicals was to attract advertisers. *Votes for Women*, the *Suffragette* and the *Vote* often urged readers to patronize their advertisers' goods and shops.[89] The *Vote* in 1911 announced prizes for readers who could present the largest number of receipts for goods bought from the firms which advertised in the paper. Taking figures for the first four weeks in October, *Votes for Women* devoted 14 per cent of its column inches to advertisements in 1908, 34 per cent in 1909, 40 per cent in 1910, 32 per cent in 1911 and 35 per cent in 1912. The W.S.P.U. issued stickers inscribed 'Votes for Women' for members to place on the bills they paid.[90] The policy must at times have been difficult to combine with the militant tactics dwelt upon elsewhere in the paper, though it is possible that circulation was spasmodically increased (and therefore presumably the attraction to advertisers) by the paper's assiduous reporting of militant exploits. Even the *Suffragette* – promoting arson, letter-burning, the breaking of shop windows and other forms of violence in the years between 1912 and 1914 – did not fail to attract its complement of advertisements: 22 per cent of the paper's total column inches in December 1912, 20 per cent in September 1913. The W.S.P.U.'s systematic raids on the windows of West End department stores in spring 1912 did not prevent Peter Robinson, Debenham and Freebody, Marshall and Snelgrove and other shops from advertising freely in its organ. Ironically, these advertisements often reinforced the ornamental, leisured image of women – with pressure to buy fashionable clothes, beauty aids and other feminine accoutrements – which the consistent feminist was beginning to subvert.

Moving from the distribution to the content of the pressure-group periodical, it performed at least three major functions: inspirational, informative and integrating. Each of these deserves some discussion. George Orwell in the 1930s asked a miner when the housing shortage first became acute in his area: 'when we were told about it', he replied.[91] The distinction between a paper's informative and inspirational rôles was never clear-cut; the columns devoted by temperance periodicals to what they called 'barrel and bottle work' or 'the fruits of the traffic' – the sufferings and brutalities resulting from drunkenness – performed both functions simultaneously.[92] Periodicals like the *Anti-Slavery Reporter*, the *Test-Act Reporter*, the *British Labourer's Protector and Factory Child's Friend* and the several papers promoted by the Anti-Corn Law League all provided readers with facts and figures which would inspire them to futher effort. It was particularly important to publicize relevant evidence collected by sympathetic parliamentary enquiries and royal commissions – a preoccupation which receives a later echo in the Fabians' popularization of Blue Book material through the columns of the early *New Statesman*. Pressure-group periodicals to some extent lived off the non-specialist press, drawing attention to favourable editorial comment, reviews and correspondence wherever they could find it.

Nowhere was the inspirational rôle of the pressure-group periodical more central than with the *English Women's Journal*, which virtually brought the British feminist movement into existence in the 1860s. The paper had not been launched with the problem of unemployment of middle-class women primarily in mind, yet it inevitably came to reflect a concern of such overriding interest to its readers. Its offices soon became indistinguishable from the premises of the Society for Promoting the Employment of Women; an advertisement in its number for 1 August 1859 said that the editors, 'finding that constant applications are made to them by ladies in want of remunerative employment . . . have determined to open a Register in connection with their Office'.[93]

In this instance the problem was so pressing that inspiration was hardly required from the periodical, but in the case of animal cruelty, awareness of the problem had to be painstakingly inculcated through stressing the kinship between animals and human beings. The Royal Society for the Prevention of Cruelty of Animals [R.S.P.C.A.] launched its *Animal World* in 1869 with stories for children which were enlivened by large engravings of animals, often in human postures, including many reproductions from Landseer. Every issue of the anti-vivisectionist *Home Chronicler* in the late 1870s contained a full-page illustration of an experiment involving vivisection designed to shock the reader into commitment. Likewise the problems of drunkenness, slavery and brutality of every kind were advertised by the speeches and writings which enlarged on these issues – though here, as with the opposition to vivisection, there was some danger that opinion would be influenced in ways quite contrary to those desired.

The objective was not simply to make converts, but to inspire the converted with the self-confidence necessary to action. Often this simply involved drawing together people who were already convinced, and encouraging them to co-ordinate efforts which would be fruitless in isolation. This was the role of the *English Woman's Journal* from the late 1850s and of the women's suffrage periodicals later. The suffragette Maud Kate Smith recently recalled being impressed by *Votes for Women*, not because it contained ideas which were unfamiliar, but because 'well, they were all my own *ideas*. I might have written the book myself . . . I did not know *anybody* understood me, and here was this woman understood it all, Christabel Pankhurst. *Well*, oooh, I knelt down by the bedside and I says "is this the purpose for which I was born" and the reply was "yes", so I knew: I couldn't turn back after that.' With Lady Rhondda, and no doubt with many others, the inspiration came first and the reading second – 'once joined I had to rationalise my emotions'.[94] The two then exhilaratingly reinforced one another when converts saw their letters or speeches reproduced in the pressure-group periodical.

Once the problem had been perceived, the periodical brought the confidence needed to tackle it. R. G. Gammage, a Chartist beleaguered in the West Country after the Frost Rising, carried off his *Northern Star*, which arrived by post every Sunday, to a 'pleasant little bower at the top of the garden, shaded from the rays of the sun by a beautiful sycamore tree. This seemed to me the height of enjoyment'. Many years later, W. E. Adams recalled how Larry the crippled shoemaker used to appear with the paper every Sunday morning 'for the purpose of hearing some member of our household read out to him and others "Feargus's letter'''.[95] Such individual or group inspiration was all the more necessary in a predominantly rural society whose reformers were often isolated from their colleagues and surrounded by the enemy; as John Bright well knew, the Tory could retire, in his unpopular moments, to the sympathy of aristocratic clubs and drawing rooms, but in his moments of unpopularity the radical – especially the rural radical – had no such resort.[96]

Information was as necessary to crusading activity as to the conversion which preceded it. The new convert required ammunition which would destroy enemies and win friends. The critics of government often lacked access to the abundant documentation enjoyed by their opponents. The London Corresponding Society's *Moral and Political Magazine* in 1796 hoped to overcome this difficulty by publishing state papers for the benefit of its working-class readers: 'the poor man, who is most interested in the progress [sc. of truth and liberty] has little opportunity of referring to them, they being generally lost in daily publications, or preserved only in large and expensive collections of such papers'. Lady Rhondda recalled how her suffragette activity 'made me take to writing', because the campaign required supporters to write indignant letters to the press; these could be worked up from the information provided by the pressure-group periodical. As a branch activist, she recalled publishing articles in the local press which were 'lifted bodily from the leading article of the organ of the W.S.P.U., *Votes for Women*'.[97] The pressure-group periodical was also valuable for providing (as the *Band of Hope Record* put it in 1858) 'a medium through which the conductors might communicate to each other methods of working; hints and suggestions on management; and, also, interesting and instructive matter which might form the subject of addresses and be useful in other ways'.[98] The *Women's Suffrage Journal* often guided readers on how to petition Parliament.[99] In 1878 it testified to the many parallels between Victorian reforming movements by reprinting an article from the *Anti-Bread Tax Circular* of 1841 which urged readers to petition parliament: 'what was true then is true now. . . . People who want a thing must ask for it, and continue to ask for it until they get it.'[100]

The pressure-group periodical experienced a tension between the need to hearten the activist and the need to enlighten the unconverted. The activist relished the news and gossip about the detailed affairs of the movement and its leaders, but such material might seem rebarbative to the potential recruit. The *Anti-Slavery Reporter* included a wealth of information about slavery and very little on the movement which had been formed to abolish it. On the other hand, the *National Temperance Magazine* in 1844 saw itself as 'a Repository of details of labour and success in the cause of Temperance' in the conviction that posterity would require 'an historical remembrancer'.[101] Something more entertaining was required to grip the attention of the newly-literate mass public of the late Victorian period, as the United Kingdom Alliance was discovering by the 1880s,[102] and the Socialist League's periodical *Commonweal* only awkwardly straddled the divide between refining socialist theory and purveying popular propaganda.[103] *Votes for Women*, and still more the *Suffragette*, became so preoccupied with the movement's day-to-day activities that they almost lost sight of the cause they were promoting. The adoption of violent tactics ensured that the *Suffragette* lavished more newsprint on justifying its methods than on indicating how these would promote the cause, let alone on precisely how the vote could promote women's emancipation.

One way of resolving the tension between the two quite distinct audiences was to devise different methods of propaganda for each: to operate a division of labour between, on the one hand, the tract, the poster, the advertisement, the procession and the open-air meeting (designed for the unconverted) and, on the other hand, the pressure-group periodical, the annual report and the branch and annual meetings (designed for the initiate). The *British and Foreign Temperance Herald* tried to combine the two in 1832 by simultaneously doing duty for periodical and tract,[104] but it lasted only four years and pressure-group periodicals usually catered primarily for the converted. The annual report was itself a periodical of sorts, designed for the subscriber and enthusiast; commitment to the cause could therefore be assumed, and the space assigned to subscription-lists, reports of meetings, obituaries and news of fellow-activists. These reports – of the R.S.P.C.A. for example, or the United Kingdom Alliance – often grew into substantial volumes. By contrast, press advertisements like the animal societies' 'Put animals into politics!' (published in national newspapers in September 1978) aimed at bringing the plight of stray dogs, ill-treated horses, factory-farmed poultry and other humane causes to the attention of a wider public which had not yet been converted.[105]

The pressure-group periodical's third major rôle was to weld together reforming movements which were in constant danger of fragmentation. Only a national periodical could raise the movement above petty local concerns, and fruitfully draw together the contrasting experiences of different localities and social groups. Only a central organ could counter the insidious pressures of an apathetic local community and insulate the new recruit against the pressure from family, relatives and friends to go along quietly. Whereas conservative and traditional values are continuously emphasized as a matter of daily, weekly, annual or generational routine – through formal occasions, ceremonial, recurring anniversaries and family functions – reformers need to reinforce themselves with processions and propaganda, campaigns and crusades.[106]

British society as constituted in the early nineteenth century made this particularly necessary. For groups too poor to travel, the newspaper provided an invaluable bond of unity; early-nineteenth-century radicalism could hardly have survived without a press of its own.[107] The cheap press was soon reinforced by the advent of the railway, so that by 1840 J. S. Mill could see the two as 'solving the problem of bringing the democracy of England to vote, like that of Athens, simultaneously in one *agora*'. He was later to describe the press as 'the real equivalent . . . of the Pnyx and the Forum', enabling representative government to function in units larger than the city-community of the ancient world[108] The Chartists were quick to take advantage of the new situation; 'I found . . . that our cause could not be held together without a paper', Thomas Cooper recalled: 'we had no organ for the exposure of wrongs'.[109] But although his *Midland Counties Illuminator* and its successors might aspire to the locally integrating rôle played by a paper like the *Northern Liberator* in the North-East, only the *Northern Star* enabled the movement to transcend local loyalties and place the Chartist leaders on their national thrones. The same two-tier reforming press reappears among the pioneer socialists; small local newspapers knit the branch together through taking up local questions, but they were reinforced by national organs which could draw the localities together and provide platforms for national leaders like Keir Hardie and Philip Snowden.[110]

At a time when so many reformers were based on the towns and needed to reach out to one another across a hostile countryside, the periodical was invaluable for ensuring that the hand was there and ready to be grasped. 'No one can work well without sympathy and encouragement from others who are likeminded', wrote the *Women's Suffrage Journal* in 1870, explaining the reasons for its existence; the journal aimed 'to extend to every isolated well-wisher the firm grasp of an outstretched hand, offering and seeking help'. At the annual meeting of the London-based anti-sabbatarian National Sunday League in 1881, a Mr Eve urged the 'wonderful effect on people in the country' to be anticipated from wider circulation of the *Free Sunday Advocate*: 'he believed there was a general desire for more freedom – an assimilation to the London Sunday', but that 'the inhabitants of small provincial towns and villages are very much under the control of the vicar, or of the ministers of the various denominations'.[111] *Votes for Women* pointed out in 1910 that without a national periodical, potential rural sympathizers might not appreciate the extent of the urban progress made by the suffragettes.[112]

In 1857 the *Alliance Weekly News* likened its circulation to the circulation of the blood: 'if the blood is not kept in constant and ample play the body must become more or less feeble and inefficient'; in 1872 the periodical had become 'the backbone of the entire organisation', the means of keeping supporters in mutual contact.[113] The *Women's Suffrage Journal* launched itself in 1870 on the hope that 'if persons interested in the movement could receive every month an account of what has been done in other places, they might be tempted to try what could be done in their own locality'.[114] This was articulating in another plane the same outlook on government that had been put forward in *Representative Government* by the feminist hero John Stuart Mill: local self-government (whether through municipal bodies or voluntary movements) could work well only if the contrasting experience of different localities was concentrated through some central agency.

A major paradox was inherent in the pressure-group periodical's integrating role, for the overall commitment to free speech which lay behind these movements did not prevent them from curbing free discussion internally, whether at the public meeting or in the correspondence-columns of their own periodical. The volume of criticism from without made it seem imperative to preserve at least the appearance of unanimity within. 'When any species of publications is patronised by political associations', William Godwin pointed out, they are scrutinized 'not to see whether what they contain is true or false, but that the reader may learn from them how he is to think upon the subjects of which they treat. A sect is generated'.[115]

The prominent prohibitionist William Saunders complained that the greater the heat generated by discussion at the top levels within the United Kingdom Alliance, 'the more rigid appears to be the exclusion of all references thereto in the columns of the *Alliance News*'.[116] One of the most significant developments within the women's suffrage movement between 1912 and 1914 was Sylvia Pankhurst's restoration of the contacts between the suffragette and labour movements on an adult suffrage basis, yet her East London Federation is virtually ignored in the *Suffragette*, the organ of her elder sister Christabel. Schismatic tendencies were reinforced when each sect within the movement had its own periodical – the London Working Men's Association with its *Commonwealth* and the Reform League with its *Bee-Hive* in the 1860s; or the Social Democratic Federation with its *Justice* rivalling the Socialist League's *Commonweal* in the 1880s. Controversies which could fruitfully have been conducted within a single movement became sterile exchanges when combatants were thus entrenched. The problem is familiar: where ideals are passionately held and where so much is thought to hang on the success of a cause – sympathizers whose dissidence gives heart to the enemy resemble traitors.

Pressure-group periodicals often acted as mere megaphones for rival leaders within the movement; Scottish Chartism, which could afford only one periodical, found itself torn apart between the *True Scotsman* and the *Scottish Patriot* for this reason, and woe betide the Chartist who chose to diverge from the line laid down by O'Connor in the *Northern Star*. 'The *Star* at once gave him and his party a general influence,' Robert Lowery recalled many years later, 'while the sayings and doings of his special favourites were regularly reported and eulogised.'[117] In mid-Victorian secularism, as in early-nineteenth-century radicalism, each leader had his own periodical to act as his mouthpiece and power base.[118] Efforts were occasionally made to create umbrella papers which would cater for all the segments of a single movement; *Women's Franchise*, for instance, tried to cater for all wings of the women's suffrage movement between 1907 and 1909. Attempts were even made to unite several distinct causes under one paper – by Joseph Livesey (with free trade and temperance) in his *Struggle* of the 1840s, for example (see plate 9); or by Ernest Jones (with Chartism, temperance and other progressive causes) in his *People's Paper* of the 1850s. But amalgamations of this type lacked the drive and focus necessary for success; commitment may have entailed sectarianism, but at least it made for vigour.[119]

3

The management of a pressure-group periodical was a hectic and often exciting business. 'Tuesdays we went to press,' wrote Mrs Swanwick of her *Common Cause* days, 'and Wednesdays there were fearful arrears of correspondence to be knocked off in the intervals of correcting page-proofs. Thursdays were an orgy of committees which had a way of slopping over into Fridays. There was no evening in the week when I was not liable to be called upon to speak.'[120] The editors of pressure-group periodicals were particularly vulnerable to the difficulty perennial in reforming movements: the postponements of long-term strategic analysis in order to cope with short-term emergencies. In a militant organization – with its conspiracies, intense loyalties and disruptions of production – this problem was still more serious, and produces in the Edwardian period one final irony in the relationship between press and pressure group before 1914; for between 1906 and 1914 the original peace-preserving aims of the pressure group and its periodical were turned upside down by the militant suffragette movement. This episode deserves a brief discussion by way of conclusion, because it brings out to the full the threat to public order latent in the manipulation of the press by the popular pressure group before 1914, and illuminates the limited impact which publicity could of itself then make on legislative change.

   The relationship between the reformer and the violence he was warding off was always complex. Although the reformer rarely himself embraced violent tactics, he traded on the claim that others were on the brink of doing so. His large processions and public meetings often seemed intimidating in their scale, and were perhaps intended to be so, and his rhetoric often maintained a precarious balance between restraining and inciting his followers. He was easily seduced from creating opinion into concentrating on creating an opinion about opinion; when this was the aim, stunts, stratagems and showy devices came to the fore. These temptations were the more dangerous by the Edwardian period because newspapers were by then much less securely in the hands of the authorities, much more alert to the sales value of sensationalism. In Christabel Pankhurst, the pressure group found a leader ready to turn this new development to her own purposes.

'Much depended, in militancy,' she later recalled, '. . . upon timing and placing, upon the dramatic arrangement and sequence of acts and events.'[121] Her unorthodox methods certainly caught the headlines, and her followers became even more closely attuned to press reactions than their reforming predecessors had been. 'Oh, my dear, what a wonderful protest,' exclaimed Leonora Cohen's hostess when she heard of Leonora's assault on the Tower of London Jewel House in 1911: 'all the news-vendors all along the Strand and all of the posters are out on the Tower of London raid.'[122] In the same year, Lady Constance Lytton justified militant tactics on the ground that the press were shutting out news of non-militant suffragism; as Mrs Pankhurst told a private correspondent in 1912, 'peaceful meetings are usually reported locally but are entirely ignored by the general Press'.[123]

Militancy placed Liberal cabinet ministers in an exceedingly difficult situation: they could hardly ignore it, yet they could not restrain it without infringing individual liberty and press freedom on a scale which their followers would find intolerable. In June 1914 the Home Secretary Reginald McKenna deplored the way the press publicized the suffragettes' efforts to petition the king: 'I hoped that the Press of all parties might be induced not to give headlines to these matters, and, if possible, not to report them at all, as I am sure that the immediate effect of the denial of all advertisement of militancy would do more to stop their actions than anything the Government can do . . . I must say I regret extremely to take up paper after paper and to notice that two or three columns are devoted simply to the advertisement of militancy, thereby carrying out for the women one of the main objects which they have in view in the commission of crime.'[124]

In October 1913 this appearance of success caused the prominent anti-suffragist Gladys Pott to bring to the attention of the leaders of the National League for Opposing Women's Suffrage her 'own firm conviction that publicity in the Press is *our greatest need* and *our opponents' chief advantage* over us'.[125] Yet this was merely to repeat the error made by many of her suffragette opponents: the failure to bear in mind the distinction made by Emily Davies (in a letter to *The Times* during 1911)[126] between influence and notoriety. There is such a thing as 'over-exposure', as we have now come to call it – particularly when violent tactics are the focus of attention. Militancy also had other drawbacks from the publicity point of view – most notably its need for continuous escalation if the element of surprise was to be maintained. As Maud Kate Smith recently recalled, '"Today's outrage". *That* put you in a mess, because you've got to see . . . you've got an outrage for the next day, you see, otherwise you don't get the placard.'[127] Furthermore, militant tactics entailed a preoccupation with means which eventually became so overriding as to cause ends altogether to disappear from view, internal debate within the organization to become ever more stringently curtailed, the structure of command to grow ever more hierarchical – with all the consequences of that for women's political participation in a democratic society. It is hardly surprising that the movement eventually moved out of contact with political reality altogether.

Since 1914, feminists have prudently refrained from stunt violence, which has been the last resort primarily of groups which can gain publicity in no other way – Blackshirts in the 1930s, the National Front in the 1970s, authoritarian movements of Right and Left. When the Campaign for Nuclear Disarmament embraced militancy in the early 1960s, Bertrand Russell justified the new move with arguments which will now be familiar: 'civil disobedience, by virtue of its news value, offers the only available method of breaking through the barrier of silence and deceit by means of which populations are being lured to their doom'.[128] John Tyndall, the National Front's chairman, pointed out in 1977 that meetings and demonstrations likely to end in riot 'are one of the few ways we have to gain a hearing'.[129]

In the case of women's suffrage, the tactic was a failure, and in perceiving this the anti-suffrage leaders showed greater insight than the conscientious Miss Pott; right up to the First World War, they knew that they could build up public support simply by pointing to suffragette conduct. 'I believe I express the opinion of everbody here present', said E. A. Mitchell-Innes from the chair at the anti-suffragists' annual council meeting in June 1913, 'when I say that I think the most valuable part of the support, the most solid and most reliable part of the support which we as a League at the present moment possess in this country, is very largely due directly to our scrupulous abstention from even a pale imitation of sensational methods.' A year later, in his presidential speech to the council meeting, Lord Curzon made comments which emphasize the delicacy of the relationship between the pursuit of publicity and changes in public opinion. His assertion reveals not only the weakness of the militant suffrage movement before 1914, but the importance of factors other than publicity and agitation in determining public policy. 'Our Society has no talent for advertisement at all', he said, 'and perhaps it is all the better for that. There is never anything very exciting in defending the *status quo*.'[130]

NOTES

1. J. Curran, 'The Press as an agency of social control: an historical perspective', in *Newspaper History from the Seventeenth Century to the Present Day*, ed. G. Boyce, J. Curran, and P. Wingate (1978), 61.

2. *House of Lords Debates* (hereafter cited as H.L.Deb.), 17 Dec. 1917, c.217; for 'safety valves', see, e.g., Lord John Russell, *Recollections and Suggestions 1813–1873* (1875), 71, 103; Henry Vincent, in *Oxford Chronicle*, 25 May 1850, 3 (a reference I owe to Raphael Samuel, of Ruskin College, Oxford). See also *Northern Star*, 20 Dec. 1851, 5.

3. R. Cobden, *Speeches on Questions of Public Policy*, ed. J. Bright and J. E. T. Rogers (1870), I, 305; E. Hodder, *Life and Work of the Seventh Earl of Shaftesbury, K.G.* (1886), I, 356. See also J. M. Winter, 'Arthur Henderson, the Russian Revolution, and the reconstruction of the Labour party', *Historical J.*, XV (1972), 771.

4. [John Bowring and an unknown collaborator], 'Education of the people', *Westminster Rev.*, VII (1827), 273 (attribution by WI). For 1831 see J. H. Wiener, *The War of the Unstamped. The Movement to Repeal the British Newspaper Tax, 1830–1836* (Ithaca, 1969), 34; J. R. M. Butler, *The Passing of the Great Reform Bill* (1914), 135; J. Hamburger, *James Mill and the Art of Revolution* (New Haven, 1963), 71.

5. Cobden, *Speeches on Questions of Public Policy*, ed. cit., I, 133; *The Collected Works of Walter Bagehot*, ed. N. St John-Stevas (1968), IV, 76, cf. 73; cf. *Anti-Bread Tax Circular*, 27 June 1843, 187, and Sheridan, quoted in A. Bullock and M. Shock, *The Liberal Tradition from Fox to Keynes* (1956), 5.

6. D. Mitchell, *The Fighting Pankhursts. A Study in Tenacity* (1967), 191;

Women's Suffrage J., 1 Aug. 1874, 110; H. Jephson, *The Platform. Its Rise and Progress* (1892), I, 546; W. F. Monypenny and G. E. Buckle, *The Life of Benjamin Disraeli* (2 vols., 1929 edn.), I, 1038.

7. B. Harrison and P. Hollis (eds.), *Robert Lowery. Radical and Chartist* (1979), 173; T. Whittaker, *Life's Battles in Temperance Armour* (1884), 373 and see generally my '"A World of Which We Had No Conception". Liberalism and the English Temperance Press: 1830–1872', *VS*, XIII (1969), 125–58; cf. R. G. Gammage, *History of the Chartist Movement 1837–1854* (repr. edn, 1969), 17.

8. W. Bagehot, *The English Constitution* (Fontana edn, 1963), 72, cf. 152; Jacob Bright, *House of Commons Debates* (hereafter cited as H. C. Deb.), 30 Apr. 1873, c. 1196; cf. Samuel Smith, *My Life-Work* (1903 edn), 477.

9. BL Add. MSS 43656 (Cobden Papers), f. 353: Cobden to Sturge, 8 Aug. 1855 (copy); Cecil in W. C. Costin and J. S. Watson, *The Law and Working of the Constitution*, II (2nd edn, 1964), 223; for Bright, see A. Kinnear, 'Parliamentary reporting', *Contemporary Rev.*, LXXXVII (1905), 370.

10. Hodder, *op. cit.*, I, 442, cf. II, 89. See also T. Clarkson, *History of the Rise, Progress, and Accomplishment of the Abolition of the African Slave Trade* (1839 edn), 217, 219; J. A. Reynolds, *The Catholic Emancipation Crisis in Ireland, 1823–29* (New Haven, 1954), 78, 84; T. M. Kemnitz, 'Chartist newspaper editors', *VPN* no. 18 (Dec. 1972), 2.

11. A. E. Dingle, 'The agitation for prohibition in England. A study of the political activity and influence of the United Kingdom Alliance,

1871–1895'(Ph.D. thesis, Monash University, 1974), 588. I am most grateful to Dr Dingle for allowing me to cite his thesis; *Jus Suffragii*, 15 Dec. 1911, 35, cf. *Common Cause*, 14 Dec. 1911, 628.

12. C. Pankhurst, *Unshackled* (1959), 70; tape-recorded interview with Mrs Helen Moyes (née Fraser) at Miranda, Sydney, Australia, 19 Aug. 1975.

13. Tape-recorded interview with Miss Cicely Hale, at Littlehampton, 6 Nov. 1974; letter from Cicely Hale to the author, 10 Jan. 1980.

14. W. T. Stead, 'The future of journalism', *Contemporary Rev.*, L (1886), 677; Harrison and Hollis, *op. cit.*, 108.

15. J. A. Hobson, *Richard Cobden. The International Man* (1919), 70–1, 78, 126–7, 131, 133, 219; J. Morley, *The Life of Richard Cobden* (11th edn, 1903), 885.

16. E. P. Thompson, *William Morris. Romantic to Revolutionary* (2nd edn, 1977), 214.

17. See, e.g., Bill Keys and Alan Fisher at the Blackpool Trades Union Congress on 6 September 1979, *Guardian*, 7 Sept. 1979, 5.

18. *Oxford Chron.*, 25 May 1850, 3 (I owe this reference to Raphael Samuel).

19. L. James (ed.), *Print and the People 1819–1851* (1976), 27, cf. 23.

20. *Northern Star*, 4 July 1846, quoted in Y. V. Kovalev, *An Anthology of Chartist Literature* (Moscow, 1956), 124. See also D. J. Rowe (ed.), *London Radicalism. 1830–1843* (1970), 197; P. Hollis, *The Pauper Press* (1970), 108.

21. *Alliance*, 8 July 1854, 1; United Kingdom Alliance, *Third Report of the Executive Committee . . . 1855*, 12.

22. British National Temperance League Archives, Sheffield: *MS Minute Books of the National Temperance League*, I (18 Feb. 1859).

23. Cobden to Collet, 5 June 1854: BL *Add. MS* 43677 (Cobden Papers), f. 49.

24. Cobden to Sturge, 4 Feb. 1853: BL *Add. MS* 43656 (Cobden Papers), f. 328; cf. f. 180: Cobden to Sturge, 11 Jan. 1851.

25. Cobden to Sumner, 23 Jan. 1862, quoted in Hobson, *op. cit.*, 361.

26. R. T. Shannon, *Gladstone and the Bulgarian Agitation 1876* (1963), 153; W. L. Arnstein, *The Bradlaugh Case* (1965), 235.

27. *Shield*, 26 Nov. 1870, 308.

28. *Storm-Bell*, no. 15 (1 June 1899); cf. E. M. Bell, *Josephine Butler. Flame of Fire* (1962), 176–7.

29. *Pall Mall Gazette*, 24 Aug. 1885, 10; cf. leader in *ibid.*, 24 Aug. 1885, 1.

30. W. T. Stead, *Contemporary Rev.*, L (1886), 678, cf. 668, 671–2, 675. See also R. L. Schults, *Crusader in Babylon. W. T. Stead and the Pall Mall Gazette* (Lincoln, Nebraska, 1972), 160, 208.

31. J. Morley, *On Compromise* (1886 edn), 33; P. Cadogan, 'Harney and Engels', *International Rev. of Social History*, X (1965), pt 1, 86; Sir M. Durand, *Life of the Right Hon. Sir Alfred Comyn Lyall* (1913), 411, but cf. Morley, *Cobden*, 767.

32. A. J. Lee, *The Origins of the Popular Press in England 1855–1914* (1976), 290–1, cf. 287.

33. D. E. Butler and A. Sloman, *British Political Facts 1900–1975* (1975), 386–7; *The Times*, 8 June 1970, 7.

34. J. A. Thomas, *The House of Commons 1832–1901* (1939), 4–7, 14–17; Lee, *op. cit.*, 115, 294–6.

35. Calculated from Lee, *op. cit.*, 294; cf. H. V. Emy, *Liberals, Radicals and Social Politics 1892–1914* (1973), 101.

36. *The Times*, 4 June 1970, 11.

37. F. E. Myers, 'British peace politics: the Campaign for Nuclear Disarmament and the Committee of 100, 1957–1962' (Ph.D. thesis, Columbia University, 1965), 201.

38. T. Cooper, *The Life of Thomas Cooper* (1872), 146, cf. 173, 197; 259.

39. P. Hesketh, *My Aunt Edith* (1966), 38–9.

40. *H. L. Deb.*, 26 Nov. 1970, c. 295.

41. C. Driver, *The Disarmers. A Study in Protest* (1964), 60; R. Rose, 'Class and party divisions: Britain as a test case', *Sociology*, II (1968), 148–9.

42. E. M. Hunt, 'The North of England agitation for the abolition of the Slave Trade, 1780–1800' (Ph.D. thesis, University of Manchester), 228–33.

43. E. P. Thompson, *The Making of the English Working Class* (Pelican edn, 1968), 691, 740; see also Lovett's evidence to the Select Committee on Public Libraries, *British Parliamentary Papers*, 1849, XVII (548), Q. 2819.

44. Reynolds, *op. cit.*, 74–7; A. Macintyre, *The Liberator. Daniel O'Connell and the Irish Party 1830–1847* (1965), 83.

45. N. McCord, *The Anti-Corn Law League 1838–1846* (1958), 182; see also Hamburger, *op. cit.*, 58–9, 275, and S. E. Finer, 'The transmission of Benthamite ideas 1820–50', in *Studies in the Growth of Nineteenth-Century Government*, ed. G. Sutherland (1972).

46. D. A. Hamer, *John Morley. Liberal Intellectual in Politics* (1968), 72–3.

47. Shannon, *op. cit.*, 49–50, 74–5, 78.

48. See my '"A World of Which We Had No Conception"', *VS*, XIII (1969), 155; H. J. Hanham, 'The problem of Highland discontent, 1880–1885', *Trans. Royal Historical Society*, XIX, 1969. 64–5.

49. Northcliffe to Lady Betty Balfour, 22 Dec. 1916: City of London Polytechnic, Fawcett Library Autograph Collection; cf. M. D. Pugh, 'Politicians and the woman's vote 1914–1918', *History*, LIX (1974), 365; B. Harrison, *Separate Spheres. The Opposition to Women's Suffrage in Britain* (1978), 118–19, 153, 205, 207.

50. Lee, *op. cit.*, 215; A. Strachey, *St. Loe Strachey. His Life and his Paper* (1930), 185ff; S. Koss, *Fleet Street Radical. A. G. Gardiner and the 'Daily News'* (1973), 75, 77.

51. S. A. Barnett, 'The press and charitable funds', *Independent Rev.* (July 1906), 64ff.

52. Harrison and Hollis, *op. cit.*, 140; H. Solly, *'These Eighty Years'* (1893), I, 346; W. Lovett, *Life and Struggles* (1876), 244.

53. Royal Commission on the . . . Contagious Diseases Act, *British Parliamentary Papers*, 1871 (C. 408), XIX, Q. 13075; Annie Kenney to A. J. Balfour, 18 Dec. 1909: BL *Add. MS* 49793 (Balfour Papers), f. 118. For

Cobden, see Morley, *Cobden*, 565.

54. *Justice*, 6 Dec. 1884, 4.

55. Schults, *op. cit.*, 156.

56. *Common Cause*, 18 Apr. 1912, 21; H. M. Swanwick, *I Have Been Young* (1935), 221 n.1.

57. *Votes for Women*, 27 Oct. 1911, 59.

58. Ray Strachey to Mrs Fawcett, 9 May 1917: Ray Strachey MSS (in the care of her daughter, Mrs Halpern).

59. K. Briant, *Marie Stopes. A Biography* (1962), 163.

60. J. Butler, *Personal Reminiscences of a Great Crusade* (1896), 402.

61. E. Glasgow, 'The establishment of the "Northern Star" newspaper', *History*, XI (1954), 65–6; G. W. Olsen, 'The Church of England Temperance Magazine 1862–1873', *VPN*, XI (1978), 39.

62. *Common Cause*, 14 Apr. 1910, 4; Women's Social & Political Union, *7th Annual Report, 1913*, 17; *Time and Tide*, 14 May 1920, 4.

63. J. R. Vincent, *The Formation of the Liberal Party 1857–1868* (1966), 58ff.

64. Circulation figures from J. A. Epstein, 'Feargus O'Connor and the *Northern Star*', *International Rev. of Social History* XXI (1976), pt 1, 97; J. F. C. Harrison, in *Chartist Studies*, ed. A. Briggs (1959), 73–4. There are circulation figures for Scottish Chartist papers in A. Wilson, *The Chartist Movement in Scotland* (1970), 270.

65. J. F. C. Harrison and D. Thompson, *Bibliography of the Chartist Movement, 1837–1976* (1978), 99 and ff.; C. D. Rice, '"Humanity Sold for Sugar!". The British Abolitionist response to free trade in slave-grown sugar', *Historical J.*, XIII (1970), 405.

66. James, *op. cit.*, 17.

67. *Quarterly Rev.*, CL (1880), 523.

68. For fuller discussion, see my '"A World of Which We Had No Conception"', *op. cit.*, 138–41.

69. R. D. French, 'Medical science and Victorian society: the Anti-Vivisection Movement' (D.Phil. thesis, University of Oxford, 1972), 265, 268.

70. Figures from *Votes for Women*, Apr. 1908, 97; 7 May 1909, 621; 1 Apr. 1910, 418; *Suffragette*, 22 Nov. 1912,

78; cf. S. Pankhurst, *The Suffragette Movement* (1931), 462.

71. Swanwick, *op. cit.*, 229.

72. Lovett, *Life*, 60; Cooper, *Life*, 145–6; Gammage, *op. cit.*, 404–5.

73. *Ballot*, 24 Dec. 1859, 2; *Justice*, 5 July 1884, 4.

74. Tape-recorded interview with Mrs Edith E. Fulford (née Pitt), at Birmingham, 9 June 1976.

75. *Suffragette*, 10 Oct. 1913, 990.

76. M. Thale (ed.), *The Autobiography of Francis Place (1771–1854)* (1972), 151; McCord, *op. cit.*, 65.

77. See my '"A World of Which We Had No Conception"' *op. cit.*, 154; Dingle, *op. cit.*, 665.

78. *Staunch Teetotaler*, (July 1867), 109.

79. Cobden to Joseph Sturge, 30 Sept. 1855: *Cobden Papers 62*, West Sussex RO (xerox copy).

80. M. Hovell, in *The Chartist Movement* ed. T. F. Tout (1918), 96; cf. J. A. Epstein, *op. cit.*, 59, 75ff, 91–2.

81. British National Temperance League, Sheffield: *British Temperance League General Purposes Committee Minutes*, 17 Dec. 1867.

82. *Justice*, 5 Apr. 1884, 5.

83. *Women's Suffrage J.*, 1 Sept. 1882, 143.

84. *Justice*, 5 July 1884, 4.

85. *Votes for Women*, 15 July 1910, 683; *Vote*, 3 June 1911, 71; *Woman's Dreadnought*, 25 July 1914, 73.

86. *Votes for Women*, 8 Oct. 1909, 29; cf. 8 Apr. 1910, 435.

87. Museum of London, typescript *Autobiography of Kitty Marion* (carbon copy) (1938), 173–4; cf. *Votes for Women*, 12 Aug. 1910, 757.

88. *Anti-Suffrage Review*, (March 1911), 47.

89. E.g. *Votes for Women*, 15 Apr. 1910; *Suffragette*, 1 Aug. 1913, 714; *Vote*, 30 Oct. 1909, 5.

90. *Vote*, 3 June 1911, 71; Museum of London 50.82/1132: typescript by E. R. Willoughby Marshall, *Suffragette Escapes and Adventures* (1947), 36.

91. G. Orwell, *The Road to Wigan Pier* (Penguin edn, 1962), 57.

92. '"A World of Which We Had No Conception"', *op. cit.*, 137–8.

93. Unpaginated advertisement page, cf.

94. Tape-recorded interview with Miss Maud Kate Smith at Solihull, 14 Jan. 1975; Lady Rhondda, *This Was My World* (1933), 125.

95. Gammage, *Newcastle Weekly Chronicle*, 31 May 1884; W. E. Adams, *Memoirs of a Social Atom* (Kelley reprint, 1967), 164, cf. 204.

96. G. M. Trevelyan, *The Life of John Bright* (1925 edn), 216.

97. London Corresponding Society *Moral and Political Mag.*, 1 (1796), vi (preface); Lady Rhondda, *op. cit.*, 130–1.

98. *Band of Hope Record*, 1 Nov. 1858, 69.

99. E.g. *Women's Suffrage J.*, 1 Mar. 1870, 5; 1 Apr. 1882, 50; 1 Feb. 1872, 27.

100. *Ibid.*, 1 Jan. 1878, 3.

101. *National Temperance Mag.*, (Jan. 1844), 30.

102. Dingle, *op. cit.*, 583–4.

103. Thompson, *William Morris*, 392.

104. *British and Foreign Temperance Herald*, (Feb. 1832), 14; for other instances, see my '"A World of Which We Had No Conception"', *op. cit.*, 129.

105. *Guardian*, 12 Sept. 1978, 2; 13 Sept. 1978, 13.

106. Cf. F. Parkin, *Middle Class Radicalism. The Social Bases of the British Campaign for Nuclear Disarmament* (1968), 38.

107. Thompson, *Making of the English Working Class*, 739.

108. J. S. Mill, 'Democracy in America', *Edinburgh Rev.*, LXXII (1840), 12; *idem, Representative Government* (Everyman edn, 1960), 180.

109. Cooper, *Life*, 171.

110. P. Thompson, *Socialists, Liberals and Labour. The Struggle for London 1885–1914* (1967), 262; K. O. Morgan, *Keir Hardie, Radical and Socialist* (1975), 139.

111. *Women's Suffrage J.*, 1 Mar. 1870, 1; *Free Sunday Advocate*, 1 Apr. 1881, 74.

112. *Votes for Women*, 23 Dec. 1910, 194.

E. M. Bell, *Storming the Citadel. The Rise of the Woman Doctor* (1953), 17, 18, 20. See also *English Woman's J.*, 1 Oct. 1860, 113ff.

113. *Alliance Weekly News*, 12 Dec. 1857; United Kingdom Alliance, *20th Report of the Executive Committee . . . 1871–2*, 64.
114. *Women's Suffrage J.*, 1 Mar. 1870, 1.
115. W. Godwin, *Enquiry Concerning Political Justice* (2nd edn, 1796), I, 290.
116. Dingle, *op. cit.*, 471.
117. Harrison and Hollis, *op. cit.*, 124, cf. 173. See also L. C. Wright, *Scottish Chartism* (1953), 208; Gammage, *op. cit.*, 205.
118. E. Royle, *Victorian Infidels. The Origins of the British Secularist Movement. 1791–1866* (1974), 201.
119. '"A World of Which We Had No Conception"', *op. cit.*, 151–2.
120. Swanwick, *op. cit.*, 209.
121. Pankhurst, *Unshackled*, 153.
122. Tape-recorded interview with Mrs Leonora Cohen at Rhos-on-Sea, 26 Oct. 1974.
123. Mrs Pankhurst to H. D. Harben, 20 Dec. 1912: BL *Add MS* 58226 (Harben MSS), f.6; cf. D. Mitchell, *Queen Christabel* (1977), 221. Lady Constance Lytton in *The Times*, 15 Mar. 1911, 8.
124. *H. C. Deb.*, 11 June 1914, c. 522.
125. Memorandum by Miss Pott, Oct. 1913, 3: India Office Library, London: Curzon MSS, MS Eur F 112/36.
126. *The Times*, 16 Mar. 1911, 8.
127. Tape-recorded interview with Miss Maud Kate Smith at Solihull, 14 Jan. 1975.
128. Myers, *op. cit.*, 162.
129. *The Times*, 23 Aug. 1977, 11.
130. *Anti-Suffrage Rev.*, (July 1913), 143; (July 1914), 110.

Aled Jones Workmen's advocates: ideology
and class in a mid-Victorian
labour newspaper system

During the early 1870s an attempt was made in some of Britain's industrial provinces to establish a national system of radical working-class newspapers. Those concerned with the enterprise sought to create an alternative network of local newspapers which would be sympathetic to the cause of labour and which could help to establish the existence of the working-class as a distinct and independent class in society. The issues which this audacious and ambitious venture raise for historians bear centrally upon the history of both organized labour and the newspaper press in the mid-Victorian period. This essay will examine some of the problems which these newspapers faced during the difficult transition from idea to precarious existence. These problems fell broadly into two closely related categories. The first concerned the difficulties of acquiring adequate financial support with which to produce and to distribute the papers. The second related to the question of ideology, and to the ways in which readers responded to the assumptions which underpinned editorial policies. The peculiarly close ties which were maintained between editors and readers make it possible to analyse the ways in which the system coped with its problems, and help to identify broadly the groups of readers who most valued its services.

The idea of an independent newspaper system was originally formulated as a twofold response, on the one hand to the employers' monopoly of control over local and national press coverage, and on the other to the exclusion of large groups of workers from the many privileges, including the craft periodicals, of skilled trade unions. Though both expressed the frustrations felt by many workers at their inability to present their own case through the press, a distinction should be made between these two responses. The former grew out of a sustained critique of the existing popular newspaper press, whilst the latter developed out of a desire prevalent among many trade unionists to possess their own means of printed communication. Advocates of the new systems argued that the

great majority of existing newspapers have leaned on the side of the employing class, if they have not directly made themselves the exponents of capitalist views, and not unnaturally that has led to the wish for journals that would place the ideas of working men fully and fairly before their own class, the employing class and the general public.[1]

Labour was felt to be stranded in a permanently disadvantaged condition, having no means with which to counter the printed arguments of employers during disputes, or to influence opinion at large. The trade associations of better-organized workers had compensated to a certain extent for this bias by producing their own journals. Owned, controlled and distributed in most cases by individual and well-established trade unions, periodicals of this genre catered for a readership which was more often than not located firmly within particular trades or industries. One prominent example of this type of periodical was the *Ironworkers Journal*, the monthly organ of the National Association of Iron, Steel, Tin, Blastfurnace and Other Workers, which was published by the union's executive committee and edited until his death in 1876 by the union's president, John Kane. Not all labour papers were so parochial in their industrial concerns, however. The *Bee-Hive*, for example, a weekly newspaper closely associated with the London Trades Council and briefly with the International Working Men's Association, was without doubt the most important working-class radical newspaper of the period.[2] Nevertheless, in spite of its wide trade union support and its evident popularity with working-class leaders in many parts of the country, the *Bee-Hive* could not always be as valuable and as relevant to a hollow-ware presser in Hanley, an agricultural labourer in Gloucestershire or a collier in Merthyr Tydfil as it was to a builder or a carpenter in the metropolis. For, like the *Ironworkers Journal*, the *Bee-Hive* also related to a specific, if rather broader, group of relatively privileged trade unionists. With some justification, therefore, many radicals considered that the great mass of working people remained outcast from Britain's 'fourth estate', and it was from amongst this silenced majority that, during the late 1860s, the demand for a 'purely working-class journal'[3] attracted its earliest adherents.

The most persistent advocate of the labour newspaper system, and the man who guided the venture from the late 1860s through to the late 1870s, was a Staffordshire potter and editor named William Owen. Born in Burslem in December 1844,[4] Owen was the grandson of a Welsh soldier and relative of Robert Owen, the co-operative socialist.[5] His father, John Owen, born in Halifax, Nova Scotia, in 1814,[6] had become a potter's printer[7] and had married a Burslem-born wife.[8] William Owen himself was apprenticed to a local pottery firm as a turner, one of the most highly paid pottery trades that a boy could then enter,[9] and in 1867, at the age of 23, he was appointed editor of the potters' own trade journal, the *Potteries Examiner*. That the newspaper system made the critical transition from an ideal to a reality, however neutered the eventual outcome, is a tribute to William Owen's farsightedness, determination and an almost cavalier attitude to the taking of risks. That the system acquired a limited degree of success within the areas in which it operated bears testimony to his shrewdness, his understanding of trade union organization and local politics and his tireless activity. The audacity of the scheme owed much to the young Owen's novel conception of what a workers' press ought to be. The goal to which he aspired, and which he articulated and shared with other like-minded colleagues, was the establishment of a daily working-class newspaper. The model for their plans was neither the kind of paper typified by the *Ironworkers Journal* nor the *Bee-Hive*, despite the obvious debts owed to each of those papers. Rather, in general shape and form, they were to emulate the familiar pattern of the popular provincial newspapers. The labour newspaper system was to be organized along lines common to many provincial dailies and weeklies, with the publication of numerous local editions of a central or parent paper. The novelty of the system was that it sought to extend this practice to the production of newspapers on a national scale, each paper being weekly local or regional editions of one national daily. As Owen explained in June 1871: 'What is needed for the working men of this country is a Times for their class – a daily newspaper representing the great industrial orders. And affiliated to that great central organ there should be local weekly newspapers in every centre of industry.'[10] In theory these editions were to be established and promoted in their various localities by interested trade unionists and by active canvassing of readers at public meetings and lectures by those who, like Owen, would be directly involved in producing the parent paper.

Again differing markedly from the craft journals, Owen helped to develop an editorial style which adhered closely to the precedent established by the local popular papers. Owen envisaged that the workers' newspapers would embody, in addition to the extensive coverage of working-class affairs, general commentaries on national and international news, serialized fiction and a certain amount of 'light relief' material extracted from the London satirical journals. This attempt to balance trade union material with an appeal to a more popular taste attracted to Owen's scheme some sympathetic radical journalists, Nonconformist ministers, local writers and intellectuals of 'advanced Liberal' views. Their contributions were to be important, even decisive, as they fused their energies into a broadly-based campaign for working-class reforms. Nevertheless, the function of the proposed system of labour newspapers was specific and understood. It was to provide a voice for those provincial workers whose interests and aspirations the provincial papers, the craft journals and even the *Bee-Hive* had ignored.

To understand why the demand for a comprehensive working-class newspaper came to be articulated at this time, and how the phenomenon itself occurred, it is necessary to look to the intense and militant working-class activity of the early 1870s. Supporters of the labour newspaper system often expressed a profound awareness of their history, regarding their work as one which continued a long and tenacious tradition of working-class journalism dating back to the struggles of radicals and republicans, Owenites and Chartists against the 'taxes on knowledge'. But an explanation of the emerging system calls for a comparison not with the newspaper campaigns of the 1830s, but with the labour unrest of the late 1880s and the early 1890s, which was also a period of great journalistic activity and the production of new radical periodicals. Like the later period of unrest, the early 1870s were characterized by the involvement of unskilled workers in attempts to build their own sometimes general, often centralized trade unions as platforms for industrial and in many cases for political action. The idea of a national system of working-class newspapers, therefore, coincided with an increased dissatisfaction with the contemporary newspaper press and with the rapid growth of trade unionism among largely non-unionized workers. The scheme which Owen and others proposed was a timely innovation whose principal aim was to provide guidance and leadership to those who were new to disciplined union organization. Moreover, that leadership would be provided in the familiar form of ordinary local newspapers rather than in numerous new trade periodicals.

The origins of the labour newspaper system, however, were firmly embedded in a long tradition of trade periodicals. Between 1867 and 1874 Owen was himself editor of a trade journal whose lineage could be traced back directly to the Owenite socialist *Potters Examiner and Workman's Advocate*. Founded by the organized potters of north Staffordshire in December 1843,[11] this paper was written by and for local potters and was owned and controlled by the United Branches of Operative Potters and printed by the trustees of the Potters Joint Emigration Society at Shelton.[12] In July 1848 the editor, William Evans, unwisely embroiled the paper and its owners in a disastrous emigration scheme. Abandoning trade unionism, Evans committed the paper, and the money of its owners, to the purchase of land to be leased to emigrants in America. Retitled the *Emigrant's Advocate*, Evans re-established the paper in an embarkation office in Liverpool. In protest, the pottery unions withdrew their support, and the paper, allegedly funded in the meantime by various shipping companies, ceased publication in February 1851. Six years later, however, the United Branches revived the idea of a trade newspaper and launched the *Potter* under their own collective editorial control. Contrary to the non-political policy pursued by its Owenite predecessor, the *Potter* in 1857 was, according to the Webbs, 'strongly Radical with perhaps a touch of Chartism remaining in it'.[13] Evans, following his return to the Potteries, undertook in 1863 to improve the *Potter* into a restyled *Potteries Examiner and Workman's Advocate*. He remained highly unpopular with many of the potters, however, and as criticism of his editorial style and conduct mounted, the United Branches removed him from the editorship in 1867.[14] To the vacant post the pottery unions appointed the young William Owen, who introduced new ambition and verve to the management of the paper. He was determined from the start to use his position as editor of the potters' journal to help create an independent workers' newspaper which transcended all sectional and parochial limitations.

Owen argued for this policy at the 1869 Trade Union Congress. The Congress showed interest and sympathy but resolved not to commit itself financially or otherwise to the creation of a provincially based 'labour newspaper system'. Failure to gain the official countenance of this infant but important representative body for the scheme threw Owen back into continued dependence on the local pottery unions. Some potters' branches had for many years levied up to 4d. per member per week for the paper's fund, and it was clear that if a network of labour newspapers was to be constructed outside the aegis of national trade unions, then the close relationship with local branches had to be maintained. The problem Owen faced was how to broaden the paper's readership without altering that close relationship, how to persuade workers of other trades not only to read and to buy the *Potteries Examiner* but also to sustain it with regular contributions from their own wages. To this end he introduced news of the activities of coalminers, ironworkers and others and promoted the paper in the heavy industrial areas of north Staffordshire by publishing local and community news items. During 1870 and 1871 this policy met with some success, and, acquiring a wider recognition, the paper was adopted as the 'official' organ of the local branches of the colliers' and ironworkers' organizations. The *Potteries Examiner*, however, remained the property of the joint financial committee of the pottery union executives. To facilitate an increase in the paper's circulation and influence, Owen became convinced that it would be necessary to extend and to diversify the ownership to include other workers' organizations. The idea of forming a broader structure of ownership was not a new one. The Hollow Ware Pressers in particular had considered enthusiastically the possibility of establishing a joint stock company to run the paper at the time of its revival in 1864.[15] But the process of restructuring the paper's financial organization and of extricating it from the control of pottery workers alone was not completed until the summer of 1871, when the pottery unions finally agreed to help establish an independent co-operative printing company. In April 1871 an *ad hoc* committee assembled to supervise sales of shares to trade union branch committees and their members, and within two months sufficient capital had been raised to start a general or jobbing branch of the company, and shortly after a newspaper printing section.[16] Ownership of the *Potteries Examiner* was then formally transferred from the old financial committee to the new executive committee of the Staffordshire Co-operative Newspaper and General Printing Society.[17] The initial success of the new arrangement convinced Owen that the embryo of a national printing and publishing company had been conceived, and that he had helped to bring into being the nucleus of a new and independent system of labour newspapers.

At this early juncture, Owen met the first signs of resistance to his newspaper and hostility to his editorial policy. He complained in the autumn of 1871 of being discriminated against by the local authority, and in particular by the Hanley school board officers, in their allocation of advertisements and public notices to local newspapers. Owen protested that the *Potteries Examiner*:

> is a trades paper, established to protect the working men's trade rights, but it is also as much a local journal as any that is published or circulated in the district . . . there would have been no objection on the part of such gentlemen . . . to advertising in the paper if it had been established to promote the interests of capital.[18]

Worse was soon to come, however. In June 1872 local employers objected to his editorial indictment of the annual hiring system which survived in pockets in some pottery firms in Longton, and Owen was sued for libel by the mayor and the presiding magistrate of Longton for damages totalling £2,000.[19] Owen was eventually fined £50 at Gloucester assizes, but not before he had received over £443 in just over three months from subscribers to the *Potteries Examiner* defence fund.[20] For in spite of growing hostility from certain quarters, Owen's strategy for extending his paper brought considerable short-term success to its circulation. Support for the paper continued to grow outside north Staffordshire throughout 1871 and 1872, with sales increasing from 2,200 a week in April to 6,650 in September 1871. In June 1871 Owen also extended its size from four to eight pages and raised its price from 1d. to 1½d.[21] At the beginning of this period of growth the North Staffordshire district of the Amalgamated Association of Miners (A.A.M.) resolved to levy each of its members 1d. per month through their branches towards the maintenance of the *Potteries Examiner,* in addition to contracting all their printing requirements to the jobbing branch of the company.[22] In May 1872 the miners of the Cannock Chase district of the A.A.M. followed this example and agreed to raise a monthly 1d. levy on their members in return for the free printing of the proceedings of their meetings in the paper and the 'general advocacy of the paper in connection with their trade'.[23] Similarly in June 1872, a conference of the South Stafforshire Trades met in Darlaston to discuss the general principle of levy-raising to support the *Potteries Examiner* and the efforts being made to extend its circulation into south Staffordshire and the Black Country.[24] Thus workers in the smaller metal trades of south Staffordshire, prominent among them being the Willenhall lock- and key-smiths, were drawn into the financial and organizational orbit of a paper which only a year earlier had been reserved exclusively for members of the pottery unions. The identification of the commitment of organized labour in Staffordshire as a whole to the *Potteries Examiner* demonstrated firstly that the paper had matured beyond being a local trade organ and, as Owen argued, had indeed 'become a journal of great importance to the class to which it belongs, and whose cause it advocates',[25] and secondly, that at the local trade union level throughout a large portion of industrial Staffordshire, Owen and his associates had won the argument for an independent workers' press, and had established firm foundations upon which a nationwide system of labour newspapers could be built.

Of the help offered by various groups of Staffordshire workers to the *Potteries Examiner,* the co-operation of the local lodges of the A.A.M. was of particular significance. Owen regarded the growing and dynamic lodges of the miners' union as the firm bedrock of financial support, guaranteed minimum sales and committed readers upon which to anchor his newspaper and to introduce it to readers in other districts. In this respect their support had been of crucial importance in both north and south Staffordshire throughout 1871 and 1872, and Owen's utilization of the network of contacts which he had established whilst selling the *Potteries Examiner* in the Staffordshire coalfields enabled him to gain friends for the paper from among workers living in distant outlying coalmining areas. Growing working-class sympathy outside Staffordshire for the idea of a labour newspaper coincided with the further expansion of trade unionism among many other groups of skilled and unskilled workers during 1872 and 1873. Owen was so impressed by the energy and the enthusiasm for organization which workers expressed in ever-increasing numbers in the Midlands, the North-West and South Wales that, in an atmosphere of heady optimism, he resolved to commence publication of a new workers' newspaper.

In June 1873 Owen and William Brown, a north Staffordshire miners' agent, began an extensive tour of the coalfields of Derbyshire, Leicestershire, Shropshire, the Forest of Dean, and South Wales. For two months they argued the case for a national working-class newspaper at lectures, public meetings, delegate meetings and miners' demonstrations, and succeeded in making arrangements with individuals to publish editions of the new paper locally. Trade union lodges were persuaded either to levy their members or to agree to purchase a minimum number of copies per week in order to enhance the circulation of the young paper. In some districts lodges agreed to do both.[26] Owen and Brown then returned to Hanley to prepare the first issue of the *Labour Press, Miners' and Workmen's Examiner*. Appearing in August 1873, this weekly paper was introduced to its readers as the working-class *Times* of which Owen had spoken in 1871. Edited and managed by Owen and printed by the Staffordshire Co-operative Newspaper and General Printing Society, the new paper was intended initially for the coalfields of Staffordshire, east Worcestershire, Shropshire, and Warwickshire, but would eventually be for general circulation in every industrial district of the United Kingdom.[27]

During the same month a network of local editions of the *Labour Press, Miners' and Workmen's Examiner* emerged in a number of important mining districts. The *Forest of Dean Examiner* was published by George Long in Cinderford, the *Cannock Chase Examiner* by Benjamin Evans in Hednesford, the *Shropshire Examiner* by John Randall in Madeley, and the *Derbyshire and Leicestershire Examiner* by R. J. Frankland in Burton. In September 1873 the *Tamworth Examiner* also appeared published by J. P. Elliot in Tamworth. A *Lancashire Examiner* was promised, but never produced.[28] The *Potteries Examiner*, whose meagre resources had long been overstretched, reverted to being principally a north Staffordshire workers' paper. Encouraged by the initial success of his venture, Owen announced that he was 'willing to make arrangements with the trade societies of any centre of industry to issue a local labour journal, in connection with the Labour Newspaper System.'[29] With the framework of the system already in existence, Owen at this point approached the national leadership of the A.A.M. for their explicit approval and assistance. In October 1873 he presented his case to their conference at Bristol, as a result of which his papers became the 'medium of general intercourse and general organ of the union'.[30] This approval, however, entailed no financial assistance nor any question of A.A.M. control over editorial policy. Following the conference three new local editions were inaugurated, the *South Staffordshire Examiner* and the *Wednesbury, West Bromwich and Darlaston Examiner*, published by Owen himself in Wednesbury from December 1873 and September

1874 respectively, and the *West of England Examiner* published in Bristol by Thomas Thomas in May 1874.

Owen's visit to South Wales, however, did not meet with the same degree of success. In June 1873 he addressed delegates supposedly representing some 30,000 or 40,000 miners and ironworkers from the whole of industrial South Wales at Merthyr Tydfil. The meeting was generally favourable to the suggestion of extending Owen's system into Wales, and a group of delegates undertook to organize the production of a *South Wales Examiner*.[31] This paper, however, never appeared. In its place J. T. Morgan, a local radical journalist and editor, produced his own independent local workers' newspaper. In September 1873 Morgan suspended the production of his two radical and quasi-republican journals, the *Merthyr Times* and the *Western Observer*,[32] and began publishing a bilingual labour paper, the *Workman's Advocate*, which purported to be the 'Official organ of the Colliers, Miners, Ironworkers etc.'[33] Following the precedent of Morgan Williams' and David John's bilingual Chartist papers published in Merthyr between 1834 and 1842,[34] Morgan responded sensitively to the linguistic complexion of industrial South Wales in general and of the town of Merthyr in particular. According to the 1891 language census only a third of Merthyr's population spoke both English and Welsh with any fluency, whilst the remaining two-thirds were thoroughly conversant in only one of the two languages in roughly equal proportions.[35] Morgan gave to this cosmopolitan working class a means of expression by dividing the *Workman's Advocate* systematically into Welsh and English sections. Other than translated editorials and some local news, Morgan in effect produced two distinct papers which were directed at the interests and the needs of linguistically defined readers.

The *Workman's Advocate* was locked into Owen's newspaper system by its chronology and by the radical and trade union activists who used it. Both the Rev. T. D. Matthias, a radical Welsh Baptist and future editor of the *Potteries Examiner*, and Phillip Harries, a north Staffordshire ironworkers' agent, are known to have circulated the *Workman's Advocate* among Welsh and other workers in the Potteries and the Forest of Dean.[36] Belatedly, Morgan even tried to reorganize his paper on the co-operative pattern of the Staffordshire Newspaper and General Printing Society,[37] and like the *Potteries Examiner*, the *Labour Press, Miners' and Workman's Examiner* and its editions, the success of the *Workman's Advocate* rested primarily on the agitation of the coalminers and on the general healthiness and vigour of their union lodges. Indeed, in August 1875 Thomas Halliday, president of the A.A.M., referred specifically to the rôle played by the *Workman's Advocate* in helping to strengthen the union in South Wales.[38] Nevertheless, Morgan zealously maintained his own editorial control over the paper, which remained independent of both trade union leaders and William Owen. The *Workman's Advocate* was expanded in the summer of 1874 to two separate penny papers, the *Workman's Advocate* which extended its circulation to Bristol and the West of England in December 1874 (see plate 4), and the Welsh language *Amddiffynydd y Gweithiwr* which published the affairs and the correspondence of workers in the coalfields of south and north-east Wales, the iron and tinplate regions of the south and west, and the slate quarrying towns of the north-west (see plate 14).

The provincial network of labour newspapers was at its most dynamic and influential during the peak of trade unionist activity in 1873 and 1874. Across the country new labour papers, many of which were quite unconnected to Owen's system, were being prepared and published. In Birmingham, for example, William Payne was busy attempting to resuscitate a scheme to issue a local labour newspaper on a co-operative basis which trade unionists in the city had prepared in 1868.[39] At the same time, miners in the coalfields of the North-East began to lend their support to another radical paper, Joseph Gould's *Miner's Advocate and Record*.[40] In February 1874 Owen's Staffordshire Co-operative Newspaper and General Printing Society started to print the *Labour League Examiner* for the executive committee of the new farmworkers' union, the Agricultural Labour League. By early autumn 1874 Owen and Morgan alone were responsible for the publication of 12 weekly labour newspapers which circulated through each industrial centre from the Potteries through the Black Country and the Forest of Dean to Bristol and South Wales. Each of these papers was financed and distributed principally by the local branches and lodges of largely unskilled and relatively recently established trade unions.

Labour newspapers provided a valuable service hitherto denied to many groups of unskilled workers. The *Potteries Examiner* published accounts, minutes or details of meetings of nearly 40 branches of the various pottery unions, 19 miners' lodges and nine branches of the ironworkers' union in the Potteries district,[41] whilst the *Workman's Advocate* in similar fashion printed the affairs of such diverse organizations as the local branches of the ironworkers' union, the A.A.M. and the general labourers, the Tin Plate Makers, the Enginemen, Firemen and Fitters and the Typographical Association. Correspondence arising from disagreements within and between branches and lodges appeared in their columns, and local public meetings, particularly those attended or addressed by union leaders, were reported in profuse detail. Furthermore, the papers' wide geographical circulation enabled workers in many districts to communicate regularly with each other, whether or not they were members of the same union. Industrial disputes were widely reported and were frequently accompanied by warnings against strike-breaking at specific works and pits. Fund-raising activities were also organized simultaneously by all the papers to help workers in dispute in other areas. They afforded to workers in many trades and occupations within a wide area the opportunity to exchange lists of wages and prices and more general information about other employers and their organizations, to learn of the condition of companies in other areas and of the experiences of workers in other local disputes. These facilities enabled rank-and-file trade unionists to initiate discussions amongst themselves and to foster their own self-confidence; they also created the impression among many employers that their workers were better organized, and could draw upon larger resources than was often the case.[42] It was in large part because of the availability of such advantageous services that trade union branches had agreed to help solve the pressing financial and distributive difficulties of the young papers.

The editors themselves, moreover, were committed to the cause of trade unionism, and used their papers as platforms from which to argue their philosophy of labour. Owen in particular was no stranger to mainstream trade unionist politics. A member of the parliamentary committee of the T.U.C. in 1873, he secured a contract with the Congress to print and publish all their official material, including the minutes of national conferences.[43] Owen's relations with the London Trades Council were also cordial, and both Lloyd Jones and George Odger accompanied him to public and union meetings to help promote the circulation of the *Examiners*.[44] He was actively involved in the trade societies of north Staffordshire and the Black Country, where he moved to edit and publish the *Labour Press, Miners' and Workmen's Examiner* in December 1874. The Rev. T. D. Matthias, Owen's successor as editor of the *Potteries Examiner* from 1875 to 1877, was a delegate to the T.U.C. conference on at least two occasions,[45] and like Owen was secretary to the Potteries Board of Arbitration and Conciliation. Similarly Morgan was president of a newly established unskilled union, the Bristol, West of England and South Wales Amalgamated Labourers Union, in 1874, and in the same year was a founding member of, and was appointed secretary to, the Merthyr Trades Council.[46]

Each editor shared the conviction that trade unionism, when it included all workers, could begin 'to make new arrangements of a social character'.[47] They preferred to think of a trade union as 'an industrial army' each member of which 'must be disciplined, must sink his own individual opinions and desires in the general movement for the good of all'.[48] A non-unionized worker, on the other hand, was a 'traitor to his class', one who allowed the employers to forge another 'link in the chain of working-class oppression'.[49] Serialized editorials, articles and letters reflecting upon the theoretical and

practical relationship between labour and capital consumed a large proportion of column space, particularly during the autumn of 1873 in the *Potteries
Examiner*, and throughout 1873 and 1874, though only sporadically in 1875,
in the *Workman's Advocate* and the *Amddiffynydd y Gweithiwr*. In general
the assumptions which underlay these discussions and exchanges, and which
informed the editorial policies of the whole network, were all elements of
what John Saville has termed 'the ideology of labourism'.[50] In its purest form
it was a theory of change without conflict, of defensive working-class self-
help resting on strong trade union organization, centralized collective bargaining and permanent negotiation. This ideology was class-conscious to
the extent that it held that labour should develop all the institutions which
capital possessed and use them to its own advantage. Owen was convinced
that working-class reforms of this nature would be 'a safety valve to the
nation, and would tend to prevent the most dangerous results from some
of those clashings between classes that appear inevitable.'[51] The editors of
these labour newspapers, therefore, were consciously engaged in a struggle
to improve the condition of labour in order to maintain a tenuous social
equilibrium between what they regarded to be the respective rights of
labour and capital.

At one level, our editors and journalists perceived themselves as working-
class custodians and popularizers of this ideology. Yet, in practice, the
advocacy of this ideology created very real problems for Owen, Matthias and
Morgan quite apart from the middle-class hostility which it aroused in some
of the provincial papers. For despite the soothingly unsophisticated nature of
the labourist argument, the mid-1870s were anything but years of class
harmony. Often, in the heat of local struggles, the force of the argument was
weakened and rendered increasingly unreal to many rank-and-file members
of trade unions, and in such circumstances editors felt that they had no
alternative but to succumb to their readers' pressures. Thus, following the
decision by the South Wales miners to ignore Halliday's advice and virtually
to renounce his leadership by going on strike in January 1875, the *Workman's Advocate* vowed to 'support the miners by every legal means within
its power, both morally and financially'.[52] Morgan also adopted an ambivalent attitude towards the work-yard riots which followed the breakdown of
out-relief in Merthyr in March 1875, which seemed to contradict his prin-
cipled aversion to public disorder and violence.[53] Similarly, when in November 1876 the Ovenmen, Kilnmen and Saggar Makers withdrew from the
Potteries Board of Arbitration and Conciliation, Matthias, who was both
secretary to the board and editor of the *Potteries Examiner*, was obliged to
accept and to support the men's decision. These issues illustrate clearly the
extent of the papers' independence from the direct control of trade union

leaders and the editors' willingness to abandon some of the fundamental tenets of their ideology, however temporarily. If editors in general 'must not offend those who have the news to give out',[54] the editors of the labour newspaper system in particular were highly sensitive to the needs, and were responsive to the pressures, of the diverse groups of trade unionists and local radicals of all hues who collectively owned, maintained, distributed, bought, read and wrote for their newspapers.

By the mid-1870s, therefore, the system of labour newspapers which Owen had initiated in 1871 had become a popular medium for working-class communication and expression which many had felt had grown as an organic institution of organized labour in much of Staffordshire, Shropshire, Gloucestershire and South Wales, and to a lesser extent in industrial and agricultural Leicestershire, Derbyshire and Warwickshire. Unskilled provincial workers had at last been given a voice, and Owen believed that the initial stage of his original scheme had been accomplished. The next step was to broaden the appeal of the papers, to loosen their dependence on local trade union branches, and to develop the papers into truly popular journals for the whole of the working class. To Owen it was 'manifest that a working-class journal has only half fulfilled its duty when it has assisted in obtaining for working men a just renumeration for their skill and toil'.[55] He and his associates believed that popular working-class newspapers would attract readers from existing middle-class local weeklies and dailies and help to foster among them the idea that they had a common working-class identity, a sense of belonging which could not be defined solely by, or remain confined to, membership of a trade union. Labour newspapers were to enter into and become involved in the whole of the social and intellectual activity of the working-class, or as Owen envisaged it: 'to be a schoolmaster to our class . . . to teach it to go down, deep into its own consciousness . . . [to] call forth latent working-class thought and . . . to find a means for the expression of that thought'.[56] The objects were to bind together the disparate components of the class and to display its political and cultural distinctiveness to the world.

Workers were encouraged by the editors of these newspapers to take a more active interest in all the areas which affected the politics of labour. The campaign against the Labour Laws which followed the Royal Commission into Trade Unions of 1867 and which threatened much of the freedom of action of trade unionists was conducted with great enthusiasm, but the involvement of these papers in debates and discussions of wider significance indicate that they aspired to more than the repeal of specific pieces of legislation. The political framework within which such working-class radicals as Owen, Matthias, and Morgan operated remained heavily influenced by Chartist tradition. Chartism had been strong in each of the areas in which the papers circulated,[57] and despite the fact that by the 1870s the movement itself had been moribund for two decades, vestiges of Chartism survived in popular memory, albeit in increasingly mythologized forms. It was customary in the Potteries, for example, for union meetings to start with the singing of Chartist songs,[58] and many of those who were involved with the labour press could recall early links with the movement. Matthias, for instance, commemorated the Chartism of his youth as 'the noblest enterprise of the nineteenth century',[59] and in 1875 announced that he had been all his life a 'Christian Chartist'.[60] Chartism's chief legacy to the radicals of the mid-1870s, however, was a language of radicalism and dissent, a vocabulary which informed much of the style of editorials, articles and letters. The subjects under discussion were usually of a more contemporary nature. The significance of the International Working Men's Association to European labour, Ireland and Home Rule and the Paris Commune were frequently dealt with, and republicanism, whilst not officially approved of, was openly discussed and often advocated by some correspondents.[61] Many of the debates, however, concerned the condition of the Liberal Party and the possibilities of initiating a Radical League within it to organize a working-class presence in Parliament, and both the *Potteries Examiner* and the *Workman's Advocate* mounted vigorous campaigns to support A. A. Walton and Thomas Halliday when they stood as 'Working-Men's candidates' in Stoke and Merthyr respectively during the 1874 general election. Indeed the Reform Act of 1867 and the possibility of a working-class intervention into national and local politics lay at the heart of their political thinking.

Unlike some contemporary papers, the short-term success of the *Examiners* and the *Workman's Advocate* did not hinge upon a 'combination of radicalism and scandal'.[62] If, as it has been shown, there was no shortage of the former, the latter was confined to the small space allotted to local police and crime reports and court news. The fiction was provided either by approved popular authors or known local radicals, and following the creation of W. F. Tillotson's 'fiction bureau' in 1873, the first systematic attempt was made to syndicate new fiction in newspapers,[63] the *Forest of Dean Examiner* published 80 'non-sensational' short stories between December 1873 and October 1877, 16 of which were serialized for two consecutive weeks or more, written by such relatively well-known writers as Eliza Meteyard, William Wilson Turnbull, Mary Howitt, and Captain Mayne Reid.[64] Fiction and many non-fiction articles were also contributed by local radicals and writers including G. T. Lawley, the Rev. Norman Glass, J. Randall, H. Wedgewood and H. M. Hunt. As in their industrial reports, labour newspapers were heavily dependent on correspondence and voluntary contributions. In the absence of a staff of professional journalists, editors encouraged their readers to provide articles on local history and geology, the history of radicalism and Nonconformity, the drink problem, and other educational material in addition to their regular letters, criticisms, reviews and poems. To hold their interest and to project the image of the papers deeper into the life of the community, the *Potteries Examiner* organized annual holiday excursions and evening concerts,[65] and the *Amddiffynydd y Gweithiwr* its poetry competitions.

One of the gravest problems which an editor faced when running a radical newspaper on a shoe-string budget was how to relate to his printers. Many provincial compositors working for radical editors evidently took little interest in their idealism, and through the records of printers' disputes it is possible to approach such editors as Owen, Matthias and Morgan not as 'workman's advocates' but as employers of labour. Printers employed by these men were notoriously cynical about their employers' methods and intentions, and there is no evidence to suggest that they enjoyed a special relationship with their managers. During a bitter dispute over the introduction of new apprentices at the *Staffordshire Sentinel* offices in 1869, it was pointed out by one striking compositor that:

> the only newspaper published in the Potteries besides the *Sentinel* was the *Potteries Examiner*, which announces on its title that it is –
> 'Devoted to the interests of labour', yet it is printed in a closed office at Newcastle, with an unlimited number of boys.[66]

Similarly many of Morgan's printers showed 'strong personal antipathy' to their editor,[67] and Morgan protested to the Provincial Typographical Association that their members in his employment were in combination with local employers 'to injure him'.[68]

Throughout the years of their publication, therefore, editors of working-class newspapers trod an uneven and at times perilous path between the rival pressures of trade union leaders, local trade union branches, extreme radicals and republicans and their own employees. Those who influenced their editorial policies most were without doubt the local trade unionists, but in spite of this healthy localism all the attempts which were made to broaden the papers into alternative, working-class community newspapers eventually failed. The failure was in large part the consequence of the economic recession which set in in earnest from the spring of 1875 and the subsequent disintegration of many of the poorer unions of the less skilled which severely weakened the financial foundations of the labour newspaper system. To survive, Owen was forced to overcome his dislike of commercial advertisements,[69] and their proportion of column space increased substantially from 7.8 per cent of the total content of the *Forest of Dean Examiner* in 1873 to 25.2 per cent in 1876, and from 6.7 per cent of the total content of the *Labour Press, Miners' and Workmen's Examiner* in 1874 to 35.2 per cent in 1877. In November 1874 Owen began to issue a new paper, the *Wolverhampton Times*, which unlike his earlier papers was directed at 'no particular class of the community',[70] but which aspired to be 'a first class family journal'.[71] By October 1877 the last of the local editions of the *Labour Press, Miners' and Workman's Examiner*, since January 1875 retitled the *Miner and Workman's Examiner*, had been terminated, and a year later the parent paper, since October 1877 again retitled the *Miner: Organ of Underground Labour*, was incorporated into the *Wolverhampton Times and Midland Examiner* and the new Liberal daily, the *Evening Echo*, only to be entirely discontinued in September 1879. The Staffordshire Co-operative Newspaper and General Printing Society, which had been established in April 1871 and which had made the newspaper system possible, was itself dissolved in September 1878, only a short period after Matthias had returned to the ministry in South Wales.[72] Following his departure, the *Potteries Examiner* slumped through successive crises, which included the threat of a Conservative takeover led by Ahmed Kenealy, son of the counsel to the Tichbourne claimant.[73] Owen returned to north Staffordshire in the winter of 1879 to find the pottery unions too weak to maintain their old newspaper any longer, and the *Potteries Examiner*, after a lively history which dated back to 1843, was sold to a joint stock company and dissolved in 1881.[74] In January 1876, only five months after the official termination of the A.A.M., Morgan also adopted a fresh course. He discontinued both the *Workman's Advocate* and the *Amddiffynydd y Gweithiwr* and began to issue an English language 'family newspaper', the *Star of the West*.[75] The new paper, however, was still-born, and Morgan left Merthyr to become manager of the Midland Liberal *West Bromwich Free Press* in June 1876.[76]

By the late 1870s the venture inaugurated in 1871 to create a national system of locally-based working-class newspapers had come to an end. Not one of the systems' newspapers had met with overwhelming success, and in the general context of the contemporary popular press their presence was ephemeral and their sales marginal. It is difficult to estimate with any accuracy the extent of their circulation, but it is clear that at no time were they in a position seriously to undermine the readership base of the more established provincial newspapers. Their appeal remained a narrow one, and they failed to become full local newspapers, among other reasons, because of the amateurishness with which they were produced,[77] and the absence of more diversified sources of revenue. Their originators had foreseen a different and a better future for their papers. They had begun with an idea firmly lodged in their minds that workers possessed an intrinsic and corporate class identity and composed a class whose forms were in every detail exact mirror images of a corresponding class of capitalists. Consequently, workers were said to require similar class institutions to those commanded by the capitalists, including an independent working-class newspaper press. Static though this analysis of class relations was, it lent immense vitality to the campaign for a labour newspaper system. The unrest and the optimism of the early 1870s added fuel to the campaign, and the editors and their associates were led to believe that vast resources of working-class energy and creativity were about to be 'moderately' and 'responsibly' released. Contrary to their expectations, however, the unrest, the prosperity and the hope proved to be only temporary phenomena.

If Owen, Matthias and Morgan genuinely sought a mass working-class readership, what in fact they encouraged and gave a comprehensive means of expression to was a radical provincial sub-culture, or groups of articulate and literate people who, despite their rejection of the revolutionary politics of the International Working Men's Association, stubbornly maintained an acute sense of class. The newspapers remained vehicles for this network of trade union activists and local working-class radicals who, if they were not personally acquainted through the usual round of conferences, union and election meetings, lecturing tours and sermons in Nonconformist chapels, were known to each other through their journalism. This network extended from the executive members of trade unions to their regional agents, branch secretaries and workplace activists, and from the agitators of the republican and political clubs to local intellectuals, amateur writers and poets. The general style and texture of the newspapers – their correspondence columns, articles, even editorials – drew heavily on a consensus of their ideas and attitudes, and the intimate relationship which was maintained between editors, contributors and readers served to inhibit the possibility of these papers being transformed into either dogmatic and distant political journals or such 'big business' radical ventures as *Reynolds'* or *Lloyd's Weekly Newspaper* which characterized the left flank of the late-nineteenth-century popular press.[78] When this core of support disintegrated in the late 1870s, the papers were found to possess no features which could distinguish them from the ordinary provincial newspapers other than their strident editorials, their lack of professionalism and their poverty. Without a politically committed readership they could not, and did not, survive.

On balance, therefore, the editors, publishers and correspondents of the labour newspaper system coped adequately with their many problems, at least for three or four years. They located and maintained a basic readership in hostile circumstances, and endured the vilification directed against them by more 'respectable' journals and the assaults of employers and the law. They were sustained by an ideology which emphasized class-consciousness as well as collaboration, and their editorial policies were informed throughout by a sense of tradition and a radical nomenclature which was manifest even in their expression of the new labourism. How influential these newspapers were in invoking a Chartist past, in prodding the 'class memory' or in helping to shape the ideology of labourism remains open to question. But what is certain is that they enabled their readers, many of whom were unskilled workers, individually and collectively to air opinions, discuss problems and communicate generally with each other, to continue a dialogue which found no analogous means of expression in either political party or trade union. In this way the labour newspaper system became an important experiment in workers' democracy and provided valuable weapons for the local armouries of workers' struggles, weapons which were wielded adroitly and often with decisive effect.

NOTES

1. *Forest of Dean Examiner*, 2 Aug. 1873.
2. For a history of the *Bee-Hive* consult S. Coltham, 'George Potter, the Junta and the *Bee-Hive*', *International Rev. of Social History*: pt 1, IX (1964) and pt 2, X (1965). For descriptions, locations, etc. of labour papers mentioned in this essay see R. Harrison, J. Woolven, and R. Duncan, *The Warwick Guide to British Labour Periodicals 1790–1970* (1977).
3. *Potteries Examiner* (hereafter cited as PE), 2 June 1871.
4. Census of England and Wales, Enumerator's Returns 1871, PRO RG 10.2852.
5. *Staffordshire Sentinel*, 14 Oct. 1912.
6. Census of England and Wales, Enumerator's Returns 1861, PRO RG 9.1929.
7. *Staffordshire Sentinel*, 14 Oct. 1912.
8. Census of England and Wales, Enumerator's Returns 1861, PRO RG 9.1929.
9. Labour Statistics: Return of Wages Published Between 1830 and 1886. Pt 1 (1887), 234.
10. PE, 2 June 1871.
11. *Potters Examiner and Workman's Advocate*, 3 July 1847.
12. *Ibid.*, 2 Dec. 1843.
13. Webb, Trade Union MSS, London School of Economics, vol. XLIV, item 3.
14. *Ibid.*
15. Record Book of the Transactions of the Executive Committee of the Hollow Ware Pressers Union, 15 Aug. 1864, Stoke City Library.
16. PE, 29 July 1871. By this date £700's worth of the available 2,000 10s. shares had been sold. See also Staffordshire Co-operative Newspaper and General Printing Society (Ltd), Instrument of Dissolution, PRO FS8/29/1426.
17. PE, 2 June 1871, 29 July 1871.
18. *Ibid.*, 21 Oct. 1871.
19. *Ibid.*, 6 July 1872.
20. *Ibid.*, 2 Nov. 1872.
21. *Ibid.*, 10 June 1871.
22. *Ibid.*, 7 Apr. 1871. For Owen and the A.A.M. see C. Fisher and J. Smethurst, 'War on the law of supply and demand', in *Independent Collier*, ed. R. Harrison (1978).
23. PE, 1 June 1872.
24. *Ibid.*, 15 June 1872.
25. *Ibid.*, 28 Sept. 1872.
26. *Forest of Dean Examiner*, 12 Feb. 1874; PE, 5 July 1873; *Miner and Workmen's Examiner*, 20 Feb. 1875.
27. *Forest of Dean Examiner*, 9 Jan. 1874.
28. *Ibid.*, 7 Nov. 1873.
29. *Ibid.*, 9 Jan. 1874.
30. PE, 18 Oct. 1873.
31. *Ibid.*, 5 July 1873.

32. These newspapers were issued between 31 March 1871 and 3 May 1873.

33. *Workman's Advocate*, 6 Sept. 1873.

34. *Advocate and Merthyr Free Press*, July 1840 – April 1841, PRO HO 41/15, 45/54; *Udgorn Cymru*, March 1840 – October 1842, PRO HO 41/45, 45/54.

35. Census of England and Wales 1891, Language of Inhabitants. Of Merthyr's 117,205 inhabitants, 34,651 spoke English, 35,244 Welsh, 39,812 were bilingual. The remainder were infants under two years, speakers of another language or those who failed to return statements.

36. *Workman's Advocate*, 17 Jan. 1874. Morgan was also subjected to abuse from more 'respectable' journals. See *Ferret*, 20 June 1874; *South Wales Daily News*, 30 Apr 1875; *Y Fellten*, 13 Nov. 1874; *Merthyr Express*, 17 July 1875; even *Tarian y Gweithiwr*, 14 May 1875.

37. Rules of the Labour Press Industrial and Provident Society (Ltd), PRO FS8/38/1934; *Star of the West*, 15 Jan. 1876. The co-operative was promoted by five local miners districts, the Merthyr ironworkers' union, the Independent Association of Tinplate Makers, the National United Association of Enginemen, Firemen and Fitters, the Bristol, West of England and South Wales Amalgamated Labourers' Union, and the Amalgamated Society of Tailors.

38. *Western Mail*, 27 Aug. 1875.

39. Prospectus, *Working Men's Paper*, Dec. 1868, Birmingham Trades Council and other allied labour organizations, circulars, leaflets etc. 1866— , 2, Birmingham City Library; *Radical Times*, 30 Sept. 1876.

40. *Miner's Advocate and Record*, 17 Jan. 1873, 31 Oct. 1874.

41. *PE*, 17 Mar. 1871.

42. Webb, Trade Union MSS, *op. cit.*

43. *Forest of Dean Examiner*, 9 Jan. 1874; Reports of Trade Union Congress 1873, 1874, refer also to payments made to Owen by Howell in T.U.C. Financial Reports 1868–76, 32–4, Howell Collection, Bishopsgate Institute. From 1877 the T.U.C. contracted its printing work to the Manchester Co-operative Printing Company.

44. *PE*, 13 Feb. 1875.

45. *Ibid.*, 16 Oct. 1875; Report of the Ninth Trade Union Congress, Sept. 1876, Howell Collection.

46. *Workman's Advocate*, 11 July 1874, 18 July 1874.

47. *PE*, 6 Nov. 1875.

48. *Ibid.*, 6 June 1874.

49. *Ibid.*, 12 Aug. 1871.

50. J. Saville, 'The ideology of labourism', in *Knowledge and Belief in Politics*, ed. R. Benewick, R. N. Berki, and B. Parekh (1973), 216.

51. *Forest of Dean Examiner*, 19 Dec. 1873.

52. *Workman's Advocate*, 1 Jan. 1875.

53. *Ibid.*, 19 Mar. 1875; reports of the Merthyr riots of 1875 in PRO HO 45/9377/41103.

54. R. de Jouvenel, *La République des camarades* (Paris, 1914), 248.

55. *PE*, 24 Feb. 1872.

56. *Ibid.*, 25 May 1872.

57. Consult H. Owen, *The Staffordshire Potter* (1901); G. J. Barnsby, *The Working Class Movement in the Black Country* (1977); D. Williams, 'Chartism in Wales', in *Chartist Studies*, ed. Asa Briggs (1959); A. V. John, 'The Chartist endurance', *Morgannwg*, xv (1971).

58. *PE*, 22 May 1875.

59. *Ibid.*, 18 Dec. 1875. Matthias also claimed to have 'followed the silent, but active, secretive Cambrian ribband-men for many a mile in our boyhood', *ibid.*, 18 Sept. 1875. A reference to the Rebecca rioters?

60. *Bee-Hive*, 22 Mar. 1873.

61. *PE*, 31 Mar. 1871, 13 Sept. 1873, 28 Mar. 1874, 10 June 1876; *Workman's Advocate*, 4 July 1874; *Forest of Dean Examiner*, 26 Feb. 1874, 6 March 1874, 20 March 1874.

62. V. S. Berridge, 'Popular journalism and working class attitudes 1854–1886: a study of *Reynolds' Newspaper*, *Lloyd's Weekly Newspaper* and the *Weekly Times*' (Ph.D. thesis, University of London, 1976), 25.

63. R. D. Altick, *The English Common Reader* (Chicago, 1957), 356–7.

64. Mayne Reid's novels and short stories were 'radical in tone . . . and bitterly hostile to Toryism': Mayne Reid to W. E. Adams, 29 Sept. 1879, in

G. Pollard, 'Novels in newspapers: some unpublished letters of Captain Mayne Reid', *Rev. English Studies*, XVIII (1942), 72–85.

65. *PE*, 11 May 1872, 14 Sept. 1872.
66. Provincial Typographical Association, Report Book of Deputations, p. 215, University of Warwick Modern Records Centre MSS 39A/TA/7/DEP/1.
67. *Ibid.*, 499.
68. *Ibid.*
69. *PE*, 15 June 1872. Owen had argued that 'No trade union journal could command advertisements because they had to contend against that class who advertised in newspapers'.
70. *Wolverhampton Times*, 4 Dec. 1875.
71. *Ibid.*
72. *PE*, 27 Apr. 1878, 18 May 1878.
73. Provincial Typographical Association, Minutes of General Council, 273, University of Warwick Modern Records Centre MSS 39A/TA/1/8.
74. Webb, Trade Union MSS, *op, cit.* Owen subsequently became editor of *Spice*, the *Watchman*, the *Daily* and the *Weekly Mail* (Burslem) in 1881, the *Staffordshire Knot* from 1883 to 1892, the *Crewe Star* and the *Weekly Star* in 1888. For a fuller biography of William Owen consult P. Anderton, 'The Liberal party of Stoke on Trent and parliamentary elections 1862–1880' (M.A. thesis, University of Keele, 1974).
75. *Star of the West*, 15 Jan. 1876.
76. *West Bromich Free Press*, 24 June 1876.
77. Lack of professionalism also characterized the later socialist press: see D. Hopkin, 'The socialist press in Britain 1890–1910', in *Newspaper History from the Seventeenth Century to the Present Day*, ed. G. Boyce, J. Curran, and P. Wingate (1978), 300.
78. V. S. Berridge, 'Popular Sunday papers and mid-Victorian society', in Boyce *et al.*, *op cit.*, 264.

12

Donald J. Gray   Early Victorian scandalous
journalism: Renton
Nicholson's *The Town*
(1837–42)

The first weekly number of Renton Nicholson's *The Town* was published on
3 June 1837, the month in which Victoria succeeded to the throne (see plates
7 and 8). It was almost too late for a periodical described by its editor in a
preface to its first volume as 'one of the most racy, spicy, and figging
productions of literature ever produced'. The principal topic of the *Town* was
an idea popular in the generation that was passing: the idea of the Town
itself, the London of Pierce Egan's *Life in London* (1821), a metropolis of
mostly night-time pleasures and a society of bucks and courtesans, gamblers,
brothel-keepers, sportsmen, policemen, pickpockets, confidence men, and
cadging beggars. In tone and matter the *Town* was habitually indecorous and
often indecent. By sometimes publishing gossip about the personal lives and
appearances of well-known and entirely obscure people, it practised a journalism of personality that early- and mid-Victorian commentators on the
press unfailingly regretted as a miserable remnant of a less dignified past. It
attacked its enemies with the invective of an old-fashioned Grub Street
satirist. It teased or flouted soon-to-be regnant notions of propriety by
running as features prurient accounts of the lives of prostitutes and famous
trials for criminal conversation, jokes and squibs that turned on sexual
double-entendre, and stories that moved by the sexual appetites of women as
well as men. As Nicholson also wrote in the preface to the first volume, in
the pumped-up style which was part of the indecorous clamour of the *Town*:

> The speculative noodles of the newspaper press have, from time to
> time, made our noble selves the subject of animadversion, because
> forsooth, we lack that maudlin sensibility and false delicacy peculiar to
> the cambric-muslin editors of the day. . . . The poisoned arrows of
> our currial foes fall pointless as they strike against our breast-plate of
> mail; and so cowardly are our assailants in heart, that we have but to
> shout, and they scamper before us like so many frightened geese.

The *Town* did survive its critics for five years; for some of these years it may even be said to have flourished in a modest way. More important, there is evidence that the primary audience towards which it was directed was made up not of young and middle-aged gentlemen enjoying or remembering the pleasures of the town, but rather of apprentices, shop assistants, clerks, and other young men of common station who were coming of age in the first Victorian decade of manifest political and social changes and chances to ride them to new social identities. The *Town* is interesting because it tells us something about the London of pleasure and exciting risk in which these readers wanted to participate, and because it allows us to guess at the service such a periodical offered to some at least of these readers who were moving out on the town and wanted to be different from their beginnings. The *Town* is also interesting because it is part of a tradition of journalism that was scandalous to the 'cambric-muslin' sensibilities of the century, and yet persisted, with some important changes, all through the Victorian period. There is no space in this essay adequately to describe the character and development of this tradition. But the *Town* may be used to suggest where its kind of journalism came from, where it went, and why the tradition and practices of scandalous journalism might interest historians of Victorian periodicals and their culture.

1

The features of early nineteenth-century scandalous journalism can be sketched in brief descriptions of three of the *Town's* predecessors: *John Bull*, established in 1820; the *Age*, which began publication in 1825; and the *Satirist* of Barnard Gregory, established in 1831. All were stamped weekly newspapers of eight pages which sold for 7d. – or, after the reduction of the duty in 1836, 6d. All published news as well as the leaders, squibs, gossip, and other features that gave them their identity and notoriety. Their prices meant that all three journals were directed primarily toward middle-class and upper-middle-class readers, and all three took political positions within the conventional structure of party and faction: *John Bull* was arch-Tory, the *Age* conservative, and the *Satirist* was hostile to Chartists and sentimentalists who supported the abolition of slavery on the plantations, but sympathetic to parliamentary reform, the diminution of the secular power and property of bishops, Daniel O'Connell, and liberal Whigs in general. Each paper was informed, in its best years, by the strong personality of its editor and principal writer: Theodore Hook of *John Bull*, Charles Molloy Westmacott of the *Age*, and Barnard Gregory of the *Satirist*. All three papers lived on after the *Town* ended publication, although by the 1840s *John Bull* had long ceased to be a scandalous journal. At least at some point in its run each was probably more successful than Nicholson's paper. *John Bull* in its first year of publication averaged a weekly sale of around 9,000 copies, and it claimed that its average weekly sale in 1825 had risen to 11,560.[1] The *Age* began unsteadily, but after Westmacott took over the editorship in 1828 it rose to a weekly sale of around 9,000–10,000 copies in the mid-1830s (it purchased 566,750 stamps between June 1834 and June 1835) before it declined to about a fifth of that sale near the end of the decade.[2] The *Satirist* was never quite so successful. Its average weekly sale from June 1834 to June 1835 was about 5,000 copies, and it was selling fewer than 4,000 copies weekly in 1840.[3] Even these latter figures were solid enough, however, in a decade in which the *Spectator* was selling between 2,500 and 4,000 copies weekly, respectable journals like the *Atlas* and the *Examiner* between 3,000 and 10,000 copies a week, and the boundaries of exceptional success for a weekly newspaper were marked by the sales of *Bell's Life in London*, which purchased over a million stamps in 1838, and the *Weekly Dispatch*, which bought over two and a half million stamps in the same year.[4]

The most obviously scandalous feature of *John Bull*, the *Age*, and the *Satirist* was their publication of gossip and abusive remarks about the personal lives, characters, and appearances of well-known persons. The writers and editors of these three papers did not invent the journalism of personality, nor were they the only journalists who practised it in the 1820s and 1830s. In 1811 Brougham complained about licentious journals which satisfied malign curiosity by marking out 'for the indulgence of that propensity individuals retiring into the privacy of domestic life, to hunt them down, and drag them forth as a laughing-stock to the vulgar.'[5] The *Palladium* (1825–6), *Paul Pry* (1830–1), the *New Satirist* (1841), and the *Crim-Con Gazette* (1838–40; later the *Bon-Ton Gazette*) – all weekly newspapers, and all but the last stamped – continued the publication of the scurrilous gossip that offended Brougham (who was often its subject) and many others, including those who frequently sued and sometimes physically attacked their editors.[6] But the unusual success of *John Bull* set it up as the model of a journal which made its mark by regularly publishing hints and revelations about the private lives of public men and women, and the long runs of the *Age* and the *Satirist* similarly established them, for imitators and critics, as exemplars of a profitable kind of journalism that lived by scandal.

John Bull was founded by friends of George IV, recently come to the throne, to counter attacks made on him and his Tory ministers by sympathizers with Queen Caroline, and by Whigs and others who used the king's attempts to divorce his wife and deny her the privileges due his queen as an occasion to embarrass or discredit the government. Most of the contents of *John Bull* were the normal matter of a stamped weekly newspaper: a gazette, foreign and imperial intelligence, legal and parliamentary reports, theatre reviews (which were sometimes reviews of the enthusiasm with which the king was greeted when he attended performances), editorials on the parliamentary debate and public controversy concerning the queen, and a lot of advertisements. But the paper immediately became known for the bite of its attacks on the partisans of Caroline. In its first number it began publishing a weekly series of comments on the women who visited the queen. It noted of the wife of Brougham, for example, that 'the advertise-ment of her marriage and that of the birth of her child followed one another much more closely than has been usual in *"well-regulated families"'*. It suggested that the motive of Lady Tankerville's visit to Caroline 'must have been one of sympathy, which the name of Caroline, *mixed up with a disgraceful and criminal affection for a menial servant*, must naturally have awakened in her breast'.[7] It was fond of recalling the prison terms served by Baron Pergami, an intimate of the queen, and others of her '*confined* circle of . . . personal friends'.[8] It frequently remarked the low social origins of some of Caroline's political supporters, such as Peter Moore, once a servant in the Fox family. It pursued Brougham, who had successfully defended Caroline in a parliamentary inquiry into her private life, in a series called 'Broughmania' in which it repeatedly asked presumably unsettling ques-tions: Did you not offer to abandon the queen if the government 'would bestow on you a silk gown or patent of preference?'; did you not in a letter to a friend remark that in your attendance on one of the queen's public appearances, 'I had great difficulty to Bring Her to the Post Sober?'[9] It mocked the intelligence and commercial connections of Joseph Hume; one writer noted that 'I had abstained from comments on your conduct to your mother, the crockery-seller at Montrose', but darkly threatened to publish 'All the Facts which led to your departure from England in 1809'.[10] Hook and his colleagues were ingenious in their grasp of the punitive uses of publicity. In addition to the series on the queen's female visitors, *John Bull* published lists of clergymen who publicly included prayers for the queen in their services. When a jury brought in a verdict of manslaughter against some soldiers who had killed two persons in the riots on the day of Caroline's funeral, *John Bull* published the names, addresses, and trades of the jurors, so that 'their customers may at their discretion reward the activity and talent they have severally displayed in the *attainment of truth and the cause of justice*'.[11]

After the death of Caroline in the summer of 1821, *John Bull* continued to champion the king and the Tory party, and to attack Whigs, radicals, republicans, *The Times* and the *Morning Chronicle*, popery, London Uni-versity, the anti-slavery movement, missionaries, and all other, in its view, levelling or sanctimonious '*humbugs* likely to militate against the interest of the country'.[12] The editorship of Hook was well concealed, both to add mystery to its notoriety and to keep him out of court and out of gaol. As late as 1827 the paper was sued for libel by an Oxford undergraduate whom it had accused of some gross vice. But by that time Hook had retreated from his energetic conduct of the paper – he himself was sentenced to prison in 1823 for financial irregularities during his term as accountant-general and treasurer in Mauritius – although he continued to draw a salary as its editor until his death in 1841. By the mid-1820s *John Bull* was, according to one of Hook's biographers, 'an ordinary Tory newspaper'.[13] That adjective is precise only when it is recognized that the ordinary journalistic manners of the 1820s still tolerated, for example, calling John Cam Hobhouse a son 'of one of that mongrel breed between the noblemen and the gentlemen, the baronets' and 'the shadow of [Sir Francis] Burdett – the zany to the mountebank – the tumbler to the quack'.[14]

The *Age* and the *Satirist* picked up the licence for slander *John Bull* allowed to lapse. When Charles Molloy Westmacott took over the *Age* in 1827, he characterized the previous proprietors as 'men of small powers of wit or satire' who 'mistook the objectionable parts of some of the successful periodicals of the day, for those which obtained those productions their reputation, and accordingly . . . converted the press into an engine of paltry pasquinade against individuals, male and female, who had never obtruded themselves on public life.'[15] Westmacott retained the conservative politics of the paper – 'We are Tory of the Tories, No popery, – No Surrender, are our watchwords'[16] – and all through the 1830s he attacked Whigs, the Roman Catholic claims, utilitarians, the Reform Bill, the anti-Corn Law movement, Chartism, the cockney sentimentality of the annuals, and the usual set of more or less liberal politicians. The *Satirist* worked the other side of the street. It made fun of William and the Lords, attacked Wellington, Peel, and Disraeli, was sympathetic to parliamentary reform and hostile to the Corn Laws, and persistently took up one of the familiar themes of radical journalists, the indifference and material riches of the ecclesiastical hierarchy.

> A Bishop am I, and I live in a stall
> And lackeys in state line my palace hall;
> I've gold in abundance, and paupers I hate,
> And dogs drive all beggars away from my gate.[17]

Gregory and Westmacott, and their staffs and contributors, prosecuted these opinions in leaders, paragraphs of straight political commentary, squibs like that on the bishops, and skits like one in which Brougham examines a black (Sambo Quashbo Hokey Pokey) and a Jew (Moses Ikey Solomon) for prizes at London University.

> Sambo: Me engaged in headwork, Massa. 'Spose two bird on a tree, and Massa fire and kill one, how many left?
> Brougham: One, of course.
> Sambo: No, massa; none left, cos de oder fly away.
> Brougham: His very Maker's image cut in ebony![18]

Like the writers of *John Bull*, Westmacott and Gregory also used gossip and other references to personal lives and identities to attack people who stood on the other side of the principles their papers espoused. The *Age* described the 'elderly smug Cockney, William Hazlitt, *alias* Bill Pimple, *alias* the Great Shabberon' as 'an old weather-beaten, pimple-snouted, gin-smelling man, like a Pimlico tailor, with ink-dyed hands, a corrugated forehead, and a *spiritous nose*'.[19] Signing himself 'a calm observer', one of its correspondents listed 'The pittances of Gaffer Grey', the pensions and sinecures held by the relatives of Earl Grey, and then swung out of his way to note that while Lord-Lieutenant of Ireland, Melbourne 'came a little into notice for an alleged *peccadillo* – a suit being instituted against him for crim.con. by the Reverend Lord Brand'.[20] One of the *Age's* ways to diminish the dignity of politicians was to imagine them eager to hurry from the discussion of great public issues to private pleasures.

> I [Russell] brought the Bylle in Parliament,
>   And after that was donne,
> I used to go to Jermyne Strete
>   To have a bytte of funne. . . .
> Oh, lette them talke about 'Reforme,'
>   Yn whyche I take such pryde,
> I'd rather clasp my Cora's forme,
>   Than alle the world's besyde![21]

The *Satirist* used the same jokes for different people. It said of Feargus O'Connor that his intentions were all very well, but 'We think, on the whole, he was just as well engaged making love to Mrs Nisbett'.[22] It made fun of 'the delicate layers of paint which graced' Palmerston's cheeks[23] and, repeatedly, of Albert's accent and supposed poverty. In a series titled 'Bastardy' it sometimes went back centuries to find an illegitimate ancestor of titled politicians it opposed, and it retailed old gossip about George IV. When one of George's former mistresses was observed in frequent attendance at the young queen's drawing rooms, the *Satirist* remonstrated with mean propriety: 'perhaps it is intended to appoint her one of the ladies of the bed chamber; and certainly she must possess some very curious information in reference to the Royal dormitories. We do not think that the profligacy of the Tories would have winked at such open indelicacy'.[24]

Unlike *John Bull*, however, and despite Westmacott's protestations, the *Age* as well as the *Satirist* also published scandalous gossip about persons who were not in public life or notice. It is almost pointless to reproduce the gossip, for it is now usually unintelligible. It is important to note that, from high to middle station, the vices are the same. 'T. M. should be more explicit as to the amour in which that "honourable" debauchee Twiselden Fiennes has been engaged', the *Satirist* wrote in one of its 'To correspondents' columns; and again: 'Is Miss Baynton aware that Vaughan is a married man? Surely she could not be or she would not expose herself in the way she does'; and yet again: 'If a Reader of the Satirist will furnish us with evidence of the "publication" on the part of the "Gin-and-water Curate residing in the neighbourhood of Dorset-square," we will make the reverend tipler repeat it'.[25] The motive of the publication of gossip like this was not politics but extortion. Gregory and Westmacott built up their papers as reckless messengers of small scandals so that the persons so found out would pay to stay out of their pages, or to be set right in them.

The papers of Barnard Gregory now at the University of illinois show how the game was worked.[26] The *Satirist* office received poems, paragraphs, inquiries, and tips from readers and contributors. 'Pray can you inform me for the good of the public', the writer of one letter (whose address was Lincoln's Inn Fields) wrote, 'how it was that in the affair of a jeweller named *Barnes* and a lady named *Hampton* . . . that Mr Chambers the sitting magistrate seemed to know so much about the *virtuous* lady's reasons for pawning her property?'[27] Some of these letters include a request for the usual payment ($1\frac{1}{2}$d. per line for prose, 2d. per line for poetry); some contributors were only hopeful ('Shd the enclosed suit you, perhaps you will desire to pay me for it with the last – if not, I am not *quite* so unreasonable as to expect it'[28]); some informants seem to have written simply out of spite or a desire for mischief. Someone from the *Satirist* office would then write or, more likely, call on the person maligned. 'The Gentleman who has been threatened with a publication concerning him in the *Satirist*, would feel much obliged if the Editor would appoint a time *today* . . . which he might wait upon him,' one letter reads. 'He is anxious to give information from respectable disinterested parties which he thinks will prove the attempt to be utterly groundless and to arise from the worst motives'.[29] The editor, however, was not likely in these conversations to be interested in or moved by testaments to character. 'As I thought', one of Gregory's colleagues wrote, 'something may be done with Bradshaw, he wd rather pay than be exposed'.[30] Bradshaw, whoever he was, bought silence in what seems to have been a usual means of payment. 'I think however if his name were not mentioned tomorrow, he will next week send a paragraph with the wherewithal to pay for its insertion.' One John Thompson of Brighton, embarrassed by an already published paragraph which claimed that his daughters had frightened a young man by asking him to dance, was apparently invited to use a variation of this device. 'I therefore request', Thompson wrote, in a handsome commercial hand, 'that you will take the earliest opportunity of correcting this unjust censure by acknowledging the error, *in the letter from your Brighton correspondent in the next number*. . . . I beg you will accept the enclosed £5 Bank Note for the trouble I now give you'.[31]

Westmacott certainly practised the same tactics with the *Age*. He had a reputation during and after his lifetime as one who 'levied blackmail without mercy',[32] and its use as a lever of extortion provides the most plausible explanation of the space given to gossip about insignificant persons in both the *Age* and the *Satirist*. Whatever the motives of its authors and readers, the effect of the publication of this gossip was to propose a social reality that was less worthy than it seemed. Its standing implication is that everyone has something to hide, some personal flaw of birth or character, some private vice or folly. Few in public life act from impulses that are entirely honest; hardly anyone, scrutinized in private life, is entirely sound. That indictment extends to the writers and readers of these revelations of the base or merely discomfiting truths about us all. On some conscious level, the pleasure of reading such scandal about the well-known and unknown must have been a guilty one. It was at least naughty to enjoy this traffic in scandalous knowledge, and while they were indulging their guilty pleasure in the imperfections of others, readers were acknowledging themselves to be gladly at home in this imperfect world. Further, it was necessary for their business that Gregory and Westmacott be known to be no better than the rest of those who made their way in the fallen order of things. It must have actually helped them to be damned by their critics as hard and brutal men who dealt with base matter and would inflict pain out of principle, as they would have it, but who were also well known to have their price.

There were two other ways in which Gregory's paper and Westmacott's gave their readers the pleasure of being scandalous. One, more important in the *Age* and the *Satirist* than it was in *John Bull*, was to maintain the tone and substance of the conversation of a gentleman intimate with the fashionable round of London. The recurrent gibes at the common social origins of prominent people was one exercise of this identity. Jokes about these personages, and jokes put in their mouths, was another. A usual feature of the *Age* and the *Satirist* was a column with a title like 'Chit-chat' or 'Facetiae' in which jokes are often started with such phrases as 'When Sam Rogers heard' and 'Her Grace of St Albans was reading an account . . .' Often the jokes that follow turn on the deficiencies or scandalous doings of some other well-known person, and often the jokes are bawdy. The account her Grace of St Albans was reading concerns the breaking of some shop windows by the cartage of long poles through the streets, and the story makes her think indelicate and seemingly well-informed thoughts about the passage of Wellesley Long Pole through these same streets.[33] The man of the fashionable world who is presumed to retail these jokes often passes on the thoughts and conversation of such forthrightly carnal-minded women.

> 'I feel I am neglected,' said a new-married bride to old Lady Cork, 'and whenever I speak of the thing to to my husband—.' 'Speak of the thing:' interrupted the antique dame; 'that is wrong, very wrong, my dear; you should always leave the thing to speak for itself!'[34]

Finally, the *Satirist* especially gave a lot of space to other pastimes of a gentleman in London – gambling, theatres, the raffish life of the debtors' prisons, the 'Noctes Downeyanae' of a young man loose on the town, the gossip of Cambridge, Brighton, Cheltenham, Leamington, and Boulogne for those on holiday or in temporary refuge from it. The effect of these jokes and reports of recreations and sprees is like that of the gossip. Someone who knows how it all really is also knows that much of experience is base and trivial, particularly in ther precincts of the affluent and powerful. The knowing response of writer and reader is amused imperturbability, and the scandalous pleasure of this response is the wicked affectation of not being shocked by what is deliberately calculated to be shocking.

The other way in which these journals were scandalous was in affecting indignant shock at the corruption and witlessness of the world. Claiming 'the liberty of the old satirist', Westmacott wrote in the preface to the collection of writings from the *Age* during the first year of his editorship:

> Was there ever a period at which the vigorous hand of the satirist was more necessary? Was there ever a period, when society from high to low needed castigation so unsparing? . . . Show us a time when swindling and gaming were so unblushingly carried on by persons in high places; when it was no disgrace to be convicted of the greatest frauds at the hazard table or the race-course? Give us a hint as to the period when seduction was so regular a trade, not a matter of passion, but a matter of pounds, shillings, and pence? or point out the period when the spirit of gambling had travelled from the Blackleg of the

West, to the British Merchant of the East; . . . when, in short, our
nobles have become traffickers in dirty lucre, and our traffickers,
swindlers and schemers.[35]

This was the rôle assumed by *John Bull* when the death of Caroline removed
its original reason for being, and Gregory too advertised his paper's 'fearless
exposure of the Black Sheep of the Law, the Mitred Shepherds of the Church,
and the Infernal Demons of the Gambling Table'.[36] For Gregory at least,
there was profit to be turned in this role too. He regularly received fees for
puffing certain gaming-houses, even as he was warning against others in
series titled 'Pandemonium' and 'Gaming hells'.

> I do not wish to know what Messrs Bonds payd you for the leading
> artile [sic] on the Hells in your paper of last Sunday but if you will
> write a Similar one for our establishment for next Sunday we shall
> feel obliged, . . . the pecuniary part of the arrangment I have no
> doubt will be settled to your satisfaction.[37]

But Gregory certainly did not expect to be paid off for his attacks on bishops,
flogging in the military, the excesses of the unstamped press, the abuses of
madhouses, the injustices of imprisonment for debt, and the incompetence or
corruption of specified lawyers and judges. (Perhaps, come to think of it,
there were opportunities for extortion in the last topic, but the *Satirist*'s long
series – it ran all through the 1830s – on 'The black sheep of the Law' often
had real bite.) Westmacott also published exposures of medical quacks and
unsteady stock companies, and after he claimed to break with the Tories
because of their truckling on the Reform Bill of 1832, he took on rich bishops
and the excesses of the aristocracy as well. In the news columns of his paper
Westmacott also paid more attention than did Gregory to sensational news
of murders, earthquakes, fires, shipwrecks, and other crimes and disasters.
That interest is important, for it suggests how the satirist's rôle adopted by
Westmacott and Gregory for their papers connects some of their scandalous
features with the conventional matter of their news.

On the one hand, it must be remembered that the bulk of the space each
week in the *Age* and the *Satirist* was given to advertisements and the kind of
political, social, financial, and other news published in other newspapers. All
the while, in the columns of jokes and gossip, the seriousness of the actors in
these newsworthy events was undercut or mocked; the real news, the editors
implied, the news only we reveal, is how these public personages talk and
what they do in private. And on the other hand, when the writers for these
scandalous journals themselves became serious about the satirist's role, they
argue that the scandal extended from private lives and persons into the

institutions on which the editors soberly reported in other columns. It was not just gin-and-water curates near Dorset Square, or blackleg gamblers in the West, or maybe even Tories and Whigs, who were the scandal. It was the Church and the City, the law and the military, medicine and politics and the system of the prisons and madhouses. The social reality proposed by these journals when their editors and writers step up to the satirist's liberties is more than base or silly. It is dangerous and fundamentally unstable, a close-in version of the world of violent crime, natural disaster, and accident which Westmacott also reported on. This too is scandalous knowledge, and it was probably titillating to take it in along with the gazette of military promotions and clerical preferments, parliamentary and financial intelligence, lists of bankruptcies, and advertisements for patent medicine. But this scandal is potentially unsettling, for it is not an amusing or denigrating addition to the news. It is rather an invitation to a dark reading of the news itself.

2

I do not want to overstate the possibility of this dark reading. I think that the possibility was there, in the journals; I do not think that my twentieth-century alertness to patterns of decay and collapse has imposed a reading on them. One of the reasons that the *Age* and the *Satirist* are interesting is that from time to time Gregory and Westmacott offered readers with a taste for scandal a perception of systemic corruption, moving from high to low, from the outlaw to the respectable, that was much like those lessons a quite different set of readers was learning in Carlyle's more expensive and re-putable essays, and yet other readers in the much less reputable penny numbers of G. W. M. Reynolds' *The Mysteries of London*. But Gregory and Westmacott were too easily deflected, or bought off, from their high satiric purposes to make their occasional realization the defining mark of their newpapers. Their journals were known and read primarily for the local thrills of their scandalous gossip and jokes, and for their general air of knowing what was happening in the great world at night and behind closed doors. 'Ask Newman tomorrow how many papers will be taken if this is inserted,' Gregory wrote on a manuscript recounting a story of an impatient women who took off most of her clothes while waiting for a clergyman to arrive to perform her wedding ceremony.[38] For Gregory, as for Westmacott, a scandalous newspaper was primarily an instrument for making money, and they did not mistake how their money was made.

The *Town* followed in this tradition, diminishing even farther the earnest and penetrating offices of satire and enlarging some of the features that had come to be expected of a scandalous journal. It too was a weekly journal of eight pages, the size, one of its advertisements noted, of the *Satirist*.

Except for a brief time near the end of its run, it was unstamped. It is, therefore, impossible to specify its sales from the records of stamp returns. In the second year of the journal Nicholson claimed its weekly sale in London was 'treble that of any stamped paper'.[39] That claim is plausible, if he had in mind only his rivals the *Age* and the *Satirist*, then buying around 2,500 or 3,000 stamps a week.[40] It seems possible that in its prime the *Town* sold 8,000 to 10,000 copies a week. It was at least successful enough to be imitated by the *Crim-Con Gazette* and for its version of scandalous journalism to be revived, in a debased form, in half a dozen journals at mid-century. The fact that it was unstamped, in any event, is central to the *Town*, and from it proceed the two most significant differences between Nicholson's journal and the *Age* and the *Satirist*.

First, because it sold at 2d., the *Town* could expect to recruit readers among the clerical and artisan classes of the city for whom a stamped newspaper at 6d. was too expensive. Certainly Nicholson seems to have tried for these readers. He published a series describing drapers' establishments, warehouses, and other big commercial firms which were nothing but remarks about the habits and dress of their proprietors and head clerks, the sort of in-house raillery that makes up the conversation, and keeps up the spirits, of the junior staff in any large organization. He published editorials remonstrating against the long hours and other hard working conditions of shop assistants, the deprivation of employment to English women by the hiring of foreigners as milliners and dressmakers, and attempts to crimp the pleasures of the poor through Sunday closing laws and other harassments. In this last cause, the writer of one editorial proclaimed. 'We are proud to be considered the organ of the working, or, as they are sometimes called, the lower classes'.[41] When the *Town* published gossip, its subjects were often persons of these classes, or the strata immediately above them:

> It is a fact that Joe Millward, the grocer's porter of Queen's-row, Pimlico, is an amorous description of individual . . .
> It is a fact that Nicholls, the Bromley omnibus-conductor, is perpetually railing against his mistress.
> It is a fact that a certain gentlemanly lawyer's clerk, residing not a hundred miles from Stockbridge, is very frequently engaged in pleading, at a certain bar in that town, in the cause of Cupid *versus* the landlady's friend.
> It is a fact that Dick Rider, the butcher of Bond-street, has a vast idea of his own powers of lady-killing politeness.[42]

This column of 'Facts and rumours', one of several titles Nicholson gave to columns of gossip, goes on to retail remarks about a tailor, the ballet-master at Covent Garden, a shopkeeper, a former dealer in marine stores who is giving himself airs, a penny baker, a piano teacher being pursued by a 'lecherous toad' in the Admiralty, a prize fighter, and an ex-carpenter who tires of matrimony because his new wife makes him dress every evening in 'a fustian jacket and ditto unmentionables'.

The second important difference between the *Town* and its rivals is that because it was unstamped for most of its career, it could not publish the political, legal, police, and other news that made up most of *John Bull* and much of the *Age* and the *Satirist*. Nor did Nicholson usually publish the commentary on current political events that was common in the unstamped radical press. Even when in 1841 he experimented for a time with a stamped edition at 4d., he did so mostly because he wanted to publish accounts of recent boxing matches, and after a few issues he announced that he was accommodating the requests of many readers and publishing both a stamped and unstamped edition of each number. Clearly, many readers of the *Town* did not come to it as Whigs or Tories or radicals, did not expect their opinions about the Church or the Law, Ireland or the Corn Laws, to be systematically exercised or confirmed in its columns. If they held one or more of the current opinions on these and other matters, they differed from the readers of *John Bull*, the *Age*, and the *Satirist* in pretty much leaving them behind to enjoy the version of the town and their time that Nicholson gave them. The *Town* is interesting, then, for the reasons that the other scandalous journals are interesting, and also because in it Nicholson worked the conventions of scandalous journalism for another set of readers, readers who came to it from an experience and perceptions of social reality and change that were different from those of the gentlemen of conventional political allegiance and secure station whom Westmacott and Gregory at least affected to address.

Specifically, Nicholson published less gossip than his two principal rivals, more fiction, much more about the night-time entertainments of the town, a great deal about the petty frauds of gamblers, quacks, stock promoters, and advertising, and a steady budget of jokes, features, and stories that swing through the prurient toward the pornographic and make his journal yet more determinedly bawdy than the *Age* or the *Satirist*. The gossip columns of the *Town* appeared intermittently and mostly concerned persons like Joe Millward and Nicholls the omnibus conductor. Gossip about better-known people occasionally appeared: 'Lord Chesterfield . . . rode a favourite pleasure mare, at Doncaster, called Laura Honey [an actress]. His beautiful filly . . . has cut him in consequence. . . . Oh, my lord, if your grandfather were alive, what would he say to your want of taste and discretion, to say nothing of your immorality'.[43] Names like Chesterfield's – Bulwer, Sir Peter Laurie,

Madame Vestris, Brougham, Albert – more often appeared in jokes, usually playing with the sexual *double entendre* that is the point of the gossip about Chesterfield. Lord Alvanley is quoted in explanation of Harriet Martineau's habit of wearing mismatched stockings: 'Why, because she does not like the *fellows* about her legs'.[44] Victoria is reported to have bribed a beautiful dancer to leave the country because Albert was winking at her.

> 'Is not one thing at a time enough for you, you dirty German prig,' said Victoria, in a rage. 'By gar, if I may not hab one ting, you shall not hab de oder,' responded the Prince; and so saying, his sulky Highness locked his German self and his German sausage in the *cabinet* all night.[45]

When Nicholson and Gregory began attacking one another in their journals in the late 1830s, Nicholson unloaded all the scandal he could think of. He called Gregory a 'common extortioner, gaming-house keeper, pimp and brothel spongee', and referred to Mother Parlby, who kept the brothel in which Gregory reportedly sponged, as 'the antiquated cyprian of whom you make use in *every way*'.[46] In a late dispute with the very successful *Weekly Dispatch*, Nicholson accused its proprietor, James Harmer, of holding financial interests in stock companies he puffed in his paper, and he attacked one of Harmer's writers, a man named Williams, in editorials and letters (including one from Mrs Williams) which claimed that he pandered his wife, customarily beat her, and executed cats on a small gallows of his own devising.[47] The motive of this vituperation was probably publicity all around. Nicholson would not have scrupled to trade in gossip as Gregory did, and he occasionally had to defend himself in the *Town* against accusations that someone claiming to represent it had tried to extort money by threatening to publish something defamatory or embarrassing. But Nicholson did not publish enough gossip about either ordinary or well-known people to make it play a large part in the economy or reputation of his journal.

He did publish a great deal of bawdy material. Like many of those in the *Age* and the *Satirist*, the jokes and some of the gossip in the *Town* often proposed a world in which everyone, from grocery porters to the royal couple, was mostly engaged in thinking about sex. Without the ballast of news and the cover of political partisanship, the *Town* itself often seems preoccupied in the same way. Its back page, especially in its last couple of volumes, was mostly made up of advertisements for the publications of H. Smith of Holywell Street, whose list included *Venus's Album, or, Rosebuds of Love, Wilson's Rum Codger*, a collection 'of the best double-entendre, flash, and comic songs', the memoirs of Harriet Wilson, the works of Paul de Kock, *Onanism Unveiled*, and *Marriage Physiologically Discus-*

sed. (Smith also advertised Lewis's *The Monk*, which had long been in trouble with the Society for the Suppression of Vice, and George Sand's *Indiana*.) Some of the *Town's* features could have gone on Smith's list. It published reports of famous trials for criminal conversation, including the inquiry into the conduct of Caroline, and extensive series of 'Sketches of courtezans', 'Brothels and brothel keepers', and 'Female sinners, aged and middle-aged'. These were rarely particularized descriptions of brothels, although Nicholson did give addresses, but were rather teasing accounts of initial seductions and subsequent liaisons, sometimes carrying a moral. 'Further detail upon this matter would be indelicate and superfluous,' the writer of a sketch of the prostitute Louisa Turner remarks, and he then moves his subject quickly to Paris, where 'jewels, carriages, and wealth are now her foot-balls . . . at the expense of that inestimable gem – *virtue*'.[48] Some of the fiction in the *Town* trembles with the usual heavy breathing of Victorian pornography.

> Close, still closer are they on that lovely bank; rich, still richer grows the colour on her cheek, and brighter, still brighter is the fire of her blue eyes – that kiss, *hissing* with the burning emotion that prompted it – that start! . . . a struggle – of pleasure or of pain – and all was quiet as the still night scene around them.[49]

Often the *Town* was simply coarse in its unrelenting play on words and phrases like 'work', 'thing', 'getting up the linen', 'working under the butler', and Albert's German sausage again (and again). Once in a while even Nicholson had second thoughts. In its first volume the *Town* published a wood engraving of an aged buck trying to kiss a chambermaid. She is holding a bedwarming pan whose handle protrudes from between his legs. 'The engraving . . . might have been construed, by persons whose ideas are anything but fastidious, into something improper,' the writer of an editorial in the next issue admitted; 'we can only say, however, that we did not study to make a *handle* for our enemies, and that, had we been prepared with another subject, probably that complained of . . . would not have been adopted'.[50]

But the tone of the *Town's* play with sexuality, although always studiedly scandalous by contemporary notions of propriety, was often more healthy than that of these tedious puns and coy suggestiveness. There was self-interest, certainly, but also good sense in the argument of one of its editorials that 'the best way to allay curiosity is by showing what it is of no consequence to conceal' and 'to do as the Spartans did of old – promote a knowledge of each other's formation, so as to render the sight as little mysterious as possible'.[51] Its provocative argument against 'The suppression of open brothels; they are as essential to the well-being of society as parish-churches'[52] was also based on its assumption that sexuality was natural, and only made vicious by convention. Sometimes an account of a famous courtesan or madame ended not in sly moral warnings but in a tribute to the sensible good temper with which she had settled into a prosperous middle age, a business success like any other. As in the *Age* and the *Satirist*, women are often as frank in their discussion and enjoyment of sex as men. One of its running jokes was about male sexual incompetence, and here women are not frail objects of seduction but very cool judges of performance. In an account of 'A grand meeting of the socialists,' for example, whom the *Town* affected to believe were interested only in un-limited sexual freedom, George Wombwell is reported to say:

> that he would carry out the principles of socialism to the fullest extent, *if he were able*. This last observation caused a general titter amongst the ladies, whisperings passed round, and we caught unconnected, sentences, 'No use' – 'Got nothing' –'Bores you to death' – 'Quite gone by' – 'About an inch' – 'Requires the rod'.[53]

This relatively robust attitude toward sexuality is also common in the most prominent fiction published in the *Town*, which were not stories of seduction but sketches of the character of the 'Cockney tales' and 'Cockney adventures', also published in 1d. weekly parts, in monthly compilations at 6d., and in a bound volume under Nicholson's name. These stories used standard farce situations (mistaken bedrooms, the country outings of city lads) and are full of the physical humour of chases, fist fights, people falling into rivers and farm ponds, tumbling in and out of and under beds, and being caught outdoors without their clothes. Sex is also physical, and fun, even in its comic embarrassments. One story begins as a middle-aged merchant's clerk starts his day by jumping back into bed with his wife after contemplat-ing her mature rotundities, moves through a drunken birthday party for a child who throws it into an uproar by announcing his discovery that the maid 'has got no dilly', and ends with the same maid's discovery the next morning of a left-over guest 'with his dress in so dishevelled a state as to leave not the slightest doubt as to his possessing the adjunct her reputed deficiency in which had caused so much confusion on the previous evening'.[54] She and the guest exploit her discovery; she gets pregnant and loses her place. But the story slides quickly past the lesson she may have learned ('We say nothing'); its point is only the raucousness of the holiday. In another story a servant and an apprentice watchmaker are secretly married and interrupted during their clandestine wedding night in the servant's bedroom by a drunken guest of a lodger in the house. Hearing her voice, the guest sings:

Fairest lady, I have come,
Through gloomy night as you suggested,
No breeks I wear upon my bum,
I'm in my shirt as you requested.

The guest is scared off by the stalwart bridegroom, agrees not to reveal their secret, and, 'being anxious to turn everything to account', converts 'his night's adventure into a recitation' for the tavern entertainments of which he is a regular patron.[55]

The *Town*'s extensive descriptions of the entertainments of the town were similarly tolerant of pleasures which were not discussed in polite company even when they were licit. In its first number it inaugurated a series of 'Characteristic sketches'; with one of the 'Man about town', a gentleman 'of no mean estate' 38 years old, single, formerly an army officer (and thus entitled to his moustaches), not by any means:

> *the monkey who had seen the world*, but the independent man of observation and intelligence. He is not the stiff-starched, pedantic observer of men and manners, who peeps into the diversions of mankind but to censure them. Our 'Man about Town' mixes with society solely with a view to its enjoyment, and remarks upon the customs of its various grades, that he may enlighten and instruct that portion of the community who are less scrutinous, or have not the time or means to make observations.[56]

Some of the London life scrutinized by the *Town* is the usual stuff of early-Victorian journalistic sketches like those of Dickens in *Sketches by Boz*: anatomies of London lodgings, outings on Thames steamers, 'Characteristic sketches' (the series ran until the very end of the journal) of London types, from clergymen and City bankers to street-sellers, billiard sharps, milliners, and Barnard Gregory himself. Most of what the *Town* attends to, however, are the entertainments and excitements that would engage a single man of means who, 38 in 1837, came on the town in the years of Egan's Tom and Jerry.

So in every issue of the *Town* a page or so is given to columns titled 'Licensed victuallers, their manners and their parlours', 'Cigar shops and pretty women', 'Free and easies', and 'The harmonic telescope', the latter two series describing taverns and night houses that offered amateur or professional singing. The *Town*'s writers are often pleased by the gentlemanly geniality of the places they visit, for Nicholson admits in his autobiography that he took payment from their proprietors to write them up in the journal.[57] Nicholson also **promoted** and epitomized in the paper the performances of the Judge and Jury Society, a series of mock trials he produced and presided over at the Garrick's Head Tavern and Town Hotel beginning in 1841, and he was quite solicitous of the fortunes of the Hippodrome, a race ground in Kensington in which he may also have had an interest. The *Town's* attention to theatre was consistent but perfunctory, and its interest in sports was sporadic, perhaps because Nicholson realized that it was difficult to be distinctive in the treatment of topics well covered in other newspapers and journals. He chose instead to make the *Town*, nearly 2,000 pages of tightly-printed, minimally illustrated copy by its close, into something of an enormous guide through a loose and well-populated network of places to drink, eat, smoke, sing, gamble, flirt with pretty women, and meet women of the town, from Crockford's, an aristocratic gaming house, to the White Conduit Gardens, a resort much favoured by the class of clerks and artisans who appear in the stories and gossip of the journal.

Another part of the excitment of the town for the readers of the *Town* was the evidence that it was dangerous. In his attention to the risks of being on the town in London Nicholson brought his journal close to the satiric prospect occasionally attained by Gregory and Westmacott of a society contaminated in every precinct. The dangers of the town, in Nicholson's journal, are rarely physical. It did not publish police news, except during its brief turn as a stamped newspaper. In its place it published such series as 'The swell mob' and 'Flats and sharps', accounts of burglars, pickpockets, confidence men, blackleg gamblers, and proprietors of mock-auctions, shell games, and other schemes in which victims were robbed without violence. Its series on Bow Street officers and London reporters often became stories of crimes and scandals recalled by shrewd men who relish the shifts and risks of the town. The sketches of courtesans and the 'Mothers' who kept brothels were also essentially stories of industrious careers outside conventional morality. All these accounts were filled with warnings to the innocent and unwary. But, as in the *Age* and the *Satirist*, the warnings were part of the pleasurable awareness of readers who were thus reminded that they had strayed beyond the respectable and safe.

Nicholson gave equally as much space to the more or less legal dodges of medical quacks, sellers of patent medicines (who advertised heavily in the journal), promoters of stock and insurance companies and loan societies, and the proprietors of dishonest employment agencies. The victims of these schemes were likely to be from among the readers of the journal, people of small means trying to lift themselves up and put something by, and it was easy, and maybe even efficacious, for the *Town* to take an earnest moral line against scoundrels who made promises they would not keep. But in the many extremely interesting columns on 'Puffery' and 'The puffing system'

Nicholson and his writers regarded the early users of advertising with a mixture of admiration and amused protest at their effrontery. They record the invention of merchants who paint their shopfronts in startling colours, construct large models of their merchandise to parade the streets, connect themselves with such popular events as the heroic deed of Grace Darling, and hire men to go around asking for their products from shopkeepers who have not yet troubled to put it in stock. The writers of the *Town* were especially fascinated by the language of advertising. In his autobiography Nicholson wrote that it was 'by the original and quaint advertisements that the popularity of the Garrick's Head was obtained' while he was managing it in the 1840s.[58] His circus poster style is still compelling. One wall poster in the London collection at the Lilly Library begins:

> Mr. Nicholson, F. A. S., D. G. F., And all that sort of thing, having felicitously accumulated renown as the Architect of his own Temple in Bow Street, a spot more Attic than the Vatican, and more renowned than the Parthenon, takes leave to treat the memories of Michael Angelo, Sir Christopher Wren, Inigo Jones, Sir John Sloane, and Mr. Wilkins with ineffable contempt, such geniuses, in comparison with Mr. Nicholson, being only Bricklayers and Plasterers. The exertion of Mr. N. are [sic] for the existing QUICK, the extant million. He submits the following programmes of Amusements to his selectest friends, the Public: 'FORTUNA AUDACES JUVAT.'

The poster then breaks into verse – 'Here you'll own in regions upper / You can get an Attic supper; / Ending, when you thence come down, / With "Bed and Breakfast, half a crown"' – lists the performances of the Judge and Jury Society and various singing ensembles for the week, and ends patriotically: 'Vivant Regina et Princeps et Kids'.[59] No one who can write like that could fail to be at once superior to and respectful of the gaudy talents apparent in the mock-sublimities of the sales catalogues of the auctioneer George Robins and verse testimonials to Warren's Blacking. The *Town* is often simply disarmed by such extravagances, taken in, for all its shrewdness, by its very awareness of the breathtaking, self-amused reach of their fraudulence.

This response to advertising is as revealing as, in another way, is the *Age's* attraction to violent crime and disaster. For the *Town* cannot draw a clear line between, say, the billiard sharps and fraudulent proprietors of mock-auctions, on the one hand, and the promotions of respectable merchants on the other, when it is so amused by the latter. The *Town* did claim the traditional rôle of the satirist. 'The galling pen of satire silences the low braggart, and regulates the manners and action of the patrician scoffer,'

Nicholson wrote in the first number, and in the preface to the fourth volume a contributor praised the *Town*'s penetration 'through the cloud and film / Thrown o'er the slippery tricks of men' as

> That light which guides incautious youth
> Far from the path of death and sin,
> And thus preserves it from the tooth
> That gnaws the guilty heart within.[60]

But when in its last volumes Nicholson several times summed up the good work done under the satiric licence of his journal, he had little to show: a few exposures of doubtful stock companies (for one of which the *Town* was successfully sued for libel), the attacks on Gregory and the *Dispatch*, a long, sometimes prurient campaign against juvenile prostitution as the protected preserve of depraved aristrocrats, some self-interested mockery of Sabbatarianism and teetotalism, and some remonstrances against penny gambling hells and gin shops, which also might hurt the business of the well-established proprietors who were Nicholson's advertisers and clients. Characteristically, the *Town* was as engaged by the frivolity and frauds it reported as it was by the ingenuity of advertisers. Its attitude fundamentally was that of the 'man about town', who scrutinizes not to censure but to enjoy a chancy, sportive world of sexual pleasure and sexual misadventure, both pathetic and comic, the delights of singing and drinking and telling dirty jokes, and the attractive dangers of sharp practice, fraud, puffery, and certain kinds of non-violent crime.

The *Town*, then, is scandalous not because, as its predecessors did in their different degrees, it looked for personal points of attack on people and events reported in other newspapers. It is scandalous mostly because it set itself up as a weekly record of ways of taking pleasure and doing business that went on in the shadows of the steadily more decorous conduct of things, and ideas about the right conduct of things, in England in the first years of Victoria's reign. The *Town* thus specifies our knowledge of the diversity of early Victorian experience, especially of those districts of it that are not criminal or sexually perverse or pushed by poverty and degradation below the immediate reality of its readers, but which were accessible to young men who presumably married and kept their jobs and perhaps rose in them to become respectable mid-Victorians. The *Town* is in fact exactly like a district in London where only the dangerous and the shrewd, like Nicholson and his fellow entrepreneurs of pleasure, really live. The others come to disport themselves and to take some not radically damaging risks. As a guide to the places and customs of this district, and as a register of a coherent and consciously unconventional attitude toward the frivolity, guile, greed, and other failings and natural pleasures of the flesh endemic in it, the *Town* is a useful document of early Victorian social history.

I am also interested in using the *Town* to make some guesses about how it and other scandalous journals served their readers. Its pose as a gentleman 'of no mean estate' is like that of the *Age* and the *Satirist*, and it is easy to see how the pose flattered the young men who could afford the *Town* and most of the entertainments it described. For 2d. and the price of a cigar in a divan and a round or two in a free and easy they could fancy themselves on the circuit of men who knew about high-priced prostitutes and had been inside Crockford's. What is complicated about the *Town* is that it also encourages these young men to take a gentleman's condescending attitude toward their own callow, upstart selves.

Although they are diffuse, the *Town* does have politics, and they are unexpectedly conservative. In its political dictionary, Tory is defined as 'The best of the "three denominations",' and a radical is 'A candidate for toryism, when fortune smiles on him'.[61] Despite its sympathy with overworked shop assistants and its antipathy toward middle-class reformers of the amusements of the lower orders, the *Town* consistently made fun of working-class and radical political organizations. For its representative man of the north of London in an early 'Characteristic sketch', it chose a popular orator of 'the ultra-radical borough of Marylebone', and the worst it could think to say about him was that he used to be a bonnet-maker.[62] It repeatedly pointed out that Thomas Wakley, the medical reformer and an M.P. for Finsbury, was a farmer's son, calling him 'Mr Cabbage Stump Wakky' and 'Artichoke Wakkey Walker'; for a while it ran a series in cockney dialect on a mock-parliament of Artichokians, 'The cabbage-stumps, the pismeres, the dandelions . . . of the great city of the cathedral, Minster-West'.[63] It described the constituents of another liberal M.P. as the 'unwashed artizans, coal-shed keepers, and potatoe-dealers of the borough of Lambeth', mixed in with a soap-boiler, 'a wide-awake watch and clock manufacturer', a plumber, and Isambard Kingdom Brunel.[64] When it visited the 'factious and brawling radicalism' of Cogers Hall, it attributed its vulgar democracy to 'the mania of our young shopkeepers and drapers' apprentices' of a class who before the French Revolution satisfied their foolish ambitions to play to an audience by trying a fling at the stage.[65]

Such political references diminish after the first year or so of the *Town*. But the journal continued to mock the pretensions of men of humble occupations who organize assemblies of the Woollen Drapers' Society, 'The Enigmatical, Poetical, Corresponding Society of St Leonard's, Shoreditch', and a literary society in Southwark with 'an imposing list of vice-presidents; at the head of which figures a name well known to Cockney excursioners, the son and heir of the celebrated ham-and-beef vendor, an affected philosopher who lectures on phrenology'.[66] When its correspondents want to review a place of entertainment unfavourably, they often note that it is patronized by 'linen drapers and tailors, shopmen, parish apprentices, milliners' or 'lads, sporting lavender-coloured kids and tall black sticks'.[67] The plots of the 'Cockney tales' commonly ridicule the manners and humiliate the affectations of the young working men and clerks who are their central characters. A journeyman fancy-harness maker starts his holiday dressed in 'a pair of very short white trowsers, dropsical Wellington boots, a yellow waistcoat, blue coat, and shining tall silk hat'.[68] Before the day is over he has stepped in cow dung, had his hat knocked off by urchins, is ducked in an ornamental fountain at the White Conduit Gardens, and loses his girl to a strong young man who is the leader of the ducking party and who finishes off the hero by knocking his hat down to his shoulders so that he looks like an *extinguished rushlight* (emphasis the *Town*'s). A muffin baker from Clerkenwell goes on a country outing with his friend, a compositor 'of very superior attainments; he could sing, imitate the bugle with his mouth, and write poetry'.[69] He is tricked by country sharpers, has his clothes stolen, is ducked in a ditch, shot 'in that part of the person usually known as the seat of honour', and eventually is arrested by the new police for loitering while making up to a servant girl. Even the steady lad who scares off the lawyer's clerk on his wedding night begins the day by taking the small wedding party to the suburbs, 'like other fashionables', where 'to display their gentility and taste' they breakfast off muffins and purl and then play games of leapfrog and hunt the slipper.[70]

The arch style of the *Town*, as knowing in specifying vulgarities of manners, dress, and occupation as in detailing the ways of pleasure and fraud, also sets the journal above the realms of experience in which it found some of its readers and to which it takes all of them.

> The sofa of David Picard, had it been capable of giving evidence, no doubt could enlighten the world as to the fitful fancies of modern voluptuaries. The high and mighty One, in His wisdom, however, has ordained that sofas should not speak, and, for the sake of morality, we are glad of it. But this is an aposiopesis.[71]

Not many readers would have understood the last line. But the purpose it completes is clear enough. They are in the company of a man who knows the secrets of voluptuaries and the uses of a sofa, but who cannot be entirely defined by this knowledge because he writes as one who knows and is so much else besides. The *Town*'s frequent use of the flash slang of the town has the same effect. After watching the lads in their lavender kid gloves casting 'long glances on the symmetrical proportions of the pretty Mrs. H.' in a cigar ship, 'we, having finished our havannah, in the plenitude of our virtuous forebearance, cut our stick'.[72] 'We' share the lads' desire, can slang with them, but clearly are not them; for 'we' can also speak like an eighteenth-century essayist and, it is intimated, could if we wished do something about our desire. The mock-heroic elevations of the prose of the *Town*, another of the conventions it inherited from Pierce Egan and his imitators, also can put it at an amused distance from its stock-in-trade. The *Town's* review of *The Swell's Night Guide*, which was directed towards its own audience, praised its illustrations for showing:

> a fidelity, a raciness, and a *goût* delicious, not only to the optics of a swell, but to those of any other style of man who has the genius to comprehend the witcheries of the magic crayon. . . . the women! ah, the women! they are gloriously executed, dished up most exquisitely; the rounded limb, the swelling bosom, the languishing eye are given with all the intense, glowing rapture of life, the true, substantial, essential, palpable, real life, not of London only, but the universe.[73]

When during their feud Gregory offered as a parliamentary candidate for Beverly after serving three months in prison for extortion, Nicholson ran an editorial as an advertisement in his own paper. He rehearsed Gregory's career: son of a woman who kept a greengrocer's shop, brother of an informer, himself an errand boy, knife cleaner, bank clerk, promoter of a bank with an auctioneer and a brewer (Puff, Froth, and Nothing), a swindler, bankrupt, 'quackdoctor, fortune teller, methodist preacher, and schoolmaster'. If such a man runs, Nicholson warned, his reputable opponent may retire in disgust from the contest. 'In that case, gentlemen,' writes Nicholson, who during some of the preceding year had signed his editorials from Queen's Bench prison, 'you will find me in the field as your redeemer'.[74]

The quality that informs this style and rôle, and the value that is fundamental to the appeal and office of the *Town* and its rivals, is that of *knowing*. The heroes and heroines of the town are Bow Street officers and reporters, successful gamblers, courtesans, and publicans, audacious advertisers, and shrewdly ironic self-promoters. These worthies are not to be taken in, not by the tricks and risks of the town, not even by their own exuberant turns in it. In the *Town* the apprentices, shopmen, and clerks who seem to have been a significant part of its audience learned this style as they learned where to go to use it. Young men on their own and maybe on the rise in London, starting out on a pound or so a week and a normal budget of appetite, curiosity, ignorance, and ambition, they were ready to learn how to *be* when they put on the clothes and attitudes that took them out of their common jobs and unremarkable lodgings for the night. The *Town* served their need. It brought the lads in their lavender gloves to the cigar divan to look on the pretty Mrs H. Then it took them behind the eyes of the man about town so that they also learned how not to behave and dress, how to feel superior to those like them who had just awkwardly entered on the town. Writers for the *Town* often emphasize how, for better or for worse, the people they write about are different from their beginnings: women seduced from respectability, working-class girls elevated to courtesans with jewels as their foot-balls, a radical orator who had put bonnet-making behind him, ordinary shopkeepers who advertised connections with the queen, the editor (and maybe two of them) of a scandalous journal running for Parliament.[75] It must have been exciting for a young man to participate, just by reading the *Town*, in this hustle of people trying to be new, rising and falling and scrambling in a world full of bubble and real possibility. And it must have been reassuring for him to feel, while reading the *Town*, that even if he had not really risen from his economic and social station, he was still somehow new, different from the others not only in his worldly knowledge of scandalous things to do after work, but also in his knowing condescension toward what he was trying hard no longer to be. If I imagine these scandalous journals as persons, as their editors liked to imagine them, the *Age* and the *Satirist* are gentlemen of diverse experience talking to their more conventional peers of the famous and favoured in the great world, and saying: 'They are really just like us, and some are worse.' The *Town* is that same gentleman, talking now to anxiously inexperienced social inferiors, and saying: 'You are just like me.'

By the mid 1840s scandalous journalism as Westmacott, Gregory, and Nicholson practised it was just about finished. *John Bull* had for nearly two decades been a standard weekly newspaper popular with the conservative clergy of the Church of England. Westmacott gave up the *Age* in 1843, conducted another paper for a while, then merged it with his former paper into the *Age and Argus* before letting it go again. The new proprietor made it into a conventional Tory newspaper renamed the *English Gentleman* because 'with all the care and expense that may be bestowed upon a journal which at any previous period may have borne an unfortunate reputation, it is almost impossible to earn for it . . . a perfectly good character'.[76] Nicholson, busy with the Garrick's Head and other enterprises, closed down the *Town* in 1842 after apologizing with characteristic spirit for an editorial 'neglect unparalleled in the history of periodical literature, and unmatched in the records of designed inattention'.[77] The *Satirist* ran until 1849. The author of the entry for Gregory in the *Dictionary of National Biography* wrote that the paper was suppressed, although I know of no agency with that authority in the 1840s. Alexander Andrews in his mid-century history of British journalism wrote that Gregory's paper was finally broken by the costs of libel suits against it.[78] In any event, Gregory had in 1847 married a woman with money, and he went into comfortable retirement.

The reasons advanced for the closing of the *Satirist* summarize the probable mixture of reasons for the subsidence of its way of scandalous journalism. Financially, these scandalous journals were a profitable but unsteady property. It was part of the piratical reputations of Gregory and Westmacott that in the 1830s they were rumored to make £5,000 or £6,000 a year from the profits of their papers and from extortion.[79] But the Gregory Papers at the University of Illinois contain many letters written in the 1830s dunning Gregory for payment of school fees for his children and costs connected with the newspaper, and the papers also contain some letters from persons whom Gregory was in turn pressing for payment for advertisements. Nicholson, who was literally starving when he found a publisher and printer for the *Town*, agreed to write 12 columns a week for £3, in addition to 'perquisites which speedily developed themselves,'[80] including fees for puffing places of entertainment and a weekly guinea paid to him by a hapless gentleman for advice and mediation in a difficult love affair. Nicholson too was always in financial trouble, and he went to prison for debt at least once during the run of the *Town* (and several times before and after) because he could not pay £250 damages won by the plaintiff in a libel suit against him. In its beginning each of these journals was published by someone other than its editor, and each editor at some point became his own publisher. That meant fewer shares in the profits. But it also meant that the editors were responsible for the expenses of the journal, including the considerable costs of defending libel actions and paying damages when they were successful. The ownership in the 1830s and 1840s of a weekly journal selling 4,000–5,000 copies or more a week and carrying at least a page of advertising probably provided a good income. But Gregory and Nicholson at least were not prudent men, and they were in a business almost as risky as any of the doubtful speculations they examined in their journals. When sales began to drop in the 1840s, their journals must quickly have become only marginally profitable.

Sales began to drop because the manners of mainstream journalism, and of the social classes it addressed, really were changing. The journalist James Grant, writing in 1837, found the *Satirist* 'full of personalities, but there is generally something so amusing, blended with good-nature in the manner in which its paragraphs are written, that even those parties at whose excesses the laugh is raised, can hardly be angry with it.'[81] But in 1843, in a generous-minded survey of Hook's life and works, J. G. Lockhart wrote in the *Quarterly Review*: 'There is little to be said in defence of the early virulence of "John Bull" . . . The trade of defamation has sunk, for many years past, into hands fit for nothing better; and when any man of mark permits himself to be betrayed into a momentary outburst of "sweltering venom" against a political rival or antagonist, he is regarded by friends with regret, and by foes as well as friends with compassion.'[82] Arguing for the elimination of the newspaper stamp to a parliamentary committee, Michael James Whitty said: 'It is a very curious illustration of the appetite of the people for what is good and correct, that the whole of London could not support even one "Satirist"; it is dead'.[83] Andrews at mid-century stated what was by then the standard, self-congratulatory opinion: the style of newspapers in the 1830s, he wrote, 'although vastly improved upon that of former times, would startle those who are accustomed to the more subdued tone and calmer language of modern newspaper controversy'.[84] By 1872, Grant had come around. Of the *Age* and the *Satirist* he wrote in his history of British journalism: 'The extinction of these journals was a positive blessing to the better classes of society,' and he continued: 'There is a tone in our weekly journalism of the present day of a much higher kind than that which characterized the London weekly newspaper of forty years ago. There were then a coarseness and virulence . . . which are happily unknown, except in cases which occur but seldom in our day.'[85]

As Grant admits, there were exceptions – 'recrudescences', in a word sometimes used to regret them – to this rule of decorum. In the late 1840s and early 1850s a knot of 1d. and 2d. imitations of the *Town* appeared: *Sam Sly, or, The Town* (1848–9), *Paul Pry* (1848–50), *Fast Life, Cheap John, Peeping Tom* (the last three journals are undated, but obviously of the same years as the others), the *Fast Man* (1850), and the *Town* revived (1849–50). The second *Town* was a four-page 1d. weekly that went right after the most interesting part of Nicholson's audience; it ran a 'Notice to the trade' that it sold to newsagents for a 1d. per dozen cheaper than the *London Journal* and *Family Herald*, popular working-class weeklies. It used the masthead of Nicholson's journal, claimed in its introductory editorial that it was continuing the good work of its namesake in revealing the vices of sexuality and dishonest trade, and was edited at first by H. G. Brooks, a member of the Judge and Jury troupe who also wrote a serial for the second *Town* that was popular enough to be reprinted separately at 2s.: 'Mrs. Lorimer Spinks, or, The married lady who was a little too gay'. But Nicholson had nothing to do with the revived *Town*. (When he tried again, it was with *Nicholson's Newspaper*, a 2½d. and later 3d. full-sized conventional weekly newspaper that emphasized sports, entertainment, and – so much for political consistency –

'the sacred cause of popular rights' like *Bell's Life in London.*[86]) Brooks' serial, a sometimes very funny melange of farcical, gothic, and nearly pornographic turns, gets something of the feel of Nicholson's *Town* at its best. But the second *Town* soon reduced itself to the kind of spicy literature Nicholson used to advertise on his back page, running almost weekly a suggestive drawing like that of the buck and the chambermaid Nicholson once apologized for, and publishing stories titled 'Recollections of a rake', 'An artist's amour', 'A curious case of Cockney crim con', and 'The mysteries of love', a translation of *Manon Lescaut.* The second *Town* was in fact published in Holywell Street, then a centre for the publication and sale of pornography. Its publisher (W. Winn) several times complained in its pages about the harassment of newsagents who sold the journal, and twice he announced a change of name – to *London Life* and *The Times We Live In* – because of a 'supposed identity with a print of bygone years, that raised for itself a special world of enemies' and 'two or three displays of petty magisterial tyranny'.[87]

All the mid-century imitation of Nicholson's *Town* followed the same pattern. *Peeping Tom*, for example, published the confessions of Lola Montes and a version of *Don Leon*, a poem about Byron which circulated regularly in the nineteenth-century underground of dirty books. *Paul Pry* and *Sam Sly* were by the end of their runs publishing two or three full pages of gossip about plumbers and grocers; the copy of *Sam Sly* in the Lilly Library includes a handbill exultantly announcing 'The death of Sam Sly' after a career in which this 'filthy publication' endeavoured 'to the extent of his powers, to annoy and perplex many respectable families'.

By mid-century, in short, this kind of journalism had unequivocally descended to the status of outlaw literature. It had become furtive and entirely illegitimate, the kind of writing the Obscene Publications Act of 1857 was directed against. The editors of scandalous journals later in the century did not always follow this move into pornography and obvious blackmail, but they and their journals were still placed outside the pale. In 1869 Grenville Murray, disappointed in his career in the diplomatic service, started the *Queen's Messenger*, a 6d. weekly. Its motto was: 'Ho, all ye who have suffered wrong!', and its intention was to reveal the incompetence and jobbery of government offices and the vice, stupidity, and senility of personages given names like 'Lord Barabbas, M.P.', a kleptomaniac and syphilitic who lives in open debauch, and 'Lord Coachington', 'a bargaining bumpkin with his pedlar's nature quite raw' who has advanced 'because a minister's mistress is an extravagant quean who wants money'.[88] Murray was physically assaulted by the son of Lord Carrington, the subject of the Coachington sketch, and fled the country to escape prosecution for perjury during the trial of his assailant. More to the point, Andrews wrote in the *Newspaper Press*, a monthly trade journal, that 'it is, happily, our simple duty to deny that Mr. Murray is a professional journalist'.[89] Adolphus Rosenberg, a stubborn and cantankerous man about whom it would be instructive to know more, published a string of scandalous weeklies in the last decades of the century, principally *Town Talk: a journal for society at large* (1878–85), edited by 'Paul Pry'. He wrote about Lillie Langtry and the Prince of Wales – referring to displays of their photographs in London shop windows, he observed that it was not pleasing 'to see Mrs. Langtry either by the side of or else beneath the Prince of Wales'[90] – and in 1879 he was sentenced to 18 months in prison for a libel against Mrs Langtry. He too complained about the harassment of newsagents who sold his journals, and after running through *Quiz: the satirist* (1879), *Rosenberg's Little Journal* (1886–7), and *Tittle Tattle* (1888), he wrote in *Town Topics* (1894) that he had learned his lesson and would settle down to make money by publishing fiction and news about entertainments. There was at least some money to be made in these late-century revivals of a now old-fashioned kind of scandalous journalism. When a short-lived weekly *Day and Night* appeared in 1871, the *Newspaper Press* quoted the disapproval of another journal: 'The *Police News* and the *Day's Doings* [it was published from 1870 to 1872] one would have thought would have sufficed for the most depraved taste. It is all very well to say such publications can never get a paying circulation. . . . The fact is that they do pay too well, and that they have now far too good a sale'.[91] Any sale would of course have been too good in the opinion of these proper judges, and the cost of even the scrambling living Rosenberg seems to have made – or the sleazy blackmailer Quintus Slide of Trollope's *Phineas Redux* (1874) – was to be made a pariah or renegade by custom, law, and professional canon.

The rightful, above-ground heirs of the purposes and audiences of the journals of Westmacott, Gregory, and Nicholson were the editors and proprietors of the society journals that were very popular in the 1860s and after. Society journalism requires a study of its own, and I touch on it here only to summarize the interest and appeal of the early-Victorian scandalous journalism that preceded it. Edmund Yates, who founded the *World* (1874–1922), was given the credit by his contemporaries for the invention of society journalism. In his autobiography Yates set out the ingredients of his successful weekly: 'all the light and gossipy news of the day' buttressed by 'good political and social articles written in a bolder, freer, and less turgid style than that in which such topics were commonly handled,' some short, light fiction, and reviews of books, plays, and music.[92] A writer in the *Newspaper Press Directory* in 1898 recognized the lineage from 'The *Anti-Jacobin Review*, the *Age*, the *Satirist*, and *John Bull*'. Yates, she wrote, 'persuaded himself that the supposed horror of the British public for what was known as "Personal Journalism" was a sham and that provided it was not vulgar or scurrillous, . . . and free from rowdyism, that it was certain to be acceptable' because of 'the insatiable demand for details, however minute, of those in authority, in affluence'.[93]

Society journalism, in short, and some closely associated journals like Henry Labouchere's *Truth* (1877–1957), with its gossip about the fashionable world and well-informed exposés of financial and political doings, seems like early-Victorian scandalous journalism to have offered the pleasures of being in the know and the useful security of guides to where to go, what to talk about, how to dress, how to entertain, and what tone to take about it all. If society journalism were to be studied, its great difference from scandalous journalism would probably prove to be in its tone. In Yates' formula society journalism looks to be determinedly light and easy. Its gossip will satisfy the reader without wounding or denigrating its subject. The entertainments to which it attends are proper; its politics are just another part of the spectacle of the world to be enjoyed; even its exposés may inform without whipping up anger or fear. For all the imperturbability of their poses as men of the world who are beyond shock, there is by comparison something raw and jumped-up in early-Victorian scandalous journalism, with its fictions of chastisement and warning and its high-spirited having at its disreputable enjoyments and enemies. These journals are, after all, of their time. They are on the back edge of changes in public manners and sensibility that were to give high value to earnestness, decorum, and the dignity and responsibility of new professions like journalism. For that reason, they also express something of the complexity and cross-currents of such changes. Their editors, writers, and readers took as their pattern and the ground of their judgments and aspirations an idea of a gentleman that came from a rigid social structure. Yet they enjoyed a steady impertinence toward persons of rank and social and institutional distinction that, as Scott Bennett points out in his essay on Gregory,[94] fits with the decline of deference in the nineteenth century toward traditional sources and signs of social authority. They studied the city of vice and danger that many were beginning to perceive as the great wen, a dark labyrinth of degradation. But like even larger numbers of people of the middle and working classes who learned to live in the city during the century, they really were not frightened of it, and enthusiastically looked out ways to enjoy it. They self-consciously set themselves against notions of refinement that were becoming important in the early-Victorian years. But they were not all that different from most of their contemporaries of their classes and occupations in their excited response to the bright, hard energies and appetites that made the 1830s and

1840s in England a time of audacious speculation and self-promotion. Above all, for all their implicit anxieties about being found out, the readers of Renton Nicholson's the *Town* especially seem to be like many of those who worked as London clerks and in crafts and small businesses in their engaging confidence that a place and time so full of fun and chance will give them their chances too to enjoy its material pleasures and profits.

NOTES

1. In the number for 31 Dec. 1821, the editors of *John Bull* stated that the paper had purchased 436,700 stamps in the first year of its publication. In the number for 1 Jan. 1826, they claimed an average weekly sale during the preceding year of 11,560. James Grant in the *The Great Metropolis* (2nd edn, New York, 1837) wrote that the weekly sale in its first years was 10,000 (II, 150); R. W. Dalton Berham, in his *Life and Remains of Theodore Edward Hook* (1849), cites the same figure (I, 204).

2. Sessional Papers, House of Commons Accounts and Papers (hereafter cited as Sessional Papers), 1835, XXXVII, 710–11. In 1839 and 1840, the *Age* purchased 105,000 and 96,000 stamps respectively: Sessional Papers, 1840, XXIX, 524–6.

3. Sessional Papers, 1835, XXXVII, 710. The *Satirist* purchased 194,027 stamps in 1840, an increase of almost 50,000 from 1839: Sessional Papers, 1840, XXIX, 524–6.

4. From June 1834 to June 1835, for example, the *Spectator* purchased 114,000 stamps, the *Atlas* 125,000 and the *Examiner* about 1750,000 (Sessional Papers, 1835, XXXVII, 710–11). In 1840 the *Spectator* was up to 194,000 stamps (the same number as the *Satirist*), and the *Examiner* to 311,825 (Sessional Papers, 1840, XXIX, 524–6). W. Weir estimated the weekly sales of the *Spectator* during October, November, and December of 1842 to be 3,850, and those of the *Examiner* to be 6,312 ('London newspapers', in *London*, ed. Charles Knight [1841–4], v, 337–52). The figures for *Bell's Life* and the *Weekly Dispatch* are from Sessional Papers, 1839, XXX, 504–6.

5. Quoted in H. R. Fox Bourne, *English Newspapers* (1877), I, 344.

6. James Grant, in the third volume of his history of British newspapers, *The Metropolitan Weekly and Provincial Press* (1872), 16–18, writes that Gregory and Westmacott used to keep on their payroll, at a guinea or so a week, 'a man of Herculean bodily appearance', preferably Irish – 'it was thought by the editors of such papers as the *Age* and the *Satirist*, that there was virtue in the genuine Irish brogue in inspiring a salutary fear of collision' – who would come forth with a cudgel under his arm when someone appeared in the office angrily demanding to see the editor, and announce that he was the editor. Alexander Andrews, in *The History of British Journalism* (1859), wrote that at one time in the 1820s there were 16 libel actions successfully brought against the *Age*, although it was impossible to collect damages from any of them; and that in 1832 the *Satirist* was successfully sued for libel by a plaintiff who then served notice of 84 separate libel actions against newsvendors who had distributed the libel by selling the paper. Andrews is a useful source of information about libel actions against the press, for one of his measures of progress in his profession is the decrease in the number of these actions.

7. *John Bull*, 17 Dec. 1820, 6. The reference here is to Lady Caroline Wrottesley, Lady Tankerville's daughter. The family of Lady Caroline sued for libel because of this squib, and were awarded £500 damages from each of the two publishers of *John Bull*.

8. *John Bull*, 31 Dec. 1820, 22.

9. *Ibid.*, 17 Dec. 1820, 7; 25 Feb. 1821, 85.

10. *Ibid.*, 11 Nov. 1821, 381.
11. *Ibid.*, 16 Sept. 1821, 316.
12. *Ibid.*, 24 June 1821.
13. Myron F. Brightfield, *Theodore Hook and His Novels* (Cambridge, Mass., 1928), 144.
14. *John Bull*, 11 June 1826, 189.
15. *Spirit of the Age Newspaper for 1828* (1829), vii–viii.
16. *Ibid.*, xvi.
17. *Satirist*, 4 Jan. 1835, 5.
18. *Ibid.*, 7 July 1839, 211.
19. *Spirit of the Age Newspaper for 1828*, *op. cit.*, 12.
20. *Age*, 13 Feb. 1831, 51.
21. *Ibid.*, 1 Jan. 1832, 6.
22. *Satirist.*, 21 Dec. 1835, 410.
23. *Ibid.*, 20 May 1838, 157.
24. *Ibid.*
25. *Ibid.*, 14 Oct. 1838, 324; 7 July 1839, 212.
26. The Gregory Papers, mostly manuscripts and letters addressed to Gregory in the first five years of the 1830s, are bound in 63 volumes. Each manuscript is numbered within the volume in which it is bound. I cite volume number and then the number of the manuscript within the volume, followed by the year in which the manuscript was written, where that is known. I am grateful to Scott Bennett and others of the University of Illinois library for their help in using the Gregory Papers. I am also grateful to Scott Bennett for allowing me to read and use a valuable unpublished essay by him on Barnard Gregory and his conduct of the *Satirist*.
27. Gregory Papers, I, 39: 1835.
28. *Ibid.*, 32, 72: 1834.
29. *Ibid.*, 32.32.
30. *Ibid.*, 10.79.
31. *Ibid.*, 4.46.
32. Frederic Boase, *Modern English Biography* (1901; repr. 1965), 1283.
33. *Age*, 30 Jan. 1831, 36.
34. *Satirist*, 7 July 1839, 213.
35. *Spirit of the Age Newspaper for 1828*, *op. cit.*, xiv–xv.
36. Gregory Papers, handbill.
37. *Ibid.*, 7.73: 1832.
38. *Ibid.*, 57.59.
39. *Town*, 2 June 1838, 417.
40. In 1838 the *Age* purchased 120,500 penny stamps, the *Satirist* 154,500

stamps (Sessional Papers, 1839, xxx, 504–6). The estimates cited by Patricia Hollis in *The Pauper Press* (1970) and by Joel H. Wiener in *The War of the Unstamped* (Ithaca, N.Y., 1969) of the scales of unstamped broadsheets and journals of police news and other sensational events are the most pertinent in guessing at the sales of the *Town*. Hollis writes: 'By the beginning of 1836 Cleave's *Gazette* was thought to have a circulation of 40,000', and she estimates the sale of Henry Heatherington's *Twopenny Dispatch* at around 20,000 (*op. cit.*, 123–4). Wiener estimates the weekly sale of *Cleave's Police Gazette* as between 30,000 and 40,000 in 1835 (*op. cit.*, 177). In her introduction to an edition of Hetherington's *Poor Man's Guardian* (New York, 1969), Hollis writes that in the early 1830s Hetherington could break even with a weekly sale of 2,500, but he did not usually pay his writers (p. xxi). Wiener estimates that a weekly unstamped 1d. paper printed on a single sheet and carrying advertisements could start making money with a weekly sale of between 3,000 and 4,000 (p. 182).
41. *Town*, 2 June 1838, 417.
42. *Ibid.*, 28 Mar. 1840, 1179.
43. *Ibid.*, 14 Oct. 1837, 153.
44. *Ibid.*, 2 Dec. 1837, 215.
45. *Ibid.*, 30 May 1840, 1249.
46. *Ibid.*, 18 Apr. 1838, 508; 4 Aug. 1838, 492.
47. *Ibid.*, 5 Oct. 1838, 980 *et seq.*
48. *Ibid.*, 3 June 1837, 7.
49. *Ibid.*, 3 Mar. 1841, 1563.
50. *Ibid.*, 27 Jan. 1838, 273.
51. *Ibid.*, 4 July 1840, 1293.
52. *Ibid.*, 22 June 1839, 856.
53. *Ibid.*, 21 Mar. 1840, 1173.
54. *Ibid.*, 9 Mar. 1839, 742.
55. *Ibid.*, 14 Apr. 1841, 1610.
56. *Ibid.*, 3 June 1837, 1.
57. *Autobiography of a Fast Man* (1863), 244.
58. *Ibid.*, 309.
59. The Lilly Library at Indiana University holds a complete run of Nicholson's *Town*, some sets of his advertisements for entertainments at the Garrick's Head, and several mid-century imitations of the *Town*, such as *Sam*

Sly, Paul Pry, and the revived *Town* in 1849. This collection, which also includes some fast-life guides to early Victorian London, was put together by Michael Sadleir and now forms part of an extensive collection of books about Victorian London designated as the London Collection by the Lilly. I am grateful for the assistance of William Cagle, the Director of the Lilly Library, and his staff in preparing this essay.

60. *Town*, 3 June 1837, 1; 30 May 1840, 1249.
61. *Ibid.*, 17 June 1837, 22.
62. *Ibid.*, 24 June 1837, 25.
63. *Ibid.*, 5 Aug. 1837, 73.
64. *Ibid.*, 12 Aug. 1837, 83.
65. *Ibid.*, 30 Sept. 1837, 137.
66. *Ibid.*, 5 July 1837, 69.
67. *Ibid.*, 16 Dec. 1837, 230; 1 June 1839, 835.
68. *Ibid.*, 3 June 1837, 4.
69. *Ibid.*, 7 Dec. 1839, 1049.
70. *Ibid.*, 14 Apr. 1841, 1610.
71. *Ibid.*, 26 Aug. 1837, 102.
72. *Ibid.*, 1 June 1839, 835.
73. *Ibid.*, 22 Sept. 1841, 1794.
74. *Ibid.*, 16 June 1841, 1685.
75. Nicholson's own life is in the pattern I see as important in the way experience is presented in the *Town*. In his *Autobiography* he mentions his parents only to say that they died when he was very young. He was brought up in London by his brother, a banker's clerk; his sisters kept a school. At 14 he was apprenticed to a pawnbroker; 'I found the business utterly antagonistic, as well as repulsive as to the growth of mind, but extremely beneficial in the accumulation of worldly knowledge' (p. 9). As an adolescent he looked older than his years, and he was on the town at 15, gradually moving up to a West End pawnbroker and the company of actors, entertainers, gamblers, and prostitutes who frequented that part of London. He was in business for himself at 20 renting and pawning jewelry, went bankrupt and into prison for debt – where 'I managed to pass for a sort of gentleman' – and then knocked around as a partner in a billiard and gambling room, proprietor of a cigar divan (with drinking and gambling illegally conducted in the back), and worked in gambling tents at race meetings. Despite his success with the *Town*, the Judge and Jury Society, and his management of *fêtes* at the Cremorne Gardens, he was bankrupt again in 1844 and as late as 1855 he was in prison for debts he ran up in these years and could never get clear of. Despite some bitterness about partners and leasors whom he thinks cheated him, Nicholson's *Autobiography* is cheerful. Yet along with his memories of the famous, skilled, and lucky he has known are recollections of those who started out with him and ended as hopeless bankrupts or suicides. It is not surprising that life in the *Autobiography* should feel like life in the *Town* – some sections of the *Autobiography* are lifted straight from the journal – but the coincidence does confirm my sense that for Nicholson the ground truth about contemporary experience was that it was open and full of promise as well as risk to those who can or must take the plunge out from their beginnings.

76. *English Gentleman*, 19 Apr. 1845, 8.
77. *Town*, 26 Jan. 1842, 1937.
78. Andrews, *op. cit.*, II, 276.
79. *Ibid.*
80. *Autobiography*, 204.
81. Grant, *The Great Metropolis*, II, 155.
82. *Quarterly Review*, XLII (1843), 80.
83. Sessional Papers, 1851, XI, 143.
84. Andrews, *op. cit.*, II, 221.
85. Grant, *The Metropolitan Weekly*, pp. 21, 89.
86. *Nicholson's Newspaper*, 18 Oct. 1851.
87. *Town*, II no. 1 [n.d.].
88. *Queen's Messenger*, 17 June 1869, 238.
89. *Newspaper Press*, III (1869), 171.
90. *Town Talk*, 30 Aug. 1879, 6.
91. *Newspaper Press*, XV (1871), 183.
92. *Edmund Yates: His Recollections*, (1884), I, 308.
93. Laura Smith, 'Society journalism', *Newspaper Press Directory for 1898*, 80–1.
94. See n.26.

13

Louis James   The trouble with Betsy: periodicals and the common reader in mid-nineteenth-century England

1

In spite of growing interest in the study of periodicals – of which this volume itself is an indication – there has been little attempt to evaluate their specific character and modality. There has been useful work on serial bibliography, on editorial history, on the political or religious orientation of particular titles. But there has been comparatively little attention given to what we might call the 'holistic' character of a journal, the way in which it possesses a specific identity through the total effect of its contents, tone and style.

In this essay I wish, first, to make some general points about the periodical as a literary genre in its own right; then to illustrate two different approaches to their evaluation. I will look at a few magazines for servants in the context of the original readership; then, working from a tabulated analysis, see what can be learnt by a structural breakdown of the contents of the *London Journal*. These are only two of many ways we may approach serial evaluation. But I wish to suggest that this task requires methodology at least as complex as that brought to the analysis of a novel or a poem.

We may start from the point that there are two ways in which to read a periodical: as a collection of individual parts, or as an entity, issue by issue, in which each element is modified by the whole. In general, it is assumed that a passage may be reprinted from a periodical with little or no change in its effect. A serialized novel is republished as a book; news items are reprinted in an anthology; a series of essays is brought together as a collection. Dickens's early periodical pieces are known only in the volume *Sketches by 'Boz'*. Yet, as Virgil Grillo has shown,[1] to get their full impact we must read them in their original context. 'The Old Bailey', for instance, is recognized as a 'landmark essay' in Dickens's discovery of 'the melancholy and the pathos, the plight of the poor'. But only if we recover the original sequence in the

Morning Chronicle can we see Dickens coming, through the topicality of his essay on 'Omnibuses' and the topographical 'Shops and their tenants', to the novelistic possibilities of London life evident in 'The Old Bailey'. We can go further than establishing an original sequence. An excellent way into Dickens's evolution as a writer is to read the different sketches in the diverse kinds of periodical that gave them birth. When placed in the jostle of business and shipping intelligence and legal news, for instance, a *Morning Chronicle* 'Sketch' gives a vivid sense of the way Dickens's art grew out of the social awareness of his time; the writing itself takes on tones missing in the abstracted, volume version.

Perhaps the most common plunder of the Victorian periodical has been the cartoon. Here surely, one may think, is an item that can stand on its own. This is not necessarily true. As we will later be considering some journalism of 1848, let us take what is perhaps the best-known cartoon on the 'Chartist scare' of this year, Leech's *Punch* caricature of 'A physical force Chartist arming for the fight'.[2] It portrays an unshaven workman – a cobbler, for a table and last lie overturned by his feet – being equipped for the class war. His wife is tying a huge tureen-cover to his chest. On his head he wears a coal-scuttle. Dangling between his legs, ready to trip him the moment he moves, there is a giant sabre. The 'message' seems clear: the middle-class satirist pours ridicule on the working-class agitators. However, this is complicated by its position in the original *Punch* issue. Specifically, it is placed opposite another full-page cartoon.[3] In this, an irascible Punch harangues the House of Commons on the eve of its recess. The government of England is reduced to tiny bodies and huge, fatuous heads. The working-class threat is juxtaposed with an equally ineffectual set of rulers, and one which is answering a crisis by going into recess. Yet another cartoon compares the bored House in session, and the animation of dissolving Parliament and getting down to the business of eating a banquet.[4]

Comparisons with the fierce portrayal of the Irish mob, and the general domestic satire, in the issues of *Punch* at this time, also reveal the satire of the working man as curiously benign. The staring eyes and tensed fingers of the cobbler might belong to a husband rehearsing for a difficult confrontation at the office; the comfortable wife busying herself with his equipment, a good wife straightening her husband's dress. The cartoon works through a juxtaposition of the ludicrous and the familiar, and Leech is as interested in the comedy of human pretensions as in making a political attack on the Chartists, although this is of course also there.

If a cartoon can change in its tone according to its context, a journal as a whole communicates through its layout, its selection, arrangement and general presentation, the use or absence of illustrations, the size of columns, paragraphs, the type itself. If a passage is altered in effect according to whether it is printed in verse form or as continuous prose, the typesetting of a news item in a paper can also change our sense of what is said. A journal's format thus becomes a tone of voice, a way of conditioning our response.

A periodical becomes identified with its specific format, as the outcry that inevitably follows any change in the style of a popular periodical testifies. A popular early-Victorian journal was called the *Novel Newspaper* (1838–48) not because it contained any news – it was entirely devoted to reprinted fiction – but because it was printed in the format of a miniature newspaper and drew on its appeal to the newspaper reader. Readers come to expect a certain style of format, and this is both personal – it becomes familiar – and social. The *Sun*, a working-class English paper, would stand out like a cloth cap and boots in an Oxford Senior Common Room, not only because of its contents but because of its incongruous cultural style. A style becomes linked to a class group, as does fairground lettering or the design of fish-and-chip counters. The dense print and cloudy photographic reproductions of the *Daily Telegraph*, as sober as a vicar's handshake, embodies the tone of the white-collar English bourgeoisie.

A periodical, because it selects and orders information in a specific way, becomes a microcosm, to a lesser or greater extent, of a cultural outlook. The format itself becomes a form of communication. Most readers will have had the experience of trying to read an unfamiliar newspaper, and feeling that there 'was little in it', even though it may have a full quota of information. Linguists tell us that our very ability to distinguish particular phonemes depends on our acculturation into a structure of language. Similarly, the pattern created by a journal's layout becomes built in, over a period of time, with our ability to read its contents. Even the paper used can be important. An academic colleague, who might be expected to read mainly for the content, cancelled her subscription to the *New Republic* entirely because she found that she did not enjoy reading it after it changed from matt to glossy paper. Alternatively, consider the experience of reading the *New Yorker* printed on coarse newsprint.

Periodicals are part of the furniture of everyday life. Books are furniture too, but only a few kinds – coffee table books, reference guides – are bought to have lying about the living room. They are bound to be read and to be stacked away, vertical. A book and a periodical demand different forms of commitment. A book requires sustained attention over a certain period of time; a periodical can be casually picked up, read, and put down in a spare moment. When I have finished with a book I rarely dispose of it, even though I may never re-read it; a journal is bought to be thrown away. Yet in effect it is more permanent than a book, always there, periodically renewed. I pay for a book, and whether or not I am pleased with my purchase, the matter ends there; in subscribing to a journal I enter into a contract by which I pay so much for the editor to provide, at regular intervals, a particular form of entertainment or information.

For these reasons a periodical is a particularly intimate form of literature. It is a community of voices, most of whom may be anonymous, but its 'dear reader' speaks with a familiarity rare in a book unless, as with the works of Dickens or Thackeray, the book itself had first appeared as a serial. Particular eras are identified with a distinctive form of literature: in the Elizabethan age, the drama; in the Augustan, verse. The Victorian age is generally seen as the great age of the novel. Yet if we allow that a significant amount of Victorian fiction appeared serially – either in journals or in number parts – we may claim that the age is also the era of the generally unrecognized genre, the periodical. This genre mediated to the era much of its finest fiction and non-fiction, and helped give both their vitality, their sense of being a dialogue between writer and reader. If we see an unprecedented development of journalism at every level of society, this is in part because its inherent intimacy and flexibility catered for its specific social context. For the Victorian age is both an age of mass movements and local-parochial groupings – groupings by region, occupation, religion, politics, class, age, sex. Carlyle noted that every little religious sect had its own periodical;[5] and this was true of most other movements, waging debates, providing entertainment, defining identities. We may compare this with the situation of the modern 'global village', which finds its natural expression in the mass medium of television. When we examine Victorian periodicals, we become aware not only of what the Victorian age was about, but how it evolved.

2

If we consider a periodical devoted to maidservants, we are hardly dealing with a sub-section of the culture. Servants are the great grey area of the Victorian culture. They formed the largest occupational group by the mid-century; the next largest section, clothing workers, was only a third as large. Yet although their work and living conditions were often appalling, they attracted no parliamentary Blue Books, no journalistic investigations. Karl Marx left them out of his analysis of capital and labour. Mayhew, in *London Labour and the London Poor*, relegated them to a note, by Bracebridge Hemyng, on prostitutes. The section concludes:

> Maid-servants live well, have no care or anxiety, no character worth speaking about to lose, for the origin of most of them is obscure, are fond of dress, and under these circumstances it cannot be wondered at that they are as a body immoral and unchaste.[6]

A major reason for this situation is that Victorian social commentators, including Marx and Mayhew, had servants of their own. Servants also had less obvious social identity than, say, mill-girls. They were isolated within their respective households, subject, in larger establishments, to a place within the domestic hierarchy. They produced no literary or social voice. But it was not only isolation that kept them from forming more identifiable sub-cultures, such as we find with other occupations. To be a maidservant was to have an ambivalent social position. One could enter service from a number of different backgrounds; if one left, one was relatively mobile socially to go into a variety of occupations. The servant was subject to her employer, yet she was also identified with the household in which she worked. If our modern concept of the English novel begins with *Pamela* (1740), her rôle as both servant and the future Lady B. reflects a fantasy rooted in the uncertain social class of her occupation.

As one might expect, this ambivalence is shown in her periodical reading. In the early nineteenth century this included a strand of fiercely 'improving' literature. Much of this came in the form of tracts. A typical Religious Tract Society publication would be *A Sunday Evening's Present to a Female Servant* (1830). Interestingly, the woodcut on the cover indicated the way in which the pamphlet should be read: the maidservant is sitting, neatly dressed and self-composed, by a frugal fire. Reading was a disciplined activity, and the contents urged the domestic to be punctual, honest, serving her mistress in the knowledge that she was thereby serving God, and preparing herself for divine service hereafter.

The *Servant's Magazine* was a monthly periodical published by the Committee of the London Female Mission from 1837 to 1866. Later the character changed markedly, and I will be considering the first three volumes. In these, the style and format had the purpose of moral instruction. 'The whole appearance [of the periodical]', the reader is told, 'reminds me of what my kind mistress used to say a servant should be, neat and lively, not showy in dress, nor light in manners.'[7] There are no illustrations for frivolous entertainment; the small format, unlike that of a newspaper, was for reading and storing tidily; the layout is clear and sober. The servant is warned that reading could be another kind of activity.

> Times have changed since the great bulk of female servants were unable to read. . . . Servants are now fond of reading, and this is well; but it is of vast importance that what they read should be adapted to promote their true welfare, to render them more useful in their station, more contented with the arrangements of a kind Providence which have placed them in it, and more alive to those

hallowed principles which can alone prepare them for the engagements and the happiness of heaven.[8]

Reading the periodical we sense the intense energy focussed within the claustrophobic world of the mistress-servant relationship. The series 'The Servant's Hall', took the form of a dialogue among Lady Christian's servants. At every moment the maid had to be concerned with saving the mistress's money. When a goose is plucked, the feathers must be kept for quills and dusters. Butter must be preserved with salt, sugar and saltpetre. Even dubious water must be made usable with alum. The reader should be at all times bound to her mistress. When Mary asks for permission to go to chapel, yet slips off to her aunt's for the evening, she is given the fearful example of the maid who fibbed her way into going to a fair, and was instantly killed by a carriage; and the apprentice who went boating when he should have been visiting his father. 'Ah! he little thought he should never see his master's face again; the boat was upset, and he and all his companions went to the bottom.'[9] This grim little magazine, offering no escape into levity or variety, is a dark image of the life – if the mistress got her way – of the servant in a middle-class evangelical household.

This atmosphere can be understood in the light of the typical servant-mistress relationship. As Walter Thornbury was to write in *The Vicar's Courtship* (1869):

> With most mistresses the ideal of a perfect servant is a strong girl who will wear ugly caps, never go out, never wish to get married and be independent, never stop working, live underground, and be perpetually willing and cheerful for eight pounds a year, without tea and sugar.[10]

Yet the relationship was a double captivity.

> It is the penalty people have to pay for civilization – the utter want of domestic and social freedom; this dwelling continually in the midst of a great army who keeps its sentinels always on the alert; this sleeping, and eating, and walking, and driving, forever surrounded by guards who are cognisant with every look; who take account of every word; who know the weaknesses, the sins, the anxieties, hopes, fears of the men and women who compose this modern inquisition . . .[11]

In this overheated emotional world the issue of sex was both taboo and dominant. We do not need to go to the long and explicit seduction of the maidservant Charlotte that provided Walter, in *My Secret Life*, with his sexual initiation,[12] to see how vulnerable the servant was to sexual pressures from the young men of the house, and sometimes the master. Here the situation of the domestic was particularly difficult: however innocent she might be of any provocation, she was under the threat of instant dismissal if implicated in any way with the sexual desires of the family. The *Servant's Magazine* approached the subject through the euphemism of flattery. Under the heading, 'The Alarum. Beware of Flattery', it warned;

> Always remember the maxim of Solomon: – 'A man that flattereth his neighbour spreadeth a net for his feet.' As you value your reputation, your peace of mind, your present and future happiness, listen not to the flattering tongue of man. Our hospitals and gaols are filled with the groans and cries of those who were once happy and respectable servants, but they harkened to the voice of flattery, not suspecting the net that was spreading for their feet. In an evil hour they were seduced, under promises which are *never performed*; and their characters lost, their prospects blighted, they recklessly rushed into deeper criminality, till they became the pitiable and wretched objects they now are.[13]

Other warnings may be even more veiled. We are told of Fanny who, allowed out one hour, stays out two, and is seen rushing home with the mistress's daughter, whose face is bright red. A passer-by hears her telling the girl, 'Be sure you don't tell; I'll take you into my room, and wash your face in cold water.'[14] The jaunt seems innocent enough – but why then, when the onlooker reports the incident to the mistress, do we hear of a prolonged moral beating up of poor Fanny, with immediate dismissal without a character? We are left with the possibility that the daughter's red face was caused by more than haste, and are never told what *did* happen.

The *Servant's Magazine* was a modest publication, with a probable circulation of about 4,000,[15] mostly in London. But its composite character gives us insights into the homes for which it was written, ranging from factual detail of household management to the imaginative aura, more cogent than a novel or a survey could provide. It is particularly useful in being focussed on a specific group of readers – although we have no indication of how much servants actually *read* the proffered gift. For, as the editor noted, it was in competition with a different kind of reading matter. 'We have too often seen in the hands of female servants . . . books . . . of a very different tendency to this . . .' What this literature might be is indicated by Augustus and Henry Mayhew in their serial novel, *The Greatest Plague in Life* (1847). The 'greatest plague' is the domestic servant, and the successive maids suffered by the narrator form a sequence of the seven deadly sins of the occupation. If Mayhew excluded servants almost entirely from *London Labour*, in this work, in spite of the comic tone, there is evidence of research.

The sins of reading are embodied in Betsy.

> And, bless your heart, she hadn't been in the house a week or so before, I declare to goodness, I don't think there was a saucepan in the place that hadn't its bottom burnt out; for there she would let, no matter what it was, boil away until there wasn't a drop of water left; for what did *she* care about the fish or the potatoes so long as she could have a quiet half-hour's cry over the 'BLACK PIRATE' or else be finding out what became of 'MARY, THE PRIMROSE GIRL'.[16]

The other novels listed are a representative selection of the periodical fiction published by Edward Lloyd in the 1840s. They include *Heads of the Headless, Marianne the Child of Charity, The Castle Fiend, The Heiress of Sackville, Children of Two Fathers, The Gipsy Boy, The Maniac Father, Lloyd's Penny Sunday Times, Emily Fitzormond, Ela the Outcast*, and a range of penny broadsheets and ballads. Notably absent are the penny periodicals such as the *London Journal* and *Reynolds's Miscellany*; this is itself an indication of Mayhew's objectivity, since in spite of their popularity, content and the correspondence columns suggest that these had a predominantly male readership.

Betsy's reading appears at first to be as wildly escapist as the *Servant's Magazine* is remorselessly disciplinary, and this mistress's reaction is typical of the employer's suspicion of romantic fiction – it took the servant's mind off work: 'Just as I might have expected, there she was, all the next day, so interested with that stupid outcast of an Ela, that she couldn't get my lamb down before the fire until it was so late, that when it came to table it was only just warmed through, and every one knows how nice underdone lamb is.'[17] But if she had looked beyond her indignation, the mistress might have seen some significance in Betsy's reading tastes. Ela was one of the most popular of Lloyd's heroines, a foundling with an aristocratic – if late-revealed – parentage. Although she cannot finally escape the consequences of her early seduction by the villain Rackett, she spends much of the long story as an heroic gipsy. Imprisoned in her kitchen dungeon, pursued by her harridan of a mistress, Betsy would have strong empathy with heroines such as Ela, even though she could only play out her resistance in her imagination.

Violence is a marked trait in Betsy's reading. She was an avid reader of murder and 'last dying confession' broadsheets. She bought Lloyd's *Penny Sunday Times*. Mayhew quotes a characteristic item from this, 'The earl in his jealous rage slaying the Lady Isoline'.[18] Describing a typical illustration, he declares: 'there was sure to be some great brute of a man, in a Spanish hat and large black cloak all flying about, striking some very grand theatrical attitude, and flourishing over his head a big carving knife, to which three or four heavy notes of admiration were hanging, while a poor defenceless woman lay at his feet, with her throat cut as wide open as a cheese, and weltering in a pool of ink'.[19] If the reference to the carving knife and the cheese are comic, how often must Betsy have looked passionately at the kitchen cutlery, and, hacking at the food she was preparing, butchered the mistress! Indeed, the layout of the *Penny Sunday Times* itself confuses the line between real and imagined violence: the fiction is placed on the front page next to the police reports. It is juxtaposed also with 'entertaining' items such as factual tit-bits and 'facetiae'. The format of the *Servant's Magazine* implies serious concentration on work; the *Penny Sunday Times* indicates fragmented interest totally alienenated from any occupation.

As we have noted, the beleaguered heroines of Betsy's reading offered an attractive fantasy for her to identify with. They were significantly different from the heroines of middle-class romance. They rarely fainted; they had the stamina and courage more generally associated with the hero in 'respectable' fiction. Heroines such as Ada,[20] and Louisa Sydney, in Reynolds's *Mysteries of London* (1845–7), disguised themselves as boys. If the heroine of the mainstream Victorian novel indicated, often directly, the domestic rôle of the woman reader, penny serial fiction reflected, indirectly, feminine rôles in which physical stamina was required for survival.

The attitude to wealth is, as we would expect, frequently ambivalent. Mayhew laughs at the exotic taste of this fiction.

> 'Hush! some one comes,' said the Count Monvaracordo to Canoni – a man of strange aspect and apparel – as they were seated in a richly decorated room at Strademoor Castle.
> 'My lord,' said the man-at-arms, 'there come three travellers through the storm, and demand admittance to the castle.'
> 'Do they proclaim their calling and degree?'[21]

Yet one can find more extravagant style in Ainsworth, and luxury is rarely portrayed to be simply indulged in, as with the 'silver fork' novel. It is generally the mask for moral decadence. Thus when we read of the Smuggler King's splendid apartment – 'tables, chairs and stools, arranged with equal taste, and of surpassing beauty, finished the superb grandeur of the whole' – the reader is prepared for his villainy. 'Here had he wrought the destruction of many of Nature's most lovely works', – the 'works' being female.[22] Wealth is fascinating and dangerous.

This ambivalence – which is of course not confined to maidservant readers, but which is particularly germane to their social status – became more overt and self-aware as the century progressed. One of the factors that broadened the mental horizons of the working-class reader was almost certainly the rapid expansion of cheap periodicals. In the mid-1840s Reynolds's penny weekly serial, *The Mysteries of London*, brought to the novel the features of the newspaper. Into the central plot Reynolds keyed thinly disguised historical facts, statistics, Mayhew-like surveys and biographies, and editorial comment on social conditions. It exchanged city houses for gothic castles, slum cellars for dungeons, and financial extortioners for the evil count or monk. Romance was becoming politicized.

In the year of the Great Exhibition, Reynolds began publishing in penny serial form *Mary Price; or Memoirs of a Serving Girl* (1851–2). In this novel, the most subdued and direct Reynolds wrote, Mary goes through seven stages of domestic service, each of which are described with some sensitivity, from maid-of-all-work to child-nursing. She is expected to keep the children in order, but she has no authority. She must be even-tempered even when exhausted by long hours of work. Her mistress projects onto her her own frustrations and insecurity. She is under sexual threat from the master of the house. Although the story ends conventionally, with Mary inheriting the Clavering estates, the serial is indicative of the way the popular reader was becoming more self-aware. No-one reading *Mary Price* could be expected to take seriously the *Servant's Magazine*.

If we are to look for what Betsy's daughter would be reading by the 1860s, we cannot do better than *Bow Bells* (1862–97) (see plate 12). Style, the correspondence columns, and other evidence suggests that it circulated widely among the young serving-maid class. Observations of the middle and upper classes are such as would interest readers who had the close knowledge only the serving classes would have. For example, 'The sorrow of gentility' lists the embarrassments faced by the mistress in keeping up appearances. It is a disaster if a visitor sees a room littered with sheets and linen. Rich relatives must be well treated: what if a rich uncle comes unexpectedly to supper and there is only cold meat or mutton chops? Above all, the lives of the ladies of the house are *dull* – they cannot ride an omnibus; their day is taken up with ornamental sewing, a decorative hippo or a 'butterfly or snail on medieval braces for a Puseyite pet parson'. If they feel emotion, they are not to express it. 'One must not be caught crying . . . over a book, or weeping during a tragedy, or in fact giving . . . way to any foolish emotion that common people are subject to.'[23]

The fiction is even more hostile to upper-class life. In 'Dora Riversdale', for instance, the eponymous heroine is the daughter of an impoverished watchmaker. She enters the service of Sir David Bridgeman as surrogate for his dead daughter Annie. We are back in the exotic castle of a Lloyd romance from the 1840s.

> 'Was she in fairy land, or in a dream?' she asked herself, as she gazed around the glistening mirrors, the magnificent paintings, and the groups of Dresden china. 'Oh how bright and beautiful was this home! Could sorrow and care ever enter so rich an abode?'[24]

She fills Annie's place, even down to fitting, Cinderella-like, her slipper, and quickly becomes educated, learning 'the works of nearly all the ancient poets and philosophers'. But the evil family doctor, Glenthorne, poisons Esther the elder sister. Sir David goes mad, and dies calling out for Plato, Zeno and Xenophon. Dora makes a high society match, but, married without love, without even esteem, what was there for Dora to hope for in such a union?'[25] She is abandoned by her husband; Dr Glenthorne pursues her; she entombs him alive, and settles down to lonely old age in an Irish castle.

Attitudes to social advancement, however, can also be ambivalent. When the first issue offered a picture of Princess Alexandra it is not, as it would have been in a Reynolds publication, in order to attack royalty, but to exploit its glamour. If some features are contemptuous of upper-class life, others showed the reader how to become a young lady. There are recipes for home-made scents, carmine, and breath-sweeteners. To make the skin white, the reader was advised to soak unripe grapes in water, sprinkle them with alum and salt, then wrap these in paper, finally roasting the packet in hot ashes. The juice, squeezed out, should be used on the face each morning: 'it will soon remove the tan'. For a depilatory, she can use two ounces of quicklime, half an ounce of sulphuret of arsenic, boiled in a pound of strong alkaline lye. These should be tested with a feather. If the flue drops off, it 'is quite strong enough'.[26]

In *The Long Revolution*, Raymond Williams sees that class identities in England became confused mainly after the Victorian period. By the 1960s, he states, such terms as 'working' or 'middle' class have 'lost any relevant meaning, as descriptions of actual social organization, but their emotional charge is no less powerful for that.'[27] For servants, as I have argued, uncertainty about class status existed not in the twentieth, but in the Victorian and earlier periods. Nor is this necessarily a matter of confusion. In one context, Betsy would have liked very much to consider herself a 'lady'; in another, she would protest against being considered middle-class. In imagination, she might wish to murder her mistress; in preparing an important dinner, she might take pride in making a good meal. A novel could not embody these conflicting structures of reality: a periodical, with its fiction, its different kinds of information, can reflect this diversity. It can provide cultural models for the Victorian reader, and for the twentieth-century researcher, in a particularly rich way.

3

— shift —

cl

In the *Servant's Magazine*, we considered a small, well-identified periodical. It has a consistent layout and an individual tone, and gives a sense of both the authors and the readers. By the 1840s, however, we find the emergence of a form of mass-circulation journalism that was to lay the foundations of the modern, more anonymous, form. The *London Journal* (1845), the *Family Herald* (1845), and *Reynolds's Miscellany* (1846) were establishing unprecedented circulations. How did they evolve? Richard Altick has described them as 'cheap periodicals which achieved and long retained immense circulations on the strength of their melodramatic fiction . . . [S]uch papers did not give conspicuous comfort to those who, a few years earlier, had felt that the welcome given *The Penny Magazine* and *Chambers's Journal* was a sure sign that the reading tastes of the masses were improving.'[28] Does this give us an accurate sense of these periodicals? Let us look closer at a series of the *London Journal* issues for 1848, at a time when the serial was moving towards a circulation of half a million (see plate 10).[29]

To do this, it is useful to analyse the balance of the contents. This method has limitations: by examining the length given to each element, we are not taking into account, for instance, that poetry takes less space than fiction, or that a useful 'filler' continued week after week at the back may take more space than a short, important, front-page article. Yet it does give us something relatively precise to work with, a guide to the balance, say, between fiction and non-fiction, and a useful 'finger-print' which shows up major changes in editorial policy, or the difference between two apparently similar journals.

Table 13.1 gives percentage of the *London Journal* contents for the ten weeks, 11 March to 13 May 1848. The journal was published each Saturday, 16 sides printed in three ruled columns, giving 48 columns in all. The size, 21 × 27 cm, was the usual one for this type of popular periodical, similar to the common broadsheet, half-way between a newspaper and a book. As was again common for this type of periodical – though not the *Family Herald* – the front page always carried a woodcut illustrating the lead feature: unlike *Reynolds's Magazine*, this was not, at this period of the *London Journal*, illustration to fiction, and consequently gives the paper a more serious appearance. The character of a sensational fiction periodical is further belied when we look behind the titles of the current features. In spite of Eugene Sue's dubious reputation and the tone of the title, 'The Seven Cardinal Sins' is a somewhat pedestrian serial, translated week by week from *Le*

Table 3.1 Contents of the London Journal, by percentage, 11 March – 13 May 1848

	11 March	18 March	25 March	1 April	8 April	15 April	22 April	29 April	6 May	13 May	Total %
'Seven Cardinal sins'	25.2	18.33	12.50	25.00	18.02	35.42	34.69	37.5	18.3	44.58	26.99
Main feature[a]	14.81	10.21	40.21	31.67	36.67	21.93	24.59	24.58	22.29	24.38	25.13
Articles[b]	29.2	22.29	39.48	60.8	28.02	0.0	33.49	4.79	8.65	21.88	11.45
French history[c]	8.75	9.48	9.48	8.54	9.27	8.96	6.47	6.46	10.62	8.02	7.50
Miscellaneous[d]	14.05	8.70	10.83	6.25	2.5	2.02	3.85	0.8	3.13	5.21	5.66
Short fiction	17.6	9.17	8.33	11.35	0.0	7.7	0.0	0.0	12.89	0.0	4.88
'Love letters of remarkable persons'	6.67	0.0	7.8	7.19	7.29	6.46	7.6	6.25	5.0	0.0	4.71
Poetry[e]	5.0	6.67	2.7	0.73	0.0	12.71	1.46	11.6	8.33	3.33	4.13
Fine art[c]	5.21	5.63	0.0	5.42	11.25	0.0	0.0	0.0	5.21	0.0	3.51
Correspondence	2.19	1.88	3.3	3.43	2.19	1.35	3.33	3.13	2.5	3.75	2.70
Advertisements	2.5	2.81	2.88	2.5	2.5	0.63	2.29	1.75	2.13	2.13	2.28
Woodcuts[f]	9.79	4.58	2.97	7.14	7.71	6.77	4.17	6.53	6.66	7.91	6.35

a Always illustrated.
b Articles include all items with separate heading not otherwise listed.
c Sometimes illustrated.
d Miscellaneous lists short items, usually single paragraphs, without headings.
e Percentage includes article on the poetry of William Thom.
f Woodcuts are listed separately, but have not been deducted from the articles they illustrate.

Table 3.2. Contents of the *London Journal*, by percentage, 8 July – 19 August 1848

	8 July	15 July	22 July	29 July	5 August	12 August	19 August	Total %
Articles[a]	38.88	31.5	43.14	63.8	28.02	4.48	37.97	34.68
Short fiction	19.90	28.06	10.63	8.33	8.33	28.96	21.25	17.92
Miscellaneous[b]	15.88	12.71	6.67	6.25	12.4	9.37	9.12	10.34
Gideon Giles[c]					28.13	20.83	19.06	.74 (22.67%, 5–19 Aug.)
Main feature[c]	8.75	8.44	7.92	10.21	8.13	8.33	10.52	8.9
French History[d]	8.75	9.48	9.48	8.54	9.27	8.96	6.47	8.70
Correspondence	5.2	4.58	5.63	3.75	2.71	6.67	4.58	4.73
Advertisements[e]	2.5	1.25	2.08	1.45	2.29	2.71	2.5	2.11
Poetry			10.83		0.73			1.65
Woodcuts[f]	9.79	4.58	2.97	7.14	7.71	6.77	4.17	6.15

a Items with separate headings not otherwise listed, including 'Essays'.
b Miscellaneous includes 'Gems of thought', 'Facetiae', 'Miscellaneous'.
c Always illustrated.
d Sometimes illustrated.
e Advertisements include one short notice of a 'Book received'.
f Woodcuts have not have been deducted from the articles they illustrate.

Constitutionnel,[30] illustrating how social evils are rooted in political injustice. 'Envy', for instance, tells of a poor man driven to violence by jealousy of the rich. 'Love-letters of remarkable persons' offers nothing more than remarkably unsensational correspondence by such historical figures as Lord Chesterfield. Although Sue's story is, by a short lead, the lengthiest item of the issues, non-fiction outweighs fiction by two-thirds to one-third, and there is attention given to both poetry and the fine arts.

The most significant movement revealed by the table is the fluctuating length of the front-page article. Although an extended analysis shows this is characteristically some 8 per cent of the issue, by March it is taking over a third or more of the total issue, at the expense, in particular, of fiction. The shift indeed reveals a major change – though brief – in the character of the *London Journal*. In general, the tone is apolitical. In the issue of 18 March, an article on 'The French defences. Calais' ended with praise to the French revolution of 1848: 'everywhere the people have succeeded; and everywhere triumph has been attendant on the clamour, *Vive la Reforme*'. Another article[31] implicitly compared the revolution of the French people to the vicious 'king and constitution' mob that had burnt Priestley's house in Birmingham in 1791. On 25 March began a series of well-documented and illustrated accounts of the 1848 revolution; the journal became partially a newspaper, and with items of French fiction and French history, strongly pro-Gallic.

A glance at the dates of the issues explains this development. The revolution in France had begun in February, and on 6 and 13 March major Chartist demonstrations, largely sparked by the insurrection across the Channel, were held in Trafalgar Square and on Kennington Common respectively. To carry news directly supporting the Chartist agitation would have been to invite attention from the government; an enthusiastic account of the social changes in France might make a similar point while appearing as history. Why did the journal suddenly become politically activated? Was this in response to popular enthusiasm, or was it due to internal editorial policy? A clue may be the Sue translation. This had its more florid romanticism excised by the translator, who added brisk notes criticizing what he considered politically inept in the story, and pointing out where Sue was particularly sharp. One can conjecture that he might in fact be G. W. M. Reynolds, who had been previously an editor of the *Journal*, and whose prolific pen and pressing financial needs might have overcome the obvious objection to supporting a rival paper to his own *Miscellany*. Reynolds was the one evident popular journalist who united expertise in French politics and French literature. Reynolds took a leading part in the pro-French demonstration of 1848,[32] and if he had already a hand in the paper through the serial, he might have extended his influence through the lead articles.

Whatever the reason for the Gallic issues, the phase ended suddenly with the 13 May issue, and the lead article was given to a remarkably undramatic article on the tragedian Macready. On 20 May, the series on 'The French Revolution of 1848' continued with an anti-populist account of the Gordon riots.[33] The ensuing editorial uncertainty is made clear in table 13.2. The lead feature lost its importance, alternating articles on actors and on topography. The main fiction serial disappeared and was not replaced, while short fiction and miscellaneous non-fiction, much of it reprinted, expanded in volume: the shorter 'fillers' were gathered under various headings, 'Miscellaneous', 'Gems of thought' and 'Facetiae'. As the serious front-page article was down-graded, poetry and fine art virtually disappeared. The editor was attempting to change the style of the paper (or was there a change of editor?) but there was little to put in its place.

On 5 August the *Journal* found a nucleus which was to give it its tone and direction through the remainder of this and through the following volume. It began a serial reprint of Thomas Miller's *Gideon Giles*. If the translator of 'The Seven Cardinal Sins' had been Reynolds, the choice of Miller would have an added significance, for he had written the continuation of Reynolds's *The Mysteries of London* after Reynolds had completed the second series. Miller, the 'basket-weaver poet', was one of the few working-class writers to make a sustained success in the main literary market. A prolific writer of children's books, romantic topography, verse, and two competent novels, his work shows a gentle, rural temperament rooted in his early Lincolnshire life. 'In a word', he wrote, introducing *Gideon Giles*, 'without speaking disparagingly of those versatile geniuses, Eugene Sue and Alexandre [sic] Dumas, I must apprise my readers beforehand that my humble table is not spread with such highly-seasoned viands as theirs. The hero of my story is of a poor, hard-working honest Englishman: the chief interest of this tale arises from his struggles to achieve a living.'[34]

Miller's tale gave the issues of the *Journal* a keynote. Not only did the contents become more Anglicized and domestic in tone, the story took a consistent central place in the format of the paper. Previously, beyond the opening article and the correspondence columns, there was curiously little attempt to give the contents a pattern: even where features ran continuously through subsequent issues, it was impossible to tell in what order they would appear. Miller's serial from the first always appeared, with a woodcut, on the right-hand middle page of the issue: page nine. The lead fiction feature was established, and it kept its place even when a second serial was introduced.

The feature on the 1848 French Revolution may have been an editorial aberration; but it is also likely to have reflected the ambivalence of the readers towards France and radicalism. Even from this brief analysis of the *Journal*, some picture of their identity and tastes begins to appear. They were reasonable educated upper working and lower middle class. They were interested in a little poetry, or the account of an historic building, but they also wanted a good story. The story, like the journal, must be lively, but not crudely sensational. They were against the aristocracy, but also wary of the mob, and if they joined in political activity, it was unlikely to be intense or sustained. The correspondence columns, if they are representative of the readers, suggests a young adult, largely male, group. When a woman writes, which is rarely, it tends to be on serious matters, such as learning botany or how to emigrate.[35] (Emigration was to form a major interest in the paper in the following volume.) Frivolous questions from women get short shrift – 'If ladies will ask questions, in mercy let them be such as ought to elicit useful replies, they will then spare themselves disappointment and us unnecessary trouble.'[36]

While this profile of the *London Journal* is accurate for this period, it would not hold true for even a decade later. By this time other shifts have taken place in the social context, in the readership, and in editorial policy. For, as even this brief study has shown, a periodical is a complex organism, constantly responding to the pressures of the times and the audience. Usually, when a serial does not respond by change – as with the *Servant's Magazine* – it is likely to do so by folding. Some exceptions occur when a periodical embodies a nostalgia for the past held by readers who feel isolated by social change. For a periodical does not embody only an editorial viewpoint; it communicates as we have suggested through both content and format: it encapsulates a style of living for particular readers at a particular time and place. All this may appear daunting to the scholar of periodicals – but it is also a challenge and an opportunity. Periodicals are cultural clocks by which we tell the times.

NOTES

1. Virgil Grillo, *Charles Dickens' Sketches by Boz* (Boulder, Col., 1974); the movement from periodical to volume form is discussed in ch. 5.
2. *Punch*, XL (1848), 101. Readers would recognize the cartoon as a gloss on the facetious account of Chartists wearing domestic implements in the preceding issue, p. 86.
3. *Ibid.*, 16, 118, 100.
4. *Ibid.*, 118.
5. Thomas Carlyle, 'Signs of the Times', *Edinburgh Rev.*, XLXIX (1829), 443.
6. *London Labour and the London Poor* (1861 edn), IV, 257–8. For some modern studies of the position of serving girls, see D. M. Stuart, *The English Abigail* (1946); E. S. Turner, *What the Butler Saw* (1962); Patricia Horn, *The Rise and Fall of the Victorian Servant* (1975); see also the excellent section on domestic servants in John Burnett's *Useful Toil* (1974)

and the first-hand information in Derek Hudson's *Munby, Man of Two Worlds* (1972).

7. *Servant's Mag.*, I (1838), 42.
8. *Ibid.*, 'Preface', III.
9. *Ibid.*, 16.
10. Walter Thornbury, *The Vicar's Courtship* (1869), I, 59.
11. Charlotte Riddell, *The Race for Wealth* (1866), II, 297.
12. Anon., *My Secret Life*, ed. G. Legman (New York, 1966), I, 39–83.
13. *Servant's Mag.*, I (1838), 31–2.
14. *Ibid.*, 50–1.
15. *Ibid.*, II (1839), 'Preface'; VI (1843), III; circulation of 6,000 claimed, 1843.
16. Augustus and Henry Mayhew, *The Greatest Plague in Life* (1847), 112.
17. *Ibid.*, 115.
18. As titles of this periodical are fragmentary, I have not been able to identify this item, but Mayhew's references are generally accurate.
19. Mayhew and Mayhew, *op. cit.*, 112–13.
20. James Malcolm Rymer, *Ada the Betrayed* (1844).
21. Mayhew and Mayhew, *op. cit.*, 112.
22. T. P. Prest, *The Smuggler King* (1844), 316–17.
23. 'The sorrows of gentility', *Bow Bells*, II (1864), 624.
24. 'Dora Riversdale', *Bow Bells*, II (1864), 354.
25. *Ibid.*, 378, 451.
26. *Ibid.*, I (1862), 15; II (1864), 349.
27. R. Williams, *The Long Revolution* (1961), 334.
28. R. D. Altick, *The English Common Reader* (Chicago, 1957), 346.
29. Henry Vizetelly, *Glances Back through Seventy Years* (1893), II, 11–12; see also Altick, *op. cit.*, 394.
30. *Le Constitutionnel*, 9 Nov. 1847–14 May 1848.
31. 'Narratives of popular outbreaks', *London J.*, VII (18 Mar. 1848), 19–20.
32. See Louis James and John Saville, entry on 'Reynolds', *Dictionary of Labour Biography* (1976), III, 146–50.
33. *London J.*, VII (1848), 161–4.
34. *Ibid.*, VII (1848), 345.
35. *Ibid.*, VII (1848), 208; VII (1848), 283; VII (1848) 272.
36. *Ibid.*, VII (1848), 367.

14

Michael Wolff *The British Controversialist and Impartial Inquirer, 1850–1872: A Pearl from the Golden Stream*

In 1967, I published an article, 'Charting the Golden Stream: thoughts on a directory of Victorian periodicals'.[1] The 'Golden Stream' in the title was derived from the name of a Baptist monthly, *Pearls from the Golden Streams: A monthly magazine of truth, incidents, and byewords*, which ran from 1861 to 1879. This particular title appealed to me because the 'Golden' suggested the richness of Victorian serials as sources of information and insight into the Victorian period and the 'Streams' suggested the tremendous outpouring of such publications (both the number of titles and the tremendous volume of pages which those titles represent). For me, the 'pearls' stood for individual newspapers, magazines, or reviews, some of them, well-known and familiar, some of them completely forgotten and perhaps even irretrievable. This essay is devoted to a particular 'pearl' which I first encountered, quite by chance, when I was trying to investigate the periodical reading-matter available to a Londoner in a given month in 1864, and realizing how hard it was even to establish what was available and how overwhelmed I was by the amount of material that I had found.

In my paper, on the basis of a relatively rapid survey of a single volume, I ventured a description of the typical reader of this particular magazine:

The *British Controversialist and Impartial Inquirer* (1850–1872) gives a complete profile of the intensely ambitious working-man who is determined to improve himself. The man for whom the *Controversialist* was published and who seems to have provided its editors with material for the debates they printed was neither socialist nor atheist; he was both utilitarian and vaguely pious; terribly anxious for education, consequent advancement, and consequent respectability. He was the man for whom Mill had such high hopes and who convinced Gladstone that he deserved the vote. Reconstruct him from the pages of the *Controversialist* and you can, in part, account for the eclipse of radical collectivism between the collapse of Chartism in 1848 and the re-emergence of socialism in the 1880s.[2]

Further intermittent study of the *British Controversialist's* 38 volumes has in no way made me regret that description, but I have become very aware of the rashness of generalizing about something as complex and extensive as the file of any journal that has, as most do, the properties of a miscellany. De Tocqueville somewhere writes that a foreigner wishing to describe a place which he has visited must do it either after he has been there only a few days or after he has become a permanent resident. It is, I believe, a condition of the study of Victorian journalism that it is very difficult to reach the point where one feels that one knows enough about a newspaper or a periodical to offer with any confidence a description which is at once thorough and short enough to be useful.

The larger challenge that this experience exemplifies lies in the submerged existence of tens of thousands of 'unknown' Victorian serials. It is not, of course, that anyone expects all those forgotten rows of volumes to become part of the common stock of information of people working in Victorian studies. One's concern is not so much to find ways of turning these 'unknowns' into 'knowns' on a par with *The Times* or *Household Words* or the *Edinburgh Review*; it is rather to raise them from obscurity to accessibility, that is, to make them available so that students know that they are there to be used and know how to make use of them.

One way to describe the potential importance of journals like the *Controversialist* is by reference to the difference which Walter Houghton's *Victorian Frame of Mind* (1957) and the *Wellesley Index* (1966—) have made to the way in which we study Victorian Britain. That work has signalled a shift in the centre of gravity of our sense of the Victorians. Compare its 'population', that is, the number of people quoted and taken seriously as mirrors of or windows on to the Victorian world, with, say, those writers one would have encountered in a survey of Victorian literature or history in the previous generation. We have moved from a world of 'major' figures to one in which both 'major' and 'minor' figures play a part. (I do not mean to suggest that this revision was accomplished single-handedly by Houghton; but he was a major influence and he, as well as anyone, 'stands for' the change.) One can see the same sort of shift operating from E. L. Woodward's *Age of Reform 1815–1870* (1938), through, say, G. Kitson Clark's *The Making of Victorian Britain* (1962) and G. F. A. Best's *Mid-Victorian Britain, 1851–1875* (1971). The 'population' of these general texts grows at each step. The number and type of Victorians who are studied for their own sake rather than as a large anonymous backdrop for 'major' figures have steadily increased.

My claim for the *Controversialist* is that it represents one set of voices, one part of the next layer of 'populations', that need to be assimilated into our sense of who the Victorians were. Just as the *Cornhill* is the 'setting' for *Culture and Anarchy* and *All the Year Round* for *Great Expectations* so the *Controversialist* and its more-or-less anonymous equivalents provide a broader setting through which we can better understand the *Cornhill* and *All the Year Round*. We have by now become accustomed to thinking of Arnold and Dickens not simply as the authors behind some major texts but as members of a set of overlapping intellectual and social circles, frequently centred around a review or magazine. Indeed it is this habit of thought that helps to explain the increased use of periodicals as primary sources rather than as mere background. But there is a larger frame of mind than the one studied by Houghton, and as the study of the 'highspots' of Victorian life and letters has benefitted from that illumination, so there is a case to be made for the even broader light cast on the Victorian world by material 'below' or beyond Houghton's that probably cannot even qualify for the label 'minor'.

The *Controversialist* is a representative of such sub-minor documentation, but its undiscriminating interests, its openness (within limits yet to be made clear) to differing points of view, its determination to nourish its readership with anything that was food for thought, allowed it to include in its pages something on almost every familiar Victorian topic and on most major and a host of minor figures and concerns.

The *Controversialist* is, then, more than a representatively unknown Victorian serial. Its over 250 monthly numbers provide a record of mid-Victorian people, events, and preoccupations, remarkable in its coverage and its perspective. The variety of treatments and opinions on so many subjects tempts me to say that if something was not noticed in the *Controversialist* it was not important. The coverage is remarkable because its founders and proprietors intended it to provide a forum for 'controversy', that is, for the clash of opinions through debate and discussion, a procedure which they believed was the best and perhaps the only way of arriving at the truth and thus serving God and the cause of national progress. ('Great is truth and will prevail' was the *Controversialist's* motto.) The editors therefore chose subjects for each month which would encourage the liveliest discussion and which would involve the most readers, either as actual participants or as audience. Its perspective is remarkable because it was trying to reach a comparatively fresh readership, part of the 'unknown public' which had made possible 'the age of periodicals'.[3] This readership, which I tried to characterize earlier, is a hard group to define and seemed primarily to consist of 'young men', who either were the sons of, or were themselves, labourers, artisans, clerks, shop assistants, or 'small' merchants, who had in common, on the one hand, that they were eager for education and self-improvement and, on the other, that they did not have the leisure or the money or the background for adequate formal schooling. They were, the editors thought, ready for every type of information and for thinking about and discussing as many timely and timeless issues as the magazine could accommodate.

My object in the body of this essay is to demonstrate as best I can the range and variety and, I hope, the usefulness of the material in the *Controversialist*'s pages. I have chosen to do this in three ways: first, by giving some basic information about the magazine, by characterizing the general nature of its contents and concerns, and by noting its particular editorial slant; second, by offering a brief catalogue of mid-Victorian particulars which it treated; and third, by looking more closely at three volumes, one each from the beginning, middle, and end of the *Controversialist*'s career.

The methodological and substantive difficulties of such a demonstration, its arbitrariness and insufficiency, are representative of the overall problem of bibliographic description for Victorian periodicals. In order to be able to solve that problem, we have to be reasonably confident that we have identified the periodicals, made them available, and given students the sort of information they need in order to find what they want and to know what they have when they have found it. All that is a long way off. Meanwhile, an effort can be made to acquaint the reader with this one magazine.

If the *Controversialist* proves to be a useful addition to the store of primary materials in any branch of Victorian studies, then it will be well to remember how accidental and idiosyncratic was the process of its emergence from uselessness. It is, along with countless (or at least uncounted) other titles, listed in the major reference works, its first issue was favourably noted by *Punch* and by the national and provincial press, it seems to have had a modest but adequate circulation, it is hardly a fugitive publication (though few libraries have complete runs); and yet it has not been, as far as I know, used by students nor has its absence from monographs or from, say, the Critical Heritage series caused a perceptible gap. There are surely among the thousands and thousands of unexplored serials, many at least as valuable as the *Controversialist*. I would contend that historiography and criticism suffer from the practical non-existence of these potentially rich documents, that additions and corrections to our understanding of the period are there for the taking if only we could bring them within our collective reach.

Once we have the *Controversialist* in our hands, we have a beginning. But, before we can fully understand it, we need a lot of internal evidence: ideally we should have absorbed its tens of thousands of pages so that we can, as it were, hear its voice, recognize its personality, and thus give tangibility and life to the data we cull from it. We also need a lot of external evidence: ideally we should have identified its owners, backers, and editors, and its hundreds of writers, and know about its finances, distribution, subscription list, reputation, and the history of its founding, its fortunes, and its end. It is then impossible to offer here a comprehensive idea, let alone a comprehensive listing, of what the *Controversialist* covers, but the flavour and some of the substance can be got from a description and from some sampling of its pages.

1

What do we know about the *Controversialist*? A prospectus was issued in January 1850 and publication began in the following May. It appeared monthly without a break until its last issue of December 1872. In 1850 it cost 3d. for 32 pages. In 1853 it went to 40 pages, in 1855 to 48 pages and a cost of 4d., in 1859 to 72 pages and 6d., and in 1862 to 80 pages with no further increase in size or cost. It is difficult to find hard data about how many copies were sold and to whom. The preface to the second volume, dated December 1851, asks for 10,000 subscribers. An article in 1871 puts the circulation in the early 1850s at 2,000 with a subsequent decline and revival. The subscribers seem to be, by and large, young men of the 'self-educating classes' and the mutual improvement and discussion societies to which they belonged. There was clearly also a scattering of 'regulars' of more middle-class circumstances, but it is impossible to say if they were a mere handful or a sizeable proportion of subscribers.

Information about the running of the magazine is also slim. After the first six volumes (1850–5), a second series was started, apparently reflecting a change in editorial control and in some aspects of policy. This second series (1856–8, six volumes in three years) led to a decline in subscriptions and influence, and the original 'conductors' resumed control with a third series, volumes I–XXVI (13–38 overall), which ended when the *Controversialist* did.

The *Controversialist* made a point of disguising the identity of its staff (in part as accepted procedure; in part, I believe, as a sign of the altruism of the undertaking). Although there is an occasional signature, most of the contributors used initials or pseudonyms. Two men were the mainstays of the *Controversialist* throughout its 21 years with the exception, it seems, only of the three years of the second series. The proprietor and editor was J. A. Cooper, a Birmingham manufacturer, author of the *Art of Writing* (reprinted from the *Controversialist*) and of *Counsels to Sunday School Teachers on Personal Improvement and Practical Efficiency*. He was 28 when the *Controversialist* began. The principal writer of leading articles, mentor and guiding spirit was Samuel Neil, a lecturer and author of text-books in self-education and logic such as the *Art of Reasoning* and the *Art of Debating* (both first published in the *Controversialist*) and of various books about Shakespeare.[4]

Title and subtitle changes help to develop the *Controversialist's* sense of itself. The first title page read 'The British Controversialist and Impartial Inquirer established for the purpose of forming a suitable medium for the deliberate discussion of important questions in Religion, Philosophy, History, Politics, Social Economy, Etc'. In 1856, at the start of the second series, it changed to 'The British Controversalist and Literary Magazine devoted to the impartial and deliberate discussion of important questions in Religion, Philosophy, History, Politics, Social Economy, Etc., and to the promotion of Self-culture and general education'. It continued in this form until the end, except that the volume for the second half of 1856 had the title 'The British Controversialist and Self-Educator'. The lengthy sub-title was dropped in 1867.

In 1855 the first series was reprinted in book form as 'A Standard Ency-clopedia of Controversy and Educational Information', describing itself as 'especially devoted to the services of the Young, who are pursuing the arduous labour of Self-Education and Mental Culture'. In 1865 the *Con-troversialist* put out an advertisement to the effect that 'It contains LEADERS equal to the Quarterlies on Logic, History, Philosophy, and Mental Culture; Impartial DEBATES on all subjects; Essays, Poetic Criti-ques, Reports of Societies, Replies to Questions, Literary Notes, &c, and it is the most useful Magazine issued for Young Men'. There was by now a reprint of 22 volumes with 'Nearly 200 Debates, 180 Leading Articles on Logic, Rhetoric, European Philosophy, Epoch Men, Eloquence, Self-Culture, and General Literature; 160 Essays on various important subjects; 600 Reviews of Books, of which many are analysed; Answers to 12,000 ques-tions; and a large amount of important matter, relating to Life, Thought, Literature, Study, Progress, and Language'. The hoped-for readership was described as 'all persons engaged in Self-Culture, Members of Debating and Mutual Improvement Societies, Students and Thinkers whose time and means are limited, and all who love impartial debate, original views, and clear expression'. The 'departments' of the *Controversialist* mentioned in the advertisement give a profile of its contents. There was always a leading article (often biographical) on some philosophical or historical subject; there were always some half dozen debates, running anywhere from 3 to 15 months, which comprised the physical bulk of the magazine (for most of the run, there was also a monthly controversy called 'The Topic'); there was always a 'Societies' Section', consisting mostly of reports from individual societies, with general pieces about such societies, and extracts from addresses to them; there was always 'The Inquirer' in which questions about matters of fact or requests for advice about some aspect of self-improvement were, in most cases, answered in subsequent issues; there was always some noticing or reviewing of recent books; within a few years, there was a department variously entitled Literary Intelligence, Literary Notes, or Literary Notices. Also after the first few volumes there were classes in various subjects which settled down to being called 'Our Collegiate Course'. For most of the life of the magazine there was something on poetry, a general section called 'The Essayist', and a variety of such miscellaneous headings as Eloquence of the Month, Laconics, and Essence of the Press.

These features had different but related functions. The leading articles were exclusively instructive, that is, they were, with a handful of exceptions, the sort of thing that one might easily find in an encyclopedia of the period. These were often monthly instalments of a comprehensive discussion of a major educational theme, such as 'The Art of Reasoning', or a set of biographies-cum-expositions such as 'Modern Logicians' or 'Epoch Men'. They were designed both to inform and to inspire, and my guess is that they were intended by both the author and the editor to serve as the printed equivalent of a monthly lecture series and as a sort of serial 'treasury' of knowledge.

The debates, of course, were also intended to be informative, but, at least at the outset, their primary purpose was rather to demonstrate the value of controversy itself, so that argument became an instrument of collaboration in pursuit of the truth. It is clear that the debates were designed to show that even very bitter disagreements could make a constructive contribution to the march of mind.

The 'Societies' Section', unlike the debates or the leading articles, constitutes, so to speak, the 'in-house' aspect of the *Controversialist*. The purpose of this section was to establish the *Controversialist* as the acknowledged organ of a healthy and flourishing educational movement which in itself had potentially unbounded social and cultural significance. The hope clearly was that this movement of mutual improvement societies and other such bodies and the *Controversialist* would both grow through mutual support. The *Controversialist* would act as a clearing-house and depository of information and would encourage the founding and expansion of such groups by letting its readers know what others were doing. The movement would help the *Controversialist* by giving its pages semi-official status and by encouraging institutional and individual subscriptions. Although, so far as I know, it is never mentioned, one can see as a sort of gleam in the eye of the *Controversialist*'s proprietors a national association of mutual improvement societies, inspired, developed, and presided over by the editors of the *Controversialist*.

'The Inquirer', 'Our Collegiate Course', 'The Young Writer's Assistant', and, occasionally, 'The Poetic Critique', depended on direct interaction between reader and staff and constituted the *Controversialist's* best effort to offer through its pages the components of a formal education – and indeed these departments closely resemble a modern correspondence course.

My guess is that the *Controversialist* had no very clear policy for its review section, so that volumes of general history, metaphysics, polemical theological pamphlets, how-to-do-it manuals for apprentices and young professionals, children's textbooks, Sunday School magazines, all seem jumbled together in notices that range from a line or two to several pages.

Finally, the Literary Notes are that part of the *Controversialist* least clearly directed toward its intended primary readership, for they consist of an extensive miscellany of middle- and high-brow literary, scholarly, and journalistic gossip, surely of little relevance to the hard-working, earnest young men who had to snatch precious minutes from their busy days, and were hardly yet at an educational level to appreciate the items in those columns.

Anyone leafing through the pages of the *Controversialist* will notice how much attention is given to religion. Religion comes first in the list of 'Important Questions' to be impartially and deliberately discussed; a high proportion of the books noticed are by clergymen or on religious subjects; and many of the incidental essays, whatever their topic, are filled with religious references and quotations. Moreover, many of the societies reported on meet in church halls, are under the sponsorship of a local clergyman, or are even explicitly connected with a congregation or a Sunday school.

From a modern perspective, such an emphasis might seem in itself to indicate a bias inconsistent with the *Controversialist's* claim to be an impartial forum for all opinions and might also suggest that the journal offers us at best a distorted glass through which to look at the 'self-teaching' classes, that is, the readership which it claims to serve. But the *Controversialist's* preoccupations with religion may well be evidence of its centrality and neutrality rather than of bias. Such a problem is historiographically fundamental and probably unresolvable, but it becomes increasingly clear that one of the adjustments which the modern student of Victorian Britain needs to make is precisely in this area of the inescapability of religion. If indeed at this time, that is, the 1850s and 1860s, religion or religiousness is still part of the cultural atmosphere of either the promoters and staff of the *Con-*

troversialist or their audience, then a neutral position between religion and 'infidelity' would be more of a distortion away from impartiality than what we actually find in the magazine.

The *Controversialist* assumed a 'frame of mind' that might be called New Testament Christianity. The very first debate, asking the question, 'Is War, under every Circumstance, opposed to Christianity?', fell almost exclusively within that frame. Moreover, in the same issue, the question 'Ought Capital Punishment to be Abolished?' was debated. The eight contributions (four pro, four con) all felt obliged to reconcile their arguments with Biblical texts and to explain away (wherever the course of the debate required it) the support given their opponents by the Bible. No one was willing to argue that, whatever the Bible might have to say on the matter, capital punishment was in itself right or wrong, although it is not hard in some cases to read this as the debater's real position with the Biblical reference as a sort of shibboleth. This latter case, however, with the apparently obligatory nature of the religious references, reinforces rather than weakens the presumption of a religious frame of mind.

The situation, however, is not uncomplicated. Whereas, in some reviews in 1851, the tone is decidedly hostile to Rationalism, Unitarianism, and Roman Catholicism, an 1853 review of a debate between G. J. Holyoake, the Secularist leader, and a clergyman on the relative merits of secularism and Christianity is respectful of both sides and quite neutral. Moreover, the journal has high praise for such major figures of anti-religious reputation as James and John Stuart Mill and G. H. Lewes; and Roman Catholic, Unitarian, and other heterodox arguments appear frequently in the debates.

Another dimension of this subject is the relationship between religious commitment and class bias. We tend to connect a religious, especially an evangelical tone, with the attempt to draw lower-class readership within the aura of a middle-class ideology. Any magazine with middle-class proprietors and contributors and a religious 'bias' which seemed directed, say, to artisan readers is assumed (according to this position) to be 'conciliationist', that is, to be seducing working-class readers away from class awareness and toward the personal ambitions of self-improvement and respectability. Such a position may have some truth to it but it ignores the possibility that the lines of social division as experienced did not so separate those who put out such a magazine from those who read it and that one of the things that joined these people rather than separated them was precisely this shared belief in New Testament Christianity. The pervasiveness of this religious point of view and, as I am arguing, its compatibility with the editorial commitment to impartiality will help account for the frequency with which religious subjects recur within the *Controversialist* as I explore it in the rest of this essay.

2

It is now time to turn to particulars, by making a selection from all the familiar and not-so-familiar mid-Victorian people and preoccupations that appeared in the *Controversialist*. The periodical's main intellectual preoccupation is with 'thought', so that scientists, philosophers, essayists, and philosophical poets and novelists crowd its pages. I have tried to convey its range in the following selection.

Among the men of letters, Carlyle, Macaulay, Dickens, Thackeray, and Tennyson are the subject of lengthy debates. The titles themselves are revealing: 'Which is the Abler Writer – Dickens or Thackeray?', 'Is the Poetry of Tennyson as Healthy in its Tendencies as that of Longfellow?', 'Is Tennyson's "Enoch Arden" Morally objectionable?', 'Is Carlyle or Macaulay the Greater Writer?'. There were other literary debates on Milton *v*. Shakespeare, Byron *v*. Scott, and 'Whether the Intrinsic Merits of Tupper's "Proverbial Philosophy" are Worthy of its Popularity' (this last is a useful reminder that, in his day, Martin Farquhar Tupper rivalled Tennyson in sales and acclaim). There were also debates on whether the perusal of fiction was proper, whether 'Sensation Novels' were superior to 'Novels with a Purpose', whether Christians could support the Stage or participate in the Shakespeare Tercentenary Movement, whether, in general, the Drama was elevating or degrading. *Controversialist* readers were also asked to discuss and decide whether 'Beauty was a Quality inherent in Objects' and whether 'Poetry declined with the Advancement of Civilization'.[5]

There was a good deal of literature in the other departments of the *Controversialist*. There were, for instance, six articles on Carlyle and reviews of his *Frederick the Great*. There was an obituary essay on Macaulay and reviews of the third and fourth volumes of his *History*. *The Idylls of the King* and *Hiawatha* were favourably reviewed, as were the early works of George Eliot.[6] There were also reviews of Clough, Thomas Hughes, and Gerald Massey, and four long articles on 'John Henry Newman's Poetry, with special reference to the "Dream of Gerontius"'. There were elaborate essays on Coleridge, Wordsworth, and De Quincey, as well as shorter ones on Byron, Shelley, and Thomas Moore. Pope, Gray, Goldsmith, Cowper, and Burns were discussed. There were many pieces on Milton and Shakespeare, some in great detail as part of a Collegiate Course, 'The Literature of England, Chronological, Biographical, and Critical'.

Several series consisted of extensive biographical and critical studies. 'Modern Historians' included Froude and Grote; 'Modern Logicians', Alexander Bain, George Boole, Hegel, Kant, George Jardine, J. S. Mill, and William Spalding; 'Modern Metaphysicians', Bacon, Charles Bray, Comte,

A. C. Fraser, William Honyman Gillespie, 'T. H. Green the Coleridgean', Hobbes, C. M. Ingleby, Lewes, and J. H. Stirling; 'Epoch Men', Chaucer, Clive, Comte again, Johnson, Loyola, Adam Smith, and James Watt; 'Toiling Upward', Sir David Brewster, Cobden, Thomas Cooper, Robert Lewis Gerrie, Douglas Jerrold, and Thorwaldsen. Arthur Hallam, Keble, Florence Nightingale, and Swedenborg were subjects of other essays. I have deliberately mixed familiar and unfamiliar names in this listing as a reminder of the selective nature of our sense of the past. For instance, the *Controversialist* thought W. H. Gillespie a major metaphysical thinker on a par with Paley.

In politics, subjects for debate ranged from franchise reform – 'Is Universal Suffrage Just or Desirable?', 'Are the Working Classes Qualified for Parliamentary Representation?', 'Is Public Agitation essential to the Attainment of Political Reform?' – to foreign affairs – 'Was the British Government Justified in Entering upon the Present War with Russia?', 'Are the Poles Justified in Endeavouring to Regain their National Independence?', 'Was Slavery the Real Cause of the American War?'. The monthly 'Topic' was dominated at appropriate times by matters of national defence, trade unionism, Italian emancipation, taxation, reform, and the American Civil War, and such particular events of immediate concern as religious revivals in the north of Ireland, the suppression of pugilism, the marriage of the Prince of Wales to Princess Alexandra (of which it was asked whether the 'Character of the Rejoicings was Worthy of the Age'), the bombardment of Kagosima, and the execution of Townley.[7]

Since the *Controversialist* saw itself as both a Christian and an impartial magazine, a great deal of attention was paid to religion. Almost every question in ecclesiastical, theological, and biblical affairs was debated – sabbatarianism, infant baptism, eternal punishment, church rates, miracles, three separate debates on the Bible and geology, a 'Topic' and three articles on *Essays and Reviews*, whether the Offertory was Preferable to the Pew-Rent System, and whether there was Sufficient Evidence apart from Scripture to believe in the Immortality of the Soul.

Under the heading 'History' there were debates over Charles I, Cromwell, Wellington, Mahomet, Mary Queen of Scots, Joan of Arc, and Queen Elizabeth. The reader of the *Controversialist* was asked about the value of the Crusades, the French Revolution, the Papacy, and the financial policy of the Nineteenth Century. There were debates on mesmerism, spiritualism, Darwinism, puritanism, scepticism, Napoleonism, non-interventionism, alcoholism, ritualism, vegetarianism, communism, and disestablishmentarianism; on the connection between crime and insanity, mind and matter, education and sensuality, national wealth and national morality; and on such a miscellany as 'Ought Horse-Racing to be Discouraged?', 'Ought the East

India Company to be Abolished?', 'Does the Country seem to be Ripening for Revolution?', 'Is Man the Creature of Circumstances?', 'Ought the Subjection of Women to be Discontinued?', 'Does the Present Multiplicity of Periodicals Retard rather than Foster Intellectual Progress?', and, of course, that annual blister, 'Ought Marriage with a Deceased Wife's Sister to be Legalized?'

Exhausting as this catalogue may be, it is far from exhaustive. Incomplete as it is, the combination here of the significant and the trivial, the famous and the obscure, shows why magazines like the *Controversialist*, if we can find a way to mine them, can lead us into the heart of the Victorian world.

3

The volumes I have chosen for a more detailed probing are those for 1851 and for the first halves of 1861 and 1871. 1851 was the *Controversialist*'s first complete year. The January issue began with an instalment of 'The Art of Reasoning', a series which had provided the leading article since the first issue in May 1850. The *Controversialist*'s sense of itself as part of the intellectual current of the time, and also of the 'rational' nature of its educational work, is shown in its choosing to lead each of its early issues with an article which was essentially a chapter in a textbook on formal logic. Another series which also ran throughout 1851 was 'The Art of Speaking', intended to teach an equally important aspect of self-education, the capacity to communicate clearly and effectively what had been acquired through reasoning.

Given their conviction that reasoning and communication were the main ingredients in the advancement both of the hitherto uneducated and of the nation as a whole, indeed, of civilization, the editors of the *Controversialist* considered controversy in the form of debate the primary mechanism for self-education, and so debate comes foremost both in the pages of the magazine and in its suggestions to young men, who are advised that the best way to self-improvement lies in joining or forming a society dedicated to mutual self-improvement.

The debates best illustrate the intention of the *Controversialist*. The choice of subjects was determined by the editors with advice from contributors and subscribers. The subjects were advertised on the wrappers of the monthly issues and submissions were invited. Recurring initials and pseudonyms suggest the existence of something like a team of regular debaters, drawn presumably from among the editors' acquaintance or from readers who wanted to try their hand in print. It is a major task of future research to try to identify these people.

One early debate was 'Can the Government Interdict the Establishment of the Roman Catholic Hierarchy consistently with the principles of Religious Liberty?' This debate coincided with the uproar over the Vatican's intentions to re-establish formal dioceses in Britain for the first time since the Reformation. It hinged superficially on the legality of that action, but in effect one side felt that national principles of religious liberty should be applied to Roman Catholicism, even though it claimed to control not only the spiritual lives of Catholics but also much of their secular lives and indeed even parts of the spiritual and secular lives of non-Catholics. The other side felt that what the Vatican was doing in proposing to appoint Wiseman Cardinal Archbishop of Westminster was indeed 'papal aggression' and that the monstrosities of Rome made impossible the ordinary application of British decency.

Another early debate was 'Have the Working Classes been Benefitted by Machinery?' The main argument of those taking the negative side was that whereas, at best, the material benefits of machinery for working people was doubtful, the more important moral consequences were clearly malign. No one doubted that mechanized production accounted for the recent notable increase in national wealth nor that machinery had increased the conveniences of civilized life and had brought new work, better wages, and a higher standard of living. But these advantages had certainly not spread through the whole of the working population, and, even among those who had benefitted materially, there had been an accompanying moral decline, a deterioration in the quality of working-class domesticity so serious that higher wages or an improved diet could not compensate for the growing dissolution of family ties. Wives and daughters were working in the factories, and as a result, home had lost its charms and had given way to the saloon, the gin palace, the theatre, and the tavern.

Machinery had caused unprecedented crowding in the cities with consequent terrible housing and a dramatic increase in disease, vice, and crime. This same movement away from the country had also severed the natural and traditionally benevolent ties between the poor and the wealthy. Manufacturers and factory overseers took advantage of their almost despotic power to abuse those who worked for them, especially the women, in ways that custom and publicity had hitherto prevented. It was a mistake to measure the prosperity of England through its productivity. An increase in the happiness of the masses could not only result from an increase in virtue, and nobody could claim that the introduction of machinery had improved the virtue of the working people. Machinery had produced great national wealth and had greatly encouraged the practical intellect, but the working classes as a whole had lost more than they gained.

The other side conceded that machinery had its costs, but the main thing was that machinery had increased the potential of the working classes for liberty. The breaking of ties with the squire and parson was a blessing rather than a curse, and it was good to be rid of those feudal relics which claimed to set boundaries on the freedoms of Englishmen of however humble a station. Many of the accusations brought against the effects of machinery had some truth to them, but this was because the new conditions of work were not yet properly understood. The freedoms which the new machinery permitted, whatever the initial problems, were essential if working people were to gain independence and self-respect. In the long run, machinery would lessen drudgery, and the very gathering of people in close quarters would make easier that education which alone could advance the general condition of the people.

In May, a debate was started on the subject, 'Ought the Government to provide a Secular Education for the People?' Everyone acknowledged that some significant increase in Britain's capacity to educate its people was needed. The opponents of the proposal made a distinction between mental instruction and true education, which included moral education. Moral education required a substantive religious component, which could not be simply or even primarily doctrinal, but would have to include genuine spiritual teaching, and this could only be done through some sort of voluntary system. Moreover, there was a connection between voluntary education and the freedom of the educated because a capacity for self-reliance and self-education would be tainted by government involvement. Secular or government education would also tend to increase dependence and mass pauperism and such symptoms of cultural decline as trashy reading material.

For those in favour of secular education the greatest enemy of liberty was ignorance. They did not want to inhibit the development of religious education, but the inability of proponents of religious education to settle their sectarian differences meant that, quite apart from the merits of secular education, something had to be done to fit the people for their growing responsibilities. In the absence of a national plan for general education, the people were being 'educated' by evil companions, natural depravity, and all the other ills of unrelieved and unsupervised ignorance.

The next debate asked, 'Is it more reasonable and beneficial to subsist on a vegetable diet than on one of flesh and vegetables?' In this debate there was a sort of stand-off about the interpretation of scriptural texts, for example, that having to do with the miracle of the loaves and fishes. The argument of those favouring vegetarianism was not only that flesh-eating was less beneficial than vegetarianism, it was that the human species was more naturally herbivorous than carnivorous, witness man's teeth, his digestive system, and his general 'nutritional economy'. Meat caused sensuality and boisterousness, while a vegetable diet helped people towards a tranquil, rational sense of joy and self-control. People were also becoming increasingly humane and merciful and public concern about the slaughter of animals for food was growing. The main argument against vegetarianism, apart from the claim that meat was nutritious and necessary for those who lived in cold climates, was that it was a fad to be lumped with Puseyism, Mormonism, Chartism, teetotalism, and Bloomerism. Rules of life were too serious a matter to be settled by discussions of what made an appropriate dinner, and young people especially should have a higher opinion of the dignity of their nature than to base their creed on such external trifles as the conditions of government or ritual or clothing or diet.

The remaining debates for 1851 were: 'Is Sectarianism Christian?', 'Was Oliver Cromwell a first-rate general, a great Statesman, and a sincere Man?', 'Does the Divine Trinity of Father, Son, and Holy Spirit exist in the Person of Our Lord Jesus Christ?', 'Is Language of Human or Divine Origin?', and 'Is Mesmerism True?'. These five debates and the four I have summarized take up only one year of the *Controversialist*'s nearly 23. It is impossible to give anything other than titles for the debates of 1861 and 1871, so these four will have to suffice as an indication of the details of the habits of thought and assumption of one segment of mid-Victorian Britain.

From the beginning, the *Controversialist* included notices of publications, though there were at the start few entries extensive enough to be called book reviews. Some 20 books were noted in 1851, all having to do with education and self-help and nearly half having some connection with religion. Typical titles from the February number are *Not the Church, not the Pope, but the Bible*; *Chapters on Policy v. Straightforwardness*; *Thoughts on the Nature of Man, the Propagation of Creeds, and the Formation of Human Character*; four volumes 'printed phonetically' (that is, in shorthand), one of them the Bible; and *Hamilton's Temperance Music Book*, which included a song called, 'A glass! a glass! but not of sherry'.

Among other 1851 books noticed were *A Progressive Course of Inventive Drawing on the principles of Pestalozzi, for the use of Teachers and for self instruction*, which is cited as an example of 'the vast increase of books for the young' and as evidence that 'everything has now its manual – from Egyptian Hieroglyphics down to the cure of corns and bunions'; *The First Steps in Chemistry*, 'a definite course of study for the self-instructed'; *The Paperhanger's and Upholsterer's Guide*; and *Gutta Percha; its Discovery, History, and Manifold Uses*. The most substantial review was given to *Christianity and its Evidence's* by the Rev. J. G. Rogers, which was highly recommended for its effort to repair the breach made by Rationalism. The reviewer's comment is worth quoting as a summary account of 'dissolvent' literature in 1851:

Rationalism is undoubtedly progressing in England. The publication of such works as Froude's 'Shadows of the Clouds,' and 'Nemesis of Faith;' Newman's 'Phases of Faith,' and 'The Soul: her Sorrows and her Aspirations;' W. J. Fox's 'Religious Ideas;' Mackay's 'Progress of the Intellect;' the extensive sale of the works of Theodore Parker and R. W. Emerson, as well as the translation of Strauss' 'Leben Jesu,' and the popularity of Thomas Cooper, the author of the 'Purgatory of Suicides,' & c., and the expounder of German rationalism to the people, – amply demonstrate this fact.

Through 'The Inquirer', readers submitted questions to be answered either by other readers or by members of the *Controversialist*'s editorial staff. Thirty-four inquiries were printed in 1851, ten asking directly for help in setting up a course of study, such as a language, mathematics, or history, with an emphasis on cheap texts. Other questioners wanted information about Saint Cecilia, or Cyrus, or the differences between two theories of electro-biology. Many questions referred to vocation, asking about mechanics and navigation, and wanting to know what were the qualifications of a skilled clerk in a solicitor's or a merchant's office, of a parliamentary reporter, how to get admitted to the Bar, and whether a self-educated young man putting in six hours a day could hope for admission to Trinity College, Dublin.

'The Inquirer' also received questions asking for aid in developing good study habits. Two questions, both elaborately answered, dealt with memory and mnemonics. There were also requests for advice about coping with weak vision, with 'wandering thoughts', and with the need for 'fixedness of purpose' in educational pursuits. A smaller set of questions were more social, asking, for instance, about correct pronunciation, about the art of conversation, and about how 'A. B., who is desirous of showing courtesy to C. D. (an equal)' with whom he 'has long held daily intercourse' should behave when C. D. has a propensity 'to insult and cast contempt on A. B., entirely *unprovoked*'.

The *Controversialist* regularly published reports from mutual improvement societies in its 'Societies' Section'. These reports contain the best clues to the nature and significance of the *Controversialist*'s actual and potential readership, and thus to its particular spot in the complicated cultural geography of mid-Victorian Britain. Thirty-two such societies reported during 1851: six from London, five from Scotland, five from Lancashire, two from Essex, and the others from Devon, Hampshire, Kent, Leicestershire, Middlesex, Monmouthshire, Nottinghamshire, Suffolk, Sussex, Yorkshire, and the West Indies. One from the Watton Mutual Improvement Society does not say whether this is the Watton in Hertfordshire, Norfolk, or that in the East Riding of Yorkshire. Typically, this report describes the Society's first anniversary *soirée* at the Lodge Room of the Crown Inn, where 190 friends, male and female, sat down to tea. The meeting was chaired by the Society's president, the Rev. A. Griffin, and speakers 'urged the necessity of increased exertion, during the coming year, in carrying the object for which the Society was formed, viz., the moral and intellectual improvement of the people'. The Society was proud to have 120 members in a town whose population was only 1,100.

Another typical report was that of the Uxbridge Young Men's Improvement Society, where the Rev. C. P. Price rejoiced that the society 'had done something in giving the youth of the town a refuge from the taproom and the gaming table'. The Society's secretary characterized it as 'a college for the people' which gave no degrees but prepared them 'to fill as they should do the station to which they have been called'. The Rev. D. Bailey, while 'glad to identify himself with the society', saw it as evidence of that general progress of society which included railways, tubular bridges, and electricity, all of which by reducing manual labour should give the people 'greater space for cultivation of the mind'. He did, however, warn its members not to mistake intellectual greatness for moral goodness.

Most of the societies conducted debates, regular classes of instruction, and a lecture series, and some of them circulated manuscript magazines. Several mention the *Controversialist*, recommending it to their members, including it in their libraries, and using it as a source of debate topics. The general impression these reports give, even in these societies presided over by clergymen, addressed by mayors, and patronized by gentlemen, is of a self-directed movement of thousands of young working men in towns and villages throughout Britain convinced that they are educating themselves into a better life and thereby contributing to national progress.

This impression is confirmed by 'The Young Student and Writer's Assistant', initiated in 1851 in response to letters from 'earnest young men eager to train their intellectual faculties and to acquire graceful and accurate powers of expression'. This was essentially a correspondence course with grading, critiques, certificates for those who did well, and prizes for those who did best. Students were obliged to write essays based on questions which were in turn derived from the leading essays of recent issues of the *Controversialist*. Instructions even included a warning about proper quotation and the avoidance of plagiarism.

We can end this survey of the 1851 volume as the editors did with the Preface which was printed with the December issue. The editors were confident that the *Controversialist* was 'no unworthy offering to be placed on the altar of our country, or to be cast at the feet of the true-progress spirit of our age'. They were proud that it had been widely and favourably reviewed by the public press of 'every shade of politics'. Most important of all, however, they were generating 'influences, that for ages yet to come, may regulate the pulsations of many a throbbing heart, and direct the aspirations of many an earnest soul'. They even went so far as to say that 'in our pages, perhaps for the first time, Truth and Error have been *fairly* brought into contact with each other'. If the realm of Error is 'thus invaded the lovers of Truth and herself thus brought into the dread presence of Reason – she must inevitably die!' The editors ended their first complete year on a practical note by telling the readership 'We are powerful only as we are popular', and by asking for 'A CIRCULATION OF 10,000 COPIES'.

4

Space will not permit, nor does a description of the *Controversialist* require, as detailed an examination of the volumes for 1861 and 1871 as I have given to that for 1851. I shall focus instead on suggesting how much continuity and how much change marked the *Controversialist*'s career during the ten-year interval between volumes.

Since 1856, when it began its Second Series, the *Controversialist* had published two volumes a year. By 1861, the monthly issue had doubled in size to 72 pages. There are three new departments: the 'Topic', the 'Essayist', and a series of short Literary Notes which end each issue. The format of the volumes is not significantly different. There are still the substantial leading articles; still the debates in religion, social economy, politics, and history; still reviews of books, the 'Inquirer', and the 'Societies' Section'. The editorial commitment seems as strong as ever, and the formal pronouncement, enshrined, so to speak, in the half-yearly Preface, is as ambitious, confident, and energetic as it was in the Preface of 1851.

Yet the *Controversialist* in its twelfth year was not the same as it was in its second. To go abruptly from 1851 to 1861 is to become aware of a change in the nature of the magazine which is not apparent in a year-by-year survey. It is idle to try to guess how much of this was the result of general changes between 1851 and 1861 and how much the effect of ten years in the life and fortunes of an editorial group and its readership. Nevertheless, in the 1851 *Controversialist*, there is, either as expectation or achievement, a sense of connection with thousands, potentially hundreds of thousands, of earnest young men throughout Britain whose intelligence and aspirations the *Controversialist* could harness. The encouragement of mutual improvement societies and their like and the provision of the needed intellectual and informational resources could make those societies a national university, training a new generation to take its deserved place in national affairs.

By 1861, some of the intensity and excitement of the early volumes has evaporated. It would be an exaggeration to say that the producers of the magazine were writing for themselves, for the *Controversialist* is still determinedly pedagogic, but it no longer conveys the impression of addressing eager and relatively ignorant minds ready to ingest enormous amounts of instruction and advice. The pace is more deliberate; the tone is more academic; the content, that is the shared world, more that of the intelligentsia. The Literary Notes, for example, which refer frequently to the Continent and America, are no different from the sort of 'Intelligence' one would find in the *Athenaeum* or the *Saturday Review*. The debates seem somehow more learned and the essays and leading articles more uniformly aimed at a knowledgeable readership.

This general difference can be seen in the 'Societies' Section', originally intended to display, under the patronage of the *Controversalist*, a growing network of local societies, contributing to the moral, spiritual, and political well-being of the nation and, by the familiar Victorian extension, of the species. By 1861, there is a noticeable dropping off of general reports of the annual meetings of local and usually unpretentious Mechanics' Institutes and Young Men's Mutual Improvement Societies. It is tempting to speculate, despite the absence of any external evidence, that the *Controversialist*'s plans for creating a momentum of interest in the magazine as a repository of such reports had not succeeded. It may be that the activity itself had subsided, though a report noting the existence of a Worcestershire Union of Educational Institutes is evidence not only of activity but of heightened collaboration clearly quite independent of the *Controversialist*.

The January 1861 entry illustrates what I mean, for, although it includes reports from Manchester of the third annual *soirée* of the Chalmer's Presbyterian Church Young Men's Association and from London of the Claylands Discussion Society of Kennington, it focusses on three quite different items: a report from Glasgow of a lecture on poetry and fiction by the Rev. Dr Caird, held in the Corporation Galleries in which 'the elegant centre gallery was quite crowded with a fashionable audience'; a report from London of a party held by Mr and Mrs C. E. Mudie to celebrate the opening of a new hall at Mudie's Library, which describes its interior decor and impressive statuary and lists the literary celebrities present; and the eighth annual report of the Manchester Public Free Libraries, which would not, I believe, have found a place in this column ten years earlier. The remaining item in the January entry, also from London, speaks of the founding of the Post Office Library and Literary Association for the benefit of employees of the General Post Office at St Martin's-le-Grand (though it is not clear what social or professional range of employees is involved). A set of lectures is announced, beginning with Anthony Trollope on the Civil Service as a profession and followed by Thomas Hughes, G. H. Lewes, George Grossmith, and T. A. Trollope, among others. This entry, which was presumably intelligible to its readers, is almost cryptic to us, for it is hard to imagine which particular employees of the General Post Office were eligible for membership in this association and which were not.

The 'Societies' Section' in 1861 began a series of general essays on the literary institutions of various cities starting with Manchester and its sixteenth-century Grammer School and relegating the category of societies in which the *Controversialist* was supposed to be most interested to a large group of 'minor "literary" Institutions, more or less public in their character, which it were useless, not to say impossible . . . to particularize'. The October entry is worth mentioning because it includes both a report of a debating club in Kandy, Ceylon, and a long first-person account by Samuel Neil of what he called a necessary health journey (to relieve the pressures of his incessant labours on behalf of the readership of the *Controversialist*) to the Midlands and the North, where he met people whom he had only known before as colleagues in the work of the *Controversialist.*

'The Inquirer' columns also changed. There were still questions asking for general advice: 'I am about to commence studying the German language without a master, would any of your readers inform me which is the best Grammar?' But more typical for 1861 is the request for specialized information such as the following from 'Antiquarian' who asks 'What were the colour, form, and material of the ancient Roman mourning costume?' or from the questioner who has a small Latin book entitled '"The Works of Johaanis Sleidani" . . . Would any reader of the *British Controversialist* let me know . . . anything concerning the author or book?'

One new regular feature does not fit clearly into these generalizations. 'The Topic' was a sort of mini-debate always on some subject of immediate interest, in which usually short selections from what must have been a substantial number of submissions were presented under affirmative and negative headings all within the one issue. In April, for instance, the 'Topic' was 'Is the Secession of the Southern States of America from the Union Desirable?'; in May it was 'Is Lord John Russell justified in Declining to Bring a Reform Bill?' These pages were always lively and by definition timely and this surely helped to multiply the number of connections between the editorial office and the readership.

The subjects debated in the January-June 1861 volume hardly differ in kind from those for 1851 and therein lies the presupposition of continuity. They were: 'Is the Christian Ministry recognized in the New Testament as A Distinct Order in the Church', 'Are the Principles of the Pre-Raphaelite

School of Painters correct?', 'Are the Modern Phenomena designated "Spiritual Manifestations" genuine? and have we in them Satisfactory Evidence of Inter-course with the Inhabitants of the Spiritual World?', 'Is the House of Lords, in its Existence and Operations, Beneficial to the Country?', 'Was the Secession of the Free Church of Scotland Justifiable?', and 'Ought the Employment of Females in Agricultural, Manufacturing, and Commercial Pursuits to be Encouraged?'

I have said that these debates were more 'learned' than those of 1851. It is not only that the level of cultivation and information is higher. In the 1851 volume, editors and their colleagues and other earnest gentlemen, united in their commitment to the general social and cultural panacea of education and the particular tool of controversy, participated in the debates partly from an interest in the subject and from pleasure in the activity itself. But another and stronger object was to attract and encourage the participation of the equally earnest young men for whom the magazine was designed.

By 1861, this second object – to inspire a socially inferior group to improve itself by imitation – seems no longer to dominate. The individual contributors to the debates concentrate on the subject itself and on the other debaters and no longer seem aware of that throng of artisans, clerks, exceptional members of the industrial and agricultural workforce, whose attraction to the *Controversialist* will lead to their own advancement and, through that, to the general progress of British society.

What the evidence rather bewilderingly suggests is that by 1861 those who read the *Controversialist* had become very much more like those who conducted it. But it was precisely the objective of the founders to appeal to a class of readers not yet educated enough to enjoy the level of amateur erudition which marks the 1861 volume. Was the *Controversialist* being increasingly read by those who were, so to speak, the 'providers' of instruction and of the material for self-education and decreasingly by the 'consumers', or had the original intended readership stayed loyal so that the ignorant 20-year-old of 1851 had become the relatively well-educated 30-year-old of 1861? It is perhaps more likely that the *Controversialist* did not catch on as vigorously as its initiators had hoped, and that there was an unconscious slide towards allowing its pages to be used by articulate and fluent people writing for each other rather than for the 'young men', whether or not the latter were still readers and subscribers.

5

In 1871, the *Controversialist* was within a year of coming to a close, but the casual or even the regular reader could easily miss any signals that the life of the magazine was threatened. Nevertheless, the signals are there.

As with the 1861 volume, the 1871 *Controversialist* is on the surface more like than unlike the 1851 volume. Each monthly issue begins with a leading article; three or four debates are in progress; and the same heading persist: the 'Essayist', the 'Societies' Section', 'The Inquirer', 'Literary Notes', all of which take their usual forms. But a closer examination reveals significant changes, although it is hard to tell whether these changes are significant only in themselves or as a response either to large-scale social and cultural changes since 1861 of which the *Controversialist*'s changes are a symptomatic reflection or to some special circumstances affecting the *Controversialist*'s staff or readership.

Hindsight tempts us to choose the latter possibility, because we now know that we are reading the penultimate volume. Moreover, the 21st anniversary issue of May 1871 included an unsigned piece called 'Past, Present, and Future', which was an account of the origins, history, current condition, and prospects of the magazine. The essay calls itself a celebration, noting how much that was original and even eccentric in 1850 has now become commonplace, in particular the very idea of controversy and 'impartial inquiry', and in general taking pride in the contribution which the *Controversialist* has made to the enlightenment of generations of young men, and through them, to that general enlightenment which, for the authors, characterizes the times in which they live. But, despite the celebration, one comes away from a reading of this essay understanding that its real purpose is to warn readers that, after 21 years as mainstay of the magazine, these two 'originators' need to hand over their responsibility to a new team. It is also clear that they are asking readers for greater support: money, contributions to the pages of the magazine, and missionary work on its behalf, particularly in urging societies to send reports of their activities.

The 'internal' importance of this article is apparent from its being cited in the volume's Preface and from its being reprinted verbatim as part of an elaborate advertisement for the *Controversialist* which, though clearly also issued independently, is bound in after the last issue. The elaborateness of the advertisement, which is tantamount to a table of contents to the previous 25 volumes, reinforces both the article's plea for support and the unspoken message that without that support the future of the *Controversialist* might well be in danger.

It is tempting to speculate that the difficulties went beyond the need of the original staff for relief. The life of a journal may well be a function of the endurance of those who started it, unless it fulfils the authentic needs of a 'special interest' or an economically significant group of readers, in which case the readers supply the life and the magazine becomes independent of the commitment and inspiration of the staff. For most of those magazines which do not catch on exhaustion seems to be reached after a few issues, or at the most, a few volumes. It may therefore be that the *Controversialist* had met and continued to meet a significant need – there is some evidence to support its continued claims to that effect – or it may be that those who began it were extraordinarily dedicated and had taken 21 years to 'burn out'.

Whatever the case, by 1871, those signs of co-operation with a network of contributors, readers, and small societies have almost entirely disappeared, and the *Controversialist* looks much more like a typical intellectual magazine and much less like a forum for discussion or a classroom in print. In this respect, the 1871 volume bears the same relationship to the 1861 volume that the latter does to the 1851 volume. The leading articles are both longer and more numerous. The 'Essayist', which had been not only shorter but on the whole lighter and more discursive than a leading article, had become sufficiently substantial to be in some months indistinguishable from the leading article. 'Toiling Upward', a new series of accounts of literary, learned, and professional men of working-class origin, provides yet another occasion for the formal essay. Even 'Our Collegiate Course' takes the form of a detailed exposition of a single literary text (in this case, Shakespeare's 'The Lover's Complaint') and entirely forgoes discussion with or reply to correspondents.

'The Inquirer' and the 'Societies' Section', which, in 1851 and to a lesser extent in 1861, had been the places in the *Controversialist* in which its role as a meeting-place of conductors and readers had been most obvious and prominent, retained their form but no longer appear in every issue and, when they do, take up a much smaller proportion of the month's pages. Moreover, their nature has changed in a way that is an extension of the difference between 1851 and 1861. In 'The Inquirer', the questions are not only on the whole far more scholarly, they are much more extensive, as are the answers. In fact, some of the answers tend towards being self-contained essays, just as many fewer of the questions are simple requests for helpful information towards self-education. A typical question for 1871 runs: 'The writer of the preface to "The Liberty and Necessity of Hobbes" speaks of "the excellent but borrowed Caryl upon Job." What ground is there for impugning the originality of the commentary of Oliver Cromwell's Chaplain in Scotland?' A not-so-typical but symptomatic answer is a seven-column, two-part disquisition telling an inquirer about the 'Westminster Scandal' (when the dean of Westminster celebrated Holy Communion to mark the start of work on a revised version of the Bible and included a Unitarian scholar whose presence on the Commission was itself a scandal to some).

The 'Societies' Section' no longer claims to retain its initial primary purpose. A few reports of mutual improvement societies are printed in 1871, but for the most part, the 'Societies' Section', again tending towards the form of the essay, is dominated by printings and paraphrases of addresses and lectures, some with no identifiable connection with any society. The very first two entries, neither of which even mentions a society, are 'Duty. A New Year's Address', which seems more appropriate to the 'Essayist', and a long piece, 'A Glimpse of "the Clapham Sect" at Home', from a lecture on Macaulay 'delivered in the Town Hall at Gult [*sic*], Ontario, U.S., by W. Morley Punshon, 1st Nov., 1870.'

The 1871 'Topic' is much like the 1871 'Inquirer' in that the whole item is characteristically less prominent; there are significantly fewer contributors, and the contributions are themselves wordier. The first 'Topic' of 1871, 'Ought Military Drill to be incorporated into Elementary Education?', does not appear until April and has only four entries each a column in length (compared to 14 entries of about half a column apiece in April 1861).

The debates in 1871 remind us of the *Controversialist*'s commitment to New Testament Christianity, for most of them deal in one way or another with religion. In additon to the two debates so classified, the education debate (a new category) is 'Should the Bible be read in Schools without Comment or Explanation?', and the history one is 'Were the Crusades Beneficial to Social Progress?' Under religion itself we have 'Is there Sufficient Evidence in the Scriptures to warrant belief in the Godhead of Jesus Christ?' and 'Ought the Authorised Version of the Holy Scriptures be Revised by a Royal Commission?' To fill out the list, under politics, the subjects are 'Ought War Organization to get the Chief Attention in our parliament?' and 'A Professional or a Popular Army – which shall we have?' Finally, under science (another new category), 'Is Man developed from the Savage State?'

The debates for 1871 show rather obviously (what is generally true for the *Controversialist*) that the editors were eager to exploit current events: the education debate derives from the consequences of Forster's Education Act; the one about revising the Bible, from the procedures which were to lead to the Revised Version; the two military debates from the Franco-Prussian War; and the science one, from the recent publication of Darwin's *The Descent of Man*.

So much, then, for the *Controversialist*'s last volume but one. If, in this glance at an early, a middle, and a late sample of the magazine, I have given the impression of a steady departure from its original purpose, I do not intend to imply that the *Controversialist* was a failure. Nearly a quarter of a century of continuous publication (a total of 272 monthly numbers) is testimony to some sort of vitality and success. The *Controversialist* had surely fulfilled the hope of its Introductory Address of May 1850 that it would provide 'an arena into which men of all sects and parties may enter to state and maintain their views, so that the impartial spectator may see the strength or weakness of every proposition, and be led to receive that truth, which, amidst the conflicts of opinion, it is hoped will be evolved'.

6

Although one of the tasks of this chapter has been to identify the uses of hitherto little-used Victorian serials, I have chosen to illustrate the value of such uses by trying to describe a single periodical at some length rather than some spectrum of a dozen or two which might be described in a few paragraphs apiece. The disadvantage of this is that as soon as one focusses on any periodical it ceases to be representative of anything more than at most a small group of titles of a particular time or place or for an audience of a particular class or belief or interest. At the extreme, the periodical becomes representative only of itself, acquiring its own special character, its own unique combination of subject-matter and editor-contributor-reader interaction.

But we should not lose the long view in which the *Controversialist* is, after all, a pearl from the Golden Stream, a typical fragment in that great expansion of serial publishing which characterizes the last two-thirds of the nineteenth century. Starting a newspaper or a magazine seems to have been part of the Victorian eagerness to create special communities at a time when the larger community seemed in jeopardy, and had become a sort of natural response for anyone who had an idea to share with anyone else.

As a journal running from 1850 to 1872 and addressing itself to the 'self-educating' classes, the *Controversialist* represents neatly a significant stage in Victorian social development, for it approximately covers that period during which not only the established classes but the most articulate voices among the clerical and lower professional classes and among the labouring classes themselves had turned from the anxieties and antagonisms of the radical and Chartist years to the milder 'assimilationist' and 'conciliationist' views which were embodied in adult education, the many varieties of institutionalized self-help, and even perhaps the political movements which climaxed in the 1867 Reform Act and the 1868 Gladstone government. And it is by the early 1870s that much of that individualistic and conformist spirit seems to have run its course and the hidden but surely persistent tensions of class division begin to re-emerge. These years are essentially those of the generation of W. L. Burn's temporary 'age of equipoise', during which, as at no other time in their century or ours, it was possible to think of there being a national frame of mind. The *Controversialist* is thus an appropriate representative of a central preoccupation of its years of existence. It would have been a far more eccentric magazine had it run from 1830–52 or 1870–92.

Moreover, it shows its appropriateness in an unusually rich way by its providing what may well be an epitome of mid-Victorian middle-of-the road opinion on scores of subjects which the mid-Victorians themselves found most pressing or significant. What in particular the controversies and essays and reports represent and how general their interpretative use will depend on an accumulation of much investigation. I hope specialists will find occasion to take a particular item in the *Controversialist* and relate it to what else is known about mid-Victorian thought and sentiment on the subject. My own view is that, whatever the result of such a series of investigations, the work would be well worth the undertaking, and my guess is that the *Controversialist* will prove to be a compendium of mid-Victorian facts and opinions, both shared and disputed, on those subjects the mid-Victorians thought most important.

If history really is not what happened but what people thought about what happened, then the *Controversialist* is an extraordinarily complicated and fruitful primary source.[8]

NOTES

1. John M. Robson (ed.) *Editing Nineteenth-Century Texts* (Toronto, 1967), 37–59; repr. *VPN*, no. 13 (Sept. 1971), 23–38.
2. *Ibid.*, 55 (*VPN*, 34).
3. 'The unknown public' *Household Words*, xviii (21 Aug. 1858), 222.
4. Frederic Boase, *Modern English Biography* (1908; repr. 1965), iv, col. 747. With this exception I have confined my discussion of the *Controversialist* to internal evidence. However, I have not run across any biographical material on Samuel Neil, who, it appears, was a resident of Glasgow and survived into the twentieth century.
5. I printed a complete list of debates in *VPN*, no. 2 (June 1968), 29–45.
6. The references to George Eliot are characteristically illuminating, from rumours that Blackwood's is planning to issue *George Eliot's Magazine* and that George Eliot is the author of the *Chronicles of Carlingford*, to the enthusiastic review of *Adam Bede* welcoming 'a thoroughly *Christian* author', an enthusiasm which the revelation of the strong-minded Miss Evans did not altogether dissipate, though there is some irritation (and a scolding comparison with George Sand) in the review of *The Mill on the Floss*. There were no further reviews of the fiction, but a long notice of the

Spanish Gipsy was full of high praise both for the poem and for the 'translator of Strauss, daughter of a dissenting, if we mistake not, a Unitarian minister, born 1820 in Belper, Derbyshire'.
7. Kagosima was a Japanese coastal town subjected to a naval shelling in 1863 in reprisal for a Japanese prince's refusal to pay compensation for the murder by his retinue of a travelling Englishman. There was considerable debate in Parliament and the press about the legality and propriety of the bombardment. In the so-called Derbyshire murder of 1863, George Townley, a respectable young man, had killed his equally respectable ex-fiancée after learning that she was to marry another. There had been conflicting evidence about his sanity, and the magistrate had been himself unclear about the legal definition of insanity. The Home Secretary's stay of execution had caused an uproar, but he later received a unanimous report from experts that Townley was indeed sane. The sentence was reinstated and commuted to penal servitude for life.
8. I am indebted to the University of Massachusetts, Amherst, and to the American Council of Learned Societies for their generous support of time spent working on this article.

Index

Academy, the, 18, 93
Acton, Lord, 3, 9, 13
Adams, W. E., 283
Age, the, 318–19, 321–32, 335–7, 340, 344; see also Age and Argus, English Gentleman
Age and Argus, 340; see also Age
Ainsworth's Magazine, 18
Alderman, Grace, 272
Alford, Henry, Dean, 11, 13
All the Year Round, 18, 369
Allen, George, 51, 57 n.2
Alliance, the, 269
Alliance News, 265, 273, 277, 279, 287
Alliance Weekly News, 286
Allingham, William, 82
Althorp, Lord, 232, plate 4
Amalgamated Association of Miners (A.A.M.), 302, 303, 304, 306, 312
Amberley, Lord, 168
Amddiffynydd y Gweithiwr, 306, 308, 311, 312
Anderton, P., 316 n.74
Andrews, Alexander, 341, 342, 344
Animals' Guardian, 278
Annan, Noel, 176
annuals, 57 n.7
Anster, John, 155
Anti-Bread Tax Circular, 284
Anti-Corn Law Circular, 279
Anti-Jacobin Review, 344
Anti-Slavery Reporter, 282, 284
Anti-Vivisectionist, 277
Argosy, 18
Argyll, Duke of, 152
Armstrong, Isobel, 109, 110 n.140, 136 n.5, 136 n.7
Arnold, Matthew, 3, 6, 9, 10, 11, 13, 14, 15, 25 n.29, 181; Culture and Anarchy, 9, 22; works in periodicals, 21–2; influence of literary criticism, 110–11, 114–17, 122, 133–5
Arnold, Thomas, 6, 25 n.15, 113
Art Journal, 47, 51; art criticism in, 79, 84, 88, 89, 91–4, 96–8, 100–3
Artists' and Amateurs' Magazine, 46, 83
Ashley, Lord, 263, 266
Asquith, Ivan, 164 n.2
Athenaeum, 18, 80, 385; art criticism in, 82–3, 85, 91–2, 94, 97
Atkinson, George, 188
Atkinson, H. G., 177
Atkinson, J. B., 89, 94
Atlas, the, 319

Bagehot, Walter, 3, 5, 6–10, 17–18, 25, n.29, 264, 265; literary criticism, 115, 117, 120, 122, 127–8, 132–5
Baines, Edward, 230
Baker, Samuel, 3
Baldwin and Craddock, 230, 232
Balfour, A. J., 275
Balfour, Betty, 273
Ballot, the, 278
Band of Hope Record, 284
Band of Hope Review, 277, plate 11
Barnett, Samuel, 274
Bastard, Thomas Horlock, 176
Bax, Belfort, 275
Bee-Hive, the, 287, 298, 299, 300, 314 n.2
Belgravia, 18, 79, 88, 102, 103
Bell's Life in London, 319, 343
Bennett, Scott, 345, 347 n.26
Bentham, Jeremy, 62, 63, 167
Bentley, Richard, 20
Bentley's Miscellany, 18
Bentley's Quarterly Review, 13
Berkeley, Henry, 266
Berridge, V. S., 315 n.62, 316 n.78
Best, G. F. A., 368
Biographical Dictionary (S.D.U.K.), 229, 232–3
Birt, Mr, 183
Black, John, 60
Blackburn, Henry, 101
Blackie, John Stuart, 152
Blackwood's Magazine, 7, 12, 18, 19, 79; De Quincey in, 21; George Eliot in, 23; art criticism, 86, 88–9, 94, 96; circulation and profitability, 235–41
Blaikie, William Garden, 147, 155, 162, 163
Blanchard, Laman, 85
Bow Bells, 358–65, plate 12
Brabant, Dr R. H., 176
Bradlaugh, Charles, 269
Bray, Charles, 176
Brewitt, Bellamy, brother of Susanna Chapman, 182
Bridges, John, 190
Bright, Jacob, 264, 265, 266, 270
Bright, John, 265–6, 284
Brignal, W. A., 204–5, 218–20
Brimley, George, 120
British and Foreign Bible Society, 230
British and Foreign Review, the, 14, 15, 16
British and Foreign Temperance Herald, 285
British and Foreign Temperance Intelligencer, see London Temperance Intelligencer

British Controversialist and Impartial Inquirer, the (1850–72), 367–92
British Critic, 12, 146
British Institution, the, 91, 92, 93
British Labourer's Protector and Factory Child's Friend, 282
British Quarterly Review, 10, 11, 12, 13, 146, 164, 170; see also Vaughan, Robert
British Temperance Advocate, 264
Broadway, 18
Brockie, William, 200, 206
Brooke, Edward, 208
Brooks, H. E., 342
Brougham, Lord, 226, 320, *plate 4*
Broughton, Rhoda, 27 n.64
Brown, William, 304
Browne, Hablot (Phiz), 17
Browning, Robert, 109–42
Builder, the, 46
Buller, Charles, 24 n.13
Bulwer-Lytton, E., 249
Bunbury, Selina, 27 n.70
Burn, W. L., 391
Burton, John Hill, 150, 152
Burton, Richard, 3
Butler, Josephine, 168–9, 269–70, 275
Buxton, T. F., 266

Cadbury, George, 274
Cairns, Rev. John, 154, 161, 162
Callaghan, James, 271
Campaign for Nuclear Disarmament, 271, 272, 290
Candlish, John, 196, 200
Candlish, Robert Smith, 148, 150
Cannock Chase Examiner, 304
Carlile, Richard, 225, 252
Carlyle, Thomas, 3, 9, 10, 14–16, 19, 25 n.29; *Sartor Resartus*, 19–20; on literature, 119, 138 n.80; review of, 140 n.145; on John Chapman, 190
Carpenter, W. B., 185
Carr, Thomas, 207
Cave, H. A., 207
Cecil, Lord Robert, 266
Chalmers, Thomas, 148, 149, 150, 160–1
Chambers's Edinburgh Journal, 79, 92, 94–5, 225, 360; circulation and profitability, 235–41, 244–5, 250
Champion, 278
Chapman, John, 13, 16, 167–90
Cheap John, 342
Christian Remembrancer, 146, 159
Church of England Quarterly, 146
Church of England Temperance Magazine (later *Chronicle*), 276, 277
Clare, John, 57 n.7
Clarion, 273
Clarkson, Thomas, 266
Coates, Thomas, 231, 233
Cobbett, William, 225, 266
Cobden, Richard, 176, 262, 264–7, 269, 275, 279
Cockburn, Henry Thomas (Baron), 8, 148, 155

Cockrane, J. G., 15, 19
Cohen, Leonora, 289
Colburn, Henry, 20
Cole, Henry, 70
Coleridge, S. T., 109, 112
Colonial Gazette, 24 n.13
Coltham, S., 314 n.2
Combe, George, 156, 170, 174, 176, 181
Common Cause, 275, 276, 278, 288
Commonweal, 285, 287
Commonwealth, 287
Constable, Archibald, 227, 228
Constable, Thomas, 148, 150, 160, 168 n.65
Contemporary Review, 6, 13, 17, 19, 80; Pater in, 21; Ruskin in, 39, 47, 48–50; art criticism, 81, 84, 86–7
Conway, Moncure, 126
Cook, E. T. (with A. D. O. Wedderburn), 30–1, 51, 54
Cook, J. D., 145
Cooper, J. A., 371
Cooper, Thomas, 272, 278, 286
Cornhill Magazine, 18, 33, 49, 369; Arnold in, 21; Ruskin in, 36, 39, 41, 47, 53
Cotton, G. E. L., 157
Country Gentleman, 274
Courtauld, Samuel, 171, 176, 177, 181–5
Cowan, Charles, 147, 149, 150
Cowen, Joseph, 200
Craik, George Lillie, 156
Cremer, W. R., 268
Crewe Star, 316 n.74
Crim-Con Gazette, 328
Croker, John Wilson, 225, 252, 253
Cruikshank, George, 17
Cunningham, William, 148, 150, 156
Curran, Eileen, 26 n.51
Curran, James, 261
Curzon, Lord, 290–1
Cuthbert, James, 208

Daily Mail, 274
Daily Mail (Burslem), 316 n.74
Daily News, 269, 274
Daily Telegraph, 31, 272, 351; Ruskin letters in, 46
Dallas, E. S., 114–15, 119, 121, 126, 134–5, 138 n.80, 152
Darwin, Charles, 176, 183; *The Origin of Species*, 7, 16
Davies, Emily, 290
Day and Night, 344
Day's Doings, the (1870–2), 344
DeGroot, H. B., 26 n.51
Delane, J. T., 145
DeMorgan, Augustus, 24 n.12
De Quincey, Thomas, 21, 150
Derbyshire and Leicestershire Examiner, 304
Despard, Mrs, 280
de Tocqueville, 15, 368
Disraeli, Benjamin, 3, 264
Dickens, Charles, 18, 115, 136 n.41, 349–50
Dixon, Thomas, 55
Donne, W. B., 193
Doxford, W. T., 211, 212

Dublin Review, 12, 146
Dublin University Magazine, 18, 23
Duncan, William, 202–3
Duns, Rev. John, 163

Eadie, Rev. John, 156
Eastlake, Charles, 48, 100
Eclectic Review, 7, 12, 16, 146
Edinburgh Review, 5, 6, 7, 8, 11–13, 15,
   17, 19, 24 n.9, 113–14, 146–7,
   270, 368; circulation, 7, 148; Coleridge
   on, 112; comparison with *North British
   Review*, 154–5; contents, 148;
   contributors, 152
Egan, Pierce, 317, 339
Eliot, George, 9, 13, 16, 17, 376, 392 n.6;
   edits *Westminster*, 168, 170–2, 174–7,
   183; writes for *Blackwood's*, 23
Ellegård, Alvar, 25 n.14
Elliott, J. P., 304
Elliott, Philip, 164 n.2
Emerson, Ralph Waldo, 20
Emigrant's Advocate, 300; see also *Potters
   Examiner and Workman's Advocate*
English Gentleman, 340; see also the *Age*
English Women's Journal, 282, 283, 286,
   287
Essays and Reviews, 11, 16
Evangelical Magazine, 146
Evans, Benjamin, 304
Evans, William, 300
Eve, Mr, 286
Evening Echo, 312
Examiner, 18, 153; Mill writes for, 59,
   60–1, 64–75, 319

Family Herald, 342, 360
Fast Life, 342
Fast Man, the (1850), 342
Fenwick, 196
Ferrier, James Frederick, 158
Flower, Edward Fordham, 176
Flower, Eliza, 73–4
Fonblanque, Albany, 60–1
Foreign Quarterly Review, 14, 15, 16, 19
Foreign Review, the, 14, 15, 19
Forest of Dean Examiner, the, 304, 310,
   312
Forster, E. M., 33
Forster, W. E., 183
Fortnightly Review, 6, 7, 13, 17, 79, 170,
   273; Arnold in, 22; art criticism in, 82,
   84–6, 88, 95; contents, 19; Pater in, 21
Fox, W. J., 12, 73, 146, 176, 177, 266; and
   the *Monthly Repository*, 163–4
Frankland, R. J., 304
Fraser, Alexander Campbell, 151–64
Fraser, James (of *Fraser's Magazine*), 19, 20
Fraser, Patrick, 161
Fraser, William (of the *Foreign Review*), 19
Fraser's Magazine, 12, 18, 20, 22, 79, 153,
   168; Arnold in, 134; art criticism in, 82,
   86–91, 95, 98, 100, 102; circulation, 7;
   contents, 19–20; Ruskin in, 39, 53–5
Free Church of Scotland, see Scotland, Free
   Church of

Free Sunday Advocate, 286
Freeman, E. A., 152, 153, 155, 156, 161
Froude, J. A., 53, 172, 177
Fulford, Edith, 279
Fulford, William, 130

Gammage, R. G., 283
Gawler, Henry, 248
Gifford, William, 112, 252
Gladstone, 3
Glass, Rev. Norman, 310
Globe, the, 153, 164 n.2
Godwin, William, 287
Goethe, 15–16
Goldstücker, Prof. Theodore, 188
Gould, Joseph, 306
Gourley, E. T., 196, 200, 209, 210, 212,
   214
Good Words, 18
Grant, Francis, 100
Grant, James, 341, 342
Grayson, Victor, 266
Greg, W. R., 49, 152, 154, 170, 172, 181
Gregory, Barnard, 318, 321–33, 336, 340–1,
   344; Gregory Papers, 341
Grillo, Virgil, 349
Gross, John, 109
Grosvenor Gallery, 103, 104, *plate 3*
Grote, George, 9, 183, 185
Grote, Harriet, 25 n.28
Guardian, the, see *Manchester Guardian*
Guardian (1819–24), ed. C. Knight, 247
Guardian (1846–1951), 18, 146, 153

Hale, Cicely, 267, 292 n.13
Halliday, Thomas, 305, 307, 310
Hamerton, P. G., 83
Hamilton, Sir William, 158–9
Hands, Charles, 267
Hanna, Rev. William, 150, 152
Hannay, James, 190
Hardie, Keir, 286
Hardy, Thomas, 20, 27 n.64
Hare, J. C., 151
Harman, Sir James, 188
Harmer, James, 330
Harney, G. J., 270
Harries, Philip, 305
Harris, Frank, 6
Harrison, Brian, 291 n.7, 293 n.49
Harrison, Frederick, 22, 31, 51, 175–6, 183,
   190
Hartley, James, 196
Havelock-Allen, Sir Henry, 207
Hayward, Abraham, 152, 154, 155, 156
Hazlitt, William, 83
Hennell, Sara, 185
Hetherington, Henry, 278
Hickson, W. E., 13, 167, 172, 177
Hill, Matthew Davenport, 227, 231, 248
Himmelfarb, Gertrude, 9
Hippisley, Mr, 183
Hodgson, Dr Ballantyne, 172, 180–1
Hollis, Patricia, 253 n.1, 291 n.7, 347 n.40
Home and Foreign Review, 13, 14, 146
Home Chronicler, 277, 283

Hook, Theodore, 318–21, 342
Hopkin, D., 316
Horner, Francis, 6
Houghton, Walter, 24 n.9, 135, 368
Household Words, 18, 368
Hovell, Mark, 279–80
Howick, Viscount, 199
Howitt, George, 210, 211, 213, 216, 220
Howitt, Mary, 310
Hudson, George, 199
Hughes, Miss Susan (sister of Dr Brabant), 176
Huish, Marcus B., 91
Hume, Joseph, 249, 320
Hunt, H. M., 310
Hunt, Thornton, 172
Hutton, Richard Holt, 21, 51, 135, 176
Huxley, T. H., 3, 9, 51, 168, 176, 185
Hyndman, H. M., 280

Illustrated London News, 79, 96
Innes, E. A. Mitchell, 290
International Working Men's Association, 298
Ironworkers Journal, 298–9

James, Louis, 292 n.19
Jeffrey, Francis, 6, 17, 19, 112, 114–17, 145
Jephson, Henry, 264
Jevons, W. A., 3
John Bull, 318–21, 322, 324, 326, 344
John, David, 305
Johnson, Andrew, 178
Jones, Everest, 288
Jones, Lloyd, 307
Justice, 278–9, 280, 281, 287

Kane, John, 298
Kaye, John William, 150, 153, 154
Kenealy, Ahmed, 312
Kennedy, William Pattison, 148, 150, 159–63
Kenney, Annie, 275
Kent, Christopher, 23 n.5, 109
Kingsley, Charles, 24 n.9, 27 n.65, 151, 153, 159
Kitson Clark, G., 368
Kitto, John, 150
Knight, Charles, 18, 227, 230–53, *plate 4*, *plate 5*
Knowles, James T., 145
Kyllman, Max, 186

Labouchere, Henry, 345
Labour League Examiner, 306
Labour Press, Miners' and Workmen's Examiner, 304, 305, 307, 312
Lambton, John George, 1st Earl of Durham, 196
Lancashire Examiner, 304
Lang, Andrew, 21
Lawley, G. T., 310
Lawson, Wilfred, 266, 268
Layard, A. H., 3
Leader, the, 18, 153
Lecky, W. E. H., 187
Lee, Alan, 164 n.2, 222 n.1, 223 nn.22, 23

Leech, John, 17, 350
Leeds Mercury, 55, 273, 276
Lefanu, Sheridan, 23
Leicestershire Mercury, 278
Leighton, Frederick, 100
Lever, Charles, 26 n.50
Lewes, G. H., 114, 126, 145, 168, 170, 178
Library of the Fine Arts, 85, 98
Literary Gazette, 8, 17, 18
Lindsay, Lord, 48
Livesey, Joseph, 279, 288, *plate 9*
Lloyd, Edward, 356
Lloyd's Weekly Newspaper, 313
Lockhart, J. G., 47, 342
Lombe, Edward, 170, 172, 176
London and Westminster Review, 6, 12, 15, 62; see also *Westminster Review*
London Corresponding Society, 284
London Journal, 342, 349, 356, 360–5, *plate 10*
London Life, see the *Town* (1849–50)
London Magazine, 21
London Review, 6, 12, 15; see also *London and Westminster Review*
London Temperance Intelligencer, *plate 6*
London Trades Council, 198, 307
London Working Men's Association, 287
Long, George (*Quarterly Journal of Education*), 246, 248
Long, George (*Forest of Dean Examiner*), 304
Longman's Magazine, 20
Lowery, Robert, 264, 267, 288
Lubbock, Sir John, 188
Ludlow, J. M., 151
Lyall, Alfred, 270
Lyell, Charles, 3
Lytton, Lady Constance, 289

Macaulay, T. B., 3, 4, 64, 140 n.145; *Essays*, 4, 17, 31
McCulloch, J. R., 3, 24 n.12
McCulloch, Mrs (of Dumfries), 280
Mackay, R. W., 172
McKenna, Reginald, 289
McLean's Monthly Sheet of Caricatures, *plate 4*
Macmillan's Magazine, 17, 18, 22, 104; contents, 19; Pater in, 21
McNeil, John, 15
Magazine of Art, 79, 84, 86, 93–4, 97, 99
Magazine of Natural History (Loudon's), 47
Maidment, Brian, 57 n.22, 58 n.23
Maitland, Edward Francis (Lord Barcaple), 149, 150
Manchester Daily Examiner and Times, 55
Manchester Guardian, 272, 273, 274
Manning, Cardinal, 3
Manwaring, George, 185, 188
Marcuse, Herbert, 268
Marion, Kitty, 281
Martineau, Harriet, 74, 248, 249; and the *Westminster Review*, 168, 170, 177, 180–5

Martineau, James, 9, 118–19; and the
  Westminster Review, 170, 172, 173–4,
  176, 177–9, 180
Massey, Gerald, 124–6, 128, 135
Masson, David, 21, 135, 150, 152, 153, 154,
  159, 162
Matthias, Rev. T. D., 305, 307, 308, 310,
  312, 313
Maurer, Oscar, 23 n.5, 27 n.64
Maurice, F. D., 151
Mayhew, Henry, 75, 274, 352; and
  Augustus, The Greatest Plague in Life,
  355–6
Mazzini, 178
Mechanics' Institutes, 7
Merthyr Times, the, 305
Meteyard, Eliza, 310
Methodist Magazine, the, 146
Miall, Edward, 266
Midland Countries Illuminator, 278, 286
Mill, James, 3, 60, 113, 117
Mill, John Stuart, 3, 6, 9, 10, 12, 13, 15, 26
  n.34, 26 n.43, 27 n.55, 286, 287; on
  poetry, 118–22; and Westminster
  Review, 167, 170–5, 178, 183, 186–90;
  writes for the Examiner, 59–77
Millais, John, 17
Miller, James, 245
Miller, Thomas, 364
Milne, Maurice, 223 n.14
Miner and Workman's Examiner, 312; see
  also Labour Press, Miners' and
  Workmen's Examiner
Miner: Organ of Underground Labour,
  312; see also Labour Press, Miners' and
  Workmen's Examiner
Miner's Advocate and Record, 306
Molesworth, Sir William, 25 n.13, 167, 172
Monetary Gazette, 46
Monthly Chronicle, 87
Monthly Repository, the, 12, 18, 146;
  under W. J. Fox, 163–4
Moral and Political Magazine, 284
Morgan, J. T., 305–13
Morley, Henry, 84
Morley, John, 4, 7, 9, 13, 25 n.28, 51, 145,
  270, 273
Morning Chronicle, 12, 60, 153, 320, 350;
  Mill writes for, 74–5; art criticism, 85
Morning Herald, 153
Morning Mail, 213, 216; see also
  Sunderland Morning Mail
Morning Star (1856–69), 265
Morris, William, 268, 280
Moyes, Mrs Helen (neé Fraser), 292
Mozley, J. B., 17
Murray, Grenville, 343, 344
Murray, John, 20, 227, 252
My Secret Life, 354

Napier, Macvey, 19
National Institution of the Fine Arts, 93
National League for Opposing Women's
  Suffrage, 289
National Review (1855–64), 5–7, 13, 146,
  176, 179–80, 187–8

National Review (1883), 82–3, 87–8, 96,
  101
National Sunday league, 286
National Temperance League, 269
National Temperance Magazine, 284
National Union of Women's Suffrage
  Societies, 266
Neil, Samuel, 372
Nevinson, H. W., 272
New English Art Club, 95
New Monthly Magazine, 18, 80; art
  criticism in, 82, 83, 87, 89, 91, 93
New Review (1889–97), 19, 21
New Republic, 351
New Society of Painters in Water-Colours
  (Associated Painters in Water-Colours),
  95
New Statesman, 272, 282
Newcastle Daily Chronicle, 195, 200, 210,
  221
Newcastle Weekly Chronicle, 200
Newman, F. W., 170, 172, 176, 180, 187
Newman, John Henry, 3, 8
Newspaper Press, the, 344
Newspaper Press Directory, the, 344
New Yorker, 351
Nicholson, Renton, 317–46
Nicholson's Newspaper, 342
Nineteenth Century, the (1877), 6, 13, 17;
  Ruskin in, 47–9, 51; art criticism in, 91
Nisard, 15
North British Review, 145–66, 170;
  circulation, 7, 148, 149, 152–3; founding,
  147–9; contents, 148; edited by A. C.
  Fraser, 151–62
North Mail, 213, 215; see also Sunderland
  Morning Mail and Morning Mail
Northcliffe, Lord, 273, 274
Northern Daily Mail, 204, 222
Northern Echo, 273
Northern Examiner, 198
Northern Liberator, 286
Northern Star, 269, 276, 279, 283, 286, 288
Northern Times, 198, 199; see also
  Sunderland Beacon and Sunderland
  Times
Novel Newspaper (1838–48), 351

Observer, the, 272
O'Connell, Daniel, 266, 273
O'Connor, Feargus, 266, 269, 276, 280,
  284, 288
Odger, George, 307
Oliphant, Margaret, 96, 113, 119
Orr, W. S., 245
Orwell, George, 282
Ottley, Henry, 91, 98
Owen, John (father of William), 298
Owen, William, 298–314
Oxford and Cambridge Magazine, 18, 110,
  129–30

Pall Mall Gazette, 49, 189; Ruskin letters
  in, 46; 'Modern Babylon', 270, 274
Pankhurst, Christabel, 264, 267, 276, 278,
  279, 283, 289

Pankhurst, Sylvia, 280
Papers of the Manchester Angling Society, 33
Parker, Theodore, 170
Parkes, Joseph, 172, 182, 230
Pater, Walter, 3, 21
Patmore, Coventry, 150
Pattison, Mark, 9, 16, 21, 183
Paul Pry (1848–50), 342–3
Payne, William, 306
Pearson, C. A., 213
Peeping Tom, 342–3
Pemberton, J. S. G., 213
Pennell, Elizabeth, 82, 85
Penny Cyclopedia, 229
Penny Magazine, 225, 226, 229, 232, 234–53, 360, *plate 5*
Penny Sunday Times, 356–7
People's Paper, 288
Pethick-Lawrence, Mr and Mrs, 278
Pictorial Times, 95
Place, Francis, 227, 249, 264
Plain Englishman, 247
Police News, 344
Pollock, Frederick, 9
Pollock, W. F., 88
Pott, Gladys, 289, 290
Potter, the, 301; see also *Potteries Examiner and Workman's Advocate*
Potteries Examiner, 299, 301–12
Potters Examiner and Workman's Advocate (later *Emigrant's Advocate*), 300
Prest, T. P., 357
Price, Bonamy, 152, 155, 157, 161
Price, W. E., 188
Prospective Review, 146, 170, 178
Punch, 45–6, 56, 57 n.22, 350, 368

Quarterly Journal of Education, 229, 235–41, 246, 248
Quarterly Review, 10–13, 17, 113–14, 132, 146–7, 174, 277, 342; circulation and profitability, 7, 235–41; contents, 11, 19; rates of payment, 159; Ruskin in, 39, 47–8
Queen's Messenger, the, 343
Quilter, Harry, 82, 87, 88
Quiz: the satirist (1879), 344

Rambler, the, 114, 146
Randall, J., 310
Randall, John, 304
Reader, the, 131
Record, the, 11, 146
Reform League, 287
Reid, Captain Thomas Mayne, 310
Religious Tract Society, 230
Reynolds, G. W. M., 327, 357–8, 363–4
Reynolds's Magazine, 360
Reynolds's Miscellany, 356, 360
Reynolds's Newspaper, 313
Rhondda, Lady, 283, 284
Rippendale, E. P., 83
Ritson, Francis, 205
Ritson, Henry, 204
Roberts, F. David, 164 n.2

Robertson, John, 150
Roebuck, J. A., 6, 63, 64, 249
Roscoe, W. C., 135
Rosenberg, Adolphus, 344
Rosenberg, Sheila, 164 n.2
Rosenberg's Little Journal (1886–7), 344
Rossetti, Dante Gabriel, 101
Rossetti, William Michael, 83, 100, 102
Rothschild, Ferdinand, 85
Royal Academy, 83–5, 90–3, 95–6, 98–100, 102, 104, *plates 1, 2*
Royal Society for Prevention of Cruelty to Animals, 283, 285
Ruddock, Richard, 200
Ruskin, John, 29–58, 83, 86, 114, 120; *Fors Clavigera*, 30–3, 36–7, 41, 51, 56, 57; *Unto this Last*, 35–6, 38, 51–3, 55; *Munera Pulveris*, 35, 38, 51, 53–4, 55
Ruskin, John James, 47, 52, 54, 58 n.23
Russell, Bertrand, 290
Russell, Charles, 205
Russell, Earl, 262
Rymer, J. M.: *Ada the Betrayed*, 357

Sadleir, Michael, 27 n.64, 347 n.59
Saffi, Aurelio, 178
St James Magazine, 18
St Pauls Magazine, 18
Saintsbury, George, 3, 23
Sam Sly, or The Town (1848–9), 342–3
Saturday Magazine, the (S.D.U.K.), 244–6, 250
Saturday Review, 13, 18, 385; art criticism in, 84–7, 89, 92, 94–5, 97, 100, 103–4; influence of, 130–2; literary criticism in, 110, 128
Satirist, the, 318–19, 321–32, 337, 340, 341, 344
Saunders, William, 287
Scott, William Bell, 83
Scotland, Free Church of, 145–66
Scottish Patriot, 288
Senior, Nassau, 3, 12, 152, 153
Servant's Magazine, the, 353–6, 365
Shairp, John Campbell, 152
Sharp, William, 82, 83
Shattock, Joanne, 26 n.38
Shee, Martin Archer, 100
Shelton, John, 86
Shields and Stockton Observer and General Advertiser, see *Sunderland Herald*
Shields Gazette, 200, 201, 202
Shropshire Examiner, 304
Sickert, William, 83
Sidgwick, Henry, 13, 22
Simcox, G. A., 93
Simey, Ralph, 205
Simon, Lady, 281
Simpson, Richard, 114, 129, 132–5
Smith, Barbara Leigh (Bodichon), 176, 190
Smith, Elder, and Co, 47, 160
Smith, H. (of Holywell St), 330–1
Smith, Herodotus (Francis Espinasse), 169–70
Smith, Julie (sister of Octavius), 176
Smith, Maud Kate, 283, 290

Smith, Octavius, 167, 176, 181, 184–5
Smith, Sydney, 6
Snowdon, Philip, 286
Social Democratic Federation, 287
Socialist (Sunderland), 199, 212
Socialist League, 285
Society for the Diffusion of Useful
  Knowledge (S.D.U.K.), 226–53
Society for Promoting the Employment of
  Women, 282
Society of British Artists, 92, 93
Society of Painters in Watercolour (the Old
  Society), 94, 95
South Staffordshire Examiner, 304
South Wales Examiner, 305
Southey, Robert, 17
'Spasmodic' controversy, 110, 136 n.8
Spectator, the, 18, 80, 153, 319; art
  criticism in, 84, 89, 92, 94, 95–6, 98–100
Speke, John, 3
Spencer, Herbert, 49, 152, 170, 174, 185
Spice, 316 n.74
Spielmann, M. H., 97, 99
Staffordshire Knot, 316 n.74
Staffordshire Sentinel, 311
Standard, the, 275
Stanley, A. P., 6, 151
Stanley, Edward Henry (15th Earl of
  Derby), 167, 170, 183–5, 186–90
Stansfield, James, 266
Stanton, Elizabeth Cady, 189
Star of the West, 315 n.37, 316 n.75
Statham, H. Heathcote, 104
Staunch Teetotaler, 279
Stead, W. T., 189, 267, 270, 273, 274
Stephen, Fitzjames, 9
Stephen, Leslie, 3, 9, 25 n.28, 26 n.29
Stephens, Frederic George, 83
Stewart, Charles (3rd Marquis of
  Londonderry), 196
Stigand, William, 111–12, 117, 122, 124
Storey, Patricia, 222 n.3, 222 n.7
Storey, Samuel, 196, 200, 202–4, 207,
  209–12, 214, 216, 218
Stow-Hill, Lord, 272
Strachey, St Loe, 274
Struggle, the, 288, plate 9
Strutt, Joseph, 230
Strutt, William, 230
Sturge, Joseph, 269
Sue, Eugène, 360, 363
Suffragette, the, 276, 278, 279, 281, 282,
  285, 287
Sun, the, 272, 351
Sunday Times, 274
Sunderland and Durham County Herald,
  see Sunderland Herald, 197
Sunderland and Durham Shipping Gazette,
  198–9
Sunderland and Hartlepool General Review
  and Advertiser, 198
Sunderland and Shields Herald, see
  Sunderland Herald
Sunderland Beacon, 197, 198–9; see also
  Sunderland Times
Sunderland Citizen, 199, 212

Sunderland Conservative Printing and
  Publishing Company Ltd, 205
Sunderland Daily Echo, 198–9, 200,
  201–7, 209–13, 215–17, plate 13; wages
  book for 1875–8, 218–22
Sunderland Daily Herald, 207; see also
  Sunderland Herald
Sunderland Daily News, 199, 200
Sunderland Daily Post, 199, 205–9
Sunderland Daily Shipping News, 199
Sunderland Echo, 194, 200; see also
  Sunderland Daily Echo
Sunderland Evening Chronicle, 199, 215,
  216
Sunderland Examiner, 198
Sunderland Herald (Shields and Stockton
  Observer and General Advertiser), 196,
  197, 198–9, 200–2, 206–7, 214–16
Sunderland Herald and Daily Post, 207,
  209–12, 213–15, 217, 221; see also
  Sunderland Herald and Sunderland Daily
  Post
Sunderland Mirror, 196, 198
Sunderland Morning Mail, 199, 212–13,
  215
Sunderland News, 198, 200
Sunderland, newspapers of, 193–223;
  development of, 194–6; politics of,
  185–6
Sunderland Sentinel, 199, 201, 204–5
Sunderland Telegram, 196, 199
Sunderland Times, 196, 197, 198–9, 200,
  201, 206, 214, 216, 219; see also
  Northern Times and Sunderland Beacon
Sunderland Weekly Echo, 198, 215, 221;
  see also Sunderland Weekly Times
Sunderland Weekly News, 199, 200, 216
Sunderland Weekly Times, 198, 206, 215,
  219
Surrey Standard, see Sussex Agricultural
  Express, Surrey Standard and Weald of
  Kent Mail and County Advertiser
Sussex Agricultural Express, Surrey
  Standard, Weald of Kent Mail and
  County Advertiser, xv
Swanwick, Mrs H. M., 275, 288

Tablet, the, 146
Tait, Archibald Campbell, 151, 152
Tait's Edinburgh Magazine, 18, 21
Tamworth Examiner, 304
Tayler, J. J., 174
Taylor, Harriet, 73, 186
Taylor, Helen (daughter of Harriet), 168
Taylor, Isaac (of Stanford Rivers), 150, 151,
  154, 155, 159–63
Taylor, John, 229
Taylor, Peter, 177–8
Taylor, William, 273
Temperance Advocate, 277
Temple Bar, 18, 23, 27 n.64
Tennyson, 11, 115, 136 n.41
Test-Act Reporter, 282
Thackeray, W. M., 22, 27 n.68, 83, 129
Thomas, Thomas, 305
Thompson, T. C., 196, 200

Thompson, T. P., 167
Thompson, William (alderman of
    Sunderland), 199
Thomson, Christopher, 251
Thomson, William (Archbishop of York),
    151, 154
Thornbury, Walter, 354
Tillotson, W. F., 310
Time and Tide, 276
Times, The, 12, 26 n.52, 49, 153, 268, 271,
    273, 320, 368; Ruskin letters in, 46, 52;
    on Mill, 61–2; Mill attacks, 66, 75,
    76 n.6; Saturday Review attacks, 131
Times we Live In, the, 343
Tinsley's Magazine, 18
Tittle Tattle (1888), 344
Town Talk: a journal for society at large
    (1878–85), 344
Town, the (1837–42), 317–46, plate 8
Town, the (1849–50), 342–3
Town Topics (1894), 344
Transactions of the Meteorological Society,
    47
Traveller, the, 59
Trollope, Anthony, 115, 137 n.41
Trollope, Thomas Adolphus, 150
Trübner, 184, 185
True Scotsman, 288
Truth (1877–1957), 345
Tulloch, John, 151, 157–8
Turnbull, William Wilson, 310
Tyndall, John, 290
Tyrwhitt, R. St John, 84, 87

United Kingdom Alliance, 266, 285, 287
Urquhart, David, 15

Van Arsdel, Rosemary, 190 n.1
Vaughan, Robert, 12
Venables, G. S., 9, 21
Verney, F. P., 81
Verulam, 278
Victoria Magazine (1863), 18
Vincent, Henry, 267, 268
Vincent, John, 276
Vote, 280, 281
Votes for Women, 275, 278–9, 280–1, 284,
    285–6

Walton, A. A., 310
Watchman, the, 316 n.74
Waterloo Directory of Victorian
    Periodicals, 23 n.3
Wayman, John, 205, 208, 209, 210, 216
Weald of Kent Mail and County
    Advertiser, see Sussex Agricultural
    Express, Surrey Standard, Weald of Kent
    Mail and County Advertiser
Wearside Star, 199
Wedderburn, A. D. O. (with E. T. Cook),
    30–1, 51, 54

Wedgewood, H., 310
Wednesbury, West Bromwich and
    Darlaston Examiner, 304
Weekly Dispatch, 319, 330, 336
Weekly Mail (Burslem), 316 n.74
Weekly Record of the Temperance
    Movement (Temperance Record), 277
Weekly Star, 316 n.74
Wellesley Index to Victorian Periodicals, x,
    xvi, 135, 368; see also under Houghton,
    Walter
Welsh, David, 147
West Bromwich Free Press, 312
West of England Examiner, 305
Western Observer, the, 305
Westmacott, Charles Molloy, 318, 321–32,
    340, 344
Westminster and Foreign Review, 16; see
    also Westminster Review
Westminster Review, 6, 7, 12–13, 16, 21,
    63, 145, 146, 148, 154, 159, 167–92, 263;
    see also Westminster and Foreign
    Review, London and Westminster
    Review
Westminster Review Company, 185, 189
Whately, Richard, 12, 151
Whewell, William, 155
Whistler, James McNeill, 81, 93
White, Blanco, 12
Whittaker, Thomas, 264
Whitty, Michael James, 342
Wiener, Joel, 291 n.4, 347 n.40
Wilberforce, William, 268
Williams, Helen Maria, 69
Williams, James (Sunderland alderman),
    199–201, 206
Williams, Morgan, 305
Williams, R. Folkstone, 88, 102
Williams, William, 204
Williams, W. S., 47, 53
Windsor and Eton Express, 247
Winn, W., 343
Wiseman, Cardinal, 113
Wolff, Michael, 20, 25 n.19, 367
Wolverhampton Times, 312 (later
    Wolverhampton Times and Midland
    Examiner)
Woman's Dreadnought, 278, 280
Women's Franchise, 288
Women's Freedom League, 280
Women's Social and Political Union, 267,
    280–2, 284
Women's Suffrage Journal, 265, 280, 284
Wood, George William, 230
Woodfall (publisher), 176
Woodward, E. L., 368
Workman's Advocate, the, 305–12, plate 14
World, the (1874–1922), 344

Yates, Edmund, 344–5

Zoophilist, the, 277